A MIND OF ONE'S OWN

Second Edition

A MIND OF ONE'S OWN

Feminist Essays on
Reason and Objectivity

Edited by Louise M. Antony and Charlotte E. Witt

Westview PRESS

A Member of the Perseus Books Group

Feminist Theory and Politics

All rights reserved. Printed in the United States of America. No part of this publication may be reproduced or transmitted in any form or by any means, electronic or mechanical, including photocopy, recording, or any information storage and retrieval system, without permission in writing from the publisher.

Copyright © 2002 by Westview Press, A Member of the Perseus Books Group

Westview Press books are available at special discounts for bulk purchases in the United States by corporations, institutions, and other organizations. For more information, please contact the Special Markets Department at The Perseus Books Group, 11 Cambridge Center, Cambridge MA 02142, or call (617) 252-5298.

Published in 2001 in the United States of America by Westview Press, 5500 Central Avenue, Boulder, Colorado 80301–2877, and in the United Kingdom by Westview Press, 12 Hid's Copse Road, Cumnor Hill, Oxford OX2 9JJ

Find us on the World Wide Web at www.westviewpress.com

A CIP catalog record for this book is available from the Library of Congress.
ISBN 0-8133-6606-2; 0-8133-6607-0 (pbk.)

The paper used in this publication meets the requirements of the American National Standard for Permanence of Paper for Printed Library Materials Z39.48–1984.

10   9   8   7   6   5   4   3   2   1

To Virginia Witt
C.W.

In memory of my mother, Elizabeth L. Antony
L.M.A.

CONTENTS

METAPHYSICS

SOCIAL AND POLITICAL PHILOSOPHY

PREFACE TO
THE SECOND EDITION

When we began thinking about a second edition of *A Mind of One's Own*, we were struck by the rapid development of feminist reflection on reason and objectivity over the past decade. While we acknowledged the impossibility of providing a comprehensive survey of the ways in which feminist philosophy has intersected with traditional philosophizing during that period, we felt that we could, nonetheless, give a good indication of the extent and nature of this fertile intermingling by supplementing the volume's original contents with new chapters that reflect some of the advances of the past decade. We were gratified by the original volume's reception, and we believe that this new edition will remain useful for feminist theorists, as well as for philosophers wanting to include feminist thought in their research or teaching.

The essays we have chosen for this second edition both enlarge the themes of the original articles and take the volume in new directions. In making our selections, we considered three points. First, we were interested in discussions that were consonant with the volume's main focus: conceptions of reason and objectivity "credentialed" within mainstream philosophy but contested within feminism. Second, we sought topics that had application beyond the narrow confines of academic philosophy. Finally, we wanted to invite a new generation of feminist philosophers to reflect on the issues treated in the first edition. Of course there are numerous topics that fit our criteria, and many new voices in feminist philosophy, but we think that the papers we have chosen especially complement and enrich the original collection.

One topic that met all our desiderata is the topic of rational choice theory. It has a long philosophical history reaching back to the political theory of Thomas Hobbes and the economic thought of Adam Smith, but it is also precisely the sort of theory that many feminists have in mind when they deplore the androcentrism of philosophical theories of rationality. Moreover, it is a theory with broad implications for economics, law, and the social sciences. The chapters by Ann Cudd and Elizabeth Anderson, which grew out of a marvelously cooperative and productive debate between the two at a meeting of the Eastern Division of the American Philosophical Association meetings, concern the question of the androcentrism of "the rational agent" assumed by rational choice theory. Their nuanced assessments of the value of rational choice theory for feminism advances our understanding in several ways. Looking at the theory through the lens of feminism sheds new light on its presuppositions and limitations. Conversely, the attempt to treat feminist values and goals within the context of rational choice theory illuminates important questions for feminist thought, like the value of autonomy. These chapters can be read profitably in connection with Jean Hampton's similarly complex treatment of contractarianism in her contribution to the original collection.

Philosophical issues posed by global feminism and multiculturalism seemed eminently appropriate for our volume, particularly those stemming from cultural practices that at least seem oppressive of women. Uma Narayan focuses on the practice of veiling in her discussion of custom, choice, and autonomy. While rejecting the idea of "group rights" or "cultural rights" adopted by some feminists and political theorists, Narayan advocates a position that recognizes the autonomy and respects the choices of many of the women who choose to participate in activities that appear repressive to many Western feminists. Her valuable contribution moves deftly between theory and practice and from culture to culture in developing a mode of understanding women unlike oneself that neither patronizes nor exoticizes. Its practical applications and real-world significance are obvious in a world where the processes of cultural globalization and cultural diversification are equally potent.

Karen Jones's essay also focuses on the issue of cultures in conflict and the challenge inherent in coming to understand and accept what may seem, from one's own perspective, to be literally unbelievable. Her case study is the asylum plea of Fauziya Kassindja, a young woman fleeing genital mutilation and forced marriage in her homeland, Togo. The U.S. Immigration judge in the case, Donald Ferlise, denied asylum on the grounds that Kassindja's story was "not credible." Jones manages to draw some useful lessons from this appalling case, developing a structure of guidelines for the evaluation of astonishing reports. In its practical orientation, its sensitivity to detail, and its feminist motivation, Jones's paper makes a useful contribution to both epistemology and feminism, and in this way seems a sterling example of the kind of "engaged" epistemological work that feminist epistemologists (including Louise Antony in her chapter in the original volume) have long been calling for. It connects clearly with feminist work on epistemic authority and the mechanisms by which some testimony is legitimated as knowledge while other testimony is dismissed as epistemically suspect. It makes a positive contribution to the feminist goal of developing more adequate, situated epistemic norms.

The work of Catharine MacKinnon on objectivity and its role in the construction and epistemology of gender remains a touchstone for feminist theory. Rachel Zuckert takes up MacKinnon's charge that objectivity, like other basic values of liberalism, codes for a male epistemological point of view and thereby contributes to the subordination of women. Zuckert argues that, ironically, MacKinnon's most persuasive criticisms of liberalism make use of the norm of objectivity in a way that is, in fact, congenial to liberal thought. This chapter can be usefully read alongside the contributions of Sally Haslanger and Elizabeth Rapaport, who also attempt to uncover MacKinnon's basic theoretical commitments and discuss the ways in which her conceptual apparatus intersects with traditional philosophical categories. The fruitfulness of this feminist engagement with foundational metaphysical issues confirms the conclusion drawn by Charlotte Witt in her first edition chapter that feminists should not and will not cease to do metaphysics.

We cannot introduce this new edition without noting, with profound sadness, the untimely death, in 1996, of Jean Hampton, whose contribution "Feminist Contractarianism" we were proud to include in the first edition. Jean's work, which married a keen analytical intelligence to a loving and wise sensibility, expressed in myriad ways the values that define feminist philosophy. She is sorely missed.

We had intended for *A Mind of One's Own* to serve as a kind of album, a set of snapshots taken at an early stage of the ongoing feminist confrontation with traditional philosophy. The added essays, then, offer glimpses of the new landscapes this fertile engagement has revealed. We hope all our readers are inspired to make forays of their own.

L.M.A.
C.W.

ACKNOWLEDGMENTS

We are grateful to the Philosophy Department at the University of New Hampshire and to the UNH Humanities Center for sponsoring a colloquium on Feminism and Rationality in September 1989 that allowed several of the contributors to this volume to meet and discuss their essays. Special thanks are due Ken Westphal in the Philosophy Department for organizing the conference and Jeannie Dutka for contributing her organizational skills and good sense.

We are also grateful to the UNH Humanities Center and to the College of Humanities and Social Science at North Carolina State University for contributing to production costs associated with the volume, and to the Women's Studies Program at UNH for their timely help. Louise Antony would like to thank the National Humanities Center and the Andrew J. Mellon Foundation for their support during her fellowship year at the Center, during which some of the editorial work for this volume was completed.

Our spouses, Joe Levine and Mark Okrent, supported this book in thought, word, and deed over the past two years. We thank them for their efforts. We also wish to acknowledge our day care providers who take care of our children so well. Louise Antony thanks Rosa Valez and Lolita Jackson at the Method Daycare Center in Raleigh, North Carolina, and Charlotte Witt thanks Karen Wilt and Darlene Drew at Westbrook College Children's Center in Portland, Maine.

Louise M. Antony
Charlotte Witt

INTRODUCTION

At the time we first conceived this project, it had been half a decade since the publication of the landmark anthology *Discovering Reality: Feminist Perspectives on Epistemology, Metaphysics, Methodology, and Philosophy of Science* (1983). In their introduction, editors Sandra Harding and Merrill B. Hintikka issued a call for a feminist philosophy that went beyond the narrowly "reformist" projects of earlier feminist work:

> The attempts to add understandings of women to our knowledge of nature and social life have led to the realization that there is precious little reliable knowledge to which to add them. A more fundamental project now confronts us. We must root out sexist distortions and perversions in epistemology, metaphysics, methodology and the philosophy of science—in the "hard core" of abstract reasoning thought most immune to infiltration by social values (ix).

Since then an extensive literature has developed in which virtually every figure, school, method, and concept of traditional philosophy has been subjected to the most searching feminist scrutiny. As Harding and Hintikka urged, the "rooting out" of "sexist distortions and perversions" has extended far beyond the document-and-deplore strategy of laying bare the explicit, but arguably excisable, sexism in this or that mainstream work. Feminist challenges have, indeed, reached into the "'hard core' of abstract reasoning" itself, with charges that the most fundamental elements of the Western philosophical tradition—the ideals of reason and objectivity—are so deeply corrupted by patriarchy that they must be greatly transformed (if not utterly abandoned) by any philosopher committed to the development of conceptions of knowledge and reality adequate to the transformative goals of feminism.

Such changes pose methodological and substantive difficulties for anyone who wishes to be both a feminist and a philosopher, but as philosophers whose concerns and methods fall squarely within the traditional philosophical paradigms under attack, we took the criticisms in a particularly personal way. Although we consider ourselves committed feminists, the import of the radical critique seemed to be that we must be mistaken—that a person cannot, at this stage of the game, be a feminist and still do that kind of philosophy.

It therefore became a pressing matter for us to achieve a better understanding of our relation to the philosophical tradition within which we worked. On the one hand, we agreed with feminist critics that the revealed misogyny of our tradition was too deep and pervasive to be simply dismissed as accidental. We also acknowledged readily that the concepts of reason and objectivity have been—and continue to be—used as potent ideological weapons in the defense of a variety of oppressive structures. Given all this, we felt that we had to take seriously the possibility that our acceptance of traditional problems and methodologies might represent a kind of false consciousness and that our continued allegiance to the tradition might even be helping to perpetuate patriarchy.

But on the other hand, reason and objectivity had a normative hold on us—we were far from convinced that these concepts either could be or ought to be abandoned. At the most general level, we viewed reason and objectivity as the tools of our trade and could not imagine what might replace them. More specifically, we felt that these concepts had important work to do in particular philosophical projects to which we felt intellectually committed. We did not share the feelings of alienation reported by some feminists with respect to these projects, although we did experience feelings of alienation from a male-dominated and sexist profession. Further, because we found reason and objectivity to be concepts that empowered rather than oppressed us, we viewed these traditional notions as potentially useful for feminist theorizing rather than antithetical to it.

Finally, we had a host of questions about the import of all these considerations for the future of philosophy and of feminist theory. Wouldn't the abandonment of reason and objectivity be self-defeating for feminists? Wouldn't we be giving up on the possibility of persuading others of the correctness of our views? If we were to dismantle traditional ideals of rational discourse and impartiality, wouldn't we be depriving ourselves of the very norms necessary to ground our own critiques? And if we disassociated feminist thought from these capacities and values claimed by men, wouldn't we be embracing and reinforcing—rather than challenging—the invidious stereotypes of femininity that are especially destructive for a woman who would be a philosopher?

As we struggled with these issues, we came to the conclusion that there were some deep and substantive disagreements among feminist philosophers that were creating counterproductive divisions among us and that it would thus be worthwhile to create a forum in which these controversies could be openly and constructively engaged. Our aim, then, in organizing this volume, was to facilitate communication between those feminist philosophers who thought the tradition was unfixable and those who were convinced that it still had much to offer. We decided to bring together a set of feminist philosophers with a variety of philosophical interests, and a variety of relationships to "the tradition," and ask them to think about reason and objectivity, with an eye toward the issues outlined above.

The resulting essays span a full range of positions concerning the value of reason and objectivity for feminist thought—from those arguing that the traditional notions are fine as is, to those who think that they need to be reconceptualized in light of feminist thought, to those who reject them altogether. Our contributors also discuss a wide variety of related topics, and we are pleased with the intellectual richness of the chapters that resulted from our original idea.

One clear issue raised by feminist readings of the history of philosophy concerns the value of the canon for feminist theory and action. One question concerning the canon that has been debated in academia recently is the question of diversity. Should we open up the curriculum to include new voices and perspectives that have been excluded, or should we continue to teach the traditional canon? Our contributors raise a different issue with regard to the traditional canon by examining it from a feminist perspective. What do the writings of the philosophers whose thought has formed the core of Western philosophy have to offer feminists? Our contributors differ in their responses to this question, but read together these essays reveal that the thought of traditional philosophers is rich with possibilities for feminist interpretations.

Because such major figures of our tradition as Aristotle and Kant defined reason in their own male image and denied women full rationality, both the ideal of reason itself and the value of Aristotelian and Kantian thought have become suspect in feminist eyes. Two contributors to this volume, Marcia Homiak and Barbara Herman, take issue with this negative evaluation of Aristotle and Kant. Homiak argues that Aristotle's ideal of rationality and the rational life is one that feminists have good reason to accept. She considers two feminist criticisms of the rational life—that it excludes the emotional side of our moral lives and that it sacrifices particular, personal ties in favor of general principles. In response, she points out that the Aristotelian rational ideal does not exclude the emotions. And she argues that caring relationships, if they are not to be oppressive to women, ought to exist within the context of an Aristotelian rational life. Herman claims that certain of Kant's views on sex and marriage are surprisingly echoed in recent feminist thought and that Kant's solution to the moral problem of sexuality is interesting and worthy of consideration. Specifically, Herman finds in Andrea Dworkin's feminist reflections on sexual intercourse an echo of Kant's concerns about the negative effects of sexual appetite on the moral status of the persons involved. If Herman is right, then feminists might find Kant's attempts to resolve the moral problems of autonomy and respect for persons created by sexual desire interesting and worthwhile rather than merely puritanical.

Feminist epistemologists have criticized both the rationalist and the empiricist strands of modern epistemology. Margaret Atherton presents an interpretation of reason in Descartes different from recent feminist interpretations, and she argues that her interpretation explains why Descartes' contemporaries like Mary Astell and Damaris Lady Masham could use his notion of reason to argue for the education of women. The fact that Descartes' contemporaries found a gender-neutral notion of reason in his thought and used it for feminist ends complicates any simple assessment of the value of Cartesian reason for feminism today. In a similar vein, Annette Baier suggests that feminists take another look at Hume's empiricism. Drawing on Hume's historical and ethical writings, as well as his essays, Baier argues that what we find is a nonindividualistic, social epistemology that harmonizes with the feminist insight that knowledge is a cooperative endeavor rather than an individual achievement.

Several of the essays in this volume explore the feminist thesis that reason and objectivity are gendered concepts associated with maleness or with men. They address the question of what it might mean to think that reason is gendered and what the consequences of that position are for feminist philosophers. Genevieve Lloyd continues the study of the maleness of reason begun in her historical essay *The Man of Reason*. Here, she argues that reason's metaphorical maleness operates on the symbolic level and that it is not a unitary phenomenon but rather a complex network of images, some relatively superficial and easily cleansed, others more profoundly embedded. Our understanding that reason is metaphorically male, and that the symbolic connections between reason and gender are complex, should lead us to appreciate the contingency of the maleness of reason rather than leading us to reject reason because it is male.

Switching the focus from the symbolic representation of reason's maleness to the social construction of gender and gender norms, Sally Haslanger explores the feminist claim that the notion of objectivity or aperspectivity is itself implicated in objectifying social relations, in particular in the objectification of women by men. What is the connection between the epistemic category of objectivity and the socially constructed gender category of being male? Drawing on the work of Catharine MacKinnon, Haslanger argues that the epistemic norm of assumed objectivity contributes to the success of functioning as a man in our culture—it contributes to the successful objectification and eroticized domination of women by men—although it falls short of being sufficient for functioning as a man.

Elizabeth Rapaport's essay is also concerned with understanding the idea of gender in Catharine MacKinnon's theory. Rapaport approaches the question of gender by contrasting MacKinnon's brand of feminist legal reasoning with that of liberal feminists and followers of Carol Gilligan. What distinguishes MacKinnon's approach to legal questions is her unique notion of gender as a socially constructed and inherently oppressive category. Rapaport explains MacKinnon's view of gender and defends it against the charge of gender essentialism.

Two contributors take a critical stance toward the value for feminists of ideals of reason or objectivity that characterize the knower as disembodied, individual, and unitary. Naomi Scheman examines the undemocratic consequences of the Cartesian conception of the knowing subject. By comparing the process through which the individual, disembodied, and unitary Cartesian subject is achieved to the process of repression and projection that Freud described as constitutive of paranoia, Scheman makes the case that the norms of modern, Cartesian epistemology both underlie oppressive social relations (like the relations between men and women) and induce a kind of epistemic paranoia in its privileged knowers. Robin Schott argues that the rejection of women's bodily existence exemplified by some postmodern and radical feminists echoes a similar rejection of material existence found in traditional philosophy. Schott argues in particular that the postmodern deconstruction of the category "women" is idealistic and is an inadequate foundation for feminist theory because it ignores the bodily condition of women that is both the basis for considering women as a group and integral to their lives and eventual liberation.

Several contributors who have worked and written extensively on philosophical topics that appear unrelated to feminist concerns—naturalized epistemology, social contract theory, empiricism in the philosophy of science, realist metaphysics—argue for the value of work on these topics for feminist theory and feminist social change. Louise Antony argues that analytic epistemology has been misunderstood by its feminist critics and that one strain of analytic thought—naturalized epistemology—actually facilitates feminist inquiry. She argues that naturalized epistemology provides a theoretical standpoint from which one criticizes the epistemic ideal of objectivity (conceived as neutrality or impartiality) without undercutting one's ability to condemn pernicious biases. In a similar vein, Jean Hampton argues that the adoption of the contractarian approach to moral and political problems is fully compatible with feminist insights. Hampton responds to the basic feminist criticism of contract theory—that the image of the contract is inadequate for relationships in the personal or private realm—by arguing that feminists should be concerned with distributive justice within the household and by acknowledging that there are aspects of human relationships that cannot be captured by the heuristic device of the contract.

Helen Longino argues that contextual empiricism (as developed in her recent book *Science as Social Knowledge*) meets the methodological needs of feminist studies of science better than the available alternatives. In particular, Longino argues that contextual empiricism provides an account of scientific inquiry that allows feminists to claim both that scientific inquiry is value laden or ideological and that it produces knowledge.

Finally, Charlotte Witt questions the antimetaphysical trend in recent feminist thought. Witt argues that there are no specifically feminist reasons for the rejection of traditional metaphysics, and she points out that both neopragmatist and postmodern metaphilosophies deprive feminist thinkers of the conceptual resources needed to critique existing social relations. Furthermore, she argues, several important feminist projects—the criticism of the philosophical tradition as phallocentric, the development of Carol Gilligan's different voice, and Catharine MacKinnon's indictment of pornography—require metaphysical investigation and argument.

We think that the chapters in this book make a substantive contribution toward clarifying the relationship between feminist thought and traditional philosophy. In particular, we are very pleased that it contains excellent essays that make the case both for and against a feminist philosophy that uses the traditional philosophical tools of reason and objectivity. We hope that the collection stimulates further debate and discussion among feminist philosophers; we envision a community of feminist thinkers that embraces serious philosophical disagreements as well as a unified political purpose.

L.M.A.
C.W.

HISTORY OF
PHILOSOPHY

I

FEMINISM AND ARISTOTLE'S RATIONAL IDEAL

MARCIA L. HOMIAK

Several years ago, as part of a meeting of the Society for Women in Philosophy, I was asked, along with two other feminist philosophers working on canonical male figures in the history of philosophy, to participate in a panel entitled "What's a Nice Girl like Me Doing in a Place like This?" The title reflected the organizers' view that there was something politically suspect about feminists working on established male figures—and something particularly suspect in this case, where the three philosophers in question (Aristotle, Hobbes, and Kant) were well-known for their benighted views on women.[1] How could we reconcile our commitment to feminism with a scholarly life devoted to the study of philosophers who explicitly describe women as inferior to men, as unfit for the best life available to human beings, as incapable of being full moral agents?[2]

In addition to these long-acknowledged problems regarding women, there have recently come to be other difficulties associated with working on Aristotle, Hobbes, and Kant. With the growing interest in revising and reorganizing the "Canon" of the humanities, so as to include works by and about not only women, but also non-Western and nonwhite peoples, devoting one's scholarly life to the study of Aristotle, Hobbes, and Kant seems to be an even more egregious departure from progressive values and ways of life. For the use and teaching of canonical works, which are predominantly white and male, has encouraged an ignorant and prejudiced view of works, writers, and subject matters outside the canon. Moreover, many of the values associated with canonical works have, historically, been used to denigrate and oppress women, nonwhite men, and the uneducated in general.[3] Thus teaching the works of the traditional canon has encouraged not only ignorance and elitism but also sexism and racism.

I have said that the values associated with the traditional canon have historically been used to denigrate women, nonwhite men, and the uneducated. One might think this historical fact renders these values themselves suspect. They may be thought skewed and incomplete or, worse yet, inherently Western, Eurocentric, or masculine. I want to explore one value in particular that is associated with most of Western philosophy and with much of the traditional humanistic canon. I am referring to the value of reason and to the value of exercising one's rational faculties. Aristotle, Kant, and Hobbes each recommends, as the best life available to human beings, a rational life, though each has a different view about what this life requires and includes. I shall discuss only Aristotle's views on these matters, and I shall argue that his picture of the rational life is neither inherently masculine nor inherently exploitative. Instead, I shall claim, his ideal is worthy of emulation by both women and men.

Ethical systems that promote rationality as an ideal have recently come under considerable criticism from feminist scholars. Much of this criticism has been influenced by Carol Gilligan's work comparing girls' and boys' ways of reasoning about ethical questions.[4] In her work *In a Different Voice*, for example, Gilligan suggests that males and females have, in general, different orientations or perspectives toward moral values and moral strategies. Women tend to adopt a "care" perspective, in which what matters to them is the preservation of relationships and connection with others; men tend to adopt a "justice" perspective, in which what matters is acting on impartial and universalizable principles. Since relationships are matters of intimacy and personal feeling, the care perspective is associated with a focus on emotion, especially on the altruistic emotions. Since impartial and universalizable principles are a result of reasoned reflection about what to do, where such reflection is carried out without the distractions of emotion and without a prejudiced concern for one's own interests or the interests of specific others, the justice perspective is associated with rationality and with the value of one's status as a rational being capable of such reflection.[5]

Thus the basis of the feminist criticism of rational ideals is that such ideals, in their application to moral questions, ignore the role of emotion and of the nonuniversalizable particularity of human life.[6] But these domains, of emotion and of specific and particular relationships, are the domains historically associated with women. Hence, the rational ideal suggests that the concerns most typical of women's lives are irrelevant to the best human life and to reasoning about what to do. Lawrence Blum has described the type of philosopher whom Gilligan's work has been used to attack, the type Blum calls the "moral rationalist": "It is the male qualities whose highest expression he naturally takes as his model. In the same way it is natural for him to ignore or underplay the female qualities as they are found in his society—sympathy, compassion, emotional responsiveness. . . . The moral rationalist philosopher thus both reflects the sexual value hierarchy of his society and indirectly gives it a philosophic grounding and legitimation."[7] Not only are the concerns of women irrelevant to the rational ideal but they also may be thought to be incompatible with it. If that is so, then the rational ideal suggests that women are not capable of living moral lives.

In effect, the rational ideal suggests that the best human life and a moral life is available only to those who engage in the kind of rational reflection necessary to determine properly how to live. We have seen how such an ideal tends to exclude women's concerns from the moral life, or women themselves from the moral life, if women are thought incapable of the necessary rational reflection. As I have mentioned, the rational ideal can also be taken to exclude other persons whose lives tend not to be associated with the rational. In Aristotle's view, for example, menial laborers are not fit to be citizens of the best state, since Aristotle believes that menial labor is a deterrent to engaging in the rational activity characteristic of human beings. More broadly, the rational ideal can be taken to exclude persons who have been associated with the body and bodily functions rather than with rational activity, however rational activity is to be understood. Oppressive stereotypes of "inferior" peoples have tended to include images of their lives as determined by what is animal or bodily. This is a way in which the rational ideal can support prejudiced views of nonwhites and uneducated people.

But the fact that the rational ideal has been, or can be, used to exclude particular groups from that ideal does not show that the rational ideal is defective. Even assuming one could establish that particular groups actually possessed the characteristics on which their exclusion was based—for example, that they were more "physical" or more "compassionate"[8]—one would have to show that their having these characteristics is incompatible with the rational ideal. And even if it could be shown that having these characteristics is incompatible with living according to the rational ideal, *that* would not be sufficient to show that the rational ideal is suspect or even that it is incomplete. The problem might lie, instead, with the way these "non-rational" characteristics are being understood. It is possible that, upon examining them carefully, they may not be found worthy of emulation. The rational ideal may emerge as a more attractive model after all.

I want to examine Aristotle's picture of the rational ideal, and to explore its worthiness to serve as a model for a good human life, by looking at three groups that fail, in Aristotle's opinion, to embody the rational ideal. These groups are menial laborers, slaves, and women of varying political status. Once we see how these people fail to embody the rational ideal, we can understand more clearly what we are committed to in living according to that ideal. Then we will be in a better position to determine whether Aristotle's rational ideal is incompatible with the traits of character typically associated with women (for example, with being more caring, more compassionate, more altruistic) and whether it is incompatible with a more "physical" or "bodily" life.

I shall argue that his ideal is not incompatible with being altruistic or with performing physical labor. But, I shall claim, if altruistic traits of character and physical work are not themselves to become oppressive, they must include precisely the activities Aristotle describes as rational. I shall treat the compatibility between the rational ideal and physical work relatively briefly, since the main focus of my concern is the relationship between caring for another and being rational, as Aristotle understands it. On the view I shall propose, being caring and compassionate must be expressed within a life lived according to the rational ideal, or else these traits become destructive and unhealthy. To explicate destructive care, I use examples of contemporary women's lives, since they are often structured so as to preclude women from exercising the rational activities Aristotle most valued. Thus some of Aristotle's reservations about women's lives are sustained, though not, of course, for the reasons he offered. If my interpretation of the rational ideal is correct, and the activities Aristotle considers rational are critical components of a nonoppressive life, then we have good reason to embrace his ideal rather than to reject it.

Psychological Freedom in Aristotle's Ideal State

Aristotle recognizes different sociopolitical classes or categories of women and men. These classes are ordered along a spectrum that reflects the different degrees to which individuals have realized the capacities and traits characteristic of human beings, where these capacities and traits are understood to be rational. To the extent that one fails fully to realize these capacities and traits, one fails to be fully human. At the extreme end of this socio-political spectrum, some individuals—namely (natural) slaves—aren't really human beings at all and hence are not women and men, properly speaking.[9] Because they lack crucial rational characteristics, Aristotle thinks they can justifiably be treated differently from other individuals who more completely realize human capacities and traits. There is, in effect, a hierarchical ordering of different human natures, according to which those who completely realize their human nature rule all those who do not or cannot.

In Aristotle's ideal state there are three broad categories of men: citizens; free persons who are not citizens, including artisans, tradesmen, and day laborers[10] (for the sake of convenience, I shall refer to these persons simply as menial or manual laborers); and persons who are neither free nor citizens (slaves). Male citizens spend the major portion of their adult lives in democratic decision-making (after serving in the military when young and before becoming priests when too old). (*Politics* [hereafter *Pol*.] 1329a2–34). They are members of the assembly, members of juries, city officials of various kinds, and so on. They take turns ruling and being ruled (*Pol*. 1332b26–27; 1295b14–27). Ruling is the activity that distinguishes these men from other groups of men in the political community. The suggestion is that through participatory democracy with other citizens like themselves, they alone fully realize their characteristic human rational capacities and traits. These rational powers, associated with the rational part of the soul (*Nicomachean Ethics* [hereafter *EN*] 1139a12), consist of deciding, choosing, discriminating, judging, planning, and so forth (*EN* 1170b10ff.).[11]

Menial laborers should not, according to Aristotle, be citizens in the best state, presumably because menial labor, in Aristotle's view, impedes the full exercise of one's rational powers (cf. *Pol*. 1277b2–6; 1278a20–21). How is this so? (i) One answer might be that menial labor involves much routine and monotonous work, in which little use is made of choosing, judging, deciding, and discriminating. There is little room for the personal style and self-expression that characterize more interesting and challenging activity. But obviously this need not always be the case. Though the sculptor Pheidias counts as a menial laborer, his work involves highly sophisticated decision-making and discrimination. If his doing manual labor impedes the full expression of his rational powers, it must do so in some other way. (ii) We must consider not only the work Pheidias does but also the conditions under which he does it. Like other menial laborers, Pheidias's decision-making powers are constrained by his need to survive. He must travel to the cities where his skills are needed, and the building projects he oversees must fit the constraints imposed by city officials or private citizens. The exercise of his rational powers is limited by, and therefore dependent upon, other people's decisions and desires. In this way he does not have complete control over his own decisions and actions.

This lack of control is evidenced in at least two ways. First, the fact that Pheidias's decisions and actions are constrained by his need to earn a living may require him to compromise his moral principles. He may be "compelled" by his superiors (cf. *EN* 1110a25) to act in ways he would not ordinarily choose. His actions are then a combination of the voluntary and the involuntary (*EN* 1110a11–19). Second, even if Pheidias is not required to take "mixed" actions (*EN* 1110a11), the fact that his decisions and actions are constrained by the desires of others means that he cannot fully express his conception of what is worth sculpting, how it is to be done, and so on. He cannot design and direct the project according to his own ideas of what is interesting and important. He must accommodate his creations to the values of others.[12]

In Aristotle's view, then, the citizen and the menial laborer (in contrast to the citizen and the slave) have the same psychological capacities. What distinguishes them are the circumstances under which they choose and decide. The menial laborer does work that often does not require much decision-making. More important, however, is the fact that the laborer's concern for economic survival constrains his decision-making, in that he does not have complete control over what work he is to do and how it is to be accomplished. On the other hand, a natural slave, in Aristotle's view lacks the very capacity for deliberation and decision (*Pol.* 1260a12). So, presumably, if he were not a slave, he would not be able to control his own life even to the extent that a menial laborer can. A slave acts wholly in the interests of another person; this is why he is not free (*Pol.* 1278b32–37). To the extent that a manual laborer lacks control over his life and must act in accordance with what others desire and require of him, his life is slavish (*Rhetoric* 1367a32–33).

Indeed, to the extent that any person's life is not the product of his own decisions and desires and is overly or improperly dependent on the desires, decisions, and opinions of other people, Aristotle deems that person's life slavish. In the *Nicomachean Ethics*, for example, Aristotle is able to say of various nonvirtuous male citizens in nonideal states that their lives are slavish. Of course, it is difficult to be precise about what constitutes "too much" or the "wrong kind" of dependence on others' decisions and desires. Surely every person who is not self-sufficient is dependent on others' actions and decisions. But many forms of dependence that arise from the absence of self-sufficiency are innocuous in that they do not undermine one's status as a rational being. I may not be able to fulfill my desire for hazelnut ice cream if there is no one to make it available to me; however, because I do not produce it myself and must rely on others to do so does not render me unable to make the sorts of decisions that serve to realize my specific rational abilities or the rational abilities I share with other rational beings. What Aristotle wants to avoid, and which he thinks only the virtuous person successfully avoids, is the kind of dependence on others that impedes, rather than encourages and extends, the full realization of one's rational abilities.

Let me illustrate with some examples from the *Nicomachean Ethics*. Aristotle tells us that the inirascible person is slavish in that he is willing to accept insults to himself and to overlook insults to his family and associates (*EN* 1126a7–8). He does not have enough self-esteem to allow himself to get angry at others' ill treatment of himself, his family, and his friends. He lacks confidence in his own judgments and perceptions and will have a tendency to accept the judgments and perceptions of others as correct. Hence, he is apt to allow others to make decisions for him. Flatterers are another example of servile persons (1125a2). They want to improve their position by gaining the favor of more privileged people (*EN* 1127a7–9). To do this, they must accept the correctness of the privileged person's desires and decisions, and thus they must accept a situation in which many of their decisions are, in effect, made for them by others. Flatterers and inirascible people are in a psychological situation analogous to that of skilled menial laborers like Pheidias.

Aristotle describes intemperate people as slavish too, but not because others make decisions for them. Indeed, intemperates may control their lives in just the ways that inirascible people and flatterers do not. They may make their own decisions, and they may be able to implement their decisions without having to accommodate others' preferences and interests. But they misuse their rational powers and undermine their development in that the activities they enjoy make too little use of these powers. Intemperate people enjoy physical sensations rather than the discriminating and choosing that surrounds tasting and touching (*EN* 1118a32–b1). Their psychological situation is like that of menial laborers whose work is routine and monotonous. There is so little decision-making going on that even natural slaves, who lack the powers of deliberation and decision, can experience the intemperate person's enjoyments (*EN* 1177a7).

In contrast to these various slavish types is the male citizen of Aristotle's ideal state. He is different even from a Pheidias who has full control over the specific sculptural projects he is engaged in. On Aristotle's view, not even such a Pheidias would have fully realized his powers of choosing and deciding. The male citizens of Aristotle's ideal state fully realize their characteristic human powers in the political activity of democratic decision-making. They realize their human powers fully in these circumstances because the deliberations involved in democratic decision-making are comprehensive and overarching. Here the exercise of the human powers is not restricted to specific decisions about what statues to sculpt, what materials to use, and so on. Rather, these are higher-level decisions about what is best for the community itself. So they would include decisions about other, more specific activities (cf. *EN* 1094a27). The exercise of the human powers is *generalized* and extended to cover virtually every aspect of human life, including, for example, questions of war and peace, finance, legislation, public works, cultural projects, and sexual matters.[13]

As far as men are concerned, then, we can determine a ranking from the complete human being who is able to actualize his powers fully because he is a politically active citizen of the ideal state, to a slave who cannot actualize the characteristic human powers because he is without them to begin with. In between are various types of incomplete, slavish persons, ranging from wealthy aristocrats (in nonideal states) to manual laborers.

What about the women who are the wives or companions of these different men, the wives of free citizens in the ideal state, the wives of free citizens in nonideal states, the wives of manual laborers, and the female companions of slaves? (I do not discuss unmarried daughters, since, for our purposes, their situations will not differ markedly from those of married women and married female slaves.)

Although Plato seems to have had moderately progressive views about some women (namely, those he thought capable of ruling the state),[14] Aristotle's views on women's nature are, without exception, objectionable. Aristotle claims that free women cannot be fully actualized human beings, no matter what their political status, since they are, like slaves, naturally defective. Although free women do not lack the capacity for deliberation and decision, as slaves do, their capacity for deliberation, Aristotle says, is not "authoritative" (*Pol.* 1260a13). Women are contrasted with (presumably male, free) children, whose deliberative capacities are merely "incomplete" (*ateles, Pol.* 1260a14). The deliberative capacity in women, then, we may assume, is permanently stunted. Unlike free, male children, no amount of education and practice in decision-making, and no change in their economic or social circumstances, will enable women to deliberate properly about what is best. They may give too much weight to what is pleasant or to what appears to be good. In effect, a woman may give over the rule of her soul to its non-rational part and thereby endanger the proper functioning of the household (cf. 1254b4ff.).[15] Hence, decisions about what is best must be made for her by men. A free woman's life will always, then, be slavish, since her life is not controlled by her own decisions.

Because natural slaves lack one of the features characteristic of human beings, they cannot, strictly speaking, be human beings, and hence they cannot be women or men—that is, they cannot be adult members of the human species. (I say they cannot "strictly speaking" be human beings, because it seems clear that Aristotle cannot actually deny that slaves are human beings. This is suggested, for example, by *EN* 1161a34ff., where Aristotle admits that there can be friendship and justice between masters and slaves "to the extent that a slave is a human being."[16]) But despite this species difference between free persons and slaves, it is hard to see the extent to which the life of any free woman is relevantly different, in regard to her departure from the ideal of fully realized human being, from that of a slave (male or female). Although a free woman presumably can deliberate about how best to carry out the decisions of her husband, or father, her actions are ultimately determined by the decisions of free men, as are those of slaves. Perhaps this is why Aristotle does not bother to discuss female slaves in any detail. As far as their legal status is concerned, it is the same as that of male slaves. As far as their psychological status is concerned, it seems no different, relative to the ideal, from that of free women.

Is Aristotle's Ideal Exploitative or Masculine?

I have sketched a view of psychological freedom in Aristotle, according to which a complete human being is one who fully realizes his characteristically human powers (the powers of judging, choosing, deciding, planning, discriminating, and so on) in the political activity of democratic decision-making. Democratic decision-making is characterized by a political structure that is egalitarian (each citizen participates equally in decision-making) and comprehensive (each citizen participates equally in the same, broad type of decision-making). Citizens participate in decisions about matters that fundamentally affect the course of their lives. These higher-level decisions influence the lower-level decisions individuals make about the specific life plans they pursue (cf. *EN* 1094a27).

Two questions arise about the life Aristotle admires and recommends. First, does the realization of this ideal life *require* that some segments of the political community exploit the labor of other segments so that they (the exploiters) have time for the decision-making involved in ruling? And, second, is this ideal life inherently masculine? If we answer either question affirmatively, we have good reason to reject Aristotle's recommendations. I think there is a fairly straightforward response to the first question. I shall indicate that briefly here.[17] Most of my attention will be directed to the second question.

Aristotle believes that the realization of the life he admires does require that rulers exploit menial laborers, since he believes that the conditions under which menial labor is performed will involve the laborer in relations of dependence that prevent the full actualization of the rational powers. Hence, rulers cannot be menial laborers. As I have suggested, Aristotle is not crazy to believe this. But it is important to distinguish between a menial life (a life whose main activity is menial labor performed under conditions of dependence) and a life that may involve menial labor but is not restricted to it. Aristotle may be correct to think that a life restricted to menial labor (where such labor can be monotonous, routine, exhausting, and carried out for the sake of an end external to it—housework is a good modern example) will demand little use of the human rational powers and will impede the development of the type of character one needs to exhibit the moral virtues. But surely he would not be correct to think that engaging in some menial labor, as part of a life that is devoted to the full expression of the rational powers, will have a devastating effect upon character. Indeed, as he notes at *Pol.* 1333a9–11: "Actions do not differ as honorable or dishonorable in themselves so much as in the end and intention of them."[18] Just as citizens take turns ruling and being ruled, then, they could take their turns at menial labor, while preserving for themselves the type of life that Aristotle considers fully human. Thus, as far as I can tell, the best kind of life, from Aristotle's point of view, does not require, even given his views about the dangers of menial labor, that some persons take up lives of menial labor to provide the necessities for others who live political lives.[19]

I have considered whether the ideal described by Aristotle is necessarily exploitative. I have argued that if citizens determine how the menial labor is to be carried out, they will not involve themselves in the dehumanizing relations of dependence Aristotle found so objectionable. And if the menial labor is distributed among the citizens in ways so as not to absorb much of any one citizen's time, then there is no reason to think that the possible monotony of some menial labor will impede the continuing exercise of the human rational powers.

One point should perhaps be emphasized. Aristotle's citizens enjoy the complete exercise of the human rational powers that participation in ruling provides. Therefore they want to avoid both the slavishness of a menial life and the slavishness of a Pheidian life. For, as we have seen, Pheidias's life, though involving sophisticated and subtle uses of the human powers, remains seriously limited and incomplete. Just as Aristotle is not crazy to think that a life of routine menial labor is incompatible with his rational ideal, so too he is not crazy to think that a "physical" life of the Pheidian type is also defective and incomplete. But this does not commit Aristotle to the view that physical activity itself is dehumanizing. There is nothing to prevent Aristotle's democratic decision-makers from being artisans and tradespeople, as well as farmers and warriors.

I now consider the second issue I raised above—that is, the issue of whether Aristotle's ideal is masculine, and, if so, whether this is reason to reject it. I take it that the ideal is considered masculine because the life considered most worth living is the life in which the characteristic human powers, considered as rational powers, are fully realized. Since, as I suggested at the outset, reason and rational deliberation have, in the history of Western thought, been associated primarily with men, and since the non-rational (which includes passions, emotions, and feelings, all of which are thought to have some relation to the body) have been associated with women, to recommend a way of life that praises and prizes reason over all else is implicitly at least to denigrate what has traditionally been associated with women. And, historically, to accept a view that prizes and praises reason above all else provides room not only for sexist views but also for racist views—views that denigrate other peoples because they have traditionally been thought more bodily or more physical than white males. Indeed, we have seen this tendency to be true of Aristotle, whose view of slaves and women as less than fully rational enables him to justify their low status in the political community.

I want to consider whether Aristotle's view of the rational, in particular, requires a devaluation of the non-rational side of the human being. This might be true if his view were a simple one, in which reason "rules" in some straightforward way over the passions, emotions, and feelings. But his view is not simple. I shall suggest, instead, that in Aristotle's virtuous person, the proper development of the nonrational side of the person can be seen to constrain and limit the operations of the rational side. In effect, it is as if to say that the rational part of the virtuous person's soul cannot work properly unless it is properly guided by the non-rational part.

Both Plato and Aristotle insist that the non-rational part of the soul (which includes appetites, feelings, emotions, and passions) must be educated—in the case of Plato, before one can begin to think sufficiently abstractly ultimately to see the Form of the Good, and, in the case of Aristotle, before one can learn how to deliberate properly about the contents of the best life (before, that is, one can acquire practical wisdom). For Aristotle, many of the individual virtues involve feeling or responding in the appropriate way. For example, it is a vice to take too much pleasure in eating, drinking, and sexual activity; it is also a vice to take insufficient pleasure in these activities. It is a vice to get too angry, or angry at the wrong times, or angry toward the wrong persons, and so on. But it is also a vice not to get angry or to exhibit anger at all, or not to do so when the situation is appropriate for anger. It is a vice to feel too much fear or not enough, or to feel it on the wrong occasions or toward the wrong persons. Reason, by itself, cannot create these feelings; nor can reason, by itself, destroy them. If reason could create or destroy feelings, then Aristotle would not be faced with the problem of *akrasia* (*EN* VII.1–3). Thus the first things to note about Aristotle's rational ideal are that it does not involve the suppression of feeling and emotion and passion and that if reason does rule over passion, its rule does not consist either in producing or in destroying passion. Nor does it consist simply in offering some general directives to the nonrational side of the soul, since there are no rules or rational guidelines for determining how much of an emotion or feeling is appropriate in different situations (*EN* 1109b21–24).

More important, however, is the psychological basis for all the different virtues. I have argued elsewhere[20] that they can be viewed as expressions of what Aristotle calls true self-love. The virtuous person is characterized by a love of what is most himself—that is, by a love of the exercise of the human rational powers, where these are the powers of judging, choosing, deciding, and discriminating that I have listed before (*EN* 1168b34–1169a3; cf. 1168a7–9 and 1170b10ff.). In enjoying the exercise of his rational powers, the true self-lover enjoys rational activity in general rather than a particular kind of rational activity. His life is therefore broadly based; it is not devoted to the pursuit of specialized goals or to the completion of specialized projects. The true self-lover enjoys the intricacies and subtleties of different intellectual endeavors and also the intricacies and subtleties of endeavors not considered intellectual: he enjoys playing, or watching, a good game of baseball or tennis; he delights in telling a story others will appreciate or in finding just the right gift for a special occasion; he enjoys pleasing and benefiting his friends.

In loving what is characteristic of himself, the virtuous person enjoys who he is and what he can do. His self-love is thus a kind of self-esteem and self-confidence. But as my examples of self-expression have indicated, true self-love is to be distinguished from the self-love that we associate with selfishness and that we normally condemn (*EN* IX.8). Given that the virtuous person enjoys rational activity in a general way, he is able to take pleasure both from the exercise of his own rational powers and from others' exercise of these powers.

The self-love Aristotle admires becomes even more generalized and more stable when a person exercises the human rational powers in political activity where decision-making is shared and evenly distributed. Self-love is more generalized because its source, the exercise of the human rational powers, is now extended to cover comprehensive, higher-level decisions, as well as decisions about activities specific to one's own life. And because the decision-making has been extended in this way, it is flexible and less vulnerable to changes in circumstance and fortune than a more specialized exercise of rational activity would be. Democratic decision-makers can adjust to changes in circumstance and can redirect the use of their abilities to meet these changes. Hence the more stable and continuous their self-esteem will be. But for someone whose decision-making powers have been focused on a particular activity, self-esteem is tied to the success of that particular activity. Hence, this person's self-esteem is precarious and easily upset. This person is like Aristotle's professional soldiers who, though (improperly) confident from past success, turn and run when circumstances are against them (*EN* 1116b15–17).

The enjoyment that a person takes in who he is and in what he does, though its source and basis is the exercise of the rational powers, is not itself an instance of such exercise. Although enjoyment may be produced by rational deliberation, the pleasure taken in rational deliberation, like the enjoyment we take in any other activity, is nonrational. This affects the extent to which my enjoyment can be altered by rational deliberation, even if rational deliberation is what I enjoy and even if that deliberation produces *rational desires* for what I enjoy. When, for example, I want to play tennis because I enjoy it, I desire to play because I find it pleasant, not because I believe playing tennis is good for my health. In this sense, my desire to play tennis is non-rational. I might also want to play tennis because I think it is good for my health, and I might have reached this conclusion on the basis of deliberation about what conduces to my good overall. The desire to play tennis that arises from such deliberation is therefore rational, and it can be altered by further such deliberation. If I cease to believe that playing tennis is good for my health, I will cease to *want* to play tennis for that reason. My newly acquired beliefs produce a rational aversion to tennis. But no such deliberations will undermine my general non-rational desire to play tennis. If I somehow come to believe (correctly) that I no longer enjoy playing tennis, my having that belief is an indication that I have already stopped liking tennis. In this case, my beliefs do not produce my non-rational aversion. It comes about in some other way. The same holds for my non-rational enjoyment of rational activity itself, which, on Aristotle's view, accounts for my having self-love.

On the assumption, then, that Aristotle's virtues require self-love and that they can be understood as different ways in which self-love is expressed, being virtuous is importantly a matter of having one's non-rational desires properly structured. Without the appropriate background of non-rational desire, the agent will not perceive correctly the nature of situations calling for practical decision and action and will thus respond in ways that Aristotle describes as non-virtuous rather than virtuous. Aristotle's notoriously vague remarks at *EN* 1144a34–36 are consistent with the idea that the structure of one's non-rational desires crucially affects one's ability to perceive practical situations correctly: "[The highest end and the best good] is apparent only to the good person; for vice perverts us and produces false views about the origins of actions."

There is a second aspect to the role of the non-rational desires in Aristotle's conception of virtue. The enjoyment taken in the expression of the human powers in cooperative democratic activity not only produces a stable self-confidence; it also produces stable feelings of friendship between the parties involved in the decision-making. Feelings of friendship arise from the fact that the democratic activity is self-expressive, that it is beneficial to the parties engaged in it, and that it is itself enjoyable (*Rhet.* 1381a30 and *EN* 1168a7–9). Friendship includes a care and concern that friends have for each other for each other's own sake (*EN* 1155b31), a tendency to rejoice and take pleasure in each other's good fortune, and a tendency to help when friends need assistance (*EN* IX.4). Feelings of friendship are maintained over time by continuing the activities that originally produced them or the comparable activities that have come to sustain them. Like enjoyment itself, friendly feelings are not produced by beliefs about what is best or about what contributes to my overall good. They thus belong to the non-rational part of the soul.

In the case of democratic decision-making, the relevant feelings of friendship are particularly stable. A combination of factors explains why this is so. First, the feelings of friendship are produced by a form of self-expression that is especially enduring in that it is overarching and generalized. They are not the product of the expression of some contingent features of the self that might disappear in a change of circumstance or fortune. Hence, the friendship is not "coincidental" and easily dissolved (*EN* 1156a14–21). Second, the democratic decision-makers share their most basic values and goals in that they are committed to engaging in cooperative activities that promote and sustain the development and exercise of the human powers (cf. *Pol.* 1280a31–34). Thus each decision-maker can view the deliberations of the others as expressions of his thinking and reasoning self (*EN* 1168b34–1169a3). Deliberators identify with each other's decisions and actions, so that each deliberator's actions become the expression of the others' rational activity. This form of self-expression, now even more generalized, is especially enduring. Citizens in the ideal state are thus tied together by feelings of friendship that are long lasting and strong.

The care, concern, and sympathetic attachment that partly constitute these ties of friendship encourage a healthy dependence among citizens. Citizens are not uninvolved with each other or contemptuous of each other in the way several of Aristotle's vicious types are (*EN* IV.3). Nor are they overly concerned with others' opinions—that is, concerned in a way that would upset their self-esteem if they were to face criticisms or obstacles. Their concern for each other does not produce a self-destructive dependence; their autonomy does not preclude enduring ties of association. Along with the self-love of virtuous citizens, these ties of friendship will influence what citizens perceive to be central to the type of life they want to maintain. They will not act to jeopardize the activities and relationships they value and enjoy.

In summary, citizens' understanding of what is best to do, their rational deliberations about how to live and act, take place within the limits imposed by educated passions and feelings. They take place within the limits imposed by a stable self-esteem that derives from an enjoyment in rational activity and within the limits imposed by strong ties of friendship that involve care and concern for other citizens for their own sakes. If this is a rational ideal, it is one in which the proper operation of reason is guided and constrained by feeling and emotion, that is, by the nonrational side of the soul.

Feminism and Reason

I have argued that Aristotle offers a picture of a rational ideal that does not exclude the emotions, passions, and feelings. In particular, the proper operation of reason is limited and constrained by the specific feelings constitutive of true self-love and civic friendship. In describing this ideal, I have not discussed the nature of the actual deliberations virtuous persons will make in specific practical contexts. But it is reasonable to suppose that virtuous persons will recognize the importance of producing and sustaining true self-love and stable ties of civic friendship that are based on enduring features of the self. When citizens come to decide how best to govern their city, these values, one would think, would be paramount in their deliberations. Specific decisions would be made with a commitment to, and appreciation of, the critical role these values play in the lives of every citizen. This does not mean that all civic decisions will be made from an "impartial" perspective, where that is taken to imply that a consideration of the specific circumstances of particular individuals is inappropriate. Nor does it mean that deliberating from such a perspective is never appropriate.

I now want to discuss in more detail the nature of the care and concern I have attributed to Aristotle's virtuous citizens. For it is "care and concern" that have come to be associated with feminist ethics and women's moral experience, where such care includes an interest in preserving relationships and commitments to others. In feminist ethics, an interest in applying impartial rules or comprehensive principles becomes secondary.

Assuming it is true that women's moral experiences focus more on questions of care and on preserving relationships and commitments, ought we to accept these experiences as a general model for our behavior toward others or as a more specific model of our moral behavior? What type of care and concern is appropriate? Is care and concern always to be preferred over more emotionally detached ways of relating to others?[21]

The care and concern that constitutes a virtuous citizen's friendship with other citizens resembles in important ways the care that Aristotle's "complete friends" have for each other. Complete friends, according to Aristotle, are virtuous, know each other well, and spend much of their time together in shared activities (*EN* IX.10). As a result, it is not possible to have many complete friends, whereas political (or citizen) friendship holds among many. Yet, even though citizen friendship and complete friendship have different characteristics, it is not hard to see a resemblance between them in regard to the care that the friends extend toward each other. For though citizen friends may not know each other to the extent that complete friends do, and though they might not spend much time together, they know each other well enough to know that they share the major aims and values that guide the decisions and practices of their community. Citizen friends perceive each other as Aristotle's complete friends do, that is, as "another oneself" (*EN* 1166a32), meaning that they value and enjoy about each other what they value and enjoy about themselves. They take pleasure, for example, in the exercise of each other's rational powers as they do in their own. In this way they are like each other and take enjoyment in the exercise of the powers they share. Each is, then, a self-lover who takes pleasure in the self-love of the other, since the exercise of self-love in one is like the exercise of self-love in the other. Their ties of friendly feeling are firm and strong and long lasting because they are grounded in the pleasure they take in who the other is as a realized human being.

The care and concern they have for each other comes from the affection that arises from their sharing in each other's rational activity. That is, they share overarching and higher-level interests and goals, and they each participate in the activities associated with these higher-level interests. This does not mean that they share each specific interest and desire.[22] The contents of their individual life-plans might be surprisingly divergent. But each has an individual plan that realizes the human powers in a specific way, and this fact is a source of enjoyment for them. So each takes an interest in the other's interests, rejoices in the other's successes, grieves with the other's losses, and so on.

None lives through the lives of the others or acquires a basis for self-esteem and self-confidence through the activities of the others. Each is independent in the sense that each enjoys the activities in her individual life-plan as well as the higher-level activities her plan shares with the plans of her friends. None is dependent on the praise and admiration of specific individuals for the maintenance of self-love, so each can endure the loss of particular friendships. Aristotle's citizens are likely to be involved in a number of relationships, since their shared general commitments and goals give them a basis for association and affection. Their emotional eggs are not all in one basket, and hence their sense of their own value and importance is not undermined by the loss of specific relationships.

The care they extend to others, then, in times of difficulty and need, is not likely to involve a sacrifice of what they take to be valuable for the sake of someone else. Care does not take the form of altruistic action, where this is thought to require self-denial or a willingness to meet another's needs without consideration for one's own. Thus, among Aristotle's citizens, one would not find relations of unhealthy dependence in which some gain a sense of their own worth only through the assistance they give to others.[23]

But in our contemporary, non-Aristotelian socioeconomic circumstances, women who live with men are often in precisely this position of unhealthy dependence in regard to them. Given the still prevailing ideology, which does not consider it deplorable that most employed women have low-paying, dead-end jobs and even that some women choose to remain unemployed, women tend to find themselves in positions of low self-esteem. Even if they are employed, they are usually economically dependent on men.[24] This dependence undermines the realization of their decision-making powers in various ways. Important family decisions, for example, are often left up to the men on whom women depend. Even women's decision-making authority over matters connected with child care and household maintenance is upset by the extent to which the market has successfully penetrated the household. Many household decisions are now made for women by men through commercials in which men promote one product or another. Women are thought to be good (that is, easily manipulated) consumers, and most commercials are directed toward women, because women often lack the self-esteem necessary to make their own decisions about how to provide the proper physical environment for their families.[25]

These problems apply to the emotional environment as well. In the context of unequal economic power, whatever care and compassion is extended to family members is likely to be distorted and unhealthy. Since family relationships are often the only means through which women obtain a sense of their own worth, preserving these relationships may take place at the cost of encouraging psychologically harmful ways of treating family members. Care within the context of unequal power relations can generate more harm than good.

In such circumstances, where the preservation of a relationship may take priority over the content of the relationship, kindness and emotional supportiveness may be offered when other emotional responses might be more appropriate. Women in these circumstances, for example, may tend not to show anger, at least toward those family members with power and control over decision-making. Women may get angry at children, since this anger does not threaten the relationships that sustain women's sense of self-worth. But women in subordinate circumstances who have little self-confidence will be much less likely to feel that they are in a position to judge adult male family members. But a belief that another has acted wrongly or improperly is part of what provokes anger; therefore, to feel angry, one must have at least enough self-esteem to be able to judge another's actions as improper.[26] But judging another in this way is difficult for persons who have survived their oppressive circumstances by encouraging calm relations with those who have power over them. A lack of confidence in their own assessments will make them tend to accept the judgments and perceptions of others as correct, just as Aristotle's inirascible persons do. Kindness in such circumstances would seem only to sustain inequality, to obscure recognition of what is best, and to undermine further the decision-making powers of the person who shows kindness.[27] In these ways, care within the context of unequal power relations can harm both the person who gives it and the person to whom it is given.

These examples suggest that altruistic actions can be damaging when undertaken in circumstances in which the altruistic person lacks self-esteem. By showing kindness and compassion when other responses might be more appropriate, the kind person can act to sustain oppressive and unhealthy ways of relating to others. Through kindness, the kind person can make the acquisition of self-esteem even more difficult. Kindness seems least likely to damage oneself or another, however, when it is offered from a position of healthy independence. But healthy independence is precisely the psychological condition of Aristotle's virtuous person, who has true self-love. Because such a person has the appropriate confidence in who he is, he need not live through the achievements of another. This kind of dependent relationship will not be of interest to him, and he will not feel the need to act in ways to develop and sustain such a relationship. If kindness can be thought of as a concern for another's good for that person's own sake and as a willingness to act to contribute to that good, then Aristotle's virtuous person will act kindly, because this is the attitude he has toward fellow citizens. Yet Aristotle's virtuous citizen knows that another's good is not equivalent simply to what another wants. He knows that another's good includes the performance of activities that will nurture and sustain the other's self-love. So Aristotle's virtuous citizen recognizes that showing concern for another's good for the other's own sake may take all sorts of forms, only some of which will look like mere behavioral niceness.

I have been suggesting that if compassion and a concern for relationships constitutes some kind of model or ideal, it is not a simple one according to which we simply act to preserve the relationship or act to help another achieve what he might want. If compassion and concern are directed toward another's good for that person's sake, then for them to be proper objects of an ideal, they must operate against the background of some sound recognition of what another's good consists in. If not, compassion and concern can serve to promote oppressive or destructive relationships. Moreover, if the compassionate person is an ideal, she must be someone whose concern for another is ungrudging and noninstrumental. Aristotle's virtuous person is most likely to offer that kind of concern, since she is secure enough in who she is not to begrudge others' successes and not to rejoice spitefully in others' losses.

Aristotle's ideal has been considered masculine because it deems the best life to be that which fully realizes the rational powers characteristic of human beings. I have argued that Aristotle's emphasis on rational powers should not deter anyone, particularly feminists, from embracing his model. Although Aristotle organizes the best life around the pleasures of rational activity, this does not commit him to a model in which the non-rational is suppressed or even subordinated. As I have argued, the realization of the virtuous person's rational powers are constrained by properly educated nonrational feelings and emotions. Moreover, Aristotle offers a way to explain how reason and emotion (and passion and feeling) can operate together to produce psychologically strong and healthy individuals—individuals who take pleasure from their own lives and from the lives of others, who are caring and concerned but not in ways that are destructive of their own self-esteem, who are independent while retaining strong and enduring ties of friendship and relationship. He offers us a view of compassion and care that is positive and constructive, not oppressive and debilitating.

There are various ways in which reason can be offered as an ideal. I think Aristotle's model of how to organize one's life around the pleasures of rational activity is worthy of emulation by both men and women.[28]

Notes

1. The title also suggests that the organizers thought it appropriate, even in this special context, to refer to the three of us as "girls." I leave aside the problems associated with the use of this term in relation to adult women.

2. For Aristotle's views on women, see *Generation of Animals* 728a17ff., 732a1ff., 775a15; *Nicomachean Ethics* [hereafter *EN*] 1162a19–27; *Politics* [hereafter *Pol.*] 1259b28–1260a24, 1277b20. For Kant, see *Observations on the Feeling of the Beautiful and Sublime*, sec. 3. For Hobbes, see *Leviathan*, chs. 19–20.

3. For a useful discussion of these issues, see Elizabeth V. Spelman, *Inessential Woman: Problems of Exclusion in Feminist Thought* (Boston: Beacon Press, 1988), esp. ch. 5.

4. See Carol Gilligan, *In a Different Voice: Psychological Theory and Women's Development* (Cambridge, Mass.: Harvard University Press, 1982). In her more recent writings, Gilligan has softened her position, to claim that though women can have the "justice" perspective as well as the "care" perspective, men are more likely to have only the "justice" perspective. See "Adolescent Development Reconsidered," in *Mapping the Moral Domain*, ed. C. Gilligan, J. V. Ward, and J. McLean Taylor (Cambridge, Mass.: Harvard University Press, 1988). For the influence of Gilligan's work on moral theory, see Lawrence Blum, "Gilligan and Kohlberg: Implications for Moral Theory," *Ethics* 98, 3 (1988): 472–491; and Eva Feder Kittay and Diana T. Meyers, eds., *Women and Moral Theory* (Totowa, N.J.: Rowman and Littlefield, 1987). For a different approach to these issues, see Owen Flanagan and Kathryn Jackson, "Justice, Care, and Gender: The Kohlberg-Gilligan Debate Revisited," *Ethics* 97, 3, (1987): 622–637.

5. See, for example, John Rawls's account of the principles of justice as chosen in special circumstances of rational deliberation in *A Theory of Justice* (Cambridge, Mass.: Harvard University Press, 1971).

6. For a discussion of the role of "particularity" in the moral life, see Lawrence Blum, "Moral Perception and Particularity," forthcoming in *Ethics* 101 (1991): 701–725, and the works cited therein.

7. Lawrence Blum, "Kant's and Hegel's Moral Rationalism: A Feminist Perspective," *Canadian Journal of Philosophy* 12 (1982): 296–297.

8. Claudia Card questions whether it is appropriate to associate care and compassion more with women than with men, and offers some helpful criticisms of the care perspective in "Women's Voices and Ethical Ideals: Must We Mean What We Say?" *Ethics* 99, 1 (1988): 125–135. See also Catherine G. Greeno and Eleanor E. Maccoby, "How Different Is the 'Different Voice'?" and Carol Gilligan's reply in *Signs* 11, 2 (1986): 310–316.

9. For considerations in favor of the view that even natural slaves are men and women for Aristotle, see W. W. Fortenbaugh, "Aristotle on Slaves and Women," in *Articles on Aristotle*, vol. 2, ed. Jonathan Barnes, Malcolm Schofield, and Richard Sorabji (London: Duckworth, 1977), p. 136.

10. For an enumeration of the various different types of non-citizens in Aristotle's ideal state and for a discussion of their legal status, see David Keyt, "Distributive Justice in Aristotle's *Ethics* and *Politics*," *Topoi* 4 (1985): 23–45.

11. What to make of Aristotle's views in *EN* X.7–8 and how to integrate them into the rest of the *EN* and *Pol.* are not matters I shall discuss here. I shall be concerned only with Aristotle's broadly based view of human good, which includes the goods of social, political, and family life (*EN* 1097b8–11), as well as various intellectual goods.

12. It should be clear that Aristotle's implied and stated reservations about manual labor are not dissimilar from some of Marx's criticisms of wage labor under capitalism, in particular, from Marx's view that such labor alienates the worker from the activity of production and from his species-being. See *The Economic and Philosophic Manuscripts of 1844*, in vol. 3 of Karl Marx and Friedrich Engels, *Collected Works* (New York: International Publishers, 1971–1978), pp. 274–277, and *Communist Manifesto*, vol. 6 of *Collected Works*, passim.

13. I discuss the nature of these higher-level decisions in more detail in "Politics as Soul-Making: Aristotle on Becoming Good," *Philosophia* 20, 1–2 (July 1990): 167–193.

14. For a helpful discussion of Plato's views on women, see Julia Annas, "Plato's *Republic* and Feminism," *Philosophy* 51 (1976): 307–321; and her *Introduction to Plato's Republic* (Oxford: Clarendon Press, 1981), pp. 181–185.

15. Fortenbaugh draws a similar conclusions in "Aristotle on Women and Slaves," p. 138.

16. I use the translation by Terence Irwin of Aristotle's *Nicomachean Ethics* (Indianapolis: Hackett Publishing, 1985).

17. I follow, in broad outline, the more detailed argument for the same conclusion offered by Terence Irwin in *Aristotle's First Principles* (Oxford: Clarendon Press, 1988), pp. 411–416.

18. As translated by B. Jowett in the Revised Oxford Translation, vol. 2, ed. Jonathan Barnes (Princeton, N.J.: Princeton University Press, 1984).

19. It is not clear that one could provide the same type of argument for Plato. This is in part, I think, because the content of the good life is less well articulated in Plato than in Aristotle and also because, however we are to understand the content of the good life, it does not include democratic decision-making as a good in itself. For the philosopher-rulers, ruling is a burden they would prefer to be without, since they would prefer to be without the responsibilities and activities that take them away from a continual contemplation and love of the Forms. They accept the burdens of ruling only because there is no other way to replicate the beauty they see in the Forms. Although it is best for the state as a whole that they rule, their interest in ruling is purely instrumental. And since menial labor is often monotonous and routine, requiring little use of the rational powers. it would be inefficient for rulers to take it up. It is therefore better left to others.

20. In "Virtue and Self-Love in Aristotle's Ethics," *Canadian Journal of Philosophy* 11, 4 (December 1981): 633–651, and in "The Pleasure of Virtue in Aristotle's Moral Theory," *Pacific Philosophical Quarterly* 66, 1 –2, (January-April 1985): 93–110.

21. See Card, "Women's Voices and Ethical Ideals"; Greeno and Maccoby, "How Different Is the 'Different Voice'?"

22. For a related discussion, see Sharon Bishop, "Love and Dependency," in *Philosophy and Women*, ed. S. Bishop and M. Weinzweig (Belmont, Calif.: Wadsworth, 1979), pp. 147–154.

23. Cf. Nancy Chodorow's description of healthy dependence in "Family Structure and Feminine Personality," in *Woman, Culture, and Society*, ed. Michelle Rosaldo and Louise Lamphere (Stanford, Calif.: Stanford University Press, 1974), pp. 43–66, esp. pp. 60–63; and in *The Reproduction of Mothering: Psychoanalysis and the Sociology of Gender* (Berkeley: University of California Press, 1978), pp. 211ff.

24. For current wage differentials between full-time working women and men, see U.S. Department of Labor, *Employment and Earnings: July 1987* (Washington, D.C.: Government Printing Office, 1987).

25. See Margaret Benston, "The Political Economy of Women's Liberation," in *Feminist Frameworks*, 2d ed., ed. Alison Jaggar and Paula Rothenberg (New York: McGraw-Hill, 1984), pp. 239–247, esp. pp. 244–245.

26. For further discussion of anger in the context of unequal power relations, see Elizabeth V. Spelman, "Anger and Insubordination," in *Women, Knowledge, and Reality*, ed. Ann Garry and Marilyn Pearsall (Boston: Unwin Hyman, 1989), pp. 263–273; and Friedrich Nietzsche, *On the Genealogy of Morals*, tr. Walter Kaufman and R. J. Hollingdale (New York: Vintage, 1967), passim.

27. For more discussion of these and related points, see L. Blum et al., "Altruism and Women's Oppression," in Bishop and Weinzweig, eds., *Philosophy and Women*, pp. 190–200; and John Stuart Mill, *On the Subjection of Women* (Cambridge: MIT Press, 1970), ch. 2.

28. I am grateful to David Copp, Jean Hampton, Janet Levin, and the editors of this volume for helpful comments on earlier versions of this paper.

2

CARTESIAN REASON AND GENDERED REASON

MARGARET ATHERTON

The concept of reason has been used in a disturbing fashion to mark a gender distinction. We have, for example, on the one hand, the man of reason and, on the other, the woman of passion. It has been the concern of many feminists to reject this distinction and, in particular, to reject the implication that women are irrational or driven solely by their emotions. For there is an evaluation built into the distinction that to be governed by reason is good, whereas being swayed by emotion is not so good. Such feminists accept a general conception of reason as the predominant human characteristic and share the positive evaluation attached to it. They have argued that the problem lies in the stereotypical understanding of the nature of women and have assumed that the concept of reason is itself gender-neutral.

More recently, however, some feminists have sought, not to reject, but to embrace such distinctions as that between reason and passion, arguing that what must be rejected is the evaluation connected with the distinction. They have argued that the problem is not so much with our understanding of the nature of women as it is with the concept of reason. Reason, they maintain, is a concept that has been constructed with a masculine bias. The characteristics of rationality are not gender-neutral but stereotypically masculine. The result has been to exclude and to denigrate women by labeling irrational those ways of thinking that are stereotypically feminine. The solution, according to these feminists, is not so much to reevaluate our understanding of women as it is to reevaluate the concept of reason itself to allow room for those characteristics that have been rejected as feminine and hence as unworthy of the man of reason. The result will be not only to allow women to gain new respect even when they make use of ways of thinking that are identified as feminine, but also to permit new methodologies into disciplines that have heretofore been restricted by masculine standards.[1]

One way to show that the concept of reason, and the standards of masculinity dependent upon it, are constructions has been to show that they are not historically invariant. Because the high evaluation given to reason is often taken to be a hallmark of seventeenth-century thought, the process that denies rationality to women is often traced back to this period and, in particular, to the work of René Descartes, whose views of reason were very influential during this time. Genevieve Lloyd has argued that Descartes's account of human thinking provided the categories that led to the separation of women and rationality.[2] Susan Bordo has claimed that Descartes's achievement was to introduce a new understanding of the nature of reason—nothing less, in fact, than a rebirth of reason in a masculine form.[3] Bordo links the process that gave rise to this masculine reconceptualization of thought with what she perceives as an increasing gynophobia during this period. According to Lloyd and Bordo, the categories of thought laid down under the influence of Descartes are said to have played a forceful and transforming role in the service of the subordination of women.

A closer study of seventeenth-century thought, however, suggests that the situation is somewhat more complicated. The seventeenth century bears witness to a very interesting, if not to say remarkable, phenomenon. An unprecedented number of women found their voices in print.[4] Many of these women chose to write on philosophical topics, and, among philosophers, it was not unusual for the great men of the period to have women as protégées. Descartes himself, for example, entered into correspondence with several women, most notably Princess Elizabeth of Bohemia. Of even greater interest, perhaps, are those women, like Mary Astell and Damaris Lady Masham, who wrote about the status of women.[5] What seems clear is that their interest in improving the condition of women was not fueled, as was the case with later feminists, by any general beliefs about equal human rights. Instead, what encouraged them to argue in support of women's intellectual capacities was precisely the concept of reason that could be found in Descartes.[6] Ruth Perry has gone so far as to call Astell a Cartesian; and Masham, although no Cartesian, employs a concept of reason not that different from the one used by Astell.[7] Thus it has been argued that it is the Cartesianism of the seventeenth century that is responsible for the feminist impulses at that time.

The question that now comes to mind is, How is it that the same texts can be said to have given rise both to a decline in the status of women and to arguments for improving their status? How can Descartes's concept of reason be seen both as having deprived women of a mind of their own and as having encouraged them to take control of their own minds? What is at stake here is the nature of the concept of reason that is being attributed to Descartes and that is claimed to have had such important effects. For linking Cartesianism with a masculine notion of reason is a loaded claim to make, and one with troubling consequences, because of the many roles Descartes plays for philosophers. On the one hand, Descartes has come to symbolize much that is thought to be central to contemporary philosophy, with its stress on carefully reasoned, rigorous argument; but on the other, Descartes's positions on particular issues have been rejected, as they have been since the seventeenth century, much more than they have been accepted.

When Cartesianism is construed broadly, as a style of argument, then for one to say that Descartes embodies a masculine form of reason is frequently taken as tantamount to saying that philosophy itself is masculine in nature, that the standards of philosophy have been constructed to exclude women. This is a point of view that makes many women who are philosophers uncomfortable. When Cartesianism is construed more narrowly, however, to include, for example, substantive claims about mind/body dualism or the essentialist nature of science, then many men are not going to find congenial the claim that they, in their reasoning processes, embody an obsolete philosophical theory. Clearly, Cartesianism and the Cartesian concept of reason can stand for different things at different times. What I propose to do first is take a look at the arguments about a gendered concept of reason as they occur in the work of Bordo and Lloyd and then see how reason is used by Astell and Masham. What I think will emerge is that Cartesianism wears a different face in each of these texts and that the gendered concepts of reason discussed by Bordo and Lloyd are not the same as the gender-neutral concept used by Astell and Masham.

I

Susan Bordo makes far-reaching claims about the importance of Cartesianism, which she supports with a detailed examination of Descartes's writing, most particularly the *Meditations.* Her work is very much influenced by Evelyn Fox Keller.[8] Keller uses two sorts of arguments to show that science, and the concept of reason that science requires, is gender-biased. Keller has produced a good deal of evidence about the metaphoric genderization of reason and science in the seventeenth century, and she has used Nancy Chodorow's version of object-relations theory[9] to argue that the character traits required by a good scientist (and a good reasoner), such as detachment and objectivity, are those that mother-centered forms of child-rearing encourage in boys but not in girls. Bordo has tried to link these two sorts of arguments by showing that the seventeenth-century attitude toward reason, as exemplified by Descartes, can be explained as a kind of psychocultural application of object-relations theory.

Bordo offers a reading of Descartes in which we are to see him as engaged, in Karl Stern's words, in a "flight from the feminine."[10] According to Bordo, Descartes's achievement was what she calls a "re-birth" of knowledge as masculine, in which the concept of reason is reshaped so that masculine traits dominate. What this reshaping amounts to, for Bordo, is the creation of a way of knowing that is characterized by distance, detachment, and purity. She sees the Cartesian method as "a program of purification and training—for the liberation of *res cogitans* from the confusion and obscurity of its bodily swamp."[11] On Bordo's account, reasoning is a matter of properly preparing the mind so that clear and distinct ideas may take possession of it. She describes the resulting theory of knowledge as follows: "A new theory of knowledge, thus, is born, one which regards all sense-experience as illusory and insists that the object can only be truly known by the perceiver who is willing to purge the mind of all obscurity, all irrelevancy, all free imaginative associations, and all passionate attachments."[12] This form of knowledge deserves the authority of being called objective, because of the way in which the knower has detached himself from the circumstances surrounding the object to be known.

In arguing that the concept of reason she finds in Descartes ought to be seen as masculine, Bordo follows Keller in relying heavily on the work of Nancy Chodorow. Although Bordo recognizes that it would be thoroughly anachronistic to apply a theory derived from the conditions of twentieth-century middle-class child rearing to Descartes, she does think that Chodorow's categories can still be used as explanatory. What Chodorow finds in the male personality structure as a result of male upbringing, Bordo finds in Descartes's intellectual products as a result of his cultural upbringing.

Bordo's argument requires her to lay heavy stress on the anxiety that she claims to find in the skeptical arguments of the First Meditation. Bordo proposes that this skepticism can best be understood when we consider the background from which the seventeenth-century view of science and the scientific world developed. According to Bordo, for medieval and Renaissance science, the world is experienced as an organic mother with which the human is united. The world of the seventeenth-century New Science is alien and mathematical, thus giving rise to profound skepticism. Descartes's theory of knowledge is a reaction formation to the anxiety caused by the loss of nature-as-mother. The pain of separation is transformed by the assertion of autonomy. Bordo writes: "The 'great Cartesian anxiety,' although manifestly expressed in epistemological terms, discloses itself as anxiety over *separation* from the organic female universe. Cartesian rationalism, correspondingly, is explored here as a defensive response to that separation anxiety, an aggressive intellectual 'flight from the feminine' into the modern scientific universe of purity, clarity, and objectivity."[13] The knower is detached from nature and in a position to dominate "her." As a result, however, of the Cartesian distinction between mind and body, nature is now identified as body, that is, as inert matter ready to be controlled, in contradistinction to the controlling mind of the knower. Bordo believes this attitude has far-reaching consequences. In particular, she thinks we are in a position "to recognize the years between 1550 and 1650 as a particularly gynophobic century."[14] She cites such events as the prevalence of witch hunts and the rise of the male obstetrician to replace the female midwife as evidence that the repression of women is closely tied to attempts to control women as childbearers. Such attempts to control women, she holds, are a product of the same reaction formation that leads to the drive to separate from and control nature.

Bordo's intricate argument relies on a number of issues, all of which deserve more discussion than I am able to provide here. Her creative application of Chodorow's psychological arguments to a cultural setting needs to be examined, and it is worth wondering whether Bordo has successfully escaped the charge of being anachronistic. Her account, moreover, depends upon a particular reading of Descartes's cultural situation, one that emphasizes those elements of Renaissance science that are bound up with the hermetic tradition from which the identification of women with nature is derived. Correspondingly downplayed is the scholasticism that is more traditionally seen as the position Descartes was working against and that, to my knowledge, does not contain the same implications for gender as does the hermetic tradition. I am a little dubious, therefore, about Bordo's account of Descartes's cultural background.

Finally, Bordo relies on a specific reading of Descartes. Her account, in order to support her claims that Descartes's project was driven by skeptical anxiety, requires her to lay heavy emphasis on the arguments of the First Meditation concerning the dream and the demon. Her final account of Descartes's reason, which emphasizes purity and detachment, is based on the assumption that Descartes's endeavor was to ensure that the mind mirrors nature and that this mirroring occurs when the purified mind is in the grip of the clear and distinct ideas. This results in a curiously passive picture of reasoning. All mental activity is expended in the purification process, at which point the clear and distinct ideas take possession of the mind. There is no mention of any epistemic properties of the clear and distinct ideas, such as their self-evidence. Bordo is trying to reveal the psychological pressures that lie behind Descartes's epistemological arguments, but by omitting reference to much of his epistemology, she produces some odd distortions. We are left with the impression, for example, that what is the matter with sensations is that they are "impure" rather than that they fail to follow deductively from the clear and distinct ideas of the essence of the body, so that a sensory idea, like red, cannot be connected with ideas of what it is to be a body.

Be that as it may, Bordo's interpretation is clearly not the only possible reading of Descartes, and there is a great deal that could be said about the strengths and weaknesses of her account. What I want to point out here is that, whatever may be said for or against her position, it emphasizes those elements of Descartes's argument that are unique to him, like the skepticism provided by the dream and demon arguments and their resolution by means of the appeal to God as the guarantor of clear and distinct ideas. I see this as problematic because Bordo's conclusions, such as her claims about the gynophobia endemic to the period, require her to apply her very specific remarks about Descartes to seventeenth-century culture generally. But the aspects of Descartes's work that she has stressed are not shared by other Cartesians, let alone by members of the seventeenth-century culture at large. So it is questionable whether Bordo can claim that her account of Cartesian reason, dedicated to purity and detachment, accurately captures a cultural phenomenon.[15]

It is in the end this fact—that Bordo's account relies on a version of reason that is very specifically tied to Descartes—that proves most troublesome to her overall endeavors. Bordo has extracted from Descartes an account of a particular way of thinking, one that emphasizes purity and detachment. She contrasts this way of thinking with another, which she calls "sympathetic thinking." This second mode of thinking, Bordo claims, was prevalent in the Renaissance and can, moreover, be characterizable by traits that are feminine. In particular, sympathetic thinking does not require detachment from the object known; instead, it trades on an identification with or sympathetic feelings for the object. Bordo's ultimate goal is to encourage use of this mode of thought, which, in her eyes, has been ruled out by Cartesian gatekeepers. But

Bordo does not supply any reasons for supposing there are only two ways of thinking, and, indeed, her method of arguing in the end suggests otherwise.

The way of thinking that Bordo derives from Descartes is, I have suggested, closely linked to elements of Descartes's thought that he does not always share with other thinkers. For Descartes, it is important that through clear and distinct ideas we are able to arrive at a knowledge of the essences of things, and this is an aspect of his thought that Bordo stresses. Other seventeenth-century philosophers, however, such as John Locke, to give just one example, were not convinced by Descartes's claim that it is possible to come to know essences and argued instead for a way of thinking that depends upon sense-experience and is more associational. Bordo is willing to grant that there are exceptions to the claim that philosophy is dominated by "Cartesian" thinkers, but by this she seems to mean that it is possible to find "sympathetic thinkers."

I am not willing to allow that Locke constitutes an exception in this sense. Sympathetic thinking is a mode of thought that seems to me to be equally foreign to Locke's way of proceeding. Instead, what I think has to be granted is that philosophers have developed accounts of more ways of thinking than just two. But once we allow that different ways of thinking may and, indeed, have proliferated, then it seems considerably less clear that any of them can be neatly associated with the stereotypically masculine or feminine. And even if Bordo could make her case that the way of thinking proposed by Descartes incorporates masculine elements, it is hard to see how this could have far-reaching consequences, since Descartes's is only one of a number of other seventeenth-century accounts of the thinking process. Bordo's argument, which assumes we can take Descartes as symbolic of an entire culture, requires that we take that culture to be far more monolithic than it in fact was. Descartes's views, although important for the period, in no sense exhaust the complexities of seventeenth-century thought. Ironically, Bordo, in making her argument that Descartes's masculine style of thought defeated a feminine style belonging to the Renaissance, seems to have been taken in by the dichotomous thinking that she herself deplores.

II

Genevieve Lloyd shares Bordo's views about the consequences of Descartes's account of reason, although Lloyd argues for these consequences on very different grounds. Like Bordo, Lloyd thinks that a particular way of thinking, derived from Descartes's theory of reason, has been associated with masculinity, and through this association, it has had the effect of suggesting that women are not fully rational. Lloyd, however, does not claim, as Bordo does, that Descartes's concept of reason is, by virtue of its inception, masculine in nature. She thinks that Descartes's own project and the motives that gave rise to it can be described in gender-neutral terms. She points out that Descartes boasted that a virtue of his proposals was that they could be understood and followed even by women. Descartes did not think that the kind of reason he described excluded women. What Lloyd does believe, however, is that Descartes's account of reason can be, and has been, used in a way that excludes women. This is because Descartes's account is sufficiently narrow that it can be taken to constitute one possible way of thinking, a masculine way, to be contrasted with another mode of thinking, conceived in opposition to his, which is feminine. Lloyd maintains that the conceptions of masculinity and femininity as we know them today were constructed by exploiting the differences in these alternative forms of thinking. The virtues connected with Cartesian reason become part of what is involved in being manly, and those virtues excluded from Cartesian reason were relegated to the feminine. Lloyd writes:

> There are aspects of Descartes's thought which—however unintentionally— provided a basis for a sexual division of mental labour whose influence is still very much with us. Descartes's emphasis on the equality of Reason had less influence than his formative contribution to a distinctive kind of Reason—a highly abstract mode of thought, separable, in principle, from the emotional complexities and practical demands of ordinary life.[16]

Lloyd's claim is that it is the concept of masculinity that has been shaped by the concept of reason, not that reason has had masculine characteristics incorporated into it. Although Lloyd's thesis is one that, historically, is a little easier to argue for than Bordo's, the result from the point of view of women is the same. Femininity, according to Lloyd, is identified as the nonmasculine, and the importance of Descartes's abstract mode of thinking is that it can be contrasted with another, nonmasculine mode. Women are again characterized by a lack of Cartesian reason.

Lloyd's account of the nature of Cartesian reason turns out to differ from that of Bordo, because Lloyd lays emphasis on different aspects of Descartes's thought. Lloyd's interpretation is not so closely linked to the *Meditations* alone, for what she identifies as important about Cartesian reason is that it is primarily a method, a set of procedures that, if properly followed, allows the knower to reach the truth. Lloyd describes this method as follows:

> In place of the scholastic disputation, which can only, he thought, obscure the mind's natural clarity, Descartes offered a few supposedly simple procedures, the rationale of which was to remove all obstacles to the natural operations of the mind. The general rubric of the method was to break down the more complex operations of the mind into their simplest forms and then recombine them in an orderly series. The complex and obscure is reduced to simple, self-evident "intuitions," which the mind scrutinizes with "steadfast, mental gaze," then combines in orderly chains of deductions.[17]

Thus, for Lloyd, what is important about Descartes's account is that he gives a recipe for clear and adequate thought. She thinks, however, that although this is a method that everyone, by virtue of their natural, rational endowment, can follow, it is nevertheless a specialized and highly abstract way of thinking. It does not represent the sort of thinking we ordinarily engage in; instead, it requires special training before proficiency can be attained. Indeed, Lloyd remarks that Descartes himself claimed to follow this method rarely.

According to Lloyd, reason becomes identified with the intellectual activity of the trained mind that engages in the kind of deductive thinking processes that constitute the sciences. Because this intellectual activity is so specialized, it can be distinguished from an alternative kind of thinking, the kind of thinking that an untrained mind engages in. This alternative, or leftover thought process, Lloyd holds, can be seen as the province of the imagination, of sense-experience, and of the emotions. These last three mental processes, significantly, differ from abstract reason, in that they all depend upon the body and are not just mental in nature. Lloyd wants to claim that Descartes's way of setting up his account of reason rests on a couple of distinctions: the distinction between the trained mind and the untrained mind, which in turn rests on the distinction between the mind and the body. These distinctions served as the basis for subsequent gender-distinctions.

To support this argument she writes:

> We owe to Descartes an influential and pervasive theory of mind, which provides support for a powerful version of the sexual division of mental labour. Women have been assigned responsibility for that realm of the sensuous which the Cartesian Man of Reason must transcend, if he is to have true knowledge of things. He must move on to the exercise of disciplined imagination, in most scientific activity; and to the rigours of pure intellect, if he would grasp the ultimate foundations of science. Women's task is to preserve the sphere of the intermingling of mind and body, to which the Man of Reason must repair for solace, warmth and relaxation. If he is to exercise the most exalted form of Reason, he must leave soft emotions and sensuousness behind; women will keep them intact for him. The way was thus opened for women to be associated with not just a lesser presence of Reason, but a different kind of intellectual character, construed as complementary to "male" Reason. This crucial development springs from the accentuation of women's exclusion from Reason, now conceived—in its highest form—as an attainment.[18]

The concept of masculinity becomes identified with those characteristics belonging to the well-trained mind. Those thought processes that are abandoned by the trained mind become the province of the female mind, certainly the quintessential untrained mind, and hence come to constitute the feminine.

Lloyd's way of describing Cartesian reason identifies elements that received ready acceptance in the seventeenth century. There was general endorsement of the view that it was possible to identify rules for right reasoning, roughly in the way Descartes had done. But for Lloyd to be able to make her case that this form of Cartesian reason was influential in shaping the categories of masculinity and femininity, it must be possible to distinguish the Cartesian reason that constitutes the masculine from some other thought process that can be identified as feminine. Lloyd achieves such a distinction by identifying Cartesian reason with trained reason, with those thought processes that belong to someone who has acquired a certain abstract-reasoning skill. This way of thinking, she argues, has come to be seen as stereotypically masculine. What is less clear, however, is that she has been able to identify, in these Cartesian resources, a way of thinking that has served to construct the feminine.

The alternative to the specific form of reasoning that she wants to call masculine seems to be that which belongs to the untrained mind. But there is little in Descartes's account of the untrained mind that seems to link with the stereotypically feminine. Lloyd's use of rather loaded terms like "sensuous" tends to obscure the fact that the untrained mind is just the mind that relies heavily and uncritically on sense-experience and on less than fully rigorous connections between ideas. There does not seem to be anything about such a mind that recalls images of the feminine. Again, aspects of this kind of thinking are characteristic of the kind of thinking described by John Locke and other empiricists. It is true that the mental processes on which the untrained mind relies all depend in some way on corporeal functions, but this rather obscure psychological fact does not seem to have entered into any notion of the feminine, any more than other corporeally based functions, like eating or sleeping, have taken on connotations of the feminine. It is worth pointing out that Lloyd herself in the passage quoted above attributes to the man of reason a "disciplined imagination." But the imagination, for Descartes, whether disciplined or not, is a faculty that works with sensory images and hence is dependent upon the body.

In general, there are difficulties in trying to make Cartesian categories, such as mind and body, fit with stereotypical views of femininity and masculinity. Even though women have been stereotypically linked with certain aspects of the body, these aspects do not seem derivable from Descartes's mind/body distinction. Neither Descartes's distinction between the mind that is skilled and the one that isn't nor his rather specialized distinction between mind and body have any obvious reflections in the categories of masculine and feminine.

Lloyd does mention certain mental processes that have come to be stereotypically associated with the feminine. She says, for example, that Descartes's Man of Reason must "leave soft emotions . . . behind." But emotions, especially soft ones, do not on their own constitute an intellectual character. There is no distinctive way of thinking that is purely emotive. If "Descartes's mode of thinking" is made sufficiently vague that it can simply feed into a distinction between reason and passion that does have stereotypical connotations of feminine and masculine, then it no longer identifies two distinct and alternative ways of thinking. If, however, Descartes's notion of reason is conceived as a specific way of thinking that can be contrasted with other ways of thinking, then it does not provide any obvious contrast with the feminine.

III

Both Bordo and Lloyd have drawn on Descartes's texts to argue that a Cartesian account of reason can be identified with masculinity and so serve as a gatekeeper to deny rationality to women. Mary Astell and Damaris Masham make very different use of these texts, for they use a Cartesian account of reason in an argument that seeks to claim rationality for women. Although Astell and Masham are writing to slightly different purposes, their claims about the nature of rationality as it affects women are sufficiently similar to warrant their being treated together.[19]

An important point that both women make is that reason is a human characteristic and therefore that the proper development of reason should not be denied to women. As Astell says:

> GOD does nothing in vain, he gives no Power or Faculty which he has not allotted to some proportionate use, if therefore he has given to Mankind a Rational Mind, every individual Understanding ought to be employ'd in somewhat worthy of it. The Meanest Person shou'd Think as *Justly,* tho' not as *Capaciously,* as the greatest Philosopher. And if the Understanding be made for the Contemplation of Truth, and I know not what else it can be made for, either there are many Understandings who are never able to attain what they were design'd and fitted for, which is contrary to the supposition that GOD made nothing in Vain, or else the very meanest must be put in a way of attaining it: Now how can this be if all that which goes to the composition of a Knowing Man in th'account of the World, be necessary to make one so? All have not leisure to Learn Languages and pore on Books, nor Opportunity to Converse with the Learned; but all may *Think,* may use their own Faculties rightly, and consult the Master who is within them.[20]

In this passage, Astell gives expression to the explicitly gender-neutral concept of reason that Lloyd found in Descartes. Reason is being identified, as it was for Lloyd, with a method of thinking. Rational thought amounts to the correct use of a faculty that belongs to all humans. As Astell emphasizes, proper thought does not require the sort of book learning that has been reserved for men. All that is necessary is to understand the character of one's reasoning faculty to ensure that it is being used appropriately.[21]

Lloyd, however, sees rational thought as the exercise of a faculty that was used only occasionally in the service of theoretical knowledge. Astell and Masham, on the other hand, present reason as intimately bound up with all human functioning. Masham, for example, writes:

> It is as undeniable as the difference between men's being in, and out of their Wits, that Reason ought to be to Rational Creatures the Guide of their Belief: That is to say, That their Assent to any thing, ought to be govern'd by that proof of its Truth, whereof Reason is the Judge; be it either Argument, or Authority, for in both Cases Reason must determine our Assent according to the validity of the Ground it finds it Built on: By Reason being here understood that Faculty in us which discovers, by the intervention of intermediate Ideas, what Connection Those in the Proposition have with one another: Whether *certain; probable;* or *none at all;* according whereunto we ought to regulate our Assent. If we do not so, we degrade our selves from being Rational Creatures; and

deprive our selves of the only Guide God has given us for our Conduct in our Actions and Opinions.[22]

The method of reasoning that Masham describes above is not all that different from what Lloyd finds in Descartes. Reason consists in the comparison of ideas, so that the connections between them can be uncovered. Astell gives rules for reasoning that are similar to the advice Descartes gives about breaking the subject down to its simplest elements and drawing no conclusion that is not distinctly present in the ideas being contemplated. But neither Astell nor Masham supposes that reason, so described, is limited in its functioning to uncovering the abstract essences of things. Instead, reason—that is, the perception of how ideas go together—is what constitutes any thinking process and is what stands as the basis for human action. Astell says, "Since the Will is blind, and cannot chuse but by the direction of the Understanding; or to speak more properly, since the Soul always *Wills* according as she *Understands,* so that if she Understands amiss, she Wills amiss."[23] What is distinctive about human conduct is that it is the result of choice. Choice requires reasons that can be more or less appropriate, valid or invalid. It is in our best interests to reason well, but it is impossible to act without engaging in some kind of reasoning.

For both Astell and Masham, an important reason why women should have a trained reasoning faculty is so that their conduct will be based on right reason, which will ensure the salvation of their souls. Reason, therefore, has a much wider scope than merely the production of theoretical knowledge. Any human action requires some sort of reasoning process, some sort of juxtaposition of ideas. As Astell writes:

> There are certain Notices which we may call the Rudiments of Knowledge, which none who are Rational are without however they came by them. It may happen indeed that a habit of Vice or a long disuse has so obscur'd them that they seem to be extinguish'd, but it does only *seem* so, for were they really extinguish'd the person wou'd be no longer Rational, and no better than the Shade and Picture of a Man. Because as Irrational Creatures act only by the Will of him who made them, and according to the Power of that Mechanisme by which they are form'd, so every one who pretends to Reason, who is a Voluntary Agent and therefore Worthy of Praise or Blame, Reward or Punishment, must Chuse his Actions and determine his Will to that Choice by some Reasonings or Principles either true or false, and in proportion to his Principles and the Consequences he deduces from them he is to be accounted, if they are Right and Conclusive a Wise Man, if Evil, Rash and Injudicious a Fool. If then it be the property of Rational Creatures, and Essential to their very natures to Chuse their Actions, and to determine their Wills to that Choice by such Principles and Reasonings as their Understandings are furnish'd with, they who are desirous to be rank'd in that Order of Beings must conduct their Lives by these Measures, begin with their Intellectuals, inform themselves what are the plain and first Principles of Action and Act accordingly.

By which it appears that there are some degrees of Knowledge necessary before there can be *any* Human Acts, for till we are capable of Chusing our Actions and directing them by some Principle, tho we Move and Speak and do many such like things, we live not the Life of a Rational Creature but only of an Animal.[24]

Thus, for Astell, reasoning is a process of some generality. There are no alternative thinking processes or ways of thinking besides the rational. A person who ceases to exhibit signs of rationality ceases to be human.

This means that for neither Astell nor Masham is reasoning something that occurs only on special occasions. They stress that reasoning is something that is apparent in *any* human thought process, no matter how trivial. Astell writes: "For the difference between a Plow-man and a Doctor does not seem to me to consist in this, That the Business of the one is to search after Knowledge, and that the other has nothing to do with it. No, whoever has a Rational Soul ought surely to employ it about some Truth or other, to procure for it right Ideas, that its Judgments may be true tho its Knowledge be not very extensive."[25] It is this that permits them to argue that women would clearly benefit from an education to improve their reason, because they already show signs of using it to good advantage in those spheres that are reserved for them. Astell says:

And that Person whose Capacity of receiving Ideas is very little, whose Ideas are disorder'd, and not capable of being so dispos'd as that they may be compar'd in order to the forming of a Judgment, is a Fool or little better. If we find this to be our Case, and that after frequent tryals there appears no hopes of Amendment, 'tis best to desist, we shall but lose our Labour, we may do some Good in an Active Life and Employments that depend upon the Body, but we're altogether unfit for Contemplation and the exercises of the Mind. Yet e'er we give out let's see if it be thus with us in all Cases: Can we Think and Argue Rationally about a Dress, an Intreague, an Estate? Why then not upon better Subjects? The way of Considering and Meditating justly is the same on all Occasions.[26]

Although Astell certainly thinks of reasoning as something that can be improved—indeed, the whole thrust of her book is to argue that women need education so that their reasoning abilities *will* be improved—she does not see the fruits of a trained reason as exhibiting a different style of thinking from that which exists ordinarily. Because women undeniably do use their reason in their day-to-day lives, we can be confident they will profit from an education to train their reason. Astell does not think that such training would produce a different way of thinking from that which an untrained mind engages in; rather, it merely makes the thinker more adept by enlarging the scope of ideas she has at her disposal. The rules of right reasoning are so general that they apply to any instance of the thinking process.

Because Astell and Masham claim that what is distinctive about humans is their capacity for rational action, they see humans as embodying a hierarchy in which the mind rules the body. But they also see the body as making contributions to human life that cannot be neglected. Astell, for example, writes:

> For I question not but that we shou'd be convinc'd that the Body is the Instrument of the Mind and no more, that it is of a much Inferior Nature, and therefore ought to be kept in such a Case as to be ready on all occasions to serve the Mind. That the true and proper Pleasure of Human Nature consists in the exercise of that Dominion which the Soul has over the Body, in governing every Passion and Motion according to Right Reason, by which we most truly pursue the real good of both, it being a mistake as well of our Duty as our Happiness to consider either part of us singly, so as to neglect what is due the other. For if we disregard the Body wholly, we pretend to live like Angels whilst we are but Mortals; and if we prefer or equal it to the Mind we degenerate into Brutes.[27]

What such a passage suggests is that talk of the soul ruling the body should not obscure the fact that it is actually impossible for humans to lead a life that is identified solely with the body, that such a life is in fact nonhuman.

Masham also seems aware that, in the human being, even corporeally based functions take place with the cooperation of reason.

> The more obviously eminent advantages accruing to us from which faculty of reason, plainly make known the Superiority of its Nature; and that its suggestions, ought to be hearken'd to by us preferably to those of Sense; where these (as it too often happens) do not concur. For did we know nothing by *Inference* and *Deduction,* both our knowledge and injoyment would be very short of what they now are; many considerable pleasures depending almost intirely upon Reason; and there being none of the greatest Enjoyments of Sense which would not lose their best Relish, separated from those concomitant satisfactions which accompany them only as we are rational Creatures.[28]

Neither Astell nor Masham sees a distinction between mind and body or a claim that the mind is superior to the body as licensing conclusions as that the life of the mind is an alternative life superior to a life based on sensation. Instead, what they emphasize is the extent to which corporeally based functions such as sensation are dependent upon reason. Sensation is not taken to be a fully independent capacity and so could not be understood as grounding an alternative way of thinking.

Similarly, it seems clear that Astell and Masham do not see a life based on reason as somehow rival to a life based on the emotions. Instead, the proper functioning of the emotions is dependent on reason. Thus Masham can argue not only that it is women's special emotional temperament that best fits them for motherhood, but also that this is a reason for increasing their rational capacities. She writes:

> For that softness, gentleness and tenderness, natural to the Female Sex, renders them much more capable than Men are of such an insinuating Condescention

to the Capacities of young Children, as is necessary in the Instruction and Government of them, insensibly to form their early Inclinations. And surely these distinguishing Qualities of the Sex were not given barely to delight, when they may, so manifestly, be profitable also, if joyn'd with a well informed Understanding: From whence, *viz.* from Womens being naturally thus fitted to take this care of their little Ones, it follows, that besides the injustice done to themselves thereby, it is neglecting the Direction of Nature for the well breeding up of Children, when Ladies are render'd uncapable hereof, through want of such due improvements of their Reason as are requisite hereunto.[29]

Masham is not just saying that women cannot perform the tasks that belong to them if they do not have the ability to think properly, although this is certainly a part of her argument. What she writes suggests that women will not, without a trained reason, be able to carry out their tasks in a soft, gentle, and tender manner. Women will not lose their emotional endowment through the acquisition of a trained reason; instead, they will be able to express their emotions appropriately.

IV

Both Astell and Masham use reason and rationality as synonymous with thinking. They do not take themselves to be describing a particular way of thinking; rather, they are giving general characteristics that underlie all thinking processes. What they have taken from Descartes's account is the idea that right reasoning and hence, more important, knowing what to do is a process that can be understood simply through introspection, without requiring the trappings of a formal education from which women were excluded. Their use of reason is gender-neutral because of its generality. If there is a single method of right reasoning that underlies all thinking, then the only sorts of notions or methods to which this can be opposed are not ways of thinking at all. To Astell and Masham, if you are not behaving rationally, then you are behaving mechanically, like an animal or a machine. There is no room within their concept of reason to construct an alternative thinking process that could be ascribed to women. Astell and Masham recognize that women may reason poorly, because they lack sufficient stock of ideas to be able to perceive how one idea may be connected with another, or that they may reason well but only in limited areas—in either case, they still reason.

Lloyd and Bordo have each argued that the concept of reason to be found in Descartes is not gender-neutral but rather describes a way of thinking that is stereotypically masculine. In making this argument, they have considerably narrowed the scope of the concept of reason, so that instead of describing a way of thinking that underlies all human activity, they pick out a particular, highly abstract form of thought—a rather different one in each case. They are thus in a position to argue that Cartesian reason constitutes only one kind of thinking, which, they claim, has been associated with masculinity. The masculine standard of rationality, then, serves as a gatekeeper to exclude feminine thought processes and, by implication, women themselves from the halls of intellectual power.

The thrust of the feminist argument, and also its strength, has lain in its plea for diversity. The idea that rational inquiry will be improved if other ways of thinking are allowed to flourish has a great deal of intuitive appeal. But it is not particularly beneficial to this line of argument to see it as directed against a single masculinist gatekeeper. I have argued that where both Bordo and Lloyd have gone wrong is with the assumption necessary to their argument—that there are only two forms of thinking, of which one is recognizably masculine and the other recognizably feminine.

In fact, as I have shown, these are conditions that cannot be readily met. Lloyd has achieved the specificity of her form of thought by identifying it as the trained rather than the untrained mind. But the operations of the untrained mind turn out to be the ones most people engage in most of the time. Thus Lloyd is contrasting an allegedly masculine way of thinking with what turns out to be, of all things, the way of thinking of the "man-on-the-street." There is nothing stereotypically feminine about such a process. Bordo's account of Cartesian thinking can be shown to differ from a way of thinking that has been associated with femininity, namely, sympathetic thinking; but her boundaries have been drawn so narrowly to achieve this distinction that her versions of Cartesian thinking contrasts with any number of different ways of thinking. Given the clear proliferation of styles of thinking that can be identified as existing in the seventeenth century and beyond, it seems difficult to make a case for a claim that one form of thought has served as a gatekeeper to exclude any other.[30]

Arguments like Lloyd's and Bordo's have, in the end, the unfortunate result of undercutting rather than encouraging diversity by narrowing attention down to only two styles of thinking. I have argued that, as far as the seventeenth century goes, insisting on the hegemony of Cartesian reason has the consequence that the quite different styles of thought proposed by John Locke or, to take a later example, George Berkeley are systematically ignored. Still further examples abound in other periods. The laudable aim of bringing about a plurality of thinking styles cannot be achieved by making it a gender issue.

The arguments of Astell and Masham, however, remind us that there is another use of reason, one that picks out whatever it is that all styles of reasoning have in common. This concept of reason has been most closely linked with the idea that there is a distinctive kind of human action based on choice. Reason, in this case, is not intended to contrast with any other form of intellectual life, and when it is forced into gender categories, the result is to suggest that women cannot think at all—they merely intuit or merely feel passion. It is this claim, failing to cohere as it does with any woman's experience of her mental capacities, that is quite properly to be resisted. So, if one construes reason narrowly in picking one or another style of thought, then appealing to gender categories is unhelpful; however, if one construes reason broadly, appealing to gender is inappropriate.[31]

Notes

1. The position that reason is a human faculty shared indifferently by men and women is a classic statement of what has been called Enlightenment Feminism, as exemplified by Mary Wollstonecraft in *A Vindication of the Rights of Women* (Baltimore: Penguin, 1975.) It is a basic premise of such works as Betty Friedan's *The Feminist Mystique* (New York: Dell, 1964), which helped initiate the most recent feminist movement, and has been defended recently by Janet Radcliffe Richards in *The Sceptical Feminist: A Philosophical Enquiry* (London: Routledge and Kegan Paul, 1980) and by Jean Grimshaw, *Philosophy and Feminist Thinking* (Minneapolis: University of Minnesota Press, 1986). Cecily Hamilton in *Marriage as a Trade* (London: Woman's Press, 1981; first published 1909) expresses very well many women's reaction to the claim that women think differently from men: "The question of the intuitive or instinctive powers of woman is one that has always interested me extremely; and as soon as I realized that my mind was supposed to work in a different way than a man's mind, and that I was supposed to arrive at conclusions by a series of disconnected and frog-like jumps, I promptly set to work to discover if that was really the case by the simple expedient of examining the manner in which I did arrive at conclusions. I believe that (on certain subjects, at any rate) I think more rapidly than most people—which does not mean, of course, that I think more correctly. It does mean, however, that I very often have to explain to other people the process by which I have arrived at my conclusions (which might otherwise appear intuitive). I can honestly say that I have never been at a loss for an explanation. I can trace the progress of my thought, step by step, just as a man can trace his. I may reason wrongly, but I do not reason in hops. And I have yet to meet the woman who does" (pp. 52–53).

In addition to the works discussed in the text, the notion that reason is gendered is explored in, for example, Evelyn Fox Keller, *Reflections on Gender and Science* (New Haven, Conn.: Yale University Press, 1985); Sara Ruddick, *Maternal Thinking: Toward a Politics of Peace* (Boston: Beacon Press, 1989); and Alison M. Jaggar, "Love and Knowledge: Emotion in Feminist Epistemology," in *Women, Knowledge, and Reality,* ed. Ann Garry and Marilyn Pearsall (Boston: Unwin Hyman, 1989),

2. Genevieve Lloyd, *The Man of Reason: "Male" and "Female" in Western Philosophy* (Minneapolis: University of Minnesota Press, 1984).

3. Susan Bordo, *The Flight to Objectivity: Essays on Cartesianism and Culture* (Albany: State University of New York Press, 1987). See also Bordo, "The Cartesian Masculinization of Thought," in Bordo, *Sex and Scientific Inquiry,* ed. Sandra Harding and Jean F. O'Barr (Chicago: University of Chicago Press, 1987), pp. 247–264.

4. See, for example, Hilda Smith, *Reason's Disciples: Seventeenth-Century English Feminists* (Urbana: University of Illinois Press, 1982).

5. The works I will be particularly considering are Mary Astell, *A Serious Proposal to the Ladies for the Advancement of Their True and Greatest Interest* (New York: Source Book Press, 1970; reprint of 1701 edition); and Damaris Lady Masham, *Occasional Thoughts in Reference to a Vertuous or Christian Life* (Printed for A. and J. Churchill at the Black Swan in Paternoster Row, London,1705).

6. Joan Kinnaird, "Mary Astell and the Conservative Contribution to English Feminism," *Journal of British Studies* 19 (1979): 53–75; Smith, *Reason's Disciples;* and Ruth Perry, "Radical Doubt and the Liberation of Women," *Eighteenth Century Studies* 18 (1985): 472–493.

7. It is also interesting that a follower of Descartes, François Poullain de la Barre, undertook to write a defense of women on explicitly Cartesian grounds. He wanted to show that beliefs about the inferiority of women did not follow from clear and distinct ideas but rather were the result of unexamined prejudice. Poullain de la Barre, *The Woman as Good as*

the Man: or, the Equality of Both Sexes, ed. Gerald M. MacLean (Detroit: Wayne State University Press, 1988).

8. See Keller, *Reflections on Gender and Science.*

9. Nancy Chodorow, *The Reproduction of Mothering: Psychoanalysis and the Sociology of Gender* (Berkeley: University of California Press, 1978).

10. Karl Stern, *The Flight from Woman* (New York: Farrar, Straus and Giroux, 1965).

11. Bordo, *Flight to Objectivity,* p. 92.

12. Bordo, "Cartesian Masculinization of Thought," p. 260.

13. Bordo, *Flight to Objectivity,* p. 5.

14. Ibid., p. 108.

15. I think there are also problems in identifying *any* particular century as especially gynophobic, given the rather rocky row women have had to hoe throughout the centuries. The period Bordo singles out seems to be neither worse nor better than many others. In addition to losing ground in some areas it is possible to point to gains in others, such as the rise of women in print, the phenomenon of the female preacher, and even the appearance of some new professions for women such as that of actress.

16. Lloyd, *Man of Reason,* p. 49.

17. Ibid., p. 44.

18. Ibid., p. 50.

19. The purpose of Mary Astell's *A Serious Proposal to the Ladies* is to argue for the need for educating women. Damaris Masham's *Occasional Thoughts* is more general, discussing the value of education for a Christian life, an area in which women have been especially neglected.

20. Astell, *A Serious Proposal,* p. 98.

21. Astell's characterization is fully consonant with Descartes's remark that even women can read his books with profit. Both Astell and Descartes would agree, however, that understanding one's reasoning faculty is an enterprise that takes much time and effort.

22. Masham, *Occasional Thoughts,* p. 32.

23. Astell, *A Serious Proposal,* p. 18.

24. Ibid., p. 62.

25. Ibid., p. 84.

26. Ibid., p. 90.

27. Ibid., p. 137.

28. Masham, *Occasional Thoughts,* p. 65.

29. Ibid., p. 190.

30. I have previously mentioned Locke as a clear and familiar example of a seventeenth-century thinker whose views on the nature of thought differed from those of Descartes. Locke, of course, had eighteenth-century descendants, such as George Berkeley, who was even more emphatically opposed to Descartes, both in his stress on the importance of sense-experience and on the fact that human mental processes rely on contingent rather than necessary connections. The success of Newtonian science at the expense of Cartesian science also served to undermine Descartes's account of rational thought. These few remarks are the beginning of a long and quite complicated story.

31. Work on this paper was supported by a Fellowship from the Center for Twentieth-Century Studies, University of Wisconsin–Milwaukee. I would like to thank Kathleen Woodward, Carol Tennessen, and the other Fellows of the Center for their help in developing the ideas that led to this paper. I would also like to thank Robert Schwartz, Virginia Valian, Joan Weiner, Elizabeth Spelman, and Louise Antony for their very helpful comments on earlier drafts.

3

HUME: THE REFLECTIVE WOMEN'S EPISTEMOLOGIST?

ANNETTE C. BAIER

We cannot reasonably expect, that a piece of woollen cloth will be wrought to perfection in a nation which is ignorant of astronomy, or where ethics are neglected.

David Hume, "Of Refinement in the Arts"

Recent feminist work in epistemology has emphasized some themes that I find also in Hume's writings on epistemology, when these are taken to include not just Book One of the *Treatise* and *An Enquiry Concerning Human Understanding* but also his claims, in his "ethical" writings, about natural abilities and their relative importance. These themes are found as well in several of his essays and throughout his *History of England* (especially in its appendixes), where his concern is with the difference between relatively "ignorant" and barbaric societies and those more-civilized societies in which the arts and sciences have made some progress. I find explored there what might be called a social and cultural epistemology, an epistemology that should be of interest to feminists. Of course, women can produce and are producing their own epistemologists and thus they do not need to turn to kindly, avuncular figures like Hume for suggestions or for confirmation of their own views. Nor do women agree with one another in their epistemological views. Many will dismiss my fondness for Hume's writings as a sure indicator of my failure to transcend my philosophical upbringing in a patriarchal tradition. Still, the very emphases that some women epistemologists, such as Lorraine Code,[1] make on the cooperative nature of our search for reliable beliefs, and our shared responsibility for successes and for failures, should incline us toward a willingness to get helpful support from any well-meaning fellow worker, alive or dead, woman or man. (And my Oxford teacher, J. L. Austin, practiced as well as preached cooperative investigations in philosophy, albeit ones with a strong leader in charge.) To dismiss as hopelessly contaminated all the recorded thoughts of all the dead white males, to commit their works to the flames, could be a self-defeating move. At the very least we should, as Hume advocated, examine each work we are tempted to burn to see if it does contain anything that is more worth saving than patriarchal metaphysics.

Hume is usually labeled an empiricist, and he does talk a lot about what experience alone can teach us. For him, this instructive experience consists in the first place in repeated pairings in a succession of lively "impressions" preserved in idea copies. It includes not merely what our senses reveal but also what our passions and their typical *expression* show us. We know from experience what makes us and others angry, and we come to know whose anger we should dread. At the start of the *Treatise,* Hume gives a sort of apology for beginning his work on human nature with an account of the human "understanding"—our capacity to retain, retrieve, relate, and use "ideas," those less lively derivative perceptions that would be more naturally attended to, he says, after prior attention to the experience whose lessons they preserve. His "excuse" for putting ideas first in his philosophy (and he is surely the first to see any need for any excuse) is that the impressions that philosophers should be most concerned with, and that he will be most concerned with, are human passions, and they usually depend on ideas, so he has to deal with thought and ideas, in at least a preliminary way, before he can do justice to feeling and action. He repeats in the *Abstract* that the reason why relations of ideas, and in particular the "natural" relations that gently select our thought sequences for us, are so important is that *"as it is by means of thought only that anything operates on our passions,* and as these are the only ties of our thoughts, they are really to us the cement of the universe, and all the operations of the mind must, in a great measure, depend on them" (*A Treatise of Human Nature* [hereafter T.] 662;[2] first emphasis mine). Theoretical reason (or should we say "imaginative curiosity"?) serves practical reason (or must we say "practical good sense"?). The reason that Hume's treatment of ideas comes before his treatment of passions and actions is precisely what may be termed "the primacy of practical reason."

The vital job of ideas is to remind us what gave pleasure or was useful to whom and at what costs and to help us to plan for the successful satisfaction of our considered experience-informed preferences. Belief "influences" passion and action, so belief matters. Lively ideas that are not quite beliefs also influence passions (suspicions, misgivings, hopes, fears), so ideas and imagination also matter, even when such ideas are not maximally lively, when they fail to carry total conviction. "Images of everything, especially of goods and evils, are always wandering in the mind" (T. 119). Such wanderers have their effects on action as well as on passion and reasoning. Poets by their eloquence can rouse our passions, even when the vivid conceptions that their tales produce in our minds do not "amount to perfect assurance" (T. 122). The whole of Hume's epistemology, in Book One of the *Treatise,* is in the service of his philosophy of passion and action in Books Two and Three. This is said at the start; it is repeated in places like "Of the Influence of Belief"; it is implied by the conclusion of Book One, whose most despairing moment took the form of a failure to be able to give any answer to the practical questions, "Whose favor shall I court, and whose anger must I dread? What beings surround me? and on whom do I have any influence, or who have any influence on me?" (T. 269); it is reiterated in Book Three's section on natural abilities and in the *Abstract*. The famous words I have just quoted from Hume's moment of despair, or feigned despair, show that it is not just practical questions but practical social ones that Humean epistemology is to serve. Not just how to get things done, but how to win friends and influence people, to placate the right superior powers, to find one's place in a web of social relations involving favor, anger, influence.

The celebrated laments in the conclusion of Book One of the *Treatise* might be read as the expression of a member of a subject race, the Scots, who had just lost their independence. Hume—speaking English with a despised Scottish accent, writing English with awareness of his own deaf ear for his own lapses into "Scotticisms," hoping for an audience with a readership who did not treat him as really one of them—might also be seen to have been in a position a bit like that of a woman trying to make her way in a profession where she is suspect from the start, a "strange uncouth monster," unlikely to win acceptance from those already securely in possession of whatever "thrones" may exist there. Admittedly, whatever Hume thought he was doing in this celebrated "conclusion of this book," he surely did not think he was merely expressing a literary Scot's frustrations, let alone putting himself into women's shoes or sympathizing with the bluestockings of his day. (Hume's relations with Elizabeth Montague, whose stockings gave us this concept, were cool.) Nevertheless it is not entirely fanciful to see him, in his unsuccessful efforts to "effect a total alteration in philosophy" and in his unsuccessful attempts to breach the academic fortresses of Scotland (the chairs of philosophy he failed to get at Edinburgh and Glasgow), as a suitable male mascot for feminist philosophers in at least the early years of feminism—those during which some feminist philosophers were feeling unappreciated, excluded, ill understood. Hume was, if you like, an unwitting virtual woman. Both his "outsider" position (in relation to the dominant culture whose favor he would have had to court if he had succeeded in his academic ambitions) and his radical goals for the transformation of philosophy should make him of some interest to twentieth-century feminists, quite independently of the interesting things he had to say about equality for women and about the means by which they might achieve it.[3]

As far as his understanding of our understanding goes, Hume is famous not merely for his empiricism but for his scepticism—for his debunking of rationalist pretensions to intuit causal necessity in individual instances and to turn reason on its own supposed workings in such a way that it articulates and endorses those pretensions, and for his challenge to rationalist pretensions to require reason to exert its quasi-divine authority to govern the motivational forces at work in human action and response. This debunking (outside a very limited domain) can be read as an attack on the whole patriarchal theological tradition and on its claims about the relative authority of various human voices—the voice of divine reason, the voice of passion, sometimes of "animal" passion, the voice of plain good sense; the voice of the backward-looking avenger of crimes on account of their odiousness versus the voice of the forward-looking magistrate inflicting punishment designed to be no more severe than necessary to produce obedience (T. 410–411); the voice of the warlike patriot condemning the enemy's devilish "perfidy" while calling his own side's treachery "policy" (T. 348) versus the voice of the impartial moral evaluator recognizing perfidy wherever she finds it; the voice of cruel inhumanity versus that of normal human sympathy; the rough masculine voice versus the soft feminine voice, and so on. But it is notoriously much easier to attack a view, and to criticize a culture based on that view, than to indicate persuasively what alternative would be, and would sensibly be predicted to be, better than the one in use. What is Hume putting in place of the rationalists' sovereign reason in all the realms where he topples its authority?

As far as validation of matter-of-fact beliefs goes, Hume's official answer, in the *Enquiry Concerning Human Understanding* (hereafter E.), is "custom or habit." After pointing out that even experience-informed reason cannot get the premises it would need to argue its way by its own rules of validity to a firm prediction about any future event, and that "there is a step taken by the mind which is not supported by any argument or process of the understanding" (E. 41), Hume goes on, "If the mind be not engaged by argument to make this step it must be induced by some other principle of equal weight and authority" (E. 41). That principle is said a page later to be custom or habit, and it is important to note that it is said to have authority, not simply to have causal influence. This may seem a disappointing answer. Indeed, we might take this to be part of the debunking enterprise, and many do read Hume's "sceptical solution" as a merely ironic one, as the final turn of his undiminished skeptical doubts about causal inference itself rather than about the rationalists' versions of it. But I do not think that he means "authority" ironically in the passage I have just quoted. He does see the natural association of events that in the past have been experienced as constantly conjoined, as carrying epistemic authority. He argues in the *Treatise* that *all* our thought moves, even the more refined and controlled of them, are "effects" of the gentle and sometimes not so gentle force of natural association working on our minds (T. 13). Thus if anything is to have epistemic authority, if any step taken by the mind is to receive normative endorsement, it cannot fail to be some sort of instance of associative thinking. What gives it its authority will indeed be a special feature not found in any and every associative thought move. The rationalists, Hume believed, had misidentified that special feature. He is offering another way of understanding epistemic authority, one that allows us to give authority to some habits that are not habits of deductive argument and to establish them as rules (T. 268).

The "habit" of trying to reduce any thought move that we regard as careful and disciplined to what Hume calls a "demonstration" of reason is a habit that Hume is doing his best to get us (or at any rate his contemporaries) to break. He offers us, as alternatives to demonstration and the habits inculcated by "our scholastic headpieces and logicians" (T. 175), his version of inductive or experienced-based "proofs," complete with eight rules for proving (Section XV of the *Treatise,* Book One, Part III), and a special sort of arithmetic for arriving at experientially based probability estimates for those cases when our experience has failed to yield constant conjunctions. These are experience-tested and experience-corrected customs. By the end of Part III of Book One, Hume is willing to call them "reason." It is, however, our human variant of "reason in animals," not some quasi-divine faculty; even the rationalists' preferred thought move, "demonstration," is treated as a human (language-mediated?) variant of rigid animal instinct. The deductive logicians' rules, and the habits they inculcate, are shown to have a narrowly restricted field of application and authority, mainly in pure mathematics, and even that authority is redescribed by Hume as a special case of the more comprehensive epistemic authority that he is suggesting that we should acknowledge. Even in our demonstrative thought moves, he claims, the necessity that we take to license and require the move to the conclusion is like causal necessity in belonging "entirely to the soul" (T. 166), a projection onto our subject matter of "the determination of the mind" (T. 166) in inference. So all inference, demonstration as well as causal inference, traces a relation whose necessity is "spread" by the mind from itself onto its subject matter. This is no retraction on Hume's part of his earlier claims that "knowledge" of a priori relations of ideas, arrived at by intuition or demonstration, is different from what we get by experience-tested "proofs." But deductive reason's authority, its ability to *require* us to reach a particular conclusion from given premises, is assimilated to that of experienced-based proofs and probabilities.

What is it that Hume believes does give authority to some habits of thought and some social customs; what is it that converts them into normative rules? My answer to this question, elaborated elsewhere,[4] is "surviving the test of reflection," where reflection has its narrow as well as its wider meaning. Not merely must we be able to keep up the custom or habit in question after we have thought long and hard about its nature, its sources, its costs, and its consequences; we must also be able to turn the habit in question on itself and find that it can "bear its own survey" (T. 620). The most authoritative survey is that of the "whole mind" of which the operation being examined will usually be merely one among others. All the operations of "the understanding"— namely, memory, demonstration, causal inference, and the use of the "fictions" of the identity of physical and mental continuants (bodies only interruptedly observed; minds, in the first-person case, observed to show a more thoroughgoing "variation" than the concept of identity is deemed strictly to tolerate)—are eventually tested by Hume by a survey that it takes the passions, including society-dependent passions, to administer. Epistemology in the usual narrow sense (and metaphysics with it) becomes subject to the test of moral and cultural reflection. The questions become, "Would we perish and go to ruin if we broke this habit? Do we prefer people to have this habit of mind, and how important do we, on reflection, judge it that they have it?" What ultimately get delegitimatized are such modes of thought or extensions of some mode of thought beyond some limited domain, as are found "neither unavoidable to mankind, nor necessary, or as much as useful in the conduct of life" (T. 225). The approved habits are seen to be useful or agreeable, or both, either to their possessors, or to their fellows, or to both (Section IV of Part III of Book Three of the *Treatise*). They are habits that "bear their own survey," the survey of "the party of humankind" who have such habits and who are concerned for the well-being of mankind.

I said that Hume shifts the source of epistemic authority from deductive reason, where the rationalists had divined it, to reflection. But of course the rationalists, and in particular G.W.F. Leibniz, had themselves given great importance to reflection in its strict sense, so it would be more accurate to say that Hume generalizes the reflective operation so that it becomes an open question whether reason is what is to be paired with reflection or whether other human psychic capacities have a better claim than deductive reason to being reflective faculties, ones capable of being turned on themselves without incoherence or self-condemnation. Both Locke and Leibniz had spoken in one breath of "reason and reflection" as what gives human persons their self-perceived special status. After Hume, the natural pairing becomes "passion and reflection," or "the moral sentiment and reflection." If Christine Korsgaard is right about Immanuel Kant,[5] he inherits a Humean pairing of morality with successful reflection, albeit with a reversion to the rationalists' conviction that reason alone, not informed sentiment, is the source of our moral capacities, both of judgment and of living in accordance with our judgments.

Hume takes passions to be intrinsically reflective, cases of a "return upon the soul" of remembered experience of good and of evil, so that the fuller reflexivity of the moral sentiment is a development of a "return upon the soul" that every ordinary passion involves. Desire for a repetition of a past pleasure, for example, depends upon the revival in memory not merely of the thought, "I enjoyed that," but of the "lively" wish for the pleasure's continuation, a wish often experienced simultaneously with the original pleasure. Desire the passion, as distinct from original instinctive appetite (which in any case soon gets mixed with and altered by the fruits of experience), is a memory-mediated will to repeat a familiar pleasure, a known good. Desires for repetition of pleasures are for minimally reflection-tested pleasures, ones whose goodness returns on the soul, ones not merely good at the time but good in retrospect, desire-generating at a later date. Ordinary experience-informed desire (the "direct" passion) is already an "impression of reflection," and its reflective success is developed and tested more stringently when it becomes the moral wish for the repetition of the special pleasure that one has got from contemplating, say, a good-humored character from a moral point of view. It becomes the wish that the character trait itself be not just an enduring one in this person but repeated in other persons, particularly in young persons whose characters are still malleable. So "reflection," that hitherto uncontested borrowing by the rationalists from the realm of sense, now gets reappropriated by an "empiricist."

To some extent it is John Locke who initiates this return of borrowed goods. Sense is reflective when "inner sense" reflects on sensation and on how we process our ideas of sense. "Ideas of reflection" are cases of sense returned on sense and on the operation whereby complex ideas of sense are constructed. Locke does not tell us enough about the "reflection" that he thinks is essential to moral responsibility and personhood, but it surely includes the primitive "return on the soul" that is involved in Humean-informed desire for repetition of familiar pleasures and includes some version of moral judgment. Locke officially takes this latter to be the ability to discern and apply a divine law, and there is no overtly reflective ingredient in his account of it.[6] He might have made recognition of divine law a reflexive turn of the human capacity for legislation, a legislation for legislators, a metalaw; but such proto-Kantian thoughts[7] are not, as far as I am aware, to be found in Locke's version of moral judgment. So although there is in Locke a doctrine of reflection that reappropriates the concept for psychic operations that are distinct from "reason," there is not a worked-out application of the concept to moral judgment. That was left for Hume (and even he leaves his readers quite a bit of the working out to do for themselves).

Now why would sensible people—in particular, sensible women—have any sympathy for this perennially popular view that authority, epistemic or moral, is ultimately a matter of having survived the challenge of reflective survey? Having become aware that Aristotle favored it ("thought thinking itself"), and that a motley crew of dead and living white males since him have also favored it, should we not just turn our backs rather than give it another hearing? I myself have raised the question[8] of whether it is not simply a fancy intellectualized version of narcissism, even in its empiricist naturalized version. I think this charge may be fair against reflection in its individualist variants (why should whatever I want to want, or love to love, be a "hyper-good" rather than a particularly stubborn and self-reinforcing craving?) But when we ask, "Why should *we* regard what we collectively, with as much information as we can get, prefer to prefer as our values?" a fair answer seems to be, "What else could they be?" We have no resources other than our own evaluations and can do no more to revise lower-level evaluations than to repeat our evaluative operations at ever higher, more informed, and more reflective levels. So until a better account of values is offered, we may have no other choice than to discover our values by collective reflection, starting from the base of our several (and collective) less-reflective desires, preferences, loves, and loyalties.

A view like Kant's makes a halfhearted gesture toward recognizing the relevance of the question, "What do *we* will to will?" Kant's own preferred question is, "What can *I* will that we all will?" But unless my metawilling is responsive to and corrected by what my fellows will to will, we will merely risk proliferating, at the metalevel, the discord and troublesome self-will that drove us in the first place to take a step away from the simple, "What do *I* want?" No coordination is to be expected, except by good luck or preestablished harmony, if each buttoned-up Kantian works out his application of the categorical imperative on his own in his private study. And Kantians do disagree about the content of the moral law. As is pretty much granted, even by those sympathetic to Kant's moral philosophy, the Kantian tests underdetermine a moral guide capable of providing any sort of coordination between actual moral agents. Kant raises individualism to a higher level. It is high-minded individualism, but one that should be left with an unchanged guilty conscience about its failure to facilitate cooperation and coordination. Its ground for guilt remains the recalcitrant self-will that it was designed to moralize and transform. As long as the contrast between duties to self and duties to others is kept sharp—so that self-respect entails the goal of self-perfection, while respect for others is paired with an obligatory regard for their happiness, not their perfection—then reasoning together can have none except formal common goals. As long as the difference between autonomy and heteronomy, between obeying "self alone" and obeying "others" (the same others whose happiness is my duty?), is left unmediated by any recognition that "I" of necessity include my reflective passions and a concern for others' agreement with me, autonomy will be in danger of deteriorating into pretend-sovereignty over compliant subjects. As long as the realm of ends lacks any procedures for shared decision making, as long as it is a "Reich," not a cooperative, then the Kantian gestures toward the need to bring some consideration of "all" into our moral and evaluative reflection and decision making will remain token and incomplete. Reflection that starts from guilty self-will seems, in Kant, to get us only as far as a higher version of self-opinionated moralistic self-will.

But is not this Kantian case one that shows how undiscriminating the test of reflection is? If the result that Kant endorses really is a product of genuine reflection,[9] then must we not conclude that we get as many different reflective "higher" values as we have differing lower level psychologies first generating the salient maxims, that is, those that get tested? Will not the guilt-haunted loner always get as his reflective outcome autonomy and his right to his private space, along with his vague dreams of an ideal realm of ends, preferably with himself playing the role of Jean-Jacques Rousseau's "legislator" while his fellow ends-in-themselves merely cast their privately arrived-at votes for or against measures on an agenda that they have had no hand in setting? Will not the sympathetic sociable Humean, naturally influenced by others' views and preferences (but a little worried about the dangers of conformism and vaguely aware of the need of gadflies), reliably get as her reflective outcome not individual autonomy but rule by "the party of humankind," a party with vague plans to safeguard freedom of the press, to protect peaceable dissenters, and to encourage a few cautious experiments in thinking and living? Will not the puritan automatically reaffirm puritan distastes and ambivalences, while the epicurean equally reliably gives normative endorsement to the way of life of *l'homme moyen sensuel*? Must we conclude: *Chacqun á son goûte réfléchi?*

Whether or not reliance on reflection will eliminate disagreements, it surely does *not* give blanket endorsement to whatever is tested. The Christian's humility, for example, can scarcely be thought to pass the test of reflection, to be something that is a virtue because it can take itself as its object. Incoherence does befall some attempts to turn an attitude of mind on itself, to make itself its own intentional object. The much-discussed problems that beset Kant's attempted demonstrations that some sort of contradiction results when a maxim such as, "If life becomes intolerable, arrange to end it," is tested by his version of reflection (if that is indeed what his tests amount to) concern the selection of the salient maxim, as well as the relationship between the universalization move and the reflexive turn. Such problems are real, on any version of "normativity as reflexivity." They are, however, more easily solvable on Hume's version of the authoritative reflection—namely, reflection by "the whole mind" rather than merely by a "sovereign reason" claiming to be its "highest" component.

Humean reflection is by the whole membership of the "party of humankind" listening to and influenced by each other's judgments. It is different from Kantian reflection by isolated individuals, let alone by ones who, in their moral judgments, follow Kant in endorsing a method of public decision making that gives no weight or very reduced weight to the opinions of the "weaker sex" and all the lower orders, such

as servants and the unpropertied. (Hume, of course, is not too much better in his political endorsements. His ideal commonwealth, however, does not explicitly exclude
women from voting or standing for office, and it has an income qualification for suf-
frage rather than a straight property qualification.[10]) "Am I willing for others to imi-
tate my example?" is a relevant question if the goal is to detect exceptions that one
might be tempted to make in one's own favor from some rule that one expects others
to follow. It is less relevant for the attempt to find out what rule one can actually expect that others will follow and that they in turn can expect one to follow. To find that
out, one must be willing to listen and discover what sort of example others are setting
or prepared to set.

As I think is recognized in Hume's account of "convention" and in his characterization of the moral point of view as building on informed sympathy, there is no substitute for listening to others' views.[11] To get from "I will . . ." to "we will . . . ," or
even to "I, as one of us, will . . . ," I must first listen to and understand the rest of us.
Trying to imagine the other's viewpoint is no substitute for hearing it expressed, and
even when all viewpoints are heard, there is still a difficult step to be taken before anyone is in a position to act or speak as "one of us." It is not so easy to act as a member of
a realm of ends, especially when there is no agreement about the constitution of that
realm. Simply to assume that what I can will others to do to me, they also can and do
will me to do to them, without verifying that assumption case by case, is to arrogate
to oneself the right to decide for others. It is to assume the pretensions of the patriarch. As, in Kant's version of an ideal commonwealth, women and servants have to
rely on propertied men to look after their interests (indeed, to say what those interests
are), so all Kantian persons, in their moral decision making, are licensed by Kant's
tests to treat all others as virtual women[12] or virtual servants, as ones whose happiness
is to be aimed at by other moral agents who are confident they know where that happiness lies. Moral decision making, for Kant, is responsible patriarchal decision making, made without any actual consultation even with the other would-be patriarchs.[13]

On the Humean alternative, norms—including norms for knowledge acquisition—are social in their genesis as well as in their intended scope. Mutual influence
and mutual criticism as the background to self-critical independence of mind are fos-
tered, not feared as threats to thinking for oneself. In his blueprint for an "ideal commonwealth,"[14] Hume includes elaborate procedures for debate at several levels and for
the prolonged consideration of measures that, though failing initially to get a majority vote of elected representatives, had obtained substantial support. There are procedures for appeal and a special court composed of defeated candidates for senator who
received more than one-third of the votes who may propose laws, inspect public accounts, and bring to the senate accusations against officials. The intricacy of the procedures for giving continued voice even to defeated candidates, the extensive provisions for debate at all levels, the division and balance of powers, are all constructive
suggestions from Hume concerning how disagreeing individuals with some conflicting interests and some differences of perception of shared interests may still constitute
a "realm." A realm must be constituted before its citizens can act as members of that
realm. "The Idea of a Perfect Commonwealth" and other essays[15] give flesh to the

rather skeletal account Hume had given in his moral philosophy proper (if that phrase is not out of place) of "the party of humankind" and how it might organize itself.

Hume's early formal account is, in several respects, more like that of Rousseau's version of the general will than is Kant's (which is more often said to show agreement with Rousseau). From the Humean moral point of view, one must have grounds to expect that other moral judges will concur with one's judgment, one must judge only on matters of general interpersonal concern (repeatable character traits, on Hume's version of this concern), and one must have freed one's mind as best one can of the canker of religious prejudice. It is not clear that Kant really recognizes any of these constraints. (His religious toleration is, like Locke's, limited to other theists, if not just to other Christian sects.) He may think that because reason is supposed to be the same in everyone, we have a priori reason to expect that we will agree. But this a priori faith comes to grief in the plain facts of the disagreement of equally rational people, especially when each person's reasoning is not submitted to her fellow reasoners for criticism. Hume, unlike Rousseau and Kant, takes the grounds on which we expect others' agreement to be our *knowledge* of their views and our sympathy with their viewpoints. Mutual influence is seen as healthy and normal. "A good natur'd man finds himself in an instant of the same humour as his company" (T. 317), and some degree of good nature is a virtue.

It is not only mood and humor but also opinion that are contagious in our species. There are "men of the greatest judgment and understanding who find it very difficult to follow their own reason or inclination, in opposition to that of their friends and daily companions" (T. 316). This psychological fact about us does not make conformism a virtue, nor does it make independence of mind an impossibility. Hume himself clearly managed to follow his own reason and inclination in opposition to that of the majority of his Presbyterian friends and companions. Freedom of thought and speech is the value invoked in the quotation from Tacitus on the title page of the *Treatise*. But Hume also believed that every person needs the reaction of fellow persons in order to test and verify privately arrived-at judgments and verdicts. The difficulty of holding on to a view when one meets not merely some dissent but also contradiction "on all sides" (T. 264), even after one has made the case for one's views, is not merely psychological—it is epistemological. The chances that one is right and everyone else is wrong are about as great as that the one who testifies to having witnessed a miracle speaks the truth. Hume's epistemology, by the end of Book One of the *Treatise*, is, like the moral epistemology he goes on to articulate, fallibilist and cooperative.

This social epistemology, launched by the end of the *Treatise*, is only slightly advanced in the *Enquiry Concerning Human Understanding*, despite the promising emphasis in its first section on the fact that "man is a sociable, no less than a reasonable being" (E. 8) and the hope expressed there that philosophy, "if carefully cultivated by several, must gradually diffuse itself throughout the whole society" (E. 10). Section X, "Of Miracles," does outline a collective procedure of evidence collection and of verification, both of laws of nature and of particular persons' or groups' reliability as witnesses. This fits with what the long footnote to Section IX, "Of the Reason of Animals," had recognized to be a source of superiority in reasoning—namely, "enlargement" of experience by information sharing (E. 107, note, point 9).

Because the *Enquiry Concerning Human Understanding* ends stuck in the book-burning mood that was merely a passing splenetic moment in the *Treatise* (T. 269), its presentation of Hume's "new turn" in philosophy is deliberately limited and partial. If it really is the case that our philosophical science should "be human, and such as has a direct reference to action and society" (E. 7), then any enquiry into the human understanding that is not part of an inquiry into human activity in society will necessarily be too "abstract." It is when Hume begins writing essays, intended for a fairly wide reading public, rather than writing inquiries, intended, perhaps (as M. A. Stewart has suggested is the case with the *Enquiry Concerning Human Understanding*), to get the author a chair of philosophy in Edinburgh (a very ill-judged means, as it turned out, to what, with the wisdom of hindsight, we can say was an unwisely chosen end), that his social action-oriented epistemology gets its best expression.

In "The Rise and Progress of the Arts and Sciences," Hume attempts to "display his ingenuity in assigning causes," the causes for what, by his own account, it is very difficult to assign causes for—namely, the flourishing of learning in some societies but not others. His question is not, as in the *Enquiry Concerning Human Understanding,* "What is it for anyone to know anything?" but rather a development of the question of the footnote to Section IX of that work: "Why do some know more than others?" What is more, the question now becomes not one about differences between one truth-seeker and another, but one about differences between different human *populations* of truth-seekers. The theses that Hume defends, with some but not enough empirical supporting material, are that "the blessings of a free government" are needed if the arts and sciences are to arise; that commerce between neighboring independent states is favorable to the improvement of learning; that once the arts and sciences have advanced, they may be "transplanted" from free states into others; that republics are the best as "nurseries" of the sciences, whereas civilized monarchies are the best "nurseries" of the arts; that in states where learning has arisen and flourished, there is an eventual natural decline to be expected, so that, as the centuries pass, such learning tends to migrate from country to country.

This "natural history" of learning may strike us as underconfirmed by the historical evidence that Hume cites. His last thesis—that "the arts and sciences, like some plants, require fresh soil"—seems overinfluenced by his agricultural or horticultural metaphor of political societies as "nurseries" and "soils" for learning. But what is striking about the whole essay is the new turn given to epistemology. That any individual's or any group's chances of accumulating a store of truths depends, in the first instance, on the authority structure of the society in which such persons live was a fairly revolutionary bit of epistemology, one that anticipates later moves in this direction by Georg Hegel, Karl Marx, Michel Foucault, Robert Brandom,[16] and Lorraine Code[17] (to name a few probably inadvertent Hume followers). As Hume writes in "The Rise and Progress of the Arts and Sciences," "To expect, therefore, that the arts and sciences should take their first rise in a monarchy is to expect a contradiction" (Es. 117). If a people are treated as slaves of their absolute ruler, "it is impossible they can ever aspire to any refinements of taste or reason" (Es. 117). "Here, then are the advantages of free states. Though a republic should be barbarous, it necessarily, by an infallible operation, gives rise to Law, even before mankind have made any considerable advance in the other sciences. From law arises security; from security curiosity; from curiosity knowledge" (Es. 118).[18] According to Hume's reformed active and social theory of knowledge, the first important human knowledge is that of jurisprudence.[19]

Hume takes the link between the structure of political authority and the prospects for epistemic progress seriously. "I have sometimes been inclined to think, that interruptions in the periods of learning, were they not attended with such a destruction of ancient books and records of history, would be rather favourable to the arts and sciences, by breaking the progress of authority, and dethroning the tyrannical usurpers over human reason. In this particular, they have the same influence, as interruptions in political governments and societies" (Es. 123).[20] This spirited defense of freedom of thought, these attacks on "blind deference," put even John Stuart Mill's *On Liberty* in the shade. Hume's linking of freedom, authority, and deference in thought with political freedom, authority, and deference is not just a speculative causal thesis; it is at the same time a transformation of the epistemological notions. The norms of thinking are no more clearly separable from the norms of human interaction than the "exchange" and "commerce" of ideas is a totally different sort of commerce from that to which Hume devotes a later essay, "Of Commerce." Mill's "marketplace of ideas" is a more competition-oriented successor to Hume's earlier discussion of intellectual exchange, including such exchange across national boundaries. If Hume gives us an early capitalist social epistemology, Mill gives a high capitalist version. The value of a theory such as Newton's, for example, is seen to be determined after "the severest scrutiny," a scrutiny made "not by his own countrymen, but by foreignors" (Es. 121). Emulation among scholars of different nations is a bit like international competition in free trade—it settles the value of any one person's or any one research team's "product." Critical scrutiny—both from competitors and from the "consumer" of the scholar's work—is, Hume argues, an essential accompaniment to freedom of thought in the rise and progress of the sciences.

In "Of Commerce" and "Of Refinement in the Arts," Hume cements the connections he had made between political, commercial, and industrial life on the one hand and intellectual life on the other. "The same age which produces great philosophers and politicians, renowned generals and poets, usually abounds with skilful weavers and ship-carpenters" (Es. 270). Hume is not saying that philosophy must guide the weavers' hands—the connection is, if anything, the opposite one: "Industry and refinement in the mechanical arts . . . commonly produce some refinements in the liberal" (Es. 270). Progress in these different aspects of a culture is mutually enhancing. The cooperation and coordination needed in the mechanical arts are also needed in the liberal arts. Their flourishing makes people more sociable, Hume argues. Once people are "enriched with science, and possessed of a fund of conversation," they will not be content to live in rural isolation; instead, they "flock into cities, love to receive and communicate knowledge, shew their wit or their breeding; their taste in conversation or living, in clothes or furniture" (Es. 271). Their tempers become refined, and they "must feel an increase of humanity, from the very habit of conversing together and contributing to each other's pleasure and entertainment. Thus *industry, knowledge* and *humanity* are linked by an indissoluble chain" (Es. 271; emphasis in original).

I have quoted liberally from these essays, because I think that they develop and give detail to the *Treatise*'s and the *Enquiry*'s claim that "man is a sociable, no less than a reasonable being" (E. 8). They have been insufficiently appreciated by the readers of Hume's first, more "abstruse" works.[21] The *Enquiry Concerning the Principles of Morals*, in the fourth appendix ("Of Some Verbal Disputes"), followed the *Treatise* in assimilating "wisdom and knowledge" to the virtues. It also disputed whether there are any virtues that are not "*social* virtues" (E. 313). But it took the *Essays* (and the *History of England*) to enrich these social-cum-intellectual virtues into political, cultural, commercial, industrial, and cosmopolitan ones. Later essays such as "Of Money" give us yet more "thick" epistemology; in particular, they advance some interesting theses about the social need and point of representations and measures of value. Money is found to be "nothing but the representation of labour and commodities, and serves only as a method of rating and estimating them" (Es. 285). But the invention of money, like the invention of contract (secured exchange of future goods), can transform a society from an "uncultivated" one into a "cultivated" one. Hume's essays on economics are about cultural epistemology as well as about economics and add to what he had already done in that area in his earlier essays.

One last point needs to be added to complete my sketch of a case for seeing Hume as a "women's epistemologist." A fairly central part of Hume's characterization of the difference between a cultivated society, in which knowledge can advance, and a "barbaric" society, in which no such advance can be expected, concerns the position of women in such societies. Hume, from his experience of the contributions to culture and to conversation of the Scotswomen and the Frenchwomen he knew, offers his non-solemn verdict that "mixt companies, without the fair sex, are the most insipid entertainment in the world, and destitute of gaiety and politeness, as much as of sense and reason. Nothing can keep them from excessive dulness but hard drinking."[22] Segregation of the sexes in social and work contexts is seen as a sign of a "rough" and "barbaric" society, whereas a social mixing of the sexes is a step toward civilization and the ending of tyranny. Hume sees all tyrannies as interconnected—the tyranny of husbands over wives, which is discussed in "Of Polygamy and Divorces," "Of Moral Prejudices," and "Of Marriage," is likened to the tyranny of absolute monarchs over subjects, which is discussed in his political essays. Neither of these tyrannies is independent of the threat of "tyrannical usurpers over human reason." Some of Hume's more apparently condescending remarks about woman's special role as a "polisher" and "refiner" of rougher and more "boisterous" male energies are distasteful to late-twentieth-century feminists. But we should not fail to appreciate the radically antipatriarchal stand that inspires them and that Hume takes throughout his philosophy. He clearly believes that men and women typically have *different* contributions to make to "industry, knowledge and humanity." What he calls the "Judgment of Females" (Es. 537) is valued as a needed corrective to that of males, as if the judgment of males is the natural place to start. But wherever we start, Hume's main message is that we all need to work together, to check each other's judgments and scrutinize each other's works, if barbarism is to be held at bay. We reflective women and men need, Hume argues, "a League, offensive and defensive, against our common Enemies, against the Enemies of Reason and Beauty, People of dull Heads and cold Hearts" (Es. 536). Such a league still has plenty of work to do.

One of the league's main tasks is to continue Hume's attempts to exhibit the links between dullness of head and coldness of heart and between "Reason and Beauty." I have followed the early Hume in using the word *reason* in a fairly narrow sense, thereby limiting its scope to what can be established by Cartesian (or Kantian) reason. Hume uses the word *reason* in shifting senses, and by the time he wrote his essays he was not willing to give the term to the rationalists; instead, he used it in a broad sense in which it no longer gets contrasted either with imagination or with passion, so it can be paired with a sense of beauty without strain. The human version of the "reason of animals," taken in Book One of the *Treatise* to include our deductive and inductive thought moves, gets further animated in Book Two when it becomes "the love of truth." In Book Three and in later writings, it comes to include also our capacity to coordinate our speaking and our actions with the speech and action of our fellows, to coordinate moral and aesthetic judgments as well as factual and mathematical ones. Hume in the end transforms the concept of reason.[23] From being a quasi-divine faculty and something that we share with God, it becomes a natural capacity and one that we essentially share with those who learn from experience in the way we do, sharing expressive body language, sharing or able to share a language, sharing or able to share our sentiments, sharing or able to share intellectual, moral and aesthetic standards, and sharing or aspiring to share in the setting of those standards.

Notes

1. See Lorraine Code, *Epistemic Responsibility* (Hanover, N.H.: University Press of New England, 1987), and *What Can She Know? Feminist Theory and the Construction of Knowledge* (Ithaca, N.Y.: Cornell University Press, 1991).

2. David Hume, *A Treatise of Human Nature* (hereafter T.), ed. L.A. Selby-Bigge and P.H. Nidditch (Oxford: Clarendon Press, 1975); *Enquiries* (hereafter E.), ed. L.A. Seiby-Bigge and P.H. Nidditch (Oxford: Clarendon Press, 1978); *Essays: Moral, Political, and Literary* (hereafter Es.), ed. Eugene F. Miller (Indianapolis: Liberty Classics, 1985). The page numbers given refer to these editions.

3. I have written about this in "Hume on Women's Complexion," *The Science of Man in the Scottish Enlightenment,* ed. Peter Jones (Edinburgh: Edinburgh University Press, 1990), and alluded to it in "Hume's Account of Social Artifices—Its Origins and Originality," *Ethics* 98 (July 1988): 757–778.

4. In Baier, *A Progress of Sentiments* (Cambridge, Mass.: Harvard University Press, 1991), especially chs. 4 and 12.

5. See Christine Korsgaard, "Normativity as Reflexivity." Talk given to the Sixteenth Hume Society Meeting, Lancaster, England, 1989.

6. See Ruth Mattern, "Moral Science and the Concept of Persons in Locke," *Philosophical Review* (Jan. 1980): 24–45.

7. Or we could also say Aristotelian, or proto-Hegelian, or proto-Brandomian. See Robert Brandom's "Freedom and Constraint by Norms," *American Philosophical Quarterly* (April 1977): 187–196.

8. "Reply to Korsgaard," Sixteenth Hume Society Conference, Lancaster, 1989.

9. Suggesting this interpretation is the formulation of the Categorical Imperative given in the *Groundwork*: "Handle nach Maximen, die sich selbst zugleich as allgemeine Naturgesetze zum Gegenstande haben Können." Similar formulations in the second *Critique* also suggest this interpretation.

10. See "The Idea of a Perfect Commonwealth." Although a minimum income is the qualification for voting, only freeholders can stand for election.

11. See Code, *What Can She Know?* ch. 7, for a discussion of the need to listen to how aggrieved social groups actually present their situations in order to be capable of properly informed sympathy with them. There she takes issue with the belief "that epistemologists need only to understand propositional observationally derived knowledge, and all the rest will follow" (p. 269).

12. Calling someone a virtual woman will be an insult in the mouth of a patriarch, a compliment in more enlightened contexts.

13. I am consciously presenting an unsympathetic reading of Kant's views in the knowledge that other contributors to this volume will present more sympathetic readings and in the confidence that their views will balance mine, so that justice can be done.

14. Hume, "Idea of a Perfect Commonwealth."

15. See "Of the Rise and Progress of the Arts and Sciences," "Of Polygamy and Divorces," "Of Refinement in the Arts," " Of Some Remarkable Customs," "Of Moral Prejudices," and "Of Suicide."

16. Robert Brandom, unpublished manuscript, 1991.

17. Code, *Epistemic Responsibility* and *What Can She Know?*

18. The need for "security" before curiosity or the love of truth can flourish, and the need for a climate of trust to give modern scientists security, is explored by John Hartwig in "The Role of Trust in Knowledge," *Journal of Philosophy* 87 (Dec. 1991): 693–708.

19. In his *History of England,* Hume develops this theme, especially when he describes the civilizing effect of the rediscovery, in 1130, of Justinian's *Pandects.* "It is easy to see what advantages Europe must have reaped by its inheritance at once from the antients so complete an art, which was itself so necessary to all other arts." (ch. 23).

20. This passage should give pause to those who want to dub Hume a conservative in politics.

21. A significant recent exception to this generalization is John W. Danford, *David Hume and the Problem of Reason* (New Haven, Conn.: Yale University Press, 1990), esp. ch. 7. See also his essay "Hume's History and the Parameters of Economic Development," in *Liberty in Hume's History of England,* ed. Nicholas Capaldi and Donald W. Livingston (Dordrecht/Boston/London: Kluwer Academic Publishers, 1990), pp. 155–194.

22. Hume, *Essays,* p. 626. This passage, originally of "Of the Rise and Progress of the Arts and Sciences," was omitted from later editions.

23. I develop this claim in *A Progress of Sentiments,* ch. 12.

This title is intended to make this paper a companion to my "Hume, the Women's Moral Theorist?" *Women and Moral Theory,* ed. Eva Feder Kittay and Diana T. Meyers (Totowa, N.J.: Rowman and Littlefield, 1987).

4

COULD IT BE WORTH THINKING ABOUT KANT ON SEX AND MARRIAGE?

BARBARA HERMAN

Kant's views on sex, women, and marriage would best be forgotten by anyone who wanted to take Kant seriously. Or so I always thought. In the discussion that follows, I hardly want to withdraw that thought in its entirety, but I have been struck by certain possibilities in Kant's later work that bear thinking about. Or so I now believe.

Our moral theories (the traditional ones, that is) have not been places one wants to go to think about morality-and-sex or morality-and-women because most discussions of sex range from uncomfortable to hostile, and traditional accounts of women are either misogynist or reflect uncritical transmissions of repressive social structures.

Some recent philosophy has responded to this and related facts, searching out the effects of male bias in our basic categories either to clear the ground for more inclusive accounts of persons or to initiate critical discussion of the features and significance of gendered human beings. Within philosophical accounts, sexuality is now well regarded—an unequivocally good thing among those so situated that they can participate in the free exchange of sexual pleasure. The body has been retrieved from rationalist disdain. And, more generally, our affective lives are taken seriously and our relationships placed at the center of the moral stage.

Some go further, arguing that we must understand that the moral agent is a person in relationships—to parents and children, friends, sexual partners—rather than an isolated individual trying to make "his" way among anonymous others. There can be no single right thing for "anyone" to do in morally demanding circumstances. What we are to do will differ as we are in different nets of relationship. Friends and lovers, associates and fellow citizens, stand differently in our moral regard than do strangers. The free and equal individual of traditional morality is now encumbered—as we all really are (and especially as most women really are). The encumbrance is not correctly understood as a burden on the life of the individual; rather, it is constitutive of our real nature as moral persons. We are not made unfree or unequal, but new and deeper meaning is given to the possible achievement of freedom and equality. There is a wider set of virtues and a much increased arena for the flourishing human life.

Adjacent to this healthy revision, there has developed a somewhat darker story. Having opened the cast of moral phenomena to feelings and relationships, it is natural to open it still further to other facts hidden or repressed in the philosophical tradition concerning class, race, and gender. But if the initial effect of the, "morality of relationships" was exhilarating, the morality of class, race, and gender may not be. It is not a complicated thought: If we are situated in and partially determined by class, gender, and race (not in the abstract, but by class, gender, and race as-we-know-them), we can be engaged in activities that are not morally acceptable, and we may not be able to "make things right" by scrupulous attention to the details of our lives and relationships.[1]

If the socialization of men and women produces deeply different mechanisms for dealing with competition and aggression, we should not be surprised that even good faith efforts at inclusion of women in institutional hierarchies leaves them at a disadvantage (in the "success" terms of the relevant organizations). Or, consider the supposed dilemmas of sexual harassment in the workplace. The premise of the most difficult claims of sexual harassment is that individual sincerity of good (or not bad) intentions is insufficient guarantor of innocence where sex (broadly construed) and inequality of power mix. So the male professor who is certain that he would never make an unwelcome sexual approach to a student or junior colleague, who is offended at the very idea that he would act without consent, cannot see that given the structure of power and authority neither he nor the recipient of his sexual advance can make it the case that their private actions are reciprocally free and equal. These are moral difficulties that do not yield to private solutions.

What has this to do with Kant? To my great surprise, I have come to believe that Kant has things to say that address these and related matters in serious ways. And I believe this in the face of his misogyny, his disdain for the body, and his unhappy status as the modern moral philosopher feminists find most objectionable.

Kantian ethics has been the object of feminist criticism because it presents the requirements of morality in terms of principle-based impartiality, because of its view that persons have moral standing in virtue of their rational nature, and because the moral regard we are to have for one another is to reflect this deep sameness—we are never to fail to treat one another as agents with autonomous rational wills. Certainly if Kantian ethics is to be viable it must accommodate a more complex account of persons and one that is not modeled on a historically specific image of men; it must also develop concepts and modes of argument that take account of the special moral facts of relationships (and of institutions and social roles as well). Whether it can do these things or whether, even if it can, it offers a compelling account of morality is open for argument.

But Kant's views about sexuality are taken to be not only not arguable but also outrageous—appropriate objects of derision, not discussion. Kant has dreadful things to say about women; his hostility toward sex, the body, and our affective lives generally is famous; and he has strongly conventional views about marriage, children, and the family.

There is some temptation to respond by deflecting these problems into the context of theory. Kant wasn't really hostile toward the body—he was arguing against a sense-based empiricism in ethics; and he wasn't really out to devalue our affective lives—his target was moral sentimentalism; and so on. Perhaps we can add that his misogyny was "merely" a misreading of what he was seeing in the socially restricted women of his culture. This gives us a more respectable dispute among theoretical positions couched in unfortunate rhetoric. Although I think Kant's targets were these philosophical positions, what he says and the views about women that he holds cannot be treated as if they did not really matter. In what way are we to take seriously the claim that the morally important thing about us is our rationality, when the exemplar of reason is found in the capacities of middle- and upper-class white males?

This is not an easy issue for me. I am in different ways unhappy with Kant and with the available alternatives to him. I am convinced that Kant gets something very right about morality (though plainly the current state of understanding of Kant does not support this view). The source of much of the difficulty with Kant, I believe, comes from our (not his) asking morality to do too much. Morality does not exhaust the normative: Substantive regulative principles of aesthetics and politics, and perhaps the personal, need to be looked at as coconstitutive of our practical lives. Even if morality is held to be supremely regulative, that fact alone does not impoverish a conception of the good life.

I also believe that there is something very right about Kant's emphasis on rationality as distinctive of "our" kind of life, though I think we get it wrong about how his conception of rationality works—what it depends on, its autonomy from other faculties or capacities, and so on.

This leaves Kant's views about women. Why are they not a definitive obstacle to taking the Kantian project seriously? Two things seem to me worth thinking about before slamming the door. Our own best views are hardly "pure": The distortions of context and ideology are not dispelled in the recognition that they must be present. There is much to be learned about how such limits are overcome—how progress is even possible—in the face of what is not (or not clearly) seen. Part of what I hope to show here is that Kant is a figure from whom such lessons can be taken. The second reason for staying with this project is Kant's insistence on human freedom as the regulative ideal for personal and social life. I do not find the idea of abandoning this ideal welcome, especially given the increase in the scope and power of the determinisms we now accept. We would do well, I believe, to attend to the details of what happens when Kant's views about women engage with matters he takes to be central to his enterprise. It is in such places that he is forced to go beyond what he otherwise casually accepts, and that is where things can get interesting.

Since I cannot argue for these convictions here, I must ask that you suspend disbelief (or is it incredulity?), if only to be able to tolerate a longish story. In what follows I want to pursue two lines of thought that presuppose that we have reason to take Kant seriously. One explores the fact that Kant's views about sexuality (not his views about women) are strikingly congruent with a strand of contemporary feminism.[2] The other considers whether and how far his solution to a moral problem he feels is inherent in sexual activity provides a way of opening rationalist moral theory to the darker side of sexual relations (dependency, power, and so on). This is also a way of introducing the larger question about the possible place of coercive public institutions in a moral theory that values individual autonomy. Both discussions either directly or implicitly engage the issue of the usefulness of this tradition in philosophy to feminist concerns.

I

The chief barrier to understanding Kant's account of sexuality and marriage comes from the custom of taking Kantian ethics to be the ethics of the *Groundwork of the Metaphysics of Morals* and his remarks on substantive issues as either belonging to the *Groundwork*'s program or, failing that, being the residue of Kant's undigested puritanical upbringing.

Generations of our students have "applied" the categorical imperative (CI) to suitable maxims describing moral situations, treating it as a universalizability test that is supposed to be completely general in its application. The history of failure to get the CI to work is the stuff of introductory philosophy courses. As everyone knows, depending upon the construction of the maxim presented, it permits or forbids too much, and both inconsistently. Worse, our maxims come already laden with moral stuff—you cannot talk about theft without property (Hegel's point), you cannot judge infidelity without a view of marriage, and you cannot even determine the wrong of acts of violence without a story about the body (and perhaps about the gendered body if we are to capture the moral wrong in rape). Yet there seems to be no way to generate "correct" descriptions or to criticize the terms of the ones employed.

If we are still inclined not to reject Kant's ethics out of hand (and it seems remarkable to me that given the prevalence of this sort of reading of Kant that this did not happen long ago), then we should suspect that we have misread the point of the *Groundwork* and the CI. And I think we have.

First of all, the *Groundwork* is not an ethical treatise. It provides neither a systematic account of the basic concepts of moral discourse nor a practical procedure for resolving moral queries and/or difficulties (despite appearances and traditional reading). Its task is to establish a connection between morality and metaphysics: If morality is to oblige (necessitate), it can do so only if the will (understood as practical reason) is free. The *Groundwork* argument motivates this metaphysical claim through an analysis of the nature of moral requirement.[3]

The four examples that are traditionally taken to illustrate a procedure for apply-ing the CI as a rule of moral judgment are rather confirming illustrations of the thesis that impermissible maxims do not have universal form. We take there to be a duty not to make deceitful promises. Analysis shows that the deceitful-promise maxim cannot be a universal law. And so on. Although it is true that every impermissible maxim does not have universal form and the CI procedure will confirm that, it does not therefore follow that the CI procedure is by itself all that is needed for moral judgment. It is easy to be misled about this since, as Kant notes, we can and do appeal directly to universalizability in informal moral deliberation (often in the familiar if misleading, "What if everyone did that?" locution).

But since we can deliberate about the permissibility of proposed action only if we are already aware of the morally salient features of our circumstances, it is the task of systematic ethics to supply the relevant descriptive concepts. In Kant's work, the contours of such a project are sketched in the two parts of the *Metaphysics of Morals*. The second part, known to us as *The Doctrine of Virtue*, establishes the basic ethical cat-egories of duty to self and others. The first part—the *Rechtslehre*[4]—argues for a set of moral institutions that provide a necessary civil framework for moral life. *This* is the location of the justification of marriage with which I will be concerned.

The general argument of the *Rechtslehre* can be looked at in either of two ways: as giving the moral defense of the State or as delineating the possible extent of what Kant calls "external freedom" (how much we can be free to do given the equal claim of all to a like liberty). The State stands in need of moral defense because its primary ac-tivity is coercive control of what we do (in the name of external freedom). But the use of force to control action disregards or manipulates the will of the agent—which is normally impermissible. The problem is to explain how, to secure such things as property and contract, State coercion is legitimate. Here we must control our cyni-cism, for we can miss something if we too quickly respond with a knowing glance at the twin pillars of bourgeois liberalism.

In the *Rechtslehre,* Kant introduces a category of moral dilemma that is created by unavoidable facts of our social lives, a kind of dilemma that cannot be resolved ei-ther through acts of unilateral good willing or by private social agreement. The dilemma has a general form: Given the conditions of human life, there are things we each *must* be able to do that are not morally possible absent certain coercive political institutions. Although his central examples are of property (real property and con-tracts), Kant uses the same form of argument to introduce the legal institution of marriage. Our need to make use of things introduces a moral requirement for (and therefore justification of) a coercive political institution of property. Our sexual need for and use of one another requires a political institution of marriage.

There is an air of paradox here, for the claim is that political institutions can be morally creative in exactly those areas where we have learned to see the role of such in-stitutions as repressive. One may think: How predictable that Kant would find a moral argument to force the institution of marriage. But just as Kant's argument for the necessity of property is not an argument for the necessity of private property, so we do well to hesitate before we jump to the conclusion that what he would justify is the institution of marriage as-we-know-it.

Consider the *Rechtslehre* argument for a political (that is, coercive) institution of property. Kant argues that (a) there cannot be legitimate moral claims to things (property) without civil society and the possibility of permissible enforcement of claims (coercion); and (b) as we must act on and with the stuff of the world and be able to possess things that we are not presently holding, we must be able to have legitimate moral claims to things; (c) therefore, given our need to act on and with the stuff of the world, we can act as we must only through the mediating civil institutions of property.

The central argument (b) goes this way: For a wide variety of the uses to which a person puts the stuff of the world—from the consumption of food to the construction of works of art—effective use of stuff requires the exclusion of others from use of it. And for any use beyond immediate literal consumption, use requires possession (title) when the stuff is not "in hand" ("possession at a distance," we might call it). It is not obvious why even stuff in hand should be unavailable for others' use—in the sense that "because I have it" is in itself a reason for you to refrain from use. It is altogether magical how stuff we are not holding or even near could be off-limits to others. Certainly the fact that we have needs or want something cannot ground permission for the use of coercive force either to get or to protect it (morality precludes that). What is missing is a *moral* connection between persons and stuff such that the exclusion of others by force or threat is legitimate.

We do not, however, stand in direct moral relation to things. Obligations are with respect to persons only. *If* persons had rights to things, we would have obligations that were in a sense with respect to things: obligations directed at persons' rights. The problem is how to get to such a right. As Kant sees it, this is a task that requires a metaphysics of morals.

We want to say that as we may repel (with force) those who would coerce or harm us, so we may repel with force those who would take what is by right ours. ("An object is mine . . . if I am so bound to it that anyone else who uses it without my consent thereby injures me" [*Rechtslehre* 51].) The only justifying reason Kant could accept is that taking what is ours is itself "a hindrance or opposition to freedom" (*Rechtslehre* 36) that may therefore legitimately be counteracted. Possession requires authority, not power.

Private individuals cannot make things property because they cannot separately or jointly create the conditions of reciprocal respect in others that render a claim of right intelligible. There is nothing about either me or the stuff, or about the relations between me and the stuff, that could by itself create a duty of restraint in others. And what I cannot do myself, we cannot do together. There is no agreement that can make things property because, as Kant sees it, the bindingness of an agreement is itself a kind of property: An agreement gives me a claim on someone else's future action. Only in civil society—in a state with the apparatus of law and enforcement—can there be authoritative rules that determine what can legitimately be claimed *and* what kind and degree of force may permissibly be used to protect what we possess. Since possession is a necessary condition of our effective external agency, and since only in civil society is possession possible, Kant argues that we are compelled (because of the nature of our agency) to create or accede to the authority of civil society.[5] This argument for property is not an argument for any particular system of property, private or communal. It is an argument to the conditions of intelligibility of the moral idea of property or right.

We have become accustomed to thinking about institutions either as they provide means to independently conceived ends or as elements in the social construction of our experience. (These roles are not mutually exclusive.) We less frequently, especially when doing moral philosophy, think of institutions as the necessary condition for moral activity. It is as if we thought we could in principle live moral lives without civil society—if only we and others were good enough. In Kantian theory some institutions are necessary not merely to compensate for our own and others' deficiencies (of goodness, strength, capacity to trust, and so on); they arise as the necessary social framework in which human beings can exercise and express their rational natures (as free and equal persons). With this in mind, I want to turn back to the official subject of this chapter: Kant on sex and marriage.

II

Kant argues that there is something about what happens in human sexual relations that leads to a condition compromising the moral standing of the partners.[6] Suppose that sexual relations led to conditions of subordinacy and dependence; that fact would introduce the presumption that sexual relations were morally impermissible (or at least morally problematic). Kant argues that there is such a sex-based moral problem and that it can be resolved only through the legal institution of marriage. He claims that within civil society it is possible to establish and secure the equality and autonomy of the partners in a sexual relationship by defining them, under the law, as husband and wife—that is, as equal juridical persons with public standing.[7] The argument for marriage follows the form of the argument concerning the necessity of the institution of property. (Of course, not just any legal institution of marriage could be cast in the role of preserving autonomy. One that regards the wife as the property of the husband only reflects the assault on autonomy that is [as Kant saw it] inherent in the sexual relation itself.)

The natural response of many to such an argument is, first, to heap scorn on the institution of marriage and, second, to claim that surely it is possible to have sex without moral difficulty—meeting in the moral state of nature, as it were, as free and equal persons sharing the pleasure of one another's bodies. Kant's argument has to be (and is) that there is something about the nature of persons and about the nature of the sexual relationship that makes a will to love well insufficient to guarantee the autonomy and equality of sexually involved persons.

The feature of sexual activity that Kant most frequently identified as the source of moral difficulty is the fact (as he saw it) that sexual interest in another is not interest in the other as a person.[8] Insofar as one is moved by sexual appetite, it is the sex (the eroticized body, the genitalia) of the other that is the object of interest. But since the body is an inseparable part of the person ("in its togetherness with the self it constitutes the person" (*Lectures on Ethics* 166)), the sexual appetite, in taking the body as the object of its interest, compels regard of the person as an object (or blocks regard for the body as the body of a person). According to Kant, the objectification of the other is both natural and inevitable in sexual activity.

Let me string together some passages from *Lectures on Ethics* to give the flavor of Kant's remarks.

> Taken by itself [sexual love] is a degradation of human nature; for as soon as a person becomes an Object of appetite for another, all motives of moral relationship cease to function, because as an Object of appetite for another a person becomes a thing and can be treated and used as such by every one.

> Because sexuality is not an inclination which one human being has for another as such, but is an inclination for the sex of another, it is a principle of the degradation of human nature, in that it gives rise to the preference of one sex to the other, and to the dishonoring of that sex through the satisfaction of desire. The desire which a man has for a woman is not directed towards her because she is a woman; that she is a human being is of no concern to the man; only her sex is the object of his desires. Human nature is thus subordinated. Hence it comes that all men and women do their best to make not their human nature but their sex more alluring and direct their activities and lusts entirely towards sex. Human nature is thereby sacrificed to sex. If then a man wishes to satisfy his desire, and a woman hers, they stimulate each other's desire; their inclinations meet, but their object is not human nature but sex, and each of them dishonors the human nature of the other. (163–164)

Talk about degradation and dishonor offends our sexually liberated ears. We might say, surely Kant confuses sexuality gone wrong with sex itself. But before yielding to the comfort of such a response, let us look at some other passages.

> There is a deep recognition in culture and in experience that intercourse is both the normal use of a woman, her human potentiality affirmed by it, and a violative abuse, her privacy irredeemably compromised, her selfhood changed in a way that is irrevocable, unrecoverable. And it is recognized that the use and abuse are not distinct phenomena but somehow a synthesized reality: both are true at the same time as if they were one harmonious truth instead of mutually exclusive contradictions. . . . By definition, she [has] a lesser privacy, a lesser integrity of the body, a lesser sense of self, since her body can be physically occupied and in the occupation taken over. By definition . . . , this lesser privacy, this lesser integrity, this lesser self, establishes her lesser significance. She is defined by how she is made, that hole, which is synonymous with entry;

and intercourse, the act fundamental to existence, has consequences to her being that may be intrinsic, not socially imposed.

It is especially in the acceptance of the object status that her humanity is hurt: it is a metaphysical acceptance of lower status in sex and in society; an implicit acceptance of less freedom, less privacy, less integrity. In becoming an object so that he can objectify her so that he can fuck her, she begins a political collaboration with his dominance; and then when he enters her, he confirms for himself and for her what she is: that she is something, not someone; certainly not someone equal.

What does it mean to be the person who needs to have this done to her: who needs to be needed as an object; who needs to be entered; who needs to be occupied; who needs to be wanted more than she needs integrity or freedom or equality? . . . The brilliance of objectification as a strategy of dominance is that it gets the woman to take the initiative in her own degradation (having less freedom is degrading) . . . she takes on the burden, the responsibility, of her own submission, her own objectification. . . . The pleasure of submission does not and cannot change the fact, the cost, the indignity, of inferiority.

This, to be sure, is not Kant. This second set of passages is from Andrea Dworkin's recent book, *Intercourse*.[9] The differences in what Kant and Dworkin say are sharp enough: Dworkin's focus is on the objectification of *women,* on the effects on women of sexuality as-we-know-it, and in particular, on the meaning and inherent violence of the act of intercourse. Still, her key ideas are, one might say, very Kantian. Sex (intercourse) turns women into things; the pleasures of sex lead women to volunteer to be treated as things; sex is not compatible with the standing of the partners as equal human beings. It was this degree of similarity with the parts of Kant that we are supposed to reject out of hand, combined with the power of Dworkin's account on its own terms, that suggested to me that adopting a different attitude toward Kant's treatment of sexuality might prove worthwhile.

Kant does see inequality as among the possible effects of sexuality, but he does not take the moral problem in sexual relations as exclusively a problem of the subordination of women. On either of the obvious interpretations of his account of sexuality, the moral costs are borne by both parties. There is the romantic version of his story: It is not the act of intercourse that by its nature subordinates women, but the ego dissolution of sexual bonding that threatens the boundaries of both persons. If persons cannot sustain the integrity of their agency in certain sorts of relations, those relations are impermissible. And there is what I take to be the central claim about mutual objectification: Sexuality involves the moral loss of self, not in terms of boundaries, but as being persons to and for one another. Dworkin too is committed to a mutual objectification (if in a master-slave sense), but it is less clear whether the cause of the objectification is intercourse per se or intercourse in the absence of sexual equality.

Objectification is plausibly problematic. If each sees the other as object—something for use—then strength (physical and social) can take the upper hand and domination follows. To treat another as a person is to take the person's interests and the conditions of rationality as grounds for moral regard—occasions for action or restraint independent of one's own wishes or interests. Objectification makes the path from sexual use to abuse open. In principle, for Kant, the direction of inequality and mistreatment could go either way, though he seems well aware that it will not.

Kant's concern for the sustenance of equality within the sexual relation is evident in his treatment of incest (see *Lectures on Ethics* 168). The only form of incest absolutely forbidden is parent-child, and that because there are independent and natural causes of inequality between parent and child. The ways that Kant imagines equality being restored to sexual partners are not available when the inequality is inherent in the relationship. There is thus nothing morally impossible in sibling incest.[10]

If there is no need to explain why Kantian ethics could not tolerate an activity in which persons are treated as objects, something needs to be offered in support of Kant's reasons for thinking sexuality is such an activity. Kant says the sexual regard is for the body or body part, not the person. The voice of erotic language often speaks of love for the beloved's body: lips, eyes, ears, feet—whatever. But must it? Is there room in sexual language for the terms of moral regard? It is a little odd to imagine sexual arousal at a moral deed—perhaps a bit less odd to be turned on by a quality of virtue, though some more than others: courage more easily than kindness (a cynic might see the marks of virility or maternity as the object here). Certainly the language and imagery of pornography support Kant's view, especially if one holds with those radical feminists who see pornography as an accurate expression of sexual reality.[11]

It is because Kant regards the sexual appetite per se as the cause of objectification that individual or private escape is not possible. Dworkin may similarly be inclined to accept a kind of sexual moral fatalism, given the asymmetry of power between men and women in intercourse. She sees no route of possible escape through private consensual acts. As she says:

> [Even visionary sexual reformers fail to face] the fundamental questions about intercourse as an act with consequences, some perhaps intrinsic. [Even with intercourse contingent on consent, and the conditions of consent the woman's desire,] the woman could not forcibly penetrate the man. The woman could not take him over as he took her over and occupy his body physically inside. His dominance over her expressed in the physical reality of intercourse has no real analogue in desire she might express for him in intercourse: she simply could not do to him what he could do to her.[12]

A similar critique of any "escape through consent" solution can be found in the work of Catharine MacKinnon, whose views about sexuality and pornography are often paired with Dworkin's.[13] MacKinnon, however, makes no comparable essentialist claim—although the alternative picture of the structure of sexual life that she draws is no more permitting of private transcendence than if she had. As she sees it, even if it is not of the nature of sexuality to objectify, objectification is a truth about sexuality as it functions in the gender structure of male dominance: "The general theory of sexuality emerging from this feminist critique does not consider sexuality to be an inborn force inherent in individuals, nor cultural in the Freudian sense, in which sexuality exists in a cultural context but in universally invariant stages and psychic representations. It appears instead to be culturally specific, even if so far largely invariant because male supremacy is largely universal, if always in specific forms."[14] The problem of objectification thus remains central to this strand of the feminist critique of sexuality as-we-know-it, whether it is in the nature of sexuality to cause objectification or whether sexual practice expresses objectifying social structures.

Suppose—in the light of this—we allow Kant's claim that the sexual appetite in itself is directed at the body. (There are of course, questions to be asked about what it might mean to think of an appetite "in itself," but we will have to leave those aside for now.) Is there any reason to think it follows that the person whose sexuality is aroused cannot see the object of sexual interest as a person? Kant's reasons for thinking it does follow can be seen in the contrast he draws between what he calls human love and sexual love.

> Human love is good will, affection, promoting the happiness of others and finding joy in their happiness. But it is clear that when a person loves another purely from sexual desire, none of these factors enter into love. Far from there being any concern for the happiness of the loved one, the lover, in order to satisfy his desire, may even plunge the loved one into the depths of misery. Sexual love makes of the loved person an Object of appetite; as soon as that appetite has been stilled, the person is cast aside as one casts away a lemon that has been sucked dry. (*Lectures on Ethics* 163)

> If . . . a man wishes to satisfy his desire, and a woman hers, they stimulate each other's desire; their inclinations meet, but their object is not human nature but sex. (*Lectures on Ethics* 164)

Why can't human love transform sexual love? Does Kant think this because he regards appetites as untransmutable original existences?

We have, one would suppose, an appetite for food per se that can be transformed into a taste for and appreciation of fine food. But the structure of an appetite for food remains: hunger and satiety marking its boundaries and, as we might say, the appetite itself remaining an appetite for food. (The possibility of the perversion or inversion of an appetite, or instinct, does not change this.) So the appetite for sex can develop into an appetite for refined or exotic sex, but it is still an appetite for sex in the sense that its object is pleasure of a certain sort to be had from the sexual use of someone's body.[15]

Human love is an interest in a person as an agent with a life (with moral capacities and so forth). Although it could include an interest in another's having sexual satisfaction as a component of a good life, it does not have as its object pleasure and so is not structured by the analogues of hunger and satiety. Kant says: "Sexual love can, of course, be combined with human love and so carry with it the characteristics of the latter, but taken by itself and for itself, it is nothing more than appetite" (*Lectures on Ethics* 163). "Carry with it" is not the language of transformation. Frequently we love as persons those we love sexually, and our concern for their well-being may control and shape the expression of sexual appetite. But for Kant this gets us no further than the fact that absent property, we might not take what was of use to someone we cared about. This would not give the loved one claim or title to the object of use, just as our human love cannot transform the object of sexual love into a subject (a person).

Kant makes the further claim that in satisfying sexual desire one party surrenders use of a part for the purposes of gain or pleasure, giving the other a right of disposal[16] over that part. And since "a human being is a unity," the right gained thereby is over the whole person. But we cannot have rights of disposal over persons because persons are not things. That is why agreement about use does not provide a remedy: The problem is not one of force. One cannot give a right of disposal over a part for it is not a right we have. Thus, Kant argues, unless it is possible to have rights of disposal over persons, sexual activity is morally impermissible.[17]

In a full treatment of Kant's views, three claims would need to be examined: first, that objectification leads to a right of disposal; second, that rights over a part of the body are in effect rights over the whole and that a right of disposal of the sexual part is a right of disposal over the person; and third, that we are not the sorts of things over which anyone (including ourselves) can have rights of disposal.

A right of disposal, I presume, is a right of free use (in the sense of having something at my disposal). We can take it as obvious that, and why, Kantian theory holds that we cannot freely use persons in this sense. But how do we get to a right of disposal from the fact that sexual interest is in and for a body (or for the pleasure to be had from sexual engagement with another's sexuality)? Kant seems to take it as given that sexual activity involves mutual surrender, so that to enjoy a person sexually is to enjoy a thing given to us. (The difficulty in getting agreement on limits of use for things we possess suggests the intuition that if an object is in my power, that I have a right of disposal over it is not without foundation.) Certainly there is much talk of possession, surrender, and use in erotic language.

In any case, I am here less interested in defending the odd metaphysics of Kant's claims about parts and wholes than I am in marking the fact that just such views about sexual use are integral to the kind of feminist argument both Dworkin and MacKinnon present. Their central programmatic task is to demonstrate that the effect of sexual regard or relationship cannot be partial—mere sex—but that the very categories of gender, of who we are as men and as women, are functions of objectifying sexual regard.

Although on Kant's view sexuality creates a morally impermissible relation between the sexual partners, it is neither desirable nor possible to forbid sexual activity. Sexual intercourse is the now standard (then necessary) means for procreation, and love relations with sexual components are essential to happiness (for many). So we have a kind of relationship that we cannot forego (as the kind of beings we are) but that is not morally acceptable. Marriage is supposed to solve the problem—resetting the moral stage so that there is a morally permissible way for sexual life to take place without inevitable moral loss or danger.

III

We have reason to be dubious about any social institution's ability to restore or preserve what may be threatened or lost in intimate relations. We have special reasons to be dubious about the institution of "marriage" as it reflects and sustains just the exploitative and agency-demeaning features of moral concern. Rather than support the institution of marriage as-we-know-it, Kantian ethics should give reasons to judge that institution impermissible.

The institution of marriage as-we-know-it involves the State's acknowledgment of only certain relationships, entered into in only certain ways, creating thereby certain State-enforced rights and liabilities. It allows the State some security about property and children—someone is responsible for getting the kids to school and in condition for minimal socialization, and property is cared for through the regulatory role of the divorce courts.[18] Marriage encourages the creation of small, isolated, economically insecure units vulnerable to the vagaries of the market. It protects the chief arena of abuse of women and children, it endorses sexual inequality (protecting the sexual and social advantages of men), and it penalizes gay men and lesbians. The institution of marriage as-we-know-it is a nasty thing. If sexuality carries a moral burden, marriage hardly seems to be the arena of its resolution.

Before thinking that what is needed is a reform of the institution of marriage, we want to wonder about the very idea of casting a social institution in this sort of morally creative role. Is it even possible to have a legal form of marriage that does not merely reinforce the moral damage of sexual relations between men and women as-we-know-them? How could the legal construction of the relationship re-create what practice has destroyed (or preserve what is endangered)? Kant has two different answers to these questions, one of which deserves some further attention.

In his *Lectures on Ethics,* Kant argues that

> the sole condition on which we are free to make use of our sexual desire depends upon the right to dispose over the person as a whole—over the welfare and happiness and generally over all the circumstances of that person. . . . [I obtain these rights over the whole person (and so have the right of sexual use of that person) I only by giving the person the same rights over myself. This happens only in marriage. Matrimony is an agreement between two persons by which they grant each other equal reciprocal rights, each of them undertaking to surrender the whole of their person to the other with a complete right of disposal over it. (167)

Now the part that does the work:

But if I yield myself completely to another and obtain the person of the other
in return, I win myself back; I have given myself up as the property of another,
but in turn I take that other as my property, and so win myself back again in
winning the person whose property I have become. In this way the two persons
become a unity of will. . . . Thus sexuality leads to a union of human beings,
and in that union alone is its exercise possible. (167)

Marriage solves the problem because each grants the other "equal reciprocal rights"
and no one loses anything. Why suppose that if I give myself and get someone else
back, that I get myself? Perhaps it goes this way: I give myself (or rights over myself)
and you give yourself; but since you have me, in giving yourself to me you give me
back to me. And so on, The idea might be this: Suppose I give you every pencil I own
or will come to own knowing that (or on condition that) you will give me every pencil
that you own or will come to own. One could say that we thereby create a community
of pencil ownership—a unity of will about pencils.

But even if this makes some sense, a unity of will out of two persons or a "union
of human beings" does not. Although one sees what Kant may have wanted—a kind
of romantic blending of self into a new and larger self—it is not possible for him to
get what he wants. If the problem with sex is that we are embodied selves, and use of
the body implies title over a self, things are not greatly improved if we become parts
of a new self that has two bodies (and sex would then be what?). The threat to the autonomous agent would seem to be increased rather than resolved in the surrender to
the new union of persons, a threat that is especially acute to women, who are not
likely to share equally in the direction of the new union.[19]

Furthermore, the account is a mess in Kant's own terms—for it does not even
make sense to "grant reciprocal rights" over a self when one's self is not the sort of
thing over which there can be rights. Nor is there any need for marriage as a public
institution, because the granting of reciprocal rights, if one had them, would be a
matter of free contract.

The argument for marriage in the *Rechtslehre* is interestingly different and possibly more fruitful. I must admit that I do not think this because of any new long account it contains (most of the *Rechtslehre*'s remarks on marriage can be read as compatible with what is said in the *Lectures on Ethics*), but because the account of marriage fits
the general pattern of argument for necessary political institutions that is the heart of
the *Rechtslehre*'s program.

The problem leading to the institution of marriage in the *Rechtslehre* is once
again the reduction of person to thing—the surrender of self (rational personhood)—
inherent in sexual activity. What goes in as individuals with an interest in reciprocal
possession of their sexual faculties comes out this time, not as a private union of wills,
but as two equal juridical persons. That is, within the State (or civil society) it is possible to reestablish and secure the equal autonomy of the partners in a sexual relationship by defining them (and so setting the conditions of their sexual relationship) under the law as equal legal persons, giving them new public natures,[20] as it were,
conventionally called "husband" and "wife." This version of Kantian marriage is not

(and cannot be) an agreement between two persons; nor can it be any other possible private act. The idea seems to be that through mediation by law, the natural tendencies to objectification, and so dominance and exploitation, in sexual relations are blocked. The institution of marriage in this way resolves the moral difficulty arising from sexual activity.

To make such an idea even intelligible, we must return to the *Rechtslehre* account of property. In a natural state (without Law), exclusion by force of anyone from use of anything is wrong; yet without the possibility of rightful exclusion, secure use is impossible. Since effective agency requires secure use, a system of rights and coercive enforcement that define conditions of legitimate possession and use is necessary and justified. We need an *institution* of property—conventions, conditions of enforcement—because there is no natural "right way" to allocate possession. But not just any institution of property will do. The justification of possession—that it is necessary for effective agency—puts constraints on the kind of institution of property that is permissible. Thus one person or one class owning everything is not.

The justification of the juridical institution of marriage should work the same way. But though it may be easy to see why property requires an institution—rules to determine legitimate possession, transfer, limits of use—it is less clear where an institution fits into the resolution of the moral problem of sexuality. We need to explain how a system of rights and enforcement could serve as the moral condition of sexual activity in a way that eliminates or resolves objectification.

Accepting a legal relation as a condition of sexual activity is to give up the freedom to act as appetite directs. But if the sexual appetite makes me regard my partner as an object, how can legal prohibition of certain sorts of use affect how I regard him? The *Rechtslehre* gives no guidance. We can, however, support the *Rechtslehre*'s claim with a somewhat conjectural answer constructed from other Kantian theses about appetite and practical rationality.

Kant sees the appetites as original (biological) springs to activity. As rational beings, we are neither constrained by the trajectory of appetitive desire nor by a conception of the object of desire as object of desire. I may be moved to play tennis because I need an outlet for aggressive energy. I may choose to play it as a pleasant social activity in which I also get exercise. Because I am a rational being, the latter interests are able to regulate my activity (controlling how and with whom I play), though there may be some tension with my natural and motivating aggressivity that needs to be monitored and controlled. Though a bit oversimplified, this example offers a model for understanding the possible role of institutions in transforming appetite-driven regard.

Morality requires that I treat other people as persons, not things. I may have and act on appetites that, if I identified with them, would lead me to regard others as things. As a rational being I need not do so. If what I desire is that you perform some useful-to-me service, morality requires that I take your voluntary participation as a condition of your action. Whatever my instrumental interest in you, I may not regard you as a mere instrument. This is not a matter of attitude or feeling. Regarding you as a person is accepting a set of constraints on my actions: I may not use force or deceit to gain your compliance with my will. Thus Kant might think: Although the sexual appetite leads me to regard and so treat another as a thing suitable to yield sexual pleasure, morality opposes this. One may grab a piece of fruit seeking its sweetness; one may not "grab" a person for sexual pleasure. That is rape.

If this is the problem of objectification, regulative *moral* principles resolve it. Why, then, does Kant think a juridical institution (marriage) is necessary? The puzzle is about the need for rules (law). In the cases of possession and contract, we must have mutually recognized property rights and mutually recognized rules governing promise and delivery. Because there is no uniquely right way to accomplish these morally necessary tasks, rules must be set; the law of property and contract will be to some extent arbitrary (the terms of "first acquisition," the conditions of adverse possession, and so on). If the justification for the institution of marriage is on parallel grounds, it must be that what is involved in regarding one's sexual partner as a person is also to some extent open.

The purpose of the institution of marriage is to block the transformation of regard that comes with sexual appetite. The point is not just to put force behind moral prohibitions on abuse (though there is that); we can treat another "well" without acknowledging his or her moral status (perhaps as a highly valued object or pet). Other appetites (for example, aggression) may tempt one to act impermissibly, but they can be deflected, regulated, or simply rejected as motives. The special problem of sexuality is that what we want is to satisfy it, even though, Kant thinks, it cannot both be satisfied and not affect the status of our regard for our partner. Then how is it possible to secure the moral status of the partners by introducing juridical marriage as the necessary moral condition of sexual activity? In order to permissibly satisfy sexual appetite, both parties must first accept a juridical relationship of rights and responsibilities. The particular rights and responsibilities (and their correlative legitimate expectations) are to some extent arbitrary, though as before, given the moral basis of the legal institution, not any set of rights and responsibilities will do the job.[21] What they are to do is to secure regard for one's partner as a person with a life, which is what the sexual appetite by itself causes one to disregard.

Marriage does not do the job of love. Human love—the concern for the life and well-being of another—is responsive to the particulars of individual need and interest. Marriage introduces rules of care and support that are, by the nature of rules, without such sensitivity. But human love will also not do the job of marriage, for the need to which the lover responds may itself undermine autonomy. The rules are not so much to restrain or oblige action as to construct moral regard. That is, they make the sexual interest in another person possible only where there is secure moral regard for that person's life, and they do this by making the acceptance of obligations with respect to that person's welfare a condition of sexual activity.

What is remarkable in Kant's account is the argument to the necessity of public rules for what we think of as the most private relationships. When sexuality and marriage are thought of as private, they are conceptually prior to any State institution of marriage that protects and regulates some but not all sexually based relations. So we get a kind of Lockean story of some consent-based relationships that are of regulatory concern to the State, usually because the family is the natural vehicle on which inheritance travels and because of children. However, it is the preexisting marital relationship that the State protects and that determines the limits of public authority. Thus the State may require the education of children (which is in its interest) and regulate the terms of divorce (which concerns the fate of property), but it may not interfere with domestic activity (which is private and prior to its concern).

With Kantian property, the State has no special problem about taxing for welfare or education since the right to property is an institution-based right, grounded in the conditions of effective human agency. If a legitimate sexual relationship can exist only within a juridical relationship, legal limitations on the form of the relationship (permissible demands, support, responsibility, and the like) would not be any invasion of privacy because the sexual relation, by its nature, is not a permissible private relation. This would not be marriage as-we-know-it. So, for example, Kantian marriage offers no conceptual barrier to defining and prohibiting spousal rape, battering, and so on. (The fact that in marriage as-we-know-it spousal rape has been held to be impossible and wife beating at times a husband's prerogative provides strong evidence in support of the objectification thesis.)[22]

IV

I must admit that at different times much of this discussion has seemed to me to be simply absurd. Then on reflection I find that I am not so sure. First there is the uncomfortable claim that sexual activity is unavoidably morally problematic. But given heterosexual sex as-we-know-it, this does not seem so farfetched. So long as sex is inter-leaved with power, so-called private sex *is* morally difficult. Date rape, battering, sexual harassment, are not aberrations. Where there seems room for argument is over our individual or joint capacity to have "good" sex (morally good, that is). Here I am sympathetic with Kant's remarks that things aren't really changed by living in a community of saints—so long as they are human saints. The structures latent in human sexual relationships set the moral machinery going. If love is not sufficient to secure respect for persons within sexuality (responsiveness to another will not do if the response may be to another's self-abnegating surrender), then perhaps the only way out is through the conventions of a healthy public culture. (This is the flip side of the feminist concern with the social construction of gender and sexuality.)

On the other hand, one might think that the very fact of sexual activity as in some sense public activity (available for scrutiny and interference), requiring a prior juridically defined relationship, would gravely distort and damage sexual life. Certainly what we know of the practice of such scrutiny is that it has been both puritanical and comfortably tolerant of the sexual abuse of women. But that is not quite the issue. I take the point rather to be this: If it turned out that violence is a natural or normal expression of the sexual appetite, and that violence is not compatible with equal moral regard for persons, then violence would be prohibited (morally) and the State could and should interfere with sex (that aspect of sexual expression). Such protection would not require bedroom police. It offers grounds for complaint, prevention, and redress on the one hand and terms of public sexual education on the other. In this sense, sexuality would indeed be distorted, if by that is meant that its permissible forms of expression are to be other than they would be without juridical rules, public education, and so forth. That does not seem to be altogether a bad thing, given the forms of sexual expression as-we-know-them. But might not there also be something of value that would be lost if sexual expression were not utterly private and spontaneous? Maybe so. But there is no argument that morality must leave everything as it finds it. If we were not drawn to act impermissibly by what we value, we would have no need for moral constraint.

There is, in Kant's account, a challenge to the inherent "goodness" of the sexual appetite that may disturb us. It is his general view of the appetites as causal impulses, neither good nor bad. Acting to satisfy them must be regulated by the principles of practical rationality independent of their capacity to give pleasure. The sexual appetite differs from the others in that its object (normally) is a person. Hunger gives us an interest in food, but the relation to the food substance falls under moral regulation only when what we would eat is someone else's property, when resources are scarce, and so on. Moral concern with sexual activity does not arise from its contingent intersection with moral requirements from other domains.

There may be deeper discomfort at the idea that moral difficulties that (appear to) arise interpersonally are not to be resolved interpersonally, but require the alienating "third term" of a juridical relationship. I do not find it hard to believe that personal "good faith" efforts can be inadequate to resolve moral difficulties that are supported by the social world in which we gain our conceptions of self and other. This, of course, does not mean that there is no difference between decency and violence in sexual relations, or that it is not worth struggling for something better. But I find myself persuaded, if not by Kant then by Dworkin and MacKinnon, that the distance between decency and violence is not the chasm we sometimes persuade ourselves it is.

The chief obstacle for me in Kant's account comes from doubt about the idea of "moral institutions"—that is, institutions that transcend the power relations that reside in the practices they "govern." What is taken to be natural—the structure of sexuality that sets the terms of the moral problem—is already a social construction. How can introducing an institution to protect the moral interests of sexual partners do other than preserve the essential social nature of those interests and the embedded relations of power and exploitation?[23] A juridical institution seems too external to the moral difficulty if what is needed is a transformation of sexuality itself. But if sexuality is not "natural," then it is less clear why the reconstruction of social relations could not be transformative—and from the "outside." Kant's failure, I would say, was in thinking (if he did) that juridical relations could secure individual autonomy without the deep transformation of social relations and the family.

That Kant's account does not resolve the problem I now think he saw surprises me far less than the discovery that at least some feminists agree that it is this problem that bears worrying about. To those who see the law as a positive avenue for radical social change, Kant may provide an unexpected source of theoretical insight and support.[24]

Notes

1. The philosophically neutral "we" should itself be a source of concern here.

2. This is not a connection I went looking for. A year and a half ago I was teaching Kant's political philosophy and participating in a study group that was reading Andrea Dworkin and Catharine MacKinnon. In the midst of a class discussion I found that I could paraphrase Kant's views of sexuality using Dworkin and MacKinnon's analysis. It seemed at once a perverse and right thing to do. I'm not sure I yet know which. This essay was supposed to help me figure that out.

3. The *Groundwork* argues this way: If obligation is possible, universalizability is the form of moral judgment (no action is permissible whose maxim cannot be willed a universal law). If the requirement of universalizability sets a possible reason for action, then the will must be free. Only a will that is free (capable of being motivated by considerations of practical rationality alone) can take universalizability as a reason for action. It remains to be shown that no other explanation of obligation is possible (a task taken up by the *Critique of Practical Reason*).

4. The main argument of the *Rechtslehre* is found in John Ladd's translation, *The Metaphysical Elements of Justice* (Indianapolis: Bobbs-Merrill, 1965), secs. 1–9. Ladd, however, omitted sections 10–35 of the original text that present the details of Kant's views on property, contract, and rights over persons. In particular, sections 24–30 contain Kant's account of marriage and the family. A nineteenth-century English translation of the complete *Rechtslehre* is available in W. Hastie's *The Philosophy of Law* (Edinburgh, 1887). Page numbers are to the Ladd translation; section numbers refer to the Hastie (and the original German). (Since this chapter was completed, Cambridge University Press has published Mary Gregor's new translation of *The Metaphysics of Morals*. It contains the complete text of the *Rechtslehre*.)

5. "[I]t is a duty of justice to act towards others so that external objects (usable objects) can also become someone's property" (*Rechtslehre*, p. 60). That is, "if it must be *de jure* possible to have an external object as one's own, then the subject must also be allowed to compel everyone else with whom he comes into conflict over the question of whether such an object is his to enter, together with him, a society under a civil constitution" (ibid., p. 65).

6. Kant is almost always talking about sexual activity between consenting adult men and women. This aspect of his critique of sexuality would apply equally to same-sex sexual relations—though Kant has other sorts of "unnaturalness" objections to them.

7. It is this—and not sexual squeamishness—that is the basis for his claim that engaging in sexual relations without marriage is not morally possible.

8. Kant, *Lectures on Ethics*, tr. Louis Infield (New York: Harper Torchbooks, 1963), p. 164.

9. Andrea Dworkin, *Intercourse* (New York: Free Press, 1987). Quotations are from pp. 122–123, 140–141, and 142–143, respectively.

10. Some recent university sexual harassment policies may reason in a similar fashion in adopting a presumption invalidating apparent consent when there are sexual relations between persons in positions of unequal power. One could understand this simply as a strong disincentive to engage in such activity. A more suggestive reading finds such policies taking to heart the impermissibility of sexual relations where conditions of equality are absent.

11. "Pornography is not imagery in some relation to a reality elsewhere constructed. It is not distortion, reflection, projection, expression, fantasy, representation, or symbol either.

It is sexual reality." Catharine MacKinnon quoted in Christine Littleton, "Feminist Jurisprudence: The Difference Method Makes," *Stanford Law Review* 41 (February 1989): 772.

12. Dworkin, *Intercourse*, p. 136.

13. Andrea Dworkin and Catharine MacKinnon together drafted and worked for the adoption of a model antipornography ordinance in Minneapolis. They share a view of pornography as a central, not marginal, aspect of sexuality, and both argue that sexual activity is an arena for the expression of masculine power and domination. Dworkin has more overtly Kantian commitments to a conception of the person that sexual practice debases.

14. Catharine A. MacKinnon, *Towards a Feminist Theory of the State* (Cambridge, Mass.: Harvard University Press, 1989), p. 151.

15. Transformations of the sexual appetite to having an object that is not the body of another can be ignored here.

16. There is some ambiguity in Kant's moral charge: Are we brought by the sexual appetite to regard our partners as objects, *as if* we had rights of disposal over them, or is it that in sexual relations we *are* objects for each other over which we do have rights of disposal?

17. "The sole condition on which we are free to make use of our sexual desire depends upon the right to dispose over the person as a whole—over the welfare and happiness and generally over all the circumstances of that person" (*Lectures on Ethics*, pp. 166–167).

18. As a law professor friend remarked, from the State's point of view, marriage is about divorce.

19. Stories such as this are the basis of Carol Pateman's critical analysis of the role of marriage in liberal political theory. See her *Sexual Contract* (Stanford, Calif.: Stanford University Press, 1989).

20. I am thinking of the idea of a "second nature" as discussed in Kant's *Conjectural Beginning of Human History*, in *On History*, ed. L. W. Beck (Indianapolis: Bobbs-Merrill, 1963), pp. 53–68.

21. Kant thinks monogamous heterosexual marriage is the only such institution, but the logic of his argument should at most establish it as one possibility or variant.

22. Since on Kant's account the moral difficulty is with sexuality per se and not male-female sex (he would see gender domination as a contingent function of strength made possible by the objectification inherent in sexual relations), same-sex relationships would also be morally possible only with marriage. And since Kant does not hold that the State has an interest in sexual activity because or only when it is procreative (see *Rechtslehre*, see. 24), there is also no conceptual barrier to same-sex marriage and a strong argument for it. Of course Kant opposes same-sex relations on the grounds that they are unnatural—as unable to promote "nature's" procreative purposes (*Lectures on Ethics*, p. 170)—so I do not mean to suggest that he would endorse my extension of his views.

23. Marx, in his *On the Jewish Question,* offers a similar criticism of the idea of the "rights of man"—which extend rights that had been the province of class privilege to all people—on the grounds that the very idea of rights protects the essential framework of private property and social isolation that stands in the way of real human emancipation.

24. My thanks to Charlotte Witt, whose insightful comments on the earlier draft of this paper helped me learn from my own project; to Margaret Radin, for teaching with me in a way that made it possible to think about new ideas in old places; and to the participants in the University of New Hampshire's symposium on "Feminism and Rationality," for two days of conversation that removed some of the sense of oppressive opposition between the ambitions of feminism and philosophy.

5

MALENESS, METAPHOR, AND THE "CRISIS" OF REASON

GENEVIEVE LLOYD

Umberto Eco, in a bemused discussion of the "crisis" of reason in his *Travels in Hyper-Reality*,[1] suggests that it is perhaps not so much reason as the notion of its "crisis" that is currently in critical condition. What exactly, he asks, is this crisis? If we feel alright, whose crisis is it? And can we clear it up? Should we be looking for a new instrument to replace reason—"feeling, delirium, poetry, mystical silence, a sardine can opener?" There is, of course, an obviously appropriate response to Eco's feigned perplexity. His facetious search for a new instrument mislocates the alleged crisis. The crisis concerns not the reliability of instrumental reason but the privileged position it has assumed.

The current "rage against reason," as Richard Bernstein has called it, is directed not at its reliability as an instrument but rather at the extent to which instrumental reason has come to dominate the traditionally rich and varied senses of the concept.[2] In Max Horkheimer's metaphor, in *The Eclipse of Reason*,[3] instrumental reason has "eclipsed" the richer dimensions of "objective" reason that traditionally expressed the ideal of a meaningful human life in a rational world. If the "fully enlightened" world is seen as radiating "disaster triumphant,"[4] it is because of what rationality has come to be in the modern world—because of the predominance of one form of reason. Such critics of reason are seeking not a new instrument but the recovery—less in forms appropriate to the modern world—of older ways of thinking of reason. Horkheimer's "objective" reason, grounding meaningful human lives, and Jürgen Habermas's "communicative" reason, articulated in the ideal of free, undistorted speech, are attempts to remedy the impoverishment of modern reason by shifting attention away from its preoccupations with instrumentality.

Eco's whimsical incredulity about the crisis does nonetheless carry a salutary message for feminists and for other contemporary ragers against reason. Some feminist dismissals of reason as male do seem to come perilously close to Eco's picture of a poignant search for a sardine can opener. The feminist critique of reason is centered on its alleged maleness, but it shares in the strengths and confusions of broader criticism of reason. And "maleness" can function in this context as a general term of disapprobation, encompassing all the negative features of post-Enlightenment reason. It should be no surprise that attempts by feminist philosophers to articulate the alleged maleness of reason evoke the same bemused responses as other articulations of the "crisis." What exactly, we may ask, is the maleness of reason, and what is supposed to follow from it? For whom is it a problem? What does it have to do with real men and women? Is the claim about reason itself or about ways in which past philosophers have talked of it? Is this maleness real or metaphorical? And, having discerned its presence in reason, what are women supposed to do? Stop reasoning? Look for another instrument?

For some feminists, accepting the maleness of reason involves trying to find or develop new female or feminine thought styles. Others have responded to these developments with dismay, seeing in them an insidious reinforcement of the old stereotypes of female irrationality. Eco's plea for clarity about what or who is in crisis is worth taking seriously, even if we think his interpretation of the issue is misguided. But, whereas Eco deplores "metaphoric irresponsibility" as exacerbating rather than illuminating the "crisis" of reason, I want to explore the issues of reason's alleged maleness not by rejecting metaphor but by trying to get a deeper understanding of how metaphor operates.

"Male" and "Female" as Metaphors

The reflections on metaphor in this chapter have been stimulated by two kinds of critical response to my book *The Man of Reason: "Male" and "Female" in Western Philosophy* (London: Methuen, 1984). On the one hand, some feminist critics have suggested that the book's treatment of the maleness of reason slides between "sex" and "gender"—between claims about the mental processes of real men and women and the social construction of masculinity and femininity in Western culture. Another kind of criticism, mostly from nonfeminists, has suggested that the book slides between the metaphorical and the literal—that it mistakes for real features of reason what are in fact mere superficial accretions of metaphor in its philosophical articulation.

Both criticisms have their point. The book directly addressed neither the sex-gender distinction nor the distinction between the metaphoric and the literal. And it does contain slides within those distinctions. But I am not at all sure that they result from a failure to observe distinctions that are in themselves unproblematic. Both sets of distinction are unstable. And the claims of the book resist encapsulation as either sex or gender, literal or metaphorical. I doubt that all the offending slides in the book result from lack of care with well-established distinctions. They come, rather, from trying to articulate—perhaps with only limited success—perceptions that those distinctions themselves help to obscure.

The distinction between "biological" sex and "socially constructed" gender has undoubtedly been useful for understanding some aspects of sex difference, providing a way of conceptualizing the rejection of biological determinism and allowing the formulation of ideals of sexual equality. But what feminists have tried to articulate as the maleness of reason cannot be readily expressed as either sex or gender. Although it does have effects for real men and women, it certainly does not pertain to them as biologically sexed beings. Can it then be treated as a feature or product of social construction? In some trivial ways, yes. Forced to choose, we would locate it with gender. Women can, of course, participate in male reason. And part of what that means can be captured in the cumbersome platitude that persons who are biologically female can exhibit character traits that are socially regarded as masculine. But there are aspects of the maleness of reason that are not captured in the idea of socially constructed masculinity. We are here dealing with the content of symbols. That, of course, belongs— if anything does—in the realm of the social. But this maleness, though it does have consequences for the social construction of gender, cannot be equated with socially produced masculinity.

Sandra Harding, in her discussion of gender in *The Science Question in Feminism,* has drawn some useful distinctions between "symbolic gender" on the one hand and "structural gender" on the other: the ways in which human activity and labor are divided by gender; and "individual gender" (that is, what counts as masculine or feminine identity and behavior).[5] My concern in this chapter is with what Harding calls "symbolic gender"—with the operations of male and female as symbols. These symbolic operations interact, of course, with gender division and with the social formation of gender identity. Masculine socialization influences which symbols male authors choose and how they operate with them. And those uses of symbols influence in turn the social formation of gender identity. But if we are to understand those interactions, there are aspects of the symbols that we must first separate from gender.

Despite their differences from biological sex, the concepts Harding calls "structural gender" and "individual gender" both apply directly to real men and women. The connections between symbolic gender and real men and women are more complex. The content of symbolic gender can be appropriated by men and women. But even though people can identify with symbolic maleness or femaleness, their proper subjects are not men and women but concepts. The maleness of reason belongs in this category of the symbolic. Equating it with gender can obscure just how different it is from the gender that has as its proper subjects real men and women, making it harder to grasp how it does interact with their biological or socially produced properties.

The distinction between sex and gender, important though it is in other contexts, can distract us from how "male" and "female" act as symbols, which is where our attention should be focused if we are to understand this aspect of reason. *The Man of Reason* was centrally concerned with male and female as symbolic content (metaphors); it was concerned with the literary dimensions of philosophical texts. This male and female symbolism is also the concern of much of contemporary French philosophy and feminist theory now being appropriated by English-speaking feminists. I suspect that the real import of this material—especially that inspired by Jacques Derrida—has been obscured by older and different concerns with sexual difference that have found expression through the sex-gender distinction.

Let me now turn to the idea of metaphor and the distinction between the literal and the metaphorical. The maleness of reason, which is sometimes, perhaps, taken all too literally by feminists, has also often been dismissed as "mere" metaphor, of no consequence for reason itself. What I want to resist in this is not the claim that the maleness of reason is metaphorical but the dismissiveness implicit in the qualification of "mereness." We can recognize this maleness as metaphorical without relegating it to the margins of truth. Like many other metaphors in the history of philosophy, this maleness is not a superficial accretion to the real being of reason. Those who talk of mere metaphor here imply that we can keep our received ideals of reason while cleaning up the offensive metaphors through which they have been articulated. But the problem goes deeper than this—not just because metaphors have their nonmetaphorical effects on our self-understanding, but also for reasons that pertain to the relations between reason and the metaphors that express it. Metaphors have their philosophical import as well as their cultural effects.

Evelyn Fox Keller has offered some illuminating accounts of the complex interactions between the metaphors of a culture and the social formation of gender, especially in relation to the collective consciousness of science.[6] My own concern is not with the processes by which social gender and symbolic gender interact but rather with getting a better understanding of symbolic maleness and symbolic femaleness independently of that interaction. This is something that can be masked by concern with the social formation of gender. It is illuminating to focus directly on it, although adequate understanding of sexual difference in relation to reason may involve bringing all the elements together again.

Contemporary French feminist theory, especially the work of Luce Irigaray, has helped bring these metaphorical dimensions of the male-female distinction into focus.[7] I want now to look at a discussion of Irigaray in a recent paper by Margaret Whitford, "Luce Irigaray's Critique of Rationality."[8] This interesting and enlightening treatment of Irigaray serves to highlight some aspects of the current use of her work that I think need close examination.

Whitford's reading focuses on Irigaray's strategy of appropriating the feminine position that has traditionally been created through the conceptualization of reason as male. Irigaray is presented as offering an alternative to what Whitford calls "exclusion" models of rationality (p. 111), although this alternative, Whitford says, is not to be understood as an "essentialist description of what women are really like," but rather as a "description of the female as she appears in, and is symbolised by, the Western cultural imaginary" (p. 114). In this respect, Whitford notes, Irigaray's work draws on that of Derrida. She uses deconstructive strategies to undermine the constraining power of male reason over its female opposites. So for Irigaray the problem is not so much that women are treated as incapable of reason as that the female has been assigned a particular function in symbolic processes. Whitford sums this process up as "to subtend them, to be that which is outside discourse" (p. 118). The female, Whitford says, is taken as representing "that original state of non-differentiation" from which distinctions and determinate identities emerge. This state outside discourse is traditionally conceptualized as female. Here, within Irigaray's "female imaginary," the laws of identity and noncontradiction do not apply. Whitford points out that all this may well sound dangerously irrationalist, but she stresses that Irigaray's point is not that *women* are irrational but that there is always a "residue" that exceeds determinate categories and that this excess has been conceptualized as female.

This description of how the female functions in Western symbolism brings out the contingency of symbolic processes and thus opens up space for questions about the relations between real women and symbolic Woman. The problem for real women, as Whitford sums it up, is that although they may be symbolized as the outside, they are not in fact outside society and its symbolic structures. We have here, she suggests, a "social imaginary"—a symbolic construction—that is taken to be real, with damaging consequences for women. Women, unlike men, find themselves homeless in the symbolic order (p. 121). What emerges from Whitford's reading of Irigaray is that sexual difference does not yet exist in the "social imaginary" of the West. Rather than being located within the operations of symbolism, sexual difference is aligned with the distinction between the symbolic and what lies outside its operation. Sexual difference symbolizes the distinction between the symbolic and what lies beyond it. Where, then, are women supposed to go from here? Symbolic meanings, Whitford stresses, cannot be altered by fiat. The symbolism cannot be simply reversed. Nor is it enough to insist that women are in fact rational, because that is not the point. The point is, rather, the relation of women to the symbolic structures that exclude them (p. 123).

There is much about Whitford's elaboration of the upshot of Irigaray's work that illuminates the operations of Woman as symbol. But I think clarification is needed of her presentation of the relations between women and symbolic Woman. Should the claim really be that women are excluded from the symbolic structures? Does this follow from the fact that Woman symbolically represents exclusion? Or has something gone awry with this application of deconstructive strategies to the understanding of women's relations to symbols? What does it mean to say that women are outside the symbolic structures? In one sense it is, of course, clearly true. It is not women but men who have created the symbolic structures we have inherited in the philosophical tradition. Men have conceptualized reason through Woman, symbolizing what is opposite to maleness and, to that extent, what is opposite to themselves as men. The symbolization of reason as male derives historically from the contingent fact that it was largely men—to the literal exclusion of women—who devised the symbolic structures. This is a symbolism appropriate to men as exclusive symbol users. If this were all that is involved in the claimed exclusion of women from the symbolic structures, it would be an uncontroversial point—and also a relatively uninteresting one. The more substantive claim concerns the ramifications of this past exclusion for women's current relations to the symbolic structures. And here the upshot of Irigaray's use of deconstructive strategies is by no means straightforward.

Irigaray herself describes her strategy in terms of mimicry or "mimesis"—a conscious appropriation of the position outside symbolism in order from this vantage point to offer readings or interpretations of texts in the Western tradition. This is supposed to yield, in her own metaphor, a jamming of the theoretical machinery. The strategy, of course, cannot but be an ironic one—it is itself an operation with symbols. And the outsideness of the speaking position also has to be metaphorical. Women as symbol users are no more outside the operations of symbols than men, whatever may be the content of Woman as symbol. Irigaray, ironically, appropriates a position outside the symbolic structures in order, by speaking from it, to make visible the role played by the projected excluded other. It is a strategy for laying bare the operations of a text; it is often a very effective one. What concerns me is a nonironic version of this deconstructive strategy that seems evident in some English-speaking versions of that strategy—as if it were literally the unspoken but real feminine that is captured through deconstruction. To be assured that this feminine is not "essential" but rather a contingent product of the symbolic structures themselves does not remove my skepticism about this vein in contemporary feminist theory.

For Whitford, what Irigaray shows is that the conceptualization of rationality in Western thought involves the domination, repression, or transcending of the symbolic female. It is, she suggests, an "exclusion" model of rationality that reflects the way the "male imaginary" deals with sexual difference. And she sees Irigaray's strategies as pointing to a more adequate conceptualization of rationality, in which the male does not repress or split off from the "unconscious" female but acknowledges or integrates it (p. 125). This issue of the connections between the use of Woman as symbol and the understanding of sexual difference needs more discussion than it has received. It is undoubtedly true that the symbolic representation of Woman has influenced the formation of gender identity in Western culture. Sexual difference provided the symbolism. And the operations of the symbolism in turn affect the constitution of sexual difference. But if we are to understand those processes of interaction and influence between symbolism and the formation of gender identity, it is important, as I stressed earlier, to first understand the symbolic operations themselves. The connections between the content of Woman as symbol and the conceptualization of sexual difference—the understanding of what it is to be a man or a woman—are, I suggest, less immediate than Whitford's application of deconstructive strategies would have us think.

What exactly is being suggested in the claim that (real) women are "homeless" in the symbolic order of Western thought? Are they homeless *in* it or *beyond* it, where the content of Woman as symbol is projected? If the point is not that (real) women are excluded from (real) rationality, why should it be any more acceptable to claim that they are excluded from the symbolic order? What does the excluded feminine have to do with real women? The ironic exercise of miming, as a real woman, the speaking position to which Woman is relegated in the symbolic order can be a powerful reading strategy. But what is supposed to emerge for the understanding of (real) sexual difference?

Whitford rightly insists that Irigaray is not prescribing what the female should be; rather, she is describing how the female functions within the symbolic operations

(p. 120); that the female imaginary is not the essential feminine common to all women but is, rather, a "place in the symbolic structures" (p. 124); and that Irigaray's *mimesis* is a strategy rather than a solution (p. 123). These are all important acknowledgments. Clearly, symbolic Woman is not to be identified with an essential feminine. What concerns me, however, is a general lack of clarity about the status of this nonessential feminine. In claiming it as a new conceptualization of both reason and the feminine are feminists perpetuating the link between sexual difference and the symbolization of reason that is the heart of the problem? Does this Irigarayan mode of criticizing the maleness of reason perpetuate a symbolic use of sexual difference that we would do better to part company with altogether?

Derrida and Deconstructive Strategies

It may help extricate us from these perplexities to focus more directly on some aspects of Derrida's deconstructive strategies that, as Whitford points out, underlie Irigaray's treatment of the symbolic dimensions of the male-female distinction and that have also had a more direct influence on contemporary feminist discussions of the maleness of reason. Susan Hekman, for example, in her discussion of Derrida in *Gender and Knowledge*,[9] presents his strategies for the displacement of traditional epistemological assumptions as providing a way of reconceptualizing the feminine in nondualistic terms. Here again my doubts about the exercise concern the swiftness of the move from understanding the operations of male and female as metaphors to the conceptualizing of sexual difference or the feminine.

Hekman makes the same important acknowledgment as Whitford: Deconstruction is not supposed to reveal an essential feminine. In Derrida's discussion, in *Spurs/Eperons*, of Nietzsche's commentary on woman, Hekman points out, Derrida makes it clear that in turning away from the "metaphysics of presence," he is explicitly embracing what the feminine has represented: qualities of multiplicity and ambiguity. But Derrida does not see this as endorsing a feminine essence. His concern is not with the elevation of a unitary feminine but with the replacement of the unitary with the multiple. What is supposed to emerge is not a feminist epistemology but a "structure that has been feminised in a metaphorical sense through the replacement of oppositions with multiplicity" (Hekman, p. 166). The content of the traditional symbolism of woman—multiplicity as against one-ness, indeterminacy as against determination—is to be exploited to break open binary oppositions. Woman as metaphor is supposed to offer a revolutionary force, a disruptive potential by which the binary logic of Western thought can be replaced. Derrida, we are told, offers a constructive way forward from the sterile debates about difference and sameness—a new option, not abandoning difference, but conceptualizing it in a new way, in terms of multiplicities and pluralities rather than polarities (Hekman, p. 174). Masculine and feminine become not opposites but representations of multiple differences. The traditional metaphorical content of Woman is used to overthrow the polarities of the metaphysics of presence. But for Hekman, Derrida's positive appropriation of the metaphor is also supposed to open a "new discourse on women and sexuality," a discourse on multiplicity that "can and should be central to feminists' attempts to reconceptualise sexual difference." This is to be a discourse that "has no center, neither masculine nor feminine," but that still does not "erase" either the masculine or the feminine (Hekman, p. 175).

It may well seem that the multiplicity of the content of Woman as metaphor in this new "decentered" but not "erased" understanding of the feminine has here reached the point of a literal, as distinct from metaphorical, contradiction. What exactly is the point supposed to be? If to affirm the content of Woman is to reject polarity in favor of multiplicity, is not that to say that the metaphor destroys itself? Why should we want to continue to affirm multiplicity—through the polarizing metaphor par excellence—as feminine? It is all very well to be told that this transformed metaphor of the feminine affirms multiplicity rather than opposition. But if multiplicity was always the content of the polarized Woman, what exactly is the content of this new, nonpolarized feminine?

The content of Woman as metaphor is, of course, closely associated with Derrida's general repudiation of what he calls the "metaphysics of presence"—the illusion of total presence of thought to object, of meaning to origin in thinking subject. Woman traditionally represents what cannot be contained or accommodated within determinate limits. It is not surprising, then, that for Derrida the metaphorical feminine should be associated with *différance*—the concept that is not a concept—through which he tries to unsettle the metaphysics of presence. *Différance* is supposed to belong neither to voice nor to writing—at any rate, not in the usual sense, which would see writing as transcription of the real bearer of meaning: self-present speech. Like Woman, *différance* connotes fluidity, endless deferral, which links it with the theme of strategy without finality. Here, Derrida says in "Différance,"[10] everything is strategic and adventurous. To talk of *différance* is to talk of what is not, of what is never present, of what is always deferred.

These connotations of endless strategy, constant deferral of meaning—blind tactics, wandering, play—can give Derrida's *différance* and the deconstructive strategies associated with it the appearance of a license to complete lack of restraint in textual interpretation, a self-indulgent free play of meanings. But it is for him part of a serious intellectual project, bringing out what lies behind the meaning of central texts in the philosophical tradition—understanding and intervening in what he sees as most irreducible about our era. It is not surprising, then, that Derrida's strategies should have been taken up by feminist philosophers. But the connections between deconstructive reading strategies and the positive evaluation of the content of Woman as metaphor are by no means clear. We are told that sexual difference should be nonexclusionary; that feminine fluidity and indeterminateness is not an irrational excess but rather a value to be defended. But what justifies the move from use of the metaphor of Woman as a reading strategy to the affirmation of its content in the understanding of sexual difference? And can it be used in this way without perpetuating stereotypes of femininity? Should it be as "feminine" that fluidity or indeterminacy are extolled? And is the identification of such values as feminine perhaps itself an implicit departure from Derrida's insistence that *différance,* if it is seen as a strategy, is one without finality? Does this idea of the feminine admit of a fixed content that would allow it to be applied to the understanding of sexual difference anymore than that could be done with the associated notion of *différance?*

Such misgivings are no doubt supposed to be allayed by the constant insistence that this is a "nonessentialist" feminine. But the identification of it as feminine at all may put at risk what is most valuable for feminism in these Derridean insights. The repudiation of essentialism here can give a false security, masking perhaps a more elusive perpetuation of damaging sexual stereotypes. The linking of the symbolism of the male-female distinction with the understanding of rationality is a contingent feature of Western thought, the elusive but real effects of which are still with us. Does the feminist appropriation of the symbolic content of Woman risk perpetuating that contingent alignment? Might not deconstructive strategies be better employed exposing that contingent link—trying to understand its operations in order to break its grip?

Seeing the maleness of reason is part of coming to understand how the symbolic structures work, realizing that there are speaking positions that, though supposedly gender-neutral, in fact depend on the male-female opposition. There can be real discomfort for women in attempting to speak from those supposedly neutral positions that have been constituted by and for male thinking subjects for whom the oppositions came naturally. But what can appropriately be said in the diagnosis of the maleness of reason does not necessarily carry over into an appropriate response to the problem. We can gain the crucial insights into the maleness of reason without appropriating the residue or "excess" as female.

The metaphor of the feminine is supposed to direct us to fluidity—to the impossibility of fixing stable contents to meaning. It is supposed to make visible a variety of "subject positions." Feminists using this Derridean approach insist that the content of the feminine here is not an essence. But should it be seen as a fixed semantic content at all? Derrida's feminine lacks determinate content in the same way that *différance* lacks determinate content. It plays a role in getting us to see what underlies all determinate content and thus alerts us to the contingency of meaning. It is misleading, then, to apply it to the understanding of what it is to be feminine, even contingently. It is not clear that this indeterminacy can be appropriated, as if it were itself a determinate meaning. It does not bring a feminine indeterminacy in from the cold to operate within the bounds of meaning.

Ironic enactments of the "unbounded feminine" can be powerful and illuminating. My concern is that nonironic enactments of feminine fluidity—as if indeterminacy were itself a determinate (though nonessentialist) meaning—perpetuate what has been objectionable in the symbolic use of Woman. Intelligent applications of the insights of deconstruction to reveal the operations of Woman as metaphor have passed over into dubious affirmations of indeterminacy in the name of the feminine. Having acknowledged that properties such as indeterminacy, vagueness, and fluidity should not be seen as the essential feminine, feminist thinkers should question whether they should be appropriated as feminine at all. There are some indications that Derrida was aware of the problem. In his own remarks about the significance of the metaphorical feminine in *Spurs/Eperons,* he warns against mistaking the perception that what will not be pinned down by truth is feminine for a claim about woman's femininity or about female sexuality.[11] But the dismissal of essentialism can too readily be taken as leaving space for a nonessential feminine. And the lure of the new Woman is strong.

The problem, however, is that in resisting the feminizing of the results of deconstruction, we risk falling back into an old posture—the affirmation of a sexless ideal of knowledge. The alleged sexlessness of reason is already part of the symbolic structure—a sexlessness that, as many feminist critics have pointed out, is often a covert form of privileging maleness. The idea of the sexless soul coexists with the maleness of reason, despite the appearance of tension. Sexlessness is here enmeshed in inherited operations of metaphor, although it may pose as a repudiation of metaphor.

These unstable and contradictory alignments of reason with the male-female distinction reach back into the conceptualization of reason in the Western philosophical tradition. Derrida has pointed out that it is not always Woman or femininity that is secondary in these oppositions. Sometimes it is the division between male and female that is secondary in relation to an ideal of mind as transcending all sexual difference. Woman has been used not only to symbolize what is opposed to male reason but also to symbolize sexual difference itself, in opposition to lack of sexual differentiation. The philosophical tradition has constructed reason as male, in opposition to female emotion, sense, imagination, and so on. But it has also constructed the soul, of which reason is the attribute, as sexless, as transcending bodily difference. And the two themes, although they may appear to be in tension, are interconnected.

Derrida, in a rather cryptic remark in an interview, referred to this inner tension in the symbolization of reason as one of the paradoxes of phallocentrism.[12] When sexual difference is determined by a Hegelian opposition, he said, the resulting war between the sexes is predetermined to a male victory, but in such a way that difference is erased. The dialectical opposition neutralizes or supersedes the difference. According to a surreptitious operation, however, phallocentric mastery is assured under the cover of neutralization every time.

Contemporary feminists have grasped this tension independently of the insights of deconstruction. Catharine MacKinnon, in her analysis of the subtle privileging of masculinity that underpins our ideas of sameness and difference, makes a similar point: Sameness means the same as men, difference means different from men.[13] Deconstructive techniques can offer some insight into the complexities of this maneuver with symbols. What emerges is not a contradiction between different ways of thinking about reason; instead, it is a complex symbolic operation in which the metaphor of maleness is both used and erased. The apparently sexless soul can be seen as itself an erased metaphor of maleness.

Deconstructive play with the representation of Woman can give us a better understanding of this spurious neutrality. The metaphors of male and female come into the conceptualization of reason in two ways. On the one hand, male reason is opposed to female, nonrational traits; on the other, sexless reason is opposed to all that pertains to body, including sexual difference. Here sexual difference is itself equated with the female. The supposed sexual neutrality of reason demands a male viewpoint—it coincides with the male position, which can take the female as its opposite. Woman therefore becomes the symbol of sexual difference.[14] In the spurious sexlessness of reason, then, we can see a shadowy maleness that is neither the full masculinity of gender nor the metaphoric maleness explicit in other constructions. This is a maleness that comes from the shedding of "feminine" sexual difference. Because sexlessness is here defined oppositionally to sexual difference, it takes on an implicit but powerful symbolic maleness. It is here that the maleness of reason is most embedded and elusive.

The interplay between the conceptualizations of reason as sexless and as male may appear to involve a contrast between literal and metaphorical treatments of reason. But it can also be seen as a complex interaction between different constructions of metaphor. There are similar interplays in other aspects of the conceptualization of reason that have been illuminated through Derrida's deconstructive reading strategies. One of his most important insights, developed especially in "White Mythology,"[15] has been into the elusiveness of the supposed separability of the metaphorical from the literal in the understanding of philosophical texts and their relations to the "writing" that is diffused through a culture. Before concluding my discussion of the metaphor of maleness, I want to try to bring out what is relevant in Derrida's treatment of metaphor by applying it to the complex play of metaphors involved in René Descartes's treatment of mental activity.

Descartes's Metaphors of the Mind in Motion

The metaphor of the mind in motion is so familiar to us—so inextricable from our thought about thinking—that it is difficult to see how we could shed it. It is a basic metaphor, like those drawn from the bodily senses, which Derrida discusses in "White Mythology"—so much part of our thought that it can be difficult to see that they are metaphorical at all. In Descartes's discussion of reason, metaphors of movement interact with metaphors drawn from sight.[16] The ideal of intellect is an attentive gaze, which leaves behind the unstable, erratic motion of inferior forms of knowledge drawn from sense and infected by the intrusions of body. The ideal is a form of stasis, with intellectual contemplation construed on the model of vision. The only real or proper activity of the mind that Descartes allows is that of the will—the mind's self-movement in response to intellectual clear and distinct perception. The other kinds of mental motion presented in the text are marks of instability—legacies of the intermingling of mind and body. But their description—as is often the case with philosophical metaphors—communicates a richness and vitality that is lacking in the preferred term in the opposition.

Temporality is here seen as a threat to selfhood, as a source of fragmentation. The benevolent and veracious God must secure the continued existence of the self through time. His sustaining causal force provides an essential continuity to mental life. The literary dimensions of the *Meditations* reinforce this theme of the temporal continuity of mental life. It is the story of a mind in motion; it is a narrative of an intellectual journey. The *Meditations* enacts an intellectual process that transcends the idiosyncrasies of any single mind. But it is nonetheless the narration of something past—the very thoughts that enabled Descartes to arrive at a certain and evident knowledge of the truth are set out to allow others to test what has convinced him, thereby convincing all.

Metaphors of sight and motion interact in this narrative. Images of darkness and light interweave with images of restlessness and turmoil. This is an arduous undertaking, Descartes says at the end of the Second Meditation; a kind of laziness brings him back to normal life. He is like a prisoner enjoying imaginary freedom while he sleeps; he dreads waking up and ending the pleasant illusion. He slides back into old opinions, fearing that peaceful sleep will be followed by hard labor, toiling not in the light but in the inextricable darkness of the problems he has raised. He feels as if he has fallen into a deep whirlpool that tumbles him around, so that he can neither stand on the bottom nor swim to the top. Even the certainty that comes from awareness of his own thinking is threatened by the movement of time. "I am, I exist—that is certain. But for how long? For as long as I am thinking. For it could be that were I totally to cease from thinking I should totally cease to exist" (Cottingham et al., vol. 2, p. 18). The way out of the instability is the cultivation of a form of mental gaze—an intellectual contemplation that will extricate him from the turmoil of change.

This refrain of emergence from instability into the stasis of intellectual contemplation recurs throughout the *Meditations*. Fixing in his mind what he has already attained is an important part of the process for Descartes. At the end of the Second Meditation, he stops to reflect on the new knowledge gained in order to fix it more deeply in his memory. And by the end of the Third Meditation, the analogies with religious contemplation are explicit and have become, indeed, rather more than mere analogy. Descartes now pauses to spend time in the contemplation of God—to reflect on his attributes and to "gaze with wonder and adoration on the beauty of this immense light, so far as the eye of my darkened intellect can bear it" (Cottingham et al., vol. 2, p. 36). This is, he thinks the same contemplation, although less perfect, that we shall have in the contemplation of the divine majesty in the next life.

Descartes's need to "fix" the mind in contemplation is frustrated by the unavoidability of time. Although our nature is such that so long as we perceive something clearly and distinctly we cannot but believe it to be true, our nature is also such that we cannot fix our mental vision continually on the same thing so as to keep perceiving it clearly. If shifting and changeable opinions are to give way to true and certain knowledge, the mind must learn to transform instability into mental vision. And this involves learning to control its motion. The mind must learn to distinguish two kinds of motion: its restless impulses to assent to what it does not understand; and the movement of assent that springs from its own true nature. Then, in a famous metaphorical passage in the Second Meditation, Descartes compares the restless mind to a wandering horse whose movements must at first be unrestrained so that one can better control it. It is surely surprising, Descartes comments, that he should have a more distinct grasp of things that he realizes are doubtful, unknown, and foreign to him than of what is true and known—that is, his own self. "But I see what it is: my mind enjoys wandering off and will not yet submit to being restrained within the bounds of truth. Very well then; just this once let us give it completely free rein, so that after a while, when it is time to tighten the reins, it may more readily submit to being curbed" (Cottingham et al., vol 2, p. 20).

The process of turning instability into the stasis of intellectual contemplation echoes Descartes's treatment in the *Rules for the Direction of the Mind* of the transformation of deduction into intuition. There, too, the distinction is drawn in terms of motion. In deduction we are aware of a movement or "a sort of sequence," he says in Rule Three (Cottingham et al., vol. 1, p. 15). And because deduction, unlike intuition, does not require immediate self-evidence, it gets its certainty, in a sense, from memory. But the movement of deduction can in the practiced mind come to approximate the superior state of intuition. We can redress the sluggishness of our intelligence and enlarge its capacity by practicing an uninterrupted movement of the imagination, Descartes says in Rule Seven, "simultaneously intuiting one relation and passing on to the next, until we learn to pass from the first to the last so swiftly that memory is left with practically no role to play, and we seem to intuit the whole thing at once" (Cottingham et al., vol. 1, p. 25). When we think of deduction as a process of inference that does not take place all at once, it seems to be a kind of movement of our minds. We are then justified in distinguishing it from intuition. But if we look on it as a completed process, it no longer signifies movement but rather the completion of a movement (Cottingham et al., vol. 1, p. 37).

Also in the *Rules,* metaphors of motion interact with metaphors of light. We can best learn how mental intuition is to be employed, Descartes says in Rule Nine, by comparing it with ordinary vision.

> If one tries to look at many objects at one glance, one sees none of them distinctly. Likewise, if one is inclined to attend to many things at the same time in a single act of thought, one does so with a confused mind. Yet craftsmen who engage in delicate operations, and are used to fixing their eyes on a single point, acquire through practice the ability to make perfect distinctions between things, however minute and delicate. The same is true of those who never let their thinking be distracted by many different objects at the same time, but always devote their whole attention to the simplest and easiest of matters: they become perspicacious. (Cottingham et al., vol. 1, p. 33)

And in Rule Two, Descartes relates the point, as he does in the *Meditations,* to memory: "Conclusions which embrace more than we can grasp in a single intuition depend for their certainty on memory, and since memory is weak and unstable, it must be refreshed and strengthened through the continuous and repeated movement of thought" (Cottingham et al., vol. 1, p. 38).

I have looked in some detail at these metaphors of mental motion in order to bring out certain aspects of philosophical metaphor that are also involved in the operation of maleness as a metaphor. There is no clear answer to the question whether the movement of the mind is literal or metaphorical. Descartes's treatment seems to "move," often imperceptibly, between the two. In some passages, as in the extended metaphor of the wandering horse, the language is straightforwardly metaphorical. But what of the passage that urges us to practice the process of deduction until we attain the state approximating intuition? Does the mind really "move" here? If not, what exactly is it that we are supposed to transform into the intellectual contemplation? Yet, surely, at some level, all talk of the mind in motion must be a metaphorical extension from the movement of bodies. Is the horse passage just a more colorful metaphor than the others? Clearly it is easier to find a nonmetaphorical rendering of what is being said into apparently more literal ways of talking of the mind's motion. But do these translations just terminate in deeper metaphors of which we cannot rid ourselves? What of the talk of the mind's activity? Is that also metaphorical? Could there be a nonmetaphorical rendering of Descartes's distinction between mental activity and passivity? Can such concepts really straddle the gap between mind and body? And if not, what are we to make of Descartes's talk of the passions of the soul as caused by the movements of bodily animal spirits? The consideration of these metaphors clearly has implications for philosophical content. They are not mere embellishment.

Our difficulty in thinking of thought without the idea of activity can make it appear that activity is the essence of thought, as if we had something that does not rest on the contingency of metaphor. But perhaps such impossibilities are always retrospective. Derrida has shown in "White Mythology" that the metaphors through which we describe thought itself are particularly difficult to think away. But his approach also stresses the contingency of metaphors, even those we cannot shed. The insight into contingency that comes with awareness of the operations of metaphor gives us valuable understanding of our ways of thinking, even where we cannot begin to articulate what it would be like to think otherwise.

What would it be to think of thought—or to think at all—without thinking of the mind as active? But the activity/passivity distinction is itself, of course, not a straightforward description of the mind's operations. It is also, like the male/female distinction with which it often interacts in philosophical texts, a vehicle of evaluation. It serves to privilege, through oppositional contrasts, some aspects of mind over others. And the privileging operates, as usual, in an unstable way. On the one hand, Descartes downgrades the "motion" of the mind. It represents an instability that must be transcended. On the other hand, the privileged state of mind is also presented as a form of activity. But this superior form of mental activity belongs to the proper nature of the soul—the movement of the will. The mental motion figured in the horse metaphor turns out to be really a form of passivity. The mind is pushed by the body into a motion not its own. The will must exert a counterforce "reining it in."

The model is fundamentally the same as that which will be elaborated in the *Passions of the Soul* through other metaphors, often military ones. The mind is rendered passive by the movements of the animal spirits. The will must fight back, exerting a counterforce through the pineal gland, redirecting the movements of the spirits. It is a struggle in which the soul is strengthened through its own "proper arms"—the determinate judgments of good and evil. The metaphors play out the privileging of one side in an oppositional contrast. And tensions in their operations reflect more than mere accidental features of the mixing of metaphors—these tensions alert us to unresolved problems in Descartes's theory of the mind and its relations with the body. Spinoza later exploits the tensions to collapse the Cartesian substantial difference between mind and body and the distinction between intellect and will to yield a different version of the contrasts between mental activity and mental passivity.

The Maleness of Reason

Let me conclude by bringing all this back to bear on the maleness of reason. Some of the symbolic operations of maleness and femaleness in relation to reason can be compared to Descartes's metaphors of the mind as a horse. Francis Bacon's metaphors of nature as a chaste bride to be wooed by male science, for example, can be shed without leaving us with nothing to say. This sexual symbolism is not merely retrospectively contingent; it is also clearly not constitutive of the thought. Other symbolic operations of male and female are more deeply embedded in the conceptualization of reason—more akin to Descartes's elusive metaphors of the mind in motion, with their slides into literal talk of mental activity. Sexual symbolism operates in this embedded way in, for example, the conceptualization of reason as an attainment, as a transcending of the feminine. Embeddedness is also a feature of the metaphors of containment that link reason and its opposites with the public/private distinction. The conceptual containment of the feminine nonrational subtly reinforces—and is reinforced by—the literal containment of women in the domestic domain. And the sexual symbolism is, of course, particularly difficult to separate from more literal claims about reason in conceptualizations of the soul as sexless, where what looks like a repudiation of metaphor can be a subtle privileging of maleness coinciding with sexlessness in opposition to "female" sexual difference.

What is interesting and important from a Derridean perspective about these slides between the literal and the metaphorical is not the discovery of metaphorical intrusions into philosophical thought—as if they should or could be shed; or as if it means the end of philosophy if they cannot. What is interesting is the tensions between different layers of metaphor and the insight these tensions give us into philosophical content. To grasp the contingency of philosophical metaphor is often to gain insight into philosophical content, even where this does not bring with it any clear idea of how we might think differently.

Feminist rage against narrowly instrumental conceptions of rationality—and against the more blatant use of sexual symbolism in formulations of ideals of reason— can distract attention from the more subtle operations of sexual symbolism in relation to reason. And the expectation that women can now come up with an alternative to male reason can reflect a lingering commitment to the primacy of instrumental reason. The maleness of reason is not a unitary representation; rather, it is a network of symbolic operations—some relatively superficial, others deeply embedded in our conceptualizations of what it is to think at all. To some of these symbolic operations, the appropriate response may well be a reevaluation and affirmation of neglected aspects of being human that have traditionally been associated with women. But I remain skeptical about the generalized affirmation of the feminine that has characterized some contemporary feminist critiques of reason. Here debate about reason joins the familiar paradoxes of other feminist debates about sameness and difference. But, as Joan Scott has argued convincingly in her excellent discussion of the relevance of deconstructive strategies, "Deconstructing Equality-Versus-Difference,"[17] all this really rests on a false choice. In some contexts, it is appropriate to demand sameness; in others, difference. And this, I think, is also the real upshot of deconstructive strategies in feminist readings of the history of philosophy. There are times and contexts in which the struggle to affirm the feminine is crucial. And there are other times and contexts in which the attempt to find feminine truth, or the truth of the feminine, is as forlorn and misconceived as Eco's feigned search for a new sardine can opener. There is, of course, room for constructive disagreement about which stance is appropriate in particular contexts.

Notes

1. Umberto Eco, "On the Crisis of the Crisis of Reason," in *Travels in Hyper-Reality,* tr. W. Weaver (London: Picador, 1987), pp. 125–132.

2. Richard Bernstein, "The Rage Against Reason," *Philosophy and Literature* 10 (1986): 186–210.

3. Max Horkheimer, *The Eclipse of Reason* (New York: Continuum, 1985).

4. T. Adorno and M. Horkheimer, *The Dialectic of Enlightenment,* tr. J. Cumming (London: Verso, 1979).

5. Sandra Harding, *The Science Question in Feminism* (Ithaca, N.Y.: Cornell University Press, 1986), p. 52.

6. See especially Evelyn Fox Keller, *Reflections on Gender and Science* (New Haven, Conn./ London: Yale University Press, 1985), pt. 2, ch. 4.

7. See especially Luce Irigaray, *Speculum of the Other Woman,* tr. Gillian C. Gill (Ithaca, N.Y.: Cornell University Press, 1985), and *This Sex Which Is Not One,* tr. C. Porter with C. Burke (Ithaca, N.Y.: Cornell University Press, 1985).

8. In M. Griffiths and Margaret Whitford, *Feminist Perspectives in Philosophy* (London: Macmillan, 1988), pp. 109–130.

9. Susan J. Hekman, *Gender and Knowledge: Elements of a Postmodern Feminism* (London: Polity Press, 1990), pp. 163–175.

10. Jacques Derrida, "Différence," in *Margins of Philosophy,* tr. Alan Bass (Brighton, Sussex: Harvester, 1982), pp. 1–28.

11. Jacques Derrida, *Spurs/Eperons* (Chicago: University of Chicago Press, 1978).

12. Jacques Derrida and Christie V. McDonald, "Choreographies," *Diacritics* 12 (1982): esp. pp, 68–72.

13. Catharine MacKinnon, "Difference and Dominance," in MacKinnon, *Feminism Unmodified* (Cambridge, Mass.: Harvard University Press, 1987), pp. 32–45.

14. Derrida describes this conceptual maneuver in his remarks in the "Choreographies" interview (p. 73) on Levinas's treatment of the symbolism of the Genesis story: A masculine sexual marking is given to what is presented either as a neutral origin or, at least, before and superior to all sexual markings. Differentiated humanity is placed beneath an undifferentiated humanity. Masculinity is left "in command and at the beginning, on a par with the Spirit." This gesture, the most "self-interested of contradiction,"

Derrida observes, has repeated itself since Adam and Eve and persists in analogous form into modernity.

15. Jacques Derrida, "White Mythology: Metaphor in the Text of Philosophy," in *Margins of Philosophy*, pp. 207–272.

16. Quotations are from *The Philosophical Writings of Descartes*, 2 vols., tr. John Cottingham and Dugald Murdoch (Cambridge: Cambridge University Press, 1985).

17. Joan W. Scott, "Deconstructing Equality-Versus-Difference, Or the Uses of Poststructuralist Theory for Feminism," *Feminist Studies* 14 (1988): 33–50.

EPISTEMOLOGY

6

ESSENTIAL TENSIONS— PHASE TWO: FEMINIST, PHILOSOPHICAL, AND SOCIAL STUDIES OF SCIENCE

HELEN E. LONGINO

In the last ten to fifteen years, feminists from various disciplines have articulated a number of challenges to conventional wisdom about the sciences. In this endeavor they have been joined by other critics both within the sciences and working in the social studies of science, although often to different ends and with different analytical tools. These differences in ends and in analytical tools provide a starting point for reflections on the relations between feminist approaches to science, philosophy of science, and social studies of science.

All three of these categories contain divergent approaches to the questions with which they engage. Nevertheless, it is possible to see feminist analysts' proposals about the role of gender and of gender ideology in the sciences as implicitly challenging at least two intradisciplinary points of consensus in philosophy of science and in social studies of science. Interestingly, these points of consensus are themselves issues of *inter*disciplinary dissensus. The normative aspirations of much philosophy of science stand in troubled tension with the descriptive results of much work in sociology, anthropology, and, to a lesser extent, history of science. Philosophy of science has taken on the task of articulating an ideal scientific method or explaining how it is that scientific inquiry produces knowledge of the natural world. Social studies of science have taken on the task of showing how social phenomena deflect actual scientific practice from the presumed ideal. Feminist science studies themselves are in disagreement over basic methodology. This disagreement has at least two sources: One, which I have discussed elsewhere,[1] is a question about the most effective strategy for undermining the hegemony of scientism; another is the inability of either strictly normative or strictly descriptive analyses of the construction of scientific knowledge to fully meet the demands of the agenda emerging from the feminist critiques. A key question raised by these critiques, then, is whether it is possible to have a theory of inquiry that reveals the ideological dimension of knowledge construction while at the same time offering criteria for the comparative evaluation of scientific theories and research programs.

I will begin this chapter with an exploration of the multiple tensions between the three bodies of inquiry mentioned in its title. I propose that a form of empiricism offers, if not a resolution of these tensions, at least a ground upon which to negotiate them. In *Science as Social Knowledge*,[2] I develop a position I call "contextual empiricism" that I wish to recommend as a feminist empiricism.[3] This form of empiricism differs in certain crucial respects from the neoclassical empiricism of David Hume and the modern empiricism of the logical positivists. Feminist, or contextual, empiricism offers an account of knowledge as partial, fragmentary, and ultimately constituted from the interaction of opposed styles and/or points of view. Rather than a foil for postmodernism, it is more appropriately understood as itself postmodernist in spirit.

Let me begin by outlining what I take the feminist agenda to be and the tensions in which it finds itself vis-à-vis the dominant traditions in philosophy and social studies of science. I will then summarize the relevant elements of the contextual empiricist account of inquiry with a view to indicating how it is possible within this account to reconcile the claim that scientific inquiry is value or ideology laden and that it is productive of knowledge. I will conclude by proposing that such an account goes further toward meeting the methodological needs of feminist science studies than current alternatives.

The Challenge to Philosophy and Social Studies of Science

Feminist scholars have developed a multifaceted critique of the sciences, addressing issues of professional structure and the experiences of women within that structure, issues of content, and issues of methodology. As regards professional structure, historians of science have documented the exclusionary practices adopted both in Europe[4] and in the United States,[5] which involve the exercise and legitimation of discriminatory policies, the channeling of women into fields that become ipso facto less prestigious, and the metaphoric appropriation of scientific inquiry as a domain of male activity.[6] Other historians have studied the experiences of individual women in the sciences, examining how gender affected their work, both its content and its career structure.[7]

As regards content, historians of science have documented the role of (male supremacist or misogynist) gender ideology in the scientific study of females and of reproduction in biology from Aristotle to Charles Darwin.[8] Both the presence and absence of women and the female in scientific research programs can reflect androcentrism. In 1990 the U.S. Congress had to pass legislation to motivate the National Institutes of Health to include women in drug trials and to attend to women's distinctive health problems. Even when women are attended to, however, the results are hardly any better. Contemporary scientists and analysts of science are continually uncovering sexist gender ideology in specific research programs in sociobiology, developmental biology, behavioral biology, and the biology of cognition; in some cases, they offer alternative approaches.[9] In addition, researchers have begun to identify the use of gendered metaphors in the description of (nongendered and nonsexed) natural processes—for example, in the analysis of intracellular processes involving the nucleus and cytoplasm.[10] Finally, several feminists both in and out of the sciences have argued that establishment science is characterized by explanatory models and frameworks that privilege relationships of control in the analysis of natural processes.[11] They argue that this represents another level of expression of gender ideology in the sciences and urge the development of other models emphasizing, not control by a relatively autonomous "master" entity, but complex interaction and mutual influence among the various factors involved in natural processes, including, for some, the researcher.

This summary survey of the multiplicity of projects carried out under the aegis of the feminist study of the sciences suggests that it has (at least) a double agenda, critical and constructive:[12]

1. Identification and elimination of masculinist ideologies in the content and methodologies of scientific inquiry, and
2. Identification and realization of liberatory or emancipatory potential in the sciences, or at least a transformation of the sciences for feminist ends.

The first of these is often presented as the task of purging the sciences of illegitimate elements introduced by the bias of practitioners; the second is presented as the task of envisioning a new science. The first, to the extent that it treats the identification of social values in a research program as sufficient to discredit it, presupposes some common criteria of evaluation according to which the influence of social values is inappropriate in the sciences. The second, focusing on research programs that privilege masculine perspectives while meeting the standards imposed by some ideal of science, envisions criteria of acceptability other than those that validate theories feminists find objectionable.

Is there an account of inquiry that makes it possible to satisfy all aspects of this agenda? Feminist scientists have looked to philosophical accounts of scientific inquiry to ground their critiques. The philosophical traditions most often invoked either explicitly or implicitly in the gender and science literature are positivist empiricism or Kuhnian holism. Positivist empiricism is deployed in defense of internalist accounts of knowledge or belief formation, and Kuhnian holism in defense of externalist ones. Philosophers have typically been concerned with the normative question of good reasons, or of what counts as a genuinely justificatory argument in the sciences. The version of Kuhn that is invoked is the one that has found its way into the social studies of science—that is, a Kuhn that licenses, or even mandates, accounts of knowledge construction that appeal to causes other than what the philosopher would recognize as good reasons.[13]

Each of these approaches can ground different aspects of the feminist enterprise. And indeed, reading feminist texts we find positivist forms of empiricism invoked to support the condemnation of masculine bias in the sciences as bad science and Kuhnian holism, or its descendants in contemporary social studies of science, invoked to support the development of alternative points of view.[14] In the first approach, critics adopt the positivist ideal of value-free or value-neutral science as a standard against which to evaluate research programs. The steps of the second approach are somewhat more complicated. The view that all research is interest or value laden supports the quest to identify masculinist interests and perspectives in "good" science and licenses the development of an alternative science grounded in other (feminist or gynecentric) interests and perspectives. Because these approaches do not represent competing programs but appear as different moments in the thinking of the same writer, these rhetorical and analytical strategies seem to put feminist science studies at odds with itself. I want to explain the resulting apparent lack of coherence as a function of inadequate philosophical views—that is, as a function of the inadequacies of the analytical traditions available to feminists.

Neither the normative tradition in philosophy of science nor the descriptive tradition in social studies of science is capable of satisfying the demands of the dual agenda in feminist science studies. One reason for this is that in spite of the vast differences between the traditions, they share a dichotomizing of the social and the cognitive. In this dichotomy, to account for belief by appeal to cognitive processes such as observation and inference is to leave no room for operation of the social in the acceptance of belief (except in the case of false beliefs), and to account for belief in terms of social and other contextual constraints is to displace cognitive processes from their traditional role in the development of knowledge, and especially from the roles assigned them in traditional philosophies of science.[15]

Is it possible to acknowledge the social and ideological dimensions of science with a theory of inquiry that also licenses the comparative assessment of (competing) research programs? This is what I take to be a central challenge of feminist science studies. As long as the dichotomizing of social and cognitive is maintained, this double agenda of feminist and other radical scientists will continue to be frustrated.

What I propose to meet the feminist challenge, then, is a much more thoroughgoing contextualism than the one that urges us to remember that scientific inquiry occurs in a social context, or even that scientists are social actors whose interests drive their scientific work. What I urge is a contextualism that understands the cognitive processes of scientific inquiry not as opposed to the social but as themselves social. Knowledge in the view I will advocate is produced not by individuals as individuals but by communities—that is, by individuals in interaction with each other. This means that normativity, if it's possible at all, must be imposed on social processes and interactions, that the rules or norms of justification that distinguish knowledge (or justified hypothesis acceptance) from opinion must operate at the level of social as opposed to individual cognitive processes.

My argument for socializing cognition is not that it meets the feminist challenge—though it does. My argument is that this move is necessitated philosophically and that it is warranted conceptually and empirically. It is philosophically necessitated by the "problem of underdetermination," the insufficiency of any given body of observational or experimental data to rule out all but one from a set of contesting explanatory hypotheses. It is conceptually and empirically warranted in that scientific inquiry is a social rather than an individual activity.

Contextual Empiricism

One of the hallmarks of scientific knowledge is said to be its objectivity. This is a notion that has come in for a great deal of criticism. Arguments offered under the banner of feminism have contended both that scientific inquiry is not as objective as it purports to be and that objectivity is a mistaken ideal reflecting masculinist preoccupations. In these polemics, objectivity itself remains insufficiently examined, a closed box hurled back and forth between rhetorical contestants. In particular, critics have assumed an identity between science and objectivity. By opening the box to illuminate its internal structure, to explore what objectivity might mean, we step aside from global accusations about science and bring feminist critique into closer contract with actual scientific inquiry. As a preliminary move, let me distinguish two senses in which we attribute objectivity to science:

1. Scientific theories provide a veridical representation of the entities and processes to be found in the world and their relations with each other.
2. Scientific inquiry involves reliance on nonarbitrary and nonsubjective (or nonidiosyncratic) criteria for accepting and rejecting hypotheses.

The claim that scientific *theories* are objective is a claim about the outcome(s) of scientific inquiry and traditionally has depended on showing that scientific *inquiry* is objective. Thus it is the second sense of objectivity that is primary and requires analysis.

What most often counts for scientists as a nonarbitrary and nonsubjective criterion is confirmation by experiential evidence. Empiricism is the philosophical elaboration of this notion into a theory of science and, more ambitiously, a theory of knowledge generally. Feminists, in spite of seemingly adopting empiricist forms of argument to condemn masculine bias, have also reviled empiricism as a form of scientism. (This seeming cross-purposedness is the subject of much of Sandra Harding's work.[16]) I think the feminist rejection of empiricism is a rejection of claims made on behalf of empiricism and on behalf of science by some proponents of empiricism. Rather than explore the literature to support this contention, I will focus on what is valuable and tenable from the empiricist tradition.[17]

A first step in articulating a form of empiricism that could be useful to feminists is to distinguish the normative functions from the descriptive functions of empiricism, as well as the two types of empiricist claim. To treat the second task first: Empiricism with respect to meaning holds that all descriptive expressions in a language must be definable in terms of sense experience. Empiricism with respect to knowledge holds that experience or experiential data are the only legitimate bases of knowledge claims. A more modest version holds that experiential or observational data are the only legitimate bases of theory and hypothesis validation in the natural sciences. This latter claim is what I take to be the commonsense core of empiricism. Notice that as I've expressed it, it is a normative claim.

Empiricism has, of course, been differently understood. Positivists and their critics gave empiricism a bad name among later thinkers about the sciences. Early critics of positivism, such as Putnam, Scriven, and Achinstein, showed that positivism or empiricism with respect to meaning (verificationism and the semantic foundationalism motivating the theory-observation distinction) collapsed upon itself. Their explorations into contemporary scientific practices, along with Hanson's and Kuhn's historical investigations, showed that the positivist account of scientific inquiry was *descriptively* inaccurate. They did not, however, offer arguments to show that empiricism with respect to knowledge was normatively incorrect (nor is it clear that they intended to). This did not stop many of us (their students) from concluding that empiricism was dead. On a more mature rethinking of these arguments, I think they show (1) that empiricism with respect to meaning is both incoherent and incapable of illuminating scientific language or linguistic practice in the sciences; and (2) that although empiricism with respect to knowledge may provide constraints on justification in the empirical sciences, it is not a description of how inquiry proceeds or how theories are developed.[18]

Simply to say that knowledge-empiricism provides constraints on justification in the sciences is not yet to articulate the principle in a way that it could be applied in that context. For example, arguments in the sciences typically go in many directions: That a hypothesis is a consequence of some theory may in certain circumstances be a good reason for accepting the hypothesis. Thus one might express the principle not in terms of exclusivity but in terms of priority: Experiential data are the least defeasible bases of hypothesis and theory validation. Although this is the formulation I prefer, there are still important obstacles to articulating the principle in a way that assures its relevance to scientific practice.

The empiricist principle, even expressed in terms of defeasibility, is articulated independently of considerations about scientific practice, logical structure, and the interfacing of these with human cognitive capacities. When empiricism is applied to scientific inquiry, such considerations impose significant constraints on its interpretation and application.

The prima facie aims of scientific inquiry, in conjunction with features of elementary logic, introduce a set of problems collectively known as the underdetermination problem. Scientific inquiry consists largely in trying to explain observed regularities in terms of postulated underlying processes. In cases of scientific reasoning serving this aim of inquiry (for example, that concerning relations between subatomic particles), hypotheses contain expressions ("muon") not occurring in the description of the observations and experimental results (cloud or bubble chamber photographs) serving as evidence for them. We need not draw on so esoteric an arena for an illustration. Hypotheses about causal processes in biology are supported by correlational data isolated from rich and complex arrays of phenomena. Relations between statements articulating hypotheses and statements articulating descriptions of data cannot be described syntactically or formally, because the two categories of statement contain different terms. To make the same point in a different way: Data—even as represented in descriptions of observations and experimental results—do not on their own indicate that for which they can serve as evidence. Indeed, phenomena as we encounter them in nature or in the laboratory are complex and susceptible to multiple descriptions. Thus certain aspects of a phenomenon may be highlighted over other aspects (for example, the speed of a reaction versus its intensity, volatility, and so on). Data are never naive but come into contact with theories already selected, structured, and organized. Hypotheses, on the other hand, are or consist of statements whose content always exceeds that of the statements describing the observational data.

In general, then, whether proceeding from hypothesis to data or data to hypothesis (or indeed, from experience to data or data to experience), there is a logical gap between them. This gap has been analyzed in various ways by various philosophers. I have argued that evidential relations are not autonomous or eternal truths but are constituted by the context of background assumptions in which evidence is assessed. These assumptions both facilitate inferences between data and hypotheses and make possible the organization of data.

Background assumptions are the vehicles by which social values and ideology are expressed in inquiry and become subtly inscribed in theories, hypotheses, and models defining research programs. If the first step in meeting the feminist challenge is finding an appropriately modest statement of empiricism, the second step is recognizing the role of background assumptions in evidential reasoning and in the analysis and organization of data. The combination of these two steps is the position I am calling "contextual empiricism." Clearly, this is a framework that can support the feminist analysis of gender ideology in a given area of inquiry. But hasn't the need for normativity been sacrificed to this descriptive need? Does not the contextualism of contextualist empiricism effectively cancel the empiricism?

An analysis that stops with the invocation of background assumptions, without criteria for ruling out, limiting, or selecting background assumptions, does put normativity and objectivity at risk. As long as the cognitive practices of science are conceived of as in principle the practices of an individual, normativity is beyond our reach, objectivity of inquiry is a delusion, and we cannot account for the stability or the success of scientific inquiry. But my conclusion is not that scientific inquiry is not objective but that the practices of inquiry are not individual but social. According to positivist empiricism, the relevance of evidence to hypotheses is secured by the formal (that is, syntactic) relation between a hypothesis and an observation report. Contextual empiricism can neither offer nor require such uncontestable certainty. We can nevertheless require that the relevance of data to hypotheses be demonstrable. Satisfaction of this criterion involves broadening the understanding of inquiry. Contextualism does not demand relativism; rather, it demands a fuller account of objectivity and knowledge from which normativity can be generated.

This fuller account, I submit, can be reached by moving from analysis at the individual level to analysis at the social level. I argued in *Science as Social Knowledge* that the objectivity of scientific inquiry is a consequence of that inquiry's being a social and not an individual enterprise.

Social Knowledge

Several sorts of argument are involved in the development of the social knowledge thesis. Empirical arguments support the claim that science just *is* a social practice; conceptual arguments support the claim that the cognitive practices of scientific inquiry are best understood as social practices; and logical and philosophical arguments support the claim that if science is to be nonarbitrary and minimize subjectivity, it must be a social practice. The empirical arguments have been best articulated by historians, sociologists, and anthropologists of science. Two recent demonstrations of the social production of knowledge that I find particularly illuminating are provided by Sharon Traweek in *Beamtimes and Lifetimes*[19] and by Peter Galison in *How Experiments End*.[20] What studies such as these show is that, in general, what gets to count as scientific knowledge is produced through social interactions. Of course, different theorists make different hay of this conclusions.[21] Articulating the philosophical import of the empirical claim requires additional analysis.

The philosophical claim that objectivity is a function of social interactions depends on making the case that the cognitive practices of science are social. I take those practices to be basically observation and reasoning. Let me say something about each.

There are several reasons to treat observation in the sciences as social. In the first place, such observation simply doesn't or can't consist in the perceptual and sensory experiences of one individual. If the point of scientific inquiry is to explain observed regularities, we want assurance that an alleged regularity actually is one. This means that we treat the descriptions of observations as intersubjectively verifiable and won't admit as potential data what is not intersubjectively verifiable. It is this requirement of intersubjectivity that grounds the principle of repeatability of observations and experiments, even though this principle may be as much honored in the breach as in the observance. The repetition of experiments often results in the modification of what we take the observed regularities to be. Furthermore, negotiation among members of an experimental group is frequently required to settle what the results of the experiment are, what counts as a genuine result, and what is rejected as an artefact of the experimental setup.[22] In both cases, then, what the data are is an outcome of experience (nature) and social interactions. To treat experiential information as constituting data or observations is to presuppose successful intersubjective verification or validation—that is, to treat them as the products of social interactions whether or not such interactions have actually taken place.

In addition, observational data, as noted earlier, do not consist in reports of any old observations but in observation reports ordered and organized. This ordering rests on a consensus as to the centrality of certain categories, the boundaries of concepts and classes, the ontological and organizational commitments of a model or theory, and so forth.[23] These social aspects of observation mean the impossibility of establishing a permanent and immutable (save by expansion) reservoir of data. To say that observational data are the least defeasible bases of hypothesis validation is to assign priority to observation and experience while allowing that the ordering, organization, and importance of their results (that is, data) can change.

How might reasoning be thought of as social? There are at least two occasions of reasoning in a context of scientific inquiry: assigning evidential relevance to a set of data, and evaluating a hypothesis or theory on the basis of such assignment. On the contextualist view outlined in the previous section, background assumptions are required in both situations. Assumptions regarding evidential relevance assert some connection between the data assigned relevance and some state of affairs described by the hypothesis to which they are assigned relevance. Assumptions involved in hypothesis acceptance include both substantive assumptions about evidential relevance and methodological assumptions about the strength of evidential support required to legitimate acceptance of a hypothesis. Just as not any old observations will do, so not any old assumptions will do either. The sorts of assumptions upon which it's permissible to rely are also a function of consensus within the scientific community, are learned as part of one's apprenticeship as a scientist, and are largely invisible to practitioners within the community.[24] Although invisible, or transparent, to the members of a community holding them, these assumptions are articulable and hence in principle public. This in-principle publicity makes them available to critical examination as a consequence of which they may be abandoned, modified, or reinforced. As in the case of observation, engaging in inferences that rely on such background assumptions presupposes their adequacy to the task. The adequacy is not (or not only) ascertained by comparison with observations for obvious reasons. What demonstrable evidential relevance amounts to in practice is a requirement that background assumptions be successfully defended against various sorts of criticism. We can read consensus in a community as signaling belief that certain fundamental assumptions have endured critical scrutiny.[25]

The intersubjective character of observation and the role of a consensual background in both observation and inference mean that critical interchange must be a part of both cognitive activities. Individuals may be motivated to engage in this interchange by any number of specific interests. What matters from an epistemological point of view is not the interests driving individuals or the affective quality of the exchange (competitive, cooperative, hostile, supportive); rather, it is that critical interchange occurs. It is not the individual's observation and reasoning that matter in scientific inquiry—it is the community's. Individual variation is dampened through critical interactions whose aim is to eliminate the idiosyncratic and transform individual opinion and belief into reliable knowledge. This solution to the problem of objectivity is not unproblematic. Criteria for the identification of appropriate critical interactions will be discussed below.

The critical interactions focused on observation are directed at the collection, analysis, and reporting of empirical data and are relevant to the claim that a given set of observations constitutes data—that is, they transform an individual's observations into data available to and accepted as such by a community. Criticism of background assumptions is included in the more general category of conceptual criticism. Conceptual criticism can be directed at hypotheses, at background assumptions facilitating inferences, and at concepts and assumptions underlying specific classifications and orderings of observational data. It can focus on their internal coherence, on their relationships with other hypotheses and theories, and on claims of evidential relevance. Criticism of background assumptions can include criticisms directed at hypotheses, as well as observations about the empirical support (or lack of it) for such assumptions and untoward consequences of accepting them.

It is just these social features of observation and reasoning that make it possible to claim some form of objectivity for scientific inquiry in the face of the problems introduced by embracing contextualism. What we're looking for in the account of objectivity is a way to block the influence of subjective preference at the level of background assumptions involved in observation and inference, as well as the influence of individual variation in perception at the level of observation. The possibility of criticism does not totally eliminate subjective preference either from an individual's or from a community's practice of science. It does, however, provide a means of checking its influence in the formation of knowledge; because as long as background assumptions can be articulated and subjected to criticism from the scientific community, they can be defended, modified, or abandoned in response to such criticism. As long as this kind of response is possible, the incorporation of hypotheses into the canon of scientific knowledge can be independent of any individual's (or homogeneous group's) subjective preferences. Their incorporation is, instead, a function in part of the assessment of evidential support. And although this assessment is in turn a function of background assumptions, the adoption of these assumptions is not arbitrary; it is (or rather, can be) subject to the kinds of controls just discussed. This does not mean that values and interests are entirely eliminated, but that idiosyncratic ones can be.

Objectivity, then, is a characteristic of a community's practice of science rather than of an individual's, and the practice of science is understood in a much broader sense than most discussions of the logic of scientific method suggest. Those discussions see what is central to scientific method as being the complex of activities that constitute hypothesis testing through comparison with experiential data—in principle, if not always in reality, an activity of individuals. What I have argued, in contrast, is that scientific method involves equally centrally the subjection of hypotheses and background assumptions to varieties of conceptual criticism and the subjection of data to varieties of evidential criticism. Because background assumptions can be and frequently are transparent to the members of the scientific community for which they are background, because unreflective acceptance of such assumptions can come to define what it is to be a member of such a community (thus making criticism impossible), effective criticism of background assumptions requires the presence and expression of alternative points of view.

We can see why some scientists would be puzzled by the charges that scientific inquiry is not objective. To the extent that members of a scientific community engage in the sorts of interactions described, they are seeking to establish the objectivity of data and inference. But they err in thinking of the individual as the sole locus of variation, idiosyncrasy, or subjectivity. Scientific communities are themselves constituted by adherence to certain values and assumptions, which go unexamined by a critical process involving only members of a community so defined.

Contextual empiricism's formal requirement of demonstrable evidential relevance (of data to hypotheses) constitutes a standard of rationality and acceptability independent of and external to any particular research program or scientific theory. The satisfaction of this standard by any program or theory is secured, as has been argued, by intersubjective criticism. The specification of demonstrability, however, will always be within a particular context. Both observational data and their evidential relevance are constituted in a context of background assumptions. This means that the empiricist principle can be applied within a context but not independently of contextual considerations. Although it is not possible to apply the empiricist principle across contexts, the requirement of demonstrability means that we can generate additional criteria for objectivity by reflecting on the conditions that make for effective criticism. These criteria operate on communities—hence, on contexts.

Earlier I invoked the idea of effective criticism. Effective criticism produces change, and a community's practice of inquiry is objective to the extent that it facilitates such transformative criticism. At least four criteria can be identified as necessary to achieve the transformative dimension of critical discourse: There are recognized avenues for the criticism of evidence, of methods, and of assumptions and reasoning; the community as a whole responds to such criticism; there exist shared standards that critics can invoke; and intellectual authority is shared equally among qualified practitioners. Each of these criteria requires at least a brief gloss.

1. *Recognized avenues for criticism.* The avenues for the presentation of criticism ought to be the same standard and public forums in which "original research" is presented: journals, conferences, and so forth. In addition, critical activities should be given the same or nearly the same weight as is given to original research. Effective criticism that advances understanding should be as valued as original research that opens up new domains for understanding; pedestrian, routine criticism should be valued comparably to pedestrian, routine original research. However, a complex set of processes in the institutions of contemporary science in the industrial and post-industrial world works against this requirement.

2. *Community response.* This criterion requires that the beliefs of the scientific community as a whole and over time change in response to the critical discussion taking place within it. What is required is not that individuals capitulate to criticism but that community members pay attention to and participate in the critical discussion taking place and that the assumptions that govern their group activities remain logically sensitive to it. The point of this criterion is that mere tolerance of criticism and dissent is not sufficient for objectivity. Criticism must play a role in shaping the

views of an objective community. Not all criticism need be accorded the same degree of legitimacy. This, among other considerations, leads to the next criterion.

3. *Shared standards.* In order for criticism to be relevant to a position, it must appeal to something accepted by those who hold the position criticized. Participants in a dialogue must share some referring terms, some principles of inference, and some values or aims to be served by the shared activity. Thus shared elements are necessary for the identification of points of agreement, points of disagreement, and what would count as resolving the latter or destabilizing the former. Similarly, alternative theories must be perceived to have some bearing on the concerns of a scientific community in order to obtain a hearing. This cannot occur at the whim of individuals but must be a function of public standards or criteria to which members of the scientific community are or feel themselves bound. Such standards can include both substantive principles and epistemic, as well as social, values. The point is not so much that individuals spontaneously act out their allegiance to these standards but that they acknowledge their relevance to the evaluation of cognitive practices in their community of inquiry. It may be possible to identify some standards that are shared by all scientific communities. Although I doubt this, some are certainly shared by several, so that scientific communities (or the sets of standards that characterize them) stand in a family relation to one another. These sets are local and they may contain elements in some tension with each other. Thus standards themselves can be criticized by appealing to other standards.

Standards do not provide a deterministic theory of theory choice.[26] Nevertheless, it is the subscription to the existence of standards that makes the individual members of a scientific community responsible to something besides themselves. It is the open-ended and nonconsistent nature of these standards that allows for pluralism in the sciences and for the continued presence, however subdued at times, of minority voices.

4. *Equality of intellectual authority.* This Habermasian criterion is intended to disqualify a community in which a set of assumptions dominates by virtue of the political (economic, physical) power of its adherents. What this criterion requires is that the persuasive effects of reasoning and argument be secured by properties internal to them (rather than by the properties, such as social power, of those who are propounding them) and that every member of the community be regarded as capable of contributing to its constructive and critical dialogue. The point of satisfying this requirement is to ensure exposure of hypotheses to the broadest range of criticism.

Whenever one mentions the intrusion of political power into scientific inquiry, the red flag of Lysenkoism is raised. But the exclusion of women and certain racial minorities from scientific education and the scientific professions in the United States also constitutes a violation of this criterion. Assumptions about race and about sex are not imposed on scientists in the United States in the way assumptions about the inheritability of acquired traits were in the Soviet Union. Many scholars have analyzed how assumptions about sex and gender structure research programs in biological, behavioral, and other sciences. Other scholars have documented the role of racial assumptions in the sciences. Yet others have studied the interaction between racial and gender ideologies in the sciences. The long standing devaluation of women's voices and those of racial minorities meant that such assumptions have been protected from critical scrutiny. Thus a community must not only treat its acknowledged members as equally capable of providing persuasive and decisive reasons and must not only be open to the expression of multiple points of view; it must also take active steps to ensure that alternative points of view are developed enough to be sources of criticism. That is, not only must potentially dissenting voices not be discounted, they must be cultivated.

Taking these criteria as measures of objectivity, objectivity is dependent upon the depth and scope of the transformative interrogation that occurs in any given scientific community. Objectivity is, therefore, a gradational property; and as the maximal fulfillment of the above four conditions, it exists only as an ideal realized more or less imperfectly in different scientific communities. Knowledge and objectivity, on this view, are identified as the outcomes of social interactions and, hence, are located not in individuals but in communities. Individuals must participate in these interactions in order that knowledge be produced; but their objectivity consists in such participation and not in any special cognitive attitude (for example, impartiality or distance) they bear to proposed objects of knowledge. Even though the sciences and scientific communities aspire to objectivity, their having aspirations should not be mistaken for satisfaction of the conditions for objectivity. Nevertheless, the community-wide process that tests background assumptions ensures (or can ensure) that the hypotheses ultimately accepted as supported by some set of data do not reflect a single individual's (or a single same-minded group's) idiosyncratic assumptions about the natural world. To say that a theory or hypothesis was accepted on the basis of objective methods does not guarantee that it is true, but it does—if anything does—justify us in asserting that it is true, for it reflects the critically achieved consensus of the scientific community. In the absence of some form of privileged access to transempirical (unobservable) phenomena, it's not clear we should hope for anything better.

Conclusion

Let me conclude by returning to the problem with which I began: finding an approach to scientific inquiry that could accommodate apparently conflicting aims of feminist science studies. I claimed that contextual empiricism (supplemented by the social account of scientific knowledge) is a philosophical approach that can meet the challenge presented by feminist science studies. The challenge is to provide an account that can ground both the critical and the constructive projects of feminism. Contextual empiricism in its extended form does so.

The normative dimension of this view mandates at one level an examination of the evidential structure of theories. Although this means looking for observational and experimental data at the outset, understanding the relevance of the data requires examining the background assumptions involved in the analysis and organization of data and the background assumptions involved in facilitating reasoning between data and hypotheses. The contextual or descriptive aspect of contextual empiricism means that discovering such assumptions, even discovering that they are laden with social values and ideology, is not grounds for condemning as bad science any work in which they play a role. There are certainly cases of bad science in research programs that feminists reject. But if they are bad, it cannot be simply because background assumptions (even value-laden ones) play a role in them; rather, it is because of methodological mistakes or perhaps because of a dogmatic attitude toward those assumptions.

Discovering such assumptions does make them available to critical examination and potentially to transformation or even rejection. As we have seen, the underdetermination of hypotheses by evidence means that there may always be other ways of interpreting and explaining a given set of data. This is not just a point about the multiplicity of logically possible, empirically equivalent hypotheses. As theories shift in one domain, background assumptions in another may also shift, requiring modification or reinterpretation of the data in that domain. Or the gratuitousness of some background assumption may become clear when it is confronted with an alternative. This occurred when physical anthropologists and primatologists questioned the universality of male dominance and the assumption that the behaviors that provided selection pressures for evolutionary change in the hominoid and hominid lines were male behaviors. The anthropological construct of "woman the gatherer" that developed out of this criticism brought new data into relief that could also then be used to challenge the original androcentric models.[27]

The community-level criteria enable us to make comparative judgments across the contexts created by research programs or traditions. Even if two such traditions treat data in incommensurable ways, it is possible to compare the social interactions involved in knowledge construction in the two contexts. It is a requirement (or an application of the requirement to our contemporary social situation) that feminists participate in the social processes that constitute knowledge construction and that the relevant research communities respond. The community-level criteria make more subtle accounts of the failure of objectivity possible. For example, in some aspects of behavioral neuroendocrinology, researchers have responded to feminist criticism by eliminating value-laden language ("sissy" and "tomboy") and by attempting to develop more rigorous data-gathering procedures.[28] For a time, however, the general community (as represented by *Science* magazine, as well as by the propounder of the claim) ignored (data-based) criticism of a claim about differences in size of the male and female corpus callosum.[29] In the first instance, the second criterion (of responsiveness) is satisfied; in the second, it is violated. The fourth criterion requires that socially significant groups be included in the scientific community to ensure criticism from all possible points of view and the incorporation into scientific debate of the broadest range of observational data possible. This criterion enables us to condemn the exclusion of women and racial minorities from the practice of science as an epistemological shortcoming and as a political injustice.

That there are standards or values apart from empirical adequacy means that not every hypothesis that can be stretched to fit some set of data is equivalent to every other hypothesis. The multiplicity of standards recognized as relevant to the assessment of theories, hypotheses, and research programs means nevertheless that at least some such other ways may be equally supportable. Indeed, in many cases alternative theoretical approaches are required to reveal the assumptions structuring a powerful or popular research program. Feminist research programs can involve selection from and recombination of traditional values and introduction of new values and standards into the study of a given bit of nature. Most accounts of objectivity work against the possibility of multiple accounts of some set of natural phenomena. The one offered here, by contrast, supports this possibility. Thus the constructive project is both licensed by and subject to the same normative constraints as license the critical project.

What it does not do is grant to some form of feminism or to any other social or political program an exclusive grant to truth of correctness. The view of inquiry outlined here means that to the extent that we speak of knowledge, it is, as I indicated at the outset, partial and fragmentary. The requirement that demonstrability be secured by intersubjective criticism has the consequence that knowledge is constituted by the interaction of opposed styles and/or points of view. Although some perspectives may be discredited (for failing to realize any of the partially shared goals of scientific communities), no single one can be privileged over the others. Within any given community, some single perspective may be privileged over others for a time, but exclusive allegiance to this perspective in the face of (inevitable) criticism violates the second criterion of objectivity for communities.

Finally, I think this approach is faithful to a fundamental insight of the feminist analysts of science: that ideological and value issues are interwoven with empirical ones in scientific inquiry. What is important is not that they be banished, but that we have (1) analytic tools that enable us to identify them, and (2) community practices that can (in the long run) regulate their role in the development of knowledge.[30]

Notes

1. Helen E. Longino and Evelynn A. Hammonds, "Conflicts and Tensions in the Feminist Study of Gender and Science," in Marianne Hirsch and Evelyn Fox Keller, eds., *Conflicts in Feminism* (New York: Routledge, 1990), pp. 164–183.

2. Helen E. Longino, *Science as Social Knowledge: Values and Objectivity in Scientific Inquiry* (Princeton, N.J.: Princeton University Press, 1990).

3. The empiricism to be developed here is not the only candidate for this denomination. Sandra Harding critiques one version of feminist empiricism in *The Science Question in Feminism* (Ithaca, N.Y.: Cornell University Press, 1986); and Lynn Hankinson Nelson develops a feminist empiricism based on the views of W.V.O. Quine in Lynn Hankinson Nelson, *Who Knows: From Quine to a Feminist Empiricism* (Philadelphia: Temple University Press, 1990).

4. Londa Schiebinger, *The Mind Has No Sex?* (Cambridge, Mass.: Harvard University Press, 1989).

5. Margaret Rossiter, *Women Scientists in America: Struggles and Strategies to 1940* (Baltimore: Johns Hopkins University Press, 1982).

6. Evelyn Fox Keller, *Reflections on Gender and Science* (New Haven, Conn.: Yale University Press, 1985).

7. Pnina Abir-Am and Dorinda Outram, eds., *Uneasy Careers and Intimate Lives: Women in Science, 1789–1979* (New Brunswick, N.J.: Rutgers University Press, 1987).

8. Ludmilla Jordanova, *Sexual Visions* (Madison: University of Wisconsin Press, 1990).

9. Ruth Bleier, *Science and Gender* (Elmsford, N.Y.: Pergamon Press, 1984); Anne Fausto Sterling, *Myths of Gender* (New York: Basic Books, 1985).

10. Gender and Biology Study Group, "The Importance of Feminist Critique for Contemporary Cell Biology," *Hypatia* 3 (1988): 61–76.

11. Keller, *Reflections on Gender and Science* also Bleier, *Science and Gender*; and Ruth Hubbard, *The Politics of Women's Biology* (New Brunswick, N.J.: Rutgers University Press, 1990).

12. There is not a single agenda that all feminists with an interest in the sciences have adopted. Some critics are concerned about what they perceive as bad science—i.e., research that is incomplete or misleading because of its omission of women subjects or its reliance on inadequate methodologies. Other critics are more concerned about what they perceive as more global problems—e.g., the privileging of reductionist over interactionist explanatory models and the reading of nature as human society. Although critics in the latter group (e.g., Evelyn Fox Keller and Donna Haraway) endorse the project to expose bad science, even though it is not theirs, some critics in the former group do not endorse the more global project. For further discussion of these tensions, see Longino and Hammonds, "Conflicts and Tensions."

13. Although Kuhn himself rejects this interpretation of his work, and although several steps of argumentation are needed to give it this interpretation, Kuhn continues to be cited as the intellectual and philosophical legitimator of the sociological approach.

14. See, e.g., Bleier, *Science and Gender*; Ruth Hubbard, Mary Sue Henifin, and Barbara Fried, eds., *Women Look at Biology Looking at Women* (Cambridge, Mass.: Schenkman, 1979).

15. Different but typical statements of the sociological approach can be found in Harry Collins, "An Empirical Relativist Programme in the Sociology of Scientific Knowledge," in Karin Knorr-Cetina and Michael Mulkay, eds, *Science Observed* (London: Sage, 1983), pp. 85–113; and Bruno Latour, *Science in Action* (Cambridge, Mass.: Harvard University Press, 1988). Statements of the philosophical approach include Larry Laudan, "The Pseudo-Science of Science," in James R. Brown, ed., *Scientific Rationality: The Sociological Turn* (Boston: Reidel, 1984), pp. 41–73; Ernan McMullin, "Values in Science," in P. D. Asquith and T. Nickles, ed., *PSA 1982*, vol. 2, (East Lansing, Mich.: Philosophy of Science Association, 1983), pp. 3–28; and Robert Richardson, "Biology and Ideology: The Interpenetration of Science and Values," *Philosophy of Science* 51 (1984): 396–421.

16. See Sandra Harding, "The Instability of the Categories of Feminist Theory," *Signs* 11, 4 (1986): 645–664.

17. There are a variety of views in contemporary philosophy claiming the label *empiricist*. The empiricism developed here is closest to that of Bas van Fraassen, *The Scientific Image* (New York: Oxford University Press, 1980), in that it both rejects the inference to the best explanation characteristic of scientific realism and treats empiricism as a prescription for, rather than a description of, hypothesis acceptance, in contrast to the epistemological naturalizers.

18. This "commonsense core" of empiricism is not the view Harding takes to task under the label *feminist empiricism* in *Science Question in Feminism*. What she criticizes is the claim that methods currently in use in the natural sciences are sufficient to eliminate masculinist or other bias in the sciences. But this core empiricism says nothing about methods in use. Furthermore, either "methods" means methods (for example, mathematical modeling, current experimental techniques, titration techniques, and so on), in which case femi-

nist empiricism is not the same as empiricism; or it means observation and inference (what philosophers mean by method). Empiricism does not claim that observation is sufficient for the validation of scientific claims; rather, it claims that it is necessary.

19. Sharon Traweek, *Beamtimes and Lifetimes* (Cambridge, Mass.: Harvard University Press, 1988).

20. Peter Gailson, *How Experiments End* (Chicago: University of Chicago Press, 1987). For a philosophical discussion of the interdependence of researchers, see John Hardwig, "Epistemic Dependence," *Journal of Philosophy,* 82 (1985): 335–349, esp. pp. 345–349.

21. E.g., some sociologists of science take the social construction of scientific knowledge to refer to the inscription of social ideologies in the content of scientific theories. The sense of "social" used in this chapter is not social in the sense of "shared" but social in the sense of "interactive."

22. The spate of attempts to replicate Pons and Fleishmann's cold fusion experiments challenged their accounts of what the regularities were. For the role of negotiation, see Michael Lynch, *Art and Artefact in Laboratory Science* (London: Routledge and Kegan Paul, 1985); see also K. Amann and K. Knorr-Cetina, "The Fixation of Visual Evidence," *Human Studies,* 11 (1988): 133–169.

23. It is in this sense that the claim that observation is theory laden makes sense; but see Mary Hesse, *Revolutions and Reconstructions in the Philosophy of Science* (Bloomington: Indiana University Press, 1980), pp. 63–110, for a careful discussion of what does and doesn't follow from the theory ladenness of observation.

24. Kuhn made this point about paradigms. I differ with him in the assessment of the accessibility of these framing elements of inquiry.

25. Obviously, such consensus can exist without its presupposition being satisfied. Consensus may be produced by processes other than critical discourse—e.g., by threat or persuasion.

26. This point was well articulated by Thomas Kuhn in "Objectivity, Value Judgment, and Theory Choice," in Kuhn, *The Essential Tension* (Chicago: University of Chicago Press, 1977), pp. 320–339.

27. See Nancy Tanner, *Human Evolution* (Cambridge: Cambridge University Press, 1981); and Adrienne Zihlman, "Women in Evolution, Part II," *Signs,* 4 (1978): 4–20. For discussion, see Longino, *Science as Social Knowledge,* pp. 104–111, 128–132.

28. Anke Ehrhardt, "Gender Differences: A Biosocial Perspective," in Theo Sonderreger, ed., *Nebraska Symposium on Motivation,* vol. 32 (Lincoln: University of Nebraska Press, 1985), pp. 37–58; and David Goldfoot and Deborah Neff, "On Measuring Behavioral Sex Differences in Social Contexts," in N. Adler, D. Pfaff, and R. W. Goy, eds., *Handbook of Behavioral Neurobiology,* vol. 7 (New York: Plenum Press, 1985), pp. 767–783.

29. Ruth Bleier, "A Decade of Feminist Criticism in the Natural Sciences," *Signs* 14 (1988): 182–195.

30. I wish to thank Louise Antony, Ernan McMullin, and Charlotte Witt for their comments on an earlier draft. I would also like to thank those who responded to its spoken versions for their helpful criticism and observations and Anne Figert for suggesting the title.

7

QUINE AS FEMINIST: THE RADICAL IMPORT OF NATURALIZED EPISTEMOLOGY

LOUISE M. ANTONY

The truth is always revolutionary.
Antonio Gramsci

I. Introduction

Do we need a feminist epistemology? This is a very complicated question. Nonetheless it has a very simple answer: yes and no.

Of course, what I should say (honoring a decades-old philosophical tradition) is that a great deal depends on what we *mean* by "feminist epistemology." One easy—and therefore tempting—way to interpret the demand for a feminist epistemology is to construe it as nothing more than a call for more feminist theorists *doing* epistemology. On this way of viewing things, calls for "feminist political science," "feminist organic chemistry," and "feminist finite mathematics" would all be on a par, and the need for any one of them would be justified in exactly the same way, viz., by arguing for the general need for an infusion of feminist consciousness into the academy.

Construed in this way, an endorsement of "feminist epistemology" is perfectly neutral with respect to the eventual content of the epistemological theories that feminists might devise. Would it turn out, for example, that feminists as a group reject individualism or foundationalism? Would they favor empiricism over rationalism? Would they endorse views that privileged intuition over reason or the subjective over the objective? We'd just have to wait and see. It must even be left open, at least at the outset, whether a feminist epistemology would be discernibly and systematically different from epistemology as it currently exists, or whether there would instead end up being exactly the same variety among feminists as there is now among epistemologists in general.

Now it might appear that the project of developing a feminist epistemology in this sense is one that we can all happily sign on to, for who could object to trying to infuse the disciplines with feminist consciousness? But now I must honor a somewhat newer philosophical tradition than the one I honored earlier, and ask, "We, who?" For though the determined neutrality of this way of conceiving feminist epistemology—let me call it "bare proceduralism"—may give it the superficial appearance of a consensus position, it is in fact quite a partisan position. Even setting aside the fact that there are many people—yes, even some philosophers—who would rather be infused with bubonic plague than with feminist consciousness, it's clear that not everyone is going to like bare proceduralism. And ironically, it is its very neutrality that makes this an unacceptable reading of many, if not most, of the theorists who are currently calling for a feminist epistemology.[1]

To see the sticking point, consider the question of whether we should, as feminists, have an obligation to support *any* project whose participants represent themselves as feminists. Should we, for example, support the development of a "feminist sociobiology" or a "feminist military science," on the grounds that it's always a good idea to infuse a discipline, or a theory, with feminist consciousness, or on the grounds that there are people who are engaged in such projects who regard themselves as feminists and therefore have a claim on our sympathies? The answer to these questions, arguably, is no. Some projects, like the rationalization of war, may simply be *incompatible* with feminist goals; and some theories, like those with biological determinist presuppositions, may be *inconsistent* with the results of feminist inquiry to date.

Bare proceduralism, with its liberal, all-purpose, surely-there's-something-we-can-all-agree-on ethos, both obscures and begs the important question against those who believe that not all epistemological frameworks cohere—or cohere equally well—with the insights and aims of feminism. Specifically, it presupposes something that many feminist philosophers are at great pains to deny, namely the *prima facie* adequacy, from a feminist point of view, of those epistemological theories currently available within mainstream Anglo-American philosophy. At the very least, one who adopts the bare proceduralist standpoint with respect to feminist epistemology is making a substantive presupposition about where we currently stand in the process of feminist theorizing. To allow even that a feminist epistemology *might* utilize certain existing epistemological frameworks is to assert that feminist theorizing has not yet issued in substantive results regarding such frameworks.[2] Such a view, if not forthrightly expressed and explicitly defended, is disrespectful to the work of those feminists who claim to have already shown that those very epistemological theories are incompatible with feminism.

So we can't simply interpret the question, "Do we need a feminist epistemology?" in the bare proceduralist way and nod an enthusiastic assent. If we do, we'll be obscuring or denying the existence of substantive disagreements among feminists about the relation between feminism and theories of knowledge. One natural alternative to the bare proceduralist interpretation would be to try to give feminist epistemology a *substantive* sense—that is, take it to refer to a particular kind of epistemology or to a particular theory within epistemology, one that is specifically feminist.

But this won't work either, for two good reasons. First, there simply is no substantive consensus position among feminists working in epistemology, so that it would be hubris for anyone to claim that his or her epistemology was *the* feminist one.[3] Second, many feminists would find the idea that there *should* be such a single "feminist" position repellent. Some would dislike the idea simply for its somewhat totalitarian, "PC" ring. (Me, I'm not bothered by that—it seems to me that one should strive to be correct in all things, including politics.) Some theorists would argue that variety in feminist philosophical positions is to be expected at this point in the development of feminist consciousness, and that various intra- and inter-theoretic tensions in philosophical inquiry reflect unprocessed conflicts among deeply internalized conceptions of reality, of ourselves as human beings, and of ourselves as women.[4] Still others would see the expectation or hope that there will ever be a single, comprehensive, "true" feminist position as nothing but a remnant of outmoded, patriarchal ways of thinking.[5]

Thus, while individual feminist theorists may be advertising particular epistemological theories as feminist theories, general calls for the development of a feminist epistemology cannot be construed as advocacy for any particular one of these. But recognition of this fact does not throw us all the way back to the bare proceduralist notion. It simply means that in order to decide on the need for a feminist epistemology, we need to look at details—both with respect to the issues that feminism is supposed to have raised for the theory of knowledge and with respect to the specific epistemological theories that have been proffered as answering to feminist needs.

This is where the yes-and-no comes in. If we focus on the existence of what might be called a "feminist agenda" in epistemology—that is, if the question, "Do we need a feminist epistemology?" is taken to mean, "Are there specific questions or problems that arise as a result of feminist analysis, awareness, or experience that any adequate epistemology must accommodate?"—then I think the answer is clearly yes. But if, taking for granted the existence of such an agenda, the question is taken to be, "Do we need, in order to accommodate these questions, insights, and projects, a specifically feminist alternative to currently available epistemological frameworks?" then the answer, to my mind, is no.

Now it is on this point that I find myself in disagreement with many feminist philosophers. For despite the diversity of views within contemporary feminist thought, and despite the disagreements about even the desiderata for a genuinely feminist epistemology, one theoretical conclusion shared by almost all those feminists who explicitly advocate the development of a feminist epistemology is that existing epistemological paradigms—particularly those available within the framework of contemporary analytic philosophy—are fundamentally unsuited to the needs of feminist theorizing.

It is this virtual unanimity about the inadequacy of contemporary analytic epistemology that I want to challenge. There is an approach to the study of knowledge that promises enormous aid and comfort to feminists attempting to expose and dismantle the oppressive intellectual ideology of a patriarchal, racist, class-stratified society, and it is an approach that lies squarely within the analytic tradition. The theory I have in mind is Quine's "naturalized epistemology"—the view that the study of knowledge should be treated as the empirical investigation of knowers.

It's both unfortunate and ironic that Quine's work has been so uniformly neglected by feminists interested in the theory of knowledge, because although naturalized epistemology is nowadays as mainstream a theory as there is, Quine's challenges to logical positivism were radical in their time, and still retain an untapped radical potential today. His devastating critique of epistemological foundationalism bears many similarities to contemporary feminist attacks on "modernist" conceptions of objectivity and scientific rationality, and his positive views on the holistic nature of justification provide a theoretical basis for pressing the kinds of critical questions feminist critics are now raising.

Thus my primary aim in this essay is to highlight the virtues, from a feminist point of view, of naturalized epistemology. But—as is no doubt quite clear—I have a secondary, polemical aim as well. I want to confront head-on the charges that mainstream epistemology is irremediably phallocentric, and to counter the impression, widespread among progressives both within and outside of the academy, that there is some kind of natural antipathy between radicalism on the one hand and the methods and aims of analytic philosophy on the other. I believe that this impression is quite false, and its promulgation is damaging not only to individual feminists—especially women—working within the analytic tradition, but also to the prospects for an adequate feminist philosophy.

The "Bias" Paradox

I think the best way to achieve both these aims—defending the analytic framework in general and showcasing naturalized epistemology in particular—is to put the latter to work on a problem that is becoming increasingly important within feminist theory. The issue I have in mind is the problem of how properly to conceptualize *bias*. There are several things about this issue that make it particularly apt for my purposes.

In the first place, the issue provides an example of the way in which feminist analysis can generate or uncover serious epistemological questions, for the problem about bias that I want to discuss will only be recognized as a problem by individuals who are critical, for one reason or another, of one standard conception of objectivity. In the second place, because of the centrality of this problem to feminist theory, the ability of an epistemological theory to provide a solution offers one plausible desideratum of a theory's adequacy as a feminist epistemology. Last of all, because the notions of bias and partiality figure so prominently in feminist critiques of mainstream analytic epistemology, discussion of this issue will enable me to address directly some of the charges that have led some feminist theorists to reject the analytic tradition.

But what is the problem? Within certain theoretical frameworks, the analysis of the notion of "bias" is quite straightforward. In particular, strict empiricist epistemology concurs with liberal political theory in analyzing bias as the mere possession of belief or interest prior to investigation. But for anyone who wishes to criticize the liberal/empiricist ideal of an "open mind," the notion of bias is enormously problematic and threatens to become downright paradoxical.

Consider feminist theory: On the one hand, it is one of the central aims of feminist scholarship to expose the male-centered assumptions and interests—the male *biases,* in other words—underlying so much of received "wisdom." But on the other hand, there's an equally important strain of feminist theory that seeks to challenge the ideal of pure objectivity by emphasizing both the ubiquity and the value of certain kinds of partiality and interestedness. Clearly, there's a tension between those feminist critiques that accuse science or philosophy of displaying male bias and those that reject the ideal of impartiality.

The tension blossoms into paradox when critiques of the first sort are applied to the concepts of objectivity and impartiality themselves. According to many feminist philosophers, the flaw in the ideal of impartiality is supposed to be that the ideal itself is biased: Critics charge either that the concept of "objectivity" serves to articulate a masculine or patriarchal viewpoint (and possibly a pathological one),[6] or that it has the ideological function of protecting the rights of those in power, especially men.[7] But how is it possible to criticize the partiality of the concept of objectivity without presupposing the very value under attack? Put baldly: If we don't think it's good to be *im*partial, then how can we object to men's being *partial?*

The critiques of "objectivity" and "impartiality" that give rise to this paradox represent the main source of feminist dissatisfaction with existing epistemological theories. It's charged that mainstream epistemology will be forever unable to either acknowledge or account for the partiality and locatedness of knowledge, because it is wedded to precisely those ideals of objective or value-neutral inquiry that ultimately and inevitably subserve the interests of the powerful. The valorization of impartiality within mainstream epistemology is held to perform for the ruling elite the critical ideological function of *denying the existence of partiality itself.*[8]

Thus Lorraine Code, writing in the *APA Newsletter on Feminism and Philosophy,*[9] charges that mainstream epistemology (or what she has elsewhere dubbed "malestream" epistemology[10]) has "defined 'the epistemological project' so as to make it illegitimate to ask questions about the identities and specific circumstances of these knowers." It has accomplished this, she contends, by promulgating a view of knowers as essentially featureless and interchangeable, and by donning a "mask of objectivity and value-neutrality." The transformative potential of a feminist—as opposed to a malestream—epistemology lies in its ability to tear off this mask, exposing the "complex power structure of vested interest, dominance, and subjugation" that lurks behind it.

But not only is it not the case that contemporary analytic epistemology is committed to such a conception of objectivity, it was analytic epistemology that was largely responsible for initiating the critique of the empiricistic notions Code is attacking. Quine, Goodman, Hempel, Putnam, Boyd, and others within the analytic tradition have all argued that a certain received conception of objectivity is untenable as an ideal of epistemic practice. The detailed critique of orthodox empiricism that has developed within the analytic tradition is in many ways more pointed and radical than the charges that have been leveled from without.

Furthermore, these philosophers, like many feminist theorists, have emphasized not only the *ineliminability* of bias but also the *positive value* of certain forms of it. As a result, the problems that arise for a naturalized epistemology are strikingly similar to those that beset the feminist theories mentioned above: Once we've acknowledged the necessity and legitimacy of partiality, *how do we tell the good bias from the bad bias?*

What kind of epistemology is going to be able to solve a problem like this? Code asserts that the specific impact of feminism on epistemology has been "to move the question '*Whose* knowledge are we talking about?' to a central place in epistemological discussion,"[11] suggesting that the hope lies in finding an epistemological theory that assigns central importance to consideration of the nature of the subjects who actually do the knowing. I totally agree: No theory that abjures empirical study of the cognizer, or of the actual processes by which knowledge develops, is ever going to yield insight on this question.

But more is required than this. If we as feminist critics are to have any basis for distinguishing the salutary from the pernicious forms of bias, we can't rest content with a *description* of the various ways in which the identity and social location of a subject make a difference to her beliefs. We need, in addition, to be able to make normative distinctions among various processes of belief-fixation as well. Otherwise, we'll never escape the dilemma posed by the bias paradox: either endorse pure impartiality or give up criticizing bias.[12]

It is here that I think feminist philosophy stands to lose the most by rejecting the analytic tradition. The dilemma will be impossible to escape, I contend, for any theory that eschews the notion of *truth*—for any theory, that is, that tries to steer some kind of middle course between absolutism and relativism. Such theories inevitably leave themselves without resources for making the needed normative distinctions, because they deprive themselves of any conceptual tools for distinguishing the grounds of a statement's truth from the explanation of a statement's acceptance.

Naturalized epistemology has the great advantage over epistemological frameworks outside the analytic tradition (I have in mind specifically standpoint and postmodern epistemologies) in that it permits an appropriately realist conception of truth, viz., one that allows a conceptual gap between epistemology and metaphysics, between the world as we see it and the world as it is.[13] Without appealing to at least this minimally realist notion of truth, I see no way to even state the distinction we ultimately must articulate and defend. Quite simply, an adequate solution to the paradox must enable us to say the following: What makes the *good* bias good is that it facilitates the search for truth, and what makes the *bad* bias bad is that it impedes it.

Now that my absolutist leanings are out in the open, let me say one more thing about truth that I hope will forestall a possible misunderstanding of my project here. I do believe in truth, and I have *never* understood why people concerned with justice have given it such a bad rap. Surely one of the goals of feminism is to *tell the truth* about women's lives and women's experience. Is institutionally supported discrimination not a *fact*? Is misogynist violence not a *fact*? And isn't the existence of ideological denial of the first two facts *itself* a fact? What in the world else could we be doing when we talk about these things, *other* than asserting that the world actually *is* a certain way?

Getting at the truth is complicated, and one of the things that complicates it considerably is that powerful people frequently have strong motives for keeping less powerful people from getting at the truth. It's one job of a critical epistemology, in my view, to expose this fact, to make the mechanisms of such distortions transparent. But if we, as critical epistemologists, lose sight of what we're after, if we concede that there's nothing at stake other than the matter of whose "version" is going to prevail, then our projects become as morally bankrupt and baldly self-interested as Theirs.

This brings me to the nature of the current discussion. I would like to be clear that in endorsing the project of finding a "feminist epistemology," I do not mean to be advocating the construction of a serviceable epistemological ideology "for our side." And when I say that I think naturalized epistemology makes a good feminist epistemology, I don't mean to be suggesting that the justification for the theory is instrumental. A good *feminist* epistemology must be, in the first place, a good epistemology, and that means being a theory that is likely to be *true*. But of course I would not think that naturalized epistemology was likely to be true unless I also thought it explained the facts. And among the facts I take to be central are the long-ignored experiences and wisdom of women.

In the next section, I will explain in more detail the nature of the charges that have been raised by feminist critics against contemporary analytic epistemology. I'll argue that the most serious of these charges are basically misguided—that they depend on a misreading of the canonical figures of the Enlightenment as well as of contemporary epistemology. In the last section, I'll return to the bias paradox and try to show why a naturalized approach to the study of knowledge offers some chance of a solution.

II. What Is Mainstream Epistemology and Why Is It Bad?

One difficulty that confronts anyone who wishes to assess the need for a "feminist alternative" in epistemology is the problem of finding out exactly what such an epistemology would be an alternative to. What is "mainstream" epistemology anyway? Lorraine Code is more forthright than many in her willingness to name the enemy. According to her, "mainstream epistemology," the proper object of feminist critique, is "post-positivist empiricist epistemology: the epistemology that still dominates in Anglo-American philosophy, despite the best efforts of socialist, structuralist, hermeneuticist, and other theorists of knowledge to deconstruct or discredit it."[14]

By the "epistemology that still dominates in Anglo-American philosophy," Code would have to be referring to the set of epistemological theories that have developed within the analytic paradigm, for analytic philosophy has been, in fact, the dominant philosophical paradigm in the English-speaking academic world since the early twentieth century.[15] This means, at the very least, that the agents of sexism within academic philosophy—the individuals who have in fact been the ones to discriminate against women as students, job applicants, and colleagues—have been, for the most part, analytic philosophers, a fact that on its own makes the analytic paradigm an appropriate object for feminist scrutiny.

But this is not the main reason that Code and others seek to "deconstruct or discredit" analytic epistemology. The fact that the analytic paradigm has enjoyed such an untroubled hegemony within this country during the twentieth century—the period of the most rapid growth of American imperial power—suggests to many radical social critics that analytic philosophy fills an ideological niche. Many feminist critics see mainstream analytic philosophy as the natural metaphysical and epistemological complement to liberal political theory, which, by obscuring real power relations within the society, makes citizens acquiescent or even complicit in the growth of oppression, here and abroad.

What is it about analytic philosophy that would enable it to play this role? Some have argued that analytic or "linguistic" philosophy, together with its cognate fields (such as formal linguistics and computationalist psychology), is inherently male, "phallogocentric."[16] Others have argued that the analytic paradigm, because of its emphasis on abstraction and formalization and its valorization of elite skills, may be an instrument of cognitive control, serving to discredit the perspectives of members of nonprivileged groups.[17]

But most of the radical feminist critiques of "mainstream" epistemology (which, as I said, must denote the whole of analytic epistemology) are motivated by its presumed allegiance to the conceptual structures and theoretical commitments of the Enlightenment, which provided the general philosophical background to the development of modern industrialized "democracies."[18] By this means, "mainstream" epistemology becomes identified with "traditional" epistemology, and this traditional epistemology becomes associated with political liberalism. Feminist theorists like Alison Jaggar and Sandra Harding, who have both written extensively about the connection between feminist political analysis and theories of knowledge, have encouraged the idea that acceptance of mainstream epistemological paradigms is tantamount to endorsing liberal feminism. Jaggar contends that the connection lies in the radically individualistic conception of human nature common to both liberal political theory and Enlightenment epistemology. In a chapter entitled "Feminist Politics and Epistemology: Justifying Feminist Theory," she writes:

> Just as the individualistic conception of human nature sets the basic problems for the liberal political tradition, so it also generates the problems for the tradition in epistemology that is associated historically and conceptually with liberalism. This tradition begins in the 17th century with Descartes, and it emerges in the 20th century as the analytic tradition. Because it conceives humans as essentially separate individuals, this epistemological tradition views the attainment of knowledge as a project for each individual on her or his own. The task

of epistemology, then, is to formulate rules to enable individuals to undertake this project with success.[19]

Harding, in a section of her book called "A Guide to Feminist Epistemologies," surveys what she sees as the full range of epistemological options open to feminists. She imports the essentially conservative political agenda of liberal feminism, which is focused on the elimination of formal barriers to gender equality, into mainstream epistemology, which she labels "feminist empiricism": "*Feminist empiricism* argues that sexism and androcentrism are social biases correctable by stricter adherence to the existing methodological norms of scientific inquiry."[20] Harding takes the hallmark of feminist empiricism (which on her taxonomy is the only alternative to feminist standpoint and postmodernist epistemologies) to be commitment to a particular conception of objectivity, which, again, is held to be part of the legacy of the Enlightenment. In her view, acceptance of this ideal brings with it faith in the efficacy of "existing methodological norms of science" in correcting biases and irrationalities within science, in the same way that acceptance of the liberal ideal of impartiality brings with it faith in the system to eliminate political and social injustice.

In Harding's mind, as in Jaggar's, this politically limiting conception of objectivity is one that can be traced to traditional conceptions of the knowing subject, specifically to Enlightenment conceptions of "rational man." The message, then, is that mainstream epistemology, because it still operates with this traditional conception of the self, functions to limit our understanding of the real operations of power, and of our place as women within oppressive structures. A genuine feminist transformation in our thinking therefore requires massive overhaul, if not outright repudiation, of central aspects of the tradition.

This is clearly the message that political scientist Jane Flax gleans from her reading of feminist philosophy; she argues that feminist theory ought properly to be viewed as a version of postmodern thought, since postmodern theorists and feminist theorists are so obviously engaged in a common project:

> Postmodern philosophers seek to throw into radical doubt beliefs still prevalent in (especially American) culture but derived from the Enlightenment . . . ;[21] feminist notions of the self, knowledge and truth are too contradictory to those of the Enlightenment to be contained within its categories. The way to feminist future(s) cannot lie in reviving or appropriating Enlightenment concepts of the person or knowledge.[22]

But there are at least two serious problems with this argument. The first is that the "tradition" that emerges from these critiques is a gross distortion and oversimplification of the early modern period. The critics' conglomeration of all classical and Enlightenment views into a uniform "traditional" epistemology obscures the enormous amount of controversy surrounding such notions as knowledge and the self during the seventeenth and eighteenth centuries, and encourages crude misunderstandings of some of the central theoretical claims. Specifically, this amalgamation makes all but invisible a debate that has enormous relevance to discussions of bias and objectivity, viz., the controversy between rationalists and empiricists about the extent to which the structure of the mind might constrain the development of knowledge.[23]

The second problem is that the picture of analytic epistemology that we get once it's allied with this oversimplified "traditional" epistemology is downright cartoonish. When we look at the actual content of the particular conceptions of objectivity and scientific method that the feminist critics have culled from the modern period, and which they subsequently attach to contemporary epistemology, it turns out that these conceptions are precisely the ones that have been the focus of *criticism* among American analytic philosophers from the 1950s onward. The feminist critics' depiction of "mainstream" epistemology utterly obscures this development in analytic epistemology, and in glossing over the details of the analytic critique of positivism, misses points that are of crucial relevance to any truly radical assault on the liberal ideology of objectivity.[24]

The second problem is partly a consequence of the first. The feminist critics, almost without exception, characterize mainstream epistemology as "empiricist." But one of the chief accomplishments of the analytic challenge to positivism was the demonstration that a strictly empiricistic conception of knowledge is untenable. As a result, much of analytic epistemology has taken a decidedly rationalistic turn. Neglect of the rationalist/empiricist debate and misunderstanding of rationalist tenets make the critics insensitive to these developments and blind to their implications.

But the misreading of contemporary epistemology is also partly just a matter of the critics' failure to realize the extent to which analytic philosophy represents a *break* with tradition. I do not mean to deny that there were *any* important theoretical commitments common to philosophers of the early modern period. One such commitment, shared at least by classical rationalists and empiricists, and arguably by Kant, was an epistemological meta-hypothesis called "externalism." This is the view that the proper goal of epistemological theory is the rational *vindication* of human epistemic practice. But if externalism is regarded as the hallmark of "traditional epistemology," then the identification of analytic epistemology with traditional epistemology becomes all the more spurious.

It was the main burden of Quine's critique of positivism to demonstrate the impossibility of an externalist epistemology, and his suggested replacement, "naturalized epistemology," was meant to be what epistemology could be once externalist illusions were shattered. As a result of the analytic critique of externalism, the notions of objectivity and rationality available to contemporary analytic epistemologists are necessarily more complicated than the traditional conceptions they replace. This is so even for epistemologists who would not identify themselves as partisans of naturalized epistemology.

In what follows, I'll discuss in turn these two problems: first, the mischaracterization of the tradition, and then the caricature of contemporary analytic epistemology.

Rationalism Versus Empiricism: The Importance of Being Partial

What I want to show first is that the "traditional epistemology" offered us by Jaggar and Flax grafts what is essentially a rationalist (and in some respects, specifically Cartesian)

theory of *mind* onto what is essentially an empiricist conception of *knowledge*. This is a serious error. Although Jaggar and Flax claim that there are deep connections between the
one and the other, the fact of the matter is that they are solidly opposed. The conception
of objectivity that is ultimately the object of radical critique—perfect impartiality—is
only supportable as an epistemic ideal on an empiricist conception of *mind*. Thus, I'll argue, the rationalistic conception of the self attacked by Jaggar and Flax as unsuitable or
hostile to a feminist point of view actually provides the basis for a critique of the view of
knowledge they want ultimately to discredit.

Much of what is held to be objectionable in "traditional epistemology" is supposed to derive from the tradition's emphasis on *reason*. But different traditional figures emphasized reason in different ways. Only the rationalists and Kant were committed to what I'll call "cognitive essentialism," a feature of the "traditional"
conception of mind that comes in for some of the heaviest criticism. I take cognitive
essentialism to be the view (1) that there are certain specific properties the possession
of which is both distinctive of and universal among human beings, (2) that these
properties are cognitive in nature, (3) that our possession of these properties amounts
to a kind of innate knowledge, and (4) that our status as moral agents is connected to
the possession of these properties. Empiricists denied all these claims—in particular,
they denied that reason had anything but a purely instrumental role to play in either
normative or nonnormative activity, and tended to be opposed to any form of essentialism, cognitive or otherwise.

Although the purely instrumental conception of reason is also criticized by feminist scholars, cognitive essentialism is the focus of one specific set of feminist concerns. It is held to be suspect on the grounds that such a doctrine could easily serve to
legitimate the arrogant impulses of privileged Western white men: first to canonize
their own culture- and time-bound speculations as revelatory of the very norms of human existence, and then simultaneously to deny the very properties deemed "universal" to the majority of human beings on the planet.

Here's how it is supposed to work: Cognitive essentialism is supposed to engender a kind of fantasy concerning actual human existence and the actual prerequisites
of knowledge. Because of its emphasis on *cognitive* characteristics, it's argued, the view
permits privileged individuals to ignore the fact of their embodiment, and with that,
the considerable material advantages they enjoy in virtue of their class, gender, and
race.[25] To the extent that the characteristics they find in themselves are the result of
their particular privileges instead of a transcendent humanity, the fantasy provides a
basis for viewing less-privileged people—who well may lack such characteristics—as
inherently less human. But since these characteristics have been lionized as forming
the essence of moral personhood, the fantasy offers a rationale for viewing any differences between themselves and others as negative deviations from a moral norm.

Recall, for example, that the particular elements of Enlightenment thought that
Flax finds inimical to feminist theory and praxis are the alleged universality, transcendence, and abstractness assigned to the faculty of reason:

> The notion that reason is divorced from "merely contingent" existence still
> predominates in contemporary Western thought and now appears to mask the

embeddedness and dependence of the self upon social relations, as well as the partiality and historical specificity of this self's existence. . . .

In fact, feminists, like other postmodernists, have begun to suspect that all such transcendental claims reflect and reify the experience of a few persons—mostly White, Western males.[26]

But moreover, cognitive essentialism is supposed to lead to what Jaggar calls "individualism,"[27] the view that individual human beings are epistemically self-suffi-cient, that human society is unnecessary or unimportant for the development of knowledge. If the ideal "man of reason" is utterly without material, differentiating features, then the ideal knower would appear to be *pure* rationality, a mere calculating mechanism, a person who has been stripped of all those particular aspects of self that are of overwhelming human significance. Correlatively, as it is precisely the features "stripped off" the self by the Cartesian method that "traditional" epistemology deni-grates as distorting influences, the ideally objective cognizer is also the man of reason. Knowledge is then achieved, it appears, not by active engagement with one's world and with the people in it, but by a pristine transcendence of the messy contingencies of the human condition.[28]

Lending support to Lorraine Code's grievance against "traditional" epistemol-ogy, Jaggar thus insists that it is this abstract and detached individualism that under-writes a solipsistic view of the construction of knowledge and precludes assigning any epistemological significance to the situation of the knower.

> Because it conceives humans as essentially separate individuals, this epistemo-logical tradition views the attainment of knowledge as a project for each indi-vidual on his or her own. The task of epistemology, then, is to formulate rules to enable individuals to undertake this project with success.[29]

It is here that the link is supposed to be forged between the Cartesian/Kantian conception of the self and the particular conception of objectivity—objectivity as pure neutrality—that is thought to be pernicious.

But the individualism Jaggar takes to unite rationalists and empiricists is not in fact a view that *anyone* held. She derives it from a fairly common—indeed, almost canonical—misreading of the innate ideas debate. Significantly, Jaggar acknowledges the existence of disagreements within the early modern period, but avers that such is-sues as divided rationalists from empiricists are differences that make no difference. Both were foundationalists, she points out, and though the foundation for rationalists was self-evident truths of reason and the foundation for empiricists was reports of sen-sory experience, "in either case, . . . the attainment of knowledge is conceived as essen-tially a solitary occupation that has no necessary social preconditions."[30]

The reading, in other words, is that whereas the empiricists thought all knowl-edge came from experience, the rationalists thought *all knowledge came from reason*. But the second element of this interpretation is simply wrong. It was no part of *Descartes's* project (much less Kant's) to assert the self-sufficiency of reason. Note that a large part of the goal of the exercise of hyperbolic doubt in the *Meditations* was to establish the reliability of sensory experience, which Descartes took to be essential to the development of adequate knowledge of the world. And although he maintained the innateness of many ideas, including sensory ideas, he carefully and repeatedly explained that he meant by this only that human beings were built in such a way that certain experiences would trigger these ideas and no others.[31]

Furthermore, Descartes himself explicitly endorses two of the very epistemic values his position is supposed to preclude. Not only does he clearly reject the sort of epistemic individualism Jaggar deplores, but he strongly upholds the necessity of acquainting oneself with the variety of human experience in order to form a just conception of the world. Expressing his contempt for the contradictions and sophistries of his learned and cloistered teachers, he recounts how, as soon as he was old enough to "emerge from the control of [his] tutors," he "entirely quitted the study of letters."

> And resolving to seek no other science than that which could be found in myself, *or at least in the great book of the world* [my emphasis], I employed the rest of my youth in travel, in seeing courts and armies, in intercourse with men of diverse temperaments and conditions, in collecting varied experiences, in proving myself in the various predicaments in which I was placed by fortune, and under all circumstances bringing my mind to bear on the things which came before it, so that I might derive some profit from my experience.[32]

And far from recommending the divestiture of one's particular concerns as sound epistemic practice, Descartes affirms the importance of concrete engagement in finding the truth, pointing to the degradation of knowledge that can result from disinterestedness.

> For it seemed to me that I might meet with much more truth in the reasonings that each man makes on the matters that specially concern him, and the issue of which would very soon punish him if he made a wrong judgment, than in the case of those made by a man of letters in his study touching speculations which lead to no result, and which bring about no other consequences to himself excepting that he will be all the more vain the more they are removed from common sense, since in this case it proves him to have employed so much the more ingenuity and skill in trying to make them seem probable.[33]

The bottom line is that rationalists, Descartes especially, did not hold the view that experience was inessential or even that it was unimportant; nor did they hold the view that the best epistemic practice is to discount one's own interests. The misreading that saddles Descartes with such views stems from a popular misconception about the innate ideas debate.

The disagreement between rationalists and empiricists was not simply about the existence of innate ideas. Both schools were agreed that the mind was natively structured and that that structure partially determined the shape of human knowledge. What they disagreed about was the *specificity* of the constraints imposed by innate mental structure. The rationalists believed that native structure placed quite specific limitations on the kinds of concepts and hypotheses the mind could form in response to experience, so that human beings were, in effect, natively biased toward certain ways of conceiving the world. Empiricists, on the other hand, held that there were relatively few native constraints on how the mind could organize sensory experience, and that such constraints as did exist were *domain-general* and *content-neutral*.

According to the empiricists, the human mind was essentially a mechanism for the manipulation of sensory data. The architecture of the mechanism was supposed to ensure that the concepts and judgments constructed out of raw sense experience accorded with the rules of logic. This did amount to a minimal constraint on the possible contents of human thought—they had to be logical transforms of sensory primitives—but it was a highly general one, applying to every subject domain in precisely the same way. Thus, on this model, any one hypothesis should be as good as any other as far as the mind is concerned, as long as both hypotheses are logically consistent with the sensory evidence.[34] This strict empiricist model of mind, as it turns out, supports many of the elements of epistemology criticized by Code, Jaggar, and others (e.g., a sharp observation/theory distinction, unmediated access to a sensory "given," and an algorithmic view of justification). I'll spell this out in detail in the next section. For present purposes, however, the thing to note is that the model provides clear warrant for the particular conception of the ideal of objectivity—perfect neutrality—that is the main concern of Jaggar and the others and that is supposed to follow from cognitive essentialism. Here's how.

Because the mind itself, on the empiricist model, makes no substantive contribution to the contents of thought, knowledge on this model is *entirely* experience-driven: All concepts and judgments are held to reflect regularities in an individual's sensory experience. But one individual cannot see everything there is to see—one's experience is necessarily limited, and there's always the danger that the regularities that form the basis of one's own judgments are not general regularities, but only artifacts of one's limited sample. (There is, in other words, a massive restriction-of-range problem for empiricists.) The question then arises how one can tell whether the patterns one perceives are present in nature generally, or are just artifacts of one's idiosyncratic perspective.

The empiricists' answer to this question is that one can gauge the general validity of one's judgments by the degree to which they engender reliable expectations about sensory experience. But although this answer addresses the problem of how to tell whether one's judgments are good or bad, it doesn't address the problem of how to get good judgments in the first place. Getting good judgments means getting good data—that is, exposing oneself to patterns of sensations that are representative of the objective distribution of sensory qualities throughout nature.

This idea immediately gives rise to a certain ideal (some would say fantasy) of epistemic location—the best spot from which to make judgments would be that spot which is *least particular*. Sound epistemic practice then becomes a matter of constantly trying to maneuver oneself into such a location—trying to find a place (or at least come as close as one can) where the regularities in one's own personal experience match the regularities in the world at large. A knower who could be somehow stripped of all particularities and idiosyncrasies would be the best possible knower there is.

This is not, however, a fantasy that would hold any particular appeal for a rationalist, despite the image of detachment evoked by a cursory reading of the *Meditations*. The rationalists had contended all along that sensory experience *by itself* was insufficient to account for the richly detailed body of knowledge that human beings manifestly possessed, and thus that certain elements of human knowledge—what classical rationalists called *innate ideas*—must be natively present, a part of the human essence.

Because the rationalists denied that human knowledge was a pure function of the contingencies of experience, they didn't need to worry nearly as much as the empiricists did about epistemic location. If it is the structure of mind, rather than the accidents of experience, that largely determines the contours of human concepts, then we can relax about at least the broad parameters of our knowledge. We don't have to worry that idiosyncratic features of our epistemic positions will seriously distort our worldviews, because the development of our knowledge is not dependent upon the patterns that happen to be displayed in our particular experiential histories. The regularities we "perceive" are, in large measure, regularities that we're *built* to perceive.

"Pure" objectivity—if that means giving equal weight to every hypothesis consistent with the data, or if it means drawing no conclusions beyond what can be supported by the data—is thus a nonstarter as an epistemic norm from a rationalist's point of view. The rationalists were in effect calling attention to the *value* of a certain kind of partiality: if the mind were not natively biased—i.e., disposed to take seriously certain kinds of hypotheses and to disregard or fail to even consider others—then knowledge of the sort that human beings possess would itself be impossible. There are simply too many ways of combining ideas, too many different abstractions that could be performed, too many distinct extrapolations from the same set of facts, for a pure induction machine to make much progress in figuring out the world.

The realization that perfect neutrality was not necessarily a good thing, and that bias and partiality are potentially salutary, is thus a point that was strongly present in the early modern period, *pace* Jaggar and Flax. There was no single "traditional" model of mind; the model that can properly be said to underwrite the conceptions of rationality and objectivity that Jaggar brings under feminist attack is precisely a model to which Descartes and the other rationalists were *opposed,* and, ironically, the one that, on the face of it, assigns the most significance to experience. And although it is the cognitive essentialists who are charged with deflecting attention away from epistemically significant characteristics of the knower, it was in fact these same essentialists, in explicit opposition to the empiricists, who championed the idea that human knowledge was necessarily "partial."

Hume, Quine, and the Break with Tradition

Let me turn now to the second serious problem with the feminist criticisms of "mainstream" epistemology: To the extent that there really is a "tradition" in epistemology, it is a tradition that has been explicitly rejected by contemporary analytic philosophy.

If the rationalists solved one problem by positing innate ideas, it was at the cost of raising another. Suppose that there are, as the rationalists maintained, innate ideas that perform the salutary function of narrowing down to a manageable set the hypotheses that human minds have to consider when confronted with sensory data. That eliminates the problem faced by the empiricists of filtering out idiosyncratic "distortions." But now the question is, How can we be sure that these biases—so helpful in getting us to *a* theory of the world—are getting us to the *right* theory of the world? What guarantees that our minds are inclining us in the right direction? Innate ideas lead us somewhere, but do they take us where we want to go?

The rationalists took this problem very seriously. A large part of their project was aimed at validating the innate constraints, at showing that these mental biases did not lead us astray. Descartes's quest for "certainty" needs to be understood in this context: The method of hyperbolic doubt should be viewed not as the efforts of a paranoid to free himself forever from the insecurity of doubt, but as a theoretical exercise designed to show that the contours imposed on our theories by our own minds were proper reflections of the topography of reality itself.

It is at this point that we're in a position to see what rationalists and empiricists actually had in common—not a conception of mind, not a theory of how knowledge is constructed, but a theory of *theories* of knowledge. If there is a common thread running through Enlightenment epistemologies, it is this: a belief in the possibility of providing a *rational* justification of the processes by which human beings arrive at theories of the world. For the empiricists, the trick was to show how the content of all knowledge could be reduced to pure reports of sensory experience; for the rationalists, it was showing the indubitability of the innate notions that guided and facilitated the development of knowledge. Philosophers in neither group were really on a quest for certainty—all they wanted was a reliable map of its boundaries.

But if one of the defining themes of the modern period was the search for an externalist justification of epistemic practice, then *Hume* must be acknowledged to be the first postmodernist. Hume, an empiricist's empiricist, discovered a fatal flaw in his particular proposal for justifying human epistemic practice. He realized that belief in the principle of induction—the principle that says that the future will resemble the past or that similar things will behave similarly—could not be rationally justified. It was clearly not a truth of reason, since its denial was not self-contradictory. But neither could it be justified by experience: Any attempt to do so would be circular, because the practice of using past experience as evidence about the future is itself only warranted if one accepts the principle of induction.

Hume's "skeptical solution" to his own problem amounted to an abandonment of the externalist hopes of his time. Belief in induction, he concluded, was a *custom,* a tendency of mind ingrained by nature, one of "a species of natural instincts, which no reasoning or process of the thought and understanding is able, either to produce or to prevent."[35] For better or worse, Hume contended, we're stuck with belief in induction—we are constitutionally incapable of doubting it and conceptually barred from justifying it. The best we can do is to *explain* it.

Hume's idea was thus to offer as a replacement for the failed externalist project of rational justification of epistemic practice, the *empirical* project of characterizing the cognitive nature of creatures like ourselves, and then figuring out how such creatures, built to seek knowledge in the ways we do, could manage to survive and flourish. In this way, he anticipated to a significant degree the "post modernist" turn taken by analytic philosophy in the twentieth century as the result of Quine's and others' critiques of externalism's last gasp—logical positivism.

Before fast-forwarding into the twentieth century, let me summarize what I take to be the real lessons of the modern period—lessons that, I've argued, have been missed by many feminist critiques of "traditional" epistemology. First, there is the essentially rationalist insight that perfect objectivity is not only impossible but undesirable, that certain kinds of "bias" or "partiality" are necessary to make our epistemic tasks tractable. Second, there is Hume's realization that externalism won't work, that we can never manage to offer a justification of epistemic norms without somehow presupposing the very norms we wish to justify. See this, if you will, as the beginning of the postmodern recognition that theory always proceeds from an "embedded" location, that there is no transcendent spot from which we can inspect our own theorizing.

The rationalist lesson was pretty much lost and the import of Hume's insight submerged by the subsequent emergence and development of neo-empiricist philosophy. This tradition, which involved primarily the British empiricists Mill and Russell, but also Wittgenstein and the Vienna Circle on the Continent, culminated in the school of thought known as logical positivism.[36] The positivists' project was, in some ways, an externalist one. They hoped to develop criteria that would enforce a principled distinction between empirically significant and empirically meaningless sentences. In the minds of some positivists (Schlick, arguably, and Ayer), this criterion would help to vindicate scientific practice by helping to distinguish science from "metaphysics," which was for positivists, a term of abuse.

The positivists were perfectly well aware of Hume's dilemma about the status of the principle of induction—similar problems about even more fundamental principles of logic and mathematics had come to light since his time. But the positivists in effect attempted to rehabilitate epistemological externalism by means of a bold move. They took all the material that was needed to legitimize scientific practice but that could not be traced directly to sensory experience, and relegated it to the *conventions* of human language. This tack had, at least *prima facie,* some advantages over Hume's nativist move: If our epistemic norms are a matter of convention, then (1) there's no longer any question of explaining how we got them—they're there because we *put* them there; and (2) there's no need to justify them because the parameter of evaluation for conventions is not truth but *utility.*

The positivists thus embarked on a program they called "rational reconstruction"—they wanted to show, in detail, how any empirically meaningful claim could be reduced, by the successive application of semantic and logical rules, to statements purely about sensory experience.j128

If such reconstructions could be shown to be possible at least in principle, then all theoretical disagreements could be shown to be susceptible to resolution by appeal to the neutral court of empirical experience. And in all of this, the positivists were committed to basically the same series of assumptions that warranted the view of objectivity that I earlier associated with classical empiricism.

But there were two things absolutely essential to the success of this project. First, there had to be a viable distinction that could be drawn between statements whose truth depended on empirical contingencies (the contentful claims of a theory that formed the substance of the theory) and statements that were true "by convention" and thus part of the logical /semantic structure of the theory. Second, it would have to be shown that the reduction of empirically contentful statements to specific sets of claims about sensory experience could be carried out. But in the early 1950s, Quine (together with Hempel, Goodman, Putnam, and others) began producing decisive arguments against precisely these assumptions.[37] The ensuing changes in analytic epistemology were nothing short of radical.

Quine's main insight was that individual statements do not have any specific consequences for experience if taken individually—that it is only in conjunction with a variety of other claims that experiential consequences can even be derived. It follows from this that no single experience or observation can decisively refute any theoretical claim or resolve any theoretical dispute, and that all experimental tests of hypotheses are actually tests of *conjunctions* of hypotheses. The second insight—actually a corollary of the first point—was that no principled distinction can be drawn among statements on the basis of the grounds of their truth—there can be no distinction between statements made true or false by experience and those whose truth value depends entirely on semantic or logical conventions.

The implications of these two insights were far-reaching. Quine's arguments against the "two dogmas of empiricism" entailed, in the first place, that the confirmation relation could not be hierarchical, as the foundationalist picture required, but must rather be holistic. Because theories have to face "the tribunal of sensory experience as a corporate body" (to use Quine's military-industrial metaphor), there can be no evidentially foundational set of statements that asymmetrically confirm all the others—every statement in the theory is linked by some justificatory connections to every other.

It also meant that responses at the theoretical level to the acquisition of empirical data were not fully dictated by logic. If experimental tests were always tests of *groups* of statements, then if the prediction fails, logic will tell us only that *something* in the group must go, but not *what*. If logic plus data don't suffice to determine how belief is modified in the face of empirical evidence, then there must be, in addition to logic and sensory evidence, *extra-empirical* principles that partially govern theory selection. The "justification" of these principles can only be pragmatic—we are warranted in using them just to the extent that they work.[38]

But to say this is to say that epistemic norms—a category that must include any principle that in fact guides theory selection—are themselves subject to empirical disconfirmation. And indeed, Quine embraces this consequence, explicitly extending the lesson to cover not only pragmatic "rules of thumb," but to rules of logic and language as well. In short, any principle that facilitates the development of knowledge by narrowing down our theoretical options becomes itself a part of the theory, and a part that must be defended on the same basis as any other part. So much for the fact/value distinction.

The reasoning above represents another of the many routes by which Quine's attack on foundationalism can be connected with his critique of the analytic/synthetic distinction, so central to positivist projects. With the demonstration that any belief, no matter how apparently self-evident, could in principle be rejected on the basis of experience, Quine effectively destroyed the prospects for any "first philosophy"—any Archimedean fixed point from which we could inspect our own epistemic practice and pronounce it sound.

But his critique also pointed the way (as Hume's "skeptical solution" did to the problem of induction) to a different approach to the theory of knowledge. Epistemology, according to Quine, had to be "naturalized," transformed into the empirical study of the actual processes—not "rational reconstructions" of those processes—by which human cognizers achieve knowledge.[39] If we accept this approach, several consequences follow for our understanding of knowledge and of the norms that properly govern its pursuit.

The first lesson is one that I believe may be part of what the feminist critics are themselves pointing to in their emphasis on the essential locatedness of all knowledge claims. The lesson is that all theorizing *takes some knowledge for granted*. Theorizing about theorizing is no exception. The decision to treat epistemology as the empirical study of the knower requires us to presume that we can, at least for a class of clear cases, distinguish epistemic success from epistemic failure. The impossibility of the externalist project shows us that we cannot expect to learn *from our philosophy* what counts as knowledge and how much of it we have; rather, we must begin with the assumption that we know certain things and figure out how that happened.

This immediately entails a second lesson. A naturalized approach to knowledge requires us to give up the idea that our own epistemic practice is transparent to us—that we can come to understand how knowledge is obtained either by *a priori* philosophizing or by casual introspection. It requires us to be open to the possibility that the processes that we actually rely on to obtain and process information about the world are significantly different from the ones our philosophy told us had to be the right ones.

Let me digress to point out a tremendous irony here, much remarked upon in the literature on Quine's epistemology and philosophy of mind. Despite his being the chief evangelist of the gospel that everything is empirical, Quine's own philosophy is distorted by his a prioristic commitment to a radically empiricistic, instrumentalist theory of psychology, namely psychological behaviorism. Quine's commitment to this theory—which holds that human behavior can be adequately explained without any reference to mental states or processes intervening between environmental stimuli and the organism's response—is largely the result of his philosophical antipathy to intentional objects, together with a residual sympathy for the foundationalist empiricism that he himself was largely responsible for dismantling.

Chomsky, of course, was the person most responsible for pointing out the in principle limitations of behaviorism, by showing in compelling detail the empirical inadequacies of behaviorist accounts of the acquisition of language.[40] Chomsky also emphasized the indefensibility of the a prioristic methodological constraints that defined empiricistic accounts of the mind, appealing to considerations that Quine himself marshaled in his own attacks on instrumentalism in nonpsychological domains.[41]

Chomsky's own theory of language acquisition did not differ from the behaviorist account only, or even primarily, in its mentalism. It was also rationalistic: Chomsky quite self-consciously appealed to classical rationalistic forms of argument about the necessity of mental partiality in establishing the empirical case for his strong nativism. Looking at the actual circumstances of language acquisition, and then at the character of the knowledge obtained in those circumstances, Chomsky argued that the best explanation of the whole process is one that attributes to human beings a set of innate biases limiting the kinds of linguistic hypotheses available for their consideration as they respond to the welter of data confronting them.[42]

Chomsky can thus be viewed, and is viewed by many, as a naturalized epistemologist *par excellence*. What his work shows is that a naturalized approach to epistemology—in this case, the epistemology of language—yields an *empirical* vindication of rationalism. Since Chomsky's pathbreaking critique of psychological behaviorism, and the empiricist conception of mind that underlies it, nativism in psychology has flourished, and a significant degree of rationalism has been imported into contemporary epistemology.

A casual student of the analytic scene who has read only Quine could, of course, be forgiven for failing to notice this, given Quine's adamant commitment to an empiricist conception of mind; this may explain why so many of the feminist critics of contemporary epistemology seem to identify analytic epistemology with empiricism and to ignore the more rationalistic alternatives that have developed out of the naturalized approach. But I think, too, that the original insensitivity to the details of the original rationalist/empiricist controversy plays a role. Anyone who properly appreciates the import of the rationalist defense of the value of partiality will, I think, see where Quine's rejection of externalism is bound to lead.

So let's do it. I turn now to the feminist critique of objectivity and the bias paradox.

III. Quine as Feminist: What Naturalized Epistemology Can Tell Us About Bias

I've argued that much of the feminist criticism of "mainstream" epistemology depends on a misreading of both contemporary analytic philosophy, and of the tradition from which it derives. But it's one thing to show that contemporary analytic philosophy is not what the feminist critics think it is, and quite another to show that the contemporary analytic scene contains an epistemology that can serve as an adequate *feminist* epistemology. To do this, we must return to the epistemological issues presented to us by feminist theory and see how naturalized epistemology fares with respect to them. I want eventually to show how a commitment to a naturalized epistemology provides some purchase on the problem of conceptualizing bias, but in order to do that, we must look in some detail at those feminist arguments directed against the notion of objectivity.

Capitalist Science and the Ideal of Objectivity

As we've seen, one of the most prominent themes in feminist epistemology and feminist philosophy of science concerns the alleged ideological function of a certain conception of objectivity. Many feminist critics see a connection between radical (i.e., nonliberal) critiques of science and feminist critiques of "received" epistemology. Such critics take as their starting point the observation that science, as it has developed within industrialized capitalist societies like the United States, is very much an instrument of oppression: Rather than fulfilling its Enlightenment promise as a liberatory and progressive force, institutionalized science serves in fact to sustain and even to enhance existing structures of inequality and domination.[43]

Although all feminists agree that part of the explanation of this fact must be that modern science has been distorted by the sexist, racist, and classist biases it inherits from the society in which it exists, feminist theorists divide on the issue of whether some "deeper" explanation is required. Alison Jaggar's "liberal feminists" and Sandra Harding's "feminist empiricists" hold that society and science are both potentially self-correcting—that more equitable arrangements of power and more scrupulous enforcement of the rules of fairness would turn science back to its natural progressive course.

But Harding and Jaggar, together with Lorraine Code and Evelyn Fox Keller, disagree with this liberal analysis. They contend that the modern scientific establishment has not simply inherited its oppressive features from the inequitable society that conditions it. Rather, they claim, a large part of the responsibility for societal injustices lies deep within science itself, in the conception of knowledge and knowers that underlies "scientific method." These critics charge that the very ideals to which Western science has traditionally aspired—particularly rationality and objectivity—serve to sanction and promote a form of institutionalized inquiry uniquely suited to the needs of patriarchy. Thus, it's argued, feminist critique must not stop at exposing cases in which science has broken its own rules; it must press on to expose the androcentric bias inherent in the rules themselves.

Thus Evelyn Fox Keller claims that any critique that does not extend to the rules of scientific method allies itself with political liberalism in virtue of its epistemology. Any such critique, she argues, "can still be accommodated within the traditional framework by the simple argument that the critiques, if justified, merely reflect the fact that [science] is not sufficiently scientific." In contrast, there is "the truly radical critique that attempts to locate androcentric bias . . . in scientific ideology itself. The range of criticism takes us out of the liberal domain and requires us to question the very assumptions of rationality that underlie the scientific enterprise."[44]

All this seems to set a clear agenda for feminist philosophers who wish to be part of the struggle for a genuinely radical social transformation: If one's going to go deeper politically and criticize the presuppositions of liberal political theory, then one must coordinately go deeper *conceptually* and criticize the presuppositions of the epistemology and metaphysics that underwrite the politics.

But does this argument work? I think that it doesn't. To see why, we need to look more closely at the epistemological position that the feminist critics take to be allied with liberalism and look in more detail at the argument that is supposed to show that such a view of knowledge is oppressive.

The "traditional" epistemology pictured in the work of Flax, Code, and Jaggar, I've argued, is an unvigorous hybrid of rationalist and empiricist elements, but the features that are supposed to limit it from the point of view of feminist critique of science all derive from the empiricist strain. Specifically, the view of knowledge in question contains roughly the following elements:

> (1) it is strongly foundationalist: it is committed to the view that there is a set of epistemically privileged beliefs, from which all knowledge is in principle derivable.
>
> (2) it takes the foundational level to be constituted by reports of sensory experience, and views the mind as a mere calculating device, containing no substantive contents other than what results from experience.
>
> (3) as a result of its foundationalism and its empiricism, it is committed to a variety of sharp distinctions: observation/theory, fact/value, context of discovery/context of justification.

This epistemological theory comes very close to what Hempel has termed "narrow inductivism,"[45] but I'm just going to call it the "Dragnet" theory of knowledge. To assess the "ideological potential" of the Dragnet theory, let's look first at some of the epistemic values and attitudes the theory supports.

To begin with, because of its empiricistic foundationalism, the view stigmatizes both inference and theory. On this view, beliefs whose confirmation depends upon logical relations to other beliefs bear a less direct, less "objective" connection to the world than reports of observations, which are supposed to provide us transparent access to the world. To "actually see" or "directly observe" is better, on this conception, than to infer, and an invidious distinction is drawn between the "data" or "facts" (which are incontrovertible) on the one hand and "theories" and "hypotheses" (unproven conjectures) on the other.

Second, the view supports the idea that any sound system of beliefs can, in principle, be rationally reconstructed. That is, a belief worth having is either itself a fact or can be assigned a position within a clearly articulated confirmational hierarchy erected on fact. With this view comes a denigration of the epistemic role of hunches and intuitions. Such acts of cognitive impulse can be difficult to defend "rationally" if the standards of defense are set by a foundationalist ideal. When a hunch can't be defended, but the individual persists in believing it anyway, that's *ipso facto* evidence of irresponsibility or incompetence. Hunches that happen to pay off are relegated to the context of discovery and are viewed as inessential to the justification of the ensuing belief. The distinction between context of discovery and context of justification itself follows from foundationalism: As long as it's possible to provide a rational defense of a belief *ex post facto* by demonstrating that it bears the proper inferential relation to established facts, we needn't give any thought to the circumstances that actually gave rise to that belief. Epistemic location becomes, to that extent, evidentially irrelevant.

Finally, the Dragnet theory is going to lead to a certain conception of how systematic inquiry ought to work. It suggests that good scientific practice is relatively mechanical: that data gathering is more or less passive and random, that theory construction emerges from the data in a relatively automatic way, and that theory testing is a matter of mechanically deriving predictions and then subjecting them to decisive experimental tests. Science (and knowledge-seeking generally) will be good *to the extent that* its practitioners can conform to the ideal of objectivity.

This ideal of objective method requires a good researcher, therefore, to put aside all prior beliefs about the outcome of the investigation, and to develop a willingness to be carried wherever the facts may lead. But other kinds of discipline are necessary, too. Values are different in kind from facts, on this view, and so are not part of the confirmational hierarchy. Values (together with the emotions and desires connected with them) become, at best, epistemically irrelevant and, at worst, disturbances or distortions. Best to put them aside, and try to go about one's epistemic business in as calm and disinterested a way as possible.

In sum, the conception of ideal epistemic practice yielded by the Dragnet theory is precisely the conception that the feminist critics disdain. Objectivity, on this view (I'll refer to it from now on as "Dragnet objectivity"), is the result of complete divestiture—divestiture of theoretical commitments, of personal goals, of moral values, of hunches and intuitions. We'll get to the truth, sure as taxes, provided everyone's willing to be rational and to play by the (epistemically relevant) rules. Got an especially knotty problem to solve? Just the facts, ma'am.

Now let's see how the Dragnet theory of knowledge, together with the ideal of objectivity it supports, might play a role in the preservation of oppressive structures.

Suppose for the sake of argument that the empirical claims of the radical critics are largely correct. Suppose, that is, that in contemporary U.S. society institutionalized inquiry does function to serve the specialized needs of a powerful ruling elite (with trickle-down social goods permitted insofar as they generate profits or at least don't impede the fulfillment of ruling-class objectives). Imagine also that such inquiry is very costly, and that the ruling elite strives to socialize those costs as much as possible.

In such a society, there will be a great need to obscure this arrangement. The successful pursuit of the agendas of the ruling elite will require a quiescent—or, as it's usually termed, "stable"—society, which would surely be threatened if the facts were known. Also required is the acquiescence of the scientists and scholars, who would like to view themselves as autonomous investigators serving no masters but the truth and who would deeply resent the suggestion (as anyone with any self-respect would) that their honest intellectual efforts subserve any baser purpose.

How can the obfuscation be accomplished? One possibility would be to promote the idea that science is organized for the sake of *public* rather than *private* interests. But the noble lie that science is meant to make the world a better place is a risky one. It makes the public's support for science contingent upon science's producing tangible and visible public benefits (which may not be forthcoming) and generates expectations of publicity and accountability that might lead to embarrassing questions down the road.

An altogether more satisfactory strategy is to promote the idea that science is *value-neutral*—that it's organized for the sake of *no* particular interests at all! Telling people that science serves only the truth is safer than telling people that science serves *them,* because it not only hides the truth about who benefits, but deflects public attention away from the whole question. Belief in the value-neutrality of science can thus serve the conservative function of securing *unconditional* public support for what are in fact ruling-class initiatives. Any research agenda whatsoever—no matter how pernicious—can be readily legitimated on the grounds that it is the natural result of the self-justifying pursuit of truth, the more or less inevitable upshot of a careful look at the facts.

It will enhance the lie that science is objective, to augment it with the lie that scientists as individuals are especially "objective," either by nature or by dint of their scientific training. If laypersons can be brought to believe this, then the lie that scientific practice can transcend its compromised setting becomes somewhat easier to swallow. And if *scientists* can be brought to embrace this gratifying self-image, then the probability of *their* acquiescence in the existing system will be increased. Scientists will find little cause for critical reflection on their own potential biases (since they will believe that they are more able than others to put aside their own interests and background beliefs in the pursuit of knowledge), and no particular incentive to ponder the larger question of who actually is benefiting from their research.[46]

Now in such a society, the widespread acceptance of a theory of knowledge like the Dragnet theory would clearly be a good thing from the point of view of the ruling elite. By fostering the epistemic attitudes it fosters, the Dragnet theory helps confer special authority and status on science and its practitioners and deflects critical attention away from the material conditions in which science is conducted. Furthermore, by supporting Dragnet objectivity as an epistemic ideal, the theory prepares the ground for reception of the ideology of the objectivity of science.

In a society in which people have a reason to believe that science is successful in yielding knowledge, the Dragnet theory and the ideology of objectivity will in fact be mutually reinforcing. If one believes that science must be objective to be good, then if one independently believes that science is good, one must also believe that science *is objective!* The Dragnet theory, taken together with propagandistic claims that science is value-neutral, etc., offers an *explanation* of the fact that science leads to knowledge. Against the background belief that knowledge is actually structured the way the Dragnet theory says it is, the *success* of science seems to confirm the ideology.

We can conclude from all this that the Dragnet theory, along with the ideal of objectivity it sanctions, has clear ideological value, in the sense that their acceptance may play a causal role in people's acceptance of the ideology of scientific objectivity.

But we cannot infer from this fact either that the Dragnet theory is false or that its ideals are flawed. Such an inference depends on conflating what are essentially *prescriptive* claims (claims about how science ought to be conducted) with *descriptive* claims (claims about how science is in fact conducted). It's one thing to embrace some particular ideal of scientific method and quite another to accept ideologically useful assumptions about the satisfaction of that ideal within existing institutions.[47]

Note that in a society such as the one I've described, the ideological value of the Dragnet theory depends crucially on how successfully it can be promulgated *as a factual characterization* of the workings of the intellectual establishment. It's no use to get everyone to believe simply that it would be a good thing if scientists *could* put aside their prior beliefs and their personal interests; people must be brought to believe that scientists largely *succeed* in such divestitures. The ideological cloud of Dragnet objectivity thus comes not so much from the belief that science *ought* to be value-free, as from the belief that it *is* value-free. And of course it's precisely the fact that science is *not* value-free in the way it's proclaimed to be that makes the ideological ploy necessary in the first place.

If science as an institution fails to live up to its own ideal of objectivity, then the character of existing science entails nothing about the value of the ideal, nor about the character of some imagined science which *did* live up to it. In fact, notice that the more we can show that compromised science is *bad* science (in the sense of leading to false results), the less necessary we make it to challenge the Dragnet theory itself. A good part of the radical case, after all, is made by demonstrating the ways in which scientific research has been *distorted* by some of the very factors a Dragnet epistemologist would cite as inhibitors of epistemic progress: prejudiced beliefs, undefended hunches, material desires, ideological commitments.

There's no reason, in short, why a Dragnet theorist couldn't come to be convinced of the radical analysis of the material basis of science. Such a person might even be expected to experience a special kind of outrage at discovering the way in which the idea of objectivity is ideologically exploited in the service of special interests, much the way many peace activists felt when they first learned of some of the realities masked by U.S. officials' pious avowals of their commitment to "human rights" and "democracy."

A materialist analysis of institutionalized science leads to awareness of such phenomena as the commoditization of knowledge, the "rationalization" of scientific research, and the proletarianization of scientists. Such phenomena make the limits of liberal reformism perfectly clear: Not even the most scrupulous adherence to prescribed method on the part of individual scientists could by itself effect the necessary transformations. But it's possible for even a Dragnet theorist to acknowledge these limits, and to do so without giving up the ideal of neutral objectivity.

I began by considering the claim, defended by several feminist theorists, that "traditional" epistemology limits the possibilities for exposing the machinations of the elite because it endorses the rules of the elite's game. On the contrary, I've argued; since a big part of the lie that needs exposing is the fact that capitalist science *doesn't follow* its own rules, the task of exposing the ideology of scientific objectivity needn't change the rules. A radical critique of science and society, *even if* it implicates certain ideals, *does not require repudiation of those ideals*.

Naturalized Epistemology and the Bias Paradox

What I think I've shown so far is that if our only desideratum on an adequate critical epistemology is that it permits us to expose the real workings of capitalist patriarchy, then the Dragnet theory will do just fine, *pace* its feminist critics. But I certainly do not want to defend that theory; nor do I want to defend as an epistemic ideal the conception of objectivity as neutrality. In fact, I want to join feminist critics in rejecting this ideal. But I want to be clear about the proper basis for criticizing it.

There are, in general, two strategies that one can find in the epistemological literature for challenging the ideal of objectivity as impartiality. (I leave aside for the moment the question of why one might want to challenge an epistemic ideal, though this question will figure importantly in what follows.) The first strategy is to prove the *impossibility* of satisfying the ideal—this involves pointing to the *ubiquity* of bias. The second strategy is to try to demonstrate the *undesirability* of satisfying the ideal—this involves showing the *utility* of bias. The second strategy is employed by some feminist critics, but often the first strategy is thought to be sufficient, particularly when it's pursued together with the kind of radical critique of institutionalized science discussed above. Thus Jaggar, Code, and others emphasize the essential locatedness of every individual knower, arguing that if all knowledge proceeds from some particular perspective, then the transcendent standpoint suggested by the ideology of objectivity is unattainable. All knowledge is conditioned by the knower's location, it is claimed; if we acknowledge that, then we cannot possibly believe that anyone is "objective" in the requisite sense.

But the appeal to the *de facto* partiality of all knowledge is simply not going to justify rejecting the ideal of objectivity, for three reasons. In the first place, the wanted intermediate conclusion—that Dragnet objectivity is impossible—does not follow from the truism that all knowers are located. The Dragnet conception of impartiality is perfectly compatible with the fact that all knowers start from some particular place. The Dragnet theory, like all empiricist theories, holds that knowledge is a strict function of the contingencies of experience. It therefore entails that differences in empirical situation will lead to differences in belief, and to that extent validates the intuition that all knowledge is partial.[48] Thus the neutrality recommended by the Dragnet theory does not enjoin cognizers to abjure the particularities of their own experience, only to honor certain strictures in drawing conclusions from that experience. Impartiality is not a matter of where you are, but rather how well you do from where you sit.

In the second place, even if it could be shown to be impossible for human beings to achieve perfect impartiality, that fact in itself would not speak against Dragnet objectivity *as an ideal*. Many ideals—particularly moral ones—are unattainable, but that does not make them useless, or reveal them to be inadequate as ideals.[49] The fact—and I have no doubt that it is a fact—that no one can fully rid oneself of prejudices, neurotic impulses, selfish desires, and other psychological detritus, does not impugn the moral or the cognitive value of attempting to do so. Similarly, the fact that no one can fully abide by the cognitive strictures imposed by the standards of strict impartiality doesn't entail that one oughtn't to try. The real test of the adequacy of a norm is not whether it can be realized, but (arguably) whether we get closer to what we want if we try to realize it.

But the third and most serious problem with this tack is that it is precisely the one that is going to engender the bias paradox. Notice that the feminist goal of exposing the structures of interestedness that constitute patriarchy and other forms of oppression requires doing more than just demonstrating that particular interests are being served. It requires criticizing that fact, showing that there's something wrong with a society in which science selectively serves the interests of one dominant group. And it's awfully hard to see how such a critical stand can be sustained without some appeal to the value of impartiality.

A similar problem afflicts the variation on this strategy that attempts to base a critique of the norm of objectivity on the androcentric features of its *source*. Even if it could be established that received epistemic norms originated in the androcentric fantasies of European white males (and I meant to give some reason to question this in section 11), how is that fact supposed to be elaborated into a *critique* of those norms? All knowledge is partial—let it be so. How then does the particular partiality of received conceptions of objectivity diminish their worth?

The question that must be confronted by anyone pursuing this strategy is basically this: If bias is ubiquitous and ineliminable, then what's the good of exposing it? It seems to me that the whole thrust of feminist scholarship in this area has been to demonstrate that androcentric biases have distorted science and, indeed, distorted the search for knowledge generally. But if biases are distorting, and if we're all biased in one way or another, then it seems there could be no such thing as an *undistorted* search for knowledge. So what are we complaining about? Is it just that we want it to be distorted in *our* favor, rather than in theirs? We must say something about the badness of the biases we expose or our critique will carry no normative import at all.

We still have to look at the second of the two strategies for criticizing the ideal of objectivity, but this is a good place to pick up the question I bracketed earlier on: *Why* might one want to challenge an epistemic ideal? If my arguments have been correct up to this point, then I have shown that many of the arguments made against objectivity are not only unsound but ultimately self-defeating. But by now the reader must surely be wondering why we need *any* critique of the notion of objectivity as neutrality. If radical critiques of the ideology of scientific objectivity are consistent with respect for this ideal, and if we need some notion of objectivity anyway, why not this one?

The short answer is this: because the best empirical theories of knowledge and mind do not sanction pure neutrality as sound epistemic policy.

The fact is that the Dragnet theory is *wrong*. We know this for two reasons: First, the failure of externalism tells us that its foundationalist underpinnings are rotten, and second, current work in empirical psychology tells us that its empiricist conception of the mind is radically incorrect. But if the Dragnet theory is wrong about the structure of knowledge and the nature of the mind, then the main source of warrant for the ideal of epistemic neutrality is removed. It becomes an open question whether divestiture of emotions, prior beliefs, and moral commitments hinders, or aids, the development of knowledge.

The fact that we find ourselves wondering about the value of a proposed epistemic ideal is itself a consequence of the turn to a naturalized epistemology. As I explained in section II, Quine's critique of externalism entailed that epistemic norms themselves were among the presuppositions being subjected to empirical test in the ongoing process of theory confirmation. This in itself authorizes the project of *criticizing* norms—it makes coherent and gives point to a project which could be nothing but an exercise in skepticism, to an externalist's way of thinking.

Naturalized epistemology tells us that there is no presuppositionless position from which to assess epistemic practice, that we must take some knowledge for granted. The only thing to do, then, is to begin with whatever it is we think we know, and try to figure out how we came to know it: Study knowledge by studying the knower. Now if, in the course of such study, we discover that much of human knowledge is possible only because our knowledge seeking does not conform to the Dragnet model, then we will have good empirical grounds for rejecting perfect objectivity as an epistemic ideal. And so we come back to the second of the two strategies I outlined for challenging the ideal of objectivity. Is there a case to be made against the desirability of epistemic neutrality? Indeed there is, on the grounds that a genuinely open mind, far from leading us closer to the truth, would lead to epistemic chaos.

As I said in section II, empirical work in linguistics and cognitive science is making it increasingly clear how seriously mistaken the empiricist view of the mind actually is. From Chomsky's groundbreaking research on the acquisition of language, through David Marr's theory of the computational basis of vision, to the work of Susan Carey, Elizabeth Spelke, Barbara Landau, Lila Gleitman, and others in developmental psychology, the evidence is mounting that inborn conceptual structure is a crucial factor in the development of human knowledge.[50]

Far from being the streamlined, uncluttered logic machine of classical empiricism, the mind now appears to be much more like a bundle of highly specialized modules, each natively fitted for the analysis and manipulation of a particular body of sensory data. General learning strategies of the sort imagined by classical empiricists, if they are employed by the mind at all, can apply to but a small portion of the cognitive tasks that confront us. Rationalism vindicated.

But if the rationalists have turned out to be right about the structure of the mind, it is because they appreciated something that the empiricists missed—the value of partiality for human knowers. Whatever might work for an ideal mind, operating without constraints of time or space, it's clear by now that complete neutrality of the sort empiricists envisioned would not suit human minds in human environments. A completely "open mind," confronting the sensory evidence we confront, could never manage to construct the rich systems of knowledge we construct in the short time we take to construct them. From the point of view of an *unbiased* mind, the human sensory flow contains both too much information and too little: too much for the mind to generate *all* the logical possibilities, and too little for it to decide among even the relatively few that *are* generated.

The problem of paring down the alternatives is the defining feature of the human epistemic condition. The problem is partly solved, I've been arguing, by one form of "bias"—native conceptual structure. But it's important to realize that this problem is absolutely endemic to human knowledge seeking, whether we're talking about the subconscious processes by which we acquire language and compute sensory information, or the more consciously accessible processes by which we explicitly decide what to believe.

The everyday process of forming an opinion would be grossly hampered if we were really to consider matters with anything even close to an "open mind."

This point is one that Quine has emphasized over and over in his discussions of the underdetermination of theory by data. If we had to rely on nothing but logic and the contingencies of sensory experience, we could never get anywhere in the process of forming an opinion, because we would have *too many choices*. There are an infinite number of distinct and incompatible hypotheses consistent with any body of data, never mind that there are always more data just around the corner, and never mind that we're logically free to reinterpret the "data" to save our hypotheses. If we really had to approach data gathering and theory building with a perfectly open mind, we wouldn't get anywhere.

This insight is also borne out by the history of science. As Thomas Kuhn has pointed out, science is at its least successful during the periods in its history when it most closely resembles the popular models of scientific objectivity. During a discipline's "pre-paradigm" phase, when there is no consensus about fundamental principles, nor even about what to count as the central phenomena, research is anarchic and unproductive. But progress accelerates dramatically when a discipline enters its mature period, marked by the emergence of a theory—a paradigm—capable of organizing the phenomena in a compelling enough way that it commands near-universal acceptance.

Kuhn emphasizes that one of the chief benefits a paradigm brings with it is a degree of closure about foundational issues, instilling in members of the community a principled and highly functional unwillingness to reconsider basic assumptions. The paradigm not only settles important empirical controversies, but also decides more methodological matters—what are the acceptable forms of evidence, what is the right vocabulary for discussing things, what are the proper standards for judging research. The fact is that all of these matters are disputable in principle—but a paradigm relieves its adherents of the considerable burden of having constantly to dispute them.

But what this means is that the practice and attitudes of scientists working within a paradigm will systematically deviate from the popular ideal of scientific objectivity: They will approach their research with definite preconceptions, and they will be reluctant to entertain hypotheses that conflict with their own convictions. Kuhn's point, however, is that the existence of such closed-mindedness among working scientists—what he calls "the dogmatism of mature science"—is not to be regretted; that it is actually beneficial to the course of scientific development: "Though preconception and resistance to innovation could very easily choke off scientific progress, their omnipresence is nonetheless symptomatic of characteristics upon which the continuing vitality of research depends."[51]

Once we appreciate these aspects of mature science, we can explain a great deal about how a fantasy of the pure objectivity of science can take hold independently of any ideological purposes such a fantasy might serve. (This is important if we want a serious, nuanced story about how ideologies work.) The fact that certain tenets of theory are, for all practical purposes, closed to debate can render invisible their actual status as hypotheses. Deeply entrenched theoretical principles, like the laws of thermodynamics or the principle of natural selection, become established "facts."[52] Similarly, the high degree of theoretical background required to translate various numbers and images into observations or data is forgotten by people accustomed to performing the requisite inferences on a daily basis.

Consensus and uniformity thus translate into objectivity. The more homogeneous an epistemic community, the more objective it is likely to regard itself, and, if its inquiries are relatively self-contained, the more likely it is to be viewed as objective by those outside the community. This suggests one fairly obvious explanation for the general perception that the physical sciences are more objective than the social sciences: Sociology, political science, economics, and psychology are disciplines that still lack paradigms in Kuhn's technical sense, Because there is still public debate in these fields about basic theoretical and methodological issues, there can be no credible pretense by any partisan of having hold of the unvarnished truth.

The kind of bias that Kuhn is here identifying is, of course, different in several important respects from the kinds of biases that classical rationalists and contemporary cognitive psychologists are concerned with. For one thing, the biases that come with belief in a paradigm are acquired rather than innate; for another, there is an important social component in one case but not in the other. The lesson, however, is still the same: Human beings would know less, not more, if they were to actualize the Dragnet ideal.

What all this means is that a naturalized approach to knowledge provides us with *empirical* grounds for rejecting pure neutrality as an epistemic ideal, and for valuing those kinds of "biases" that serve to trim our epistemic jobs to manageable proportions. But it also seems to mean that we have a new route to the bias paradox—if biases are now not simply ineliminable, but downright *good,* how is it that *some* biases are *bad?*

I'm going to answer this question, honest, but first let me show how bad things really are. It's possible to see significant analogies between the function of a paradigm within a scientific community, and what is sometimes called a "worldview" within other sorts of human communities. Worldviews confer some of the same cognitive benefits as paradigms, simplifying routine epistemic tasks, establishing an informal methodology of inquiry, etc., and they also offer significant social benefits, providing a common sense of reality and fostering a functional sense of normalcy among members of the community.

But what about those outside the community? A shared language, a set of traditions and mores, a common sense of what's valuable and why—the very things that bind some human beings together in morally valuable ways—function simultaneously to exclude those who do not share them. Moreover, human communities are not homogeneous. In a stratified community, where one group of people dominates others, the worldview of the dominant group can become a powerful tool for keeping those in the subordinate groups in their places.

The real problem with the liberal conceptions of objectivity and neutrality begins with the fact that while they are unrealizable, it's possible for those resting comfortably in the center of a consensus to find that fact invisible. Members of the dominant group are given no reason to question their own assumptions: Their worldview acquires, in their minds, the status of established fact. Their opinions are transformed into what "everybody" knows.[53] Furthermore, these privileged individuals have the power to promote and elaborate their own worldview in public forums while excluding all others, tacitly setting limits to the range of "reasonable" opinion.[54]

Because of the familiarity of its content, the "objectivity" of such reportage is never challenged. If it were, it would be found woefully lacking *by liberal standards*. That's because the liberal ideal of objectivity is an *unreasonable* one; it is not just unattainable, but unattainable by a long measure. But because the challenge is *only* mounted against views that are aberrant, it is *only* such views that will ever be demonstrated to be "non-objective," and thus *only* marginal figures that will ever be charged with bias.[55]

Lorraine Code makes a similar point about the unrealistic stringency of announced standards for knowledge.[56] She rightly points out that most of what we ordinarily count as knowledge wouldn't qualify as such by many proposed criteria. I would go further and say that as with all unrealistically high standards, they tend to support the status quo—in this case, received opinion—by virtue of the fact that they will only be invoked in "controversial" cases, i.e., in case of challenge to familiar or received or "expert" opinion. Since the standards are unreasonably high, the views tested against them will invariably be found wanting; since the only views so tested will be unpopular ones, their failure to pass muster serves to add additional warrant to prevailing prejudices, as well as a patina of moral vindication to the holders of those prejudices, who can self-righteously claim to have given "due consideration" to the "other side."

But what are we anti-externalist, naturalized epistemologists to say about this? We can't simply condemn the members of the dominant class for their "bias," for their lack of "open-mindedness" about our point of view. To object to the hegemony of ruling-class opinion on this basis would be to tacitly endorse the discredited norm of neutral objectivity. "Biased" they are, but then, in a very deep sense, so are we. The problem with ruling-class "prejudices" cannot be the fact that they are deeply-held beliefs, or beliefs acquired "in advance" of the facts—for the necessity of such *kinds* of belief is part of the human epistemic condition.

The real problem with the ruling-class worldview is not that it is biased; it's that it is false. The epistemic problem with ruling-class people is not that they are closed-minded; it's that they hold too much power. The recipe for radical epistemological action then becomes simple: Tell the truth and get enough power so that people have to listen. Part of telling the truth, remember, is telling the truth about how knowledge is actually constructed—advocates of feminist epistemology are absolutely correct about that. We do need to dislodge those attitudes about knowledge that give unearned credibility to elements of the ruling-class worldview, and this means dislodging the hold of the Dragnet theory of knowledge. But we must be clear: The Dragnet theory is not false because it's pernicious; it's pernicious because it is false.

Whether we are talking in general about the ideology of scientific objectivity, or about particular sexist and racist theories, we must be willing to talk about truth and falsity. If we criticize such theories primarily on the basis of their ideological function, we risk falling prey to the very illusions about objectivity that we are trying to expose. I think this has happened to some extent within feminist epistemology. Because so much of feminist criticism has been oblivious to the rationalistic case that can be made against the empiricistic conception of mind at work in the Dragnet theory, empiricistic assumptions continue to linger in the work of even the most radical feminist epistemologists. This accounts, I believe, for much of the ambivalence about Dragnet objectivity expressed even by those feminist critics who argue most adamantly for its rejection.

This ambivalence surfaces, not surprisingly, in discussions about what to do about bad biases, where positive recommendations tend to fall perfectly in line with the program of liberal reformism. Lorraine Code's discussion of stereotypical thinking provides a case in point.[57] Code emphasizes, quite correctly, the degree to which stereotypical assumptions shape the interpretation of experience, both in science and in everyday life. But despite her recognition of the "unlikelihood of pure objectivity,"[58] the "unattainability of pure theory-neutrality,"[59] and her acknowledgment of the necessary role of background theory *in science,* her recommendations for reforming everyday epistemic practice are very much in the spirit of liberal exhortations to open-mindedness. She sees a difference between a scientist's reliance on his or her paradigm, and ordinary dependence on stereotypes:

> It is not possible for practitioners to engage in normal science without paradigms to guide their recognition of problems, and their problem-solving endeavours. Stereotype-governed thinking is different in this respect, for it is both possible and indeed desirable to think and to know in a manner *not* governed by stereotypes.[60]

But it's by no means clear that it *is* possible. I sense that Code has not appreciated the depth of human reliance on theories that cannot be shown to be "derived from the facts alone." In characterizing certain kinds of background belief and certain forms of "hasty generalization" *as stereotypes,* she is presupposing a solution to the very problem that must be solved: viz., telling which of the background theories that we routinely bring to bear on experience are *reliable* and which ones are not.

The liberal epistemological fantasy, still somewhat at work here, is that there will be formal marks that distinguish good theories from bad. The empiricist version of this fantasy is that the formal mark consists in a proper relation between theory and "fact." In this case, the good theories are supposed to be the ones that derive in the proper way from the data, whereas the bad ones—the biases, the prejudices, the stereotypes—are the ones that antedate the data. But once we realize that theory infects observation and that confirmation is a multidirectional relation, we must also give up on the idea that the good theories are going to look different from the bad theories. They can't be distinguished on the basis of their formal relation to the "facts," because (1) there are no "facts" in the requisite sense, and (2) there are too many good biases whose relation to the data will appear as tenuous as those of the bad ones.

But what's the alternative?

A naturalized approach to knowledge, because it requires us to give up *neutrality* as an epistemic ideal, also requires us to take a different attitude toward bias. We know that human knowledge requires biases; we also know that we have no possibility of getting *a priori* guarantees that our biases incline us in the right direction. What all this means is that the "biasedness" of biases drops out as a parameter of epistemic evaluation. There's only one thing to do, and it's the course always counseled by a naturalized approach: *We must treat the goodness or badness of particular biases as an empirical question.*

A naturalistic study of knowledge tells us biases are good when and to the extent that they facilitate the gathering of *knowledge*—that is, when they lead us to the truth. Biases are bad when they lead us *away* from the truth. One important strategy for telling the difference between good and bad biases is thus to evaluate the overall theories in which the biases figure. This one point has important implications for feminist theory in general and for feminist attitudes about universalist or essentialist theories of human nature in particular.

As we saw in section II, much of the feminist criticism raised against cognitive essentialism focused on the fact that rationalist and Kantian theories of the human essence were all devised by men, and based, allegedly, on exclusively male experience. Be that so—it would still follow from a naturalized approach to the theory of knowledge that it is an *empirical* question whether or not 'androcentrism' of that sort leads to bad theories. Partiality does not in general compromise theories; as we feminists ourselves have been insisting, all theorizing proceeds from *some* location or other. We must therefore learn to be cautious of claims to the effect that particular forms of partiality will inevitably and systematically influence the outcome of an investigation. Such claims must be treated as empirical hypotheses, subject to investigation and challenge, rather than as enshrined first principles.

So what about universalist or essentialist claims concerning human nature? I have argued that there really are no grounds for regarding such claims as antipathetic to feminist aspirations or even to feminist insights regarding the importance of embodiment or the value of human difference. Suggestions that essentialist theories reify aspects of specifically male experience, I argued, involve a serious misunderstanding of the rationalist strategy. But notice that even if such charges were true, the real problem with such theories should be their *falseness,* rather than their androcentrism. A theory that purports to say what human beings are like essentially must apply to *all human beings;* if it does not, it is wrong, whatever its origins.

In fact, I think there is excellent evidence for the existence of a substantial human nature and virtually no evidence for the alternative, the view that there is no human essence. But what's really important is to recognize that the latter view is as much a substantive empirical thesis as the Cartesian claim that we are essentially rational language-users. We need to ask ourselves *why* we ought to believe that human selves are, at the deepest level, "socially constructed"—the output of a confluence of contingent factors.[61]

Another thing that a naturalized approach to knowledge offers us is the possibility of *an empirical theory of biases*. As we've already seen, there are different kinds of biases—

some are natively present, some are acquired. An empirical study of biases can refine the taxonomy and possibly tell us something about the reliability and the corrigibility of biases of various sorts. It may turn out that we can on this basis get something like a principled sorting of biases into good ones and bad ones, although it will be more likely that we'll learn that even a "good" bias can lead us astray in certain circumstances.[62]

One likely upshot of an empirical investigation of bias is a better understanding of the processes by which human beings design research programs. What we decide to study and how we decide to study it are matters in which unconscious biases—tendencies to see certain patterns rather than others, to attend to certain factors rather than others, to act in accordance with certain interests rather than others—play a crucial role. We can't eliminate the biases—we shouldn't want to, for we'd have no research programs left if we did—but we can identify the particular empirical presuppositions that lie behind a particular program of research so that we can subject them, if necessary, to empirical critique.

One important issue is the *saliency* of certain properties. Every time a study is designed, a decision is made, tacitly or explicitly, to pay attention to some factors and to ignore others. These "decisions" represent tacit or explicit hypotheses about the likely connection between various aspects of the phenomena under study, hypotheses that can be subjected to empirical scrutiny.

Imagine a study purporting to investigate the development of human language by examining a sample of two hundred preschoolers. Must the sample, to be a valid basis for extrapolation, contain boys and girls? Must it be racially mixed? How one answers this question will depend on the empirical assumptions one makes about the likely connection between parameters like gender and race, on the one hand, and the language faculty on the other. To think that gender or race must be controlled for in such studies is to make a substantive empirical conjecture—in this case, it is to deny the rationalistic hypothesis that human beings' biological endowment includes a brain structured in a characteristic way, and to make instead the assumption that cognitive development is sensitive to the kinds of differences that we *socially* encode as gender and race.

Such an assumption, laid out this baldly, seems pretty dubious. Indeed, it's hard to see what such an assumption is doing other than reflecting sexist, racist, and classist beliefs to the effect that social groupings are determined by biological groupings. Realizing this is a necessary first step to countering the genuinely pernicious "essentialist" theories of Jensen, Herrnstein, and the human sociobiologists and to exposing the racism and sexism inherent in their programs of "research." Such "research" is precisely at odds with rationalist methodology, which only invokes human essences as a way of explaining human *commonalities*—and then, only when such commonalities cannot plausibly be explained by regularities in the environment.

Consider, for example, the claims that blacks are "innately" less intelligent than whites.[63] In the first place, we must point out, as we do, that race is not a biological kind, but rather a *social* kind. That is to say that while there may be a biological explanation for the presence of each of the characteristics that constitute racial criteria— skin color, hair texture, and the like—the *selection of those characteristics as criteria* of membership in some category is *conventionally* determined. Here is where the empiricist notion of "nominal essence" has some work to do: race, in contrast to some other categories, is socially constructed.

The second step is to point out that if such classifications as race fail to reflect deep regularities in human biology, and reflect instead only historically and culturally specific interests, then there is no reason, *apart from racist ones,* to investigate the relation between race and some presumably biological feature of human beings. Again, it takes an extreme form of empiricism to believe that brute correlations between one arbitrarily selected characteristic and another constitutes *science*—but even from such a perspective it must be an arbitrary choice to investigate one set of such correlations rather than another. Why intelligence and *race?* Why not intelligence and number of hair follicles?

It is this point that really gives the lie to Herrnstein's repugnant invocation of "scientific objectivity" in defense of his racist undertakings.[64] The fact that there is no empirical grounding for the selection of race as a theoretical parameter in the study of intelligence utterly defeats the disingenuous defense that such "science" as Herrnstein is engaged in is simply detached fact gathering—callin' 'em like he sees 'em. The decision to use race as an analytical category betrays a host of substantive assumptions that would be exceedingly hard to defend once made explicit. How could one defend the proposition that race and intelligence are connected without confronting the embarrassing fact that there's no biologically defensible definition of "race"? And how could one defend the proposition that human "mating strategies" will receive their explanation at the biological level, without having to explicitly argue against the wealth of competing explanations available at the social and personal/intentional levels?[65]

In sum, a naturalized approach to knowledge requires us, as feminists and progressives, to be critical of the saliency such categories as gender and race have *for us.* The fact that such parameters have been egregiously overlooked in cases where they are demonstrably relevant shouldn't make us think automatically that they are always theoretically significant. The recognition that selection of analytical categories is an empirical matter, governed by both background theory and consideration of the facts, is in itself part of the solution to the paradox of partiality.

The naturalized approach proceeds by showing the empirical inadequacy of the theory of mind and knowledge that makes perfect neutrality seem like a good thing. But at the same time that it removes the warrant for one epistemic ideal, it gives support for new norms, ones that will enable us to criticize some biases without presupposing the badness of bias in general. The naturalized approach can therefore vindicate all of the insights feminist theory has produced regarding the ideological functions of the concept of objectivity without undercutting the critical purpose of exposing androcentric and other objectionable forms of bias, when they produce oppressive falsehoods.

The End

I began this essay by asking whether we need a "feminist" epistemology, and I answered that we did, as long as we understood that need to be the need for an epistemology informed by feminist insight, and responsive to the moral imperatives entailed by feminist commitments. But I've argued that we do not necessarily need a conceptual transformation of epistemological theory in order to get a feminist epistemology in this sense. We need, in the first instance, a *political* transformation of the society in which theorizing about knowledge takes place. We've got to stop the oppression of women, eliminate racism, redistribute wealth, and *then* see what happens to our collective understanding of knowledge.

My bet? That some of the very same questions that are stimulating inquiry among privileged white men, right now in these sexist, racist, capitalist-imperialist times, are *still* going to be exercising the intellects and challenging the imaginations of women of color, gay men, physically handicapped high school students, etc.

I'm not saying that we should stop doing epistemology until after the revolution. That would of course be stupid, life being short. What I am saying is that those of us who think we know what feminism is, must guard constantly against the presumptuousness we condemn in others, of claiming as Feminist the particular bit of ground upon which we happen to be standing. We need to remember that part of what unites philosophers who choose to characterize their own work as "feminist" is the conviction that philosophy ought to matter—that it should make a positive contribution to the construction of a more just, humane, and nurturing world than the one we currently inhabit.

I have argued that contemporary analytic philosophy is capable of making such a contribution and that it is thus undeserving of the stigma "malestream" philosophy. But there's more at stake here than the abstract issue of mischaracterization. Attacks on the analytic tradition as "androcentric," "phallogocentric," or "maleidentified" are simultaneously attacks on the feminist credentials of those who work within the analytic tradition. And the stereotyping of contemporary analytic philosophy—the tendency to link it with views (like the Dragnet theory) to which it is in fact antipathetic—has turned feminists away from fruitful philosophical work, limiting our collective capacity to imagine genuinely novel and transformative philosophical strategies.

I acknowledge both the difficulty and the necessity of clarifying the implications of feminist theory for other kinds of endeavors. It's important, therefore, for feminist theorists to continue to raise critical challenges to particular theories and concepts. But surely this can be done without the caricature, without the throwaway refutations, in a way that is more respectful of philosophical differences.

Let's continue to argue with each other by all means. But let's stop arguing about which view is more feminist, and argue instead about which view is more likely to be true. Surely we can trust the dialectical process of feminists discussing these things with other feminists to yield whatever "feminist epistemology" we need.[66]

Notes

1. A possible exception may be Jean Grimshaw, who comes closer than any other thinker I've encountered to endorsing what I'm calling a "bare proceduralist" conception of feminist philosophy: "There is no particular view, for example, of autonomy, of morality,

of self, no one characterisation of women's activities which can be appealed to in any clear way as the woman's (or feminist) view. But I think nevertheless that feminism makes a difference to philosophy. The difference it makes is that women, in doing philosophy, have often raised new problems, problematised issues in new ways and moved to the centre questions which have been marginalised or seen as unimportant or at the periphery." From Grimshaw, *Philosophy and Feminist Thinking* (Minneapolis: University of Minnesota Press, 1986), p. 260.

2. Naomi Scheman made this point in a letter to members of the Committee on the Status of Women of the American Philosophical Association in 1988, when she and I were serving on the committee. Her letter was partly a response to a letter of mine raising questions about whether our charge as a committee should include the promotion of "feminist philosophy."

3. For discussions of epistemological frameworks available to feminists, see Sandra Harding, *The Science Question in Feminism,* (Ithaca, N.Y.: Cornell University Press, 1986), especially pp. 24–29; Mary Hawkesworth, "Feminist Epistemology: A Survey of the Field," *Women and Politics* 7 (1987): 112–124; and Hilary Rose, "Hand, Brain, and Heart: A Feminist Epistemology for the Natural Sciences," *Signs* 9, 11 (1983): 73–90.

4. See Mary E. Hawkesworth, "Knowers, Knowing, Known: Feminist Theory and Claims of Truth," *Signs* 14, 3 (1989): 533–557.

5. See, for example, Sandra Harding: "I have been arguing for open acknowledgement, even enthusiastic appreciation, of certain tensions that appear in the feminist critiques. I have been suggesting that these reflect valuable alternative social projects which are in opposition to the coerciveness and regressiveness of modern science. . . . [S]table and coherent theories are not always the ones to be most highly desired; there are important understandings to be gained in seeking the social origins of instabilities and incoherences in our thoughts and practices—understandings that we cannot arrive at if we repress recognition of instabilities and tensions in our thought" (*Science Question in Feminism,* pp. 243–244).

6. See Naomi Scheman, "Othello's Doubt/Desdemona's Death: The Engendering of Skepticism," in *Power, Gender, Values,* ed. Judith Genova (Edmonton, Alberta: Academic Printing and Publishing, 1987); and also Scheman's essay in this volume. See also Evelyn Fox Keller, "Cognitive Repression in Physics," *American Journal of Physics* 47 (1979): 718–721; and "Feminism and Science," in *Sex and Scientific Inquiry,* ed. S. Harding and J. O'Barr (Chicago: University of Chicago Press, 1987), pp. 233–246, reprinted in *The Philosophy of Science,* ed. by Richard Boyd, Philip Gaspar, and John Trout (Cambridge, Mass.: MIT Press, 1991).

7. For example, see Catharine A. MacKinnon, *Towards a Feminist Theory of the State* (Cambridge, Mass.: Harvard University Press, 1989).

8. This is not quite right—the ideology of 'objectivity' is perfectly capable of charging those *outside* the inner circle with partiality, and indeed, such charges are also crucial to the preservation of the status quo. More on this below.

9. Lorraine Code, "The Impact of Feminism on Epistemology," *APA Newsletter on Feminism and Philosophy* 88, 2 (March 1989): 25–29.

10. Lorraine Code, "Experience, Knowledge, and Responsibility," in *Feminist Perspectives in Philosophy,* ed. by Morwenna Griffiths and Margaret Whitford (Bloomington: Indiana University Press, 1988), pp. 189ff.

11. Code, "Impact of Feminism on Epistemology," p. 25.

12. It might be objected that there is a third option—that we could criticize those biases that are biases against our interests and valorize those that promote our interests. But if we are in fact left with only this option, then we are giving up on the possibility of any medium of social change other than power politics. This is bad for two reasons: (1) As moral and political theory, egoism should be repugnant to any person ostensibly concerned with justice and human well-being; and (2) as tactics, given current distributions of power, it's really stupid.

13. 1 have defended a kind of non-realist conception of truth, but one which maintains this gap. See my "Can Verificationists Make Mistakes?" *American Philosophical Quarterly* 24, 3 (July 1987): 225–236. For a defense of a more robustly realist conception of truth, see Michael Devitt, *Realism and Truth* (Princeton, N.J.: Princeton University Press, 1984). (A new edition is in press.)

14. Code, "Impact of Feminism on Epistemology," p. 25.

15. Significantly, these theories are not all empiricist, and the theories that are most "postpositivist" are the least empiricist of all. I'll have much more to say about this in what follows.

16. See, e.g., Helene Cixous, "The Laugh of the Medusa," tr. by Keith Cohen and Paula Cohen, *Signs* 1, 4 (1976): 875–893; Luce Irigaray, "Is the Subject of Science Sexed?" tr. by Carol Mastrangelo Bove, *Hypatia* 2, 3 (Fall 1987): 65–87; and Andrea Nye, "The Inequalities of Semantic Structure: Linguistics and Feminist Philosophy," *Metaphilosophy* 18, 3–4 (July/October 1987): 222–240. I must say that for the sweepingness of Nye's claims regarding "linguistics" and "semantic theory," her survey of work in these fields is, to say the least, narrow and out-of-date.

17. See, e.g., Ruth Ginzberg, "Feminism, Rationality, and Logic" and "Teaching Feminist Logic," *APA Newsletter on Feminism and Philosophy* 88, 2 (March 1989): 34–42 and 58–65.

18. Note that the term "Enlightenment" itself does not have any single, precise meaning, referring in some contexts to only the philosophers (and *philosophes*) of eighteenth-century France, in other contexts to any philosopher lying on the trajectory of natural-rights theory in politics, from Hobbes and Locke through Rousseau, and in still other contexts to all the canonical philosophical works of the seventeenth and eighteen centuries, up to and including Kant. I shall try to use the term "early modern philosophy" to denote seventeenth-century rationalism and empiricism, but I may slip up.

19. In Alison Jaggar, *Feminist Politics and Human Nature* (Totowa, N.J.: Rowman and Allenheld, 1983). p. 355.

20. In Harding, *Science Question in Feminism,* p. 24.

21. Jane Flax, "Postmodernism and Gender Relations in Feminist Theory," *Signs* 12, 4 (Summer 1987): 624.

22. Ibid., p. 627.

23. Never mind Kant, who, apart from this note, I'm going to pretty much ignore. Virtually nothing that Flax cites as constitutive of the Enlightenment legacy can be easily found in Kant. He was not a dualist, at least not a Cartesian dualist; his opinions regarding the possible existence of a mind-independent reality were complicated (to say the least), but he clearly thought that it would be impossible for human beings to gain knowledge of such a world if it *did* exist; and the reading of the Categorical Imperative—how does it go? "Treat others as ends-in-the ruse Ives, never merely as means"?—that has Kant coming out as ignorant or neglectful of human difference seems to me to be positively Orwellian.

24. Harding is an exception, since she acknowledges Quine, though nothing after Quine. Code does allude to there being some changes in mainstream epistemology since the heyday of positivism, but says that the changes are not of the right nature to license the questions she thinks are central to feminist epistemology. Alison Jaggar, too, acknowledges that positivism has lost favor but says nothing about the sahape of the theories that have succeeded it. See Jaggar, *Feminist Politics.*

I think it's particularly regrettable that feminist critics of mainstream epistemology have failed to see connections between their concerns and those of Alvin Goldman. Goldman has been one of the chief advocates of a version of epistemology called "reliabilism," which makes the actual circumstances of belief production an essential part of their justification. See his *Epistemology and Cognition* (Cambridge, Mass.: Harvard University Press, 1986). It is also terribly unfair to Goldman to be lumped together with all other epistemologists and criticized for neglecting the social dimensions of knowing. Goldman, at least, takes it as a truism that knowledge has a social component and that the study of knowledge requires consideration of the social situation of the knower: "Most knowledge is a cultural product, channeled through language and social communication. So how could epistemology *fail* to be intertwined with studies of culture and social systems?" (p. 1).

Jaggar, too, acknowledges that positivism has lost favor, but says nothing about the shape of the theories that have succeeded it. See Jaggar, *Feminist Politics.*

25. Cognitive essentialism generally gets associated with another thesis singled out for criticism—namely, dualism, the view that the mind is separate from the body and that the self is to be identified with the mind. Although dualism is not exclusively a rationalist view (Locke is standardly classified as a dualist), it is most closely associated with Descartes, and it is Descartes's *a priori* argument for dualism in the *Meditations* that seems to draw the most fire. Cartesian dualism is seen as providing a metaphysical rationale for dismissing the relevance of material contingencies to the assessment of knowledge claims, because it separates the knowing subject from the physical body, and because it seems to assert the sufficiency of disembodied reason for the attainment of knowledge.

In fact, dualism is a red herring. It's an uncommon view in the history of philosophy. Many people classically characterized as dualists, like Plato, were surely not Cartesian dualists. And on top of that, the dualism does not work. Being a dualist is neither necessary nor sufficient for believing that the human essence is composed of cognitive properties.

26. Flax, "Postmodernism," p. 626.

27. "Individualism" as Jaggar uses it is rather a term of art. It has a variety of meanings within philosophical discourse, but I don't know of any standard use within epistemology that matches Jaggar's. In the philosophy of mind, the term denotes the view that psychological states can be individuated for purposes of scientific psychology, without reference to objects or states outside the individual. This use of the term has *nothing* to do with debates in political theory about such issues as individual rights or individual autonomy. A liberal view of the moral/political individual can work just as well (or as poorly) on an anti-individualist psychology (such as Hilary Putnam's or Tyler Burge's) as on an individualist view like Jerry Fodor's.

28. See also Naomi Scheman's essay in this volume.

29. Jaggar, "Postmodernism," p. 355.

30. Ibid.

31. See, for example, the excerpts from *Notes Directed against a Certain Program,* in Margaret Wilson, ed., *The Essential Descartes* (New York: Mentor Press, 1969).

32. Ibid., p. 112.

33. Ibid. One passage from one work should, of course, not be enough to convince anyone, and Descartes is clearly fictionalizing his own history to some extent (like who doesn't?). I do not have the space here to provide a full defense of my interpretation, but I invite you to read the *Discourse* on your own.

34. A little qualification is necessary here: The empiricist's requirement that all concepts be reducible to sensory simples does count as a substantive restriction on the possible contents of thought, but it's one which is vitiated by the reductionist semantic theory favored by empiricists, which denies the meaningfulness of any term which cannot be defined in terms of sensory primitives. See the discussion of this point in Jerry Fodor, *Modularity of Mind: All Essay on Faculty Psychology* (Cambridge, Mass.: MIT Press, 1983).

Also, the empiricists did allow a kind of "bias" in the form of innate standards of similarity, which would permit the mind to see certain ideas as inherently resembling certain others. This innate similarity metric was needed to facilitate the operation of *association,* which was the mechanism for generating more complex and more abstract ideas out of the sensory simples. But the effects of a bias such as this were vitiated by the fact that associations could also be forged by the contiguity of ideas in experience, with the result once more that no effective, substantive limits were placed on the ways in which human beings could analyze the data presented them by sensory experience.

35. David Hume, *An Enquiry Concerning Human Understanding* (Indianapolis: Hackett, 1977), p. 30. For a different assessment of Hume's potential contributions to a feminist epistemology, see Annette Baier's essay in this volume.

36. I have been much chastised by serious scholars of early-twentieth-century analytic philosophy (specifically Warren Goldfarb, Neil Tennant, and Philip Kitcher) for here reinforcing the myth that logical positivism was a uniform "school of thought." I guess I should thank them. The view that I am labeling "positivism" is the usual received view of the movement, but it may have belonged to only some of the more flatfooted and marginal members of the group (like A. J. Ayer) and certainly was not the view of the most important philosopher in the movement, Rudolf Carnap.

Still, the version of positivism I am outlining is the version that Quine attributed to his predecessors, and the version that he was reacting against. Moreover, even if Carnap was not an externalist in the sense of seeking a metaphysical vindication of scientific practice (as Michael Friedman argues in "The Re-evaluation of Logical Positivism," *Journal of Philosophy* 88, 10 [October 1991]: 505–519), he still was committed to a sharp separation between contentful and merely analytic statements, which is enough to generate the kinds of difficulties that I'm claiming beset positivism generally. My thanks to Marcia Homiak for calling my attention to the Friedman article.

37. Here are some of the most important works: W.V.O. Quine, "Two Dogmas of Empiricism," reprinted in Quine, *From a Logical Point of View* (Cambridge, Mass.: Harvard University Press, 1953); Carl G. Hempel, "Problems and Changes in the Empiricist Criterion of Meaning," *Revue Internationale de Philosophie* 11 (1950): 41–63, and "Empiricist Criteria of Cognitive Significance: Problems and Changes," in Hempel, *Aspects of Scientific Explanation and Other Essays in the Philosophy of Science* (New York: Free Press, 1965): Nelson Goodman, *Fact, Fiction, and Forecast* (Cambridge, Mass.: Harvard University Press, 1955); and Hilary Putnam, "What Theories Are Not," reprinted in Putnam, *Mathematics, Matter, and Method: Philosophical Papers,* Vol. I (Cambridge: Cambridge University Press, 1975).

38. Quine and J. S. Ullian catalog these principles—which they refer to as the "virtues" of hypotheses—in an epistemological primer called *The Web of Belief* (New York:

Random House, 1970). Quine and Ullian employ a strikingly Humean strategy in trying to explain the epistemological value of the virtues.

39. W.V.O. Quine, "Epistemology Naturalized," in Quine, *Ontological Relativity and Other Essays* (New York: Columbia University Press, 1969), pp. 69–90.

40. See Noam Chomsky, "Review of B. F. Skinner's *Verbal Behavior*," *Language* 35, 1 (1959): 53–68.

41. See Noam Chomsky, "Quine's Empirical Assumptions," in *Words and Objections: Essays on the Work of W. V. Quine,* ed. by D. Davidson and J. Hintikka (Dordrecht: D. Reidel, 1969). See also Quine's response to Chomsky in the same volume.

I discuss the inconsistency between Quine's commitment to naturalism and his *a prioristic* rejection of mentalism and nativism in linguistics in "Naturalized Epistemology and the Study of Language," in *Naturalistic Epistemology: A Symposium of Two Decades,* ed. by Abner Shimony and Debra Nails (Dordrecht: D. Reidel, 1987), pp. 235–257.

42. For an extremely helpful account of the Chomskian approach to the study of language, see David Lightfoot's *The Language Lottery: Toward a Biology of Grammars* (Cambridge, Mass.: MIT Press, 1984).

43. I take this to be an established fact. There's a mountainous body of scholarship on this issue, much of it the result of feminist concerns about specific ways in which women have been excluded from and damaged by institutionalized science. The whole area of biological determinist theorists provides an excellent case study of the ways in which science both supports and is distorted by social stratification. *Genes and Gender II*, ed. by Ruth Hubbard and Marian Lowe (New York: Gordion Press, 1979), is a collection of now classic articles critically examining alleged biological and ethological evidence for the genetic basis of gender differences. For a more current analysis of similar research in neurophysiology and endocrinology, see Helen Longino, *Science as Social Knowledge* (Princeton, N.J.: Princeton University Press, 1990), ch. 6. Two excellent general discussions of the interactions among politics, economics, ideology, and science as exemplified by the growth of biological determinist theories are Stephen Jay Gould, *The Mismeasure of Man* (New York: W. W. Norton, 1981); and R. C. Lewontin, Steven Rose, and Leon J. Kamin, *Not in Our Genes* (New York: Pantheon Books, 1984).

44. Evelyn Fox Keller, "Feminism and Science," in Boyd, Gaspar, and Trout, eds., *Philosophy of Science,* p. 281. In this passage, Keller is also remarking on the tendency of (what she views as) the liberal critiques to focus on the "softer" biological and social sciences, and to leave alone the "harder" sciences of math and physics.

45. Carl R. Hempel, *Philosophy of Natural Science* (Englewood Cliffs, N.J.: Prentice-Hall, 1966). See especially pp. 10–18.

46. There's a good case to be made that scientists actually have *disincentives* to ponder such questions. The structure of incentives in academia necessitates rapid generation and publication of research, and research requires securing long-term funding, usually from a government agency or a private corporate foundation. Scientific research is thus heavily compromised at the outset, whatever the ideals and values of the individual scientist. For a detailed discussion of the ways in which academic and economic pressures systematically erode "objectivity" in science, see William Broad and Nicholas Wade, *Betrayers of the Truth: Fraud and Deceit in the Halls of Science* (New York: Simon and Schuster, 1982).

47. This follows from a general point emphasized by Georges Rey in personal conversation: It's important in general to distinguish people's theories of human institutions from the actual character of those institutions.

48. This despite the fact that the Dragnet theory supports a strong context of discovery/context of justification distinction. On empiricist theories, the justification of an individual's belief is ultimately a relation between the belief and the sensory experience of that individual. Location matters, then, because the same belief could be justified for one individual and unjustified for another, precisely because of the differences in their experiences.

49. This is not to say that there are no puzzling issues about moral ideals that are in some sense humanly unattainable. One such issue arises with respect to the ideals of altruism and supererogation, ideals which it would be, arguably, *unhealthy* for human beings to fully realize. See Larry Blum, Marcia Homiak, Judy Housman, and Naomi Scheman, "Altruism and Women's Oppression," in *Women and Philosophy,* ed. by Carol C. Gould and Marx W. Wartofsky (New York: G. P. Putnam, 1980), pp 222–247. On the question of whether it would be good for human beings to fully realize any moral ideal, see Susan Wolf, "Moral Saints," *The Journal of Philosophy* 79, 8 (August 1982): 419–439.

50. Jerry Fodor, *Modularity of Mind* (Cambridge, Mass.: MIT Press, 1983); Noam Chomsky, *Reflections on Language* (New York: Random House, 1975); David Mart, *Vision: A Computational Investigation Into the Human Representation and Processing of Visual Information* (San Francisco: W. H. Freeman, 1982); Susan Carey, *Conceptual Change in Childhood* (Cambridge, Mass.: MIT Press, 1985); Elizabeth Spelke, "Perceptual Knowledge of Objects in Infancy," in J. Mehler, E.C.T. Walker, and M. Garrett, eds., *Perspectives on Mental Representations* (Hillsdale, N.Y.: Erlbaum, 1982); Barbara Landau and Lila Gleitman, *Language and Experience: Evidence from the Blind Child* (Cambridge, Mass.: Harvard University Press, 1985); Steven Pinker, *Learnability and Cognition: The Acquisition of Argument Structure* (Cambridge, Mass.: MIT Press, 1989).

51. Thomas S. Kuhn, "The Function of Dogma in Scientific Research," (1963), reprinted in Janet A. Kourany, *Scientific Knowledge* (Belmont, Calif.: Wadsworth, 1987), pp. 253–265. Quotation is from p. 254.

52. This phenomenon affects even as sensitive and sophisticated a critic of science as Stephen Jay Gould. Responding to creationist charges that evolution is "just a theory," Gould insists: "Well, evolution *is* a theory. It is also a fact. And facts and theories are different things, not rungs in a hierarchy of increasing certainty. Facts are the world's data. Theories are structures of ideas that explain and interpret facts. Facts do not go away while scientists debate rival theories for explaining them. . . . [H]uman beings evolved from apelike ancestors whether they did so by Darwin's proposed mechanism or by some other, yet to be discovered." Stephen Jay Gould, "Evolution as Fact and Theory," *Hen's Teeth and Horse's Toes* (New York: W. W. Norton, 1980), pp. 253–262. Quotation from p. 254.

Gould's point, I believe, is that the world is as it is independently of our ability to understand it—a position I share. But if facts are part of the mind-independent world, they cannot also be "the world's data." "*Data*" is the name we give to that *part* of our theory about which we can achieve a high degree of interpersonal and intertheoretic agreement; however, there can be as much contention about "the data" as about "the theory." Gould concedes as much in the next paragraph when he writes: "Moreover, 'fact' does not mean 'absolute certainty.' . . . In science, 'fact' can only mean 'confirmed to such a degree that it would be perverse to withhold provisional assent.'" If *that's* what "facts" are, then they can and do sometimes "go away while scientists debate rival theories for explaining them." Ibid., p. 255.

53. Notice that we don't have to assume here that anyone is knowingly telling lies. Clearly, in the real world, members of the ruling elite *do* consciously lie, and they do it a

lot. But here I'm trying to point out that some of the mechanisms that can perpetuate oppressive structures are epistemically legitimate.

54. See Edward Herman and Noam Chomsky, *Manufacturing Consent* (New York: Pantheon, 1988); Noam Chomsky, *Necessary Illusions: Thought Control in Democratic Society* (Boston: South End Press, 1989), esp. ch. 3 ("The Bounds of the Expressible"); and Martin A. Lee and Norman Solomon, *Unreliable Sources: A Guide to Detecting Bias in News Media* (New York: Carol Publishing Group, 1990).

55. This explains some of what's going on in the so-called "debate" about so-called "political correctness." Most of what's going on involves pure dishonesty and malice, but to the extent that there are some intelligent and relatively fair-minded people who find themselves worrying about such issues as the "politicization" of the classroom, or about "ideological biases" among college professors, these people are reacting to the *unfamiliarity* of progressive perspectives. Those foundational beliefs that are very common within the academy—belief in a (Christian) god, in the benignity of American institutions, in the viability of capitalism—generally go without saying and are thus invisible. *Our* worldviews are unfamiliar, and so must be articulated and acknowledged. Precisely because we are willing and able to do that, while our National Academy of Scholars colleagues are not, we become open to the charge of being "ideological."

It's the very fact that there are so *few* leftist, African-American, Hispanic, openly gay, feminist, female persons in positions of academic authority that accounts for all this slavish nonsense about our "taking over."

56. Lorraine Code, "Credibility: A Double Standard," in *Feminist Perspectives*, ed. Code, Mullett, and Overall, pp. 65–66.

57. Ibid.

58. Ibid., p. 71.

59. Ibid., p. 73.

60. Ibid., p. 72.

61. Ironically, the preference among many feminist theorists for "thin" theories of the self, like postmodernist constructivist theories, is itself a vestige of an incompletely exorcised empiricism in contemporary feminist thought. It is a specifically empiricist position that the groupings of objects into kinds effected by human cognition are not keyed to "real essences," but are rather reflections of superficial regularities in experience that persist only because of their pragmatic utility.

62. We know, for example, that some of the built-in rules that make it possible for the human visual system to pick out objects from their backgrounds—so-called structure from motion rules—also make us subject to certain specific kinds of visual illusions. See A. L. Yuille and S. Ullman, "Computational Theories of Low-Level Vision," in *Visual Cognition and Action*, ed. by Daniel N. Osherson, Stephen M. Kosslyn, and John M. Hollerbach, vol. 2 of *An Invitation to Cognitive Science*, ed. by Daniel N. Osherson (Cambridge, Mass.: MIT Press, 1990), pp. 5–39.

63. I am here reiterating the arguments Chomsky mounted against Herrnstein's apologia for Jensen's theory of race and intelligence. See Noam Chomsky, "Psychology and Ideology," reprinted in Chomsky, *For Reasons of State* (New York: Random House, 1973), pp. 318–369; excerpted and reprinted as "The Fallacy of Richard Herrnstein's IQ," in *The IQ Controversy*, ed. by Ned Block and Gerald Dworkin (New York: Random House, 1976), pp. 285–298.

64. See Herrnstein's reply to Chomsky, "Whatever Happened to Vaudeville?" in Block and Dworkin, eds., *IQ Controversy*, esp. pp. 307–309.

65. These considerations also help defeat the charge, hurled against critics of biological determinist theories, that we progressives are the ones guilty of "politicizing" the debate about nature and nurture. The Herrnsteins and E. O. Wilsons of this world like to finesse the meticulously arrayed empirical criticisms of their work by accusing their critics of the most pathetic kind of wishful thinking—"Sorry if you don't *like* what my utterly objective and bias-free research has proven beyond a shadow of a doubt. You must try to be big boys and girls and learn to cope with the unpleasant truth." For examples, see Herrnstein, "Whatever Happened to Vaudeville?" in Block and Dworkin, eds., *IQ Controversy*; and E. O. Wilson, "Academic Vigilantism and the Political Significance of Sociobiology," reprinted in *The Sociobiology Debate,* ed. by Arthur L. Caplan (New York: Harper and Row, 1978), pp. 291–303.

66. I must here acknowledge a terrible error in the first edition of this book. In note 24 I had earlier claimed, quite falsely, that Lorraine Code never cited or discussed any analytic epistemologist other than Alvin Goldman in "either of her two books." In fact, at the time of my writing, the books in question, *Epistemic Responsibility* and *What Can She Know? Feminist Theory and the Construction of Knowledge,* contained substantive discussion of, and numerous references to, many analytic epistemologists. I apologize most sincerely to Professor Code and hope that she will accept my assurances that this false allegation was the result of egregiously sloppy scholarship rather than malice. In any case, I deeply regret the mistake.

Much of the preliminary work for this essay was done during a fellowship year at the National Humanities Center, and I wish to thank both the center and the Andrew J. Mellon Foundation for their support. The essay is based on a presentation I gave at the Scripps College Humanities Institute Conference, "Thinking Women: Feminist Scholarship in the Humanities," in March 1990. I want to thank the institute, especially Norton Batkin, for the invitation to think about these issues. I also want to thank my co-participants at the conference, especially Naomi Scheman, to whom I owe a special debt. I have enjoyed an enormous amount of stimulating and challenging conversation and correspondence with Naomi about all the issues in this essay. It's a tribute to her sense of intellectual fairness and her commitment to feminist praxis that she and I have managed to conduct such an extended dialogue about these issues, given the intensity of our disagreements. I also want to make it clear that while I had the benefit of reading Naomi's essay before completing my own, I did not finish mine in time for her to react to any of the points I raise here.

Many other people have helped me with this essay. I want to thank Judith Ferster, Suzanne Graver, Charlotte Gross, Sally Haslanger, Barbara Metcalf, and Andy Reath for hours of valuable conversation. Marcia Homiak, Alice Kaplan, and Georges Rey supplied extremely useful comments on earlier drafts; David Auerbach did all that *and* extricated me from an eleventh-hour computer crisis, and I thank them heartily. Very special thanks to my co-editor, Charlotte Witt, for her excellent philosophical and editorial advice and for her abundant patience and good sense. I cannot fully express my thanks to Joe Levine for all he's done, intellectually and personally, to help me complete this project. Thanks as well to my children, Paul and Rachel, for their patience during all the times I was out consorting with my muse.

8

THE POLITICS OF CREDIBILITY

KAREN JONES

1. Introduction

Two central themes in feminist epistemology are the importance of epistemic dependency and the role of our epistemic concepts, such as knowledge, justification, objectivity, and rationality, in generating and reinforcing authority by supporting norms of credibility that function to authorize some agents as knowers, while deauthorizing others.[1] These two themes unite most explicitly in the epistemology of testimony, which is the subject of this chapter. My task, however, is not to address the distinctively theoretical questions surrounding testimony, such as whether testimony is a source of knowledge on a par with memory and perception or whether it can be reduced to other, more fundamental, modes of epistemic access to the world.[2] Instead, my project can be understood as an exercise in practical epistemology, conceived of as analogous with practical ethics: I want to investigate how to approach a subclass of testimonial utterances, namely, astonishing reports. Two questions immediately arise: why *practical epistemology*? and why astonishing reports in particular?

Broadly construed, practical ethics aims to investigate concrete, contested, moral issues such as abortion or medical confidentiality. Analogously, practical epistemology aims to investigate concrete, contested, epistemological questions. Although there is a large body of work, both feminist and nonfeminist, that can be described as practical epistemology,[3] practical ethics is a recognized philosophical area whereas practical epistemology is not. The reason for this, I suspect, is more sociological than philosophical: Practical ethics flourishes in the context of addressing questions that arise in specific professions, such as medicine, business, law, and research.[4] However, since we are all equally inquirers of one sort or another, there is no corresponding

group of professionals to demand that philosophers turn their hand to practical epistemology.

The reasons that motivate practical ethics also motivate practical epistemology.
Each area of inquiry promises to help us understand a matter of practical importance,
and each promises to enrich our understanding of its corresponding theoretical domain. Just as practical ethics should not be thought of merely as the application to
particular problems of moral rules or relatively determinate principles that are defended either directly by reflectively endorsed intuition or indirectly by appeal to ethical theories, neither should practical epistemology.[5] This "engineering model" of
practical ethics overlooks the interpretive work that is required before rules or principles can be brought to bear on a concrete problem.[6] Furthermore, it assumes that a
complete picture of right judgment in these areas can be achieved by a proper appreciation of rules and principles. Practice, both moral and epistemic, turns out to be more
complicated that this picture allows.[7] Indeed, in this chapter I will argue that being a
wise recipient of testimony to the astonishing requires capacities that cannot be fully
captured in rules, though some rules can be offered to guide the conscientious inquirer.

Inquirers seek methods that will enable them to form true beliefs and avoid
forming false beliefs. Accordingly, the rules are defended by showing that they enable
an inquirer to purchase an increase in the ratio of true to false beliefs without paying
an unacceptable cost in terms of the ability to form beliefs at all. The notion of an
"unacceptable cost" is necessarily vague, but rules that require too much cognitive effort relative to available resources, or that too frequently generate the answer "withhold judgment" in areas where judgment is needed, carry unacceptable costs.[8]

Although the rules I will defend can offer some guidance, it turns out that some
of the capacities needed to apply them correctly will be affective and perhaps even
moral capacities, such as the capacity for empathy, which appears important for
achieving the appropriate self-trust and trust in others so essential for wise judgment
concerning the acceptance of astonishing reports. Thus paying serious attention to
concrete epistemic problems has a theoretical payoff—it reveals the importance of an
investigation into the connection between affective and cognitive capacities and between epistemic virtues and moral virtues.

Granted that practical and theoretical considerations motivate the project of
practical epistemology, why focus on astonishing reports in particular? To understand
their importance for feminist epistemology, we first need to get clearer about the role
of trust and the role of background beliefs in identifying and accepting or rejecting
astonishing reports.

It is a commonplace that the credibility we ascribe to reports should be a function of the trustworthiness of the testifier, or testifiers, and the plausibility of what
they say in the light of what else we believe.[9] Let's follow Locke's terminology and call
these the two "foundations" or "grounds" of credibility.[10] When it comes to astonishing reports, there is a reason not to accept what is said, namely, that it conflicts with,
or seems surprising in the light of, our understanding of how the world works. But
there is also something to be said in favor of accepting it, namely, that by testifying to

it someone has vouched for its truth. When a trustworthy witness reports that an improbable event took place, the two "grounds of credibility" pull in opposite directions.

How are we to think of testimony as a ground of credibility? What is it to testify that *p*? To testify that *p* contrasts with arguing that *p* insofar as it is the testifier *herself* who vouches for the truth of *p*. In arguing that *p*, one presents reasons for public consideration, reasons that can be evaluated and accepted or rejected.[11] Testimony replaces argument when the audience can't assess the cogency of the reasons given or when it can't have the right sort of access to those reasons (e.g., when the witness alone saw the event). Testimony is accepted (if it is) on account of the audience's accepting that the testifier is in a position to vouch for the truth of *p*. Hence the connection between testimony and trust: we must trust the testifier because she *herself* is warranting the truth of *p* (unlike the arguer, who can let the arguments provide warrant for the truth of *p*). When we accept testimony, we stake our bets on the trustworthiness of the testifier. However, the trustworthiness we bet on need not be global; what we care about is local, namely, trustworthiness with respect to this exchange of information regarding *p*. Thus we might trust an informant to give us directions, but not to tell us about something that requires specialist knowledge. The domain-specific nature of the trust that we have in informants parallels the domain-specific nature of the other sorts of trust that we have in persons: trust is to be analyzed *not* as the two-place relation it might appear to be ("A trusts B"), but rather as a three-place relation: A trusts B to do Z.[12]

The trustworthiness of informants has two components: competence with respect to the truth of *p* and veracity with respect to this exchange. Competence with respect to the truth of *p* can be understood in terms of counterfactual tendencies to reach correct judgment: if *p* were the case, then the informant would tend to believe that *p*; if *p* were not the case, then the informant would tend not believe that *p*.[13] Trustworthy informants need not be right on every occasion (and, indeed, can be wrong on the occasion in question and yet still be trustworthy. It would be too much to demand infallibility from a trustworthy scientist, for example.) Certain outlier circumstances might make a trustworthy informant supply false information—perhaps she is an entirely nonculpable victim of conspiracy—but she will use methods and mechanisms for acquiring belief that will tend to make her get it right.

The second component in the trustworthiness of informants is veracity. Although we are concerned with veracity in respect to this particular exchange, in the typical case, we are willing to bet on the testifier's local trustworthiness on account of having views about her trustworthiness beyond this particular exchange, including beliefs about her general veracity with regard to the kind of question at issue, or at any rate her veracity, in this domain, toward people like us. Indeed, the least we can suppose, if it is to be reasonable for us to find the testifier locally trustworthy, is that she would be honest in relevant alternative exchanges indistinguishable from this one, else we could not be sure that she was trustworthy in this one. Such judgments about local trustworthiness are often routine and based on *no particular evidence* about the person: we expect persons in general to be reliable and honest in giving simple directions; social scientists, on the other hand, expect less than candid answers to questions about sexual practices and carefully design their surveys to control for this.

The second ground of credibility is plausibility in the light of what else we take ourselves to know. An astonishing report is, other things being equal, less credible than a nonastonishing one. How astonishing a report is admits of degrees, and we can construct an ordered series ranked according to how improbable it is that the event testified to occurred or occurred in the way it was alleged to have occurred. At one extreme are reports of miracles—events, or ways events are produced, that contradict the laws of nature as we take them to be on the basis of past experience and our best available theories.[14] (These have been the focus of most mainstream philosophical discussion of astonishing reports.) At the other end are reports of events, or ways events are produced, that are merely surprising. We can see what causal mechanisms would be needed to bring about such an event, in the way it is alleged to have been brought about, but it seems surprising to us that the confluence of causal mechanisms required to bring it about should have occurred. In between, there are reports of events or ways events are produced that are marvelous. We can grasp what causal mechanisms would be required to bring about such an event in the way it is alleged to have been brought about, but we think either that there are no such mechanisms in operation in the relevant circumstance, or that it is *extremely* unlikely that the mechanisms required should have converged in the way needed to bring about the event. Locating a particular report with respect to this scale must be done in the light of our theoretical assumptions about the way it works and the casual mechanisms that are in operation in it. Thus, for example, Augustine found it "inconceivable" that there could be antipodes, or "men on the opposite sides of the earth, where the sun rises when it sets to us, men who walk with their feet opposite ours."[15] He reasoned that even if, as some hypothesized, the world were round, there just wasn't enough time after the flood for humans to have traveled such a great distance.

That we rank reports on this scale in the light of our background beliefs has important political consequences, consequences that have been overlooked in mainstream work on testimony.[16] Given that experience affects our beliefs, and that in societies characterized by relations of dominance and subordination different social groups can be expected to have different experiences, it is not surprising that some reports that seem astonishing to members of some groups will seem highly likely to members of other groups. Recall, for example, how African Americans and whites disagreed about O.J. Simpson's guilt because they disagreed about how likely it was that he was the victim of a police frame-up.

Just as assessments of the plausibility of the content of reports can differ on account of different social locations, so too can assessments of the trustworthiness of witnesses. Because accepting testimony requires that we assess the testifier as being trustworthy (with respect to this exchange, but where this is typically based on broader trustworthiness judgments), prejudice influences whether we will accept testimony even more readily than it influences whether we will accept argument. Testimony is thus even more vulnerable to prejudice than argument is. Should we routinely underestimate the trustworthiness of a class of reporters, we risk cutting ourselves off from the possibility of learning from them. Testifiers who belong to "suspect" social groups and who are bearers of strange tales can thus suffer a double disadvantage. They risk being doubly deauthorized as knowers on account of who they are and what they claim to know. If we operate with norms of credibility that do not take into account the influence of background beliefs and of prejudice on our credibility judgments, there is a very real risk of committing epistemic injustice.[17]

This epistemic injustice—unfair in itself—also functions to maintain substantive social injustice. For example, how credible you think a particular report of incestuous sexual abuse is depends on your understanding of male sexuality and of the role and structure of the patriarchal family and, in addition, on your beliefs about the ability of women and girls to understand their experiences (think of seduction-fantasy theory) and report them truthfully. Likewise for reports of, and statistics regarding the prevalence of, sexual harassment, race-based police harassment, torture, human rights abuse, and so on. For this reason, and independently of any theoretical benefits that accrue from investigating astonishing reports, such reports merit philosophical reflection.

2. A Case Study

Since my task is practical epistemology, let's begin with a case study. Take Fauziya Kassindja's now well-known story.[18] Fauziya Kassindja fled her native Togo in October 1994, escaping a forced polygamous marriage and female genital mutilation. Her father was opposed to FGM and, while alive, protected her and her sisters from it. But when he died, Kassindja's aunt became her guardian and forced her mother to leave the family home. When Kassindja's mother learned of the aunt's plans for Kassindja, she sent Kassindja's sister to help her, giving her $3,000 to leave the country. Kassindja's sister drove her to the airport in Ghana, where Kassindja boarded the first flight leaving that evening. The flight took her to Germany. Knowing no one in Germany and not speaking German, Kassindja wandered around the airport until she struck up a conversation with a German stranger named Rudina Gergs. Gergs believed Kassindja's story and offered her a place to stay. Kassindja remained with Gergs until another chance encounter took place, this time with a Nigerian man, Charlie, whom she met on a train. Charlie sold her his sister's passport, which she then used to travel to the United States. Rather than enter illegally, Kassindja gave herself up to the INS, claiming asylum as a refugee from FGM. Her case was heard by Judge Donald Ferlise of the Immigration and Naturalization Service, who, on August 25, 1995, denied Kassindja's application for asylum. Though told the same story Gergs believed, Ferlise found it incredible: "I have taken into account the lack of rationality, the lack of consistency and the lack of inherent persuasiveness in her testimony and have determined that this alien is not credible."[19]

What went wrong and how could it have been avoided, supposing—as is almost certainly not the case—that Ferlise had wished to be epistemically responsible?

3. Three Rules Governing Astonishing Reports

In his judgment, Ferlise acknowledges the two Lockean grounds of credibility—he recognizes the importance of reaching a final verdict based on a trustworthiness measure ("consistency," "rationality") and a plausibility measure ("inherent persuasiveness"). Reaching a final verdict is a matter of determining the relative strength of the two grounds and the direction—for or against belief—in which they pull.

This leads naturally to rule 1, the independence rule: Conduct *separate* assessments of the trustworthiness of the witness and the plausibility or probability of what they say; then, and only then, determine the credibility of the statement or story given that it is testified to by that witness.[20]

If we approach a testifier with a low initial assessment of her trustworthiness—perhaps because she is a member of a suspect class, or because she has a motive for lying—and we do not follow the independence rule, we can be led to assign a lower plausibility rating to the content of her testimony than we otherwise would. In this way, the low trustworthiness rating gets to count twice over: first in its own right and second insofar as it depresses the value of the prior probability assigned to the content of what is said, where the prior probability is the probability assigned to the truth of what a witness says independently of her so testifying.

It is easy to underestimate the importance of the error that we can get ourselves into if we fail to separate these two evaluations. Most discussions of testimony, including Bayesian accounts, talk about a speaker asserting a single arbitrary proposition, p. In such cases, all we risk is assigning too low a value to the prior probability of the truth of p. However, most testifiers testify not just to the truth of single sentences, but to the truth of stories, whether an expert's tale of causal interactions between items in the world or a refugee's tale of desperate flight from political repression. When the testifier is telling a story, an initial low assessment of trustworthiness affects how we will interpret that story. When we are suspicious of a testifier, we interpret her story through the lens of our distrust. It is a commonplace that trust and distrust are self-fulfilling, distrust even more strongly so than trust. If, as I have argued elsewhere,[21] trust and distrust contain an affective component, then this should come as no surprise. Distrust puts in place a suspicious cognitive set that colors how we will interpret the words of another. It leads us to look for signs of deception, irrationality, or incompetence and thus leads us to seek out evidence of inconsistencies, to magnify those we suppose ourselves to have found, and to focus on them in our assessment of the story as a whole. It also leads us to overlook the ways in which any inconsistencies that we take ourselves to have found can be explained away. Thus a low initial trustworthiness rating, if not insulated from affecting the assessment of the prior probability of the report, can give rise to *runaway* reductions in the probability assigned to a witness's story.

This dynamic can be seen at work in Donald Ferlise's judgment in the Kassindja asylum case. Ferlise was known not to be sympathetic to female asylum seekers.[22] We can suppose that this lack of sympathy might have manifested itself in a tendency to view such requests with suspicion. In his judgment, Ferlise fastened on to three things that he saw as indicative of "the lack of rationality, the lack of consistency, and the lack of inherent persuasiveness" that led to his adverse credibility finding: Kassindja did not know the current whereabouts of her mother. She claimed to be unable to avoid FGM should she return to Togo, while Ferlise doubted that the practice could be so pervasive if her sisters had avoided it and she had escaped it up until now. And she was able to survive in Germany and get to the United States because of the help of two total strangers. I will return to the question of whether Ferlise should have found any of these facts improbable, but for now what is interesting to note is that of the three, only the second, her claim to be unable to avoid FGM should she be repatriated, strictly bears on the merits of her asylum request. But perceived implausibility in the parts was taken to undermine the plausibility of the whole and thus the trustworthiness of the witness. Moreover, taken individually, none of these elements of her story seems sufficient to cast doubt on the whole—for example, Kassindja could explain how her father's protection had enabled her to avoid FGM despite the practice's prevalence. It thus seems likely that Ferlise took these considerations to undermine Kassindja's credibility only because he viewed them through a lens of distrust that was already in place. During the appeal, the INS used relatively inconsequential and readily explained inconsistencies in Kassindja's story to argue that her credibility required further examination. These inconsistencies included whether FGM was performed by an old man or an old woman—something that, as the appeal judges ruled, a teenager protected from FGM might well be confused about and something that hardly matter to the case—and whether Kassindja actually was married to or would be forced to marry an older man. (A marriage certificate had been signed by her aunt and her "husband," but Kassindja had refused to sign it and may have been confused as to her own marital status.)

Ferlise's decision shows that not only can assessments of the trustworthiness of witnesses lead to runaway reductions in assessments of plausibility when their testimony is viewed through the lens of distrust, but also that assessments of low plausibility, when permitted to infect assessments of trustworthiness, can lead to a two-way mutually reinforcing loop. Our low initial trustworthiness rating leads to a reduction in the plausibility rating we would have given to the content of the story, and this in turn confirms our initial assessment of untrustworthiness, which in turn make us only the more confident in our low plausibility ratings. Small wonder, then, that Kassindja should have failed to convince Ferlise. When we violate the rule for the independence of assessments of trustworthiness and of plausibility, there is little the doubly epistemically disadvantaged can do to persuade us—we make it impossible for them to convince us by *words* of the truth of what they say. Only very strong—sometimes dramatic—external corroboration can break us out of such a mutually reinforcing loop. Often the form that this external corroboration has to take is the word of members of a "nonsuspect" group who are eyewitnesses to the event or who have seen physical evidence that strongly corroborates the story. When questions arose concerning the veracity of the slave narrative, *The History of Mary Prince*, white abolitionists sought confirmation by writing to other white abolitionists requesting that they verify that Mary Prince had scars consistent with her story of abuse.[23] In a more recent case, Patricia

Williams's first-person account of being turned away from a Benetton boutique because of her race was substantially altered by a law review editor and all references to the company were deleted because "they were not in the habit of publishing things that were unverifiable." Williams wonders "what it would take to make my experience verifiable. The testimony of an independent white bystander?"[24]

It might be objected that there's nothing wrong with violating the independence requirement in the typical case. Don't we usually take the untrustworthiness of a witness to cast doubt on their story and, further, take the implausibility of a story to support the hypothesis that the witness is untrustworthy? If Ferlise's reasoning was actually as described, there is something pathological about it; however, the objection continues, the pathology lies not in violating a spurious independence requirement but in allowing there to be formed a tight, mutually supporting loop that resists external corroborating evidence. And that's the vice of arrogance, not this newfangled vice of failing to separate questions of trustworthiness from questions of plausibility.

This objection fails to take seriously the problem *as viewed from the perspective of the inquirer herself*. It is easy for us to see how corroborating evidence could have broken Ferlise out of this loop; indeed, on appeal, counsel for Kassindja produced a corroborating affidavit from a world-renowned anthropologist supporting each of her contentions about her likely fate should she be repatriated. In the light of his testimony, Kassindja's claims are shown not to be astonishing at all. But once you have convinced yourself, however prematurely, that a witness is untrustworthy and that what she says is unlikely anyway, it becomes hard to see why you would need to seek out such corroborating evidence: all the evidence you have points in the same direction and just confirms what you knew anyway. Worse yet, you can have in place an interpretative schema capable of incorporating all the available evidence. This happened during the European witchcraft trials: the recantation of an accusation that might have corroborated someone's innocence was taken to be just what you would expect a witch to cause and so a further sign that the accused was guilty.[25] If Kassindja had had an experienced lawyer,[26] the lawyer would have been able to force Ferlise to revise his plausibility and trustworthiness ratings by confronting him with strong corroborating evidence. In this respect judges have an advantage over ordinary inquirers, insofar as ordinary inquirers usually do not have anyone to force them to confront new evidence. All the more important, then, that our ratings not be illicitly depressed.

There are two further objections to consider: (1) what the envisaged separation amounts to in practice is obscure, and, on some readings, the separation risks depriving us of tools we routinely use in assessing trustworthiness and (2) the independence rule places a counterintuitively large burden on someone who would reject testimony to the astonishing.[27]

It seems that we frequently take the fit between the things someone tells us and that which we independently believe as grounds for judging her trustworthy. And we are willing, on account of this, to extend our trust to her testimony on new but related matters. Thus we are more disposed to accept the views of someone with whom we have a track record of shared judgment when those views extend beyond our own beliefs (and even when they extend beyond our competence to assess) than we are to accept the views of someone whose track record of judgments diverges from our own. We might even, following Philip Kitcher,[28] use such agreement to calibrate our witnesses much as we calibrate instruments—think, for example, of movie reviewers. (But, as Tony Coady points out, we shouldn't think of the calibration process as giving us anything like a credibility ratio, where we understand this on the model of a die's tendency to roll six. A fair die's tendency to roll six is unaffected by context, excluding contexts that prohibit rolling altogether, such as gravity-free environments). Things are otherwise with persons. Few persons have a general, domain-unspecific tendency to veracity and none a general, domain-unspecific tendency to competence.[29] Still, while holding *domain fairly constant* we can make some rough generalizations from past track record. Am I seriously proposing that we ignore such evidence?

This forces a clarification of how the independence rule is to be interpreted. It enjoins us against using the implausibility of a person's *current* utterance, whose truth is still the subject of investigation, to tell against her trustworthiness with respect to it, and recommends that these two lines of inquiry be pursued independently. But it says nothing against using our assessments of *past* divergence in judgment as grounds for attributing a low trustworthiness rating to the witness on matters of this kind. But the discussion does recommend caution in how we do this, since people do not have a quasi-mechanical, domain-independent tendency to utter truths and falsehoods in a fixed ratio.

What else may go into an investigation of the witness's trustworthiness? Demeanor, body language—though this is notoriously variable across cultures—formal credentials, character witnesses, the presence or absence of motives for deceit, among other things. Inconsistency may enter too, but not the inconsistencies imagined or overestimated because of assumed untrustworthiness.

At this point, the next objection emerges. Am I advocating that one conduct this sort of detailed investigation into trustworthiness in each case, and won't that sometimes place an unreasonable burden on those who would reject astonishing reports? If so, then, while the rule may purchase an increased ratio of true to false beliefs, it will do so at an unacceptable cost. Thus it might appear that the rule is inconsistent with good epistemic practice for inquirers governed by the goal of seeking truth, but with limited time and resources to use in the pursuit of that goal. Indeed, we dismiss a range of tales without subjecting their bearers to much, if any, investigation for trustworthiness. Examples include tales of cures by psychic surgery, stories of astral travel, and reports of alien abduction. In these sorts of cases it seems that we are using our assessment of the implausibility of what the testifier says to assign such a low trustworthiness rating that we feel entitled not to pursue the matter any further. And if we are doing this, then we violate the independence requirement.

I think that such cases can be adequately handled within the bounds of the independence rule. It is true that the content of the witness's utterance is affecting our trustworthiness rating in cases of this kind, but this need not imply that it is the *implausibility* of the content that is affecting it. Recall that some of the factors that legitimately may enter assessment of trustworthiness include whether the testifier's competence or veracity might be undermined by self-interest or by psychological distortions such as wish fulfillment or fantasy. Whether such factors operate *in a particular context* can only be determined by considering the content of what the speaker says, since what someone says alerts us to the reasons why (in the context) she might say it other than its being true. In the cases we are correct to dismiss quickly, such alternative explanations are easy to find. Note that two equally implausible reports might be unequal in the extent to which they suggest alternative explanations for why someone might utter them: what leads us to discount the trustworthiness in the one case but not in the other isn't implausibility as such. Thus sometimes we need not bother to seek out further corroborating evidence of trustworthiness on account of being able to ascribe a low trustworthiness rating to a speaker because the content of what she says supports the hypothesis that truth is not what explains her saying it.[30]

But there must be limits on the legitimacy of such shortcuts in determining trustworthiness, or else why couldn't Ferlise defend his low trustworthiness rating as being a natural response to the existence of explanations, other than truth, for Kassindja's story? Perhaps it is reasonable to suppose asylum seekers distort the truth in ways designed to help their cause. And why couldn't Ferlise claim that there was not enough evidence of trustworthiness to warrant his believing despite his initial low plausibility rating? Just demanding that inquirers separate their assessments of trustworthiness from assessments of plausibility does not set in place enough safeguards against unfairly dismissing a report. What additional brakes do inquirers need, and when do they need them?

We can make a first pass at articulating the additional rules, by looking at what, intuitively, we would be inclined to say about what separates Ferlise's too ready dismissal of Kassindja's story from our ready, but not too ready, dismissal of tales of, for example, psychic surgery. Intuitively, the difference seems to lie in the *reasonableness* of the trust that we can place in our distrust and in our trust. It would have been reasonable for Ferlise to distrust his own tendencies to distrust witnesses of this type, but it is not similarly reasonable for us to distrust our tendencies to distrust those who report strange cures. Similarly, it is not reasonable for Ferlise to trust the completeness or accuracy of the background beliefs that he brought to bear in assessing the plausibility of what Kassindja said. As Karen Musalo, Kassindja's appeal attorney, stated, "Judge Ferlise's credibility determination is based on a set of incorrect assumptions about the cultural norms and practices in Togo, and the inappropriate use of the judge's own concept of 'common sense.'"[31] In contrast, self-distrust need not undermine our assessments of the plausibility of tales of surgery performed without anesthetic that cures immediately and leaves no scars.

What sort of difference should self-distrust make? If self-distrust is not to license believing anything at all, then it is best thought of as shifting evidential burdens, rather than as enjoining us to trust anyone our distrust of whom we cannot trust. In the ordinary case, apparent untrustworthiness or apparent implausibility establish a presumption against acceptance analogous to a legal presumption of innocence. Such presumptions can be outweighed: juries can come to believe that there is enough evidence to convict. Likewise, we might come to believe a report that seemed astonishing if we come to have excellent evidence of the trustworthiness of the reporter. Consider Sister Dianna Ortiz's claim that her Guatemalan torturers were supervised by someone from the United States named "Alejandro." What disturbs the officials of the U.S. embassy in Guatemala is the high trustworthiness many are willing to ascribe to nuns, a trustworthiness that can make it seem reasonable to accept her story even for those who believe that the United States has a basically benevolent, human rights–driven foreign policy. Similarly, we might come to believe a report from a witness we distrusted if we came to have very substantial corroborating evidence that supported the truth of what she said. But it takes a great deal of evidence to outweigh the presumption against acceptance that implausibility and untrustworthiness establish.

Suppose, in contrast, that we cannot trust our distrust or cannot trust the background theories in the light of which we judge the report implausible; then self-distrust *rebuts* the presumption against accepting such reports. Such rebutting *cancels*, rather than outweighs, the presumption against acceptance. When such a presumption is rebutted, that does not mean we are entitled to go ahead and accept the report—that would be a recipe for gullibility. Instead it shifts the weight we give to evidence: with no presumption against acceptance in place, it will take much less evidence of trustworthiness for us to be warranted in believing an astonishing report than it takes when we can trust the background theories in the light of which we find the report astonishing. The amount of corroborating evidence we need when we should distrust our distrust of the witness is likewise reduced. Return to the example of Dianna Ortiz: if we cannot trust our trust in the background assumptions about U.S. foreign policy against which Ortiz's report seems surprising (and, arguably, these cannot be trusted), then we should be willing to accept the report with comparatively less corroborating evidence. If one can come to accept Ortiz's testimony, and the testimony of others like her, then one has the starting point for revising one's background beliefs about the trustworthiness of the U.S. government. Accepting testimony can thus be the starting point for radical change in one's background beliefs but does not have to presuppose that such changes are already in place. Self-distrust makes one open to them.

In addition to rebutting the presumption against accepting an astonishing report, self-distrust also recommends that we be more cautious in reaching a final judgment on credibility and thus requires us to search for more corroborating evidence of the story reported, of the speaker's trustworthiness, and of the background beliefs relative to which the story looks more or less plausible. In his adverse credibility finding, Ferlise not only violated the independence rule but made two additional mistakes. He discounted the corroborating evidence available to him, a discounting warranted only on the assumption that self-trust was justified, and he failed to call for further corroborating evidence, assuming instead that he was well placed to assess the plausibility of Kassindja's story.

The discussion so far can be summed up with two further rules. Rule 2 (self-trust and the weighing of evidence) is, Let the presumption against accepting an apparently astonishing report or believing an apparently untrustworthy witness be rebutted when it is reasonable to distrust one's own distrust or judgments of implausibility.

Rule 3 (self-trust and the burden of evidence seeking) is, Let the burden of seeking corroborating evidence of trustworthiness vary inversely with how reasonable it is to trust one's own tendency to trust witnesses of this type; and let the burden of seeking corroborating evidence for the likely truth of *p* vary inversely with how reasonable it is to trust the background knowledge one brings to bear in assessing plausibility.

4. Reasonable Metatrust and Distrust

Clearly, much depends on how the word "reasonable" is to be understood as it occurs in the rules governing the weighing of evidence and the burden of evidence seeking. From *our* perspective it is easy to see the mistakes Ferlise made and it is easy to feel confident that we are not making the same mistakes when, for example, we quickly dismiss tales of psychic surgery. Ferlise, however, was probably as confident in his judgment as we are in ours. If an inquirer is unable to make judgments of reasonableness, then the rules threaten not to be first person accessible. Thus it becomes important to address the questions, What makes it reasonable to adopt a metastance of trust or distrust and how can an inquirer tell which is appropriate and when?

On the one hand, the notion of "reasonableness" cannot be cashed out in terms of whether one's metadistrust or trust identifies objectively mistaken first-order trust or distrust. Cashed out in this way, judgments of reasonable metastance would have to be consequent on judgments of the objective correctness of the first-order stance, and thus the notion of reasonable metastance would pull no independent weight. Furthermore, it can be reasonable for an inquirer to trust her trust even though she is in error. For example, an inquirer, through no lack of care, or reflection, might not have access to the fact that the testifier is honestly conveying her true belief that *p* (think of the boy who cried wolf). If objective success is the criterion for reasonableness, then the rules will not be first person accessible. On the other hand, the criterion cannot be merely that the adopted metastance is consistent with, or supported by, the inquirer's existing beliefs about the likely success of her first-order trust and distrust. Perhaps inquirers sometimes rush to conclusions about metatrustworthiness that are not, in fact, consistent with what they hold about likely reliability, and further reflection would lead them to abandon their initial assessment. However, if objective success is too thick a requirement, mere consistency is too thin. Inquirers can form metastances consistent with their beliefs about the likely contours of their reliability and yet have been irresponsible in the formation of those very beliefs. Perhaps they are prone to being overly confident in their assessment of their own epistemic performance. Thus, although mere consistency meets the first-person accessibility requirement, it is too weak to capture the kind of epistemic fault that needs to be captured. The right understanding of "reasonableness" must, therefore, lie somewhere between a fully objective and a merely subjective account. This suggests that the notion of a reasonable metastance should be cashed out in terms of the metastance that a *responsible* epistemic agent, similarly situated to the actual agent, could be expected to have—the significance of the "similarly situated" will become clearer in a moment. Among the things that responsible inquirers need to do in determining appropriate metastance with respect to their trustworthiness assessments is reflect on the patterns in their own tendencies to trust and distrust persons of certain kinds. One might discover, for example, that one routinely underestimates the trustworthiness of people of different races and so come to think that what explains one's distrust is not sensitivity to markers of untrustworthiness but rather racist stereotypes. Return to Ferlise: intuitively, what separates his distrust of Kassindja from our distrust of bearers of tales of psychic surgery is that we can reasonably trust our trust and Ferlise cannot. To this claim it might be objected that the selfsame grounds that make our distrust reasonable also make his, namely, the existence of explanations, other than truth, for why they report what they report. Wish fulfillment coupled with charismatic charlatans' deceptive practices can explain tales of astonishing cures. But, equally, it seems, the desire to enter the United States can explain why Kassindja should have told the story she told.[32] Aren't Ferlise and ourselves on all fours in this respect? The difference is this: Ferlise had a *pattern* of underestimating the trustworthiness of those requesting asylum. He routinely finds more instances of untrustworthiness among women who appear before his court than his colleagues find among women appearing before their courts.[33] Perhaps the explanation is bad luck: there just are more untrustworthy women appearing before his court. But why should this be so, given the way cases are randomly distributed for hearing? Perhaps the explanation is Ferlise's superior ability to detect untrustworthiness among women. Perhaps. But why should he have superior ability in this regard to his equally trained peers? A responsible epistemic agent pursuing this reflection ought to arrive at a metastance of distrust in her distrust. To be sure, this should not lead her, without further evidence, to believe that the witness is trustworthy, but, as explained, a metastance of distrust in distrust does not require that first-order distrust be replaced with first-order trust. Instead it shifts the weight of evidence and the requirements for evidence seeking.

It takes judgment to examine patterns in our trust and distrust and to calibrate these in the light of the performance of other inquirers and in the light of our theories about what is likely to make for error and what for success. The fact that one has patterns of trust and distrust that are at odds with those of other inquirers need not lead to a metastance of distrust. For example, a feminist academic might find that she has a pattern of trusting the intellectual competence of women more readily than her nonfeminist colleagues. However, she has available an explanation for this divergence in judgment that reveals why, in the light of pervasive sexism, her patterns of trusting might be more nearly correct than those of her nonfeminist colleagues. Ferlise might attempt a similar explanation and claim that his patterns in trust diverge from those of his peers because he is genuinely objective, while they are influenced by "political correctness." It takes judgment to know which explanations to accept and which to reject. However, this should not be thought of as vitiating the usefulness of the metastance rules. The rules are able to shape debate in controversial cases in ways that accord with what seems to be good epistemic practice. In the final section I return to the question of what additional skills are needed to apply the rules correctly.

Reflection can also help the responsible inquirer begin to grasp the likely contours of her own ignorance and error. For example, thinking about how ideology leads to systematic distortions in belief can be the starting point for the kind of self-distrust that shifts evidential burdens. Reflection can also alert the inquirer to the possibility that she has judged a reported event to be astonishing when she was better advised to form no judgment on the matter at all. We should distinguish between cases where an event seems astonishing in the light of the inquirer's past experience, previously accepted testimony, and best theories about available causal mechanisms, from cases where past experience, testimony, and theory are silent on the matter. Ferlise, like the King of Siam,[34] formed beliefs in the light of which a report seemed astonishing, when neither experience nor theory committed him to such beliefs. Augustine, in contrast, being a biblical literalist, had a theoretical reason for thinking it impossible that there should be people on the other side of the world. Thus, provided that Augustine was responsible, given his social location, in being a biblical literalist (and arguably he was, since the evidence against such literalism was not then available) a metastance of trust in his confidence in the background beliefs he bought to bear in assessing plausibility was reasonable for him, though not reasonable for either Ferlise or the King of Siam. Note, however, that epistemically responsible agents will not now be biblical literalists; hence reasonableness is to be cashed out in terms of the metastance that a responsible epistemic agent, *similarly situated to the actual agent*, could be expected to have.

This list of things responsible inquirers need to consider is not intended to be exhaustive. It is offered, instead, in response to the objection that the metastance rules, with their appeal to "reasonableness," will not be first-person accessible. The rules face other objections: (1) Why not formulate a simpler first-order rule to govern assessments of trustworthiness? (2) If we are forced to second-order trust, then why aren't we forced to third and higher order stances, without limit? (3) Will these rules, with their appeal to reasonable metatrust, help subordinates—who may be especially prone to self-distrust—truth track? I will address each of these objections in turn.

If one of the problems in the Kassindja credibility finding was that Ferlise approached Kassindja with distrust and viewed her testimony through the lens of that distrust, then a solution simpler to that contained in the weighing of evidence rule suggests itself: why not advocate a default stance of trust in witnesses and require positive evidence of untrustworthiness to move from the default of trust? (Where, in accordance with the independence rule, the fact that what the witness is saying appears astonishing does not, in itself, count as evidence for untrustworthiness.) Beginning with a default of trust would counteract tendencies toward dismissing the testimony of witnesses who belong to "suspect" social groups more effectively than a rule formulated in terms of the reasonableness of metatrust.

A default stance of trust enjoins us to trust without further evidence of trustworthiness; thus, advocating such a stance toward witnesses asks us to overlook what we know about how both competence and veracity are domain-sensitive. Given that the two components of trustworthiness are domain-sensitive, it follows that our default stance should likewise be domain-sensitive.[35] Moreover, a rule that recommends "trust, unless . . ." preempts discussion of the burden of evidence seeking, since, if one starts with trust in place, then it seems—absent the positive signs of untrustworthiness that would rebut the default stance—there is no apparent burden of evidence seeking to be discharged. Ascending to the metalevel lets us investigate the patterns in our tendencies to trust and distrust, and it is these patterns that are crucial for determining whether the first-order trust is likely to be going astray.

That metatrust lets us track patterns in our first-order trust also provides the key to understanding how to answer the regress objection: if second-order assessment is required, then why not third-order, and so on, without limit? The answer is that only in rare cases are there patterns to be tracked at the second-order and thus that need to be captured with third-order trust. (An example might be the patterns of distrust in distrust of distrust that white liberal guilt can generate. Suppose a white person, despite repudiation of such attitudes as racist, nonetheless tends to distrust persons of color. She might appropriately respond to such distrust with distrust. However, she might also wonder whether such distrust is itself to be trusted: wouldn't she distrust anyone in circumstances like these?) Third- and higher-order levels, in contrast, seem not to have patterns that conscientious inquirers need to track. Thus, although there exists the theoretical possibility of an ever ascending hierarchy of self-reflexive trust and distrust, the hierarchy gets no practical purchase.

The third objection calls for considering whether the rules assist those in subordinate social positions to truth-track when it comes to reports that seem astonishing in the light of *their* experiences and background beliefs and in the light of their reasonable stance toward their own patterns of trust. Perhaps the rules, with their references to self-trust, are tailored to the epistemic needs of those who occupy dominant social positions. This objection can be developed in two ways, one emphasizing the psychological consequences of occupying a position of social subordination and one emphasizing the epistemological consequences of such social locations.

According to the first way of developing the objection, the problem lies in how the rules will be applied—because of an understandable greater tendency toward self-distrust on the part of those who occupy subordinate social positions, subordinates will take themselves to have reason for self-distrust more readily and thus more frequently than will dominants.[36] True, the rules do not enjoin an inquirer to adopt a metastance of self-distrust when she *believes* that such distrust is warranted, but rather when it is *reasonable* to so believe. However, in applying the rule, all an inquirer has to go on is her own best take on when it is reasonable so to believe. And this is true even if the inquirer seeks the advice of others, for she must still decide which advice to accept, which to reject. Thus, if as a matter of psychological fact, subordinates routinely underestimate their epistemic capacities, then the rules will fail the test of enabling them to truth-track. This objection cannot simply be dismissed as being a problem, not with the rules themselves, but with how they are applied in less than ideal circumstances. Epistemic rules, ideals, heuristics, and so on must be tailored for the kinds of epistemic agents that we are. It is no use recommending a procedure if, given how we are constituted, the attempt to follow that procedure will lead us further from our truth-seeking goal.[37]

The second way of developing the objection is epistemological: greater self-distrust on the part of subordinates than on the part of dominants is warranted. The possibility that greater self-distrust is *warranted* for subordinates is endorsed by Louise Antony:

> Let us suppose the correctness of some broadly reliabilist account of knowledge according to which a person counts as knowing a proposition p only if there are, for that person, no ineliminable salient defeaters of p. . . . A social consensus against p may count, legitimately, as a salient defeater of p, one that, on this account, we must be able to defeat in order to be properly said to *know* that p. Against such an epistemic background, it seems to me to be the case that any member of a group whose cognitive abilities are *generally* deemed to be less trustworthy than others will have less secure knowledge, at least in certain domains, than members of dominant groups.[38]

Mainstream rival accounts to the background beliefs that subordinates bring to bear in their plausibility judgments will be salient to subordinates, but rival accounts from subordinate perspectives may not be salient to dominants. Perhaps subordinates have extra epistemological work to do in defending their position against salient rival accounts than do dominants.

One way of responding to this objection, in both psychological and epistemic forms, is to restrict the class of inquirers whose epistemic practice the rules are supposed to govern. Antony argues that dominants and subordinates may require different epistemic norms if they are to be able to truth-track, with dominants following norms that give greater weight to social factors and subordinates following more individualistic epistemic norms.[39] However, I think that there are reasons to resist this move. The rules I have defended are intended to guide epistemic practice in all cases involving astonishing reports, only a subclass of which involve members of "suspect" social groups. Moreover, most inquirers are sometimes members of dominant social groups, sometimes members of subordinate social groups and sometimes members of both at once. Consider, for example, the response of some white feminists to the O.J. Simpson trial. Some white feminists objected to the racial focus of media analyses of the trial, claiming that the trial was not about race, but about gender. But the trial was about *both* race *and* gender. It will not do to think that white feminists should have one metastance with respect to background beliefs that grow out of their feminist practice and another toward those background beliefs that concern race. The problem with this move is that it asks us to treat race and gender as two independent variables, a move that much recent feminist scholarship renders problematic.[40] If we propose one set of rules for dominants and one for subordinates, which set are white feminists supposed to follow? For these reasons, I take the suggestion that the rules themselves should build in reference to the social location of the rule follower and thus be designed to be applied by some knowers, but not others, to be a move of last recourse. Better, if we can, to find rules for any inquirer.

Return first to the epistemological way of developing the objection. Consider the problem from the perspective of subordinates: subordinates have available to them a reasonable explanation for why they might be more reliable across certain domains than members of dominant groups. Subordinates often have the sorts of experiences that undermine belief in ideologically driven accounts of how the social world works.[41] (Think, for example, of black experiences of police harassment.) Thus the mere presence of available alternatives to one's theory need not be undermining when one has an explanation for the spread of those theories and an account of why one might be in a better position to truth-track. Now consider dominants: does the mere fact that an alternative is not salient to a member of a dominant group lighten their epistemological burden? It seems to me that the answer depends on why the alternative fails to be salient. Appeal to salient defeaters is motivated in part by the desire to cordon off skeptical hypotheses so that they need not undermine day-to-day knowledge claims: if someone can know that *p* only when she can rule out all hypotheses that entail that not-*p*, then she will know nothing about the external world unless she can rule out skeptical brain-in-a-vat hypotheses. Intuitively, it seems that responsible inquirers can proceed without brain-in-a-vat hypotheses being salient. In contrast, I would claim that members of dominant social groups cannot responsibly ignore the rival social explanations advocated by members of subordinate social groups. What matters is not just whether the defeater is in fact not salient, but whether it is *responsible* to allow it not to be salient. The answer to that is, of course, going to depend on the kind of defeater and the reasons why it might or might not be readily salient.

What of the objection in its psychological form? Is it not plausible to suppose that subordinates will tend to be less confident than they should be and so will tend to misapply the rules? And, given I've conceded the importance of rules that are rules for *us*, in the sense of rules for the kinds of cognitively limited, embodied, socially located inquirers that we are, such tendencies toward misapplication cannot be dismissed. How serious they are, though, depends on a number of factors. I want to argue that the lesson to be drawn from the possibility of misapplication is not that the rules need to be changed, but rather that we need to investigate what—besides the rules—is needed for inquirers to do well in their acceptance or rejection of apparently astonishing reports. It is to that question that I now turn.

5. The Limitations of Rules

The three rules are not algorithms for how to arrive at a judgment regarding a particular report—indeed, they are entirely silent on the question of how to form an all-things-considered judgment regarding a report. Instead, they tell you how to go about forming the trustworthiness and plausibility assessments that feed into final assessments of credibility. Sometimes, in the course of working out those trustworthiness and plausibility measures, the question of all-things-considered credibility becomes obvious. For example, an inquirer might undertake a burden of evidence seeking which leads to the discovery that the witness is quite likely to be trustworthy with respect to that which she is testifying and that what she is saying is not anyway as astonishing as it first seemed. In such cases, a final verdict will be easily reached. In other cases, however, a final verdict may be a matter of considerable controversy. The two grounds of credibility may pull in opposite directions and they may seem about equally balanced. In such cases, reaching a final verdict will be a matter of delicate judgment, and one not reducible to rules that can determine decision.[42]

Not only are the rules not algorithms for reaching an all-things-considered verdict as to credibility, they are not algorithms for reaching the assessments of trustworthiness and plausibility that feed into such final verdicts; thus, judgment is required in at least two levels. For example, there is room for debate and nice judgment regarding whether self-trust or self-distrust is reasonable and regarding whether there is enough additional supporting evidence to outweigh an initially adverse trustworthiness assessment. How is it, then, that one develops the capacity for right judgment in the application of these rules?

The second and third rules appeal to the notion of self-trust. On the one hand, appropriate self-distrust can make you receptive to testimony, even when such testimony has the potential to lead to a radical revision in your background beliefs. On the other hand, inappropriate self-distrust can lead you to accept false views. It is the capacity for *appropriate* trust and self-trust that helps us truth track. How, then, is such a capacity created and sustained? This is an empirical question, but some hypotheses concerning the social and psychological features that support appropriate trust and self-trust suggest themselves. Recent history shows that among the important social conditions is the existence of political movements for liberation, such as feminism and antiracist movements. Furthermore, making knowledge producing and certifying institutions such as the academy and the media more inclusive also helps. I want, however, to focus on the affective capacities of an agent that help her truth-track, for these are nicely illustrated by the central example of this paper.

Ferlise is a person of little empathy, as the court record shows. Kassindja was unable to speak when Ferlise first asked her if she understood that her asylum request had been denied. He twice said "Hello?" when her response still could not be heard.[43]

Compare Ferlise with Miss Rufel in Shirley Williams's novel *Dessa Rose*. At first Miss Rufel refuses to believe the story of Dessa's abuse at the hands of her mistress, suspecting that the tale is fabricated to play on her sympathies. She wants to see the scars: "This the first thing flashed in my mind when Nathan told me she wanted to see them scars, that Miz Lady had to *see* the goods before she would buy the story."[44] In the end, Miss Rufel does get to see the scars, though inadvertently. But what made her capable of coming to believe a tale she had an overwhelming interest in not believing, since it disrupted her understanding of the world and threatened her place within it, was the capacity for empathy. Miss Rufel finds herself responding to the run-away slaves who have taken to living on her property as if they were "just people." She does this despite her professed belief that, of course, since they are runaways and she is white, she can assume they are nothing like her. Furthermore, what made her capable of coming to distrust her own need for proof of Dessa's story was being able to see that need through the eyes of others:

"The mistress have to see the welts in the darky's hide, eh?"

"Ye—" His tone implied that her desire for proof was mean and petty and she flushed hotly, as the image of herself inspecting the wench's naked loins flashed vividly to life in her mind.[45]

There is reason to believe that these examples are representative. For example, John Bigelow and Karen Green argue that the defenders of witches accused during the European witchcraft craze were not distinguished from the witch burners by their ability to formulate and argue against rival explanatory hypotheses. Individuals on both sides displayed such reasoning capacities in about equal measure, but the defenders were more sympathetic and had more appropriate trust in their fellow human beings. If empathy is indeed required to sustain appropriate trust and self-trust, then the capacities needed to be able correctly to apply the rules governing astonishing reports will include affective capacities. Far from it being the case that Ferlise's coldness made him better able to truth-track—as some popular conceptions of the distorting effects of emotion imply—it stood in the way of his ability to have the appropriate trust and self-trust required for epistemic success. Furthermore, the affective capacities that sustain appropriate trust and self-trust are central to recognized *moral* virtues such as kindness and respect. This opens up the possibility that some moral virtues may provide the grounds for epistemic virtues.

Notes

Earlier versions of this chapter were presented at Dartmouth, Eastern SWIP, Johns Hopkins, and Monash. Each audience contributed to its final shape. Special thanks to Louise Antony, Carl Ginet, Brian Keeley, Scott MacDonald, Philip Pettit and Jennifer Whiting, for written comments and helpful discussion.

1. The feminist bibliography on these themes is lengthy. Important contributions include Genevieve Lloyd, *The Man of Reason: "Male" and "Female" in Western Philosophy* (Minneapolis: University of Minnesota Press, 1984); Catharine MacKinnon, *Feminism Unmodified* (Cambridge: Harvard University Press, 1987); Helen Longino, *Science as Social Knowledge* (Princeton: Princeton University Press, 1990); Lorraine Code, *What Can She Know?* (Ithaca, N.Y.: Cornell University Press, 1991). Recent mainstream epistemology has likewise become interested in both epistemic dependency and norms of credibility. Some recent accounts of knowledge begin from an assumption of epistemic dependency, arguing that we have the concept of knowledge in order to be able to identify who can function as a reliable informant—a person we can reasonably depend on if we want to find out whether or not *p*. It is argued that this dependency sets constraints on an adequate account of knowledge. See Michael Welbourne, *The Community of Knowledge* (Aberdeen: Aberdeen University Press, 1986); Edward Craig, *Knowledge in the State of Nature* (Oxford: Oxford University Press, 1990); Richard Miller, "The Norms of Reason," *Philosophical Review*, April 1995, pp. 205–245.

2. For discussion of these issues, see C. A. J. Coady, *Testimony: A Philosophical Study* (Oxford: Oxford University Press, 1992); and Elizabeth Fricker, "Against Gullibility," in *Knowing from Words*, ed. B. K. Matilal and A. Chakrabarti (Dordrecht: Kluwer, 1994), pp. 125–161.

3. For example, concrete feminist critiques of scientific practice fall under this heading. For a sample of these critiques, see Ruth Bleier, ed., *Feminist Approaches to Science* (New York: Pergamon, 1986). Recent examples of practical epistemology include chapters 10–16 of Coady, *Testimony*; much of Alvin Goldman's *Knowledge in a Social World* (Oxford: Oxford University Press, 1999); and Brian Keeley, "Of Conspiracy Theories," *Journal of Philosophy*, March 1999, pp. 109–126. The best known exercise in practical epistemology is Hume's discussion of miracles in *An Enquiry Concerning Human Understanding*, sec. 10, "Of Miracles" (1778; reprint, LaSalle, Ill.: Open Court, 1988).

4. This may be to the detriment of practical ethics, as it allows practical ethical questions that are not tied to the professions to be relatively overlooked.

5. The distinction between rules and principles seems to be this: Rules are more directly action guiding than principles, though principles aim to articulate considerations (e.g., "respect autonomy") that must be taken into account in determining what, all things considered, one should do.

6. For a critique of this model of practical ethics, see Arthur Caplan, "Can Applied Ethics Be Effective in Health Care and Should It Strive to Be?" in Caplan, *If I Were a Rich Man Could I Buy a Pancreas?* (Bloomington: Indiana University Press, 1994), pp. 3–17.

7. In moral theory, witness, for example, the resurgence of interest in the virtues even among those who do not think virtue ethics provides a comprehensive theory of morality that is a rival to consequentialist and deontological theories. In epistemology, see Linda Zagzebski, *Virtues of the Mind* (Cambridge: Cambridge University Press, 1996).

8. See Louise Antony, "Sisters, Please, I'd Rather Do It Myself: A Defense of Individualism in Feminist Epistemology," in *Feminist Perspectives on Language, Knowledge, and Reality*, ed. Sally Haslanger, *Philosophical Topics*, Fall 1995, pp. 59–95, for discussion of how to defend epistemic norms and heuristics. For a discussion of epistemic power as a virtue, see chapter 6 in Alvin Goldman, *Epistemology and Cognition* (Cambridge: Harvard University Press, 1986).

9. This is accepted by Locke, bk. 4, chap. 16, sec. 9 in *An Essay Concerning Human Understanding* (1689; reprint, Oxford: Oxford University Press, 1975), p. 663; F. H. Bradley, "The Presuppositions of Critical History," in *Collected Essays* (1935; reprint, Oxford: Oxford University Press, 1969); and Coady, *Testimony*.

10. Locke, *Essay Concerning Human Understanding*, p. 663.

11. For this formulation of what it is to testify that-p, see my "Second-Hand Moral Knowledge," *Journal of Philosophy*, February 1999, p. 57; for a contrasting conception, see Coady, *Testimony*, p. 43.

12. For a discussion of trust as a three-place relation, see Annette Baier, "Trust and Anti-Trust," *Ethics* 96 (1986): 231–260.

13. We do not require that if p were not the case the informant tend to believe that not-p, for it is enough for her not to misinform us—assuming veracity—if she has no false beliefs.

14. Some reports of miracles concern events, such as resurrections, that contradict the laws of nature; other reports of miracles concern events, such as a house being spared by a tornado, that do not themselves contradict the laws of nature (houses *are* spared by tornadoes) but are reported to have been produced by mechanisms, such as divine intervention, that are supposed not to be governed by the laws of nature.

15. Augustine *City of God* 16.9.

16. There are feminist exceptions; notably Lorraine Code, "Incredulity, Experientialism, and the Politics of Knowledge," in *Rhetorical Spaces: Essays on Gendered Locations* (New

York: Routledge, 1995), pp. 58–82; and Miranda Fricker, "Rational Authority and Social Power," *Proceedings of the Aristotelian Society* 98, 2 (1998): 159–177.

17. For the notion of epistemic injustice, see Fricker, "Rational Authority," p. 171.

18. There are disadvantages to using a legal case—perhaps the judge's decision is an artifact of the specifically legal presuppositions in play—presumptions against asylees, for example—however, ordinary knowers are not obliged to defend their credibility judgments, whereas judges are. Legal sources can thus provide useful records of reasoning, usually omitted in other contexts. I think in this particular case Ferlise's judgment of incredibility was not affected by legal presumptions and thus can be used to provide a starting point for our discussion. Obviously, it will be useful to use other examples to test the rules that emerge from a discussion of this one.

19. U.S. Department of Justice, Board of Immigration Appeals, "In re Fauziya Kasinga [sic]." File A73 476 695. Interim Decision 3278. Fauziya Kassindja's name is misspelled in the court documents and initial press releases about her case.

20. This separation requirement is in the spirit of Hume's discussion in "Of Miracles." It is endorsed by Elizabeth Fricker: "Note, however, that the prima facie incredibility of what a speaker asserts by an utterance is not best treated as evidence against her trustworthiness with respect to it. . . . We need to separate the evidence for 'P' stemming from the fact that it has been asserted by a trustworthy speaker, from other evidence for or against 'P'. Where these conflict, there will ensure a Humean battle between them in the belief-updating process of a rational hearer. To represent this battle most perspicuously, it is the *ex ante* estimate of the trustworthiness of a speaker that we should take; not one revised downwards in the light of her prima facie incredible utterance" ("Against Gullibility," p. 135).

The rule is compatible with, but does not require, a Bayesian interpretation. Bayes's Theorem tells us how to update beliefs in the light of new evidence and can be applied to belief updating in the light of testimonial evidence. Let A be an astonishing event, T be testimony to that event, and K be background beliefs, then if A and -A are mutually exclusive and jointly exhaustive relative to K (the set of background beliefs) and Pr(T/K)—that is, the value of the denominator—is not equal to 0 (the probability of the testimony occurring, given background beliefs) then

$$Pr(A/T\&K) = \frac{Pr(T/A\&K).Pr(A/K)}{Pr(T/A\&K).Pr(A/K) + Pr(T/-A\&K).Pr(-A/K)}$$

It is alleged that Bayes's theorem recommends counterintuitive credibility ratings when it comes to testimony. Jonathan Cohen, "Can Human Irrationality Be Experimentally Demonstrated?" *Behavioral and Brain Sciences* 4 (1981): 317–370, presents an example concerning the credibility that should be assigned to a witness's report that a taxicab of a certain color was involved in an accident. The distribution of taxicabs and the reliability of witnesses can be such that Bayes's theorem recommends discounting testimonial evidence as to the color of a cab involved in an accident. But ordinary inquirers do not discount in the way the theorem recommends. Some see such counterintuitive credibility ratings as counting against Bayes's theorem and others as showing that we attribute too much weight to testimony. However, David Owen, "Hume *Versus* Price on Miracles and the Prior Probabilities: Testimony and the Bayesian Calculation," *Philosophical Quarterly* 37, 147 (1987): 187–202, argues that the example is underdescribed and fails to disambiguate the meaning of the reliability ratio assigned to the testifier. Commonsense thinking is charged with irrationality on the assumption that the accuracy figure given is, as we might put it intuitively, a fact-to-witness ratio; that is, if a fact holds, the witness is right 80 percent of the time. If, however, the reliability ratio is interpreted as a witness-to-fact connection, then it is correct to discount the prior probabilities, for such a connection asserts that if a witness says it holds, then 80 percent of the time it does hold. Thanks to Philip Pettit and Fred Schick for this reference.

21. See Karen Jones, "Trust as an Affective Attitude," *Ethics*, October 1996, pp. 4–25.

22. See Fauziya Kassindja and Layli Miller Bashir, *Do They Hear You When You Cry?* (New York: Delacorte, 1998), p. 342.

23. See March 28, 1831, letter from M. Pringle to Mrs. Townsend, appendix to *The History of Mary Prince: A West Indian Slave, Related by Herself* (London: Pandora 1987), pp. 119–120. This need to see evidence written on the body is a theme of slave narratives and of fiction. For another example, see Shirley Ann Williams, *Dessa Rose* (New York: Berkley, 1986) discussed in section 5 below.

24. Patricia Williams, "The Death of the Profane," in *The Alchemy of Race and Rights* (Cambridge: Harvard University Press, 1991), p. 47. Also cited by Code in "Incredulity," p. 69; and Fricker, "Rational Authority," p. 170.

25. For a discussion of this sort of reasoning pattern in the European witchcraft trials, see John Bigelow and Karen Green, "Does Science Persecute Women? The Case of the 16th–17th Century Witch-hunts," *Philosophy* 73 (1998): 195–217.

26. One of Kassindja's grounds for appeal was that an unsupervised law student prepared her case. See Karen Musalo, "Brief for the Respondent," U.S. Department of Justice Executive Office of Immigration Review, Board of Immigration Appeals, Falls Church, Virginia, File A73 476 695.

27. In addition, it might be objected that we have to take plausibility into account in determining the trustworthiness of a testifier insofar as we have to take it into account in working out whether the person is indeed *testifying* and not, for example, making a joke. Thus when someone says something deeply implausible such as "pigs fly," we know that she is joking. However, I don't think that it is in recognizing the *im*plausibility of what someone says that we recognize the joke; since, after all, we recognize jokes in plausible and even in tautological statements ("No, my yacht is not longer than it is") just as readily as in implausible ones. How jokes are recognized is a complex matter and something notoriously culturally sensitive. Plausibility may play a role, but it seems that context, vocal and bodily clues, and flagrant violations of conversational rules of relevance are among the chief means by which jokes are distinguished from serious assertions.

28. Philip Kitcher, "Authority, Deference, and the Role of Individual Reason," in *The Social Dimensions of Science*, ed. Ernan McMullin (Chicago: Notre Dame Press, 1992), pp. 244–271.

29. For references to the empirical literature supporting this claim, see Coady, *Testimony*, p. 211.

30. Louise Antony has suggested to me that there might be exceptions to the independence rule. One possible exception concerns cases of a one-off encounter with a witness testifying to something incredible. Because of the one-off nature of the encounter, it might be thought that it is legitimate to let judgments of incredibility affect judgments of trustworthiness, since there is nothing else to go on in assessing trustworthiness. However, even in one-off cases, I would argue that we typically do have something to go on in assessing trustworthiness—we can call on our background theories about human motivation and our understanding of demeanor and body language (is the person drunk, on drugs, or genuinely distressed, for example). In one-off encounters with persons who report appar-

ently incredible events there will, however, typically not be enough evidence of trustworthiness to outweigh the presumption against accepting such reports.

31. Musalo, "Brief for the Respondent," p. 15.

32. Kassindja was advised by Charlie to claim asylum immediately on arrival, so the fact that she did not enter illegally is compatible with this explanation.

33. Compare the explanation of why Peter, who finds fewer instances of sexism than others, should distrust his trust is given in my "Second-Hand Moral Knowledge," p. 74.

34. "And as it happened to a Dutch Ambassador, who entertaining the King of Siam with the particularities of Holland, which he was inquisitive after, amongst other things told him, that the water in his country, would sometimes, in cold weather, be so hard, that men walked upon it, and that it would bear an Elephant, if he were there. To which the King replied, *Hitherto I have believed the strange things you have told me, because I look upon you as a sober fair man, but now I am sure you lye.*" Locke, *An Essay Concerning Human Nature*, p. 657.

35. For an argument that the domain sensitivity of testimonial trustworthiness means that testimony is not a unified epistemic kind, see Fricker, "Against Gullibility."

36. In support of this claim, see Sandra Bartky's discussion of the double ontological shock of feminist consciousness, "On Psychological Oppression," in *Philosophy and Women,* ed. Sharon Bishop and Marjorie Weinzweig (Belmont, Calif.: Wadsworth), pp. 33–41.

37. For a discussion of the sorts of abstractions that are and are not legitimate, see Antony, "Sisters, Please," p. 62.

38. Antony, "Sisters, Please," p. 88.

39. Antony, "Sisters, Please," pp. 89–90.

40. Some important contributions to this topic include Cherie Moraga and Gloria Anzaldúa, eds., *This Bridge Called My Back: Writings by Radical Women of Color* (Watertown, Mass.: Persephone, 1981); María Lugones and Elizabeth Spelman, "Have We Got a Theory for You: Feminist Theory, Cultural Imperialism, and the Demand for 'The Woman's Voice,'" *Women's Studies International Forum* 6 (1983): 573–581; bell hooks, *Feminist Theory from Margin to Center* (Boston: South End, 1984); Elizabeth Spelman, *Inessential Woman* (Boston: Beacon, 1988).

41. See Nancy Hartsock, "The Feminist Standpoint: Developing the Ground for a Specifically Feminist Historical Materialism," in *Discovering Reality: Feminist Perspectives on Epistemology, Metaphysics, Methodology, and Philosophy of Science*, ed. Sandra Harding and Merrill Hintikka (Dordrecht: Reidel, 1983), pp. 283–310.

42. We might be able to state maxims such as "Believe the proposition best supported by evidence," but they can offer no concrete help.

43. Kassindja, *Do They Hear You When You Cry?* p. 368.

44. Williams, *Dessa Rose*, p. 205.

45. Williams, *Dessa Rose*, p. 147.

9

THOUGH THIS BE METHOD, YET THERE IS MADNESS IN IT: PARANOIA AND LIBERAL EPISTEMOLOGY

NAOMI SCHEMAN

When you do not see plurality in the very structure of a theory, what do you see?
María Lugones, "On the Logic of Pluralist Feminism"

Somewhere every culture has an imaginary zone for what it excludes, and it is that zone we must try to remember today.
Catherine Clément, *The Newly Born Woman*

In an article entitled "The Politics of Epistemology," Morton White argues that it is not in general possible to ascribe a unique political character to a theory of knowledge.[1] In particular, he explores what he takes to be the irony that the epistemologies developed by John Locke and John Stuart Mill for explicitly progressive and democratic ends have loopholes that allow for undemocratic interpretation and application. The loopholes White identifies concern in each case the methods by which authority is granted or recognized.

Neither Locke nor Mill acknowledges any higher epistemic authority than human reason, which they take (however differently they define it) as generic to the human species and not the possession of some favored few. But for both of them, as for most other democratically minded philosophers (White discusses also John Dewey and Charles Sanders Peirce), there needs to be some way of distinguishing between the exercise of reason and the workings of something else, variously characterized as degeneracy, madness, immaturity, backwardness, ignorance, passion, prejudice, or some other state of mind that permanently or temporarily impairs the development or proper use of reason. That is, democracy is seen as needing to be defended against "the excesses of unbridled relativism and subjectivism" ("Politics," 90).

The success of such a defense depends on the assumption that if we eliminate the voices of those lacking in the proper use of reason, we will be eliminating (or at least substantially "bridling") relativism. This, I take it, can only mean that those whose voices are listened to will (substantially) agree, at least about those things that are thought to be matters of knowledge, whether they be scientific or common-sense statements of fact or fundamental moral and political principles or specific judgments of right or wrong. To some extent this assumption is tautological: It is frequently by "disagreeing" about things the rest of us take for granted that one is counted as mad, ignorant, or otherwise not possessed of reason. But precisely that tautologousness is at the root of what White identifies as the loophole through which the antidemocratic can pass: Moral, political, and epistemological elitism is most attractive (to the elite) and most objectionable (to others) when the nonelite would say something different from what gets said on their behalf, allegedly in the name of their own more enlightened selves.

White argues that the democratic nature of an epistemology cannot be read off its face but is in part a matter of its historically specific application:

> Whether such a philosophy will be democratic in its effect depends on the ease with which the ordinary man may attain the privileged status described in the epistemology or the moral philosophy of the democratically oriented thinker. Where, because of social conditions, large numbers of persons in the community are not thought by such a philosopher to be able to see what their moral duties and rights are because they lack the attributes of a fully equipped moral judge, then the democratic intentions stand a good chance of being subverted ("Politics," 91–92).

It's unclear to me why White thinks that the antidemocratic subversion of an intentionally democratic epistemology depends specifically on philosophers' beliefs about who can exemplify their theories. Surely, such subversion depends at least as much on the ways in which that theory is understood and applied by others and on the beliefs of those others about who does and does not satisfy the philosopher's criteria of enfranchisement. Such beliefs may even, as I will argue is the case with René Descartes, contradict the philosopher's own explicit statements. Authorial intent is not determinative of how democratic an epistemology is: Having constructed a loophole, theorists do not retain the authority to determine what can pass through it.

White's own unselfconscious use of 'man' in what I assume he intends to be a generic sense is, ironically, a case in point. As has been argued by many feminist theorists,[2] masculine nouns and pronouns do not, in fact, have genuinely generic senses. Rather, in designating the masculine *as* generic, they designate the feminine as different, thereby requiring an act of self-estrangement on the part of female readers who would take themselves to be included in their scope. And all too often (frequently despite the stated beliefs of philosophers themselves), women have *not* been included among the rational, the mature, the unprejudiced. Historically, more often than not, in the real worlds in which philosophers' theories have been interpreted, the vast majority of women—along with many men—have been barred from or thought incapable of attaining "the privileged status described in the epistemology or the moral philosophy of the democratically oriented thinker[s]."

A striking feature of the advance of liberal political and epistemological theory and practice over the past three hundred years has been the increase in the ranks of the politically and epistemically enfranchised. It would seem, that is, that the loopholes have been successively narrowed, that fewer and fewer are being relegated to the hinterlands of incompetence or unreliability. In one sense, of course, this is true: Race, sex, and property ownership are no longer explicit requirements for voting, officeholding, or access to education in most countries. But just as exclusionary gestures can operate to separate groups of people, so similar gestures can operate intrapsychically to separate those aspects of people that, if acknowledged, would disqualify them from full enfranchisement. We can understand the advance of liberalism as the progressive internalization—through regimes of socialization and pedagogy—of norms of self-constitution that (oxymoronically) "democratize privilege."

Thus various civil rights agendas in the United States have proceeded by promulgating the idea that underneath the superficial differences of skin color, genitalia, or behavior in the bedroom, Blacks, women, and gays and lesbians are really just like straight white men. Not, of course, the other way around: Difference and similarity are only apparently symmetrical terms. In the logic of political identity, to be among the privileged is to be among the same, and for the different to join those ranks has demanded the willingness to separate the difference-bearing aspects of their identity, to demonstrate what increasingly liberal regimes were increasingly willing to acknowledge: that one didn't need, for example, be a man to embrace the deep structure of misogyny. It is one of my aims to argue that the norms that have structured modern epistemic authority have required the internalization of such exclusionary gestures, the splitting off and denial of (or control over) aspects of the self that have been associated with the lives of the disenfranchised, and that those gestures exhibit the logic of paranoia.

This process of "democratizing privilege" is inherently unstable. Materially, it runs up against the requirement of capitalism for significant numbers of people who are outside the reasonably affluent, paid labor force: the vast majority of people in the Third World, as well as those in affluent countries who are unemployed or marginally employed or who work only in the home—that is, those whose bodies literally are the foundation on which privileged subjectivity rests. As more and more of those Others lay claim to stand on the ground that their bodies have constituted, that ground gets predictably unstable.[3] Ideologically, expanding the ranks of the same runs up against the rise of the wide varieties of nationalisms and identity politics that have followed on the recognition by large numbers of people that they have all been attempting to impersonate a small minority of the world's population, and that it might instead be both desirable and possible to claim enfranchisement as the particular people they happen to be. Recent work in epistemology and philosophy of science, much of it explicitly influenced by Ludwig Wittgenstein or W. V. Quine (neither of whom would embrace either the explanations or the political agenda at issue here), can be seen as responsive to the need, given these challenges, for an epistemology that breaks with the structures of modernity by eschewing the homogenization of foundationalism and allowing for the democratic enfranchisement of explicitly and irreducibly diverse subjects. Knowledge rests not on universally recognizable and unassailable premises but on the social labor of historically embodied communities of knowers.

Part of my aim is to provide an account of what I think underlies this shift in mainstream Anglo-American epistemology and philosophy of science, to place that shift in social and historical context. But I am also concerned with the extent to which much work is still captive to older pictures, notably in the continuing dominance of individualism in the philosophy of psychology. A fully social conception of knowledge that embraces diversity among knowers requires a corresponding conception of persons as irreducibly diverse and essentially interconnected. The individualism of modern personhood entails a denial both of connection and of individuality: Modern subjects are distinct but not distinctive. Philosophers have taken this subject as theirs: It is his (*sic*) problems that have defined the field, the problems of anyone who takes on the tasks of internalizing the norms of privilege. As these norms change, so must the corresponding conceptions of personhood.

It is in this light that I want to examine the influence of Descartes's writings, works of intentionally democratic epistemology that explicitly include women in the scope of those they enfranchise. I have argued elsewhere, as have many others,[4] for the undemocratic nature of the influence of Cartesian epistemology, an influence that extends even to those epistemologies standardly treated as most antithetical to it (notably, empiricism). In particular, I want to argue that the structures of characteristically modern epistemic authority (with science as the central paradigm) normalized strategies of self-constitution drawn from Cartesian Method. The discipline that is meant to ensure that proper use of the Method will not lead to "unbridled relativism and subjectivism," although intended by Descartes to be both liberatory and democratic, has come to mirror the repressions that mark the achievement of privilege. Those strategies find, I believe, a peculiarly revelatory echo in the autobiographical writings of Daniel Paul Schreber and in their use in Freud's theory of paranoia.[5] Ironically, by the very moves that were meant to ensure universal enfranchisement, the epistemology that has grounded modern science and liberal politics not only has provided the means for excluding, for most of its history, most of the human race but also has constructed, for those it authorizes, a normative paranoia.

I
Schreber

> The pedagogical conviction that one must bring a child into line . . . has its origin in the need to split off the disquieting parts of the inner self and project them onto an available object. . . . The enemy within can at last be hunted down on the outside.[6]

[Anti-Semites] are people who are afraid. Not of the Jews, to be sure, but of themselves, of their own consciousness, of their instincts, of their responsibilities, of solitariness, of change, of society, and of the world—of everything except the Jews. . . . Anti-Semitism, in short, is fear of the human condition. The Anti-Semite is a person who wishes to be a pitiless stone, a furious torrent, a devastating thunderbolt—anything except a human being.[7]

Daniel Paul Schreber, a German judge, was thrice hospitalized for mental illness. After a brief confinement in a Leipzig clinic in 1884–1885, he recovered sufficiently to serve as *Senatspräsident* (head of a panel of judges) in Dresden. He was rehospitalized in 1893 until 1903, when he left the asylum after succeeding in a legal suit for his release from "tutelage" (that is, involuntary state guardianship). He returned to the asylum in 1907 and remained there until his death in 1911, the same year Freud published the case history based on the *Memoirs of My Nervous Illness*, which Schreber published in 1903 to draw attention to what he took to be happening to him.

Subsequent discussions of Schreber's case and of the *Memoirs* have taken issue with Freud's account. Sam Weber, in his introduction to recent republications (in German and English) of the *Memoirs*, gives a Lacanian reading of the text; and Morton Schatzman, in *Soul Murder: Persecution in the Family*,[8] takes Schreber's account as a transformed but intelligible description of what was done to him as a child by his father, Daniel Gottlieb Moritz Schreber. The elder Schreber was a renowned doctor whose theories of child rearing were exceedingly influential in the development of some of the more extreme forms of what Alice Miller describes as "poisonous pedagogy,"[9] by which she means the accepted, even normative, use of coercion and violence against children supposedly "for their own good." I find helpful correctives to Freud both in Weber's Lacanian remarks and, especially, in Schatzman's antipsychoanalytic analysis"[10] (to which I will return); but I want to start with Freud's account, in part because its logical structure mirrors that of the *Meditations* and the *Discourse on Method*.

Freud suggests that central to symptom-formation in paranoia is the process of projection, but that this process can't be definitive of paranoia, in part because it appears elsewhere—for example, "when we refer the causes of certain sensations to the external world, instead of looking for them (as we do in the case of others) inside ourselves" (*SE*, 12:66). He expresses the intention of returning to a general theory of (nonpathological as well as pathological) projection, but he never does. I want to suggest that the account he does give—of projection as a mechanism of paranoia—is closer to such a general theory than he thought it to be, because the relationship to the external world that was epistemically normative in his time and in ours is, by that account, paranoid.

Paranoia, for Freud, starts with the repression of a homosexual wishful fantasy— that is, for a man, sexual desire for another man.[11] In paranoia, as in all cases of repression more generally, there is a detachment of libido: What is previously cathected becomes "indifferent and irrelevant" (*SE*, 12:70). In paranoia this decathexis spreads from its original object to the external world as a whole, and the detached libido attaches itself to the ego, resulting in megalomania.[12] It is the subsequently megaloma-

niacally recreated world that is permanently hostile to the paranoid: "The human subject has recaptured a relation, and often a very intense one, to the people and things in
the world, even though the relation is a hostile one now, where formerly it was hope-
fully affectionate" (*SE,* 12:71).

The hostility of the re-created world is a function of the mechanism of projection. The repression of the fantasy of loving a man takes the form of its contradiction,
"I *hate* him," which is transformed by projection into "*he* hates—and persecutes—*me,*
which justifies my hating him." Freud says only that the "mechanism of symptom-
formation in paranoia requires that internal perceptions—feelings—shall be replaced
by external perceptions" (*SE,* 12:63). Presumably an account of just why such replacement should be required was to await the never-delivered general account of projection, but the mechanism isn't very mysterious: Placing all the initiating feeling out
there, on what had been its object, is a far more effective way of shielding the ego
from the acknowledgment of its own forbidden desires than would be a simple transformation of love into (inexplicable) hate.

The hostile forces in Schreber's world—God and his "rays"—are unequivocally
male, and he believes that part of their plan is to transform him into a woman. The
meaning of the transformation is twofold. Men, according to Schreber, have "nerves of
voluptuousness" only in and immediately around their penises, whereas women's entire bodies are suffused with such nerves (*Memoirs,* p. 204). God is directing toward
Schreber, who has captured all of God's attention, rays that stimulate these nerves, requiring Schreber to "strive to give divine rays the impression of a woman in the
height of sexual delight" by imagining himself "as man and woman in one person
having intercourse with myself," an activity that Schreber insists, obviously protest-
ing too much, "has nothing whatever to do with any idea of masturbation or anything
like it" (*Memoirs,* p. 208). The rays also impose demands, in the form of compulsive
thinking, on Schreber's "nerves of intellect," and he is forced to strike a balance between intellectual thought and sensual ecstasy. But, most important, he must attempt
always to be engaged in one or the other:

> As soon as I allow a pause in my thinking without devoting myself to the cul-
> tivation of voluptuousness—which is unavoidable as nobody can either think
> all the time or always cultivate voluptuousness—the following unpleasant con-
> sequences . . . occur: attacks of bellowing and bodily pain; vulgar noises from
> the madmen around me, and cries of "help" from God. Mere common sense
> therefore commands that as far as humanly possible I fill every pause in my
> thinking—in other words the periods of rest from intellectual activity—with
> the cultivation of voluptuousness. (*Memoirs,* pp. 210–211)

In addition to being provided with soul-voluptuousness, God's other aim in
"unmanning" him was eventual "fertilization with divine rays for the purpose of creating new human beings." Schreber was cognizant of the humiliating aspects of his
position: The rays themselves taunted him, saying such things as, "Fancy a person
who was a *Senatspräsident* allowing himself to be f . . . d." He initially entered into

complicity with his transformation into a woman at a time when he believed that he was the only real person existing: "All the human shapes I saw were only 'fleeting and improvised,' so that there could be no question of any ignominy being attached to unmanning" (*Memoirs*, p. 148). He subsequently defends the essential honor of his position as an accommodation with necessity and with God's will: "Since then I have wholeheartedly inscribed the cultivation of femininity on my banner. . . . I would like to meet the man who, faced with the choice of either becoming a demented human being in male habitus or a spirited woman, would not prefer the latter" (*Memoirs*, p. 149).

The logic of Schreber's madness seems to me not that of homosexuality, repressed or otherwise. His delusions mirrored his treatment as a boy at the hands of his father, and his madness indicts that treatment even while preserving the idealization of the powerful father who administered it. What that combination of terror and enthralled submission in the face of remembered or imagined male power does reflect is the logic of male homophobia. 'Homophobia' is often used as though it meant the same thing for women as for men; but, given the very different social constructions of female and male sexuality, there is no reason to think this should be so. In particular, male homophobia attaches with greatest force not to the general idea of sexual desire for another man but to the specific idea of being in the receptive position sexually. Given a culturally normative definition of sexuality in terms of male domination and female subordination, there is an understandable anxiety attached to a man's imagining another man's doing to him what men are expected to do to women: Real men, *Senatspräsidenten* or not, are not supposed to allow themselves to be fucked. (Thus in men's prisons, the stigma attaches not to rapists but to their victims.)

Male homophobia combines this anxiety with its corresponding desire, that of being, as we might say, ravished,[13] or swept away. It's notoriously difficult to speak—or think—clearly about such desires or pleasures, a difficulty made apparent by the intertwinings of rape and rapture (which themselves share a common Latin root) in the *Oxford English Dictionary*'s definition of 'ravish.' The story seems to be the bad old one of the woman falling in love with the man who rapes her, a staple of pornography and Gothic romance and barely veiled in Freudian accounts of normative femininity and in fairy tales. (Did Sleeping Beauty consent to the Prince's kiss?) Part of what is so insidious about these stories is that they link violence and domination to the pleasures of release—for example, the pleasure that sneezing can be, the sudden unwilled flood of sensation. Not, that is, *against* our will, inflicted upon us and a threat to our integrity, but *un*willed, a respite from will, a momentary reprieve from the exigencies of bodily discipline, an affront not to our humanity but to our solemnity, not to our self-respect but to our self-conceit. (The unlinking of such pleasure from the sadomasochistic structure of normative sexuality—the uncoupling of rape from rapture—is a fairy tale worth believing in, even if we can't quite tell it clearly.)

Schreber enacts both the anxiety and the desire: His body and mind are wracked by the struggle to resist what he ultimately succumbs to—being "unmanned" in the name of perpetual feminine "voluptuousness." His compensation for being subjected to such humiliating pleasure is the knowledge both that God has singled him out to receive it and that from his feminized loins will issue a new race of humans to re-create the world. Homophobia thus gets joined to another venerable fantasy structure: the usurpation by men of women's reproductive power. At least as far back as Socrates, men have taken the imagery of childbirth to describe their allegedly nobler, sublimated creative activities. Schreber's fantasies expose the homophobic anxieties that underlie the use of this imagery: You can't give birth without being fucked.

II
Descartes

They are, in essence, captives of a peculiar arrogance, the arrogance of not knowing that they do not know what it is that they do not know, yet they speak as if they know what all of us need to know.[14]

Cartesian philosophy is a paradigmatic example of White's thesis about the subversion of the democratic intent of an epistemology, although not because of Descartes's own views about who it authorized. Descartes's explicit intent was the epistemic authorization of individuals as such—not as occupiers of particular social locations, including the social location of gender.[15] Most important, Descartes wanted to secure epistemic authority for individual knowers, who would depend on their own resources and not on the imprimatur of those in high places, and, he argues, those resources could only be those of mathematized reason, not those of the senses. Only such a use of reason could ensure the sort of stability that distinguishes knowledge from mere opinion. Descartes's Method was designed to allow anyone who used it to place him- or herself beyond the influence of anything that could induce error. Human beings, he argues, were not created as naturally and inevitably subject to error: God wouldn't have done that. What we are is finite, hence neither omniscient nor infallible. But if we recognize our limits and shield ourselves from the influence of what we cannot control, we can be assured that what we take ourselves to know is, in fact, true.

The Method is a form of discipline requiring acts of will to patrol a perimeter around our minds, allowing in only what can be determined to be trustworthy and controlling the influence of the vicissitudes of our bodies and of other people. Purged of bad influences, we will be struck by the "clarity and distinctness" of truths like the cogito.[16] We will have no real choice but to acknowledge their truth, but we ought not to find in such lack of choice any diminution of our freedom. Because the perception of truth comes from within us, not "determined by any external force," we are free in assenting to it, just as we are free when we choose what we fully and unambivalently want, even though it makes no sense to imagine that, given our desire, we might just as well have chosen otherwise.[17]

Freedom from determination by any external force requires, for Descartes, freedom from determination by the body, which is, with respect to the mind, an external force. Thus when Descartes invokes the malicious demon at the end of the First Meditation to help steel him against lazily slipping back into credulity,[18] his efforts are of a piece with his presentation at the end of *The Passions of the Soul* of "a general remedy against the passions."[19] Passions are no more to be dispensed with entirely than are perceptions (or, strictly speaking, *other* perceptions, given that passions are for Descartes a species of perception). But no more than other perceptions are passions to be taken at face value: They can be deceptive and misleading. Still less are they to be taken uncritically as motives to act, whether the action in question be running in fear from the dagger I perceive before me or assenting to its real existence. In both cases, I (my mind) need to exercise control over my perceptions or, at least, over what I choose to do in the face of them. Seeing ought *not* to be believing in the case of literal, embodied vision, but when ideas are seen by the light of reason in the mind's eye, assent does and should follow freely.[20]

The individualism of Cartesian epistemology is yoked to its universalism: Though we are each to pursue knowledge on our own, freed from the influence of any other people, what we come up with is not supposed to be our own view of the world—it is supposed to be the truth, unique and invariable. When Descartes extols, in the *Discourse*,[21] the greater perfection of buildings or whole towns that are the work of a single planner over those that sprang up in an uncoordinated way, he may seem to be extolling the virtues of individuality. But what he finds pleasing are not the signs of individual style; it is the determining influence of reason as opposed to chance. Individualism is the route not to the idiosyncrasies of individuality but to the universality of reason.

This consequence is hardly accidental. Scepticism, which was a tool for Descartes, was for some of his contemporaries the ultimate, inevitable consequence of ceding epistemic authority to individual reason. If epistemic democratization was not to lead to the nihilism of the Pyrrhonists or the modesty of Montaigne, Descartes needed to demonstrate that what his Method produced was knowledge, not a cacophony of opinion.[22] It could not turn out to be the case that the world appeared quite different when viewed by people differently placed in it. More precisely, everyone had to be persuaded that if it *did* appear different from where they stood, the remedy was to move to the Archimedean point defined by the discipline of Cartesian Method. Those who could not so move were, in the manner of White's discussion, relegated to the ranks of the epistemically disenfranchised.

Descartes himself does not, so far as I know, consider the possibility that not everyone of sufficient maturity could actually use his Method: The only disqualifying attribute I know he explicitly discusses is youth.[23] He does, of course, briefly consider in the First Meditation the possibility that he is mad or asleep and dreaming, but his aim there is to argue that it makes no difference: The cogito would still be true and knowable. Later, when he needs to go beyond those confines to areas in which sanity and a certain degree of consciousness can be presumed to make a difference, he needs, for the sake of his argument, to rely on first-person accessible signs that his mind is in working order: There's no way in which the judgment of others could be allowed to undercut the agent's own sense of being epistemically trustworthy.

It is central to Descartes's project, as it is to the social and political significance of that project, that no one and nothing other than agents themselves can confer or confirm epistemic authority (despite God's being its ultimate guarantor: His guarantee consists precisely in our each individually possessing such authority). Epistemic authority resides in the exercise of will that disciplines one's acts of assent—principally to refrain from assenting to whatever is not perceived clearly and distinctly.[24] And the will, for Descartes, is not only equally distributed among all people but is also, in each of us, literally infinite: What is required is not the acquisition of some capacity the exercise of which might be thought to be unequally available to all; rather, it is the curbing of a too-ready willingness to believe.

Of course, such restraint will lead only to the avoidance of error; in order actually to acquire knowledge, one has also to clearly and distinctly perceive ideas to which one will, freely and inevitably, assent. But even such acquisition is, for Descartes, not reserved for the few, and even it is more a matter of disciplining the interference of distracting and misleading influences from the body, and from the external world through the body, than it is a positive matter of access to recondite truths. We need to train ourselves to quiet the ceaseless chatter of inner and outer perception, to curb, for example, the wonder we feel at the appearance of what seems to us unusual and extraordinary. A certain degree of wonder is useful for retaining in memory what we might otherwise fail to register sufficiently, but wonder, if unchecked, draws our attention hither and yon, when we should be intentionally directing it along the lines of thoughtful investigation. In his discussion of wonder Descartes does distinguish among people who are "dull and stupid," or "ignorant" because "not naturally inclined to wonder," or inclined to excessive, distracting wonder because "though equipped with excellent common sense, [they] have no high opinion of their abilities."[25] But none of these differences are differences in *intellect:* In our active capacities as knowers we are all, for Descartes, absolutely equal, and by disciplining our overactive wills, we can all bring our problematic (and unequal) bodies into line.

But, as I argued above, there is no reason why philosophers' own views about who can and cannot fully exemplify their requirements of epistemic enfranchisement should carry any special weight when the question concerns the democratic or antidemocratic effect of their theories, especially as those theories have been influential far beyond those philosophers' lifetimes. Descartes is a paradigmatic case in point.

The Cartesian subject was revolutionary. The individual bearer of modern epistemic authority became, through variations on the originating theme of self-constitution, the bourgeois bearer of rights, the self-made capitalist, the citizen of the nation-state, and the Protestant bound by conscience and a personal relationship to God. In Descartes's writings we find the lineaments of the construction of that new subject, and we see the centrality of discipline to its constitution. Such discipline is supposed in theory to be available to all, not only to those whose birth gave them a privileged place in the world. If one was placed where one could not see the truth, or obtain riches, or exercise political or religious freedom, the solution was to move to some more privileged and privileging place. The "New World" was precisely constituted by the self-defining gestures of those who moved there from Europe and who subsequently got to determine who among those who followed would be allowed to take a stand on the common ground. (That constitution of the "New World" is one reason why the people who already lived there merited so little consideration in the eyes of those who invaded their home. The relationship the Indians took—and take—themselves to have to the land, a relationship grounded in their unchosen, unquestionable ties to it, was precisely the wrong relationship from the perspective of those who came to that land in order to define themselves anew by willfully claiming it, unfettered by history.)

With the success of the revolutions prefigured in the Cartesian texts, it became clear that the theoretical universalism that was their underpinning existed in problematic tension with actual oppression. Those who succeeded in embodying the ideals of subjecthood oppressed those whose places in the world (from which, for various reasons, they could not move[26]) were (often) to perform the labor on which the existence and well-being of the enfranchised depended and (always) to represent the aspects of embodied humanness that the more privileged denied in themselves.

The 'often' and 'always' in the preceding sentence reflect differences in the form taken by the oppression of various groups and the concomitant applicability of various methods for explaining that oppression. With respect to certain groups, most clearly the working class but also many women and people of color, oppression has been in large measure a matter of exploitation. Members of privileged groups benefit directly from the labor done by the exploited, whose oppression is a function both of the theft of their labor and of the ideological representation of that labor as disenfranchising. Such labor is disenfranchising either positively, in that its nature (for example, the bearing and rearing of children) is taken to be incompatible with intellection, or negatively, in that it doesn't allow for the leisure to cultivate the "higher" capacities that authorize the enfranchised.

For other oppressed groups, notably gay men, lesbians, and the disabled, the element of exploitation is either missing or at least far less evident, and an economic analysis of why they are oppressed is less evidently promising. It is striking, however, that such groups share with the others the representation of their supposed natures as incompatible with full social, political, and epistemic authority. For various reasons they are portrayed in hegemonic discourses as incapable of full participation in public life: They are put into one or more of the categories of disenfranchisement that White discusses. All the oppressed—the obviously exploited and the others—share in the minds of the privileged a defining connection to the body—whether it is seen primarily as the laboring body, the sexual body, the body insufficiently under the control of the rational will, or some combination of these. The privileged are precisely those who are defined not by the meanings and uses of their bodies for others but by their ability either to control their bodies for their own ends or to seem to exist virtually bodilessly. They are those who have conquered the sexual, dependent, mortal, and messy parts of themselves—in part by projecting all those qualities onto others, whom they thereby earn the right to dominate and, if the occasion arises, to exploit.

Exploitation and oppression are, of course, enormous and enormously complicated phenomena, and there is no reason to believe that one theory will account for all their aspects and ramifications, all their causes and effects.[27] There are also reasons for being generally suspicious of the felt need for, what are called by their critics, grand or totalizing theories or master narratives.[28] It is certainly not my intent either to give or to invoke any such theory. Rather, as Sandra Harding argues,[29] we (those who would seek to understand these phenomena with the aim of ending them) need to embrace not only methodological pluralism but even the "instabilities and incoherencies" (*Science Question,* p. 244) that come with theorizing during times of large-scale intellectual, social, and political change. In that spirit, I see this essay as part of what we might call the social psychology of privilege, an examination not of the apparently economically rational grounds for exploitation-based oppression, but of the deep springs that feed such oppression as well as the oppressions that seem on their face less rational.

Privilege, as it has historically belonged to propertied, heterosexual, able-bodied, white men, and as it has been claimed in liberal terms by those who are variously different, has rested on the successful disciplining of one's mind and its relation to one's body and to the bodies and minds of others. The discourses of gender, race, class, and physical and cognitive abilities have set up dichotomies that, in each case, have normalized one side as the essentially human and stigmatized the other, usually in terms that stress the need for control and the inability of the stigmatized to control themselves. Acts of violence directed against oppressed groups typically are presented by their oppressors as preemptive strikes, justified by the dangers posed by the supposedly less-civilized, less-disciplined natures of those being suppressed. Workplace surveillance through lie detectors and drug testing (procedures in which subjects' bodies are made to testify to the inadequacies of their minds and wills), programs of social control to police the sexual behavior of homosexuals, the paternalistic disempowerment of the disabled, increasing levels of verbal and physical attacks on students of color by other students, and the pervasive terrorism of random violence against women all bespeak the need on the part of the privileged to control the bodies and behavior of those who are "different," a need that both in its targets and in its gratuitous fierceness goes beyond securing the advantages of exploitation.

Cartesian strategies of epistemic authorization, viewed through the lens of Schreber's paranoia, are illuminating here. As the authorized subject constitutes himself by contrast with the disenfranchised others, so he constitutes himself by contrast with the world that is the object of his knowledge. He also, by the same gestures, reciprocally constitutes that world. Freud, in his discussion of Schreber, quotes Goethe's *Faust:*

> Woe! Woe!
> Thou hast it destroyed,
> The beautiful world,
> With powerful fist!
> In ruins 'tis hurled,
> By the blow of a demigod shattered!
> . . . .
> Mightier
> For the children of men,

More splendid
Build it again,
In thine own bosom build it anew![30]

The gesture is not only Schreber's; it is, of course, Descartes's. Like Schreber, Descartes imaginatively destroys the world through the withdrawal of his attachment to it (he becomes agnostic about its very existence), and like Schreber, his ego is thereby aggrandized and goes about the task of reconstituting the world, or a semblance of it, under the problematic aegis of an all-powerful father. This reconstituted world is perceived as hostile—made up as it is of everything the ego has split off—and as permanently in need of vigilant control. It is also perceived, and needs to be perceived, as independent of the self as the self needs to be perceived as independent of it. There can be no acknowledgment of the self's complicity in the constitution of the world as an object of knowledge: "Indeed," as Paul Smith puts it, "it is the desired fate of both paranoia and classical realism to be construed as interpretations of an already existing world, even though the world they both create is their own."[31]

Smith notes the need of the paranoiac (or that of the humanist intellectual—he has in mind, in particular, hermeneutically inclined anthropologists such as Clifford Geertz) "to objectify or *realize* a reality and yet to proclaim the 'subject's' innocence of its formation" (*Discerning the Subject,* p. 87; emphasis in original). Not only as hostile—or exotic—but as real, the world has to be regarded as wholly independent of the self. And the very activity of securing that independence has to be repressed; the subject and the world have to be innocent of each other, unimplicated in each other's identity.[32]

Despite Descartes's genuinely democratic intentions, as his epistemology was taken up by those who followed him, it authorized those—and only those—whose subject positions were constituted equally by their relationship to a purportedly objective world and by their relationship to the disenfranchised Others, defined by their inescapable, undisciplined bodies.

III
Paranoia, Discipline, and Modernity

Whatever we seek in philosophy, or whatever leads us to ask philosophical questions at all, must be something pretty deep in human nature, and what leads us to ask just the questions we do in the particular ways we now ask them must be something pretty deep in our tradition.[33]

The most influential theorist of surveillance, discipline, and control is Michel Foucault. His *Discipline and Punish: The Birth of the Prison* traces the development and deployment of characteristically modern systems of power as pervasively applied to the bodies of the subjugated; his *The History of Sexuality,* volume 1, looks at those systems largely as they shape subjectivity, desire, and knowledge.[34] In both cases power is not the simple possession of certain individuals or groups; rather, it is omnipresent, constitutive as much as constraining, expressed through the tissue of our personal and institutional lives.[35] But whereas the forms of administrative power discussed in *Discipline and Punish* construct individuals as objects, the discursive constructions of sex construct us as subjects in what we take to be our freedom, the expression of our desire. As we struggle against what we have learned to call repression, we speak our desire in terms that construct it—and us—according to a distinctively modern regime, even as we take ourselves to be striving toward the liberation of timelessly human wants and needs.[36]

I want to use Foucault to bring together Descartes and Schreber. With the success of the economic, social, cultural, and political revolutions that empowered the Cartesian subject,[37] the discipline Descartes called for moved from being the self-conscious work of self-constituting radicals to finding expression in the pedagogy of the privileged.[38] The soul-shaping regimes of the elder Schreber are a particularly stark version of that pedagogy, which finds coded expression in the *Memoirs* of Freud's Schreber and a chilling critique in the works of Alice Miller.

Morton Schatzman's *Soul Murder* is a detailed argument for the thesis that Schreber's *Memoirs* recount in coded form what his father did to him when he was a child. Daniel Gottlieb Moritz Schreber wrote prolifically about child-rearing regimes aimed at suppressing a child's will and replacing it with automatic obedience to the will of the parent while simultaneously inculcating in the child enormous powers of self-control, which the child was to exercise over his or her own body and desires. That is, the goal was not an attitude of subservient obedience, such that children would have no idea of what they were to do until commanded by their parents. Rather, the child's will was to be replaced by the will of the parent in such a way that the child would not notice (or, at least, would not remember[39]) that this was done and would henceforth act "autonomously," as though the now-internalized commands came from her or his own true self. And that commanding self needs precisely not to be weak and unassertive, charged as it is with keeping under control the child's unruly body, emotions, and desires.

Not surprisingly, prominent among the desires and unruly impulses that need to be kept under control are those connected with masturbation and sexual curiosity. Foucault's characterization of modern Europe as hardly silent about sexuality is borne out by Miller's examples of instructional techniques for extracting from children confessions of masturbation (*For Your Own Good,* pp. 18–21) and of arguments that sexual curiosity needs to be (albeit perhaps fraudulently) satisfied, lest it grow obsessive. One recommended means is to have children view naked corpses, because "the sight of a corpse evokes solemnity and reflection, and this is the most appropriate mood for a child under such circumstances" (*For Your Own Good,* p. 46). J. Oest, whose advice this was in 1787, also advised "that children be cleansed from head to foot every two to four weeks by an old, dirty, and ugly woman, without anyone else being present; still, parents should make sure that even this old woman doesn't linger unnecessarily over any part of the body. This task should be depicted to the children as disgusting, and they should be told that the old woman must be paid to undertake a task that, although necessary for purposes of health and cleanliness, is yet so disgusting that no other person can bring himself to do it" (*For Your Own Good,* pp. 46–47).

Miller quotes extensively from the elder Schreber as well as from these and other, similar eighteenth- and nineteenth-century pedagogues who counseled parents on how, for example, "exercises can aid in the complete suppression of affect" (*For Your Own Good,* p. 25; the counsel comes from J. Sulzer, whose *Essay on the Education and Instruction of Children* was published in German in 1748). The same theorist made it clear that such suppression of autonomy was not intended only or even primarily for those whose place in society was subordinate: "Obedience is so important that all education is actually nothing other than learning how to obey. It is a generally recognized principle that persons of high estate who are destined to rule whole nations must learn the art of governance by way of first learning obedience. . . . [T]he reason for this is that obedience teaches a person to be zealous in observing the law, which is the first quality of the ruler" (*For Your Own Good,* pp. 13–14).

The choreography of will breaking and will strengthening has one additional turn: The shaping fiction of the enterprise is that the unruliness of children, however omnipresent, is nonetheless unnatural. In Schreber's words, "The noble seeds of human nature sprout upwards in their purity almost of their own accord if the ignoble ones, the weeds, are sought out and destroyed in time."[40] Thus the parental will that replaces the child's is in fact more truly expressive of the child's true nature than was the "bad" will the child took to be her or his own. It is not just that children should come to think so.

All this is, of course, much more reminiscent of Kant than of Descartes. It is Kant who argued that our passions are not expressive of our true, autonomous selves and, hence, that acting on them is neither morally right nor autonomous, and that those categories—the lawbound and the free—are actually identical. It is Kant who most clearly taught us to control our passions[41] and to identify with a self that we experience not as idiosyncratic but as speaking in the voice of impartial reason. Descartes, on the other hand, seems far more human, more playful, more respectful of the body and the emotions, more intrigued by the diversity in the world around him, more—and this is the crucial difference—antiauthoritarian than Kant.

As, of course, he was. He was in the midst of making the revolution that the pedagogues and Kant inherited, and it was a revolution precisely against entrenched authority, a revolution waged in the name of the individual. There is an exhilaration that even today's undergraduates can find in reading Descartes; he can speak, for example, to the woman student who is in the midst of discovering for herself that she has been systematically lied to about the world and her place in it, that authorities she had trusted disagree with each other and that none of them seems to have it right, and that even her own body can be untrustworthy: She may, for example, find food repulsive because even as she becomes emaciated she sees herself as hideously fat, or she may have learned from a sexual abuser to desire her own humiliation.

But, I want to argue, the Descartes we have inherited (and, more broadly, the liberal politics his epistemology partially grounds[42]) is a problematic ally for this young woman, as he is for the other women and men who have been the excluded Others. Though he is not Kant, let alone Schreber (either the paranoid son or the "paranoidogenic"[43] father), the discipline of the Method that lies at the heart of Descartes's constitution of himself as epistemically authoritative bears the seeds of paranoia, seeds that germinated as the revolution he helped to inaugurate moved from marginality to hegemony.

As Freud argues, the central mechanism of paranoia is projection, that process by which something that had been recognized as a part of the self is detached from it (a process called "splitting") and reattached onto something or someone other than the self. An underlying motivation for such splitting is narcissism: What is split off is incompatible with the developing ego. But it is significant to note that one obvious effect is the diminution of the self—it no longer contains something it once did. One consequence of that recognition is that it provides a motivation for thinking of that which is split off as wholly bad, perhaps even worse than it was thought to be when it was first split off. It has to be clear that the self really is better off without it.

This is one way of thinking about the fate of the body in Cartesian and post-Cartesian epistemology. The self of the cogito establishes its claim to authority precisely by its separation from the body, a separation that is simultaneously liberating and totally isolating. Although Descartes goes on, under the protection of God, to reclaim his body and to place himself in intimate and friendly relation to it, the loss to the self remains: René Descartes, along with all those who would follow his Method, really is a *res cogitans,* not a sensual, bodily person. One can glimpse the magnitude of the loss in Descartes's attempts to theorize his relationship to the body he calls his own, an attempt he ultimately abandons,[44] but the full force of it is found elsewhere, when the demand that one separate from and control one's body is joined both to Christian associations of the body with sin and to the pedagogical practices that replaced Descartes's self-conscious self-constitution.

It became impossible to empower the mind without disempowering and stigmatizing the body, or, in Foucauldian terms, anatomizing, administering, scrutinizing, and disciplining it. The body Descartes regains and bequeaths to his heirs is mechanical, not the lived body but the object of scientific practices, a body best known by being, after its death, dissected. It became the paradigmatic object in an epistemology founded on a firm and unbridgeable subject-object distinction.[45] And it became bad—because it had once been part of the self and it had had to be pushed away, split off, and repudiated. So, too, with everything else from which the authorized self needed to be distinguished and distanced. The rational mind stood over and against the mechanical world of orderly explanation, while the rest—the disorderly, the passionate, the uncontrollable—was relegated to the categories of the "primitive or exotic . . . two new interests in bourgeois society, to compensate for the estranged experience of the bourgeois self."[46]

The Cartesian God—the poisonously pedagogical parent, seen by the successfully reared child as wholly benevolent—conscripts the infinite will of the privileged son and sets it the task of "autonomously" disciplining the body, the perceptions, and the passions, with the promised reward being the revelation of guaranteed truths and the power that goes with knowledge. Evelyn Fox Keller is discussing Francis Bacon, but she could as well be discussing Descartes—or the paranoid Schreber:

> What is sought here is the proper stance for mind necessary to insure the reception of truth and the conception of science. To receive God's truth, the mind must be pure and clean, submissive and open—it must be undefiled and

female. Only then can it give birth to a masculine and virile science. That is, if the mind is pure, receptive and submissive—female—in its relation to God, it can be transformed by God into a forceful, potent and virile agent—male—in its relation to nature. Cleansed of contamination, the mind can be impregnated by God and, in that act, virilized—made potent and capable of generating virile offspring in its union with nature.[47]

Such a self, privileged by its estrangement from its own body, from the "external" world, and from other people, will, in a culture that defines such estrangements as normal, express the paranoia of such a stance not only through oppression but, more benignly, through the problems that are taken as the most fundamental, even if not the most practically pressing: the problems of philosophy. Those problems—notably, the mind-body problem, problems of reference and truth, the problem of other minds, and scepticism about knowledge of the external world—all concern the subject's ability or inability to connect with the split-off parts of itself—its physicality, its sociability. Such problems are literally and unsurprisingly unsolvable so long as the subject's very identity is constituted by those estrangements. A subject whose authority is defined by his location on one side of a gulf cannot authoritatively theorize that gulf away. Philosophers' problems are the neuroses of privilege; discipline makes the difference between such problems and the psychosis of full-blown paranoia.

IV
Beyond Madness and Method

The new *mestiza* copes by developing a tolerance for ambiguity. . . . She has a plural personality, she operates in a pluralistic mode—nothing is thrust out, the good, the bad and the ugly, nothing rejected, nothing abandoned.[48]

The alternative to relativism is partial, locatable, critical knowledges sustaining the possibility of webs of connections called solidarity in politics and shared conversations in epistemology.[49]

The authorized subject thus achieves and maintains his authority by his ability to keep his body and the rest of the world radically separated from his ego, marked off from it by policed boundaries.[50] Within those boundaries, the self is supposed to be unitary and seamless, characterized by the doxastic virtue of noncontradiction and the moral virtue of integrity. The social mechanisms of privilege aid in the achievement of those virtues by facilitating splitting and projection: the unity of the privileged self is maintained by the dumping out of the self—onto the object world or onto the different, the stigmatized Others—everything that would disturb its pristine wholeness.

Various contemporary theorists are articulating alternative conceptions of subjectivity, conceptions that start from plurality and diversity, not just among but, crucially, within subjects.[51] From that starting point flow radically transformed relationships between subjects and between subjects and the world they would know.

One way to approach these discussions is to return to Freud. Mental health for Freud consisted in part in the acknowledgment by the ego of the impulses of the id: "Where id was, there ego shall be."[52] The German is more striking than the English: The German words for 'ego' and 'id' are 'ich' and 'es';[53] the sense is "Where *it* was, there *I* shall be." One can take this in two ways. Under the sorts of disciplinary regimes that constitute epistemic privilege, the exhortation has a colonizing ring to it. The not-I needs to be brought under the civilizing control of the ego; the aim is not to split it off but to tame it. Splitting represents the failure of colonization, the loss of will for the task of domestication. The healthy ego is unified not because it has cast out parts of itself, but because it has effectively administered even the formerly unruly outposts of its dominion. Or so goes the story one is supposed to tell. (Any splitting goes unacknowledged.)

There is another way to take Freud's exhortation. The aim might be not to colonize the "it" but to break down the distinction between "it" and "I," between object and subject. "Where it was, there I shall be," not because I am colonizing it, but because where I am is always shifting. As Nancy Chodorow puts it, in giving an object-relational alternative to the classical Freudian account, "where fragmented internal objects were, there shall harmoniously related objects be."[54] Moving becomes not the installment of oneself astride the Archimedean point, the self-made man taming the frontier of the "New World," but the sort of "world" travel María Lugones discusses as the ground of what she calls, following Marilyn Frye, "loving perception."[55] By putting ourselves in settings in which we are perceived as—and hence are able (or unable not) to be—different people from who we are at home, we learn about ourselves, each other, and the world. And part of what we learn is that the unity of the self is an illusion of privilege, as when, to use Lugones's example (from a talk she gave at the University of Minnesota), we think there is a natural, unmediated connection between intention, will, and action, because if we are privileged, the world collaborates with us, making it all work, apparently seamlessly, and giving us the credit. As Frye puts it, we are trained not to notice the stagehands, all those whose labor enables the play to proceed smoothly.[56]

What is problematic about Descartes's Faustian gesture is not the idea that the world is in some sense our creation. Rather, it is on the one hand the individualism of the construction (or, what comes to the same thing, the unitary construction by all and only those who count as the same, the not-different) and on the other the need to deny any construction, to maintain the mutual independence of the self and the world. Realism ought not to require such independence on the side of the world, any more than rationality ought to require it on the side of the knowing subject, if by realism we mean the recognition that the world may not be the way anyone (or any group, however powerful) thinks it is and if by rationality we mean ways of learning and teaching that are reliably useful in collective endeavors.

Philosophical realism has typically stressed the independence of the world from those who would know it, a formulation that, at least since Kant, has been linked with the intractability of scepticism. But it's hard to see exactly why independence should be what is required. A world that exists in complex interdependence with those who know it (who are, of course, also part of it) is nonetheless real. Lots of real things are not independent of what we think about them, without being just what anyone or any group takes them to be—the economy, to take just one obvious example. The interdependencies are real, as are the entities and structures shaped by them. One way we know they are real is precisely that they look different to those differently placed in relation to them. (There aren't a variety of diverse takes on my hallucinations.) The only way to take diversity of perspectives seriously is to be robustly realistic, both about the world viewed and about the material locations of those doing the viewing. Archimedean, difference-denying epistemology ought to be seen as incompatible with such a robust realism: How could there possibly be one account of a world shaped in interaction with subjects so diversely constituted and with such diverse interests in constructing and knowing it?

A specifically Cartesian feature of the conception of the world as independent is the world as inanimate, and consequently not reciprocally engaged in the activities through which it comes to be known. Thus, for example, the social sciences, which take as their objects bearers of subjectivity and the entities and structures they create, have been seen as scientifically deficient precisely because of the insufficiently independent status of what they study. (The remedy for such deficiency has typically been the dehumanizing objectification of the "subjects" of the social sciences, an objectification especially damaging when those subjects have been otherwise oppressed.) But it's far from obvious that being inert should make something more knowable: Why not take 'subject' and 'object' to name not ontological categories but reciprocal, shifting positions? Why not think of knowledge emerging paradigmatically in mutual interaction, so that what puzzles us is how to account not for the objectivity of the social sciences but for the intersubjectivity of the natural sciences?[57]

In a discussion of the problems from an African-American perspective, with the critical legal theorists' rejection of rights, Patricia Williams suggests that rather than discarding rights,

> society must *give* them away. Unlock them from reification by giving them to slaves. Give them to trees. Give them to cows. Give them to history. Give them to rivers and rocks. Give to all of society's objects and untouchables the rights of privacy, integrity, and self-assertion give them distance and respect. Flood them with the animating spirit that rights mythology fires in this country's most oppressed psyches, and wash away the shrouds of inanimate-object status.[58]

One might respond similarly to the suggestion from postmodernist quarters that we discard subjectivity and agency; rather, we should profligately give them away and invest the things of the world with subjectivity, with the ability and interest to return our gaze.[59] Realism can mean that we see ourselves as inhabiting a world in which the likes of us (whoever we may be) are not the only sources of meaning, that we see ourselves as implicated in, reciprocated by, the world.

The world as real is the world as precisely not dead or mechanistic; the world as trickster, as protean, is always slipping out from under our best attempts to pin it down.[60] The real world is not the world of our best physics but the world that defeats any physics that would be final, that would desire to be the last word, "the end of the story, the horizon of interpretation, the end of 'the puzzlement,'" a desire Paul Smith calls "claustrophilic."[61] Donna Haraway imaginatively sketches an epistemology for the explicitly partial, fragmentary, ununified knowers we are and need to be if we are to move within and learn from the complexities of the world and the complexities of how we are constructed in it. As she puts it, "Splitting, not being, is the privileged image for feminist epistemologies of scientific knowledge" ("Situated Knowledges," p. 586).

A trickster reality is thus matched by a trickster subjectivity, a subjectivity that finds expression in African and Afro-American oral and written traditions. In *The Signifying Monkey,* Henry Louis Gates, Jr., builds "a theory of African-American literary criticism" (the book's subtitle) on the ground of Afro-American vernacular traditions.[62] Literature, the written word, was the privileged site for the attainment and display of Enlightenment rationality, the place for former slaves and the descendants of slaves to stake a claim to full membership in the human community. The signifying monkey and other traditional African trickster figures from oral traditions are for Gates a way of exploring the simultaneous appropriations and subversions of the site of writing, the attempts of Afro-American writers not to mimic the texts of the masters but to write themselves and their communities into history and culture by transforming the nature of writing itself, by giving voice to the written word. Gates's central trope of "Signifyin(g)" complexly spins a story about the multivocality of Afro-American texts, the weaving of vernacular voices into literature, and the subversions, parodies, and appropriations of earlier texts. Even when the singular voice is seen as a desirable ideal, its achievement is never a simple matter, never seen as a birthright; there are always other voices playing around the edges of the text.

The unity of privileged subjectivity is mirrored in the demand that language be transparent, a demand most explicit in the now-discredited ideal languages of the logical positivists but lingering in the demands of present-day analytic philosophers for (a certain picture of) clarity, as though the point of language was to be seen through. When June Jordan writes of Black English that one of its hallmarks is "clarity: If the sentence is not clear it's not Black English," she might seem to be endorsing such a demand, but the clarity she extols is contextual and "person-centered": "If your idea, your sentence, assumes the presence of at least two living and active people, you will make it understandable because the motivation behind every sentence is the wish to say something real to somebody real."[63] The clarity of analytic philosophy, by contrast, is best exhibited in argumentative contexts, detached from the specificities of anyone's voice, in avoidance of ad hominem and other genetic fallacies. The clarity of Black English, Jordan explains, is grounded in the rhythms and intonations of speech, in the immediacy of the present indicative, and in an abhorrence of abstraction and the eschewal of the passive (non)voice: It is the clarity of illumination, not of the transparent medium. In contrast to the language of philosophy, which assumes its adequacy as a vessel for fully translatable meaning, Black English does not take its authority for granted. It is a language "constructed by people constantly needing to insist that we exist, that we are present."[64] It aims not at transparent representation but at subversive transformation; it is an act of intervention, used by communities of resistance and used within those communities for collective self-constitution.

There are many other theorists of trickster subjectivity. Gloria Anzaldúa, for example, in *Borderlands/La Frontera* writes in a combination of English and Spanish, refusing the demand to choose one or another "pure" language, as she moves along and across the borders that are supposed to define and separate, finding/creating herself by refusing the definitions and separations.

Teresa de Lauretis finds in some women's films a challenge to the unity of the subject. For example, Lizzie Borden's *Born in Flames* discomfits some privileged women viewers precisely in its not addressing them alone, in its not (re)presenting the women of color in the film *to* them but, rather, addressing an audience of women as diverse as the women on the screen. There is no unitary viewer for the film, a move that de Lauretis takes to express the feminist understanding "that the female subject is en-gendered, constructed and defined in gender across multiple representations of class, race, language, and social relations; and that, therefore, differences among women are differences *within* women."[65]

In *The American Evasion of Philosophy,* Cornel West finds in pragmatism a challenge to the Enlightenment that can make room for a historical subject constituted otherwise than by the norms of European epistemology.[66] He sees what he calls "prophetic pragmatism" as an intellectual stance for liberationist struggles, in part because of its inheritance from earlier pragmatists, notably Dewey, of a rejection of foundationalism and individualism and an openness to the "fluidity, plurality, and diversity of experience" (*American Evasion,* p. 91). Knowledge and the knowing subject emerge together from continuous engagement with the world; such engagement (with our actual lives at stake) and not the abstractions of epistemology ought to be the stuff of our reflection.[67]

There is, however, an obvious problem with taking splitting and internal multiplicity as the hallmarks of liberatory subjectivity. The most striking and clear-cut cases of internal multiplicity are cases of multiple personality, a pathological condition typically caused by severe childhood abuse, that is, by the most poisonous of pedagogies.[68] Recent clinical work with people with multiple personalities suggests such multiplicity is a means of coping with the terror and pain of the child's situation.[69] Part of that coping consists in a protective amnesia of what the child can neither stop nor understand nor tell anyone about. Consequently the lines of communication between the different selves become blocked, and some of the relations between them become antagonistic as some of the selves adopt coping strategies that are at odds with those of others. Multiple personality, on such a view, is a comprehensible, perhaps even rational, response to an intolerable situation, a way of maintaining some degree of agency in the face of profoundly soul-destroying attacks on one's ability to construct a sense of self. Such construction, throughout life, but especially when one is a child, proceeds interactively. We all are, to use Annette Baier's term "second persons,"[70] and when those we most trust to mirror us abuse that trust, the conditions for wholeness are shattered.

In reflecting on the experiences of "multiples," Claudia Card (to whom I owe much of this discussion) suggests that we can see the main difference between them and the rest of us as lying not in their internal multiplicity but in the amnesia that both guards it and keeps it at odds. Therapy can succeed not by integrating all the personalities into one, or by making all but one go away, but by creating the possibility for respectful conversation among them, facilitating their mutual recognition and acceptance. Analogously with oppressed communities, Card argues, multiples are internally in strife, unable to confront those who have damaged them, needing not seamless unity but effective alliance building.[71] They need from trusted others a mirror of themselves not as unitary but as united, which requires, in part, that those others be committed to the joint survival of all the selves they are and to at least some of the projects in which those selves might engage, either jointly or individually, with mutual respect.

Such an account parallels María Lugones's account of her experiences as a "multiplicitous being," a U.S. Latina lesbian who could not be unitary without killing off a crucial part of who she is, without betraying both herself and others with whom she identifies and for whom she cares.[72] Without identification with and engagement in struggle within *la cultura hispana Nuevomejicana,* the imperiled community in which she "has found her grounding," she risks becoming "culturally obsolete," but as a lesbian within that culture, she is not a lover of women—she is an "abomination." Needing to be both of the very different people she is in the *Nuevomejicana* and lesbian cultures, she works not for unity but for connection, for the not-to-be-taken-for-granted understanding of each of her selves by the other, understanding that is cultivated by work in the "borderlands," "the understanding of liminals." Victoria Davion contends that it is such connection that can ground a conception of integrity that does justice—as she argues any usable feminist notion of integrity must—to the experiences of multiplicitous beings,[73] and it is just that connection that it would seem multiple personalities need to acquire within/among themselves.

Thus we can see the splitting characteristic of multiple personality as a response to oppression that needs resolution by the achievement not of unity but of mutual respect, an achievement that requires the loving collaboration of others. On this view, such splitting is the most striking example of a far more common phenomenon, seen also in experiences such as those María Lugones theorizes. I want to suggest that, without blurring the specificities of such experiences, we can recognize that the experiences even of those who identify with dominant cultures can lead, in different ways, to multiplicitous identities. Gloria Anzaldúa, for example, stresses the importance for *mestizas* of the acceptance of all of who they are, "the white parts, the male parts, the queer parts, the vulnerable parts."[74] But she equally calls for such self-acceptance on the part of the privileged, as the only alternative to the splitting and projection that underwrite domination: "Admit that Mexico is your double, that we are irrevocably tied to her. Gringo, accept the doppelganger in your psyche. By taking back your collective shadow the intracultural split will heal" (*Borderlands/La Frontera*, p. 86).

Erica Sherover-Marcuse suggests that all children are subject to what she calls 'adultism', a form of mistreatment which targets all young people who are born into an oppressive society.[75] Such mistreatment, she argues, is "the 'training ground' for other forms of oppression," a crucial part of the socialization of some as oppressor, some as oppressed, and most of us into complex combinations of both. Central to such socialization is its normalization, the denial of its traumatic nature, the forgetting of the pain; and central to emancipation is "a labor of *affective remembrance*."[76] Alice Miller argues similarly in *For Your Own Good* that only those who have been abused become abusers, and her account focuses on the mechanisms of splitting and projection: "Children who have grown up being assailed for qualities the parents hate in themselves can hardly wait to assign those qualities to someone else so they can once again regard themselves as good, 'moral,' noble, and altruistic" (p. 91).

The abuse of which Alice Miller writes, which ranges from the normative to the horrific, shares the requirement of amnesia, which means that the split-off parts of the self, whether they be the survival-ensuring "alters" of the multiple or the stigmatized Others of the privileged, are empathically inaccessible. What Sherover-Marcuse calls "an emancipatory practice of subjectivity" (*Emancipation and Consciousness,* p. 140) requires memory, connection, and the learning of respect for the Others that we are and for the Others outside of us. Schreber, as privileged jurist and as incarcerated madman, emblematizes the victimized child who grows up to become the dominating adult, the possessor of power—power that is real enough (as is the privilege it secures) but that rests on a history of abuse. As long as we hold on to the ideal of the self as a seamless unity, we will not only be marginalizing the experiences of those like María Lugones and Gloria Anzaldúa, for whom such unity could only be bought at the price of self-betrayal, but we will be fundamentally misrepresenting the experiences of even the most privileged among us, whose apparent unity was bought at the price of the projection onto stigmatized Others of the split-off parts of themselves that they were taught to despise.

As Quine has persuasively argued,[77] epistemology cannot come from thin air: To naturalize epistemology is to acknowledge that we need to study how actual people actually know. But one thing we ought to know about actual people is that they inhabit a world of systematic inequality, in which authority—centrally including epistemic authority—is systematically given to some and withheld from others. If our interest is in changing that world, we need to look critically at the terms of epistemic authority. Certainly there is no reason why those who have historically been dominated by the epistemology of modernity—the objects to its subjects—should accept the terms of that epistemology as the only route to empowerment.

That epistemology presents itself as universal, a universal defined by precisely that which is not different in the ways that some are defined as different: women (not men), people of color (not white people), the disabled (not the able-bodied), gays and lesbians (not heterosexuals). To again echo Foucault, none of these categories is natural or ahistorical, and they all came into existence as strategies of regimentation and containment. They all represent aspects of the multiple, shifting, unstable ways that people can be, aspects that have been split off from the psyches of the privileged, projected onto the bodies of others, and concretized as identities. The privileged, in turn, having shucked off what would threaten their sense of control, theorize their own subjectivity (which they name generically human) as unitary and transparent to consciousness and characterized by integrity and consistency. Not only is such subjectivity a myth; its logic is that of paranoia.[78]

Notes

1. Morton White, "The Politics of Epistemology," *Ethics* 100 (October 1989): 77–92.

2. For one of the earliest and most thorough of such arguments, see Janice Moulton, "The Myth of the Neutral 'Man,'" in *Feminism and Philosophy,* ed. Mary Vetterling-Braggin, Frederick Elliston, and Jane English (Totowa, N.J.: Littlefield, Adams, 1977).

3. I have argued for this dependence in "Your Ground Is My Body: Stratagien des Anti-Fundamentalismus," tr. L. Pfeiffer, in *Paradoxien, Dissonanzen, Zusammenbrüche: Situationen offener Epistemologie,* ed. Hans Ulrich Gumbrecht and K. Ludwig Pfeiffer (Frankfurt: Suhrkamp, 1991).

4. See Genevieve Lloyd, *The Man of Reason* (Minneapolis: University of Minnesota Press, 1984); Susan Bordo, *The Flight to Objectivity: Essays on Cartesianism and Culture* (Albany: SUNY Press, 1987): my "Othello's Doubt/Desdemona's Death: The Engendering of Scepticism," in *Power, Gender, Values,* ed. Judith Genova (Edmonton, Alberta: Academic Printing and Publishing, 1987); and Jacquelyn Zita, "Transsexualized Origins: Reflections on Descartes's *Meditations,*" *Genders* 5 (Summer 1989): 86–105.

5. Daniel Paul Schreber, *Memoirs of My Nervous Illness,* tr. and ed. Ida Macalpine and Richard A. Hunter (Cambridge, Mass.: Harvard University Press, 1988); Sigmund Freud, "Psycho-Analytic Notes upon an Autobiographical Account of a Case of Paranoia (Dementia Paranoides)," *Standard Edition* (hereafter SE), 12:9–82 (London: Hogarth Press, 1958).

6. Alice Miller, *For Your Own Good: Hidden Cruelty in Child-Rearing and the Roots of Violence,* tr. Hildegarde Hannum and Hunter Hannum (New York: Farrar, Straus, and Giroux, 1984), p. 91.

7. Jean-Paul Sartre, *Anti-Semite and Jew,* quoted in Erica Sherover-Marcuse, *Emancipation and Consciousness: Dogmatic and Dialectical Perspectives in the Early Marx* (Oxford: Basil Blackwell, 1986), p. 158.

8. Morton Schatzman, *Soul Murder: Persecution in the Family* (New York: Random House, 1973).

9. Miller, *For Your Own Good.*

10. It is antipsychoanalytic in the manner of Jeffrey Moussaieff Masson's later but better known work, *The Assault on Truth: Freud's Suppression of the Seduction Theory* (New York: Farrar, Straus, and Giroux, 1984), i.e., in reading patients' reports and symptoms as expressions not of fantasies but of what was actually done to them as children.

11. Freud's account is almost entirely in masculine terms, but here, as elsewhere, he took his analysis to apply also to women, *mutatis mutandis.* As I will go on to argue, the phenomena he describes are, in fact, wholly gender inflected and are grounded in distinctively masculine experiences.

12. Freud gives two reasons for the attachment of the libido to the ego: that, detached from the entire external world, it has nowhere else to go (*SE,* 12:65), and that narcissism is the stage at which paranoids are characteristically fixated; hence, it is the stage to which they regress (*SE,* 12:72). This latter view is connected to Freud's notorious association of homosexuality with narcissism, a stage intermediate between autoeroticism and object-love (*SE,* 12:60–61).

13. The term 'ravished' comes from a conversation with Gary Thomas about music and sexuality: 'ravishing' seems the best word for the effect on us of certain, especially Romantic, music.

14. Molefi Kete Asante, *The Afrocentric Idea* (Philadelphia: Temple University Press, 1987), p. 4.

15. Cartesian philosophy was, in fact, influential on and in some ways empowering for contemporary feminists. See Ruth Perry, "Radical Doubt and the Liberation of Women," *Eighteenth-Century Studies* 18 (1985): 472–493.

16. It is a frequently remarked problem that the original argumentative role of the cogito depends on the absolute uniqueness of its claim to our credulity, yet it is then supposed to stand as a paradigm for other successful claimants.

17. Descartes, Meditation 4, in *The Philosophical Writings of Descartes,* 2 vols., tr. John Cottingham and Dugald Murdoch (Cambridge: Cambridge University Press, 1985), p. 40 (hereafter C&M).

18. Meditation 1, C&M, 2:15.

19. Descartes, *The Passions of the Soul,* pt. III, sec. 211, C&M, 1:403. I owe the suggestion to look again at *The Passions of the Soul* to Adam Morton, who may, however, have had something else entirely in mind.

20. Evelyn Fox Keller and Christine R. Grontkowski provide an excellent account of the role and fate of vision in Cartesian dualism in "The Mind's Eye," in *Discovering Reality: Feminist Perspectives on Epistemology, Metaphysics, Methodology, and Philosophy of Science,* ed. Sandra Harding and Merrill B. Hintikka (Dordrecht: D. Reidel, 1983).

21. Descartes, *Discourse on the Method,* pt. II, C&M, 1: 116–117.

22. On Pyrrhonist and Montaignean skepticism, see Richard Popkin, *The History of Scepticism from Erasmus to Descartes* (New York: Humanities Press, 1960).

23. See e.g., part 2 of *Discourse on the Method,* C&M, 1:123.

24. See Margaret Dauler Wilson, *Descartes* (London: Routledge and Kegan Paul, 1978), pp. 17–31.

25. Descartes, *Passions of the Soul,* pt. II, sees. 75–79, C&M, 1:354–356.

26. The most heinous case of such oppression is slavery, and the U.S. slave trade, of course, required the movement of slaves from their homes. But such movement was the denial rather than the expression of those people's will, and it served to confirm what, in the nonliteral sense, was their place in the world as defined by Europeans and Euro-Americans, part of which was that they had no say over where, literally, their place in the world was to be.

27. For a helpful discussion of the intertwinings of oppression and exploitation, see Marilyn Frye, "In and Out of Harm's Way: Arrogance and Love," in *Politics of Reality: Essays in Feminist Theory* (Freedom, Calif.: Crossing Press, 1983), pp. 52–83.

28. The literature on these disputes is vast and growing. For an introduction and overview, see Sandra Harding, *The Science Question in Feminism* (Ithaca, N.Y.: Cornell University Press, 1986), pp. 163–196; and Linda Nicholson, ed., *Feminism/Postmodernism* (New York: Routledge, 1989). For some of us, myself included, the later Wittgenstein is an in-

dependent source of a deep skepticism toward theories, though not necessarily toward the activity of theorizing. For a discussion of that distinction, see Barbara Christian, "The Race for Theory," *Cultural Critique* 6 (Spring 1987): 51–63.

29. Harding, *Science Question in Feminism,* and "The Method Question," *Hypatia* 2, 3 (Fall 1987): 19–35.

30. Freud, "Notes on a Case of Paranoia," *SE,* 12:70. The quote is from Part I, Scene 4 of *Faust.*

31. Paul Smith, *Discerning the Subject* (Minneapolis: University of Minnesota Press, 1988), p. 98. Smith's parallels between paranoia and what he calls "humanist epistemology," which I came across in the final stages of writing this paper, are very similar to mine, as is his aim to articulate a conception of human subjectivity and agency that is politically and socially usable.

32. See my "From Hamlet to Maggie Verver: The History and Politics of the Knowing Subject," *Poetics* 18 (1989): 449–469; and "Missing Mothers/Desiring Daughters: Framing the Sight of Women," *Critical Inquiry* 15 (1988): 62–89.

33. Barry Stroud, *The Significance of Philosophical Scepticism* (New York: Oxford University Press, 1984), p. x.

34. I owe this juxtaposition of the two books to a suggestion by Michael Root. See Hubert L. Dreyfus and Paul Rabinow, *Michel Foucault: Beyond Structuralism and Hermeneutics,* 2d ed. (Chicago: University of Chicago Press, 1983), pp. 143–183.

35. Feminists and others have expressed concern that despite the attractiveness of Foucauldian theory we need to be wary that by following him we risk losing politically indispensable notions like oppression and power (as something some people have unjustly more of). It is similarly unclear how in Foucauldian terms to formulate effectively coordinated strategies of resistance. See, e.g., *Feminism and Foucault: Reflections on Resistance,* ed. Irene Diamond and Lee Quinby (Boston: Northeastern University Press, 1988); and Cornel West, *The American Evasion of Philosophy: A Genealogy of Pragmatism* (Madison: University of Wisconsin Press, 1989), pp. 223–226. I share this concern but find some of Foucault's analyses helpfully illuminating: I want to "go a piece of the way with him," a notion I owe to an unpublished paper by Angelita Reyes, "Derridada . . . Don't Leave Home without Him, or, Going a Piece of the Way with Them."

36. The unspecified 'we' in these sentences is a reflection of one thing many feminists and other liberationist theorists find problematic in Foucault—the homogenization of subject positions. It is striking to me how difficult it is not to do this, to be always conscious of the diversity of different people's experiences. Philosophy as a discipline makes such consciousness especially difficult, because the philosophical subject is defined precisely by its (alleged) universality.

37. See, e.g., Francis Barker, *The Tremulous Private Body: Essays on Subjection* (London: Methuen, 1984), for an account of the emergence of the distinctively modern subject.

38. The echo of Paulo Freire's *Pedagogy of the Oppressed* is intentional. Freire's aim is to develop an explicit pedagogy that will be empowering to those who are currently oppressed; I want to examine the implicit pedagogy that actually empowers the currently privileged.

39. Alice Miller stresses the importance for the success of "poisonous pedagogy" that its victims not have any memory of what was done to them, that they never see their parents as anything other than good and loving. My discussion draws heavily on her *For Your Own Good.*

40. Quoted in Miller, *For Your Own Good,* p. 90; from Schatzman, *Soul Murder,* p. 19, quoting Schreber.

41. But we should not obliterate them. Kant suggests, for example, that we should visit places that house the poor and the ill to reinvigorate in ourselves sympathetic feelings that can be enlisted on the side of motivating us to do what duty commands. Immanuel Kant, *The Doctrine of Virtue: Part II of the Metaphysics of Morals,* tr. Mary J. Gregor (Philadelphia: University of Pennsylvania Press, 1964), see. 35, p. 126.

42. This is as good a place as any to note that what I find problematic in Cartesian epistemology is not peculiar to him or even to rationalism. The gender associations are, in fact, far clearer in Bacon. (See Evelyn Fox Keller, "Baconian Science: A Hermaphroditic Birth," *Philosophical Forum* 11, 3 (Spring 1980): 299–308; reprinted in Keller, *Reflections on Gender and Science* (New Haven, Conn.: Yale University Press, 1985). For a fuller statement of what I take to be in common in views that the usual accounts of the history of philosophy put in opposition, see my "Othello's Doubt/Desdemona's Death."

43. The term is Schatzman's, *Soul Murder,* p. 137.

44. For the attempt, see Descartes, Meditation 6, C&M, I : 56–57; the Fourth Set of Replies (to Arnauld), C&M, 2: 60; Sixth Set of Replies (to Mersenne), C&M, 2: 297–299. For further attempts and, in the face of Princess Elizabeth's persistent questioning, his abandonment of the possibility of getting a rationally grounded theoretical account of the union of mind and body, see Descartes's Letters IX (a and b) and X (a and b) to Princess Elizabeth, in *Descartes: Philosophical Writings,* ed. Elizabeth Anscombe and Peter Thomas Geach (Indianapolis: Bobbs Merrill, 1954).

45. Barker, *Tremulous Private Body.* See also my "From Hamlet to Maggie Verver."

46. Donald M. Lowe, *History of Bourgeois Perception* (Chicago: University of Chicago Press, 1982), p. 22.

47. Keller, "Baconian Science," p. 304.

48. Gloria Anzaldúa, *Borderlands/La Frontera: The New Mestiza* (San Francisco: Spinsters/Aunt Lute, 1987), p. 79.

49. Donna Haraway, "Situated Knowledges: The Science Question in Feminism and the Privilege of Partial Perspective," *Feminist Studies* 14, 3 (Fall 1988): 584.

50. Firm ego boundaries are typically taken as a measure of mental health: One is supposed to be clear about where one's self leaves off and the rest of the world begins. An alternative view—that part of mental health, or of an adequate epistemology, consists in the acceptance of a sizable intermediate domain—has been developed by the object relations theorist D. W. Winnicott. For a discussion of the relevance of his work to feminist theory, see Keller, *Reflections on Gender and Science,* pp. 83, 99–102; and Jane Flax, *Thinking Fragments: Psychoanalysis, Feminism, and Postmodernism in the Contemporary West* (Berkeley/Los Angeles: University of California Press, 1990), pp. 116–132.

51. Sandra Harding and Donna Haraway are two such theorists, who also give excellent overviews of work in this area. See, especially, Haraway, "Situated Knowledges," 575–599; and Harding, "Reinventing Ourselves as Other: More New Agents of History and Knowledge," in Harding, *Whose Science? Whose Knowledge? Thinking from Women's Lives* (Ithaca, N.Y.: Cornell University Press, 1991), pp. 268–295. See also three papers in which María Lugones develops a pluralistic theory of identity: "Playfulness, 'World'-Traveling, and Loving Perception," *Hypatia* 2, 2 (Summer 1987): 3–19; "Hispaneando y Lesbiando: On Sarah Hoagland's *Lesbian Ethics,*" *Hypatia* 5, 3 (Fall 1990): 138–146; and "On the Logic of Pluralist Feminism," in *Feminist Ethics,* ed. Claudia Card (Lawrence: University Press of Kansas, 1991), pp. 35–44.

52. Freud, *New Introductory Lectures on Psychoanalysis,* SE, 22:80.

53. See Bruno Bettelheim, *Freud and Man's Soul* (New York: A. A. Knopf, 1983). The *New Introductory Lectures* were originally written in English, but the point still holds: Freud used the English of his translators.

54. Nancy Chodorow, "Toward a Relational Individualism: The Mediation of Self Through Psychoanalysis," in *Reconstructing Individualism: Autonomy, Individuality, and the Self in Western Thought* ed. Thomas C. Heller, Morton Sosna, and David E. Wellbey (Stanford, Calif.: Stanford University Press, 1986), pp. 197–207.

55. Lugones, "Playfulness, 'World'-Traveling, and Loving Perception"; Frye, "In and Out of Harm's Way."

56. Frye, "To Be and Be Seen," *Politics of Reality,* pp 167–173.

57. For a start on such an account, as well as an argument for why we should seek one, see Lorraine Code, *What Can She Know? Feminist Theory and the Construction of Knowledge* (Ithaca, .N.Y.: Cornell University Press, 1991), esp. chs. 3 and 4; and Sandra Harding, *Whose Science? Whose Knowledge?* esp. ch. 4.

58. Patricia J. Williams, *The Alchemy of Race and Rights: Diary of a Law Professor* (Cambridge, Mass.: Harvard University Press, 1991), p. 165.

59. See Rainer Maria Rilke's "Archaic Torso of Apollo": "There is no place / that does not see you. You must change your life." *Translations from the Poetry of Rainer Maria Rilke,* tr. M. D. Herter Norton (New York: W. W. Norton, 1938).

60. Haraway, "Situated Knowledges," p. 596.

61. Smith, *Discerning the Subject,* p. 98.

62. Henry Louis Gates, Jr., *The Signifying Monkey: A Theory of African-American Literary Criticism* (New York/Oxford: Oxford University Press, 1988).

63. June Jordan, "Nobody Mean More to Me than You/And the Future Life of Willie Jordan," in *On Call: Political Essays* (Boston: South End Press, 1985), pp. 129–130. Such accounts make evident the Eurocentrism of deconstructive sorties against such notions as presence, voice, and authorship. See, for example, Jacques Derrida, "Plato's Pharmacy," in his *Dissemination,* tr. Barbara Johnson (Chicago: University of Chicago Press, 1981).

64. Jordan, "Nobody Mean More to Me than You," p. 129.

65. Teresa de Lauretis, "Rethinking Women's Cinema: Aesthetics and Feminist Theory," in *Technologies of Gender: Essays on Theory, Film, and Fiction* (Bloomington: Indiana University Press, 1987), p. 139.

66. West, *American Evasion of Philosophy.*

67. George Herbert Mead has also inspired theorists of subjectivity concerned with sociality and internal diversity. See, in particular, Karen Hanson, *The Self Imagined: Philosophical Reflections on the Social Character of Psyche* (New York: Routledge and Kegan Paul, 1986); and Catherine Keller, *From a Broken Web: Separation, Sexism, and Self* (Boston: Beacon Press, 1986).

68. Thanks to Louise Antony for stressing the importance of dealing with these issues.

69. "Dissociative Disorder," *Diagnostic and Statistical Manual of Mental Disorders,* 3d ed., rev. (Washington, D.C.: American Psychiatric Association, 1987), 269–279.

70. Annette Baier, "Cartesian Persons," in *Postures of the Mind: Essays on Mind and Morals* (Minneapolis: University of Minnesota Press, 1985), pp. 74–92. See also the chapter on "Second Persons" in Code, *What Can She Know?* pp. 71–109.

71. Claudia Card, "Responsibility and Moral Luck: Resisting Oppression and Abuse," manuscript, 1989.

72. Lugones, "Hispaneando y Lesbiando."

73. Victoria M. Davion, "Integrity and Radical Change," in Card, ed., *Feminist Ethics*, pp. 180–192.

74. Anzaldúa, *Borderlands/La Frontera*, p. 88.

75. Sherover-Marcuse, *Emancipation and Consciousness*, p. 139.

76. Ibid., p. 140. Emphasis in original.

77. W. V. Quine, "Epistemology Naturalized," *Ontological Relativity and Other Essays* (New York: Columbia University Press, 1969).

78. Louise Antony's detailed and erudite response to an earlier draft was a model of friendly, feminist criticism: It is a rare thing to have one's writing so thoroughly disagreed with and at the same time taken so seriously and with so much care. Ruth Wood was, as usual, of enormous help in clarifying the convolutions.

METAPHYSICS

IO

ON BEING OBJECTIVE AND BEING OBJECTIFIED

SALLY HASLANGER

1. Introduction

One of the common themes in feminist research over the past decade has been the claim that reason is "gendered": more specifically, that reason is "male" or "masculine." Although feminists have differed in their interpretations of this claim and the grounds they offer for it, the general conclusion has been that feminist theory should steer clear of investments in reason and rationality, at least as traditionally conceived. For example, we should avoid an epistemology that privileges reason or the standpoint of reason; we should avoid theories of the self that take rationality to be a defining trait; and we should avoid endorsing moral and political ideals that glorify reason and the reasonable "person" (read: man).

The feminist resistance to ideals of reason has at least two different strands. On one strand, giving reason prominence is problematic by virtue of what it leaves out; our views (and our lives) are distorted by a failure to recognize and properly value what has traditionally counted as "feminine." It is not that reason is inherently objectionable, but allowing ourselves to be preoccupied with the significance of reason reflects a bias toward men, or the "masculine," which feminism ought to challenge.[1] Thus we might aim in our theorizing to integrate "feminine" perspectives and attributes that have been contrasted with reason, or we might recognize an alternative "feminine" reason in addition to the more traditional "masculine" reason.[2]

On the other strand, reason itself is more deeply implicated in our oppression; the problem is not one that can be solved by a shift in emphasis—in short, by a new appreciation of the feminine. Offering a positive characterization of this second strand is tricky, for there are markedly different views about how reason is implicated and what we should do about it. But the core idea is that a rational stance is itself a stance of oppression or domination, and accepted ideals of reason both reflect and reinforce power relations that advantage white privileged men.[3] On this view, the point is not to balance the value of reason with feminine values, but to challenge our commitments to rational ideals.

On the face of it, it may seem misguided for feminists to pursue these challenges. It has long been a feminist project to resist the association between women and the "feminine," and even to question the very categories of "masculine" and "feminine." If feminists now take up the project of revaluing the feminine, aren't we reinforcing rather than combating traditional stereotypes? Should we not be wary of ideals of femininity that have been defined in the context of male dominance?[4]

Moreover, although it is clear that the rhetoric of reason is often used to marginalize and silence women, an appeal to the value of reasoned debate is also a way of opening up a discussion to criticism of standard assumptions. Because an important element in the traditional conception of reason is the value it accords to honest public debate and self-criticism, women's insistence on standards of reason should be one way to combat the dogmatism that fuels patriarchy. If we reject the value of rational reflection and reasoned discussion, then what acceptable methods are left to criticize entrenched positions and to mediate between conflicting points of view? How are we to construct and evaluate our own feminist positions? Even if there are flaws in traditional accounts of reason, must we conclude that they are hopelessly flawed?[5]

This brief glance at some of the issues that arise in considering the claim that reason is gendered shows that we face two huge stumbling blocks: the first is the concept of reason, the second is the concept of gender. Both are highly contested concepts: attempts at their analysis spark profound disagreement. Often it is unclear in the context of debate what account of reason or gender is under discussion, making it unclear who is speaking to whom, where there is disagreement and where there is not. Given the vast amount of interdisciplinary literature on the issue, literature drawing from different traditions and speaking to different audiences, the task of sorting through the discussion seems intractable.

In what follows I will pursue the following strategy. In the first part of the essay, I consider what it is for a concept or a point of view to be "gendered." Drawing on the idea that gender should be defined in terms of social relations, I begin with the idea that concepts or attributes are gendered insofar as they function as appropriate norms or ideals for those who stand in these social relations. After modifying and elaborating this idea, I turn to ask whether and to what extent the norms of rationality are specifically appropriate to the role defining the social category of men. To make progress in answering this question, we need at least a working definition of gender.

In the second part of the essay, I begin by considering Catharine MacKinnon's proposal for defining the social relations that constitute gender. On her view, gender is defined in terms of sexual objectification: roughly, women as a class are those individuals who are viewed and treated as objects for the satisfaction of men's desire. In short, women are the sexually objectified, men the objectifiers. She argues, moreover, that rationality, construed as a stance of objectivity, is an ideal that sustains the inequality of power on which sexual objectification depends. MacKinnon's account of gender has often been criticized for focusing too narrowly on a specific form of gender oppression. But even allowing that there are a plurality of different relations which constitute gender, MacKinnon's work still provides a compelling analysis of one of them. Moreover, working with MacKinnon's concrete analysis of gender enables us to explore in some detail the connections between objectification and objectivity.

Drawing on MacKinnon's critique of objectivity, I undertake to explicate a set of epistemic and practical norms that would, under conditions of social hierarchy, legitimize and sustain objectification. I argue that there is an ideal recommending "neutrality" and "aperspectivity" whose satisfaction both contributes to success in the role of objectifier and is sufficient for functioning as a collaborator in objectification. However, I argue against MacKinnon's stronger claim that satisfaction of this ideal is sufficient for functioning in the social role of a man. I conclude that the ideal is contextually "gendered" and so a proper target for feminist concern, though it is not in the strong sense "masculine."

Before continuing, let me emphasize that for the bulk of the essay I will try to remain as neutral as possible on the issue of what counts as reason or rationality. My strategy here is to approach the question of whether reason is gendered by way of a better understanding of gender. If there are some epistemic or practical ideals that are gendered, we should determine what they are; whether these ideals are "really" what has traditionally been meant by 'rationality', or whether they are currently what we mean by 'rationality', is an important question but not my immediate concern.

I should also note that to my mind, there is something peculiar about engaging in discussion and reasoned debate over the value, or legitimacy, or reality, of reason and rationality. If there is something wrong with our commitments to reason, I doubt we'll find it this way (and I don't know what we could do about it if we did). But this is just to say that in this essay, I will be assuming that at least some minimal conception of reasoning and some minimal norms of rationality are not at stake in the discussion.

2. Gender and Social Construction

In order to understand the charge that reason is "masculine" or "gendered," it is important to sketch some of the background work that has been done on gender.[6] It is no easy task, since there are deep disagreements among theorists about what specific account we should give of gender or whether we should seek to give an account at all. Some of the concerns have even prompted the suggestion that the concept of gender is no longer a useful theoretical tool, and this in turn has raised the specter of "post-feminism."[7] The project of this essay is (thankfully) a few steps back from that cutting edge, for the charge that reason is "gendered" or "masculine" arises from feminist views which allow that the notion of gender is at least dialectically appropriate. So I will begin by working briefly through some of the distinctions and themes that the critique of reason draws upon in order to situate the more detailed discussion that will follow.

Sex and Gender

For the time being, let us restrict ourselves to speaking of human beings. Let us use the terms 'male' and 'female' to indicate a classification of individual human beings on the basis of anatomical difference. For our purposes it is not important to specify exactly what anatomical differences count, though primary sex characteristics are a place to start. Let us allow that the distinction between males and females is neither exhaustive nor exclusive and that the terms may be vague—that is, given that human beings display a range of anatomical diversity, we can allow that there are individuals who do not fall neatly within either class and that there are others who fall within both. Further, let us leave it open whether such an anatomical classification is "natural" or "social," "real" or "nominal." And let us say that two individuals are of different *sex* just in case each falls within one and only one of the two classes, and they don't fall within the same class.[8]

It is commonplace in feminist research that we must distinguish sex from *gender*.[9] In keeping with this research, let us use the terms 'man' and 'woman' to indicate gender difference (allowing that boys may fall within the gender *man* and girls within the gender *woman*). Although it *might* be that the distinctions of sex and gender are extensionally equivalent—that is that all and only females are women and all and only males are men—the basis for the gender classification is not anatomical; rather, its basis lies in social relations.

To see the general point, it is useful to consider other straightforward examples of distinctions based in social relations. Consider a scapegoat. An individual is a scapegoat not by virtue of their intrinsic features but by virtue of their relations to others: anyone, regardless of their bodily features, character, and so on can function as a scapegoat in the right circumstances. What makes you a scapegoat is the role you play in a social group. Consider a landlord. One is a landlord by virtue of one's role in a broad system of social and economic relations which includes tenants, property, and the like. Even if it turned out as a matter of fact that all and only landlords had a closed loop in the center of their right thumbprint, the basis for being counted a landlord is different from the basis for being counted as having such a thumbprint. Likewise for gender, one is a woman, not by virtue of one's intrinsic features (for example, body type), but by virtue of one's part in a system of social relations which includes, among other things, men.[10] Gender is a relational or extrinsic property of individuals, and the relations in question are social.[11] If gender rests in this way upon the organization of social life, we should at least entertain the possibility that just as a change in social relations could have the result that there are no landlords and tenants, a change in social relations could have the result that there are no men and women, even if there continue to be males and females.

It is natural to ask next: What are the social relations that constitute gender? Here things become theoretically difficult, for although it seems plausible that gender difference appears cross-culturally and trans-historically, we must at the very least allow that the specific social relations constituting gender differ from culture to culture. But the recognition of broad social differences raises the question whether gender can be understood as a unitary phenomenon at all.[12] Moreover, there is a theme among feminists that the social relations that give rise to gender distinctions are relations of domination; in particular, they are oppressive to women.[13] However, gender oppression does not typically occur in isolation from other forms of oppression; the social relations that constitute gender will be part of a system of social relations, and such systems also serve to ground other distinctions such as race and class. What distinguishes those social relations that constitute *gender*? On what basis (if any) can we meaningfully isolate gender from other hierarchical social distinctions, and gender oppression from other forms of oppression? Are anatomical facts concerning sex and reproduction important for distinguishing gender from other social categories, and gender oppression from other oppressions?[14]

Gender-Norms

There are several strategies for addressing the questions just raised which have been proposed and criticized in the feminist literature. Before I return to the issue of specifying what relations constitute gender, we need to consider a related distinction between "gender-norms": *masculinity* and *femininity*. Gender-norms are clusters of characteristics and abilities that function as a standard by which individuals are judged to be "good" instances of their gender; they are the "virtues" appropriate to the gender.

Because the notion of a "norm" is used in different ways, an example will help illustrate the notion I am relying on. Consider a paring knife. Something counts as a paring knife only if it has features that enable it to perform a certain function: it must be easily usable by humans to cut and peel fruits and vegetables. We can distinguish, however, between something's marginally performing that function and something's performing the function excellently. A good paring knife has a sharp hard blade with a comfortable handle; a poor paring knife might be one that is so blunt that it crushes rather than cuts a piece of fruit, it might be too large to handle easily, and so on. Those features that enable a paring knife to be *excellent* at its job, are the "virtues" of a paring knife. (Something that functions as a good paring knife may function as a poor screwdriver and, when nothing else is available, a good screwdriver may function as a poor paring knife. Although having a sharp pointed blade is a virtue in a paring knife, having such a blade is not a virtue in a screwdriver.) In general, our evaluation of the goodness or badness of a tool will be relative to a function, end, or purpose, and the norm will serve as an ideal embodying excellence in the performance of that function.

Likewise, masculinity and femininity are norms or standards by which individuals are judged to be exemplars of their gender and which enable us to function excellently in our allotted role in the system of social relations that constitute gender. Although I won't be able to make these ideas perfectly precise, the leading idea is that at least some roles have a point or a purpose; to name a few fairly clear examples, consider the roles of teacher, cook, doctor, firefighter, rabbi, pilot, waitress, plumber. For each role there are performances that would count as successes and others that would count as failures; in general, one can do a better or worse job at them. The suggestion is that gender roles are of this kind; gender-norms capture how one should behave and what attributes are suitable if one is to excel in the socially sanctioned gender roles.

In the traditional privileged white Western scenario, to be good at being a man (that is, to be masculine), one should be strong, active, independent, rational, handsome, and so on; to be good at being a woman, one should be nurturing, emotional, cooperative, pretty, and so on. For example, I am a woman because I stand in various gender-constitutive relations to others (often whether I choose to or not); however, I am not in the traditional sense a "good woman" because I don't live up to this ideal of femininity. Judged against the standard of such traditional gender-norms—that is, judged in terms of how I function in the traditional role of woman—I do not excel. Although I don't aspire to satisfying this ideal, this doesn't prevent others from judging me in its terms.

I noted above that there are difficulties in specifying the social relations that constitute gender, especially if we seek to understand it as a cross-cultural phenomenon; these difficulties are echoed and amplified in the project of specifying the content of gender-norms. We should be wary of postulating a single gender-norm for women across cultures or even within a cultural group:

> A glance at women's magazines, for example, reveals a range of often competing subject positions offered to women readers, from career woman to romantic heroine, from successful wife and mother to irresistible sexual object. These different positions which magazines construct in their various features, advertising, and fiction are part of the battle to determine the day to day practices of family life, education, work, and leisure.[15]

Moreover, gender-norms vary markedly with race, class, and ethnicity. To use a particularly apt example in the context of this essay, there are studies that suggest that although developed capacities for abstract thought and intellectual activity are part of a masculine gender-norm for some privileged groups of men in Western communities, these elements of the masculine norm do not persist across class.[16]

Because our values and the structure of our lives have an impact on each other, the norms and the roles tend to adjust to each other. The acceptance of new roles for women can result in the recognition of new "women's virtues," and the appeal of new norms can result in changes in social roles.[17] But we should keep in mind that norms and roles can also fall desperately out of sync when the norms remain rigid while social roles change; gender-norms "often take on complex lives and histories of their own, which often bear little resemblance to their functional roots."[18] In the course of these complex histories, norms can become internally contradictory, making it impossible to live up to them or to structure a coherent life around them.[19] Such incoherence in the norms may indicate that they no longer reflect the allotted social roles, or it may reflect an incoherence in the roles themselves.

In contexts where gender roles are well entrenched, the corresponding norms function *prescriptively:* not only do they serve as the basis for judgments about how people ought to be (act, and so on), but also we decide how to act, what to strive for, what to resist, in light of such norms.[20] This prescriptive force is backed by social sanctions. In aspiring to a gender-norm, you aim to conform your behavior to those ideals that make you especially suited to your allotted role; if you don't aspire to the norm or if you don't manage to conform, you can expect censure, sometimes mild, sometimes severe. Moreover, those social relations that constitute gender (including, for example, the organization of parenting) provide a context in which children tend to internalize the locally endorsed gender-norms.[21] Thus conformity to our proper gender role comes to seem right and good, and perhaps most significantly, internally motivated rather than socially enforced. As a result, we should expect that socially endorsed gender-norms will *reflect and reinforce* the local pattern of gender relations.

However, we should also note that the properties constituting the norms can also function *descriptively:* some individuals have the properties in question and others do not. In a society where gender-norms are generally agreed upon and well entrenched, and where individuals are fairly successful in living up to them, corresponding generalizations about the differences between men and women, even about males and females, may be descriptively adequate.[22] Noting such generalizations, there is an unmistakable tendency to conclude that a woman is "by nature" or "essentially" feminine (and a man masculine). In short, the prescriptive role of the norms is not acknowledged, and gender differences are taken to be natural or inevitable.[23] But this inference is mistaken: Even if the generalizations are accurate, their accuracy may simply reflect the impact of the norms and the pattern of social relations that underwrites the acceptance of those norms.[24]

In contrast, the theoretical framework I have sketched emphasizes the prescriptive role of gender-norms and highlights the fact that gender is grounded in broad social arrangements. Particular traits, norms, and identities, considered in abstraction from social context, have no claim to be classified as masculine or feminine. The classification of features as masculine or feminine is *derivative,* and in particular, depends on prior *social* classifications. For example, consider the claim that sensitivity to interpersonal relationships is a feminine trait. In considering this claim we must not suppose that such sensitivity is inherently feminine or that its status as feminine is determined biologically, or psychologically, or by virtue of its inclusion in an extrasocial (be it "natural" or "metaphysical") archetype of Woman. Not only does such reification fail to accommodate the broad cultural differences in the content of gendered ideals; worse still, the reliance on such archetypes masks the fact that the status of ideals as masculine or feminine rests upon an organization of social life in terms of "proper" roles and functions.[25] The ideals are gendered because the roles for which they count as ideals constitute gender.

I stress this dependence of gendered ideals on social arrangements because it highlights one issue in the problematic of justifying social arrangements. Ideals present themselves as standards or excellences to be valued; if we assume that the "right" ideals are given by authority (for example, by nature or God), then it is tempting to justify a distribution of social roles by virtue of the opportunities they provide to achieve the given ideals. If nurturing is an inherently feminine excellence and bravery is an inherently masculine excellence, then it might seem justified to distribute social roles in a way that facilitates women's opportunities to nurture and men's opportunities to be brave. But if we allow that ideals are functionally rooted in roles and activities, this strategy loses its force. An excellent slave is one who is obedient; an excellent master is one who exercises control. But such ideals of slavishness and mastery do not justify the institution of slavery because the ideals gain their prescriptive force only in a context where we assume the appropriateness (or inevitability) of the social roles of master and slave. In short, an ideal is appropriate only insofar as we are justified in endorsing the social role for which it functions as the ideal; the ideal does not, in turn, justify the role.

This argument is aimed primarily at those who would claim that naturally or transcendentally "given" ideals of masculinity and femininity warrant a gendered division of social life. But it is also intended to motivate the concern that the value we accord to masculinity or femininity cannot be easily separated from the value we accord the corresponding gender roles. If the gender roles are oppressive and constitute a system of male domination, then we should be cautious in theoretically appropriating either masculine or feminine virtues, even if our intention is to construct a revised ideal of human virtue.

3. Masculine Rationality

Within the Western philosophical tradition, the capacity to reason has been crucial to accounts of the self, and ideals of rationality have been construed as important elements in normative accounts of knowledge and morality. It is also clear that these ideals of rationality and rational selves have typically been defined in contrast to what are assumed to be characteristic features and capacities of women: Women are guided by emotion or feeling rather than reason; women are not capable of impartiality or abstract thought; women are more intuitive and closer to nature than men, and so on.[26] Moreover, anyone who displays a tendency to diverge from rational ideals (or virtually anything that does so) counts as feminine.[27] It is striking that even very different accounts of rationality agree on the contrast with assumed "feminine" attributes. The significance of this contrast supports the hypothesis that in spite of efforts to cast rationality as a "human" ideal, it is in fact a masculine one. That rationality is masculine is explicitly stated by some philosophers, and this assumption also forms a backdrop to common Western conceptions of gender difference that have a deep influence on everyday life.

Insofar as allegedly gender-free accounts of knowledge, morality, and personhood offer ideals defined by their contrast with femininity, patriarchy turns one of its neatest tricks. The reification of masculine ideals as human ideals ensures that one's efforts to be feminine will consistently undermine one's efforts to realize the ideal for persons (and similarly the ideals for morality and knowledge). Women face an impossible choice that carries censure either way: be a good person but fail as a woman, or be a good woman and fail as a person. This is no small consequence. As Judith Butler notes,

> The social constraints upon gender compliance and deviation are so great that most people feel deeply wounded if they are told that they exercise their man-

hood or womanhood improperly. In so far as social existence requires an unambiguous gender affinity, it is not possible to exist in a socially meaningful sense outside of established gender norms. . . . If human existence is always gendered existence, then to stray outside of established gender is in some sense to put one's very existence into question.[28]

Initially it is tempting to think that the mistakes of this tradition can be easily remedied by excising the problematic claims about women and femininity. One might propose, for example, that conceptions of rational selves and the ideals of rationality need not be defined in contrast to femininity; they can stand on their own as ideals for both men and women. This proposal acknowledges that rational ideals have been associated with men and are assumed to be masculine; but it goes on to claim that we should simply reject these associations and assumptions. The traditional conceptions of femininity were misguided: To be a good woman (or a good man) just is to be a good person (in one or another of the traditional senses). In short, the sexism of the tradition is not inherent in its accounts of the self or the role of reason; rather, its sexism lies in a failure to see that, as a matter of fact, the accounts apply equally well to all of us.

But feminist work on gender raises doubts about this apologetic strategy. If rational ideals have been defined in contrast to feminine ideals, then there is reason to think that underlying these ideals we will find a division of gender roles. As I've already argued, norms are not gendered simply by being associated with men or women; they are gendered by providing ideals that are appropriate to the roles constituting gender.[29] Masculine norms are excellences appropriate to men's social role, and masculine identities are conceptions of self and world that justify one's place and activities in this role by presenting the activities as appropriate, good, natural, or inevitable. If we simply extend masculine norms to everyone and take the masculine conception of self and world to apply generally, we would seem to be committed to the view that everyone should occupy the social role (and so take up the perspective on social life) that was once granted only to men. In effect, this move assumes that what was a model for life within one social category among others can (and should) become a model for all of us.

The initial worry is that if reason itself is masculine, then simply granting that rational ideals properly apply to everyone, regardless of gender, reflects a bias toward men. We might ask, If the ideals of rationality are ideals appropriate to men's social role, by what right do we extend these ideals to "human" ideals? What are we to make of the ideals appropriate to women's social role, particularly those that are defined in contrast to rationality? Likewise, if philosophical accounts of self and world only reflect how things seem from the social position of boys and men, and *not* how things seem from the social position of girls and women, then by what right do we expect everyone to endorse these conceptions? The concern is that masculine ideals appear to offer, at best, only a partial model of human life. One pressing question is how, or whether, we might remedy such a partial model. Should we aim to integrate the different perspectives?

We can extend and deepen these questions by noting that it is by no means obvious whether it is warranted to extend men's social role, and its corresponding rational ideals and excellences, to everyone. Whether such an extension is even possible will depend, of course, on how one conceives of gender and, in particular, how the ideals of rationality are grounded in gender. But the worry gains focus if we attend to the hypothesis mentioned above that gender roles are defined relationally and hierarchically—for example, just as someone is a landlord by virtue of standing in a certain (hierarchical) relation to another who is a tenant, someone is a man by virtue of standing in a certain (hierarchical) relation to another who is a woman. Because gender roles are situated within complex social arrangements, we cannot simply assume that it is possible or warranted to generalize masculine roles or to integrate masculine and feminine ideals.

For example, we cannot coherently extend some social roles to everyone: it is not possible for everyone to take up the role of being a free slave-owner. For different (very material) reasons, it is not possible for everyone to live the life of pure contemplation, "unsullied" by menial labor and uninterrupted by the needs of the young, the sick, and the elderly.[30] Although some other roles can be generalized, we should hesitate to do so: Even though it is possible for everyone to function as a scapegoat with respect to some group of others, proposing that everyone should function in the role of scapegoat and endorse its corresponding ideals would be misguided. So we should ask, What are the roles for which rationality is an appropriate ideal? What roles are motivated and authorized by a conception of rational selves? In particular, if rationality is an ideal for men's social role, and if gender is defined relationally, then can we coherently endorse rationality without also endorsing those social relations that constitute gender and without also endorsing a contrasting ideal for women?

It is important to note that these questions have correlates concerning feminine norms and ideals. For example, if feminine norms such as "intuitiveness," "partiality," and "situatedness" offer ideals particularly suited to the gender roles of women, we should question whether these feminine norms can be "de-gendered" to free them from their links to social arrangements of gender oppression. This shift of focus from masculine ideals to feminine ideals raises doubts about the strategies of "gynocentric" feminists who seek to remedy the Western tradition's emphasis on reason by revaluing what are traditionally conceived as feminine virtues.[31] Understanding that gender and gender-norms are grounded in social relations, we may have reason to challenge not only masculine norms and identities but also feminine ones. If masculine and feminine ideals can be realized only in social contexts organized by gender relations, or if their realization functions to sustain existing gender relations, then if gender relations are relations of domination, those who seek to end gender oppression should reject both masculine and feminine ideals.

At this stage of the discussion, I have not yet offered an argument which shows that reason is gendered. The point noted early in this section—that traditional accounts of rational ideals characterize them in contrast to femininity—lends plausibility to the claim that such ideals are gendered. But it remains to be shown in what sense, and to what extent, an endorsement of reason functions to sustain oppressive gender roles. In order to provide such an argument, we will need to look at a more detailed account of gender and reason. We will turn to this task shortly. Before doing so, however, we must consider in more detail the relationship between norms and roles.

The questions raised above suggest two underlying suspicions. The first is that those situated in certain oppressive or problematic roles succeed (for example, their activities are furthered and sustained) by satisfying the ideals of reason. The second is that those who satisfy the ideals of reason thereby function in a problematic or oppressive social role; that is, simply satisfying the ideals of reason is enough to situate you in the role of oppressor. Plausibly, in both cases we would have grounds to question the value of reason if we are concerned to promote social change. Moreover, these suspicions become specifically feminist if the oppressive social roles in question are gender roles. But these two suspicions need further clarification before we can make a compelling case against the ideals of reason.

So far I have repeatedly suggested that norms or ideals are "suitable" or "appropriate" to specific social roles. Admittedly, these notions remain obscure; as a start toward clarification, it will help to introduce a couple of distinctions that will play a role in the arguments that follow. As indicated above, I am assuming that some roles have a point or a purpose and that certain performances in these roles count as successes and others as failures. Further, I will assume that excellence in an ongoing role will require a reliable disposition to perform successfully. Drawing on these ideas we can say that a norm is *appropriate* to a social role just in case those functioning in the role will have a greater chance of success (in that role) if they satisfy the norm; in other words, satisfying the norm would make for, or significantly contribute to, (reliable) success in the role. So, an "appropriate" norm for a role is one whose satisfaction will, other things being equal, take you from merely meeting the minimal conditions for the role to doing a better, or even excellent, job at it.

Promoting excellence in oppressive social roles is something we should aim to avoid; we should not assume, however, that the value of a norm can be judged simply in light of its contribution to excellence in a given social role. Consider, for example, the roles of master and slave. Plausibly, "good" masters are those who (among other things) are kind and compassionate toward their slaves. Such kindness on the part of good masters may help sustain the social institution of slavery by encouraging slaves' loyalty and hard work. But the fact that kindness contributes to success in the role of master should not lead us to reject the value of kindness in general; nor should we even conclude that it is wrong for those who are masters to be kind and compassionate toward their slaves, suggesting, perhaps, that they should be cruel and heartless instead. We can continue to value kindness, even the kindness of masters, while acknowledging that it is a norm appropriate to an oppressive social role. Nevertheless, we must acknowledge that a master's kindness is worrisome insofar as it functions to perpetuate the institution of slavery. And there is something clearly wrong in encouraging individuals to be good masters: In order to be a good master, one must also be a master, and this role we have reason to reject.

As a step toward sorting through these complications, we can note that some norms are separable from the social role for which they are appropriate and some aren't. One may have features that would contribute to success in a particular role without functioning in that role and without that role even being socially available. For example, suppose we were to characterize a good tenant as one who pays the rent on time and is considerate of others (does not disturb their neighbors, does not destroy others' property, and so on). These features are appropriate to the role of tenant: They contribute to success in being a good tenant, and they serve as standards by which tenants are evaluated.

However, one of the elements in this specified tenant ideal, namely, being considerate of others, is separable from the relations constituting the social category of tenant. Satisfying this norm does not entail one's participation in the role of tenant because one can be considerate of others without being a tenant. In contrast, the condition that one pay one's rent on time is not separable in this way. One can satisfy the condition of paying one's rent on time only if one is a tenant; in satisfying this norm, one thereby satisfies the conditions for being a tenant. If one is not a tenant, then not only is the ideal inappropriate, but there is no way to satisfy it short of becoming a tenant. Similarly, a good teacher reliably informs and guides others in learning, listens carefully, and encourages enthusiasm for the subject. Listening carefully is separable from the role of teacher, but reliably informing and guiding others in learning is not. Satisfying the latter plausibly entails that one functions as a teacher (assuming, of course, that one need not be a teacher by profession to be a teacher).

These examples illustrate two points. First, some norms are such that satisfying them entails one's participation in a particular social role; these norms are *constitutively grounded* in a social role; but in the case of conjunctive norms or ideals, even if as a whole they are constitutively grounded in a social role, they may have elements that are separable from the role.[32] Second, if a norm is constitutively grounded in a social role that is defined relationally—for example, as the role of tenant is defined in relation to landlords—then satisfying the norm will require that social arrangements provide for such relations. Because of the relational character of the role of tenant, satisfying the tenant ideal requires that someone is a landlord. If the tenant ideal is appropriate to some, then there is a landlord ideal appropriate to others. Thus commitment to a norm that is constitutively grounded in a relational social role presupposes the appropriateness of a contrasting and correlative ideal.

We should note, however, that there is a middle ground between norms that are constitutively grounded in a particular social role and ones that are wholly separable from the given role. As I characterized the conditions for the constitutive grounding of a norm in a role, it is (conceptually) necessary that anyone who satisfies the norm functions in that role—necessarily, anyone who pays their rent on time is a tenant. However, we should note that whether and how one is situated in a role will often depend on contextual factors; therefore, satisfying a norm may be sufficient for functioning in a role in some contexts but not in others.[33]

Consider first a relatively straightforward example: the ideal life of pure contemplation mentioned above. There is nothing about satisfying this ideal, in and of itself, that makes one dependent on the work of others for one's sustenance and survival. The life of pure contemplation is not constitutively grounded in the role of dependent by virtue of the concepts employed in the ideal: angels could satisfy it without function-ing in a dependent role. And yet as a matter of fact, given the material conditions of human life, any adult who comes even close to satisfying this ideal will, in doing so, function in a dependent role. That is to say, given certain background conditions, sat-isfying the ideal is sufficient for functioning in the social role of a dependent.

In the case of pure contemplation, the background conditions that we just as-sumed—for example, the human need for food and shelter—are general and, at least to some extent, apply to all of us; but other background conditions will be socially specific. Consider the ideal for an investigative journalist. Plausibly, in order to be an excellent investigative journalist, one should "relentlessly" pursue and publicize information of concern to the general public. Note, however, that the social roles of those who satisfy this norm will vary greatly depending on their social context. Someone who satisfies this norm under a dictatorship where such journalistic efforts are prohibited by law will thereby function in the role of a criminal and will be subject to prosecution. (More im-portant, perhaps, those who satisfy the norm in such contexts take up a role of resist-ance.) However, satisfying this journalistic norm will not be sufficient for being a crimi-nal, or for resistance, under a democracy where journalistic freedom is legally protected. Thus one could realize the same ideal, even in substantively the same way, in two differ-ent social contexts and yet in doing so function in very different social roles.[34]

Let us say (roughly) that a norm or an ideal is *contextually grounded* in a social role just in case, given specified background conditions, satisfying that norm is or would be sufficient for functioning in that role.[35] No doubt determining whether an ideal is contextually grounded in a particular social role will be a difficult project that will rely on controversial assumptions about the context in question. These contextual complications are not typically a focus of attention in evaluating norms or ideals; in-stead we describe the ideals in ways which are largely indeterminate with respect to who or what satisfies them, and with respect to how and when they are satisfied (though, as feminist work has shown, often sexist background assumptions play a cru-cial role in our evaluations). We may grant that in evaluating a norm it is important to determine the variety of possible ways that it can, in principle, be realized and the conceptual limits on its realization. But it is only by considering how norms and ideals are realized *in context* that we can effectively determine their consequences, and their value, for our thoroughly situated lives.[36]

As I mentioned above, our evaluation of norms goes hand-in-hand with an eval-uation of the roles in which they are grounded. On the face of it, we might think that if a norm is grounded in a socially problematic role, then we should reject the norm; in rejecting the norm, we often hope to discourage others from assuming the role. However, if a norm is contextually grounded in a problematic social role, the appro-priate move may not be to give up the norm; rather, it may be warranted instead to change the background conditions connecting the norm with the role. For example, plausibly in those contexts in which realizing the ideal of investigative journalist ren-ders one a criminal, we should continue to endorse the role of investigative journalist and its norms but work to change the social conditions that are responsible for a jour-nalist's criminal status.

Having noted these differences in the way in which norms and ideals might be "appropriate to" or "grounded in" social roles, we can now gain clearer focus on the task of showing that reason is masculine, or gendered. In section 2, I suggested that traits are "gendered" insofar as they make for excellence in socially endorsed gender roles. Although this captures part of the idea, the discussion in this section expands and develops the initial suggestion. I have proposed that a norm is *appropriate to* a social role just in case satisfying that norm would make for or significantly contribute to successful functioning in that role. Further, broadly speaking, a norm is *grounded in* a social role just in case (allowing restricted background conditions) satisfying the norm is sufficient for functioning in the role, perhaps successfully, perhaps not. Let us say that a norm is *weakly gendered* just in case it is appropriate to a gender role, and that it is *strongly gendered* just in case it is grounded—either constitutively or contextually—in a gender role.

We can now reconsider the two "underlying suspicions" that prompted this discussion. The first suspicion was that those situated in oppressive social roles succeed—and, further, their roles are perpetuated—because they satisfy the ideals of reason. The second was that satisfying the ideals of reason was itself enough to situate you in an oppressive social role. If we assume that men's role is problematic—that it is oppressive to women—then these two suspicions correspond respectively to the charges that the ideals of reason are weakly gendered and that they are strongly gendered.[37] But the arguments I've offered show that we must be careful in drawing broad conclusions about the value of reason, or lack of it, based on the claims that it is gendered.

If we find that the norms of rationality are weakly gendered (that their satisfaction contributes to success in men's social role), this does not establish that we should reject them wholesale; it may be, for example, that satisfying the norms of rationality is separable from gender roles and has independent value. Nevertheless, there is significant political import in showing that the norms of rationality are weakly gendered. Consider again the example of a kind master. However laudable individual acts of kindness on the part of masters may be, insofar as these acts contribute to the perpetuation of slavery as an institution, the political consequences of these acts are abhorrent. It is a sad fact about social life that the good we manage to accomplish may, in a broader context, sustain much more severe harm; and this harm is all too often masked by the good deeds that sustain it. If satisfying the norms of rationality enables men to excel in their social role, and does so specifically in a way that perpetuates male dominance, then knowing this is an important factor in unmasking the forces that prevent social change.

Moreover, if we find that rationality is weakly gendered, it does not follow that those who are rational stand in oppressive gender relations; nor does it follow that promoting ideals of rationality also promotes oppressive gender roles.[38] (One can promote kindness without promoting slavery.) However, if the norms of rationality are strongly gendered, say, if they are grounded in men's social role, then one who satisfies these norms thereby functions socially as a man. If the grounding is contextual, we should look hard at both the norms and the particular background conditions that link the norms with the role. But if men's social role is a role of domination, then on finding that rationality is grounded in this role, we can then insist that under the specified background conditions, satisfying the norms of rationality is offensive.

I'll now turn to consider a series of arguments designed to show that there is an ideal of objectivity that is both weakly and strongly gendered—in particular, masculine. The arguments I consider are based largely on an interpretation of Catharine MacKinnon's work, though there are points at which I employ a rather free hand in reconstructing the main line of thought. My goal is not to do justice to the full complexity of MacKinnon's views, but to draw on her insights in developing a critique of one conception of objectivity. I begin by explicating MacKinnon's account of the relation that constitutes categories of men and women. I then turn to consider what norms are appropriate to the role defined for men. Following MacKinnon's lead, I argue that there is a cluster of epistemic and practical norms, an ideal I label "assumed objectivity," that contributes to success in men's role and helps sustain a gendered division of social life. This shows that the ideal is weakly masculine. I then consider her further claim that this ideal of assumed objectivity is contextually grounded in men's social role; in particular, I ask whether satisfying this ideal is sufficient, under conditions of male dominance, for functioning as a man. I argue that it is not. Though I do not believe that MacKinnon's arguments accomplish the goal of showing that assumed objectivity is strongly masculine, I suggest that this ideal is contextually grounded in a different, but still problematic, social role.

4. Gender Relations: MacKinnon on Gender

In sketching some of the distinctions that play a role in recent feminist theory, I intentionally skirted controversial issues which now need attention. In particular, if we are to give substantive content to the claim that reason is gendered, we need an account of the social relations that constitute gender. Allowing that the category of gender is contested within feminist theory, is it possible to chart a path through some of the controversies?

There is a growing trend in current feminist research which recommends that although we should employ the concept of gender in our theorizing, we should not treat gender as a unified category.[39] On this "pluralistic" approach to gender, we acknowledge that gender is constituted through a variety of social relations, without aiming to specify what these relations have in common (perhaps opting for Wittgensteinian "family resemblances"?). In effect, we take gender relations to comprise an irreducibly disjunctive class.[40] Whether or not we accept this as our final conclusion, it is reasonable to grant that, at least at this stage, our theoretical efforts are best spent in exploring the range of relatively determinate relations that constitute gender; further, we may grant that it is not a criterion of success in our inquiry that gender can be given a unified analysis.

In keeping with this strategy, our emphasis should be on the task of proposing and employing admittedly partial, temporary, and context-sensitive gender distinctions. As a result, the charge that reason is gendered will not have a unique substantive content; its interpretation will depend on what gender relations are at issue. In the discussion that follows I will evaluate one instance of this charge, employing MacKinnon's account of gender as constituted by sexual objectification. To simplify my discussion I will often gloss over these limitations, speaking as if the account offers a definition of the relation that constitutes the social categories of men and women as such. I trust that given the allowances just sketched, we can proceed with an acknowledgment of the relevant qualifications.

Catharine MacKinnon's work on gender and objectivity is part of a large systematic project with broad repercussions for ongoing political and legal debates.[41] Her work is deeply grounded in a commitment never to lose sight of the terrible concrete reality of sexual violence against women. MacKinnon's account of gender falls largely within the specific theoretical framework I sketched above: Gender categories are defined relationally—one is a woman (or a man) by virtue of one's position in a system of social relations.[42] So one's gender is an extrinsic property, and assuming that we can survive even dramatic changes in our social relations, it is not necessary that we each have the gender we now have, or that we have any gender at all. MacKinnon's account adds to this background three main claims: (1) The relations constituting gender are, by definition, hierarchical. That men dominate women is not a contingent truth; relations of domination *constitute* the categories of man and woman. (2) Gender relations are defined by and in the interests of men. (3) Gender is "sexualized."[43] To quote MacKinnon:

> Male and female are created through the eroticization of dominance and submission. The man/woman difference and the dominance/submission dynamic define each other. This is the social meaning of sex and the distinctively feminist account of gender inequality.[44]

> Gender emerges as the congealed form of the sexualization of inequality between men and women.[45]

> A theory of sexuality becomes feminist methodologically, to the extent that it treats sexuality as a social construct of male power: defined by men, forced on women, and constitutive of the meaning of gender.[46]

To put the point bluntly: One is a man by virtue of standing in a position of eroticized dominance over others; one is a woman by virtue of standing in a position of eroticized submission to others.[47] The modes and forms of dominance, submission, and eroticization may vary from culture to culture, context to context[48]; moreover, it is not necessary that one be anatomically female to be a woman or anatomically male to be a man, though, of course, this is the norm.[49]

But this blunt statement of the point is incomplete, for we need some better understanding of "eroticized dominance/submission" in order to connect it to the idea of objectification, and men's power to define the terms. As I interpret MacKinnon's position, if dominance/submission is eroticized, then the submissive participant must be viewed, at least by the dominant participant (though often by both participants), as being an object for the satisfaction of the dominant's desire. This desire presents her submissiveness to him, and his domination of her, as erotic. (We should keep in mind that on MacKinnon's view it is not because of some "purely natural" male urge toward domination or female impulse toward submission that subordination in its various forms is found erotic or stimulating. Desire is socially conditioned; locally, the most extreme and effective vehicle of this conditioning is pornography.[50])

So how is eroticized dominance/submission connected to objectification? For our purposes there are two points to highlight: First, if dominance/submission is eroticized, then the submissive participant is both *viewed as* and *treated as* an object of the dominant's desire.[51] Second, the submissive participant is viewed in functional terms: She is *for* the satisfaction of his desire. Let us concentrate here on the first point. (I will return to the second point in the next section.) On MacKinnon's view, the relation of objectification that constitutes gender requires both attitude and act. Gender is a distinction of power that is *read into* and *imposed upon* women: "Men treat women as who they see women as being."[52] The category of women is, in a sense, that group of individuals onto which men project and act out their desire.

However, we must take special note of the act, for the dominance inherent in gender is not just in the content of the desire—for example, a wish for dominance. Nor is the dominance merely a matter of projection: of viewing certain individuals through the lens of one's desire to dominate them. For this projection "is not just an illusion or a fantasy or a mistake. It becomes *embodied* because it is enforced."[53] On MacKinnon's view, one who objectifies another has the power to enforce compliance with his view of them.[54] The power and the force are socially real: In the United States during 1989, according to Federal Bureau of Investigation (FBI) reports, a woman was raped on average every six minutes, and nine out of ten women murdered were murdered by men;[55] and according to the National Coalition Against Domestic Violence, a woman was beaten on average every fifteen seconds.[56]

In individual cases, the dominant party who sexually objectifies another need not exercise this power directly; the force behind the submissive participant's compliance may have been exercised in other contexts and in indirect ways. Moreover, the dominant party may have, and may maintain, the power to enforce compliance even if in some cases he attempts force and fails; power doesn't guarantee success. But the fact of the dominant participant's real power is a necessary condition for objectification. Because this inequality of power is a condition of objectification, and because gender is defined in terms of objectification, gender is, by definition, hierarchical: Those who function socially as men have power over those who function socially as women.

Although gender is defined relationally in terms of social roles which in principle could be taken up by different individuals at different times (and no doubt in individual cases are), socially these roles have "congealed": it is a particular group of individuals who are assigned the status "man" and another group the status "woman." Broadly speaking, men are male, women are female, and males have the power to dominate females.[57] However, it is important to note that objectification is not "the cause" of male dominance. That males objectify females presupposes that males have power over females; this follows from the conditions on objectification. Moreover, objectifying *attitudes*—for example, attitudes representing females as "sex objects"—may function socially to sustain inequality of power, but having such attitudes does not, by itself, give one power. MacKinnon's analysis of gender is not intended to provide a causal account of the origins of male dominance. Rather, it is an account which locates gender within a system of hierarchical social relations; as we shall see, one point of highlighting objectification is to explain how, in certain contexts, male dominance is self-sustaining.

So, in MacKinnon's terms, the social category of women is that group of individuals who are viewed functionally as objects for the satisfaction of men's desire, where this desire is conditioned to find subordination stimulating, and where men have the power to enforce the conformity of those they so perceive to their view of them.[58] Male supremacy grants a particular group of individuals this power over others. It is important to note that on this account women are *not* defined as those who *are* submissive, or as those who *actually* satisfy men's conception of what is desirable; nor are women defined as those who have a feminine identity or who satisfy the norms of femininity (though this account will enable us to explain why many women will). In effect, what we share, as women, is that we are perceived and treated as sexually subordinate. Our commonality is in the eye, and the hand, and the power, of the beholder.

This last point becomes evident through an analogy between the concept of gender and the concept of meat. What counts as meat varies from culture to culture; the distinction between meat and not-meat is not marked simply by what animal flesh humans can digest (though in some cases the distinction may be coextensive with this). The class of things that count as meat for a given group of people is determined by their attitudes, desires, and appetites. What do the deer, the tuna, and the lamb have in common that the horse, the dolphin, and the kitten lack? The former are (at least locally) objects of socially trained human appetite; they are viewed and treated as objects for human consumption, and their lives are endangered as a result. The category of meat is not a "natural" category; like gender it is social, relational, and hierarchical. Like gender, the category of meat is a "fiction" which humans have the power to enforce and so to make all too real through practices of domestication, hunting, and fishing. As (many) vegetarians aim for a day when nothing will fall within the category of meat, (many) feminists aim for a day when no one will fall within the category of women.[59]

MacKinnon's account of gender, like others that define gender hierarchically, has the consequence that feminism aims to undermine the very distinction it depends upon. If feminism is successful, there will no longer be a gender distinction as such—or, allowing that there are a plurality of relations that serve to constitute gender and a plurality of feminist projects, we can say that one goal of feminism is to fight against the sexual subordination that constitutes these categories of men and women. "The refusal to become or to remain a 'gendered' man or woman . . . is an immanently political insistence on emerging from the nightmare of the all-too-real, imaginary narrative of sex and race."[60] "To refuse to be a woman, however, does not mean that one has to become a man."[61]

5. Objectivity and Objectification

Working with MacKinnon's account of gender and her conception of the social relations that constitute men and women, can we construct an argument for the claim
that reason is gendered or, more specifically, masculine? As I sketched above, I will divide this question in two[62]: First, is rationality weakly masculine? That is, considering those who function as men, does it make for or specifically contribute to their success as men? If so, how does it do so? Second, is rationality strongly masculine? That
is, does one who satisfies the norms of rationality thereby function socially as a man?

MacKinnon does not often use the term 'rationality', though when she does, it
appears that she takes it to be equivalent to 'objectivity'. And most often she applies
the terms to stances or points of view: One's point of view is rational, iff it is objective,
iff it is "neutral," "distanced," or "non-situated."[63] In a compressed, though typical,
statement of her position, MacKinnon claims:

> The content of the feminist theory of knowledge begins with its criticism of
> the male point of view by criticizing the posture that has been taken as the
> stance of "the knower" in Western political thought. . . . [That stance is] the
> neutral posture, which I will be calling objectivity—that is, the non-situated,
> distanced standpoint. I'm claiming that this is the male standpoint socially,
> and I'm going to try to say why. I will argue that the relationship between ob-
> jectivity as the stance from which the world is known and the world that is ap-
> prehended in this way is the relationship of objectification. Objectivity is the
> epistemological stance of which objectification is the social process, of which
> male dominance is the politics, the acted-out social practice. That is, to look at
> the world objectively is to objectify it. The act of control, of which what I have
> described is the epistemological level, is itself eroticized under male su-
> premacy.[64]

Here MacKinnon claims that the stance of objectivity is the stance of those who function socially as men.[65] This would seem to commit her to the claim that one functions
socially as a man if and only if one satisfies the norms of objectivity. Given my readings of her arguments, I think we can charitably recast her point in terms of the conditions for weak and strong gendering: Objectivity is strongly masculine because satisfying the norms of objectivity is sufficient, at least under conditions of male
dominance, for being a sexual objectifier. And objectivity is weakly masculine given
that those who function as men are successful in this role, at least in part, because they
are objective.

In the next several sections I will concentrate on the charge that objectivity is
weakly masculine; I will then turn to the question whether objectivity is strongly
masculine. So the question now before us is this: Given someone who is a sexual objectifier, what would make for their (reliable) success in that role?[66] (In answering this
question, my emphasis will be on what makes for an ideal objectifier, bracketing the
fact that men are not just objectifiers but are *sexual* objectifiers. When we turn to the

charge that objectivity is strongly masculine, I will then consider how sexuality figures in the picture.)

The Epistemology of Objectification

As outlined above, if one objectifies something (or someone), one views it and treats it as an object for the satisfaction of one's desire; but this is not all, for objectification is assumed to be a relation of domination where one also has the power to enforce one's view. Objectification is not just "in the head"; it is actualized, embodied, imposed upon the objects of one's desire. So if one objectifies something, one not only views it as something which would satisfy one's desire, but one also has the power to make it have the properties one desires it to have. A good objectifier will, when the need arises—that is, when the object lacks the desired properties—exercise his power to make the object have the properties he desires. So if one does a "good" job in objectifying something, then one attributes to it properties which it in fact has. Thinking alone doesn't make it so, but thinking plus power makes it so. "Speaking socially, the beliefs of the powerful become proof [proven?], in part because the world actually arranges itself to affirm what the powerful want to see. If you perceive this as a process, you might call it force."[67] Or, as Monique Wittig puts it: "They are *seen* black, therefore they *are* black; they are *seen* as women, therefore they *are* women. But before being *seen* that way, they first had to be *made* that way."[68]

This suggests that an ideal objectifier is in the epistemic position of (at least) having some true or accurate beliefs about what he has objectified.[69] Such beliefs attribute to the object properties that it has, and these (post hoc) attributions would seem to be as empirical and as publicly accessible as you like.[70] We must note that the possibility of accurate description is not what distinguishes the objectifier's position, or the objective stance, from others: "Because male power has created in reality the world to which feminist insights, when they are accurate, refer, many of our statements will capture that reality, simply exposing it as specifically male for the first time."[71] So we may allow that there is *something* accurate about an (ideal) objectifier's view of things; moreover, one need not be an objectifier in order to acknowledge such claims as accurate or, more generally, to make accurate claims oneself.

As I read MacKinnon's view of objectification, however, there is an aspect of illusion in objectification that we have not yet captured. The illusion on the part of the objectifier (an illusion often shared by the objects of his objectification) is that these post hoc attributions are true by virtue of the object's *nature* and not by virtue of having been enforced. The important distinction here is between properties that are part of (or follow from) an object's "nature," and those that are mere accidents. This distinction has a long and complex history in Western philosophy, but there are three themes relevant to our purposes here:[72] (1) All objects have a nature or essence; to be an object is (in some significant sense) to have a nature; it is by virtue of their nature that objects are members of kinds or species. This allows that there are also other legitimate classifications of objects in terms of accidental similarity or shared properties, but we should distinguish these classifications from those that group things in accordance with their natures. (2) Natures determine what is normal or appropriate—what is natural—for members of the kind. Natures serve to explain the behavior of the object under normal circumstances. (3) An object's nature is essential to it—that is, the object cannot exist without having those properties which constitute its nature.

Returning to objectification, if one objectifies something, one views it as an object for the satisfaction of one's desire. The suggestion I am pursuing is that in objectifying something one views it as *having a nature* which makes it desirable in the ways one desires it, and which enables it to satisfy that desire.[73] For example, if men desire submission, then in objectifying women men view women as having a nature which makes them (or, under normal circumstances, should make them) submissive, at the same time as they force women into submission. The illusion in successful objectification is not in the reports of its consequences—the women who have been forced to submit do submit; the illusion is in, so to speak, the modality of such claims—women submit *by nature*.[74]

Hence, the point that men view women *as objects* is not simply the point that men view women as something to use for their pleasure, as means and not ends. To view women as objects is to view women as a (substantial) kind; it is to view individual women as having a Woman's Nature. As the objectifier sees it, it is distinctive of this (alleged) kind that those features he finds desirable or arousing in women are a consequence of their nature, and so under normal circumstances women will exhibit these features. As we will consider further below, it follows from this view that women who fail to have those features men find desirable should be considered as deviant or abnormal. And if women are to develop in accordance with their nature, we should provide circumstances in which they will have those features. From the point of view of the objectifier, his view of women captures their individual nature; MacKinnon's aims to unmask this illusion: "See: what a woman 'is' is what you have *made* women be."[75]

So what is the epistemic position of one who successfully objectifies something? A successful objectifier attributes to something features that have been forced upon it, and he believes the object has these features "by nature."[76] In the relevant cases, this latter belief concerning the nature of the object—let us call this his "projective belief"—is false. But then what role does that belief play? Answering this takes us to the issue of neutrality.

Neutrality and Aperspectivity

As I've indicated, MacKinnon claims that "neutrality" and "distance" or "nonsituatedness" characterize the stance of objectivity, and that this stance functions as the norm for those who objectify others. This gives us little to go on, Neutrality between what? Distance from what? Drawing on several themes in MacKinnon's work, I will aim in this section to motivate an ideal of objectivity, consisting of a cluster of epistemic and practical norms, which is appropriate for the role of successful objectifier.[77]

What we are seeking is that set of norms that would effectively and reliably guide a successful objectifier's beliefs and actions, and whose general endorsement would sustain his position of power. We may assume that one in this role is situated in a position of power; success in this role requires maintaining the power to objectify others in an ongoing way.

Consider the objectifier's projective belief that the object of his domination has the properties "by nature" which, in fact, he has enforced. Two questions will guide the discussion: First, what role does this belief play in sustaining the objectifier's position of power? Second, what kind of justification could an ideal objectifier offer for this belief? Clearly these questions are closely connected, for if an ideal objectifier guides his beliefs and actions in accordance with a set of principles that legitimate them, then one would expect that in a social context where the principles are generally endorsed, his behavior would seem appropriate and his social position would be (relatively) safe. This allows that in contexts where the principles are not generally endorsed, a good objectifier might still guide his actions by these principles, but his position of power would be more tenuous insofar as others would challenge the principles guiding his behavior.

In following the thread of MacKinnon's discussion, I will pursue the following suggestion: (1) If the accepted norm for practical decision making is to adapt one's actions to accommodate natures, and (2) if the accepted epistemic norm for determining a thing's nature is to read it off of observed regularities, and (3) if in seeking regularities we are enjoined to deny or ignore our own contribution to the circumstances we observe, then the objectifier's beliefs and actions will appear "legitimate" and the unequal distribution of power that sustains objectification will be preserved.

As mentioned above, the belief that objects have natures plays a significant explanatory role: an object behaves as it does, under normal circumstances, because of its nature. So, regular patterns in the behavior of objects can and should be explained, at least in part, by reference to qualities of the objects themselves. Moreover, it is not possible to change something's nature. An object's nature is essential to it; a change with respect to an object's nature destroys the object. This suggests that in practical decision making we ought to be attentive to things' natures. It won't do to try to fry an egg on a paper plate; there's no point in trying to teach a rock how to read. Because the world is not infinitely malleable to our wants or needs, reasonable decision making will accommodate "how things are," where this is understood as accommodating the natures of things, the background conditions constraining our action.[78]

But of course it is a difficult matter to figure out what the natures of things are. If natures are responsible for regular behavior under normal circumstances, it is a plausible strategy to begin by inferring or postulating natures on the basis of observed regularities. Given the assumption that practical decision making should accommodate "the nature of things," this epistemic strategy has practical repercussions; it also leaves some important issues unaddressed. First, it will matter whose observations count (for example, only "normal" observers?), how we adjudicate disagreement, and what terms are classed as "observational." Second, if the point is to find natures, the strategy of inferring or postulating natures on the basis of actual observed regularities assumes that ordinary (observed) circumstances are "normal." Allowing for the possibility that current circumstances are not, broadly speaking, normal—that things are not expressing their natures in their regular behavior—accommodating regular behavior may *not* be justified by the need to cope with the real constraints the world presents.

The procedure of drawing on observed regularities to set constraints on practical decision making would appear to be a paradigm of "neutral," "objective," or "reasonable" procedure. And yet the ideal objectifier exploits this combined epistemic and practical norm—and its gaps—to his advantage. I'll offer here only a sketch of how this is done. We are asked to begin by assuming that actual circumstances are "normal." Looking around us, we discover rough generalizations capturing differences between men and women; more women than men satisfy the (contextually specific) norms of femininity and have a feminine gender identity internalizing those norms. Considering those gender categories of men and women constituted by sexual objectification, there are notable differences between men and women in line with the corresponding norms of dominance and submission.

However, if we take such existing gender differences as evidence for the different "natures" of men and women, and so structure social arrangements to accommodate these natures, then we simply reinforce the existing gendered social roles—that is, we sustain those social arrangements in which men dominate and women submit. "Once power constructs social reality . . . the subordination in gender inequality is made invisible; dissent from it becomes inaudible as well as rare. What a woman is, is defined in pornographic terms; this is what pornography does. If [we] look neutrally on the reality of gender so produced, the harm that has been done will not be perceptible as harm. It becomes just the way things are."[79] Once we have cast women as submissive and deferential "by nature," then efforts to change this role appear unmotivated, even pointless. Women who refuse this role are anomalies; they are not "normal" observers, and so their resistance, recalcitrant observations, and even their very efforts to speak may be ignored. Strangely, against this backdrop it is of no help to insist that women are rational agents capable of freely deciding how to act, for then it simply appears that women, by nature, rationally choose their subordinate role.[80] As a result, there is even less motivation for social change.

These reflections suggest that what appeared to be a "neutral" or "objective" ideal—namely, the procedure of drawing on observed regularities to set constraints on practical decision making—is one which will, under conditions of gender hierarchy, reinforce the social arrangements on which such hierarchy depends. But the argument for this conclusion is still incomplete, for one could object by claiming that observed regularities do not support the claim that women are, by nature, submissive. Straightforward empirical research would appear to show that many of the features the objectifier attributes to women "by nature" are a product of contingent social forces.

This is where the objectifier must resort to a norm of "distance," to a claim of aperspectivity. Initially it is plausible to offer this as a meta-norm that dictates what claims you, as an effective objectifier, should make about your results: (1) claim that your observations are not conditioned by your social position (though the claims of the subordinate are); and (2) claim that you have had no impact on the circumstances you are observing—you see what is happening without being part of it. If you can get others who already accept the proposed norms of neutrality to accept these claims about your standpoint, then your position of power is (relatively) safe.

In effect, if you are going to be successful in objectifying others, the best way to do it is to present the results of your objectification as "how things are," not to be evaluated and changed, but to be accepted as part of the circumstances we all must accommodate in steering a course through life. The norm of aperspectivity, at least in this context, functions to mask the power of the objectifier, thereby reinforcing the claim that the observed differences between men and women are a reflection of their natures. By this move the objectifier casts gender differences as asocial and amoral: We aren't responsible for things' natures, so morality has no foothold.[81] And because we cannot change something's nature, there is nothing to be done about it anyway.

So what epistemic and practical role does the objectifier's projective belief play in the process of objectification; or, in other words, what is the role of those beliefs that attribute to the object her enforced properties "by nature"? In general, such beliefs concerning the nature of things function as a linchpin to convert observation to practical justification; under conditions of gender hierarchy they enable the objectifier to use the observable consequences of his domination to justify his continued domination. But the objectifier's projective claims can function to reinforce his position of power over others only because he works in a context where norms of epistemic and practical neutrality are generally endorsed, and where he has convinced others of his aperspectivity (at least with respect to the object of his domination).

Assumed Objectivity

Should we conclude from this argument that theoretical positions committed to "natures" are politically suspect? Should we conclude that those who accommodate empirical regularities in deciding how to act objectify others? I don't think so; but to see why not we need to make the argument a bit more precise. In stating the norms of neutrality and aperspectivity at issue, it would be desirable to offer more substantive detail than I will here; such detail can make a difference to the arguments. But in the context of this essay my concern is to state the basic ideas that form the basis for a more precise formulation, not to provide that formulation.

What exactly is the ideal of objectivity at issue, and how is it connected to objectification? Let us take *absolute objectivity* to consist (roughly) of three norms:

- *epistemic neutrality:* take a "genuine" regularity in the behavior of something to be a consequence of its nature.
- *practical neutrality:* constrain your decision making (and so your action) to accommodate things' natures.
- *absolute aperspectivity:* count observed regularities as "genuine" regularities just in case: (1) the observations occur under normal circumstances (for ex-

ample, by normal observers), (2) the observations are not conditioned by the observer's social position, and (3) the observer has not influenced the behavior of the items under observation.

The point of absolute aperspectivity is to limit application of the norm of epistemic neutrality—only those observations that satisfy the aperspectivity conditions (1) through (3) are a legitimate basis for drawing conclusions about the nature of things. We should note, however, that because the objectifier's projective beliefs are not based on observations satisfying the constraints of absolute aperspectivity, they are not justified by the principles of absolute objectivity. At the very least the objectifier fails to satisfy conditions (2) and (3). But the ideal objectifier gets around this by relying on a supplemental principle of aperspectivity:

- *assumed aperspectivity:* if a regularity is observed, then assume that (1) the circumstances are normal, (2) the observations are not conditioned by the observers' social position, and (3) the observer has not influenced the behavior of the items under observation.[82]

Assumed aperspectivity entitles us to claim that any regularity we observe is a "genuine" regularity and so reveals the nature of the things under observation. In effect, we may apply the principle of epistemic neutrality to any regularity we find, because assumed aperspectivity bridges the gap between observed regularities and genuine regularities. It is this norm of assumed aperspectivity which enables the objectifier to conclude that his observations (which themselves may be accurate) are a guide to things' natures; in effect, the norm provides a basis for his projective beliefs. Let us call the ideal of objectivity which consists of absolute objectivity supplemented by the norm of assumed aperspectivity the ideal of *assumed objectivity*.

The broad question before us is whether and to what extent this ideal of assumed objectivity is gendered—more specifically, is it either weakly or strongly gendered. Let us ask first: Is this ideal *appropriate* to the role of men—that is, to what extent does it contribute to excellence in men's social role; and second, is the ideal *grounded in* men's social role—that is, is this an ideal whose satisfaction is sufficient for functioning as a man?

As I read MacKinnon's argument, we should conclude that the ideal of assumed objectivity is weakly masculine. It is appropriate to the role of objectifier in two ways: First, an objectifier who satisfies this ideal will reliably form the projective beliefs required for objectification and will act accordingly; moreover, a commitment to the ideal would provide him with principles to guide and legitimate his objectifying behavior. Second if the ideal is broadly endorsed, then it is at least likely that the objectifier's position of power, necessary for his continuing objectification, will be preserved. (We may assume that if the ideal is appropriate to the role of objectifier, it is appropriate to the role of sexual objectifier.)

To see these points, remember that we are considering how one who meets the minimal conditions as an objectifier might sustain a practice of successful objectification and so become an "excellent" objectifier. It is perhaps easiest to judge individuals' excellence in this role, as in many others, by whether they conform to principles that consistently recommend and justify their objectifying behavior. Objectifiers who conform to the norms of assumed objectivity will qualify, in this sense, as excellent. A man, for example, who objectifies women will view them and treat them as having a nature which makes them what he desires them to be; but he must also have the power to enforce this view. As discussed above, objectification occurs under conditions of inequality where some individuals have power over others. It is plausible that under such conditions there will be consequences of inequality evident in observable and regular differences between the unequal parties. But then, assuming that men will be witness to these regularities, those men who satisfy the norm of assumed objectivity will have reason to view women and treat women as they appear under the conditions of inequality—that is, as subordinate. The norms tell us to observe the differences and behave accordingly: see, women are subordinate (submissive, deferential, . . .), so treat them as subordinate (submissive, deferential, . . .). By the standards set by assumed objectivity, such objectifying beliefs and actions are justified. Those objectifiers who conform to these standards will reliably and consistently fulfill their role, given the social power to do so.[83]

Moreover, assumed objectivity contributes to sustaining that social power, at least in contexts where its norms are broadly endorsed. It is plausible that insofar as you are in a position to justify your behavior in light of broadly shared epistemic and practical norms, your social position is relatively secure. The relevant regularities that provide the basis for the objectifier's projective beliefs are generally accessible and, we may assume, accurate. So if the ideal of assumed objectivity is generally endorsed, then the inference to the projective belief and the consequent practical decisions will be broadly recognized as legitimate. Thus a general endorsement of the ideal of assumed objectivity reinforces the objectifier's position of power and contributes to his ongoing success.

The considerations just offered suggest that the ideal of assumed objectivity is weakly masculine, because satisfying the ideal contributes to success in the role of objectifier and, therefore, to success in the role of sexual objectifier. Should we also conclude that the ideal is strongly masculine? Let me begin by asking whether it is grounded more broadly in the role of objectifier: Is satisfying the ideal sufficient for objectifying others? MacKinnon suggests that it is: "to look at the world objectively is to objectify it."[84] Let us recall that an ideal might be grounded in a social role either constitutively (if it is not possible to satisfy the ideal without functioning in that social role) or contextually (if given specified background conditions satisfying the ideal is sufficient for functioning in the role). I think we may grant that satisfying the ideal of assumed objectivity is not constitutively grounded in the role of objectifier; our focus should be on contextual grounding.

In considering the ways in which the ideal of assumed objectivity contributes to the success of an objectifier, we saw that under conditions of gender inequality, one who observes regular differences between men and women and who satisfies the ideal will view women as subordinate, treat women as subordinate, and be justified, by those standards, in doing so. But this is not sufficient, in general, to be an objectifier or, more specifically, to sexually objectify women. I propose that the ideal of assumed objectivity is contextually grounded, not directly in the role of objectifier, but in the role of collaborator in objectification.

To explain, remember that one objectifies something just in case one views it and treats it as an object that has by nature properties which one *desires* in it and, further, one *has the power* to make it have those properties. (Sexual objectification adds to each of these two further conditions: The desire in question is an erotic desire, and the desire is for dominance/submission.) Let us say that one *collaborates in objectifying* something just in case one views it and treats it as an object that has by nature properties which are a consequence of objectification, that is, properties which are a consequence of the forces sustaining social hierarchy. Collaboration differs from objectification insofar as one may collaborate in objectifying something without viewing it in terms of one's projected desire: One may not find the properties attributed to the object desirable—they may be viewed as undesirable, perhaps simply "natural" or "inevitable." Collaboration also differs from objectification insofar as one who collaborates need not have the power to force her view of things upon them. Nevertheless, collaboration is not simply a passive process of allowing others to carry on with their objectification; a collaborator shares with both sorts of objectifiers a pattern of thought and action. A woman who views women as weak and inferior by nature, and acts accordingly, collaborates in objectification, though in doing so she need not objectify women.

So if we consider a context of gender inequality—let's say a context where male dominance is widespread—we may assume that there will be generally observable differences between men and women that are a consequence of men's forcing their view of women on women. Individuals in this context who are aware of these differences and who satisfy the norm of assumed objectivity (at least with respect to these observed regularities) will view the differences as "natural" and will act to accommodate gender difference. This, I take it, is sufficient to function in the role of a collaborator in objectification. In short, the ideal of assumed objectivity is contextually grounded in the role of collaborator; the relevant background conditions for this grounding are that the one who satisfies the ideal (a) does so in a context of social hierarchy, (b) is aware of the observable consequences of this hierarchy, and (c) applies the norm to these observations.

I state these background conditions in terms of social hierarchy rather than gender hierarchy, because we may allow that there are other forms of objectification besides sexual objectification (for example, racial objectification); correspondingly, there are other forms of collaboration. The argument just offered suggests that the ideal of assumed objectivity is sufficient for functioning in a specific collaborative role relative to the social context and one's application of the norms. For example, in a context where both racial and sexual domination are in place, one who observes both racial and sexual differences, and who satisfies the norms of assumed objectivity with respect to both, will collaborate in both racial and sexual objectification; if one satisfies the norms only selectively, one may, for example, collaborate in racial but not sexual objectification or in sexual but not racial objectification.

We should not conclude however, that any and every case in which one satisfies the ideal of assumed objectivity, even under conditions of social hierarchy, is sufficient for functioning as a collaborator. This is to say that all three of the above-stated background conditions (a) – (c), not just the first, must be met before drawing the connection between assumed objectivity and collaboration. This is because there are contexts, even under conditions of social hierarchy, in which one observes a regularity in something's behavior, assumes that it is a consequence of its nature, and acts to accommodate this nature, without thereby collaborating in objectification.

For example, I observe that watering begonias with ammonia kills them; I assume that this is a consequence of their nature, and I adjust my actions so that I water begonias with ammonia only if I want to kill them. I don't try to change the fact that begonias die when watered with ammonia. In this case, the relevant property of begonias is not a consequence of objectification; that they have this property is not due to social coercion. I satisfy the ideal of assumed objectivity with respect to my observations of begonias, but I don't collaborate in objectifying them. It is central to objectification that social facts are treated as natural facts and so are cast as immutable; assumed objectivity legitimates this error. But where the observable regularities used as a basis for drawing conclusions about natures are not the result of social coercion or force, there is no objectification and so no collaboration in objectification.

Similarly, if I observe that people regularly die when deprived of food and shelter for an extended period, and I take this to be a result of their nature, and also accommodate this fact in deciding how to act, I don't collaborate in objectification. Again, that there are conditions under which we cannot survive is not a consequence of objectification. The important point to note here is that one objectifies someone (or something) only if the properties one takes to be part of her nature are properties she has as a consequence of social forces. The fact that a human organism will stop functioning under conditions of physical deprivation is not plausibly a result of social forces. Again, the element of illusion—the masking of social/moral facts as natural facts—is missing; this illusion is a crucial element of both objectification and collaboration.

Objectivity and Sexual Objectification

The argument I have just offered for the conclusion that assumed objectivity is contextually grounded in the role of collaborator, falls considerably short of the thesis that satisfying this ideal of objectivity is sufficient for being a sexual objectifier. It falls short in two important ways. First, I have argued that in a limited variety of cases, satisfying the norm of assumed objectivity is sufficient for functioning as a collaborator, not as an objectifier. Second, I have left sexuality virtually out of the picture. To be fair, I should acknowledge that MacKinnon does sketch an argument for the claim that in being objective one functions as a sexual objectifier.

Let us grant that we are considering whether assumed objectivity is contextually grounded in the role of men under conditions of male dominance. Further, let us say that one takes up an *objectivist stance* toward something, just in case on the basis of assumed objectivity, one views it as an object having certain properties "by nature," and takes this as a constraint in deciding how to act. The hypothesis under consideration is that if you are an objectivist in this sense, then your relationship to the object is one of sexual objectification. What must be shown is that if one takes up such an objectivist stance toward something, then (1) one views it and treats it as having by nature properties one desires, (2) one has the power to force it to have these properties (and sometimes exercises this power), and (3) one desires subordination and finds force erotic.

MacKinnon's argument for this claim relies on three controversial premises (my numbering indicates a link with each of the required points above):

1 +. In general, to view something as an object is to view it as having, by nature, certain properties that one finds useful or desirable: "The object world is constructed according to how it looks with respect to its possible uses."[85]

2 +. One's stance toward an object is objective only if one has made (or makes) it have the properties one attributes to it: "What is objectively known corresponds to the world and can be verified by being pointed to (as science does) because the world itself is controlled from the same point of view."[86]

3 +. All domination or control is eroticized: "The act of control . . . is itself eroticized under male supremacy."[87]

So the picture is this: In taking up the objectivist stance toward something, you project your needs/desires onto it (taking the desired properties to be part of its nature, even if it doesn't currently exhibit them); you make it have the properties you project; and you find this control erotic. One thereby sexually objectifies the "object" of this stance. If the social role of men is the role of sexual objectifier, then taking up the objectivist stance is sufficient for being a man.

Although I have only indicated the barest outline of MacKinnon's argument, I will not undertake to explicate it further here. I offered some examples in the previous section which suggest that at least premises (1 +) and (2 +) are seriously overstated. Even more effective counterexamples to these claims could be easily constructed. Further, if we accept MacKinnon's premises, then we lose the distinction between objectification and collaboration; as sketched above, a collaborator is an objectivist who conforms her beliefs and actions to the objectifier's projected reality. But she need not find this reality desirable and she need not have the social power to enforce it. If MacKinnon's premises are accurate, this is not an available position: On her view an objectivist not only desires objects to have the properties she takes to be part of their nature, but is in a position to make them conform to her view. Yet it is mysterious, for example, why taking up an objectivist stance should be thought sufficient for having such power.

More important, however, I think the basic strategy of MacKinnon's argument—a strategy all too common among feminist theorists—is deeply flawed. The strategy is to take a powerful analysis of how the social world has been shaped by male power and desire, and to extend this analysis to the world as a whole. For example, take a powerful account of pornography as a mechanism by which the social category of women is constructed, and suggest that there are analogous accounts for all categories. But such generalization, rather than strengthening MacKinnon's position, weakens it.

MacKinnon's analysis of gender and sexual objectification is important and effective because it vividly captures the very real power that men have over women, power backed by violence and hatred and law. In spite of the horror of it, it is empowering to recognize that the threat of male violence has significantly formed the social world as women know it and live it. What has been done can maybe be undone. If we claim however, that the power that has determined gender categories is *the same power* that has determined all categories, then we deflate the social analysis of this power with the simple thought that much of what the world is like is not within the control of people, societies, cultures, languages, etc. In short, in the effort to generalize our insights we lose the contrast between what we do have significant control over and what we don't. Fortunately we are not omnipotent; we don't have the power "to force the world to be anyway [our] minds can invent."[88] Men don't have this power; neither do women; neither do "cultures," etc. The fantasy of such power may be useful in casting our current categories as open to critique, but believing in the fantasy, I submit, is as dangerous as supposing that our current categories capture Nature's "givens."

The analysis of gender categories as socially constructed succeeds as a critique of traditional ideas about men and women in part because it targets the specific mechanisms of social control that are responsible for the observable differences between men and women. It is the contrast between these mechanisms of control and naturalistic or deterministic causal mechanisms—for example, mechanisms that are responsible for the observable differences between, say, water and ammonia—that lends support to the hope that social change is possible. There may be a complex social analysis of why we are interested in the difference between ammonia and water and why we are keen to distinguish them, but it is implausible to suggest that specific mechanisms of social control are responsible for their difference. If we insist that the mechanisms responsible for any apparent natural differences are the same mechanisms that are at work in constructing gender difference, we lose our focus on what social power consists in.

If we suppose, for example, that the explanation of gender difference should apply in explaining all differences, then it is plausible to seek a common denominator in the variety of explanations offered. But seeking such a common explanatory strategy distracts the effort for social change; there are two temptations that lead us astray. On the one hand, if we note the significance of causal explanation in understanding regular patterns in things' behavior, it is tempting to resort to a social or psychological determinism in explaining gender; thus it becomes obscure, once again, how the power that constructs gender is both optional and, more important, subject to moral appraisal. On the other hand, it is tempting to relocate the source of gender oppression in a "pattern of thought" common to all efforts at differentiation—for example, a pattern that attributes natures to things. This shifts our attention from a concern with the concrete mechanisms of social control and relocates the problem "in our heads"— as if domination and abuse would end if we just stopped the bad habit of thinking that things have natures (or if we stopped distinguishing things or postulating unified categories). Worse still, taking our thoughts to be the problem can lead to an intellectual nihilism that deprives us of the resources for constructing viable alternatives to existing social arrangements.

Analyses of categories that purport to be natural in terms of hierarchical social relations (for example, analyses of gender, race, sex) have highlighted the political import of the distinction between the social and the natural; and plausibly such analyses should prompt us to reevaluate all our judgments about what is natural and what is social. But even if systematic doubt and extra caution are warranted *for every case*, this does not support a wholesale denial of the distinction between natural categories and social categories. Nor does it give us grounds for thinking that a commitment to things having "natures" is antifeminist; in particular, recognizing that I am not by nature a woman leaves untouched the broader question of whether I have a nature and, strange as it may sound, whether my nature is natural or not.[89] Generalizing the strategy behind a social analysis of gender across the board may seem a promising way to combat a dogmatic insistence on the immutability of life as we know it. But concrete analyses of socially constructed categories do not warrant sweeping conclusions about "all language" and "all categories," and the hasty generalization of our analyses both theoretically and politically weakens the force of our position.

6. Conclusion

Thus far I have argued that there is a complex epistemic and practical norm—what I have called the ideal of "assumed objectivity," which is appropriate to the role of objectifier: realizing this ideal enables objectifiers to be better objectifiers, and its endorsement perpetuates objectification. If there is a social category of men defined by the relation of sexual objectification, then (assuming that someone can be a good sexual objectifier only if they are a good objectifier) the ideal is appropriate to at least one significant gender role for men. From this we should conclude that the ideal of assumed objectivity is weakly masculine.

I have also argued that the ideal of assumed objectivity is contextually grounded in the role of collaborator in objectification. Under conditions of social hierarchy, those who observe the consequences of inequality and apply the norms in assumed objectivity to their observations will function socially as collaborators. I also argued, however, that one can satisfy the ideal of assumed objectivity under these specific background conditions and not function as an objectifier or as a sexual objectifier. Thus we should conclude that the ideal, at least with respect to these conditions, is not grounded in men's social role and so is not strongly masculine. Of course, this leaves open the question whether there are other gender roles, and other background conditions, with respect to which the ideal is strongly masculine.

What should we make of these conclusions? To what extent do they offer reason to reject the ideal of assumed objectivity? We should begin by noting that the ideal of assumed objectivity is a cluster of principles; it consists of assumed aperspectivity, along with the principles in absolute objectivity (epistemic neutrality, practical neutrality, and absolute aperspectivity). The arguments I have considered, even if they pose a challenge to the value of the ideal as a whole, do not offer grounds for rejecting *all* of the constituent principles in the ideal; nor do they offer grounds for deciding which constituent principle, or principles, to reject. What problems the ideal may cause are a consequence of the principles being employed in conjunction.[90] This is important, for it shows that one cannot plausibly use the argument I have outlined against those who endorse something less than the full conjunction of principles. The argument is ineffective, for example, against those who accept that things have natures which we must accommodate in our decision making, but who deny that we can read off natures from just any apparent regularity; it is also ineffective against those who make quick inferences to natures but who think there's no general imperative to accommodate or respect them.

In introducing the charge that rationality is gendered, I suggested that its being so would constitute a challenge to the Western philosophical tradition's emphasis on ideals of reason and rational selves. Given the arguments just offered, have we a basis for claiming that the traditional commitments of epistemology and metaphysics are male biased or that they sustain male domination? Certainly we cannot answer this question without a detailed examination of the philosophical positions that have been offered. I would suggest, however, that it is difficult to situate the charge that assumed objectivity is gendered as a critique of traditional epistemology and metaphysics.

Undoubtedly philosophers have relied on the ideal of assumed objectivity in constructing accounts of human nature and in offering moral, political, and epistemological theories; moreover, they have relied on it in ways that are politically problematic. But we must also acknowledge that the norm of assumed objectivity does not capture a broad range of philosophical ideals of rationality; and it does not do justice to the sensitivity philosophers have shown concerning the problem of postulating natures. Those working within a (broadly) empiricist tradition are happy to rely on observed regularities in forming their theories, but they are notoriously opposed to attributing natures to things; those working within (broadly) Aristotelian and rationalist traditions are happy to attribute natures to things, but they do not do so on the basis of observed regularities alone. Thus it would seem that important figures in the traditional philosophical canon not only explicitly reject the ideal of assumed objectivity, but also offer resources for demonstrating its weaknesses and for constructing alternatives.

However, even if the conclusion that assumed objectivity is gendered does not provide a direct indictment of those pursuing traditional projects in epistemology and metaphysics, neither can we rest content, thinking that these projects have been vindicated. For example, we should ask: In what cases does the explicit rejection of assumed objectivity belie a deeper reliance upon it? What are the alternatives to assumed objectivity? Are there other conceptions of objectivity—conceptions offering weakly or strongly gendered ideals—playing a role in philosophical theorizing? And are there additional ways that norms and ideals can be gendered beyond those we have discussed?

Having noted some limitations of the arguments considered, we still face the more difficult question of how these arguments bear on our evaluation of assumed objectivity. Given that the ideal of assumed objectivity is weakly masculine and contextually grounded in the role of collaborator in objectification, should we reject the ideal? Let us return to the examples (discussed above) of the kind masters, and the journalists whose excellence renders them criminals. In these cases, it seemed plausible that we should continue to value kindness and the virtues of journalists, but work to change the circumstances that made for their offensive consequences. Is assumed objectivity an ideal like these? Should we broadly endorse, even abide by, its norms, but work to undermine the social hierarchy that makes for its offensive consequences?

I submit that we should reject the ideal of assumed objectivity—at least in the unqualified form we've considered it—for the suggestion that we might endorse it while working to undermine the existing social hierarchy leaves us in an unmanageable position. There are two issues to address: First, should we accept the ideal of assumed objectivity as binding on us—should we accept its norms to guide our attitudes and actions? Second, should we support and value the activities of others who live by those norms, even if we don't? In answering these questions, it matters who is included in the "us," who counts as "we." The "we" I am speaking of, and to, is culturally and historically situated. We live under conditions of social hierarchy, a hierarchy in which one has power by virtue of being, for example, male, white, straight. More important, I am assuming that we are committed to changing this.

If we accept the norms of assumed objectivity as binding on us, then our efforts at social change would be, by its lights, not only unmotivated but unjustified. Because we live under circumstances of social hierarchy and are aware of the consequences of this hierarchy, the ideal of assumed objectivity would instruct us to collaborate in the existing patterns of objectification: we should view and treat the subordinate as subordinate. In short, our circumstances satisfy the background conditions under which assumed objectivity renders one a collaborator. But in committing ourselves to social change we reject these attitudes and these actions, viewing them as wrong and unjustified. Such a conflict is unmanageable. Faced with such a conflict, assumed objectivity is clearly the commitment to revise. Moreover, if we allow that others, also situated under conditions of social hierarchy, legitimately guide their attitudes and actions by the ideal of assumed objectivity, then this legitimacy will extend to their collaborative activities. But then it becomes obscure on what basis we demand that they change.

In these respects the ideal of assumed objectivity is unlike kindness and unlike journalistic excellence; in those cases there is no conflict between valuing the ideals and being committed to social change. Admittedly, there are actual cases in which satisfying the ideal of assumed objectivity is not offensive, even when its constituent norms are employed in conjunction. And there are times and places in which the background conditions are not those of social hierarchy, so satisfying the ideal will not render one a collaborator. But unfortunately, we are not in such a time or place, and endorsing unrestricted application of the ideal will only keep us from getting there.

Notes

I would like to thank Elizabeth Anderson, Louise Antony, Susan Brison, Susan Donaldson, Cynthia Freeland, Beth Hackett, Elisabeth Lloyd, Will Kymlicka, Maria Morales, Laura Murphy, Jay Wallace, Alison Wylie, and Stephen Yablo for their encouragement, comments, and helpful discussion on the topics of this essay; for this, as well as valuable editorial assistance, special thanks to Charlotte Witt. Thanks also to Wayne Sumner and the Philosophy Department at the University of Toronto for their generosity in making available to me the resources of the university while I was on leave from the University of Pennsylvania.

1. There is an enormous amount of feminist research offering critiques of male bias in traditional disciplines. Important anthologies focusing on critiques of traditional philosophical projects include Sandra Harding and Merrill B. Hintikka, eds., *Discovering Reality: Feminist Perspectives on Epistemology, Metaphysics, Methodology, and Philosophy of Science* (Dordrecht: D. Reidel, 1983): Carol Gould, ed., *Beyond Domination: New Perspectives on Women and Philosophy* (Totowa, N.J.: Rowman and Littlefield, 1984); Carole Pateman and Elizabeth Gross, eds., *Feminist Challenges: Social and Political Theory* (Boston: Allen and Unwin, 1986); Eva Kittay and Diana Meyers, eds., *Women and Moral Theory* (Totowa, N.J.: Rowman and Littlefield, 1987); Ann Garry and Marilyn Pearsall, eds., *Women, Knowledge, and Reality* (Boston: Unwin Hyman, 1989); Alison Jaggar and Susan Bordo, eds., *Gender/Body/Knowledge: Feminist Reconstructions of Being and Knowing* (New Brunswick, N.J.: Rutgers University Press, 1989).

2. A paradigm example of this latter project is Carol McMillan's *Women, Reason, and Nature* (Princeton, N.J.: Princeton University Press, 1982). See also Sara Ruddick, "Maternal Thinking," *Feminist Studies* 6 (Summer 1980): 342–367. This general strategy has been widely pursued in the context of theories of moral reasoning, often inspired by Carol Gilligan's *In a Different Voice: Psychological Theory and Women's Development* (Cambridge, Mass.: Harvard University Press, 1982).

3. This line of thought is relatively common among French feminists and feminist postmodernists. See, e.g., Elaine Marks and Isabel de Coutivron, eds., *New French Feminisms: An Anthology* (Amherst, Mass.: University of Massachusetts Press, 1980); Luce Irigaray, *Speculum of the Other Woman,* tr. Gillian C. Gill (Ithaca, N.Y.: Cornell University Press, 1985); Susan Bordo, "The Cartesian Masculinization of Thought," *Signs* 11 (1986): 439–456; Jessica Benjamin, "Master and Slave: The Fantasy of Erotic Domination," in *Powers of Desire,* ed. A Snitow, C. Stansell, and S. Thompson (New York: Monthly Review Press, 1983): 280–299; Evelyn Fox Keller, *Reflections on Gender and Science* (New Haven, Conn.: Yale University Press, 1985). Helpful commentaries explicating important themes in this line of thought include Toril Moi, *Sexual/Textual Politics* (New York: Methuen, 1985); and Chris Weedon, *Feminist Practice and Poststructuralist Theory* (Oxford: Basil Blackwell, 1987). For a different approach to the same issue, see also Susan Griffin, *Woman and Nature: The Roaring Inside Her* (New York: Harper and Row, 1978); and Mary Daly, *Gyn/ecology: The Metaethics of Radical Feminism* (Boston: Beacon Press, 1978).

4. Many feminists have cautioned against theorizing an alternative "feminine" kind of reason. These include Genevieve Lloyd, *The Man of Reason: "Male" and "Female" in Western Philosophy* (Minneapolis: University of Minnesota Press, 1984), esp. 105; Robert Pargetter and Elizabeth Prior, "Against the Sexuality of Reason," *Australasian Journal of Philosophy,* supplement to vol. 64 (June 1986): 107–119; Jane Flax, "Postmodernism and Gender Relations in Feminist Theory," in *Feminism/Postmodernism,* ed. Linda Nicholson (New York: Routledge, 1990), 39–62; Christine DiStefano, "Dilemmas of Difference," in Nicholson, ed., *Feminism/Postmodernism,* 63–82. One alternative to the idea of "feminine reason" has been to locate instead a "feminist standpoint" that offers an alternative to the ideal of "masculine reason" as well as a critique of femininity. See, e.g., Nancy Hartsock, *Money, Sex, and Power* (Boston: Northeastern University Press, 1984); and Alison Jaggar, *Feminist Politics and Human Nature* (Totowa, N.J.: Rowman and Allenheld, 1983). This

strategy too has received sustained criticism. See Sandra Harding, *The Science Question in Feminism* (Ithaca, N.Y.: Cornell University Press, 1986).

5. Important work in evaluating feminist critiques of rationality and in reconstructing conceptions of reason include Helen Longino, "Feminist Critiques of Rationality: Critiques of Science or Philosophy of Science," *Women's Studies International Forum* 12 (1989): 261–269, and *Science as Social Knowledge* (Princeton, N.J.: Princeton University Press, 1990); Mary Hawkesworth, "Feminist Epistemology: A Survey of the Field," *Women and Politics* 7 (Fall 1987): 115–127, and "Knowers, Knowing, Known: Feminist Theory and Claims of Truth," *Signs* 14 (1989): 533–557; Sandra Harding, "The Instability of Analytical Categories in Feminist Theory," *Signs* 11 (1986): 645–664, and *The Science Question in Feminism* (Ithaca, N.Y.: Cornell University Press, 1986); Susan Hekman, "The Feminization of Epistemology: Gender and the Social Sciences," *Women and Politics* 7 (Fall 1987): 65–83; Judith Grant, "I Feel, Therefore I Am: A Critique of Female Experience as a Basis for Feminist Epistemology," *Women and Politics* 7 (Fall 1987): 99–114; Donna Haraway, "Situated Knowledges: The Science Question in Feminism and the Privilege of Partial Perspective," *Feminist Studies* 14 (Fall 1988): 575–599; Seyla Benhabib, "Epistemologies of Postmodernism: A Rejoinder to Jean-François Lyotard," *New German Critique* 33 (1984): 104–126; Iris Young, "The Ideal Community and the Politics of Difference," *Social Theory and Practice* 12 (Spring 1986): 1–26.

6. Useful papers include Joan Scott, "Gender: A Useful Category of Historical Analysis," *American Historical Review* 91 (December 1986): 1053–1075; Jane Flax, "Gender as a Social Problem: In and For Feminist Theory," *Amerikastudien/America Studies* 31 (1986): 193–213, and "Postmodernism and Gender Relations"; Donna Haraway, "'Gender' for a Marxist Dictionary," in her *Simians, Cyborgs, and Women: The Reinvention of Nature* (New York: Routledge, Chapman, and Hall, 1991), 127–148. For important early attempts at defining gender in terms of social relations, see also Gayle Rubin, "The Traffic in Women: Notes on the Political Economy of Sex," in *Toward an Anthropology of Women,* ed. Rayna Rapp Reiter (New York: Monthly Review Press, 1975), 157–210; and Sherry Ortner, "Is Female to Male as Nature to Culture?" in *Women, Culture, and Society,* ed. Michelle Rosaldo and Louise Lamphere (Palo Alto, Calif.: Stanford University Press, 1974), 67–87.

7. See, e.g., Susan Bordo, "Feminism, Postmodernism, and Gender Scepticism," in Nicholson, ed., *Feminism/Postmodernism,* 133–156; and DiStefano, "Dilemmas of Difference," esp. 73–78.

8. The suggestion that sex may not be a binary classification and that it may be socially constructed appears, of course, in Michel Foucault; see, e.g., *The History of Sexuality, Vol. 1: An Introduction,* tr. Robert Hurley (New York: Vintage/Random House, 1980). This suggestion has also been endorsed by many feminist theorists. For useful discussions, see Monique Wittig, "One Is Not Born a Woman," *Feminist Issues* 1 (Winter 1981): 47–54, "The Category of Sex," *Feminist Issues* 2 (Fall 1982): 63–68; Judith Butler, "Variations on Sex and Gender: Beauvoir, Wittig, and Foucault," in *Feminism as Critique,* ed. S. Benhabib and D. Cornell (Minneapolis: University of Minnesota Press, 1987), 128–142; and Donna Haraway, "A Manifesto for Cyborgs: Science, Technology, and Socialist Feminisms in the 1980's," in her *Simians, Cyborgs, and Women,* 149–181.

9. This "commonplace," however, is not as straightforward as it may seem, and it is not accepted across the board. The distinction between sex and gender has been challenged as presupposing and reinforcing a problematic contrast between "nature" and "culture." See, e.g., Moira Gatens, "A Critique of the Sex/Gender Distinction," in *Beyond Marxism? Interventions after Marx,* ed. J. Allen and P. Patton (Sydney: Intervention Publications,

1983), 143–163; Haraway, "'Gender' for a Marxist Dictionary," esp. 133–134; and Butler, "Variations on Sex and Gender." However, it is by no means obvious that in drawing the distinction between sex and gender, one is thereby committed to saying that sex is a natural category; my concern here is to emphasize the social character of gender, allowing that sexual difference must also be given a social analysis, one plausibly interdependent with the analysis of gender.

10. Roughly, an intrinsic property of x is one that x has simply in virtue of itself, regardless of the properties of other things—e.g., x could have that property even if it were the only thing existing. Intrinsic properties need not be essential and may be temporary. An extrinsic property of x is one that x has not simply in virtue of itself; x's having the property depends on the properties of other things as well.

11. At this point, in saying that the relations are "social" I mean simply to indicate that they concern certain relations that hold between individuals by virtue of their place in a social system. My point is completely neutral on the issue of whether or not we should be realists about properties or think that all properties and relations are "merely conventional." Any plausible nominalism or conventionalism will have the resources to distinguish social properties and relations from others in the sense intended. See Ian Hacking, "World-Making by Kind-Making: Child Abuse as an Example," in *How Classification Works,* ed. Mary Douglas (Edinburgh: University of Edinburgh Press, 1992), especially sec. 1–2.

12. Important works discussing the ethnocentric and imperialistic tendencies in feminist accounts of gender include Cherrie Moraga and Gloria Anzaldúa, eds., *This Bridge Called My Back: Writings by Radical Women of Color* (Watertown, Mass.: Persephone, 1981); bell hooks, *Ain't I a Woman: Black Women and Feminism* (Boston: South End Press, 1981); Audre Lorde, *Sister/Outsider* (Trumansburg, N.Y.: Crossing Press 1984); Maria Lugones and Elizabeth Spelman, "Have We Got a Theory for You: Feminist Theory, Cultural Imperialism, and the Demand for 'The Woman's Voice,'" *Women's Studies International Forum* 6 (1983): 573–581; Elizabeth Spelman, *The Inessential Woman: Problems of Exclusion in Feminist Thought* (Boston: Beacon Press, 1988); Elizabeth Weed, ed., *Coming to Terms: Feminism, Theory, Politics* (New York: Routledge, Chapman, and Hall, 1989); Gayatri Spivak, "Explanation and Culture: Marginalia," in *In Other Worlds: Essays in Cultural Politics,* ed. Gayatri Spivak (New York: Routledge, Chapman, and Hall, 1988), 103–117, and her "Feminism and Critical Theory," in Spivak, ed., *In Other Worlds,* 77–92. For a useful discussion of ethnocentric bias in the feminist critique of rationality, see, e.g., Uma Narayan, "The Project of Feminist Epistemology: Perspectives from a Nonwestern Feminist," in Jaggar and Bordo, *Gender/Body/Knowledge,* 256–269.

13. For an important discussion of this claim, see Catharine MacKinnon, *Feminism Unmodified: Discourses on Life and Law* (Cambridge, Mass.: Harvard University Press, 1987), ch. 2. See also Flax, "Postmodernism and Gender Relations," esp. 45, 49; Monique Wittig, "The Straight Mind," *Feminist Issues* 1 (Summer 1980): 103–111, "Category of Sex," and "One Is Not Born a Woman." It is important to note that not all social relations are hierarchical (e.g., being a friend is not), and not all hierarchical relations are relations of domination (e.g., although plausibly the relations of doctor-patient, mother-daughter, and so on are hierarchical, they are not themselves relations of domination). Unfortunately, the distinctions between social, hierarchical, and dominance relations are sometimes conflated.

14. For a discussion of the political interplay between categories of sex and gender, see references in notes 8 and 9 above. See also Evelyn Fox Keller, "The Gender/Science System; or, Is Sex to Gender as Nature Is to Science?" *Hypatia* 2 (Fall 1987): 37–49.

15. Weedon, *Feminist Practice and Poststructuralist Theory,* 26.

16. See, e.g., Jean Grimshaw, *Philosophy and Feminist Thinking* (Minneapolis: University of Minnesota Press, 1986), 62.

17. For example, in some affluent Western communities the ideal of the "supermom" has replaced the ideal of the "homemaker" as a gender-norm for women (is this a new "femininity"?). We should also note that gender-norms may function differently if women take control of defining the social relations that constitute gender—i.e., being a "good woman" within a women's community may require satisfying very different norms than those traditionally counted as feminine. Note that feminist resistance to the claim that gender categories are constituted by relations of domination is sometimes supported by the thought that the category of women should be defined *by* and *for* women in terms of a more empowering self-conception; such a definition would plausibly not employ relations of domination. This constructive project is highly contested, for there is a clear danger of replacing one set of oppressive gender roles (and gender-norms) with another. One alternative is to resist the construction of gender categories altogether, likewise resisting the consolidation of (at least binary) gender-norms. We might instead recommend a "subversive recombination of gender meanings" (see Judith Butler, "Gender Trouble, Feminist Theory, and Psychoanalytic Discourse," in Nicholson, ed., *Feminism/Postmodernism,* 333). See also Theresa de Lauretis, "Feminist Studies/Critical Studies: Issues, Terms, and Contexts," in her *Feminist Studies/Critical Studies,* (Bloomington: Indiana University Press, 1986), 1–19.

18. DiStefano. "Dilemmas of Difference," 70.

19. E.g., the idea that a "good" woman is asexual, combined with the idea that a "good" woman is responsive to men's sexual desire, offers women little room to negotiate a coherent relation to sexuality. For a discussion of such contradictions in the context of moral evaluation, see Kathryn Morgan, "Women and Moral Madness," *Canadian Journal of Philosophy,* supplementary vol. 13 (Fall 1987): 201–225.

20. However, we should note that norms may entail features that are not in any obvious way under our control; hence, our strivings to satisfy the accepted norm may be pointless and even tragic. Self-mutilation and self-starvation are not uncommon consequences of the felt need to satisfy accepted gender-norms.

21. A broad range of feminists have been keen to incorporate the suggestion that our conceptions of self and world bear the marks of gender, largely due to the influence of early childhood experience. In internalizing the relevant gender-norms, we develop "gender identities"; these gender identities represent reality—self and world—in a form that motivates our participation in the assigned gender role. The literature on this is enormous. Important examples include Nancy Chodorow, *The Reproduction of Mothering: Psychoanalysis and the Sociology of Gender* (Berkeley: University of California Press, 1978); Dorothy Dinnerstein, *The Mermaid and the Minotaur: Sexual Arrangements and Human Malaise* (New York: Harper and How, 1976); Jane Flax, "Political Philosophy and the Patriarchal Unconscious: A Psychoanalytic Perspective on Epistemology and Metaphysics," in Harding and Hintikka, eds., *Discovering Reality,* 245–281; Keller, *Reflections on Gender and Science;* Naomi Scheman, "Individualism and the Objects of Psychology," in Harding and Hintikka, eds., *Discovering Reality,* 225–244. For an important critical discussion of this work, see Butler, "Gender Trouble."

22. It is important to note, however, that when gender-norms are well-entrenched, individuals are often interpreted as living up to them even when they don't: a woman may be assumed to be nurturing, weak, or dependent even when she isn't. (Others may make these assumptions about her, and she may also make these assumptions about herself.)

23. Another temptation prompted by generalizations that women are feminine and men are masculine is to define the social categories of gender in terms of conformity to idealized gender-norms—i.e., to take the social class of women to consist of those who are feminine. This, too, is a mistake, but for different reasons. On this view, it is rightly acknowledged that gender differences are the result of social forces; but in taking femininity to be the mark by which one qualifies as a woman, the analysis loses much of its power as a critique of patriarchy's assumptions about women. Delimiting the class of women in terms of the standards of femininity treats unfeminine women as not "really" women at all and ignores the possibility of women's resistance to the norm; worse still, because socially endorsed conceptions of "femininity" will reflect race, class, heterosexual, religious, and ethnic bias, by defining women as those who are feminine we are in danger of repeating the exclusion and marginalization that feminism is committed to redressing.

24. This point has been made repeatedly over the centuries. See, e.g., John Stuart Mill, *The Subjection of Women,* in *Essays on Sex Equality,* ed. Alice Rossi (Chicago: University of Chicago Press, 1970). We will discuss later some of the mechanisms that all too often obscure this point.

25. For a convincing and engaging discussion of this point, see Christine Delphy, "Protofeminism and Antifeminism," in *French Feminist Theory,* ed. Toril Moi (Oxford: Basil Blackwell, 1987), 80–109. See also Iris Young, "Is Male Gender Identity the Cause of Male Domination," in *Throwing Like a Girl and Other Essays in Feminist Philosophy and Social Theory* (Bloomington/Indianapolis: Indiana University Press, 1990), 36–61.

26. See Lloyd, *Man of Reason.*

27. Just about anything can be (and has been) interpreted as exemplifying the norms of femininity and masculinity. Useful examples of the projection of gender-norms onto individuals of other kinds is available in feminist work in science (especially biology). See, e.g., Helen Longino and Ruth Doell, "Body, Bias, and Behavior: A Comparative Analysis in Two Areas of Biological Science," *Signs* 9 (1983): 206–227; and Haraway, *Simians, Cyborgs, and Women,* esp. pts. I–II.

28. Butler, "Variations on Sex and Gender," 132.

29. Unfortunately, many feminist theorists speak as if a concept is masculine simply by virtue of being "associated" with men: "The basic thesis of the feminist critique of knowledge can be stated very simply: the privileging of the rational mode of thought is inherently sexist because, at least since the time of Plato, the rational has been associated with the male, the irrational with the female" (Hekman, "Feminization of Epistemology," 70). As should be clear from my discussion thus far, I find this "simple statement" of the thesis too weak to do justice to the depth of the feminist critique; at the very least, more needs to be said about the nature of the association, showing it to be more than "mere" association, in order to sustain the feminist challenge.

30. For a wonderful discussion of whether and to what extent philosophical conceptions and ideals of self can be extended to include women, see Susan Okin, *Women in Western Political Thought* (Princeton, N.J.: Princeton University Press, 1979).

31. For a valuable discussion and defense of "gynocentric" feminism that is sensitive to these concerns, see Iris Young, "Humanism, Gynocentrism, and Feminist Politics," in her *Throwing Like a Girl,* 73–91.

32. Note that in defining constitutive grounding in terms of entailment, I am not distinguishing between cases in which the entailed conditions are presupposed by the entailing conditions (as might be claimed of the tenant example) and those in which they are not presupposed but in which they count as more straightforward sufficient conditions (as

in the teacher example). For classic attempts at characterizing the difference between presupposition and entailment, see, P. F. Strawson, *Introduction to Logical Theory* (London: Methuen, 1952), and "Reply to Mr. Sellars," *Philosophical Review* 63 (1954): 216–231.

33. We should note that in determining whether a norm is *appropriate to* a role, parallel issues arise: Is satisfying the norm required in any context in order to excel at the role? Or does satisfying the norm contribute, in a given context, to excellence in the role. Because it is relatively common to acknowledge the contextual factors in determining a norm's appropriateness to a role, my discussion here will focus on the constitutive/contextual distinction with respect to grounding.

34. Clearly the journalistic ideal mentioned may be satisfied in a variety of different ways and by a variety of different actions. Two journalists may end up in different social roles because they realize the norm through different courses of action. My point here, however, is that even if a journalist were to pursue the same course of action as in fact she does, but under different background conditions, she could be cast in a different social role.

35. In offering this condition it is important to note that there has been significant philosophical attention devoted to the problem of articulating and evaluating conditionals that depend upon the specification of relevant background conditions. A classic statement of the problem appears in Nelson Goodman, "The Problem of Counterfactual Conditionals," *Journal of Philosophy* 44 (February 1947): 113–128; also his *Fact, Fiction, and Forecast,* 2d ed. (Indianapolis: Bobbs-Merrill, 1965) See also Roderick Chisholm, "Law Statements and Counterfactual Inference, *Analysis* 15 (April 1955): 97–105; J. L. Mackie, "Counterfactuals and Causal Laws," in *Analytical Philosophy,* ed. R. J. Butler (New York: Barnes and Noble, 1962), 66–80. It remains a standing problem how to set limits on the assumed background conditions so that the conditional yields a substantive requirement; in this case, the problem is how to set constraints on the background conditions to avoid the result that any norm whatsoever is grounded in a given social role, yet without describing the constraints so that the conditional in question trivially holds. I will not undertake to solve this problem here. I trust that the argument I will discuss below does not depend for its plausibility on working through the details of this issue.

36. It is important to keep in mind that the contextual grounding of a norm in a role need not contribute to success in that role and that the norm need not count as part of an ideal "for" that role, in the ordinary sense. For example, what makes you an excellent journalist may, under certain conditions, result in your being a criminal without making you a good criminal. Nevertheless, noting that norms are not only constitutively but also contextually grounded in roles highlights the fact that our "virtues" may unexpectedly cast us in roles for which they were never intended.

37. There is, however, one qualification we must add. It is a complicated matter to determine whether the features that promote success in a social role are responsible for perpetuating the role. Consider doctors: A successful doctor is one who heals her patients. It is tempting to say that healing patients, although required for a doctor's success, is not responsible for perpetuating the role of doctor; it's the fact that people get sick, in spite of good doctors' efforts, that perpetuates this role. But we should also note that people getting sick can't be all that is responsible for sustaining the social role of doctor, since it is easy to imagine how in contexts where all doctors are bad at their job, the role might lose credibility and eventually disappear. Thus I suggest that the features that contribute to success in a role will, at least indirectly, perpetuate the role.

38. This theoretical possibility is important, for it allows us to claim that there may be ideals appropriate to women's social role that are, nevertheless, separable from this role.

Just as satisfying some traditionally masculine ideals may not be sufficient to cast one in a man's role, satisfying some traditionally feminine ideals may not be sufficient to cast one in a woman's role. We may hope that this will allow us to endorse some of the traditional feminine ideals without supporting social arrangements of gender oppression.

39. See, e.g., Haraway, "Manifesto for Cyborgs" and "Situated Knowledges"; Butler, "Variations on Sex and Gender" and "Gender Trouble"; and de Lauretis, "Feminist Studies/Critical Studies."

40. For example, consider the relation "is a mother of." Employing a pluralistic approach to mothering relations, we might claim that one can be a mother of someone either by contributing the ovum from which they developed, by giving birth to them, by adopting them, or by playing a certain role in their parenting; in effect, we would claim that the conditions for being a mother are irreducibly disjunctive and heterogeneous.

41. MacKinnon develops her position on gender and objectivity in "Feminism, Marxism, Method, and the State: An Agenda for Theory," in *Feminist Theory: A Critique of Ideology,* ed. Nannerl O. Keohane, Michelle Z. Rosaldo, and Barbara C. Gelpi (Chicago: University of Chicago Press, 1982), 1–30 (hereafter FMMS-I) (originally published in *Signs* 7 [1982]: 515–544); "Feminism, Marxism, Method, and the State: Toward Feminist Jurisprudence," *Signs* 8 (1983): 635–658 (hereafter FMMS-II); *Feminism Unmodified;* and *Towards a Feminist Theory of the State* (Cambridge, Mass.: Harvard University Press, 1989).

42. I say that MacKinnon's account falls "largely" within the framework, because she is more critical of the distinction between sex and gender than I have been here. Claiming that sex and gender are interdependent, she chooses to use the terms 'male' and 'man' and the terms 'female' and 'woman' interchangeably. See her *Feminism Unmodified,* 263(n5), and FMMS-II, 635(n1). Although I will continue to use the man/woman terminology when speaking of gender, in quotations I will leave her terminology as is.

43. See, e.g., MacKinnon, *Feminist Theory of the State,* 113. Note that this third element in the analysis of gender—i.e., that gender is "sexualized"—is what distinguishes MacKinnon's analysis from a broad range of others. Many of the accounts are inspired by the thought that the category of women is defined as "other" to men; as I interpret these analyses, they share with MacKinnon both the idea that gender is irreducibly hierarchical and that our "otherness" is projected onto women by and in the interests of men. As has been frequently noted in the literature, however, there are "other others" besides women. MacKinnon's emphasis on sexuality seems to offer a way of distinguishing the hierarchical categories of gender from other hierarchical categories, such as race, class, and so on. But this way of distinguishing gender (and gender oppression) won't work if, as MacKinnon sometimes suggests, all hierarchy is "sexualized."

44. Ibid., 113–114. See also *Feminism Unmodified,* 50.

45. MacKinnon, *Feminism Unmodified,* 6.

46. MacKinnon, *Feminist Theory of the State,* 128.

47. It is important to note that on MacKinnon's analysis, eroticized domination/submission is the definition of sex, or at least "sex in the male system"—i.e., under male supremacy. (See ibid., 140.) So sex is the relation in terms of which MacKinnon defines the social categories of man and woman. However, it is also important to recognize that on her view not all loving physical intimacy is sex (ibid., 139) and that many other interactions "from intimate to institutional, from a look to a rape," can qualify as sex on her terms (ibid., 137). Although I recognize the importance of MacKinnon's strategy to define sex in terms of domination, here I am downplaying her account of sexuality and pornography in

order to highlight other aspects of her account. I regret that in doing so, my exposition fails to reflect many of the important connections she draws.

48. MacKinnon herself does not endorse the pluralist approach just sketched; rather, she takes her account of gender to capture the basic structure of all gender relations. She does allow, however, that there are cultural variations in the way this structure is instantiated. See MacKinnon, *Feminist Theory of the State,* 130–132, 151; *Feminism Unmodified,* 53; and FMMS-I, 24(n55).

49. MacKinnon quotes C. Shafer and M. Frye, "Rape and Respect," in *Feminism and Philosophy,* ed. Mary Vetterling-Braggin et al. (Totowa, N.J.: Littlefield, Adams, 1982), 334: "Rape is a man's act, whether it is a male or female man, and whether it is a man relatively permanently or relatively temporarily; and being raped is a woman's experience, whether it is a female or male woman and whether it is a woman relatively permanently or relatively temporarily." MacKinnon comments: "To be rapable, a position that is social, not biological, defines what a woman is" (*Feminist Theory of the State,* 178, 179). See also *Feminism Unmodified,* 52, 56.

50. For further discussion of these issues in connection with MacKinnon's analysis, see Andrea Dworkin, *Pornography: Men Possessing Women* (New York: Perigee, 1981), and *Intercourse* (New York: Free Press, 1987).

51. On the issue of the intentionality in sexual abuse, see Hacking, "World-Making by Kind-Making." Hacking's essay is very useful in understanding that social categories are those which depend, at least in part, on being viewed as categories. He argues convincingly that it is problematic to extend social categories to other times and contexts if there is reason to doubt whether the relevant concepts were available for conceptualizing the categories in question. So, one might argue, in contexts where concepts such as desire, submission, and the like are not available, there is no gender. MacKinnon seems to be sensitive to this issue in claiming (contra the Freudians) that infants "cannot be said to possess sexuality" in her sense (*Feminist Theory of the State,* 151).

52. MacKinnon, *Feminism Unmodified,* 172.

53. Ibid., 119.

54. For an especially clear statement of this claim, see ibid., 233–234(n26). MacKinnon contrasts objectification, which requires actual power to dominate, with stereotyping, which need not: "Objectification is the dynamic of the subordination of women. Objectification is different from stereotyping, which acts as if it is all in the head" (ibid., 118, 119). See also ibid., ch. 2. I take it that individual women can stereotype men, but women do not objectify men (at least not normally or as easily) because we don't have the social power. Although an analysis of social power is important to flesh out MacKinnon's account of gender, I will not offer one here.

55. Federal Bureau of Investigation, *Uniform Crime Reports for the United States, 1989* (Washington, D.C.: GPO, 1990), 6, 15. According to this report, there were 94,504 forcible rapes (p. 10), with forcible rape defined as "the carnal knowledge of a female forcibly and against her will. Assaults or attempts to commit rape by force or threat of force are included, however statutory rape (without force) and other sex offenses are excluded" (p. 14). Needless to say, rape often goes unreported. Credible estimates of rapes far surpass the FBI statistics; some suggest we should multiply the FBI numbers by as much as ten.

56. National Coalition Against Domestic Violence, Fact Sheet, in "Report on Proposed Legislation S2754," 27. On file with the Senate Judiciary Committee.

57. On MacKinnon's view, pornography is at least locally responsible for conditioning the particular sexual dynamic within which the domination of *females* is erotic. Yet she says surprisingly little about why it is that females, on the whole, have been marked as women. Her idea seems to be that because dominance is rationalized by biological difference, women's bodies come to be the "location" for gender to play itself out (see, e.g., *Feminist Theory of the State*, 54–59); however, because there is a general tendency to rationalize domination biologically, other embodied differences (race, age, weight, and so on) can and do provide alternative locations (*Feminist Theory of the State*, 179).

58. Using the relation of sexual objectification, the structure of this definition of gender seems to be (roughly) as follows: x *is a woman* iff there is a y such that y sexually objectifies x; x *is a man* iff there is a y such that x sexually objectifies y. It is more tricky to define male supremacy. We might begin by considering this: A social system S *is a system of male supremacy* iff for all female x and male y in S, x's being female licenses (via S's norms, institutions, divisions of labor, and so on) any y's sexual objectification of x, and it is not the case that y's being male licenses any x's sexual objectification of y.

59. This is not intended as an argument that a consistent feminist should also be a vegetarian (though I do believe that eating animals is, in most circumstances, wrong). Nor am I suggesting that the analogy is perfect; there are admittedly important differences between women and meat. Nor am I arguing that one should never view and treat things as objects for the satisfaction of one's desires; it will surely depend upon what sorts of things and what sorts of circumstances are in question. The analogy, however, does raise the possibility that, as explicated, MacKinnon's account fails to provide a sufficient condition for being a member of the category of women: If one finds cooking erotic, then it may be that one sexually objectifies food. But if we define women as the sexually objectified, this, I take it, would be an undesirable consequence. MacKinnon mentions that sex is like cuisine, though she doesn't suggest that a meal can function socially as a woman (*Feminist Theory of the State*, 132). One strategy to begin solving this problem would be to add conditions to the analysis of sexual objectification that require intentionality (i.e., the having of attitudes) of the subjugated participant.

60. Haraway, "'Gender' for a Marxist Dictionary," 148.

61. Wittig, "One Is Not Born a Woman," 49.

62. It is important to keep these steps distinguished. Even if we are able to establish the strong claim that if one is a man, then one is a "good" or "successful" man *just in case* one is rational, we still cannot conclude that if one is rational, then one functions as a man—namely, that rationality is grounded in men's social role. The latter claim requires a separate argument.

63. For MacKinnon's uses of the term 'rationality', see, e.g., *Feminist Theory of the State*, 96–97, 114, 162, 229, 232; FMMS-II, 636(n3), 645. For the connections between objectivity, neutrality, and aperspectivity see, e.g., *Feminism Unmodified*, 50; *Feminist Theory of the State*, 83, 97, 99, 114, 162–164, 211, 213, 232, 248. I will assume that one is objective iff one's stance is objective if one satisfies the norms of objectivity.

64. MacKinnon, *Feminism Unmodified*, 50.

65. See also MacKinnon, *Feminist Theory of the State*, 114, 121–124, 199, 213, 248–249; *Feminism Unmodified*, 50–52, 54–55, 150–151, 155; FMMS-I, 23–25, 27; FMMS-II, 636, 640, 644–645, 658.

66. There are several points we should be attentive to in considering the ideal objectifier. First, given that objectification requires both thinking and acting, excellence at objectification will require that one meet standards governing both thought and deed. Thus

we should expect that the norm of objectivity in question will contain both epistemic and pragmatic elements. Second, one most fully realizes the ideal for those roles that are defined in terms of a *power* to act when one is *exercising* that power—e.g., a doctor is one who is able to heal others, but a doctor is most fully a doctor when she is actually healing someone. Moreover, one who excels at such a role should reliably have the power to act and should be able to sustain her power—e.g., a good doctor reliably heals her patients and sustains this power to heal. Third, one is more likely to succeed in roles that require sustaining a course of action (and a set of attitudes) if one's actions (and attitudes) are guided by norms or principles that legitimate them—e.g., even though a good doctor may sometimes rely on hunches or guesses, this works only against the backdrop of her reliance on medical knowledge and practice. This last point is important, for we evaluate actions and attitudes themselves as "good" or "warranted" in light of their relation to principles that are used to justify them.

67. MacKinnon, *Feminism Unmodified,* 164.

68. Wittig, "One Is Not Born a Woman," 48–49.

69. It is interesting to consider whether being a successful or ideal objectifier places one in a privileged epistemic position with respect to the consequences of one's objectification. Consider an argument that such an objectifier is incorrigible: S is incorrigible with respect to p iff (necessarily) if S believes p, then p is true. Suppose S is a successful objectifier, and S, in objectifying x, views x as F. Because S, by hypothesis, is ideally successful, if x is not F, then he exercises his power to make it the case that x is F; so S's belief that x is F is (or will soon be) true. So it would seem that (necessarily) if S is an ideal objectifier with respect to x, and S believes x is F, then x is F. In short, if S believes that x is F, and x is not (at least eventually) F, then S must not be an ideal objectifier. Admittedly, there are temporal qualifications that disrupt the argument and divert us from the standard notions of incorrigibility, but the suggestion provides food for thought.

70. See MacKinnon, *Feminist Theory of the State,* 100: "Of course, objective data do document the difficulties and inequalities of woman's situation."

71. MacKinnon, *Feminism Unmodified,* 59; *Feminist Theory of the State,* 125.

72. An important source for this conception of natures is Aristotle. See, e.g., *Physics* I–II and *Metaphysics* VII–IX. A wonderful commentary on Aristotle's conception of natures is Sarah Waterlow, *Nature, Change, and Agency in Aristotle's Physics* (Oxford: Oxford University Press, 1982).

73. Although MacKinnon rarely puts the point in this way, I think making explicit the objectifier's commitment to natures helps in understanding her position. For example, she describes pornography (and some of its horrors) in these terms: "Women's bodies trussed and maimed and raped and made into things to be hurt and obtained and accessed, *and this presented as the nature of women*" (my emphasis) (MacKinnon, *Feminism Unmodified,* 147). See also MacKinnon, *Feminist Theory of the State,* 138.

74. This modality is ambiguously expressed (or obscured) in the verb 'to be'. The verb 'to be' is notoriously ambiguous; there are two uses at issue here. Consider the claim: women are submissive. It could be used to express an empirical generalization: As a matter of fact, all (or most) women are submissive. It could express a fact about women's nature: All individual women are, by their nature, submissive. MacKinnon's arguments highlight problems that arise when this ambiguity is not acknowledged (see, e.g., MacKinnon, *Feminism Unmodified,* 55, 59, 154, 166, 174; and *Feminist Theory of the State,* 98, 122, 125, 204). MacKinnon also suggests a potential ambiguity in the claim: Women are equal to men. Again the modality of the verb 'to be' is an issue: To claim that women *are* equal ob-

scures the fact that women are *not* actually equal; nevertheless we may allow that women *should be* equal (see, e.g., MacKinnon, *Feminism Unmodified,* 39–40, 59, 171, 178–179; and *Feminist Theory of the State,* 163, 231, 240, 242).

75. MacKinnon, *Feminism Unmodified,* 59. It is important to keep distinct the objectifier's view of women from MacKinnon's own account of gender. Consider a particular woman, Rachel. On the objectifier's view, Rachel is a woman by nature; this is her essence which explains why, under normal circumstances, she is feminine. If she is not feminine (submissive, sexually desirable), it is because circumstances are frustrating and inhibiting her true nature. On MacKinnon's view, Rachel is a woman because she is viewed by an objectifier as having a nature that is responsible for those features he finds desirable and is treated accordingly. MacKinnon's move is subtle—it uses the intended or perceived definition of a kind to function in the definition of an accident: Men take women to be submissive by nature; those whom men take to be submissive by nature (and whom they force into submission) constitute the category of women; but no woman is a member of that category by nature.

76. Of course, the objectifier need not formulate explicitly the commitment to "natures," in particular, to a "Woman's Nature." In the next section I will indicate the epistemic role of an objectifier's projective beliefs; I hope this will be sufficient to illustrate what sort of beliefs might qualify.

77. My reconstruction of MacKinnon's argument draws primarily from the following chapters in *Feminism Unmodified:* "Desire and Power" 46–62; "Not a Moral Issue," 146–162; and "Frances Biddle's Sister," 163–197; and from *Feminist Theory of the State:* "Consciousness Raising," 83–105: "Method and Politics," 106–125; "The Liberal State," 157–170; and "Toward Feminist Jurisprudence," 237–249. Some of the arguments in these chapters originally appeared in MacKinnon, FMMS-II.

78. On the idea that reasonable decision making should accommodate "how things are" and that we should "conform normative standards to existing reality," see, e.g., MacKinnon, *Feminism Unmodified,* 34, 164–166, 176, 178; and *Feminist Theory of the State,* 162–164, 218–220, 227, 231–232.

79. MacKinnon, *Feminism Unmodified,* 59. See also ibid., 52–53, 59, 155, 166; and *Feminist Theory of the State,* 94, 99–100, 104, 117–118, 124–125, 128, 163–164, 198, 204, 218–220.

80. See, e.g., MacKinnon, *Feminism Unmodified,* 172; and *Feminist Theory of the State,* 153–154, 174–175, 209.

81. Although strictly speaking we aren't responsible for things' natures, within the broadly Aristotelian tradition we are thought to be responsible for seeing that things exemplify their natures as fully as possible. For example, if it is part of a woman's nature that she bear children, then she *ought* to, and we should "facilitate" her doing so. Thanks to Charlotte Witt for this point.

82. Although there is considerable vagueness and obscurity in the principles I have suggested, there is one qualification that deserves special note. In my statement of the principles of absolute aperspectivity and assumed aperspectivity, I have relied on the notion of an "observed regularity." In the philosophical literature a "regularity" is typically taken to be a true universal generalization, and an "observed regularity" to be such a generalization for which we have observational evidence. However, as I am using the term I mean to allow that there are regularities that fall short of being universal generalizations, either because they don't strictly hold of all members of the class or because they only hold for cases that have actually been observed up to a point in time. Those who prefer to re-

serve the term 'regularity' for the stricter usage might instead think in terms of "observed patterns."

83. Because here we are concentrating on what is required for being a "successful" or "excellent" objectifier, we must allow that there are objectifiers who meet the minimal conditions for objectification but who aren't guided by and don't satisfy the ideal of assumed objectivity. They do it, but they don't do it "well." Objectifying well requires mastering the "art" of objectifying in a sustained and reliable way. If the argument I've sketched is convincing, one won't be an ideal objectifier unless one's projective beliefs are based on observable regularities. "Poor" objectifiers may be highly imaginative, or they may work under conditions in which there isn't an established social hierarchy, so the relevant differences between dominant and subordinate are missing. But without (publicly accessible) justification, it will be more difficult to sustain a practice of objectification, and one's power will be more easily challenged. In short, good objectification may depend on a developed practice of objectification that has established the regularities needed to be effective.

84. MacKinnon, *Feminism Unmodified,* 50 (quoted above).

85. Ibid., 173; see also 307(n17).

86. MacKinnon, *Feminist Theory of the State,* 122.

87. MacKinnon, *Feminism Unmodified,* 50 (also quoted above). See also her *Feminist Theory of the State,* 137–138, 147.

88. MacKinnon, *Feminist Theory of the State,* 122.

89. It is important to note that one may be committed to natures without being a "naturalist." Although the term 'naturalist' covers many different views, typically naturalists are committed to thinking that natural science has a privileged status in finding natures; moreover, naturalists privilege physical properties over others. But the idea of a "natural" property is ambiguous between a physical property that natural science studies and a property that is part of, or follows from, something's nature. Plausibly, Catholicism is committed to natures, but it is not committed to naturalism.

90. Admittedly, one might argue that each of the principles are weakly masculine because in contexts where the other principles are realized, they contribute to success in the role of men. This illustrates both the difficulty and the importance of having clear criteria for what can count as "background conditions." See note 35 above.

11

GENERALIZING GENDER:
REASON AND ESSENCE IN THE
LEGAL THOUGHT OF
CATHARINE MACKINNON

ELIZABETH RAPAPORT

Catharine MacKinnon's work has been a shaping force in the development of feminist legal theory as well as on the course of legal reform. Although few feminist scholars accept her views on gender and sexuality in their entirety, her preeminent contribution to feminist legal theory is generally acknowledged.[1] MacKinnon's most signal legal reform success has been in identifying sexual harassment as a form of sex discrimination prohibited by federal employment law. More recently, attended by greater controversy and less material success, she has been active in the feminist antipornography campaign. This chapter has two objectives. The first is simply the journeywoman task of understanding MacKinnon's theory of gender and especially the methodology she employs. The second objective is to defend an aspect of MacKinnon's methodology that has of late come under political and philosophical attack. She has been accused of gender essentialism, a vice that is variously defined but is most commonly understood to mean treating the concept of gender as a transcultural and transhistorical universal.

The price of gender essentialism, according to its critics, is the imposition of false uniformity on the disparate experience of women of different classes, races, ethnicities, and sexual orientations. Privileged white intellectuals read their own experience as that of women as such. In doing so we falsify the experience of those whom we call sisters but whose voices we ignore. In my view, these deplorable consequences do not necessarily overtake the theorist who seeks to generalize about gender. The impulse that animates MacKinnon's work, the desire to formulate a theory that speaks from and to the experience of all women, should not be easily relinquished. Generalizing about gender, at least in the modest form in which it is done by this bold theorist, need not be philosophically or politically pernicious.

I

There are at least three well-established models of the interplay among reason, gender, and the law in the work of various contributors to the rich, variegated, and burgeoning field of feminist jurisprudence.[2] I will briefly characterize two in order to situate and discuss a third—that of Catharine MacKinnon. No feminist legal theorist would resist the characterization of the law as male if what is meant by the masculinity of the law is that it systematically reflects and advances the interests of men at the expense of women. There are, however, distinct feminist orientations toward the nature and uses of reason in the law.

Liberal feminist legal theorists treat reason as unproblematic (that is, ungendered), a neutral tool well adapted to pressing demands for legal reform. Liberal feminist strategy relies heavily on pressing for vindication of the legal system's own norms of rational adjudication. Chief among these is the principle of formal equality: Like cases should be treated alike; differences of treatment should reflect genuine and relevant, as opposed to mythic-stereotypical or irrelevant, differences between the sexes. Significant victories can be credited to the ability of feminist lawyers to expose the irrationality, when measured against the legal system's own norms, of sexist legal doctrines.

Consider an example, or set of examples, from the important domain of constitutional equal protection adjudication. In a series of cases beginning in 1971, liberal feminists were encouraged in their reliance on appeals to accepted norms of legal rationality by the action of the Supreme Court. The Court embarked upon a course of striking down legislation that relied upon gender stereotypes as a basis for conferring or withholding benefits and burdens. Thus the Court sustained a challenge to federal law that allowed male members of the armed forces an automatic dependency allowance for their wives but required servicewomen to prove that their husbands were in fact dependent.[3] In 1976 it announced the standard to be applied in determining whether gender classifications were consonant with the Fourteenth Amendment's equal protection guarantees: Government was barred from relying on gender classifications unless they served important government objectives and were substantially related to the achievement of those objectives.[4] The Court would no longer allow traditional gender stereotypes to stand proxy for germane bases of classification.[5]

It may be important to note that although liberal feminists have no quarrel with the principles of rationality at work in the legal system, they do not necessarily look to the courts with great hope of achieving further significant reforms. Wendy Williams, a leading liberal feminist litigator and theorist, expresses skepticism about the ability of courts to engage in stereotype-discarding analysis in areas that go beyond what was achieved in the first decade of equal protection cases. By 1980, issues were reaching the Supreme Court that went beyond challenging the separate spheres of male and female activity, home, and the wider world. When confronted with equal protection challenges to a male-only draft registration law and a statutory rape law making sex with an underage partner criminal for a male but not a female, the Court reached what Williams called its "cultural limits."[6] It was not prepared to scrutinize the basis for treating men as inherently aggressive and women as unsuitable for war or unlikely to initiate sex. Williams does not expect the courts to be precocious wielders of rationality in exploding such basic cultural stereotypes. Change at so fundamental a level, if it comes, will, she believes, come as a result of legislative enactment responsive to feminist political success.

Other feminist legal scholars, applying the work of Carol Gilligan to law, argue that the feminine voice has been devalued in and excluded from the legal system. They see the influx of women into the legal profession in the past two decades as creating an opportunity to introduce female styles of lawyering and adjudication into legal institutions.[7] These feminists regard legal rationality as male in the sense that it embodies norms of deliberation and judgment that are characteristic of men but not women. Carol Gilligan's germinal work in psychology criticized Lawrence Kohlberg for offering as a universal model of moral development one that was derived from the study of male subjects and (at best) applied only to men.[8] Measured on the Kohlbergian scale, females as a class proved to be deficient in mature moral reasoning capacity.[9] Gilligan became persuaded that Kohlberg's model was yet another in a long Western tradition that privileges predominantly male styles of deliberation and judgment as at once male and practical reasoning as such. The result has been not only the denigration of women but also the loss to society (in spheres wider than that to which women have been consigned) of the advantages of women's distinctive styles of analysis and judgment. Gilligan's own work seeks to uncover the distinctive characteristics of female moral experience and reasoning.

Feminist legal scholars who have been influenced by Gilligan's work argue for the reception into legal institutions of female styles of lawyering and adjudication. Some argue for female reasoning styles as supplementation and enrichment; others regard Gilligan's work as illuminating the road to models of legal reasoning superior to those that seek to capture the virtues of male rationality. The programmatic implications of the Gilligan critique of law are largely still to be worked out and are in any case more encompassing than the present focus on legal rationality. Writing explicitly about legal reasoning, both Katharine Bartlett and Suzanna Sherry have argued that feminist practical reasoning pays more attention to context and is likely to be suspicious of the vices of excessive abstraction and generalization.[10] Judith Resnik has been critical of impartiality as a judicial virtue. She argues that monitoring interest and cultivating empathy with the parties at risk and in the toils of the law can be seen from a feminist perspective to be not only a different but also a superior model of the virtue of the judicial stance.[11]

Catharine MacKinnon does not take rationality in the law as she finds it, as do liberal theorists; nor does she seek to enrich or improve legal institutions by legitimating female styles of adjudication and lawyering. Her interest in rationality, which for her is the central legitimizing norm of liberal legalism, is entirely critical.[12] For MacKinnon, rationality is an enemy to be unmasked and destroyed. In what follows I will first articulate her critique of liberal legalism's male concept of rationality. I will then present her account of gender, which seeks to explain what legal rationality works to conceal. Finally, I will defend MacKinnon's methodology, insofar as she treats generalizing about gender as a legitimate conceptual tool of feminist theory.

MacKinnon's critique of legal rationality, as well as her theory of gender, can probably best be understood as an effort to come to terms with Marxism, to retain what is sound or can be turned to the uses of feminism, and to discover what needs to be discarded in the interest of furthering feminist theory and practice. MacKinnon's critique of rationality has two intimately related aspects targeted at the epistemological stance of liberal legalism and the basic substantive norms, especially the constitutional norms, that are paradigmatically virtuous, true, or correct from the liberal point of view.

Rationality—or in MacKinnon's usage, its synonym, objectivity—is the central epistemological norm of liberal legalism. In her words: "Objectivity is liberal legalism's conception of itself. It legitimates itself by reflecting its view of society, a society it helps to make by so seeing it, and calling that view, that relation, rationality. Since rationality is measured by point-of-viewlessness, what counts as reason is that which corresponds to the way things are."[13] MacKinnon has two criticisms of liberal legalism's "objectivism." First, MacKinnon, following Marx, denies that there can be theory that escapes (1) historical determination and limitation or (2) perspective—that is, partiality for the social interest the theory expresses.[14] All thought is in this sense ideological. The epistemological error of liberal legalism is to suppose that its own or any other thought could transcend its historical situation and partiality.

Second, liberal legalism claims objectivity for norms that foster, reflect, impose, and sanction male supremacy. But again, just as the bourgeois political philosophy—democratic republicanism—dissimulates its relationship to capitalism, and is innocent of the deception, liberal legalism believes itself to be committed to gender neutrality.[15] For MacKinnon, the liberal state—like all states, including the socialist state—is male in that it "authoritatively constitutes the social order in the interests of men as a gender."[16] The state is "jurisprudentially male": It conceals and legitimizes male power by presenting gender inequality as occurring despite, not in part because of, the legal regime.[17] MacKinnon finds this to be "especially vivid" in constitutional law.[18] Her critique of the neutrality of constitutional law resembles Marxist critiques of such supposedly neutral legal regimes as contract before wage and hour legislation were permitted.[19] She finds formal equality or equal liberty concealing and maintaining substantive inequality, replacing, mutatis mutandis, "class" with "gender."

MacKinnon's criticism of the accepted interpretation of the First Amendment's protection of freedom of speech can serve as an example of her constitutional critique. The First Amendment has occupied her in connection with her efforts to brand pornography as a form of legally redressable gender discrimination.[20] MacKinnon was in the forefront of a movement to enact municipal ordinances that make pornography a discriminatory practice amenable to redress as a civil rights violation. She was the principal author of the first and model ordinance enacted in Minneapolis in 1983. MacKinnon defines pornography as "the graphic sexually explicit subordination of women, whether in words or pictures."[21]

Among the several harms pornography causes, in MacKinnon's view, is the harm to all women that results from its propagation of the idea that women are only fit for, and enjoy, subordination. Pornography, MacKinnon argues, is a central practice of male domination through which both men and women learn to regard women as fit only for exploitation and abuse and to hone and deepen the sadomasochism that—increasingly, due to the good offices of pornography—is the specific content of sexuality in our culture. Pornography is the site at which gender identity and a sexuality of dominance and submission are fused.[22]

MacKinnon's indictment of pornography is controversial in all its details among feminists. Yet, as one of MacKinnon's critics among feminist legal theorists, Robin West, has noted, most women experience pornography as primarily "victimizing, threatening and oppressive."[23] Because of the chord struck, she has been able to bring yet another aspect of sexual exploitation from the trivialized margin to the center of cultural discussion and political debate.

Indianapolis enacted a version of the antipornography ordinance in 1984. The Federal Court of Appeals held that the Indianapolis ordinance violated the First Amendment. Judge Easterbrook's opinion concedes much to antipornography feminism.[24] He concedes that pornography is a practice that socializes both sexes to accept and relish male supremacy, that it produces "bigotry and contempt" as well as "acts of aggression" against women. Easterbrook refuses to engage in facile and implausible distinctions between mere impotent ideas of a reprehensible nature and socially undesirable or criminal action. He insists that beliefs are potent, that they cause and shape behavior. However, having conceded that pornography is political speech, Easterbrook then accords it the dignity constitutionally mandated for the expression of any political viewpoint, none of which may be proscribed. Antipornography feminism must confront male supremacy in the arena of the marketplace of ideas. On pain of extinguishing freedom of speech and setting itself up as an arbiter of truth, the government may not take the part of what appears to be embattled enlightenment against pernicious error.

MacKinnon's critique of pornographic expression as protected speech mobilizes well-known arguments against the futility of legal formalism. Her argument is premised upon the claim that the free speech of pornographers can only be protected at the price of silencing women. When women rise to protest pornography, the contempt in which pornography helps to hold them prevents them from being heard. Judge Easterbrook reasons that the Constitution requires the government to be neutral with respect to the political expression of male supremacists and antipornography feminists. For MacKinnon, this neutrality is specious. Easterbrook's analysis requires that we assume that absent unjustified government regulation, all social groups enjoy free speech. But once the profound and pervasive powerlessness of women in the social status quo is acknowledged, governmental abstention is exposed as reinforcing the lack of free speech and lack of access to other channels of political action for women. From MacKinnon's point of view, Easterbrook's interpretation of the protection the Constitution grants to pornography affords but one more instance of the invisibility and unreachability of gender oppression from the standpoint of legal liberal rationality. Thus does formal equality conceal and justify substantive inequality.[25] The invalidation of an ordinance aimed at redressing the inequality must be seen not as maintaining governmental neutrality but as siding with the status quo of male supremacy.[26]

MacKinnon's epistemological critique, like liberal feminist critique, addresses itself to specious generalizations about gender. She aims to expose the substantive content of pseudo-formal principles and the overweening claims to an unattainable objectivity of authoritative male law, morality, and science. For liberal theorists, the target of critique is bad science; for MacKinnon, it is also what critical Marxists sometimes call scientism—that is, ideology tricked out as timeless universal truth.

MacKinnon, critic of the specious universality of liberal legalism, has been in turn accused of trafficking in universals: She is charged with purveying a theory of gender that distorts and ignores the disparate experience of women unlike herself. It is to MacKinnon's theory of gender that I now turn.

II

For MacKinnon, the baseline theory with which she begins is not liberalism but Marxism. It is of Marxism that she asks, Is it adequate to the project of feminist critique of society in general and law in particular? MacKinnon finds Marxist methodology inadequate for the task of feminist theory construction in three respects:

1. MacKinnon rejects the proposition that class is more fundamental than gender. Therefore, she denies that the best accounts of gender oppression explain it reductively by reference to class phenomena and that a politics dedicated to class struggle on behalf of workers will encompass an adequate address to gender oppression. Gender is for MacKinnon the fundamental theoretical term in autonomous feminist theory.[27]

2. MacKinnon rejects the temptation to engage in feminist reductionism, to treat gender as the fundamental social division that underlies and illuminates all other social antagonisms. In addition to rejecting the primacy of class analysis, she rejects the search for an all-encompassing theory of social conflict. She does not reduce class to gender, and she regards other forms of social oppression, notably racism, as also requiring autonomous theoretical explanation and political mobilization. She is consistently Marxist, as she herself describes Marx's own work, in claiming no objectivity or transcendence of standpoint for feminism. All that feminism claims for itself is to uniquely represent women's point of view, a point of view neither derivable from nor reducible to that of any other social category—for example, the human individual of liberal theory or Marxism's working class. It is a point of view that claims epistemologically privileged access to that which it represents—women's experience—and that is dedicated to furthering the interests of women as a class.[28]

3. MacKinnon also distinguishes feminism from Marxism on the grounds that feminism employs—and, because of the profoundly isolating and mystified conditions of women's oppression, had to invent—a distinctive method. Its method is consciousness raising and its derivatives, all of which center on women sharing their experience with other women. The theory of gender emerges from and is tested against the experience of women as we have come to understand it in listening to and talking to each other.[29]

MacKinnon, who with succinct audacity calls her theory of gender simply "feminism," adopts as her own the Marxist conception of the work of theory, the uncovering of the hidden roots of power in social relations. Although she renounces the goal of one all-encompassing theory of social conflict, she aspires to a comprehensive theory of gender as a system of social oppression. The secret of gender relations that feminism reveals is the sexual dominance of women by men. "Sexuality is to feminism," MacKinnon hypothesizes, "what work is to marxism."[30] "Sexuality is the social process that creates, organizes, expresses, and directs desire," and in so doing it socially constructs men and women.[31] The nature of woman as constructed is the gratification of male desire, although there are as many variations in the meaning of erotic gratification as there are distinct cultures: "As the organized expropriation of the work of some for the use of others defines the class, workers, the organized expropriation of the sexuality of some for the use of others defines the sex, woman."[32]

I would like to focus attention on six aspects of MacKinnon's sexual-domination-based account of gender.

1. Gender distinctions, like class distinctions, are hierarchical; to be gendered is to be socially assigned to one of a pair of complementary superior and inferior groups.

2. Gender embodies as it serves the sexual domination of men over women. Crucial to MacKinnon's theory of gender is the claim that socially constructed female nature—that is, gender as distinct from the biological substratum that for MacKinnon has no interesting social effects—is nothing but the projection of that which answers male desire, always including the subordination and inferiority of the female object of desire to the male sexual subject. MacKinnon theorizes that sexual exploitation—men's invidious pursuit of sexual pleasure—is the dynamic force that drives and sustains the subordination of women in all its facets. Female gender is an artefact of male lust and power.[33]

3. Therefore, women exist for men. Traits common to us as a class bespeak our subordination rather than our authentic interest or volition.[34] MacKinnon's work is profoundly anti-utopian. For MacKinnon, feminism is an engine of critique and resistance to women's victimization. Feminist theory reveals that currently there is no well-founded basis for projecting positive values for women to aspire to live by, either counterculturally, in zones or pockets of resistance to male supremacy, or as an attractive vision of a post-male supremacist world to strive to bring into being. In her view, the positive traits, the distinctively female values and culture around which feminists such as Gilligan would center an affirmation of female worth, are nothing more than the traits assigned to women in order to serve men. Here is MacKinnon's description of Gilligan's mistake:

I do not think that the way women reason morally is morality "in a different voice." I think it is morality in a higher register, in a feminine voice. Women value care because men have valued us according to the care we give them. . . . Women think in relational terms because our existence is defined in relation to men.[35]

Further, the powerlessness of women in male supremacist society produces a profound silence; it prevents women not just from "being heard" but also from "having anything to say."[36] Women's speech in more ample sense requires that women acquire more power than we have now. The liberatory work of feminist criticism is purely destructive; the positive work of social transformation would begin when there is a critical mass of awareness of the systemically exploitative nature of gender relations.

4. Just as MacKinnon sees women as victims of the male supremacist order, she sees men as its beneficiaries. Individual men may choose to renounce male power and privilege because they disdain to be oppressors and wish to enlist in the forces of liberation. However, MacKinnon offers men qua men no inducement to do so.

5. MacKinnon hypothesizes that both men and women in contemporary society experience male domination and female subordination as sexual, indeed, as the sine qua non of sex. The dominance and submission structure of sexual desire is a defining feature of male dominance in contemporary culture.[37] Absent sexual domination, our culture would know no sexual desire.

6. MacKinnon proposes "a new paradigm" of the social experience of sex in our civilization, one in which coercion is the norm and genuine consent and mutuality the exception.[38] The new paradigm follows from MacKinnon's sexual-domination-based theory of gender: If women exist in order to serve male desire, and sex is enjoyed as a consummation of domination, then it follows that the typical man in a typical sexual encounter will either tend to presume his "partner's" consent, be indifferent to her wishes, or actively seek to impose himself upon her. Although MacKinnon is often erroneously understood to be arguing that all sex is rapelike, she does not regard all men as rapists or all sex as coerced. On her view, some of us lead atypical lives and some who lead typical lives experience atypical interludes of sex unmarred by domination. Most of us do not.[39]

MacKinnon's blurring of the distinction between consensual sex and rape is controversial among feminists and anathema to nonfeminists. Yet one need not share her vision in order to recognize that it has enabled her to identify coercive sexuality as endemic in a broad range of circumstances that were until recently all but culturally invisible and whose victims have been outside the bourn of the law's protection. In no small part due to her theoretical and reform efforts, coercive sexuality and the law's tolerance of it have gained recognition as critical problems for the feminist agenda. We can no longer think of rape by the unknown assailant as an experience radically distinct from everyday intimacy; the realm of the sexually ordinary has been revealed to include marital, date, and acquaintance rape, incest and child abuse, workplace and schoolhouse sexual harassment.[40]

MacKinnon's coercion paradigm can be seen as an elegant but terrible application of the central insight of feminist legal theory to the arena of sexuality. Feminist legal theorists have argued that the law both reflects and is constitutive of a fundamental social division between the public and the private realms, a division injurious to women in a myriad of ways. The private realm of family and intimate relationships has been left largely unregulated by law—in contrast to the public sphere—as a matter of deep structural social policy. The presumptions underlying the private/public distinction include, as the current law reflects, the (male) supposition that sexual relations are normally governed by free and mutual consent. The coercion paradigm of sexual relations provides a powerful means of challenging the privileging of the private realm as a domain in which mutuality and harmony of interests make regulation unnecessary. If women experience coerced sex as either typical or even substantially more common than the male view of social reality supposes it to be, then through maintenance of the private realm the law helps to render female gender a status of sexual victimhood.

I do not myself find MacKinnon's thesis that sexual exploitation is the life force or linchpin of gender inequality persuasive. Although sexual relations may commonly exhibit the dominance and submission patterning she describes, MacKinnon has not shown why sexual exploitation should be regarded as the primary cause rather than an effect of gender hierarchy. In my view, sexuality is also a domain of great variety and fluidity, as well as an area of life where men and women experience each other as peers in vulnerability and power—an equality that tends to be eroded as sexual relationships are folded into social and economic institutions that support male dominance. However, one need not accept MacKinnon's general theory of gender in its entirety to learn from what she has used it to bring into high relief: that women in our society share the experience of vulnerability to sexual victimization in a wide range of circumstances that the current legal order either ignores or condones. One need not hold with MacKinnon that to be a woman is to be a sexual victim *and nothing else* in order to accept that susceptibility to legally invisible or unreachable sexual victimization is a defining feature of female gender in our society. Further, the coercion paradigm can be explored and developed and its utility tested independent of the general theory by the standard feminist methods endorsed by MacKinnon, searching for commonalities in the self-reported experience women share with each other, as well as by conventional social science.

III

MacKinnon has pursued a style of theorizing that has come increasingly into disfavor among feminist scholars. She has striven to develop a "linchpin" theory, a comprehensive explanation of gender exploitation in an era in which postmodernist trends in philosophy, social theory, and jurisprudence have led to skepticism about the legitimacy of theorizing on such an ambitious scale.[41] Feminist theorists in particular have become increasingly critical of claims to discern transhistorical and transcultural universality, of claims to find a concept of gender, whether rooted in biology or cultural universals, that serves to explain the condition of all women.[42] Even more urgently, because of its immediate relevance to contemporary feminist politics, feminist theorists have resisted efforts to develop and impose a unitary feminism that speaks for women of every class, race, ethnicity, and sexual orientation. The weight of feminist opinion today rests with those who have cautioned that feminism must be pluralistic. These critics have argued that the quest for the essentially female has led to the privileging of white middle-class women's experience as women's experience as such and the silencing—yet again, but this time by their elite sisters—of the voices of women of color and working-class women. I will below defend the value of MacKinnon's approach against excessively pluralizing tendencies in feminist theory.

I understand *strong* gender essentialism to hold that women share certain characteristics that have been invariant in all the historically and culturally diverse manifestations of human society and that either (1) account for women's distinctive moral (in the broadest sense) traits, or (2) explain women's subordination by men, or (3) both. Biologically based accounts that interpret women's social existence as elaborations of our reproductive role—whether narrowly construed (as by Shulamith Firestone) or broadly construed (as by Nancy Chodorow)—are clearly of this type.[43] MacKinnon eschews biologism, insisting that men and women are pure social constructs and that there is no well-founded reason to suppose that purely biological gender would map on to traits that have social significance in the absence of a system of male domination.

There are passages in her work where MacKinnon speaks the language of strong essentialism.[44] If MacKinnon is to be consistent, however, strong essentialism is barred to her by her method. MacKinnon's method requires that we begin with and test theory against the experience of women, She asserts that feminist method is a historical advance in that it democratizes social theory; it gives at least a portion of control over the problems focused upon and the content of theory to those whose interests social theory seeks to advance. This grounding in women's experience is a constraint that prohibits social theory from sweeping too broadly to employ feminist method. A feminist may speculate about the grand sweep of history, but she cannot theorize about it without violating the canons of feminist method. Moreover, MacKinnon has no need to make transhistorical claims for her theory of gender domination. Her goals require only what might be called *weak* essentialism, or less paradoxically, the search for (warranted, not underinclusive) generalizations about the experience and condition of women in our society. The principle of parsimony urges suitable restraint. I understand MacKinnon, then, to be asserting that, within the frame of modern European industrial culture and despite the varieties and particularities of experience of women of different social classes, races, or ethnicities, the concept of gender yet powerfully helps recover, focus, and organize common experience of self-identity and moral outlook, or of oppression, or both.

However, of late, MacKinnon's commitment to constructing genderwide theory, even though pursued within a methodological framework that countenances only socially and historically contextualized generalizations, has been enough to call forth criticism from feminists persuaded that the attempt to generalize about the experience of all women is doomed to failure for at least two reasons. First, theories about gender such as MacKinnon's invariably treat the experience of some women—the white middle-class women from whose ranks theorists typically come—as the experience of all women. Such "white solipsism" is self-defeating and offensive to those whom it excludes.[45] Second, MacKinnon supposes that it is possible to extract without distortion or falsification from the complex experience of, for example, a black woman, that portion of experience of self and of victimization attributable to her gender rather than to her race. This supposition is not borne out by black women's accounts of their own experience. Black legal feminist theorist Angela Harris and other feminists of color contend that their experience cannot be so fragmented without fatal loss of meaning; race and gender oppression are experienced as fused and inseparable.[46] They argue that the experience of gender by white women is profoundly different from that of women of color. White middle-class women do not suffer from multiple sources of oppression; indeed, as whites we are beneficiaries of and often participate in racism. MacKinnon's unconscious expression of racism is to ignore, in violation of the strictures of feminist method, black women's own accounts of their experience.

In a powerfully instructive article exposing the poverty of white solipsism, Angela Harris rejects MacKinnon's coercion paradigm; she finds that MacKinnon's universalizing reading of rape ignores and distorts the experience of women of color: "This . . . is an analysis of what rape means to white women masquerading as a general account; it has nothing to do with the experience of rape of black women. For black women, rape is a far more complex experience, and an experience as deeply rooted in color as in gender."[47]

The crux of MacKinnon's analysis of rape is that legally redressable rape is but one—relatively infrequent at that—form of coerced sex. Sex seen as consensual from the male perspective is often, even usually, coerced sex from the feminist perspective. We may here include forced sex that is indistinguishable from rape except that the man has a privilege that blocks legal responsibility (marital rape) and acquaintance rape, which is usually legally unreachable because the prosecution cannot establish lack of consent in a court of law. Child abuse and incest are similarly legally invisible when victims are unable to see redress or are incompetent to give testimony. We may also include sex that does not involve force but is more rapelike than consensual in that the woman's compliance is induced by her dependence rather than by sexual desire.

Harris criticizes MacKinnon for failing to recognize—because she failed to listen to the voices of black women themselves—that black women's experience is qualitatively different from that of white women: MacKinnon, writes Harris, treats "'black,' applied to women [as] an intensifier. . . . If things are bad for everybody (meaning white women), then they're even worse for black women."[48] Harris discusses three features of black women's experience of rape that illustrate the distortion wrought by the leaching out of color and the application of MacKinnon's paradigm: (1) If whites think of stranger rape first when they think of rape, black women's historical experience focuses as much on rape by white owners and domestic employers. (2) The rape of a black woman in slavery was not a crime. Even after emancipation the law was seldom used to protect black women from the depredations of men, black or white. Criminal rape only happened to white women; "what happened to black women was simply life."[49] (3) Finally, a primary signification of rape for black men and black women is the brutalization of black men accused of raping white women, a brutalization in which white women were complicit when they failed to acknowledge their willing roles. Harris summarizes as follows:

> Thus, the experience of rape for black women includes not only a vulnerability to rape and a lack of legal protection radically different from that experienced by white women, but also a unique ambivalence. Black women have simultaneously acknowledged their own victimization and the victimization of black men by a system that has consistently ignored violence against women while perpetuating it against men. The complexity and depth of this experience is not captured, or even acknowledged, by MacKinnon's account.[50]

There are two questions that I would like to raise about Harris's analysis of the black rape experience and her critique of MacKinnon. I will proceed from the premise that Harris's analysis of the cultural meaning of rape to black women is completely accurate.[51]

(1) It appears to me that the validity of Harris's analysis of the black rape experience and MacKinnon's coercion paradigm are entirely compatible. MacKinnon need not, and I think would not, deny that black female experience is unique and qualitatively distinctive in just the ways that Harris claims it to be. MacKinnon denies over and over again any desire to homogenize the experience of oppression: "What we have in common is not that our conditions have no particularity in ways that matter."[52] MacKinnon claims only that along with the particularity of distinctness there is common experience of rape, common experience of various forms of coerced sex that the male paradigm of stranger rape obscures. The first question I would like to ask black women is this: Do you recognize the commonality of experience of powerlessness and of legal invisibility in black and white marital rape, or in sex forced on an Irish domestic servant in Boston with nowhere to go except to another potentially equally dangerous household, or in sex forced on a black domestic in Atlanta or New York? MacKinnon, I believe, helps us to understand what these varieties of otherwise culturally and historically differently conditioned experience share: Although from the point of view of feminism they are varieties of rape, from the point of view of the law they are cases where consent is presumed and where the law does not concern itself with whether or not consent was in fact withheld.

(2) Harris has explained that for black women rape has as a primary signification "the terrorism of black men by white men, aided and abetted . . . by white women."[53] The question I would ask my black sisters is this: Does Harris here conflate the *experience* of rape with the *politics* of rape? I believe this may be the case. Let me amplify. I suspect that what may be of fundamental concern to Harris is resisting white feminist demands that she choose her gender over her race in circumstances in which Harris and other women of color are torn by the conflicting pulls of facets of their multiplic-

itous identity. Commitment to the struggle against racism as well as the experience of unredressable rape by whites in a white supremacist system surely impel black women to refuse to lend legitimacy to any antirape campaign that is insensitive to the need to challenge the white paradigm of rape—that is, the strange black man who jumps out of the bushes. Here I must say I see no in-principle division of political interests between black and white women. All women have an interest in challenging the stereotypical notion that rape is something that men of an alien and despised social group inflict on our (fill in the blank) women. Rape is predominantly a same-race, not a racial crossover, crime.[54]

Nonetheless, MacKinnon and other white feminists may be guilty of blithely presuming that the form of oppression from which we suffer makes the most powerful claim in all circumstances on the political loyalties of all our sisters. Harris takes MacKinnon to task for her analysis of the case of a Pueblo woman who married a Navajo man and whose children were denied inheritance rights in communal Pueblo land.[55] The Pueblo ordinance granted such rights to children of mixed marriages when the father was Pueblo but not when the Pueblo parent was the mother. MacKinnon condemns the tribal ordinance because if forces female but not male Pueblos to choose between their gender and tribal identity. Harris criticizes MacKinnon for making the assumption that a woman of color should always choose her gender over her race and therefore analyzing Julia Martinez's case without finding it necessary to inform herself concretely about the specifics of the issues as understood by the Pueblos of Santa Clara.[56]

The defects of MacKinnon's analysis of the Santa Clara Pueblo case are not properly attributed to her feminist theory. MacKinnon's feminism is not reductionist. She is not committed to the view that gender identity or gender oppression has political primacy. MacKinnon can maintain with perfect consistency that all women share as women certain common traits or experiences; that the proper tactical or strategic response to multiple oppression cannot be determined a priori and should not be presumed to be the same in every context; and that it is not for white women to tell black or Native American women where their duty or interest ties in circumstances of conflict. MacKinnon is committed by her standpoint epistemology to recognize that blacks and other oppressed groups must in turn ground social theory and political choice in their own experience and interests as they understand them. MacKinnon's feminism claims neither to be the only nor to be the fundamental theory of the oppressed.

Despite MacKinnon's theoretical boldness and ambition, her gender generalizing is actually of a quite modest variety. She is best read as seeking warranted generalizations about women's lives in modern industrial society rather than speaking for all ages. Further, she does not hold that women's oppression is more fundamental than that suffered by others; nor does she hold that addressing gender oppression should necessarily take priority over other social issues. She apparently regards the generalizing theorist—herself—as bearing the burden of proof that her theory is sufficiently inclusive to describe the experience of all women. Finally, MacKinnon acknowledges that even if gender has common meaning, it also has distinctively contextualized meanings for women with different cultural histories, one among which is that of the white middle class. Should this modestly framed insistence on the possibility of making genderwide generalizations be rejected? In her recent extended philosophical critique of essentialism, Elizabeth Spelman argues that any instance of what might be called "pure feminist theory" falsifies and distorts as it attempts to abstract gender traits from the particularities of women of diverse races and classes. I would like to briefly consider two arguments that Spelman makes in her refutation of essentialism.

(1) Spelman argues that essentialists, whether mainstream apologists or dissonant critical theorists like MacKinnon, confound the categories employed by their theories to describe or explain the social world with reality itself; essentialists reify the social categories of whatever conceptual scheme has them in its sway. Spelman argues that classifying people may be done in an indefinite number of ways that reflect the purposes and interests of those doing the classifying. The criteria used to sort people into social groupings reflect the varied and often antagonistic purposes theory serves rather than the essential racial, gender, or class properties of the people classified.[57] Spelman's argument brings to bear against essentialism a watershed insight common to several overlapping philosophical traditions whose progenitors include John Dewey, Ludwig Wittgenstein, and Rudolf Carnap: The world can be described in alternative ways bespeaking distinctive theoretic purposes. We confuse the social ontology of our theories with the way the world really is only to the detriment of our understanding of both theory and the world.

For those of us who share enough philosophical common ground with Spelman, her argument is irresistible against (strong) gender essentialism, clearly the doctrine she had in view in making the argument. It does not address the gender generalizing of a theorist like MacKinnon, who does not claim to describe fundamental or unchanging reality and who acknowledges and wants to learn from other perspectives. MacKinnon is not susceptible to the criticism that she confuses the social ontology of a favored viewpoint with an objective and uniquely accurate view of obdurate reality.

(2) Spelman also argues that essentialists are proponents of what she calls "additive analysis" or "a version of personal identity we might call tootsie roll metaphysics":

> Each part of my identity is separable from every other part, and the significance of each part is unaffected by the other parts. On this view of personal identity (which might also be called pop-bead metaphysics), my being a woman means the same whether I am white or Black, rich or poor, French or Jamaican, Jewish or Muslim. As a woman, I'm like other women: my difference from other women is only along the other dimensions of my identity. Hence it is possible on this view to imagine my being the same woman even if my race were different—the pop-bead or tootsie roll section labeled "woman" is just inserted into a different strand or roll.[58]

Spelman's philosophical critique of additive analysis, like Harris's critique of white ignorance of and indifference to black women's experience, provides a wealth of insight into the pitfalls—and pratfalls—of white solipsism. Nevertheless, Spelman uses her critique of "additive analysis" too extravagantly: In forbidding any generalization along purely gender lines, Spelman has lost the thread of her first argument considered above. She is treating a useful theory or generalization (additive analysis distorts) as a uniquely correct description of social reality (it is never useful to, it is always a distortion to, generalize along purely gender lines). Spelman's critique is a potent tool to accomplish certain purposes: to expose white solipsism, to insist on proper attention to the voices of all women, to call attention to the interplay among race, class, and gender in the formation of personal identity or the way in which people are treated. But there are other purposes. One such is *to attempt* to abstract commonalities from the diversity of women's experience for the sake of better understanding and pursuing common objectives. Attention to common experience—if such there be—like attention to diversity, is a methodological virtue worth cultivating.[59] Kaleidoscopic pluralism, like excessive abstraction, poses dangers to feminist theory and effective political action on behalf of the interests of women.

The search for a "total" theory of gender such as MacKinnon seeks may prove elusive or even illusory. This eventuality would not detract from the utility of theoretical illuminations of aspects of women's common experience. I submit that MacKinnon's coercion paradigm is just such an illumination of women's common experience and its encounter with the dissonant stance of the law.

Notes

I would like to thank Katharine Bartlett, Sally Haslanger, Christine Littleton, and Charlotte Witt for their illuminating comments on earlier drafts of this paper.

1. See MacKinnon's *Sexual Harassment of Working Women* (New Haven, Conn.: Yale University Press, 1979), *Feminism Unmodified* (Cambridge, Mass.: Harvard, 1987), and *Towards a Feminist Theory of the State* (Cambridge, Mass.: Harvard, 1989). The latter two collections make MacKinnon's essays and speeches of the past decade readily available. Her influence, as well as the critical assessment of her role in the development of feminist jurisprudence, can be traced in Katharine Bartlett, "MacKinnon's Feminism: Power on Whose Terms?" 75 *California Law Review* (1986); Christine Littleton, "Feminist Jurisprudence: The Difference Method Makes," 41 *Stanford Law Review* (1989); and Frances Olsen, "Feminist Theory in the Grand Style," 89 *Columbia Law Review* (1989).

2. A fourth approach, postmodernism, will be discussed in part III of this chapter. I make no claims to an exhaustive or definitive discussion of the strands that contribute to contemporary feminist legal theory. See Katharine Bartlett, "Feminist Legal Methods," 103 *Harvard Law Review* (1990), on the development of feminist legal theory during the past decade. See also Susan Okin, "Sexual Difference, Feminism, and the Law," 16 *Law and Social Inquiry* (1991).

3. Frontiero v. Richardson, 411 U.S. 677 (1973).

4. Craig v. Boren, 429 U.S. 190 (1976).

5. See Wendy Williams, "The Equality Crisis: Some Reflections on Culture, Courts, and Feminism," 7 *Women's Rights Law Reporter* (1982).

6. In Rostker v. Goldberg, 453 U.S. 57 (1981), and Michael M. v. Superior Court, 450 U.S. 464 (1981), respectively. See Williams, "Equality Crisis," p. 183.

7. Carrie Menkel-Meadow, "Portia in a Different Voice: Speculation on a Women's Lawyering Process," 1 *Berkeley Women's Law Journal* (1985).

8. Carol Gilligan, *In a Different Voice: Psychological Theory and Women's Development* (Cambridge, Mass.: Harvard, 1982), p. 18.

9. Ibid.

10. Bartlett, "Feminist Legal Methods," p. 849; Suzanna Sherry, "Civic Virtue and the Feminine Voice in Constitutional Adjudication," 72 *Virginia Law Review* (1986), p. 605.

11. Judith Resnik, "On the Bias: Feminist Reconsiderations of the Aspirations for Our Judges," 61 *Southern California Law Review* (1988).

12. The term *liberal legalism* is Karl Klare's. See his "Lawmaking as Practice," 40 *Telos* (1979). MacKinnon, like writers associated with the critical legal studies movement, uses it as a convenient label for both the legal system we have and liberal jurisprudential understandings of it.

13. MacKinnon, *Towards a Feminist Theory of the State,* p. 162.

14. MacKinnon distinguishes between the theory of ideology of Marx, which she accepts, and the Marxism of Engels and the Second International, which lapsed into objectivism, claiming that dialectical materialism could yield transcendent truths (ibid., pp. 107–108).

15. See Karl Marx, "On the Jewish Question," in David McLellen, ed., *Karl Marx: Selected Writings* (Oxford: Oxford University Press, 1977).

16. MacKinnon, *Towards a Feminist Theory of the State,* p. 162.

17. Ibid., p. 163.

18. Ibid.

19. One need not be a Marxist to motivate this style of critique. Justice Holmes, for example, makes the same kind of critique in his dissent in Lochner v. New York, 198 U.S. 45 (1905). Of course, some Marxists would argue that wage and hour legislation provides merely the illusion of reform, further disguising while perpetuating capitalist exploitation. MacKinnon apparently regards genuine legal reform as a legitimate goal of the feminist movement.

20. See "Pornography," chaps. 11–16 of *Feminism Unmodified,* pp. 127–205.

21. *Feminism Unmodified,* p. 262.

22. Ibid., p. 148.

23. Robin West, "The Feminist-Conservative Anti-Pornography Alliance and the 1986 Attorney General's Commission Report on Pornography," 1987 *American Bar Foundation Research Journal,* p. 686.

24. American Booksellers v. Hudnut, 771 F.2d 323 (7th Cir. 1985), *aff'd* Hudnut v. American Booksellers, 475 U.S. 1001 (1986).

25. MacKinnon applies to the arena of gender an argument against the possibility of government neutrality in the marketplace of ideas that has been the subject of debate among legal scholars, philosophers, and political scientists for some time. The classic defense of the value of neutrality in constitutional law is Herbert Wechsler, "Toward Neutral Principles of Constitutional Law," 73 *Columbia Law Review* (1959). See also Eric Hoffman, "Feminism, Pornography, and the Law," 133 *University of Pennsylvania Law Review* (1985); Robert Post, "Cultural Heterogeneity and Law: Pornography, Blasphemy, and the First Amendment," 76 *California Law Review* (1988); and Cass Sunstein, "Pornography and the First Amendment," 1986 *Duke Law Journal.*

26. MacKinnon's critique of the specious gender neutrality of the law does not settle, but rather sets the stage for, the intrafeminist controversy about the wisdom of pressing for legal regulation of pornography. At the strategic level, the most important division among feminists with respect to pornography is between those who hold the harms of pornography to be sufficiently great, and sufficiently reachable through regulation, to outweigh the potential harms of regulation, and those who do not. Critics of regulation argue that to invite the state to suppress pornography will result in the use of state power to reinforce conservative gender stereotypes to the detriment of women and the fragile progress we have made. See "Feminist Anti-Censorship Taskforce Brief in American Booksellers v. Hudnut," 21 *Michigan Journal of Law Reform* (1987–88); and West, "Feminist-Conservative Anti-Pornography Alliance."

27. See MacKinnon, *Towards a Feminist Theory of the State,* "A Critique of Marx and Engels," pp. 13–36.

28. MacKinnon, *Towards a Feminist Theory of the State,* "Methods and Politics," pp. 106–125, esp. 115–116. See Bartlett, "Feminist Legal Methods," pp. 872–877, on the need for a feminist critique of feminist standpoint epistemology.

29. See MacKinnon, *Towards a Feminist Theory of the State,* "Consciousness Raising," pp. 83–105. "Experience" is, of course, a problematic and theory-laden category; I make no attempt to analyze it here.

30. MacKinnon, *Feminism Unmodified,* p. 48.

31. Ibid., p. 49.

32. Ibid.

33. MacKinnon's theory lacks a genetic or etiological dimension. MacKinnon does not attempt to account for how it is that there are men and women or how men came to dominate women.

34. Misogynist art provides some rich examples that can serve to illustrate MacKinnon's notion of female gender as the objectification of male sexual desire. Recall that in D. H. Lawrence's celebration of sexuality, *Lady Chatterley's Lover,* Mellors, the gamekeeper, instructs his paramour that the completely feminine sexual partner ought not to achieve orgasm; she should be solely engrossed in her lover's satisfaction. Or consider Fellini's *8 1/2*—in the hero's fantasy, the women of his household have to "go upstairs" at the age of 30; when they are no longer sexually interesting to him they disappear or perhaps cease to exist.

MacKinnon makes it clear that although the dominance of men over women has established the social meanings of male and female gender, biological males and females can play either gender role. Gender hierarchy patterned on heterosexual relations is for her typical of homosexual and lesbian life. Similarly, women sometimes assume the male role in intimate relationships with men or in society's range of hierarchical institutions. Far more unusual than decoupling the standard combination of biological sex and social gender is the achievement of unexploitative sexual and other social relationships.

35. MacKinnon, *Feminism Unmodified,* p. 39.

36. Ibid.

37. Ibid., p. 148.

38. Ibid., p. 6.

39. On this point, see Littleton, "Feminist Jurisprudence," p. 777, and Olsen, "Feminist Theory in the Grand Style," pp. 1156–1157.

40. Substantially more women are raped by persons known to them than by strangers. Based on survey interviews collected from a sample of 60,000 households, the

National Crime Survey (NCS) finds the following incidence of rape in 1988 among women over 12:

Relationship to victim:	
Stranger	53,310
Nonstranger	74,050
spouse	8,145
other relative (not parent)	4,443
well known but unrelated	33,322
casual acquaintance	26,140

See U.S. Department of Justice, *Criminal Victimization in the US. in 1988* (Washington, D.C.: GPO, 1990).

Authoritative estimates on the prevalence of rape are difficult to obtain. The NCS also estimates that 8 percent of American women are raped in the course of their lives. We can probably take this estimate as a lower bound: Women surveyed may well not have appreciated that various forms of coercive sex they had experienced would count as rape and/or they may not have been willing to report such incidents to the interviewers. In *Rape in Marriage* (Bloomington: Indiana University Press, 1990), Diana Russell finds, based on a sample of 930 women in San Francisco, that 44 percent of women are raped at least once during their lifetime. This estimate in Russell's controversial study could be taken, at the current juncture of inquiry, as an upper bound.

41. "Sexuality," writes MacKinnon, in summarizing her theory, "is the linchpin of gender inequality" (*Towards a Feminist Theory of the State*, p. 113).

42. See Bartlett, "Feminist Legal Methods," pp. 847–849; and Nancy Fraser and Linda Nicolson, "Social Criticism without Philosophy: An Encounter between Feminism and Postmodernism," in *Universal Abandon?* ed. Andrew Ross (Minneapolis: University of Minnesota Press, 1988).

43. See Shulamith Firestone, *The Dialectic of Sex* (New York: Morrow, 1970); and Nancy Chodorow, *The Reproduction of Mothering: Psychoanalysis and the Sociology of Gender* (Berkeley: University of California Press, 1978).

44. See, for example, MacKinnon, *Towards a Feminist Theory of the State*, p. 105; or *Feminism Unmodified*, pp. 166–167.

45. The phrase is Adrienne Rich's; see "Disloyal to Civilization: Feminism, Racism, Gynephobia," in *On Lies, Secrets, and Silence* (New York: W. W. Norton, 1979), quoted by Angela Harris, "Race and Essentialism in Feminist Legal Theory," 42 *Stanford Law Review* 588 (1990).

46. Harris, "Race and Essentialism," p. 588.

47. Ibid., p. 598.

48. Ibid., p. 596.

49. Ibid.. p. 599.

50. Ibid., p. 601.

51. There are other important critiques of the inattention to women of color in mainstream feminist theory, including that of Kimberle Crenshaw. In her "Demarginalizing the Intersection of Race and Sex: A Black Feminist Critique of Antidiscrimination Doctrine, Feminist Theory and Antiracist Politics" in 1989 *University of Chicago Legal Forum,* Crenshaw argues persuasively that women of color experience distinctive forms of oppression because of their membership in two subordinated groups. She argues that their oppression has been ignored by both antisexist and antiracist movements, neither of which

can achieve its formal objectives until the interaction between race and gender subordination is acknowledged, understood, and addressed.

52. MacKinnon, *Feminism Unmodified,* p. 76. See also MacKinnon's "Feminism, Marxism, Method, and the State," 8 *Signs* 520(n7) (1983), in which MacKinnon draws out the implications of her conception of feminist method with respect to reports of their experience by women of color that differ from those of whites: "I aspire to include all women in the term 'women' in some way, without violating the particularity of any woman's experience. Whenever this fails, the statement is simply wrong and will have to be qualified or the aspiration (or the theory) abandoned."

53. Harris, "Race and Essentialism," p. 599.

54. In 1987 more than 70 percent of black rape victims reported that the men who raped them were black; more than 78 percent of white victims reported that the men who raped them were white. U.S. Department of Justice, *Criminal Victimization in the United States in 1987* (Washington, D.C.: GPO, 1989).

55. Santa Clara Pueblo v. Martinez, 436 U.S. 49 (1978).

56. See "Whose Culture? A Case Note on Martinez v. Santa Clara Pueblo," in MacKinnon, *Feminism Unmodified,* pp. 63–69; and Harris, "Race and Essentialism," p. 594.

57. Elizabeth V. Spelman, *Inessential Woman* (Boston: Beacon Press, 1988), p. 148.

58. Ibid., pp. 136–137. See, generally, chs. 5 and 6, pp. 114–159.

59. See Susan Bordo, "Feminist Skepticism and the 'Maleness' of Philosophy," 85 *Journal of Philosophy* (1988), who, working largely from within the perspective of continental philosophy, expresses similar concerns.

I2

MACKINNON'S
CRITIQUE OF OBJECTIVITY

RACHEL ZUCKERT

Catharine MacKinnon describes herself as a radical feminist, one who practices, she writes, "feminism unmodified." MacKinnon thus takes her theory to be fundamentally, formatively a feminist one, unlike Marxist or liberal feminist theories, which are mere adaptations of preexisting theories to accommodate women's concerns. But MacKinnon also understands her radical feminism as a political and theoretical attack on the liberal establishment at its roots, in its most fundamental nature, at a deeper level than disagreements within liberalism (or Western political philosophy more generally) right and left. MacKinnon's objections to liberalism are multiple and complex: she criticizes liberalism, for example, on the grounds that it endorses "individualism, naturalism, voluntarism, idealism, and moralism."[1] But MacKinnon identifies the core of her objections to liberalism as a "political-methodological" or "political-epistemological" critique of liberal "objectivity." Her most ambitious political, epistemological, and even metaphysical claim against liberalism is her argument that there is an intrinsic link between "objectivity" as the purportedly neutral but actually male epistemological point of view expressed in or presupposed by liberalism, and "objectification" as the social-sexual process that subordinates women.[2] To the degree to which liberals are committed to objectivity, MacKinnon argues, so too are they inevitably committed to the subordination of women.

In this chapter, I shall investigate and evaluate this most ambitious of MacKinnon's criticisms of liberalism. I analyze MacKinnon's critique of liberal objectivity as comprising three different, and escalating, types of criticism: (1) an internal criticism of specific liberal claims (that liberals are less objective than they claim), (2) a metaphysical criticism (that there is no such thing as objectivity), and (3) a moral/political criticism (that objectivity is in itself an immoral norm). I shall argue in each case that MacKinnon's successful criticisms of liberalism and objectivity, despite her own descriptions of them, and despite liberal antagonism toward her, should be understood to lie largely within the liberal tradition and its norms, both moral/political and epistemological.

A Few Caveats and Sketchy Definitions to Start

Liberalism, objectivity, and objectification are all controversial and broad terms for which MacKinnon herself gives no hard and fast definitions. Because MacKinnon's claims are at a somewhat high level of abstraction, directed at whole traditions within philosophy, I do not provide strict definitions for these terms either. But I wish to indicate here (in a sketchy manner) how I will take them in this chapter.

I take objectification, first, to mean the treatment of a person as an object, as merely a means to one's own ends (the satisfaction of the objectifier's needs or desires). According to MacKinnon (following Dworkin), the objectification of women in our society takes a variety of forms,[3] but it is largely embodied in, and enforced by, sexual practices and our social understanding of them (manifested most clearly in pornography). The male objectifier objectifies women first and foremost as a means to the satisfaction of his *sexual* desires. Sexual objectification, further, constitutes a moral or political wrong, according to MacKinnon and Dworkin, in that it "ranges from dehumanizing women as sexual things and commodities to torturing and maiming women as sexual acts. The dehumanization is fundamental to the subordination and the precondition for the more explicit violence."[4] Thus men's objectification of women includes, or at least makes possible and legitimates, certain abuses of or injustices against women. But for MacKinnon objectification *itself* is already a harm (not merely a precondition for other harms) because it is "dehumanizing," that is, it treats a human being without recognizing that human being's dignity or (in liberal terms) autonomy.[5]

As is attested by Kant's second formulation of the categorical imperative, liberals agree with MacKinnon that treating human beings as means to one's own ends is in itself wrong.[6] This view, expressed in terms of "rights" or of "autonomy," is shared by all forms of liberalism, usually on the grounds that all human beings are rational and ought to be allowed as much as possible (rationally) to choose their own ways of life, to be self-determining. This view is often conjoined with a certain agnosticism about what a substantively good life is[7] (except that it ought to be chosen by the individual herself). In other words, the two guiding norms of liberalism are freedom and equality: liberals believe that all individual human beings ought to be treated as free, and equally so. Further, according to liberals, government is legitimate if and only if it serves to guarantee these freedoms (i.e., to prevent the infringement of individuals' autonomy by others), and is not to dictate to individuals how to lead their lives except to prevent harm to others (the government too ought not to infringe upon individuals' autonomy). (Correspondingly, individual citizens have an interest in, and owe duties to, a legitimate government because their rights are thus protected by the government.) Legitimate government (on the liberal view) must, thus, be universalist and egalitarian (treat all human beings as having these rights; no one is exempt from the law). Finally, and importantly in the context of MacKinnon's views, the liberal values of autonomy and equal rights ground the liberal condemnation of discrimination, as ill-founded, coercive treatment of an individual as unequally free, or the infringement upon that person's autonomy (or right to self-determination).

Last, I take objectivity as a norm of scientific inquiry (or of inquiry more broadly), a norm not strictly synonymous with truth. (Thus I mean to preclude an obvious, but wrong, rejoinder to MacKinnon: if you don't believe in objectivity [truth], how can you claim that your views are true/objective? One can, at least in principle, criticize objectivity but retain some other conception of truth or epistemological method.) If one endorses objectivity as the norm of scientific inquiry, one admits that it is always a subject, a human being, who is inquiring and any result obtained from this inquiry will be stated by that human being. (There is no ultimate "real world" to which we can refer or about which we can know in terms other than our own terms.)[8] Objective knowledge, or the aim of this inquiry, is then defined by contrast to subjective opinion, perspective, interest, or perceptions—it might be (loosely) defined as what any (ideal) knower, any subject, would find to be true of the object investigated. In seeking for objective knowledge, one tries to find various methods or criteria by which one could tell whether one's interests, prejudices, preferences, wishful thinking, and so on, have or have not influenced the results of inquiry. For example, Edward Donnerstein (a psychologist whose research on pornography and its effects MacKinnon cites) invokes repeatability of experiments as a criterion agreed upon in the scientific community for the objectivity of the results of these experiments—any experimenter would find the same, the results were not dependent on some special conditions, for example, the prejudices or moods of the experimenter or (in Donnerstein's case) the particular film he chose to use in his experiments (*IHW* [Donnerstein testimony], p. 52).[9]

I further wish to emphasize three aspects of objectivity, thus broadly construed. First, objectivity is properly to be understood as a *norm* according to which inquiry is conducted or the results of inquiry are judged; inquirers can aim to be objective but may fail actually to be so. Second, objectivity is typically defined in contrast to subjectivity (another highly controversial concept) and thus, as a norm, may well imply or include the norms of "distance," "neutrality," or "impartiality" that MacKinnon attributes to it. Finally, most defenders of objectivity take objectivity to be attainable in some sense through reason, as universal or nonsubjective (as opposed to interests, emotions, perceptions, etc.).

I now turn to the question of why MacKinnon (or anyone) should consider liberalism and objectivity to be connected to each other. Certainly liberalism and objectivist epistemology are conjoined historically; for example, Kant introduced "objectivity" to epistemological terminology, and he is a liberal moral/political philosopher.[10] But I wish to dismiss out of hand a reading of MacKinnon that would have her base her views on such flimsy, contingent grounds. MacKinnon is not arguing that liberalism is in male interests purely because liberalism has not had a perfect record historically of recognizing women's rights (and certainly has not eliminated the subordination of women). Similarly, MacKinnon is not arguing that objectivity as a norm of inquiry (or reason, which is closely tied to objectivity as suggested above) subordinates women simply because it has been traditionally (in the male-dominated philosophical tradition) been attributed to men and denied to women. Though both of these facts are indeed to be lamented (as MacKinnon does), such simplistic arguments are unworthy of MacKinnon, who is after an intrinsic, conceptual link between liberalism, objectivity, and objectification.[11]

I suggest, rather, that liberal political norms and the objectivity norm are connected (not merely historically) because they are both values grounded in valuing reason and universality: liberals ground the rights of human beings in the human capacity for rationality; objectivity theorists endorse the rational subject as the correct kind of scientific inquirer. Correspondingly, both liberals and objectivist epistemologists tend to be proceduralists. On both views, we have no sure, automatic, self-verifying, intuitive knowledge of the right way of life or of the world. Thus we must rely on some rational method or procedure to try to adjudicate which interests ought to be served or protected, which claims are true of the world. Both liberals and objectivists endorse rationality both as descriptive (of human beings, at their best) and as normative (as the aim to which we ought to aspire, how we ought to treat other human beings). Thus, though MacKinnon does not (to my knowledge) articulate the connection between liberalism and the norm of objectivity in these terms, I believe that the tight connection she draws between liberalism and objectivity is largely justified.

MacKinnon does, however, discuss more explicitly (and critically, as I shall discuss below) the ways in which liberalism as practiced relies on the norm of objectivity (and, correspondingly, of universality and disinterest) to establish what the "facts" of the situation are, in order to determine whether and in what way its norms of liberty and equality ought to be enacted in the particular case in question. For example, on the liberal view, one needs to have an objective view of the facts of the case to decide whether an action (e.g., a landlord evicting a tenant) is a case of discrimination (e.g., on the basis of race) or a legitimate eviction (e.g., on the grounds that the tenant disturbed other tenants). Alternatively, a landlord might be judged to be objective in her disapproval of a tenant when her reason is the tenant's troublesome behavior, and not to be objective when her "reason" is the tenant's race. (Though the tenant's race is in some sense an objective fact about him, it is not in itself an objective reason for eviction—the color of one's skin [like the color of one's hair] does not entail that one will fail to pay rent, create unhealthy conditions for other tenants, etc.)[12] Thus objectivity plays two roles in the practice of liberalism: as a way to establish how things are (so that we know what we need to do) and as a norm of correct behavior (very broadly speaking; this norm is closely tied to the liberal norm of equality, as suggested above, since the aim of objectivity is the aim to act as any subject would, to avoid self-interest, and to treat all [other] subjects equally).[13]

With these vague definitions and caveats in hand, I shall now present my three versions of MacKinnon's claim against liberalism and objectivity.

I. False Claims of Objectivity

Members of the liberal establishment claim that their judgments are objective, but they are wrong. Instead, their judgments are either false or influenced by their interests (here male interests), or both.

Despite MacKinnon's claims to the contrary, much of her criticism of liberal "objectivity" seems to be interpretable as this sort of claim, a claim that does not criticize the norm of objectivity at all. Instead, this sort of claim constitutes an endorsement of the norm of objectivity, combined with arguments that particular claims are not in fact objective. Most obviously, MacKinnon argues in just this way when she uses Donnerstein's and Malamuth's research on the effects of pornography to combat the establishment claim that pornography is "harmless," "only fantasy," or even cathartic of bad sexual impulses.[14] In these arguments, MacKinnon is pointing to objective, scientific research (or the closest-to-objective, most well researched evidence we have at the moment) as evidence that certain claims are false and self-interested.

Most of MacKinnon's implicit invocations of the objectivity norm are subtler, however. For example, MacKinnon's repeated claims that women have been silenced or rendered "invisible"[15] seem assimilable to such an interpretation. In pointing out that women's experiences (e.g., how many women have been abused by pornographers or by men influenced by pornography) have not been noticed, MacKinnon is pointing out, first, that there is significant "data" out there that has not been gathered.[16] Again, this data could serve to falsify the claims that pornography is harmless—could show that these claims are based on bad data.[17]

Second, MacKinnon points out that the categories according to which we judge the data may themselves be influenced by male-dominated interests. As Haslanger notes, MacKinnon's analysis of rape law provides a good example of this type of point.[18] Not only is rape, supposedly the crime of violating a *woman's* sexual or bodily integrity, defined in many of these laws exclusively with reference to what sex is for [many] men (i.e., penetration); these laws also define rape as against a woman's "consent" or even define rape as sex when the *perpetrator knows* that the woman hasn't consented. They thus implicitly assume that women need only consent to (not actively desire) sex for it not to be rape, and that it is the man's perceptions of the event that count, not the woman's. Thus the very definitions or distinctions used to determine the putative facts of the case are "interested," based on a male understanding of sexuality, and are biased in favor of the male perpetrator. These laws thus tend to make it very difficult to convict rapists, thus legitimating rape and serving (at least some) male interests in being able to rape with impunity.

MacKinnon's criticisms here fit quite well within a discourse governed by the general norm of objectivity as sketched above. First, she is arguing that inquiry and/or definitions as to what is inquired about have not been objective enough. Second, her etiology of this failure has much in common with the liberal/objectivist explanation of epistemological error: it is the interests of the inquirers, lawmakers, or judges (here their particular, subjective character as men) that has prevented them from attaining truly "objective" results.[19] MacKinnon does not here fundamentally challenge the liberal objectivist position, which grants that it is quite difficult to attain objectivity in inquiry, particularly about social, psychological, or political facts.[20] The liberal or objectivist obsession with procedure (and reason) is partially due to the liberal recognition that interests are hard to overcome, and strongly held interests, or interests "close to home," are even harder to get around.[21] MacKinnon's attacks on pornography as dangerous because it appeals to, or subconsciously conditions, (irrational) male sexual desire sound quite Kantian; for example, MacKinnon writes, "so-called speech that works as a sex act is not an argument. An orgasm is not an argument."[22] It is precisely such overpowering irrationality that makes many liberal philosophers so suspicious of the emotions, passions, and sexual drives; we need rational procedures, rational self-examination, to guard against interests that may overpower our judgment even without our awareness of such interests.

MacKinnon adds sophistication to this account of error by emphasizing the difficulty of obtaining some of the data required due to social power relations. The "data" about women's experiences of sexuality are not easily available because women are "silenced," intimidated by the unequal power relations that subordinate them in society. Thus this "data" is not simply lying around out there to be found, but is "invisible," not openly challenging the accepted categories or distinctions we use to understand sexuality or sexual politics (except as, e.g., MacKinnon and Dworkin have given this silence two very powerful voices). To the degree to which women are objectified in our society, this objectification may contribute to the difficulty in "gathering this data." Not only will the official, public culture, if it believes that women are (in some way) like objects, without (sexual) wills of their own, but it will fail to realize that women have voices and sexual desires of their own (need not merely consent), and, more generally, fail to recognize that women have opinions of their own, worth listening to. And to the degree that women internalize this societal judgment, women will censor themselves (again, particularly in the context of sexuality) and be unwilling to offer (or to consider as legitimate) any of their own experiences or opinions.[23]

Similarly, MacKinnon adds needed complexity to the account of how male interests influence inquiry or supposedly objective views about gender and sexuality in particular. Liberal attempts at objectivity may, for example, assume too frequently that interests, prejudices, or perspectives are subjective in the narrow sense, that is, as peculiar to *this* man. MacKinnon's point is that many men (and some women) may share the *same* blinding, prejudicial interests, and thus these interests may be hidden (or seem not to be interests at all) because they are shared by so many inquirers. Likewise, to return for a moment to the landlord-tenant example I gave above: my landlord may not herself realize that her decision to evict her tenant was discriminatory, nor may an "unbiased," third party discern that discrimination, because both of their perceptions of the tenant's behavior may be informed by societal, discriminatory practices and prejudices against male African Americans (that they are troublesome, violent).[24] Such shared, "normalized," prejudices are one of the potential problems in liberal methodology that MacKinnon criticizes under the heading of "individualism."

MacKinnon thus calls attention to the hidden pervasiveness of discriminatory interests, particularly the male interest to keep women subordinated, its entrenchment even in the terms we commonly use or the distinctions we make, the complications involved in extricating ourselves from prejudiced, male-dominated mind-sets, its conditioned presence even in our bodies, and so on.[25] She reveals how the liberal discourse of neutrality and impartiality can serve to mask or legitimate these (actually) partial or self-interested views. MacKinnon thereby makes a useful contribution to rational discourse and to liberal attempts at fostering freedom and equality, aiming at the norm of objectivity and (true) impartiality about the complicated issue of gender inequality.

None of these remarks (at least so interpreted), however, constitute a criticism of the norm of objectivity *itself*. They merely point out that supposedly objective claims may not be so objective after all. To prevent such a reading of her views, MacKinnon emphasizes (as noted above) that she practices "feminism unmodified," that is, she is not speaking for women from a liberal or objective view point, but is speaking from the "women's point of view" (e.g., *FU*, pp. 15–6, 60; *TFTS*, p. 117). She takes herself, that is, to be making a much stronger claim against liberalism and objectivity, to which I now turn.

II. All Claims of Objectivity Are False

Everyone is always speaking in terms of his or her own interests or as influenced by power relations; objectivity is impossible (and any claims to it necessarily hypocritical).

MacKinnon indicates that this is her view not only in the kind of slogan quoted above but also in her allusions to Heisenberg's uncertainty principle (e.g., *TFTS*, pp. 122–123). The idea here seems to be that because the inquirer or observer is always already in some position or other, with some prejudices or interests, or at least with some perspective or other, this inquirer never can become "distanced," "neutral," or "aperspectival," as is (putatively) required by the objectivity norm (e.g., *TFTS*, pp. xvi, 101). This kind of claim seems somewhat dubious about scientific (e.g., physical) inquiry about objects in the natural world. Even Newtonian physics (in the complicated ways in which one must fix frames of reference and allow for the physical position of the observer vis-à-vis the observed events) recognized that the observer or inquirer or subject is part of the physical world that she is investigating, and that her place in the world influences her observations.[26] (We did not need Heisenberg to tell us this.) As sketched above, objectivity as a norm of scientific inquiry does not require that the subject eliminate herself from the world entirely but rather that nothing particular, subjective, distorting, whatever, enter her picture of the world. Hence those elaborate, rational calculations of frames of reference in Newtonian physics, and hence the "objective" applicability of Heisenberg's uncertainty principle for all inquirers: it predicts mathematically and with accuracy *how (any) subject* will influence subatomic particles and their behavior.

Yet when inquiry concerns the political, psychological, or social, MacKinnon's claim is more persuasive.[27] Politics is about power and interest, and it intrinsically involves self-understandings and relations of people to one another—any "facts" in politics concern such issues. Thus it may be particularly difficult, or even impossible, to isolate oneself from one's interests in political inquiry, since political or social factors form one's desires, self-conceptions, and identity in pervasive, deep ways. In the case of sexuality in particular, the subordination of women has been a part of the power structure in all Western societies (thus we are presented with no comparison points, no "outside" perspective) and, as formative of our sexual identities, reaches so intimately and pervasively into one's being that the societal or political influences on one's perspective on questions about gender inequality may be well nigh inescapable.[28]

MacKinnon's focus on sexual matters may also reinforce her doubts about our ability to remove ourselves from our own subjective perspectives, perceptions, or feelings.[29] Not only are sexual desires overpowering and irrational, but sexual activities or events are in many respects themselves subjective phenomena, even in the narrow sense of subjective as particular to individual subjects. Again MacKinnon's discussions of rape law provide a good example of this point. Rape is not, strictly speaking, an event separable from the "subjective" perceptions or feelings of the two people involved. As noted above, some rape laws take the perpetrator's subjective perceptions (in fact, his [subjective] perceptions of her [subjective] perceptions or attitudes) into account. And at least part of the "fact" that a woman was raped is her *feeling* of pain, her *feeling* of violation. One might be led to conclude that there is no "outside" non-subjective perspective to have, or judgment to be made, about this event. As MacKinnon puts it, for him, the event *was* sex and pleasure; for her, the event *was* violence, coercion, and pain. In a way different from the usual meaning of this statement, MacKinnon suggests, perhaps rape is (metaphysically) "her word against his" (*FU*, p. 90). Another person asked to determine the nature of this event cannot take both these (mutually exclusive) viewpoints into account and come up with a third, "objective" view—one *or* the other account has to be taken as true.

Given the power relations in our society, his word counts for much more, MacKinnon adds. His word, in fact, can become "objectively" true due to these power relations.[30] He believes that he did not commit a rape. And because society legitimates his view, does not convict him, he is right—he did not (in the eyes of society) commit rape; it was indeed sex. And her word, correspondingly, is judged and made to be "subjective." For, according to MacKinnon, because society tends to view women as objects for sexual use by men, the woman's word does not have credibility, particularly when she says she doesn't want to be sexually used. And once her word is not believed, her word is then presented as "merely subjective." Despite the "facts," she still feels violated—sees the facts only through the "distortion" of her own feelings or subjective perceptions. And then she will further internalize her objectification: even she herself will not take her subjective feelings to be important.[31]

Thus MacKinnon's argument would run something like this: social relations, particularly social-sexual relations, intrinsically involve different points of view or "subjective" perceptions, feelings, and so on. There is no way to understand those social relations as what they are while ignoring the "subjective" perceptions of those involved (which include the investigators, as everyone is involved in social relations). Given power differentials (particularly between women and men) and the current sexual practices in our society (as increasingly violent), these "subjective" perceptions are drastically different from one another, even directly contradictory. Anyone trying to judge these sexual relations will thus have to choose one set of subjective perceptions or interests over the other. There is no alternative and, specifically, no objective disinterested position to take (one must support someone or other's interests).[32]

This is a perfectly consistent position for MacKinnon to hold (again: one need not make the easy objection against her that she contradicts herself by claiming to speak the truth, i.e., that there is no truth). She is, indeed, quite upfront, admitting that she is speaking in her own—women's—interests. For example, she writes that "feminism is the first theory to emerge from those whose interest it affirms" (*TFTS*, p. 83). On this view, she is not really speaking for everyone "objectively" or otherwise, but she is speaking for women, in our interests, trying to get some power for us; that's all there is to do. She wants, she says, "to increase women's power over sexuality, hence over our social definition and treatment. I think that means decreasing the pornographer's power over it" (*FU*, p. 140). Only power and interests are "real" (in social/political matters) and it would indeed be in women's interests if we were to be able to gain more power in society, to be able to convict more rapists and stop sexual abuse and so on. And this argument, if successful, would indeed be a critique of objectivity[33] and any liberal claims to objectivity that go beyond the internal critique that liberalism claims to be universal, objective, and nonpartial but really is not.[34]

Yet this is also an extremely dangerous position for MacKinnon to take, for it would detract from her powerful moral rhetoric of justice. It would, again, be consistent for her to try to mobilize a group of people in her own interests (and theirs) to try to obtain power, and perhaps the rhetoric of justice is the most powerful rhetoric, the most likely to reach people and mobilize them, given that our society's expressed norms are of justice, liberty, and equality.[35] But if her position is that only power exists, so let's get some power for ourselves, then her rhetoric of justice is, at heart, merely rhetoric. Her criticism of liberalism and/or objectivity loses much of its bite here, since she is saying that partiality is all there is. The liberal establishment may exhibit partiality toward male interests, but such partiality is now revealed as not unjust but merely inconsistent; all they have to do is admit that they do act in their own—male—interests, but such action would seem perfectly justified, for that's all one can ever do anyway.

Thus, though MacKinnon does endorse Claim II at certain points, it is not, I think, ultimately conducive to or (more strongly) consistent with her moral and political passion to change society on behalf of women (nor, thus, the real source of her criticism of the ruling norms of liberalism or of objectivity). Not only (as I have just argued) would her rhetoric of justice be (ultimately) ineffectual if it were to be understood as an expression of group interest. But also such description of her project would, more deeply, falsify and denigrate her own motives and aims. For MacKinnon, like Dworkin, seems sincerely to believe that domination, violence, and abuse are wrong, not just that they happen not to be in women's interests when they are directed against women. She does a disservice, that is, to her own aims for real justice and true equality[36] when she describes her aims as expressions of women's group interest alone.[37]

Here again, MacKinnon's passion on behalf of harmed women (like Dworkin's, more obviously) seems based on broadly liberal concerns. According to liberals, the primary, overriding concern of justice (and, as suggested above, the legitimation of government) is the prevention of harms, or of infringements upon individuals' liberty or rights, which on any liberal view would include rights to bodily integrity or to protection from assault. As suggested above, because liberals are agnostic about the nature of the good human life, they tend to concentrate on securing the conditions for each individual to choose his or her way of life.[38] On these grounds, a liberal ought to judge that the violation of someone's bodily integrity is wrong and cannot be redeemed or excused by pleasure on the part of the violator. This is the positive side of liberal individualism, much slighted by MacKinnon. For liberals, every individual's rights count, and rights not to be harmed count *first*. Liberals ought, similarly, to experience the kind of outrage and disgust deeply felt by both MacKinnon and Dworkin at someone whose pleasure *consists in* violating someone else's integrity and rights.

Nor does MacKinnon even, epistemologically or methodologically speaking, (ultimately) propose a true alternative to objectivity that would better address the metaphysics of power in politics. She recognizes that her view might imply that anything a woman says is thereby (because uttered by a woman) right if one endorses the interests of women. Such a view would be dangerous (if not impossible) for MacKinnon to endorse, for the simple fact that there are many women who disagree with her.[39] MacKinnon not only needs to be able to defend her view as correct against these objectors but also to explain why any women would disagree. After all, if one believes (according to this political "metaphysics of power") that every individual merely expresses the interests or interested perspective of his or her gender (gender being the power relation that forms or determines the interests and perspectives on the issues about which we are trying to judge here), and MacKinnon's views *do* express the interests of women (as she claims that they do), how can any woman disagree?

MacKinnon's explanation of such disagreement, interestingly enough, turns out to be self-interest, the central liberal explanatory device for error or disagreement (as discussed above). Some women have been so thoroughly trained to be submissive and to value their submissiveness as necessary for their survival as women in a male-dominated society that they endorse submissiveness (MacKinnon's reading of "care") as a "feminine" ethic or, worse, they come to sexualize submission—as "female" masochistic desire—and "consent" to their own violation and abuse (self-interest in the form of survival instinct).[40] Other women are so afraid that they will lose any of the respect, goods, and so on, that they have managed to wring out of the male establishment by taking on male roles, that they won't attack the male establishment (e.g., *FU*, p. 217) (self-interest at the expense of less fortunate women). MacKinnon reserves the most scorn for those who refuse to criticize male sexuality because they want to take on the sexually dominant role and therefore explicitly endorse sex as violence as pleasure (sexual self-interest).[41] In tune with liberal or objectivist explanations of error, MacKinnon sees her opponents as so (however understandably) misled, misguided, and biased by their self-interest that they cannot be "objective" about the position of women in society.

MacKinnon herself explicitly endorses "consciousness raising"[42] as the feminist method by contrast to objectivity as the male-dominant method. It is difficult, however, to see exactly where consciousness-raising differs from objectivist method (to the degree to which consciousness-raising is an epistemological method, rather than a political grass-roots movement). Consciousness-raising certainly served an important epistemological (as well as political) purpose for feminism in that in consciousness-raising, women's isolation in their separate homes (and consequent powerlessness) was broken down.[43] Thus not only did consciousness raising facilitate the gathering of "data" about women's experiences (data that had been neglected or, more strongly, "silenced," as noted above), but it also served to convince and reassure women that their experiences indeed reflected "objective" truths about social reality, i.e., were legitimate. Thus women came to realize that they shared an unjust position in society, or formed a "gender consciousness" something like a Marxist class consciousness: they came to see that their (common) problems were the result of political and social oppression of women and thus worth fighting against—not merely the result of some subjective moods, perceptions, or particular situations of individual women (*TFTS*, p. 100). As noted above, however, these epistemological (rather than political) benefits of consciousness raising are assimilable to description under the norm of objectivity.

But MacKinnon appears, further, to see consciousness-raising as a distinctive method because it involves community, or the interchange of opinions, perceptions, life-experiences, etc., among individuals, out of which interchange the individuals involved can come to see the truth of women's situation or indeed can come to "redefine truth" in general (*TFTS*, pp. 87, 101). MacKinnon appears to contrast the communal process in consciousness-raising with the self- or (individual) subject orientation of objectivist epistemology. The original defenders of objectivity in the Western epistemological tradition endorsed "methodological solipsism," namely, the view that one ought to start with the subject and its experiences and build knowledge out from there.[44] These philosophers nonetheless take it to be good evidence that one's judgments might be objective (given critical wariness about interests, prejudices, etc.), that other subjects agree with one's judgments, and most of them explicitly endorse public, rational debate as the only way to progress toward objectivity or rationality (without such debate, one is liable to fail to see the weaknesses of one's own positions).[45] Such agreement, or the possibility of such agreement, in fact operates as the same sort of confirmation that it is not something peculiar to oneself that caused one to believe whatever it is, as consciousness-raising served women. It is unclear in what way their views about epistemology (promulgated almost exclusively in the context of discussion of natural scientific subject matters) would apply to inquiry about, for example, moral, political, social, and subject matters. But certainly they would think that data in these realms would include reports of the experiences and attitudes, and so on, of subjects other than themselves.[46]

To return to the earlier example of rape and rape law, MacKinnon ultimately suggests (despite her rhetoric) that there *is* a (more) objective understanding (available to us)[47] of an event like rape, as expressed in her (somewhat scanty) positive recommendations to change rape law. She suggests, for example, that rape laws stop defining rape as intercourse that involves "more than the normal amount of force," which, as she points out, indicates that we as a society have pretty odd ideas about what "normal, consensual" intercourse is supposed to involve. Rather (presumably), she believes that one piece of evidence that the woman's point of view is the right or objective point of view is that (some) force was involved (e.g., *FU,* pp. 88–90; *TFTS,* p. 112). This suggestion, I think, would allow that there are ways of adjudicating accusations of rape without merely choosing between different interests.[48]

Thus MacKinnon does not (decisively) reject objectivity as a norm of scientific inquiry (nor, thereby, liberalism and its other norms) on these "metaphysical" grounds. I now turn to MacKinnon's final criticism of liberalism and objectivity—a moral or political criticism.

III. Objectivity Is a Peculiarly Male, Peculiarly Dominating Norm

The norm of objectivity itself is intrinsically dominating, objectifying, and unjust. (To transmute a famous aphorism of Wallace Stevens, *A scientist looks at the world the way a man looks at a woman.*)

MacKinnon's moral or political objection to liberal objectivity has two, somewhat paradoxical, sides. On the one side, she argues that liberalism is (purposefully) impotent against the power structures that exist in society due to its "neutrality"; correspondingly, objective scientific inquiry falsely presents the (political) world as fixed, unchanging, and thus impervious to any political activism. On the other side, she suggests that liberalism and objectivity secretly privilege, enact, or promote attitudes of domination and violence against the world (including other people) as the "correct" or "free" stance toward the world (e.g., *TFTS,* p. 107).[49]

I shall take the second of these claims first, as I believe that it is actually less important than the first for MacKinnon (and is less persuasive). This view, that objectivity is morally wrong because it endorses or simply is dominance, is the one that most closely links objectivity to objectification (itself a mode of, and support for, domination). As already noted, (unjust) social processes that objectify women can make objective judgments about women more difficult to come by. Such objectification may make women less credible (both to themselves and to others) and make their views (paradoxically) seem "merely subjective." Thus in both cases, objectification contributes to the difficulties involved in becoming objective about sexuality. Here, however, MacKinnon, and more explicitly Dworkin, want to say that (endorsing the norm of) objectivity is *itself* objectifying.

Like a number of other post-Enlightenment thinkers,[50] MacKinnon suggests that modern science and its methods embody an attitude of domination and mastery toward the world. Many of these thinkers point, for example, to Bacon's slogans in support of "new," modern science (that modern scientists aim at the "mastery and

ownership of nature" and do so by putting "nature to the rack") and to the proliferation of technology, or the harnessing of nature to serve our interests, which has accompanied modern technology as evidence for the domineering or mastery-loving tendencies in the modern scientific attitude. Dworkin[51] makes a similar point by
emphasizing that Sade was an Enlightenment figure who endorsed (and practiced)
both rational Enlightenment and sadism.

In MacKinnon's articulation of this view, for example,

> the feminist approach to consciousness revealed a relation between one means
> through which sex inequality is produced in the world and the world it pro-
> duces: the relation between objectification, the hierarchy between self as being
> and other as thing, and objectivity, the hierarchy between the knowing subject
> and the known object. (*TFTS*, p. xi)

MacKinnon's idea here seems to be that the methodological solipsism associated
with defenders of objectivity establishes a self separate from the world, as metaphysically
more real than the world, or at least as epistemologically prior to the world.[52] The
world, then, is considered (as a whole) as an object, as raw material to be tested, known,
mastered, re-formed, by this self or subject (*TFTS*, p. 108). Such a metaphysical or epistemological view has moral consequences in that those who consider themselves in this
way will consider the people they encounter to be, as parts of the world, objects that passively lie "out there" to be manipulated like raw materials, to be mastered, to be made to
serve the self's needs. When and if these "selves" have social power (e.g., are white, educated men in Western society), they can enforce such objectification on other, powerless
human beings (e.g., women), whom they consider objects (*FU*, 55). Again, not only will
women thus be forced to fill the role of objects (e.g., for sexual gratification), but women
will internalize this role and come to consider it legitimate or appropriate. Thus, MacK-
innon writes, male power is a "seamless" system: it sees women as objects and treats
women as objects; women then see themselves as objects and act accordingly (thus confirming the original male judgment).

Such arguments about the nature of modern science are rather complicated, and I
cannot enter into them here (though I have indicated above that the self-as-utterly-sepa-
rate-from-the-world characterization of modern science seems inaccurate). I will note
merely that feminists should not necessarily be quick to endorse such views about modern science and its mistreatment of nature. Once it starts thinking of the world as raw
material (taking physics and mathematics to be the foundational sciences), modern science also becomes quite suspicious of natural kinds and teleological understandings of
the order of nature. Arguments against modern science may, by contrast, rely on a certain romanticism about nature that includes a romanticism about women as nature or
about women's nature (or about some supposed originary nature of human social-sexual
relations). Feminists ought to be very wary of such allies.

Further, even if one were to grant that this characterization of modern science
and its aims and methods were correct (and that it is immoral or intrinsically dominating to treat nature the way modern science does), it is not at all clear that the

conclusion, as it relates to MacKinnon's political concerns, follows. That is, even if one were to grant that modern scientists treat nature as a passive object or as raw material, they do not thereby necessarily believe that other human beings are such passive objects. Modern science or modern philosophy more generally, in its denial that the "truth" about the world is intuitively available, to be read off the world (or received from God), privileges agreement or community with other *subjects*, other selves, other knowers in its endorsement of objectivity as the aim of scientific inquiry. (Despite, perhaps, the misleading term, "objectivity.") As suggested above, objectivity is frequently understood as that which could be agreed upon by all subjects, as a norm that guides a scientific community (as in the repeatability of experiments criterion discussed above).[53]

Correspondingly, it would be more appropriate to consider the Enlightenment (understood as an endorsement of both liberal political philosophy and objective modern science) as the movement that identified the love of mastery over other people as morally and politically wrong (an infringement on their rights as rational beings).[54] If liberal objectivists endorse the mastery of nature, to the degree that they do, it is as distinguished from their condemnation of the mastery of other people (precisely on the grounds that other people are also subjects, i.e., rational and self-determining, unlike raw material or objects).[55] It is in fact because liberals or objectivists set up this "distance" between nature (even human nature) and the self (endowed with freedom, rationality, or autonomy) that they can counteract claims that nature determines what is right for human beings, that (in particular, say) the "objective" or natural fact that women bear children determines next to nothing about the normatively correct role of women in society.

This is not to deny that, in fact, liberal males in authority or male scientists have objectified women. Nor, more generally, that scientists have objectified or exploited people (as, e.g., unconsenting "subjects" for medical or psychological experimentation) in the name of "objective," scientific results. (Just as painters and novelists have exploited and objectified people in the name of beauty and artistic expression; values and norms can often be used, intentionally or unintentionally, to justify self-interest and self-promotion.) Scientists, particularly those who transplant the methods of the natural sciences to the social sciences, may well be tempted (wrongly) to see other human beings as objects or as raw material rather than as other subjects, other potential knowers endowed with human dignity. I deny that the modern, objectivist, epistemological stance as such entails the objectification of women. As I have suggested, this objectivist stance may, rather, have been a precondition for the development of feminism, for it allowed one to conceive of women as human beings or subjects first and foremost, rather than as biologically, naturally determined organs for reproduction.

Thus the first moral objection to objectivity seems unjustified. MacKinnon is more interested in the former (and, I think, more persuasive) of these claims about liberalism and objectivity, namely, the accusation that these norms collaborate with domination precisely because they endorse "neutrality" or "distance." MacKinnon's word for this problem with liberalism is "formalism," which reflects the proceduralist commitments both of liberalism and of the defenders of objectivity.

This criticism is composed of two interrelated elements, which MacKinnon inherits from Marx.[56] First, as presented by MacKinnon, liberals seem to believe that the only power exerted in society is exerted by the government.[57] They are, therefore, obsessively concerned with limiting government power to its legitimate functions but refuse to recognize (much less to enlist the government, or invest the government with power, against) power exerted by any other societal force (most pressingly, for MacKinnon, the social power exerted by pornographers against women). According to MacKinnon (following Marx), this attitude amounts to the claim that nongovernmental power relations ought to be left alone (or at least left alone by the government). Second, the way in which liberals limit government power is to require that the government must be universalist, formalist, neutral, or proceduralist in order to be legitimate; it must treat individuals abstractly and equally. It must not enforce its substantive views of the right way of life on individuals. The government thereby treats individuals, formally or universally, as if they are equal—even though in matter of fact, these individuals are not equal due to the non-governmental powers at work in society. Thus the government reinforces the inequality perpetrated in civil society; for its formal (non-interfering) treatment of individuals just reproduces whatever [power, or lack thereof] individuals "came in" with. The liberal commitment to "formalist" equality, that is, suffers from "idealism," according to MacKinnon: it does not face the "real" power and subordination present in society, but pretends idealistically that such power does not exist, acts "as if" all citizens are in fact equal (*FU*, pp. 35–37).

Correspondingly, those who endorse objectivity as a norm of scientific inquiry endorse formalist, rationalist procedures for discovering the "content" out there in the world. Thus the norm of objectivity concerns only the limitation or regulation of the scientist's activity; it does not urge the inquirer to evaluate or even change the status quo.[58] Inasmuch as liberals are committed to objectivity, they are concerned primarily to limit or to make ineffectual interest, passion, or emotion, not to endorse activism, particularly governmental activism.[59]

This criticism correctly identifies the aims of liberalism and objectivity, and the reasons for the rational proceduralism both positions espouse. It expresses a legitimate frustration on MacKinnon's part that our society, which espouses norms of freedom and equality, is far from being a society of free and equal citizens.[60] Though this appears to be a criticism of liberals' or objectivists' hypocrisy (they only pretend to be unbiased or to be disinterested or to care about equality), like the criticisms discussed above, MacKinnon's point here is somewhat different, questioning the liberal commitment to the norm of objectivity itself. MacKinnon is arguing that liberal, objectivist formalism or proceduralism, even when carried out as well as possible, as disinterestedly as possible, is an immoral political stance (at least in our society, where there are such strong social power structures and widespread inequality) because it precludes change, activism, or involvement. According to MacKinnon, liberal proceduralism is complicit with whatever the prevailing social power structure is. And therefore only those who are already in power (men, mostly) would be inclined to endorse such a political, moral, or even scientific program. MacKinnon appears to be making this sort of claim when she says that women tend not to be bothered by skepticism about the external world (or, by extension, methodological concerns about how to find out the truth about it) because "it hits us in the face" (*FU*, p. 57; *TFTS*, p. 123). MacKinnon's point here seems to be that only if one has a sufficient amount of (social and political) power can one have the luxury to be (worried about being) neutral or distanced, only if one has a decently good social position can one be worried only about *government* infringements upon one's liberties. Liberalism, that is, may have begun as a revolutionary movement but, now that it is established, it has become a position of complacency, of collaboration with whatever there is out there, purposefully impotent—at best naive about, and at worst collaborative with, existing social power conditions.[61]

Thus MacKinnon may be making a familiar argument from contemporary moral philosophy against (at least some) liberal moral/political philosophers: we need to supplement respect for others (as rational beings, as equal under the law, etc.) with compassion in order to behave in a truly moral way. Though this is probably a good criticism of some forms of liberal political philosophy, MacKinnon's more potent point against liberalism is that by its own proceduralism it fails to implement its own norms of freedom and equality. Liberals may very well claim that all people ought to be treated equally. But if they prevent themselves from acting to make that so in reality (through self-restriction to formal measures or limitation of governmental power alone), they will never accomplish the reality of those norms. Or, to put it another way, the inactivity of liberal government is itself an activity that legitimates (unjust) social power structures.

This characterization of MacKinnon's argument may sound somewhat odd, for MacKinnon argues that her conception of equality differs from that espoused in liberalism, and she very rarely endorses the norm of liberty or freedom. Freedom (of speech, in particular) is the banner under which MacKinnon's opponents march (particularly in the controversy about MacKinnon's antipornography ordinance). Because MacKinnon takes this invocation of freedom to be (in essence) a claim that men ought to be allowed (freely) to abuse, exploit, and objectify women, she avoids the vocabulary of "freedom" in expressing her views. Rather, she characterizes her project as an attempt to limit the claims of freedom by endorsing claims of equality. So, MacKinnon writes, in deciding how or whether to protect freedom of speech, "there is no requirement that the state remain neutral as between equality and inequality" (*OW*, p. 107).[62]

But she might well have said that liberals are not, supposedly, neutral about liberty, particularly so-called negative liberty, either. MacKinnon describes the failure of proceduralist liberal government with respect to gender inequality as follows:

> [Liberal] sex equality law has been . . . ineffective at getting women what we
> need and are socially prevented from having on the basis of a condition of
> birth: a chance at productive lives of reasonable physical security, self-expres-
> sion, individuation, and minimal respect and dignity. (*FU*, p. 32)

MacKinnon's list of the ways in which women should be—but are not in fact—treated equally can be restated quite well in terms of negative liberty. First, here and elsewhere, MacKinnon calls attention to a vast range of citizens (women) whose liberties, whose bodily integrity and basic security against assault and violence from others, are not being protected. Second, MacKinnon is also invoking a broader norm of freedom shared by many, if not all, liberals.[63] Most, if not all, liberal theories are grounded in the view that individual human beings have, and ought to be treated as having, dignity, as individual, rational beings who can (and ought to be allowed to) choose or direct their own lives. No individual, correspondingly, ought to be denied such individuality and dignity because of "conditions of birth," whether membership in a group (women) or physical capabilities that do not prevent rational choice (e.g., the ability to be pregnant). Insofar as liberals are committed to the norm of treating each (rational or potentially rational) human being as worthy of respect, as equally worthy of the opportunity to exercise her freedom or autonomy, liberals ought—like MacKinnon—to condemn discriminatory social (or legal) practices that make such "individuation" and "self-expression" impossible as wrong, unjust, and as requiring change.[64] For liberals, as for MacKinnon, the government's failure to protect individuals from bodily harm and from others' infringement on their autonomy is wrong; for, as discussed above, according to liberals, government is legitimate only insofar as it protects citizens from such infringement, rights, or autonomy, and protects them all, equally.[65] Liberals ought not be "neutral" about such equality.[66]

That is, liberals are committed to some substantive norms (freedom and equality), and are committed to these norms *as* norms, as moral/political standards by which one can judge whether society and government as they stand are just or not. The agnosticism within liberalism about substantive views of the (morally) good life or the value that (some) liberals place on a plurality of goods and life choices in society[67] may tend to obscure the fact that liberals are thus agnostic, thus value plurality *because* they *are* committed to the goals of freedom and equality as *necessary* (though generally not sufficient) conditions for just or moral human life.[68] Liberals need not or even ought not, I think, simply assume that individuals *are* free and equal in society, but rather that they *ought* to be so treated (by the government and by other individuals or groups within society).

In regard to the aspect of liberalism with which MacKinnon is here taking issue, liberals ought to remember that they are not committed to rational proceduralism for procedure's sake or not committed to objectivity just to find out what's true out there, as legal liberals especially seem to believe.[69] Rather, liberals are committed to procedure because it is supposed to guarantee or promote freedom and equality for all citizens (from the government, but also from others), to objectivity as a means toward the realization of such norms. Liberal proceduralism ought to be seen, I suggest, as an active choice that liberals or liberal government make in order to realize the norms of freedom and equality—not merely as a guarantee that the government will remain inactive (as, ironically, both MacKinnon and her fiercest opponents interpret it). MacKinnon's objection, therefore, that due to its formalism and idealism, liberal proceduralism fails to realize the norms of freedom and equality, and indeed even reinforces and legitimizes inequality and coercion is a serious one for liberals.

In defense of liberal proceduralism and its "idealism," one may say that the liberal norms of objectivity, freedom, and rationality (including their formalism) seem to be intrinsic to the attempt to combat the dangers of oppression and inequality on the basis of "conditions of birth" (even if they are pervertible by power and interest in the ways that MacKinnon describes). The formalism or irreality of reason and rational proceduralism allow one to see that how things are is not how things have to be, that how things are is not how they *ought* to be. (Or is the best way or is the only way available for us to try to get beyond our own strictly selfish interests, submerged or subconscious as they may be.) MacKinnon repeatedly raises the question of how women ever could have become critical of their subordination, given the strong societal forces to keep women in their place and their "thingification in the head," most often concluding that it is in a sense mysterious how this ever could have happened (e.g., *TFTS*, p. 103). Normative critique or rational freedom, provided in part by the very formalism (or "distance" from real conditions) MacKinnon criticizes, however fleeting, transitory, potentially misguided it is, seems to be a better explanation than a shrug of the shoulders (as MacKinnon in fact seems to admit in *FU,* p. 218, in a rare moment of praise for freedom).

But there are dangers in liberal "formal" or "ideal" proceduralism as well, as MacKinnon powerfully argues, and such dangers are not merely contingently related to the liberal commitment to objectivity or rationality. The liberal commitment to idealism, formalism, and "pure" rational consideration of human beings may allow the liberal objectivist to gain enough distance from actual social conditions to judge that they are unjust, that (for example) a woman's ability to get pregnant is irrelevant to her full normative status as a human being. But this very same rational distance, this very same "idealist" point of view, can indeed engender the sorts of legal decisions MacKinnon criticizes under the heading of "formalist" equality. For if the ability to be pregnant is irrelevant to the normative status of women as rational human beings worthy of respect, then legal accommodations for pregnancy look like special, even discriminatory, treatment; human beings "as such" do not get pregnant. As a result of the liberal disallowal of such accommodations (as "discriminatory" or irrelevant to equality), MacKinnon argues, women as women, due to a "condition of birth," reap disadvantages and harms in the workplace with (seemingly) no legal recourse (*TFTS*, p. 222).

Is liberalism absolutely committed to such "formalist" conceptions of equality in its practice, as the only way in which one can (try to) instantiate its norms of freedom and equality? I do not believe so. Certainly liberal government, at least as originally designed and legitimated, did not, need not, and ought not stop with the "objective" recognition of inequalities and infringements on liberty as abstractly, formally, or normatively defined. According to liberals, government is licensed to do something about these harms; for example, the abolition of slavery, a "social institution" that instantiated and promoted inequality, was not only permissible but was a necessary action on the part of a government guided by liberal ideals. And if government action to protect rights and liberties limits the freedom of others (as, e.g., slaverholders' freedoms are limited), such limitation is perfectly consistent with the basic principles of liberalism: the government legitimately restricts individuals from harming others or infringing on their rights.

Further, some liberals at least have seen that the government must act more broadly to ensure that all citizens can truly exercise their freedom (rather than merely treat them "as if" they are already in the position to do so), that is, to ensure that all individuals are provided with (true or real) equality of opportunity, not just equal protection under the law in a more formalistic sense.[70] For example, liberal commitments to public education, to minimum wage laws, and to ensuring access to public life and work for those with physical disabilities (widely shared positions) are commitments to acting to promote equality, to provide the "real" conditions under which true autonomy for each individual would be possible (however ineffectual these are in the current state of things). And it seems to me to be consistent with liberal norms, even or indeed especially of "objectivity," to recognize that women have different positions in society from men, have different needs from men, and require different guarantees in order for us to be capable of enjoying our negative liberties and exercising our freedom. So, for example, women may need legal, institutional support during pregnancy and child care; such institutional support would be a recognition of objective facts about women—that pregnancy and childcare can impede women's autonomy in the workplace and that socially institutionalized workplace (or more broadly economic) practices can impede women's autonomous choices to bear and care for children. Such institutional support would, then, serve to ensure the "real" conditions under which women could attain and exercise autonomy. More importantly still, pregnancy and child care are, in different ways, *themselves* preconditions for the possibility of the existence and upbringing of autonomous adult human beings in society. Thus a liberal society ought to provide provisions and support for women, who are crucial to the existence of autonomous human beings.[71] The norms of freedom and equality are indeed universal norms that commit liberals to guaranteeing everyone's rights and autonomy; but the universality of such norms (I believe) does not mean that one need to assume that all people have such autonomy already or to ignore the fact that people are unequally positioned to exercise their autonomy. Such universality ought, rather, to require that one ought to act so that all people will indeed have such autonomy.

How to guarantee such "real" freedom and equality is, obviously, a vexed question for women, muddied and charged (as MacKinnon shows) by its entanglement with sexuality. But it is a question posed *within* liberalism—and one that must be posed by liberals. J. S. Mill's *On the Subjection of Women* is testimony that a liberal can advocate governmental activism to promote broad legal, social, and political change of the institutions that permeate society and subordinate women. Given the widespread, entrenched, sexualized subordination of women in our society MacKinnon portrays so passionately, it is indeed imperative for liberals, by their own normative standards of justice, to do the same, not to hide behind "proceduralism" or governmental inactivity as the only recourse. Normative commitments ought not to be mere ideals, but should be ideals by which we try, actually, to live, that we try, actively, to instantiate in reality. And we are so far from where we ought to be.

In conclusion, despite her self-understanding, MacKinnon is doing exactly what is needed for the liberal, objectivist project. She calls public attention to "data" that is consistently ignored, unmasks pervasive and strong interests that skew purportedly objective judgments, illustrates the irrationality or nonneutrality of our definitions, and should reawaken us to the normative urgency of the currently prevalent injustice in our society. In the strongest of her arguments against liberalism and its claims to objectivity, MacKinnon ought at the very least to reinvigorate the liberal project, jolting liberals out of the danger of purposefully impotent, collaborative "complacency of the privileged" (*FU*, p. 2).

Notes

I would like to thank Denise Schaeffer, for introducing me to MacKinnon's work, as well as Charlotte Witt, Michael Zuckert, and especially Martha Nussbaum for comments on this chapter.

1. *Feminism Unmodified {FU}* (Cambridge: Harvard University Press, 1987), p. 137.

2. See, e.g., *Towards a Feminist Theory of the State {TFTS}* (Cambridge: Harvard University Press, 1989), pp. ix, xi, 114, 120–121; *FU*, 54–60.

3. E.g., violability, fungibility, possessibility, etc. MacKinnon here is following Dworkin, who presents the various aspects of male objectification of women in *Pornography: Men Possessing Women* (New York: Plume, 1989), pp. 13–30. (Dworkin actually presents the various forms of male power, but these correspond to forms of objectification of women.) The various meanings of objectification are outlined clearly by Martha Nussbaum in "Objectification," *Philosophy and Public Affairs*, Fall 1995, pp. 256–265.

4. Catharine MacKinnon and Andrea Dworkin, eds., *In Harm's Way: The Pornography Civil Rights Hearings {IHW}* (Cambridge: Harvard University Press, 1997), "Memo on Proposed Ordinance," p. 255. All citations to *IHW* are to MacKinnon's introductory essay or her own testimony or remarks unless otherwise noted.

5. A misogynist (and consumer of pornography) in my acquaintance illustrated MacKinnon's point admirably in objecting to her claim that men objectify women: "We don't treat women as objects; I mean, we have to buy them dinner, and we have to say that they're beautiful [to get "them" into bed]. We don't have to do that with objects." He may have a very small point here: Donnerstein's research (as reported in *IHW* [Donnerstein testimony], p. 48) indicates that men are aroused much more by pornography that represents women "enjoying" being raped than by pornography that shows women being raped *simpliciter* (without expressions of "enjoyment"). For these men, the fact that women are subjects or human beings, not objects, is relevant to their sexual desires. Thus, as has often been objected against MacKinnon, her characterization of (male) sexual desire may not always be sufficiently sophisticated or complicated. It remains troubling (to say the least), in all of the ways MacKinnon describes, that so many men find such "rape myth" pornography arousing.

6. In the context of this chapter I shall (mostly) take it as given that both "sides" of the debate are in agreement here; I shall return to discuss this issue in my final section. Liberals may not agree with MacKinnon that sexuality in our culture is objectifying or that the source of women's subordination is (specifically or primarily) sexual objectification or (even more probably) that pornography is the main mechanism of the sexual objectification of women, and thereby of the subordination of women in America or (finally) that MacKinnon's pornography ordinance would be the correct (or even an effective) way to address gender inequality. I cannot consider these issues here, but (again) shall assume general agreement that (some or many) men objectify women sexually, in a morally problem-

atic way, and that this objectification does facilitate sexual violence against women (leaving aside the question of whether this is the primary process that subordinates women in society).

7. Judge Easterbrook, in his opinion reaffirming the unconstitutionality of the Indianapolis pornography ordinance written and promoted by MacKinnon and Dworkin, expresses just such a liberal view: "But the Constitution does not make the dominance of truth a necessary condition of freedom of speech. To say that it does would be to confuse an outcome of free speech with a necessary condition for the application of the amendment. "A power to limit speech on the ground that truth has not yet prevailed and is not likely to prevail implies the power to declare truth. . . . If the government may declare the truth, why wait for the failure of speech?" (*IHW* [appendix, Easterbrook opinion], p. 474).

8. This, I think, is what Haslanger means by "weak [discursive] social construction" ("Ontology and Social Construction," *Philosophical Topics*, Fall 1995, p. 99). Since she endorses the truth of this weak social construction, I am baffled by the concluding sections of this article, in which she seems to assume that it is nonetheless meaningful to talk about the real world, independent of our (means of) access to it, and that objectivity is a meaningless or completely debunked scientific norm.

9. I take this account to be largely consistent with MacKinnon's characterization of objectivity in *TFTS* (pp. 97–98), except for MacKinnon's emphasis on "aperspectivity" as a requirement for objectivity. As I indicate below, I believe that this is a mistaken characterization of modern science and its conception of objectivity.

10. Though Locke's epistemology is often taken to be opposed to Kantian epistemology, Locke is probably the originator of many of these positions (broadly taken); he did not, however, use the term "objectivity" to describe the aim of scientific inquiry.

11. See Charlotte Witt's chapter in this volume for a nice discussion of the inadequacy of a merely historical argument to discredit the concepts and practice of philosophy within the philosophical tradition.

12. It has unfortunately been argued that race could be a relevant fact for a landlord's consideration insofar as the race of a tenant bothers other (racist) tenants; offense or discomfort at others' differences from oneself is not, however, a legitimate harm on standard liberal views (see, e.g., J. S. Mill, *On Liberty*, chaps. 2 and 4). MacKinnon herself arguably reflects a similar view about the difference between "offensiveness" and real, legitimate harm in her attempts to redescribe the harms of pornography: pornography is not, she argues, "offensive" as obscenity law (mis)describes it; pornography is, rather, *harmful*. See *Only Words {OW}* (Cambridge: Harvard University Press, 1993), pp. 88–89.

13. Such a connection between rational objectivity, proceduralism, and equality is reflected in Rawls's proceduralist theory of justice, particularly in the construct of the original position: The just society, according to Rawls, is one that you would choose no matter who you ended up being or what position in society you would end up having, i.e., one that *any* (rational) subject could or would choose.

14. See, e.g., her endorsement of Donnerstein's research and generally of "progress" in science (*IHW*, p. 7 n. 22, p. 14).

15. MacKinnon makes this point frequently throughout her work; see, e.g., *OW*, pp. 6, 9, 19, 72.

16. This kind of criticism is similar to Gilligan's criticism of Kohlberg's methodology (that he never included girls in his experimental pool) or current criticisms of medical research that it has focused exclusively on (e.g., drug effects on) men. It is similar to methodological criticisms within the scientific community. See the chapters by Louise

Antony and Helen Longino in this volume for more detailed discussion of this sort of internal criticism of the scientific establishment within feminist epistemology and philosophy of science.

17. Similarly, MacKinnon claims that pornography promulgates false claims, particularly the false claim that women enjoy being raped, on the grounds (really) that these claims are not objective, as they are *not* claims that any subject, e.g., a woman who is raped, would assent to. Although pornographers claim that they are speaking (making claims) and thus protected by the First Amendment, they do not tend to claim that their speech is "objective" (rather, it's "fantasy" or untrue, unreal, they claim). They are not therefore MacKinnon's immediate targets when she criticizes objectivity claims (except insofar as they encourage their customers in believing falsities about the world).

18. "Ontology and Social Construction," pp. 108–111.

19. I take this to be the content of MacKinnon's claims, such as the following. Generalized discourse, she says, "assimilated [particularities] to a false universal that imposed agreement, submerged specificity, and silenced particularity. . . . [Her opponents] face losing the advance exclusivity of their point of view's claim to truth—that is, their power" (*TFTS*, p. xvi).

20. Thus, for example, MacKinnon's arguments (as expressed in "Difference and Dominance") about the way in which "same" or "equal" often implicitly or explicitly really means the same as (white) men, equal meaning measuring up to a (white) male standard have also been made by Susan Okin, a liberal feminist, who in turn has (to some degree) persuaded Rawls that some aspects of his allegedly neutral procedurism mask injustice against women. MacKinnon's arguments of this sort thus seem quite assimilable to, or consistent with, liberal political philosophy, for example, Okin's discussions of pregnancy and health/disability coverage. Okin, *Women in Western Political Thought* (Princeton: Princeton University Press, 1979), pp. 269–721. In regard to divorce law, see *Justice, Gender, and the Family* (New York: Basic, 1989), pp. 138–139, 160–161; Rawls, "The Idea of Public Reason Revisited," *University of Chicago Law Review* 64 (1997).

21. A problem Mill explicitly recognizes with respect to the subordination of women. *On the Subjection of Women,* in *On Liberty and Other Writings,* ed. Stefan Collini (Cambridge: Cambridge University Press, 1991), p. 128.

22. *OW*, p. 63. MacKinnon makes this point in the context of arguing that pornography is not speech but behavioral conditioning. Leaving aside the argument that pornography should not be protected speech, this view about the irrationality and power of sexual desire and interest plays a role in MacKinnon's very liberal-like account of why women's subordination persists in liberal society, despite our explicit normative commitment to equality: "sexual self-interest." In fact, MacKinnon claims to answer the implicit question Mill asks about why the subordination of women should be so persistent, the source of its "peculiar durability" as MacKinnon puts it (*FU*, p. 7)—sexual desire or interest is a very strong one, very liable to counteract objective, rational considerations.

See Barbara Herman's chapter in this volume for extensive, persuasive connections between the views of Kant, MacKinnon, and Dworkin on sexuality.

23. MacKinnon's more extreme versions of this claim may not be so easily assimilable to an objectivist view, as she implies that there simply are no such data to be collected. That is, MacKinnon sometimes claims not only that women are silenced, but that women do not have (or are not allowed to have) opinions, perspectives, etc. of their own *at all*. MacKinnon's point here is that the prevailing paradigms of male dominance are so prevalent and so powerful (so enforced by social conditions) that they not only act as non-gov-

ernmental censorship of opposing views but also that women, as powerless, are forced to conform with these views, not to formulate their own, different views. (This protective adaptation or survival strategy of women is a theme Wollstonecraft and Mill also emphasize.)

Though MacKinnon is pointing to a very real phenomenon (again perhaps particularly real in social-sexual relations), she overstates her point. Though we may not be able quite to imagine what sexual relations would be were they stripped of the male-dominant paradigms (e.g., of pursuer and pursued, male initiation of intercourse, etc.) that MacKinnon is attacking, women's pain and dislike of pornography (see, e.g., Pauline Bart's survey about pornography in *IHW* [Exhibits], pp. 216–220) are indeed "out there" to be found if one takes care to look. Similarly, MacKinnon and Dworkin have both struck chords of recognition in their listeners; they are not expressing views that are alien to many women's experiences.

24. See Louise Antony's chapter in this volume for a perceptive discussion of this dynamic as part of a "serious, nuanced study of how ideologies work."

25. MacKinnon argues that though race discrimination and gender discrimination have a great deal in common, gender discrimination is more deep-seated, powerful, and irrational than race discrimination because it is sexualized. See, e.g., *OW*, pp. 60–64.

26. Thus I take MacKinnon's criticism of objectivity as requiring that an inquiring subject be at no "time or place" (*TFTS*, p. 98) to be mistaken. Louise Antony (in her chapter in this volume) argues similarly (and in more detail) that early modern (and analytic) epistemologies recognize the knowing subject's place in the world in a variety of ways (as she quite helpfully delineates).

27. She herself (*FU*, p. 57) explicitly states that her claims apply much more tellingly to the political world than to the natural world. And she remarks that it may not be very straightforward to apply the scientific methods used in natural science to social and political phenomena. Liberals have traditionally thought this, given their distinctions between the "ought" of moral/political relations and the "is" of natural science.

Haslanger devotes a great deal of attention to analyzing MacKinnon's claims in the context of scientific knowledge in both of her articles on MacKinnon ("Ontology and Social Construction," and her chapter in this volume). As indicated above, I find her reversion to naive realism in "Ontology and Social Construction" highly problematic, but on the whole I endorse her distinctions between various ways of construing the role of social construction and the male-interested-ness of objectivity. Similarly, her point that science may serve our interests or we may decide to pursue a line of inquiry because we want or need to know (e.g., in medicine) but we may nonetheless obtain objective results in that inquiry is well taken. Nonetheless, I believe that it is more profitable to discuss MacKinnon's arguments in the context of social science than to criticize her by adverting to natural science or simple observation statements like "the pavement is wet" as Haslanger does (despite her expressed disdain for verificationist epistemology).

28. Feminism, MacKinnon says, "inquires into an intrinsically social situation, into that mixture of thought and materiality which comprises gender in the broadest sense" (*TFTS*, p. 83).

29. Difficult as it may be to determine "objectively" whether divorce laws, or job remunerations, are equitable, they seem much more amenable to impartial consideration than (e.g.) pornography—as must be eminently clear from the nasty, disrespectful treatment MacKinnon and Dworkin have received, and not just from the pornographers whose profits they threaten.

30. Haslanger analyzes this dynamic quite well in "Objectivity and Being Objectified" in this volume. On her analysis, objectifiers in power can *make* their supposedly objective statements be objective or be accurate about women's "natures" because they have the power to enforce women's compliance with these statements or judgments. I do not consider my account to be in conflict with Haslanger's, but as her account is so complete, I do not see the need to rehearse it here.

31. See, e.g., *TFTS*, 178–179, for MacKinnon's description of the various ways in which women come to devalue their own feelings, experiences, or viewpoints.

32. One might take this argument as MacKinnon's version of the (now familiar) philosophical attack on the distinction between facts and values: there is no possible value-free, interest-free description of the "facts" in, for example, a rape case. Thus the liberal attempt to establish the objective facts and then judge or evaluate them is fundamentally, inevitably mistaken (or, as I shall explain in the next section, inevitably in collaboration with the powerful).

33. Perhaps one could still, on this view, continue to use objectivity as a norm, even if it were understood to be unattainable; it depends on one's view as to the meaningfulness of necessarily unattainable ("heuristic") norms. In any case, one could not consistently believe that any particular claim could be objective.

34. See *TFTS*, p. 121, for a particularly forceful statement of her position as going beyond internal criticism of liberalism and/or objectivity as partial and thus hypocritical.

35. MacKinnon is after all a political activist, and thus part of her aim is to mobilize and unite a sufficiently large "interest group" (in order to gain enough power to change things), as she suggests in *TFTS* (e.g., pp. 9, 87). Hence, for example, her statements that the "woman in the pornography is you" (e.g., *FU*, p. 228). MacKinnon's point here is not only that liberal (middle- and upper-class, professional) women are misguided if they think that they escape the sexual stereotyping that underlies the abuse of less fortunate women. She is also trying to evoke compassion, literally "feeling with," the comradeship necessary to underlie a broad political movement. Thus her invocation of liberal values could be a way of drawing a potentially recalcitrant set of sympathizers to her side.

MacKinnon has been accused of "essentialism" on the grounds that she is trying to find commonalities in all women's experiences (primarily by focusing on sexuality rather than economics or education). Elizabeth Rapaport argues in her chapter in this volume, rightly I think, that such accusations are unfounded and that MacKinnon is to be praised, politically speaking, for trying to bring women together in a common cause.

36. As MacKinnon suggests when she says that "we do not seek dominance over men. To us it is a male notion that power must dominate. We seek a transformation in the terms and conditions of power itself" (*FU*, p. 23). She seeks legitimate or just exercise of power.

37. I am in considerable sympathy with Louise Antony's and Charlotte Witt's arguments (in their chapters in this volume) with respect to feminists who appeal to postmodern or perspectival notions of justice, meaning, or truth in general. I could not agree more that (as Witt writes) a postmodern "metaphilosophy [that] does not countenance the possibility of real, universal norms" constitutes a "self-defeating strategy for feminists who would criticize the tradition for gender bias" (p. 279).

38. Locke might be a good example from the history of liberalism. Pain, he believes, is much more powerful and important in human life (as something to avoid) than pleasure. (His view seems to be, consistent with the liberal position as I have sketched it, that preventing pain is easier than securing pleasure, as well as being a first priority in matters of

justice.) (See, e.g., *Essay Concerning Human Understanding* 2.20.6; *Second Treatise* 2.10; see also Mill, *On Liberty*, chapter 1, for a classic statement of such priorities in the liberal conception of government and justice.)

MacKinnon's own emphasis on the "experience" of women (e.g., *TFTS*, pp. 88–91) as a distinctive "methodological" standpoint, and her attempts to show how *bad* women's lives *are* while leaving open what women might want to make of their lives (once freed of subjection), reflects a similar desire to privilege pain over pleasure (first get rid of pain, then worry about what the positively good life would be like).

39. MacKinnon recognizes such a problem, e.g., *TFTS,* pp. 102–103, 115, though she states her position in somewhat less confrontational terms than I have done here. She does not say that she needs to show that other women are *wrong* morally or epistemologically. Rather, she shows how these other views are "as justified by aspects of women's experience as a feminist perspective would be" (*TFTS*, p. 102). Nonetheless, I think her position, ultimately, must be that women who disagree with her (however understandably and however much we ought to respect individuals' or individual women's opinions and experiences—a good liberal view) are mistaken and, in the case of those who desire sexual dominance themselves, immoral.

40. See, e.g., *TFTS*, pp. 99–100, 102, 177, 181; *FU*, p. 54, for such an etiology of women's collaboration with male, objectifying dominance (women's "thingification in the head"). MacKinnon here attacks liberal individualism and (particularly) "voluntarism," head-on: even a woman's consent or desire, she suggests at points, cannot excuse violent sex or participation in pornography. Her pornography ordinance includes the proviso that "proof of the following facts or conditions shall not constitute a defense: . . .". That the person signed a contract, or made statements affirming a willingness to cooperate in the production of pornography" (reproduced in *IHW*, 442–443). To many liberals, MacKinnon's position here sounds quite dangerously radical (or perhaps extremely conservative; MacKinnon is hard to fit into the political spectrum as we know it). Should not individual women be allowed to choose to express their sexual desires, whether MacKinnon approves of them or not?

The nature, origin, and benignity (or not) of (female) masochistic desire are complicated issues that lie outside the scope of this discussion. I shall merely note that MacKinnon's view deserves to be taken seriously by liberals. All classical liberals share the view that some choices are not consistent with the liberal, normative status of human beings as rational self-determining beings; the clearest case is slavery. "Consent" to slavery is self-contradictory (determining oneself to be determined by another) and a violation of one's own human dignity. It cannot excuse the wrong of slavery. Desires for sexual slavery and submissiveness might be more problematic for the liberal position than an easy voluntaristic position recognizes. Herman's discussion of Kant's views on marriage and sexuality (in her chapter in this volume) nicely explicates the way in which sexuality may (inherently?) present such problems for liberal political theory.

41. *FU*, p. 14. I do not mean, necessarily, to endorse MacKinnon's understandings of any of these branches of feminist thought. I merely wish to point out that her way of explaining or discrediting them is quite consonant with liberal/objectivist "methodology."

42. *TFTS*, pp. 7, 83–105.

43. See, e.g., *TFTS*, p. 86. Consciousness-raising, and the public or communal nature of the women's movement that grew of it, challenged another liberal value—privacy. Feminists including MacKinnon have shown the way in which this value has (at least) collaborated with male domination of women in Western society. See Mill, *On the Subjection of*

Women, pp. 128–129, for a good discussion of the role of "privacy" in the subordination of women.

44. Many epistemologists in the modern tradition, e.g., Descartes, Locke, Hume, and Kant, make such broad assumptions as part of their methodologies.

45. See, e.g., Kant, *Critique of Pure Reason* (e.g., A793–4/B821–22); Kant, *Prolegomena* Ak. 298–299; Kant, "What Is Enlightenment?" in *Foundations of the Metaphysics of Morals*, trans. L. W. Beck (Englewood Heights, N.J.: Prentice-Hall, 1995), especially pp. 84–85.

46. Consciousness-raising also led women to unite in a *political* project to fight against shared oppression. This, I suggest, is a political result of the recognition of objective facts rather than a sort of communal epistemological method that is an alternative to the objectivity norm.

47. I bracket these terms to indicate that one ought to take objectivity as a continuing enterprise, and any claims to objectivity (in definitions or judgments) as subject to criticism and revision.

48. Similarly, although we ought to follow MacKinnon in suspicions about social scientific methodology and the criteria used by social scientists, we might still believe that there are ways objectively to study "subjective" phenomena (i.e., as psychology aims to do). For example (though MacKinnon does not suggest this), if a rapist scored high on Zillman's Sex Callousness scale (a measure employed by Donnerstein in his empirical psychological work on pornography and its effects), then it would be reasonable to believe that his subjective perceptions about whether his victim "liked it" are mistaken, given his systematically misguided, inaccurate, or unjust views about women—his incapability to discern whether a woman does desire sex or not. This would, I suggest, constitute a reasonably objective way to determine that "his word" is not worth very much. (MacKinnon may have a similar point in mind when she endorses the introduction of defendants' past sexual histories into rape cases; *FU*, 113.)

49. I have a hard time reconciling these two views of objectivity, although they are united as being (putatively) in the service of male power, or expressions of male power, according to MacKinnon. Similarly, MacKinnon's assimilation of objectivity and "naturalism" seems somewhat suspect. How can those who endorse objectivity, and its attempts to master nature, object to "naturalism," or the view that nature has some fixed content that ought to be left alone? Maybe MacKinnon does not need to reconcile these two into one consistent position but can merely say that male power comes in different forms. In any case, I do not try here (much) to explain how they can come together.

50. E.g., Heidegger, "The Question Concerning Technology," in *Basic Writings*, ed. David Farrell Krell (New York: Harper & Row, 1977), pp. 298–300; Levinas, "Philosophy and the Idea of Infinity," *Revue metaphysique et de morale* 62 (1957): 241–253; Horkheimer and Adorno, *Dialectic of Enlightenment*, trans. John Cumming (New York: Continuum, 1998), e.g., p. 93.

51. *Pornography*, pp. 70–100; cf. Horkheimer and Adorno, *Dialectic*, pp. 181–191.

52. Descartes's *cogito ergo sum* as the first, indubitable item of knowledge on which all other knowledge is based (or on the model of which all other potential knowledge is judged) is the most obvious example of such a move in epistemology. Because this claim is an existence claim, it might also be read as a claim to metaphysical priority as well.

53. This is not to say that modern science, or this privilege of the subject as separate from the world, is the correct way to understand our epistemological relation to the world. Nor is it to say that this modern scientific worldview has not been used to the detriment of

women. For example, the camera is indeed a powerful mechanism (both literally and figuratively) in the objectification of women as operated by pornography. The camera stands for the eye of the viewer, and it is identified with the male viewer as the self for whom the world presented by the camera (in pornography, primarily women's bodies, women's sexuality) is the object *to be used* for masturbation. There is no intersubjectivity or recognition of a community of subjects, as there may well be in at least some encounters between real human beings. As J. M. Coetzee points out, the camera stands between the male viewer and the woman viewed disallowing reciprocity—the woman doesn't look back. "The Harms of Pornography: Catharine MacKinnon," in *Giving Offense: Essays on Censorship* (Chicago: University of Chicago, 1996), pp. 68–71.

However, both MacKinnon and Dworkin make much broader claims. They take modern science/objectivity to be intrinsically tied to vision or seeing, and thus in entirety (somehow) to be implicated in this visual objectification through pornography (see, e.g., *TFTS*, pp. 114–115). As MacKinnon notes, the visual metaphor for knowledge has been used frequently in Western philosophy since Plato. MacKinnon and Dworkin take visual pornography to be particularly powerful in conditioning male sexual desire. (They are also troubled by photographic pornography because it requires using real women to make the pornography, but this, I think, is a quite different concern.) Vision is thus a common metaphor in (objectivist, and most other) epistemology and is involved in women's objectification through pornography. *Perhaps* the visual metaphor in epistemology hints at some connection between epistemology and objectification. But it is not at all clear what this connection is supposed to be. What mechanism in seeing is responsible for the domination involved, supposedly, in both objectivity and objectification?

54. As, for example, attested by Locke in his works on education, (some) classical liberals are fully aware that human beings are tempted by the love of mastery. Some of them at least, including Locke, saw the need to reeducate this love of mastery into pride in one's own self-mastery or rational autonomy. See *Some Thoughts Concerning Education*, ed. Grant and Tarcov (Indianapolis: Hackett, 1996), pp. 31–34, 55–57.

55. As Dworkin herself makes clear in her discussion of Sade, he was only contingently related to the French Revolution and its ideals. (He was not thrown in jail—as legends about Sade aver—because he endorsed liberal views but because he had abused women and children.)

Barbara Herman, in her chapter in this volume, very nicely explicates this fundamental liberal distinction between human relations to other human beings and human relations to material objects in her discussion of Kant's special difficulties when he turns from the topic of property (the possession of material objects or physical nature) to the topic of sexual relations and marriage.

56. E.g., "On the Jewish Question," in *Early Writings*, trans. and ed. T. B. Bottomore (New York: McGraw-Hill, 1964), esp. pp. 30, 36.

57. Or so MacKinnon claims. Liberalism encompasses, however, a broader spectrum of views than MacKinnon recognizes (which spectrum I too am guilty of obscuring in the wide sweep of this chapter). J. S. Mill, in *On the Subjection of Women* and even in *On Liberty* (used often as a philosophical authority by MacKinnon's opponents), recognizes powerful, dominating forces within society apart from the government, i.e. (respectively), the male power structure (as instantiated in educational and familial institutions) and majority opinion and custom. The liberal defense of free speech in general (the liberal view MacKinnon has found most intolerable) stemmed at least in part from the liberal desire to defuse the sociopolitical power of religious institutions. MacKinnon does, however, identify a

strong trend in liberalism, and I shall be concerned primarily with that aspect of liberalism here as well.

58. This view of objectivity does connect the "formalism" and the "naturalism" MacKinnon attributes to liberalism/objectivism. Many individuals from minority groups who receive less, and inferior, education are indeed, objectively speaking, less qualified for certain jobs. One might therefore be led to think that "by nature" such individuals are inferior. I put this argument in a footnote because it seems to be based on a patently bad inference. Nonetheless, it has been made (famously in the *Bell Curve*); similarly, MacKinnon has been faced with arguments that men's sexuality just *is* dominating by nature, thus any attempts to change that or to resist it are futile or wrong because they would be contrary to nature (a view that seems to be gaining more and more currency, unfortunately, especially as articulated in evolutionary psychology). As I indicate below, however, even if these arguments were good arguments, they are not true to the spirit (I think) of liberalism, and its statement of normative goals (as distinct from statements of [putative] facts).

59. A certain strand in liberalism, e.g., that represented by Adam Smith, is probably not assimilable (directly) to such a description, for on this view, one ought to encourage interests, even the self-interests of entrepreneurs, so that such interests can serve the greater good by strengthening the economy. As indicated above, I am here indeed leaving out many of the complexities and disagreements within liberalism itself; this sort of liberalism would (I believe) still endorse the limited, "objective" exercise of governmental power, though they are not (as I say) concerned to eliminate all interests en masse.

60. MacKinnon's frustration comes out clearly in her responses to a certain set of objections against her and Dworkin's pornography ordinances: that there are "already laws on the books" that criminalize sexual abuse, rape, coercion, and so on, and even prohibit "obscenity" (pornography). If these laws were effective or enforced, then indeed (she says) we would not need the pornography ordinances she defends. But since these laws are not enforced, not effective, they hardly count as real protection of women against the harms the laws *say* (but only or merely say) are wrong.

61. A good example of the naivete and complacency involved in this liberal attitude is Gayle Markel's testimony (*IHW*, p. 395). She argues that women who oppose pornography should "vote with their pocketbooks." As if it is women who are the consumers of pornography that make pornography the profitable business that it is; as if the women for whom MacKinnon and Dworkin are pleading can "vote" for much of anything with their pocketbooks.

62. See MacKinnon's third essay in *Only Words* ("Equality and Speech") for her sustained argument that freedom (of speech) ought to be limited by equality concerns (as under the Fourteenth Amendment).

63. Even Isaiah Berlin (from whom I borrow these distinctions between positive and negative liberty), a strong proponent of quite limited, negative liberty as a liberal norm in order to limit governmental action, argues that all conceptions of liberalism rely to some degree on such broader conceptions of liberty, or of the dignity of an individual as a normative, substantive goal. Berlin, "Two Concepts of Liberty," in *Four Essays on Liberty* (Oxford: Oxford University Press, 1990).

64. Thus I share Witt's view (as argued in her chapter in this volume) that MacKinnon "in her claim that pornography dehumanizes women . . . appeals to the notion that human beings are characterized (or perhaps ought to be characterized) by the power of self-definition" (285) despite MacKinnon's claims (of the sort I have been discussing) that "there is no such thing as human nature" (284). I differ from Witt in being more hesitant

to characterize such a concept of human nature as a "metaphysical" one—I take her parentheses "(or perhaps ought to be characterized)" as accurate, and as marking a difference between normative and metaphysical conceptions of humanity. I wish to make a stronger connection between specifically liberal commitments to, or conceptions of, such normative views about human nature and MacKinnon's views. (On this last point I am, I think, closer to Herman, whose sense of the similarity between Kant and MacKinnon/Dworkin I share.)

65. Thus I find some of MacKinnon's claims, such as the following, rather puzzling; "The individual concept of rights which this [liberal] theory requires . . . produces the tension between liberty for each and equality among all, [which] pervades liberal feminism, substantiating the criticism that feminism is for the privileged few" (*TFTS*, p. 7). Perhaps this comment is true about liberalism as practiced, but that would only show that liberalism as practiced has not accomplished the actual goals of liberalism—the protection of everyone's rights.

66. In these remarks, I do not mean to say (necessarily) that the specific social practices identified by MacKinnon as responsible for women's subordination (i.e., primarily pornography) must be recognized as so responsible by liberals, nor that MacKinnon's specific, suggested remedies (i.e., her antipornography ordinance) must be adopted by liberals. Liberals ought to consider these arguments, for there is no separate reason to support government protection for free speech other than that the government ought to protect individuals' liberties. Such protection, as all classical liberals argue, involves limitation of the freedom of each individual (i.e., individuals ought not to be free to harm others); pornography or other forms of discriminatory speech could fall into the category of action that harms others and therefore would rightfully be limited.

67. E.g., Rawls, *Theory of Justice* (Cambridge: Harvard University Press, 1971), e.g., pp. 522–526; J. S. Mill, *On Liberty,* chap. 3.

68. Such, I would say, is the basic "moralism" underlying the liberal position, a "moralism" not to be confused (I think) with that to which MacKinnon refers in her criticism of liberalism. Though MacKinnon does not fully explain what she means by this criticism, I take her to mean that political (conservative) moralism (about sexual matters in particular) is hypocritical—political moralists claim to care about moral issues, but actually they are trying to further male interests (e.g., for each man's possession of particular women to the exclusion of other men). Second, MacKinnon argues that moralism about sexuality is dangerous because it makes sexual matters, particularly sexual violence, "taboo" and thereby makes sexual violence even "sexier" (e.g., *FU*, p. 162). I think MacKinnon is right about this point but cannot argue for that here (Coetzee discusses this dynamic more fully). I do not, however, take this sort of sexual morality to be intrinsic to (all) liberalism (as evinced by the serious disagreement about such issues in this country) in the way that the liberal commitment to freedom for all individuals is.

69. Again Judge Easterbrook, in his opinion on MacKinnon's pornography ordinance, is a good example of such proceduralism for procedure's sake.

70. Others try to refine or perfect procedures so that they will not simply perpetuate injustice—an attempt, one might argue, that is the center of Rawls's project.

71. Though I do not endorse all of her positive recommendations, Susan Moller Okin's *Justice, Gender, and the Family* presents excellent arguments for such institutional legal support for women based on a liberal understanding of justice and rights. She makes plausible practical recommendations as to how such support could be incorporated into our liberal political order.

13

FEMINIST METAPHYSICS

CHARLOTTE WITT

I am a feminist by political conviction and an Aristotelian metaphysician by school-
ing and inclination. My double self makes perfect sense to me, or so I have thought for
many years. True, in the tiny world of Aristotelians there is rarely a mention of his misogyny, or rather, mention and dismissal of the topic are virtually simultaneous. And
equally true, in feminist philosophical circles mention of Aristotle and metaphysics
are more likely to end a conversation than to begin one. I used to think that the antagonism between metaphysicians and feminists was a result of mutual ignorance, and
I used to think that there was no real conflict between the two groups because one was
primarily concerned with political theory and the other with metaphysical issues.
And, because there is no direct and obvious connection between political and metaphysical questions, there is no compelling reason for feminist theorists and Aristotelian metaphysicians to enter into debate, either rancorous or friendly.

   In this essay I explore the contrary thesis, the traditional idea that there might
be an important connection between political theory and metaphysics. In particular I
explore the idea that political theory—in this case, feminist theory—does have consequences for metaphysics.[1] What sort of consequences? Two claims, it seems to me, are
particularly important to consider. The first is the idea that every acceptable feminist
theory is inherently anti-metaphysical.[2] I suspect that this claim (even where it does
not receive explicit articulation) explains some of the mutual antagonism between
feminists and metaphysicians. On this view, then, the contribution of feminist theory
to metaphysics is the metaphilosophical position that one ought to stop doing metaphysics in order to theorize in an appropriately feminist manner. The second major
claim is that feminist theory makes a distinctive contribution to metaphysics. Here
the point is the reverse of the first: Not only is feminism not inherently anti-metaphysical, but it contributes significantly to our understanding of at least some meta-

physical issues.³ The challenge in this regard is to explain how feminist theory, rooted as it is in existing concrete political conditions, could have an impact upon our most abstract reflections concerning the structure of reality.

What are the metaphilosophical consequences of feminism? In Part One I argue that there are no specifically *feminist* reasons for rejecting metaphysics. My argument has two stages. Because it would be impossible to devise an argument in principle concerning the implications of every possible antimetaphysical position for feminist theory, I consider the positions of Richard Rorty and Jean-François Lyotard, whose views have currency in feminist circles today. I show that their views neither originate in feminist concerns nor provide an adequate basis for social change. I next examine a historical argument that might be thought to provide the specifically feminist motivation for the critical stance toward traditional philosophy codified in the anti-metaphysical positions considered earlier. I end Part One by arguing that the feminist claim that the history of philosophy—including metaphysics—in the Western tradition is phallocentric, or male-biased, requires showing not only that women have been excluded from traditional categories but also that their inclusion makes a conceptual difference. So I conclude that feminists who are developing a gender critique of the tradition (with which I am sympathetic) must also engage in the project of reconceiving traditional categories; they ought to do metaphysics. That is, rather than providing the specifically feminist reasons for adopting an anti-metaphysical metaphilosophy, the historical critique itself turns out to require metaphysical supplement.

In Part Two I take up the second issue, the question of what the feminist perspective could contribute to metaphysics. The problem is to understand how a political theory could influence an abstract inquiry like metaphysics. If there is any such influence, it is likely to be most accessible in those areas of metaphysical reflection with direct and obvious political bearing, such as our understanding of human nature. From Aristotle to Kant the tradition has linked questions of political and ethical life to ontological questions concerning the nature of a human being.⁴ I argue that feminist theory has developed several analyses of human nature that purport to modify in different ways our traditional understanding of what it is to be human. If this is so, then it is true that the history of metaphysics is phallocentric and that it need not be so. It also follows, of course, that any adequate account of human nature must consider feminist theory; it is not enough simply to include women (the obligatory "he or she") in the population of human beings; one must also consider in what way their inclusion might alter our conception of what it is to be human.

All of the terrain in this essay is disputed. Feminists disagree over the existence and nature of feminist theory just as for centuries metaphysicians have differed over the nature of metaphysics. What do I mean by feminist theory? And what do I mean by metaphysics? For the purposes of this essay, my approach to both of these questions is the same. I do not provide definitions of either term, and I prefer to proceed by example. The question of human nature is an example of a metaphysical question; Gilliganism and Feminism Unmodified are examples of feminist theories.

I said that the question of human nature counts as a metaphysical question, and earlier I remarked that traditional philosophers like Aristotle and Kant anchored their ethical and political theories in their accounts of human nature. These remarks ignore a basic difference concerning how the two philosophers conceptualize what is to count as the ontological basis for their ethics and political theory. So, while it is true that both Aristotle and Kant base their ethical theories in ontology, they do not agree on what the relevant category is. Aristotle's ethics is based on the distinctive rational nature and function of human beings (and on the ontological fact that they have natures and functions), while Kant rejects this naturalistic description of moral agents and substitutes the category of persons for Aristotle's human beings. My point is that if an Aristotelian human nature of a Kantian person reflects a covert appeal to the male standard, then feminist reflection on what it is to be human or a person might force us to reconsider those concepts.

Part One: Feminist Theory and the Rejection of Metaphysics

Let us begin with the claim made by some feminists that metaphysics ought to be rejected root and branch because it is an inherently masculine and oppressive enterprise. As I see this issue, the central question is whether there are any specifically feminist reasons for rejecting the metaphysical project. By a feminist reason I mean either a reason that is clearly and directly related to the situation or experience of women or a reason that is needed to explain or to ameliorate that situation. If, for example, you used the historical claim that the metaphysical tradition is male-biased to explain why women are thought to lack the power of transcendent reason in our culture, then you would be giving a feminist reason in my sense of the term. It seems to me that there are no feminist reasons to accept the current philosophical views that reject the metaphysical enterprise. Further, and most important, these positions lack the theoretical resources required for an adequate feminist criticism of patriarchy's ideology and institutions. So, although the antimetaphysical stance may be compatible with some varieties of feminist theory, there are no compelling feminist reasons to adopt it. A philosopher is not a feminist because and insofar as she rejects the possibility or desirability of metaphysics.

Let us consider these points in relation to the recent anti-metaphysical trend in philosophy on both sides of the Atlantic. Feminist theorists Nancy Fraser and Linda Nicholson describe what American pragmatism and Continental postmodernism have in common:

> Writers like Richard Rorty and Jean-François Lyotard begin by arguing that Philosophy with a capital "P" is no longer a viable or credible enterprise. From here, they go on to claim that philosophy, and by extension, theory more generally, can no longer function to *ground* politics and social criticism. With the demise of foundationalism comes the demise of the view that casts philosophy in the role of *founding* discourse vis-à-vis social criticism.[5]

The idea common to both Rorty and Lyotard is that philosophy must give up its self-image as engaging in a unique type of foundational inquiry and accept a new status as one form of inquiry among others. But to think of metaphysics, for example, as just one kind of inquiry into reality among others, on a par with poetry or sociology, is to reject the discipline in its traditional self-image.

Rorty and Lyotard differ with regard to their reasons for rejecting metaphysics and the other traditional subdivisions of philosophy. Rorty rejects what he calls "representationalism" because it assumes the possibility of a correct set of representations or a privileged description on the one hand and reality, that which is to be represented or described, on the other hand. Rorty's rejection of this foundationalist picture of philosophy is a result of his pragmatist metaphilosophy: "Anti-representationalists do not think such efforts (of representationalists like Thomas Nagel) insane, but they do think that the history of philosophy shows them to have been fruitless and undesirable."[6] In other words, Rorty's view is that metaphysics has outlived whatever usefulness it once had and so it should be retired like an outmoded piece of technology.

Lyotard shares Rorty's rejection of philosophy as foundational for other discourses or disciplines. He appears to do so not because he shares Rorty's pragmatist metaphilosophy, but because the idea of a "metadiscourse," like philosophy, no longer has legitimacy in our times, the postmodern period. Lyotard defines postmodernism as "incredulity toward metanarratives" and contrasts the postmodern attitude toward the project of justification with the modern attitude: "I will use the term *modern* to designate any science that legitimates itself with reference to a metadiscourse of this kind making an explicit appeal to some grand narrative, such as the dialectics of Spirit, the hermeneutics of meaning, the emancipation of the rational or working subject, or the creation of wealth."[7] Metaphysics, as traditionally conceived, is a paradigmatic "grand narrative" insofar as it attempts to provide universal foundations (in Lyotard's vocabulary, "legitimization") for science, ethics, and political theory. Why do postmoderns no longer believe in metanarratives—not just particular metanarratives like those of Hegel, Marx, or the Enlightenment but the entire project? According to Lyotard, it is because every discourse (or language) is embedded in continent, historical practices (its rules): "Any consensus on the rules defining a game and the "moves" playable within it *must* be local, in other words, agreed on by its present players and subject to eventual cancellation."[8] If *all* discourse, *all* language games, *must* be local, then metanarratives are really just pretentious local narratives that happen to be widely believed. Lyotard has abandoned the foundational philosophical project not for Rortyan pragmatic reasons, but because he deems it impossible—given the nature of language.[9]

It is certainly possible that a feminist theorist might find Rorty's or Lyotard's rejection of traditional philosophy including metaphysics intrinsically plausible. One might think with Rorty that metaphysics has served its function and just doesn't do anyone any good: "Whatever good the ideas of 'objectivity' and 'transcendence' have done for our culture can be attained equally well by the idea of a community which strives after both intersubjective agreement and novelty—a democratic, progressive, pluralistic community of the sort of which Dewey dreamt."[10] Or one might agree with Lyotard that the hallmark of our age is the realization that all descriptions of reality are context-bound and perspectival and that, therefore, no discourse can claim to transcend its own perspective and context. Further, Rorty's pragmatism and Lyotard's postmodernism might be compatible with some directions in feminist theory.

It is clear, however, that there are no particularly feminist reasons for accepting either explanation of the petering out of metaphysics. For, whatever their intrinsic philosophical plausibility, neither theory reflects feminist insights and neither explains the status of women or their exclusion from culture. And, perhaps most important, neither view provides an adequate theoretical basis for significant conceptual or social change.[11] The latter point deserves fuller consideration.

Rorty's celebration of modern, liberal democracy and his rejection of the utility of any deep criticism of existing social categories ought to make feminists who accept his metaphilosophical views on their intrinsic merit reconsider them in the light of their political implications. Rorty is a metaphilosophical radical, but a political moderate; his metaphilosophy only allows for a critique of patriarchy based on pragmatic concerns. But surely feminists want to do more than claim that gender bias based on biologism is not useful; surely we would want to claim that it is false or even immoral. After all, biologism (the idea that gender roles are grounded in biology) might be a very useful theory for a patriarchal culture like our own. No sense in arguing with nature, is there?

In a recent paper entitled "Feminism and Pragmatism," Rorty describes pragmatism's resources for feminism in different terms.[12] He argues that prophetic feminists like Catharine MacKinnon and Marilyn Frye are engaged in a process of invention; they are creating women as full human persons rather than discovering that that is what they really are and have been all along. For the pragmatist there is nothing that women (or slaves or homosexuals) really are and have been all along. The process of liberation for these groups is a process of creating a new vocabulary and new social structures that describe them and acknowledge them as fully human. Initially Rorty's description of prophetic feminism as creating a new reality rather that merely discovering and articulating the biases and limitations of traditional descriptions of reality seems attractive and innocuous. But it is important to read the fine print. In following Rorty and replacing talk of discovery with talk of invention, feminists must also relinquish "the notion that the oppression of women is *intrinsically* abominable" and "the claim that there is something called 'right' or 'justice' or 'humanity' which has always been on their side making their claims true."[13] Indeed, feminists who are good pragmatists cannot advocate for feminism or explain its success by appeal to its truth or moral rightness.[14] To return to the example of biologism, pragmatist feminists could not argue against it because it is (was and always will be) a false view and because it is (was and always will be) an immoral view. Pragmatism's seductive metaphors of creativity turn out to disarm feminism by forbidding the kinds of criticisms that feminists of all types do make, and ought to make, of patriarchy.

Similarly, feminists who find the arguments of postmodernism intrinsically convincing should consider the implications for political theory and political change of postmodernism's thoroughgoing relativism.[15] Postmodernism provides meager resources for thinking about political change. Consider the example of biologism again. If all discourse is radically contextualized and local (made entirely relative to historical groups or cultures), then feminist critiques of oppressive, patriarchal theories themselves are contextualized. But if this is so, what grounds are there to claim that patriarchal discourse (the language game of male power that is our local lingo) ought to change? In particular, what grounds are there to contest the biologistic language of patriarchy, the idea that terms like *man* and *woman* refer to biological categories?

All of this makes perfect sense, of course. Why should philosophical theories developed entirely independently of feminist concerns themselves constitute the feminist metaphilosophical perspective? At this point some feminist anti-metaphysicians might object that I have told only half of their story, and it is the other half that provides the *feminist* reasons for the rejection of metaphysics. The claim, then, is that the kinds of metaphilosophical positions outlined above only become necessary for feminist theorizing if they are adopted for feminist reasons. So we need to ask again whether there are any feminist reasons for adopting an anti-metaphysical metaphilosophy.

The major feminist argument against traditional metaphysics is historical. Drawing upon the work done by feminist historians of philosophy that shows the tradition to be male-biased and even misogynist, some feminist thinkers have argued for the rejection of traditional philosophy as a whole. Commenting upon the modern period in philosophy, Iris Young says:

> Recent feminist analyses of modern political theory and practice increasingly argue that the ideas of liberalism and contract theory, such as formal equality and universal rationality, are deeply marred by masculine biases about what it means to be human and the nature of society. If modern culture in the West has been thoroughly male dominated, these analyses suggest, then there is little hope of laundering some of its ideals to make it possible to include women.[16]

Given the male bias at the core of the tradition's understanding of what it is to be human—in particular the ideal of universal rationality—Young thinks that there are good reasons for a "break" with modernism.

Other feminist philosophers have extended the reach of male bias back to the origins of the philosophical tradition in the West.[17] In *The Man of Reason,* for example, Genevieve Lloyd makes a historical argument that the concept of transcendence, the ability of reason to transcend material and temporal limits, is male centered; transcendence *means* overcoming nature, matter, the feminine. "Rationality has been conceived as transcendence of the feminine; and the 'feminine' itself has been partly constituted by its occurrence within this structure."[18]

What are the implications of the fact that metaphysics, the transcendence of reason, was historically conceived of in relation to men and not women? There are three possibilities: (1) One could argue for a clean break with the tradition, a rejection of metaphysics. (2) One could argue that the feminist understanding of the tradition gives good reasons for engaging in a reconception of the central categories of metaphysics like reason and transcendence. (3) One could argue that all that is required in order to address the evident male bias in traditional philosophy is the explicit inclusion of women in the domain of reason.

It is clear that the historical argument does not necessitate drawing the first conclusion. There are three objections facing those who would draw the first conclusion. First, it does not follow from the fact that metaphysical categories have reflected male experience in the past that they need do so in the future. Second, the case for male bias cannot be made based on the historical evidence alone, because we need to show not only that women were excluded in the tradition but also that their exclusion has made a conceptual difference. Third, the historical argument (whether supplemented by a conceptual investigation or not) is insufficient to discredit metaphysical inquiry itself.

This last point, that the historical argument is not powerful enough to discredit metaphysical inquiry, does not concern the ideas generated by metaphysical reflection but rather the activity itself. There may be arguments to the effect that reflective philosophy is a waste of time or inherently elitist, but the feminist criticism of the philosophical tradition is not such an argument—for it criticizes the fruits of philosophy and not the activity itself.[19] So, although the historical critique of metaphysics, unlike Rortyan pragmatism and Lyotard's postmodernism, is explicitly feminist and therefore is a necessary element in any feminist theorizing about the history of philosophy, it does not provide the missing conceptual link between the metaphilosophical arguments against metaphysics we have considered and feminist theory.

And, in fact, although some feminist theorists appear to want to reject traditional philosophy altogether by proposing a "break with modernism," what some envision is a project of reconceptualization of the kind suggested in option (2) above. "Male-biased (or patriarchal) conceptual frameworks must be replaced by ones that are not male-biased."[20] I take it that to undertake a reconception of basic metaphysical categories is to do metaphysics. In the end, then, feminist criticisms of male-centered metaphysical categories should motivate theoretically inclined feminists to reform or revolutionize metaphysics rather than to abandon metaphysics altogether. If feminists do not engage in this project, then they are left with option (3)—the idea that the traditional metaphysical categories are fine as they are and that women simply need to be included explicitly. This is, I believe, the attitude of many (male) philosophers today who would challenge feminists to show how feminist theory has anything to contribute to traditional philosophy other than a legitimate demand for inclusion.

Let me draw together the themes of this section by considering how a feminist thinker might bolster the historical argument with a deconstruction of metaphysics. The historical story shows that women have been excluded from traditional philosophy in several ways and, consequently, that the values of traditional philosophy (like reason) really reflect male values and norms. These values are purportedly universal, but their simple extension to women seems suspect. Why should we accept male norms as the norms? I have suggested that we feminists need to rethink the traditional categories. Another feminist, however, impressed by the duplicity of our tradition, might embrace a total deconstruction of the claim to universal norms—that is, she might adopt a Rortyan or Lyotardian metaphilosophy. In doing so, however, she undercuts herself. For she wants to claim that the universal norms of the tradition are illegitimate and ought to be rejected, but neither metaphilosophy provides grounds for her claim. If your metaphilosophy does not countenance the possibility of real, universal norms, then how can you criticize the tradition for not furnishing them? This is a self-defeating strategy for feminists who would criticize the tradition for gender bias.

I said that as things stand we could conclude from the historical argument either that traditional categories need to be thought through again or that we need merely include women in their domain. In order to show that the stronger conclusion is correct it is necessary to show not only that women have been excluded in the tradition but also that their inclusion makes a conceptual difference. For, if their inclusion does not make a conceptual difference, then what is meant by calling the tradition "phallocentric," or "male-biased," is uncontroversial and relatively easy to correct. So, not only does the gender critique of the tradition not provide a conclusive argument against metaphysics, it actually needs to be supplemented by a conceptual project with the goal of establishing that the inclusion of our perspective makes a conceptual difference.

Part Two: Feminist Theory and the Question of Human Nature

What difference does a feminist perspective make on the way we theorize about human nature? In what follows I discuss two different answers to this question proposed by recent feminist theory. The first answer, which I will call "Gilliganism," focuses on the idea of reason and argues that the traditional notion of reason is inadequate to capture women's distinctive voice.[21] Because reason is the basic ingredient in the traditional concept of a human being, the latter concept is also flawed and ought to be reconceived in a way that incorporates an enriched notion of reason corresponding to the experience of women as well as men.

A second feminist perspective, called "Feminism Unmodified" by its creator Catharine MacKinnon, criticizes the entire enterprise of theorizing about the nature of human beings or persons.[22] The enterprise as a whole is mistaken because it ignores or even conceals the central analytic tool of any feminism deserving the name: the concept of gender. To talk about ungendered human beings, to think of persons as a metaphysical category, is to blur the two categories that any feminist should recognize as basic: the categories of male and female. Examining the notion of a human being or a person through the lens of gender reveals a structure of male domination whose primary locus is heterosexuality and its institutions. "Male" and "female" refer to positions in the structure of domination—males" have power, "females" do not. Although MacKinnon situates her views on the question of human nature within a historicist, contextualist framework (a Lyotardian perspective), I argue that her criticism of existing categories and institutions (for example, pornography) requires a normative concept of humanity. Hence, I argue that although MacKinnon may be right in emphasizing the importance of understanding institutions in terms of their history and social context, she would unnecessarily deprive feminism of a powerful tool and would undercut her own argument if she were to reject the possibility of metaphysics.

Gilliganism questions the narrowness of the traditional concept of a human being and argues that it should be reconceived to accommodate women's experience; Feminism Unmodified questions the legitimacy of the concept itself by arguing that all understanding begins with an understanding of gender and power. In what follows, I develop each position in turn and show that each offers a rethinking of the question of human nature for feminist reasons; hence, each counts as a feminist contribution to the metaphysical inquiry into the nature of human beings.

Carol Gilligan's *In a Different Voice* describes the way in which women speak and reason and argues that their different voice has been unheard in standard psychological studies of children's moral reasoning. Since its publication in 1982, *In a Different Voice* has enabled women scholars to "hear" a distinctive female voice in a wide range of academic areas including philosophy, science, literary studies, and the law. Although Gilligan formulated her theory in the context of research in developmental psychology, it can be transferred to a wide variety of disciplines precisely because it concerns a distinctive, feminine style of reasoning. It concerns a way of reasoning rather than either a subject matter or a set of conclusions. Further, a recent application of Gilligan's ideas to Justice Sandra Day O'Connor's legal reasoning shows that the method of reasoning is feminine rather than feminist.[23] In her fascinating article, Suzanna Sherry uses the disagreements between Justice O'Connor and her ideological soul mate, Chief Justice Rehnquist, to isolate a feminine style of jurisprudence that favors community over individual rights and stresses contextual decision making. The feminine voice is a way of thinking that women share and not a substantive, political stance adopted by feminists committed to social change.

Gilliganism makes two claims: (1) that there is a feminine form or method of reasoning, and (2) that this "voice" has been drowned out or silenced by traditional (male) reasoning. Let us consider each of these claims in turn. The first important point is that Gilliganism does not claim that there is a feminine logic or that inference patterns are different for women and men. Instead, it uses the notion of reasoning in a broader sense that includes, for example, the way that one chooses and formulates premises in thinking through a problem. In this broader sense of reasoning, the feminine voice is distinguished by two features: the tendency to view interpersonal relations as a basic feature of reality and a high degree of concern for the details of a situation or problem. Feminine reasoning is concrete rather than abstract; it does not operate by smoothing away the details of a problem but tries to accommodate them in their variety and richness. Feminine reasoning assumes relatedness rather than individuality in its descriptions of situations, thus adding to the complexity of the task of reason in cases of moral conflict.

The feminine voice has not been heard, according to Gilliganism, because theorizers have been trained to listen to the masculine voice, a style of reasoning that is a kind of abstract chess game played with unrelated pawns. The dominant voice is one that limits details and context in its desire for abstraction; it sees reason as applying abstract, general principles to a domain of unconnected individuals. If one identifies this species of thought with reasoning as a whole, if one makes it the norm, then feminine reasoning will either not show up at all or will appear to be defective. The theory argues for an inclusion of both voices, for an enriched notion of reason and reasoning.

Gilligan's ideas have been as controversial as they have been influential. Critics have questioned her research methodology, interpretation of data, and conclusions.[24] Critics, for example, have questioned whether or not there is a significant gender difference on the Kohlberg scale, a central claim of Gilligan's book. If there is no measurable difference between the two genders, then doubt is cast on both the idea that the two genders reason differently and that the male voice has drowned out the female one. In addition, feminist theorists have questioned the political utility of resurrecting and confirming the sexist stereotype of distinctively feminine thought patterns.[25]

How does Gilligan respond to these points? As I presented the two voices, they are identified with different genders, but Gilligan herself is elusive on this point. Although she clearly associates the different voice with women, she shies away from any essentialist claims. "The title of my book was deliberate; it reads, 'in a *different* voice,' not 'in a *woman's* voice.' In my introduction I explain that this voice is identified not by gender but by theme."[26] In other words, she holds neither that all (or most) women reason this way nor that all (or most) men do not. But this official disclaimer, required perhaps by her limited empirical base, is not consistent with her view that the feminine voice has been excluded from theoretical discourse because those theories have been developed by men about men. "But I do not see it as empowering to encourage women to put aside their own concerns and perceptions and to rely on a psychology largely defined by men's perceptions in thinking about what is of value and what constitutes human development."[27] Because it seems to me that Gilligan's theory does require a strong, though perhaps not essentialist, identification of the feminine voice with women, I have referred to that view as "Gilliganism" and I leave it open whether or not Gilligan herself adheres to that position.

Gilliganism argues for a unique feminine style of reasoning and holds that the feminine voice has been either absent or devalued in traditional accounts of reason and reasoning. Gilliganism provides a positive account of what gets left out if one patterns reasoning, the distinctively human capacity, on a male model. It is, therefore, an example of the kind of project of reconceptualization that I argued in Part One is required in order to persuade us that more than inclusion of women under existing concepts of the human being is possible, desirable, or mandatory. As things stand, however, Gilliganism has yet to establish its central empirical claim—namely, that there are two distinct reasoning styles strongly associated with women and men. Further, even if the empirical case were established, a number of important philosophical issues need to be addressed. In the first place, it needs to be shown by argument that the different voice is one that should be included in our normative concept of a human being. Perhaps, as Catharine MacKinnon and other feminists argue, the different voice is an imposition upon women whose ultimate value is highly questionable. The second major conceptual task would be to consider how the two "voices" Gilliganism claims to have discerned can be integrated. Is each voice appropriate to a different human context, so that we should all strive to be bilingual? Or does Gilliganism envision a new ideal of reason emerging from a blending of the two voices?

Catharine MacKinnon's Feminism Unmodified appears initially to agree with Gilliganism, for she argues that the traditional concept of a human being, a genderneutral human being, is really that of a male human being. A genderneutral concept, like that of a human being, really refers to the male standard. "Think about it like those anatomy models in medical school. A male body is the human body; all those extra things women have are studied in ob/gyn. It really is a case in which more is less."[28] Because MacKinnon emphasizes that allegedly neutral legal concepts like equality incorporate a hidden reference to the male standard—just as Gilligan points out the male standard for excellence in moral reasoning—one might expect MacKinnon to argue for a recognition of a legal counterpart to the different voice of Gilliganism. But she does not. A discussion of MacKinnon's criticisms of Gilliganism will allow us to see the distinctive perspective of Feminism Unmodified on the question of the traditional concept of a human being. It will allow us to see the very different moral MacKinnon draws from the feminist critique of reason and human nature in the philosophical tradition.

MacKinnon's basic criticism of Gilliganism raises the question of the value of the feminine voice, the different voice that we are urged to respect and to integrate into our notion of what it is to be human. She questions whether the characteristics that distinguish the feminine voice from its masculine counterpart are either inherently valuable or inherently female:

> I do not think that the way women reason morally is morality "in a different voice." I think it is morality in a higher register, in the feminine voice. Women value care because men have valued us according to the care we give them. . . . Women think in relational terms because our existence is defined in relation to men. Further, when you are powerless, you don't just speak differently. A lot, you don't speak. . . . All I am saying is that the damage of sexism is real, and reifying that into differences is an insult to our possibilities.[29]

The retrieval of a different voice, its legitimacy by women for women, is really the retrieval of a false voice (a falsetto) that has been imposed on women by men for their own purposes. MacKinnon's criticism of Gilliganism reveals the central concepts of her own analysis of the human being question: the importance of male supremacy in constructing our notions of gender, and the denial that the question of human nature has a valid, genderless interpretation. From MacKinnon's perspective, Gilliganism's vision of a blending of male and female voices in a new, richer notion of reason—and hence a new, fuller notion of a human being—amounts to a validation of the status quo—a social situation in which men have power and exercise it over women.

There are two basic claims underlying the position of Feminism Unmodified. The first is that there is no legitimate genderless interpretation for the question of human nature. The second is that the categories of male and female, the categories that one must refer to when considering human beings, are defined by men in their own interest. Let us consider these claims in turn.

MacKinnon discusses the concept of a human being in connection with the idea that pornography is wrong because it is dehumanizing. She comments:

> But "human being" is a social concept with many possible meanings. . . . In a feminist perspective pornography dehumanizes women in a culturally specific and empirically descriptive—not liberal moral—sense. In the same act, pornography dispossesses women of the same power of which it possesses men: the power of sexual, hence gender, definition. The power to tell one who one is and the power to treat one accordingly. Perhaps a human being, for gender purposes, is someone who controls the social definition of sexuality.[30]

MacKinnon insists that feminist theory must use the notion of gender as its central analytic tool. By using the notion of gender in connection with the traditional concepts of a human being, feminists can see that a purportedly universal concept is really modeled on males of a certain class. Moreover, concepts of gender are socially and historically constructed rather than based on biology or any other form of essentialism. "Sexuality to feminism is, like work to marxism, socially constructed and at the same time constructing."[31] But if sexuality or gender is socially constructed rather than a given, we can and must raise the questions of power and domination. Further, if we notice that women and men are equally different from one another but not equally powerful, the central question of feminism emerges—a question that concerns dominance or the power relations between the socially constructed categories of men and women rather than the question of difference. Gilliganism entirely misses this point and, indeed, serves to obscure it.

In relation to the question of what a human being is, the domination of men over women translates into the idea that men (human beings) specify "the social definition of sexuality." In other words, MacKinnon urges us to go beyond merely realizing that the notion of a human being has been modeled on male human beings, to the realization that the ability to define—a profound power supposedly granted to all human beings—is really granted to males. And the socially determined gender categories, including Gilligan's different voice, define women as subservient to men. That is their entire function, their raison d'être.

Pornography serves as a concrete illustration of how the female gender is defined in a way that expresses and confirms male control and domination. "Pornography purports to define what woman is."[32] And the pornographic definition of what a woman is is that she exists for male pleasure. Further, pornography eroticizes domination specifically in a society in which respect for persons, including self-respect, is a major ingredient in the concept of a human being. "In this way women's sexuality as expressed in pornography precisely negatives [sic] her status as a human."[33]

Feminism Unmodified would seem to leave nothing standing with regard to the traditional question of what it is to be a human being. The theory insists at the outset that that question be inspected through the lens of gender; what emerges is a notion of human nature that mirrors what it is to be male in our culture. As it turns out, however, concepts of gender are not themselves fixed and biological; rather, they are social through and through:

> By the way, I mean the word male as an adjective. The analysis of sex is social, not biological. . . . By male, then, I refer to apologists for these data; I refer to the approach that is integral to these acts, to the standard that has normalized these events so that they define masculinity, to the male sex role, and to the way this approach has submerged its gender to become "the" standard.[34]

Neither human beings, nor men and women, constitute natural kinds. The notion of a human being gives way to reveal its meaning in terms of gender (for example, as purportedly universal but really gender specific). Male and female, in turn, are seen to be merely social constructs that serve a particular social function—namely, to consolidate and perpetuate male domination.

The radical antibiological and antiessentialist analysis of male and female is both interesting and controversial; it challenges a deep intuition according to which differences between the two genders are at least partially anchored in biology. Moreover, MacKinnon's position appears to be so thoroughly antirealist that it leaves little purchase for metaphysics, for speculations about human nature. There is no such thing as human nature, really; there is no such thing as male and female really. Unmodified Feminism does not appeal to concepts like human nature and male and female; indeed, it explicitly disavows them. If anywhere, it appears that in MacKinnon's thought we have found a dismissal of the traditional inquiry into human nature; moreover, it is a dismissal on feminist grounds.

In fact, however, MacKinnon's critical posture concerning existing power relations requires a covert appeal to some normative notion of a human being. As we saw above, her rejection of liberal political theory's criticism of pornography as "dehumanizing" (that is, immoral) questioned the adequacy of the liberal concept of a human being. Presumably MacKinnon finds the liberal critique of pornography—which sees pornography as dehumanizing to its user because it excites his animal nature—to be inadequate because it is male-centered both in its analysis of the harm of pornography and in its notion of what a human being is.

But MacKinnon's own analysis of pornography also turns on the idea that pornography is dehumanizing in a different sense of the term. Pornography's real harm is that it defines women as for the pleasure of men, for their use. It removes from women their power of self-definition and places it in the hands of men. If we ask the question, What is wrong with this? the answer must be that it is dehumanizing, that part of what it is to be human is to have the power of self-definition. I am suggesting that it is possible to eke out of MacKinnon's criticisms of current oppressive social (sexual) structures a normative notion of what it is to be human. In fact, I am suggesting more; in order for MacKinnon to make the kind of criticism she does make of current sexual institutions—the loci of power, in her view—she must make an appeal to some notion of humanity that these institutions damage in women. Both in her idea of what is important and of value in human beings (the power of self-definition) and in her persuasive articulation of the central position of sexuality and its institutions in the social structure and construction of gender, MacKinnon's ideas have value for those who speculate on the question of what it is to be human.

There is a tension in MacKinnon's thought.[35] In her insistence on the social construction of gender and its institutions (like pornography), MacKinnon appears to embrace a metaphilosophy resembling Lyotard's. If all languages are local, then all criticism must be internal and use local jargon. As I pointed out at the end of Part One, a metaphilosophy like Lyotard's provides no underpinning for MacKinnon's claim that liberalism's views of pornography are immoral and ought to be rejected. In two respects, however, MacKinnon actually rejects this position in her criticisms of the "language" of pornography. In the first place, she criticizes pornography in terms that are not drawn from the local language (that is, the language of patriarchy). She explicitly rejects the terms of the standard criticisms of pornography and uses instead the new language of Feminism Unmodified. Second, in her claim that pornography dehumanizes women she appeals to the notion that human beings are characterized (or perhaps ought to be characterized) by the power of self-definition. Feminism Unmodified is right to claim that gender is a social and historical category (not a biological given); but it also ought to reject the politically powerless claim of Lyotardian postmodernism that the languages of gender are local and untranslatable.[36]

In my discussion of Gilliganism and Feminism Unmodified I have made two points. First, I have shown the way in which even feminist critics of traditional ways of approaching the question of what it is to be human need to confront that very question themselves. Second, by outlining two directions in feminist reflection on the question of human nature, I have described several proposals concerning how we ought to reconceive the notion of a human being. It seems to me that these proposals ought to receive critical attention from both feminist theorists and their more traditional philosophical brethren.

I argued in Part One that feminist theorists need not reject metaphysics, and I suggested that the anti-metaphysical stances of Rorty and Lyotard provided scant resources for the critical projects of feminism. In Part Two these ideas were illustrated by considering Catharine MacKinnon's analysis of pornography. A careful look at the terms of her critique showed that she does use (and must use) categories that transcend their historical and social niche in her criticism of the current, patriarchal understanding of pornography. Although I have not claimed that all feminist theories must engage in metaphysical reflection, I have argued this for feminist critiques of the history of philosophy, for Gilliganism, and for Feminism Unmodified.

It is hard to envision a philosophical community in which feminist theory is fully integrated. In part this is because feminism is a political movement as well as a theoretical one. Political movements, no matter how well justified and necessary, create waves of dissension and conflict. And so it is unlikely that Aristotelians and feminists will see any relationship between their respective philosophical concerns in the near future. In contrast, I see the philosophical tradition as continuous, and this chapter sketches one portrait of it in which feminist reflections concerning what it is to be human find a place alongside those of Aristotle.[37]

Notes

1. Some feminists might object that I am referring to an entity called "feminist theory" that (does not exist. There are many feminist theories, and the very notion of theoretical unity is one that has been criticized by feminists for its essentialist tendencies. For a development of this point, see Elizabeth V. Spelman's *The Inessential Woman: Problems of Exclusion in Feminist Thought* (Boston: Beacon Press, 1988). I agree that there are many feminist theories floating around; indeed, I discuss two of them in Part Two of this chapter. On the other hand, although I cannot defend the point here, I see nothing wrong with thinking about feminist theory the way we think about Marxism or liberal political theory, as referring to a variety of theories united by a shared perspective.

2. The position that postmodernism's rejection of traditional metaphysics and epistemology is (with a few modifications) the appropriate perspective for feminist theorizing is articulated in many of the essays (and the introduction) of Linda J. Nicholson, ed., *Feminism/Postmodernism* (New York: Routledge, 1990). A genuine rarity in feminist philosophy is Ann Garry and Marilyn Pearsall, eds., *Women, Knowledge, and Reality: Explorations in Feminist Philosophy* (Boston: Unwin Hyman, 1989), which contains three essays under the heading "Feminist Metaphysics."

3. I am treating these two positions as mutually exclusive—but are they? Perhaps the criticism and eventual rejection of metaphysics itself constitutes a kind of contribution to metaphysics. If, for example, we come to see the metaphysical tradition as permeated by misogyny, or if we come to adopt an ironic perspective toward it, don't these attitudes contribute to our understanding of metaphysics *without* continuing the metaphysical project? Feminist criticisms of the history of philosophy do indeed help us to understand it in a new way, and they can do so without doing metaphysics. But, as I argue in Part One of this essay, feminist criticisms of the history of philosophy are neutral with regard to the question of the rejection of metaphysics; I would not consider a critique of sexism in Aristotle, for example, to be equivalent to a rejection of metaphysics.

4. For a recent, feminist effort along these lines, see Jean Hampton's chapter in this volume.

5. Nancy Fraser and Linda Nicholson, "Social Criticism Without Philosophy: An Encounter Between Feminism and Postmodernism," in *The Institution of Philosophy,* ed. by Avner Cohen and Marcelo Dascal (La Salle, Ill.: Open Court, 1989), 285.

6. Richard Rorty, *Objectivity, Relativism, and Truth* (Cambridge: Cambridge University Press, 1991), 7.

7. Jean-François Lyotard, "The Postmodern Condition," *After Philosophy,* ed. by Kenneth Baynes, James Bohman, and Thomas McCarthy (Cambridge: MIT Press, 1987), 73.

8. Ibid., 89.

9. In "Cosmopolitanism Without Emancipation: A Response to Jean-François Lyotard," in *Objectivity, Relativism, and Truth,* Rorty provides a helpful discussion of the differences between his thought and Lyotard's.

10. Rorty, *Objectivity, Relativity, and Truth,* 13.

11. For a discussion of this point see "Social Criticism Without Philosophy" (289–290).

12. Richard Rorty, "Feminism and Pragmatism," *Michigan Quarterly Review* 1, 2 (Spring 1991).

13. Ibid., 237.

14. Ibid., 250.

15. Rorty argues in "Postmodernist Bourgeois Liberalism," in *Objectivity, Relativity, and Truth,* that postmodernism is not relativistic. "To accuse postmodernism of relativism is to try to put a metanarrative in the postmodernist's mouth. One will do this if one identifies 'holding a philosophical position' with having a metanarrative available" (202). Rorty makes this comment in response to the charge that postmodernism is relativism and that relativism is self-refuting. In this essay. Rorty labels himself a "postmodernist" and defends his view from the charge of relativism (and self-refutation). But it is unclear that this defense will work for Lyotard. For Lyotard—insofar as he holds that all languages are necessarily local (an apparently absolute statement)—does embrace relativism and is open to the charge of self-refutation. For a criticism of Lyotard's thought as inadequate for progressive political change, see Seyla Benhabib, "Epistemologies of Postmodernism: A Rejoinder to Jean-François Lyotard," in Nicholson, ed., *Feminism/Postmodernism,* 107–130.

16. Iris Young, "Impartiality and the Civic Public: Some Implications of Feminist Critiques of Moral and Political Theory," in *Feminism as Critique,* ed. by Seyla Benhabib and Drucilla Cornell (Minneapolis: University of Minnesota Press, 1987), 58.

17. For a survey of works on reason and gender in the philosophical tradition, see Karen J. Warren, "Selected Bibliography on Western Philosophical Conceptions of Reason, Rationality, and Gender," *APA Newsletter on Feminism and Philosophy* 88, 2 (March 1989).

18. Genevieve Lloyd, *The Man of Reason* (Minneapolis: University of Minnesota Press, 1984), 104. For a survey of the different ways in which feminists have described reason as male, see Karen J. Warren, "Male-Gender Bias and Western Conceptions of Reasons and Rationality," *APA Newsletter on Feminism and Philosophy* 88, 2 (March 1989).

19. An objection to the distinction between "fruits" and "activity" is that the male bias is implicated not just in the fruits of metaphysical reflection (i.e., the substantive doctrines or theories) but also in the kinds of questions metaphysicians have traditionally raised. But the fact that some (or all) of the questions that have been asked are male-biased does not show that the activity itself is male-biased. A feminist metaphysician might ask very different questions but still be engaged in fundamentally the same philosophical activity.

20. Warren, *Male Gender Bias,* 52.

21. The locus classicus is Carol Gilligan, *In a Different Voice* (Cambridge 1982). The term *Gilliganism* was coined by Sally Haslanger.

22. Catharine A. MacKinnon, *Feminism Unmodified* (Cambridge, Mass.: Harvard University Press, 1987).

23. Suzanna Sherry, "Civic Virtue and the Feminine Voice in Constitutional Adjudications," *Virginia Law Review* 72 (1986): 543.

24. See, e.g., "On *In a Different Voice*: An Interdisciplinary Forum," *Signs* 11, 2 (1986).

25. See Claudia Card, "Women's Voices and Ethical Ideals: Must We Mean What We Say?" *Ethics* 99, 1 (1988).

26. *Signs* 11, 2 (1986): 327.

27. Ibid., 333.

28. MacKinnon, *Feminism Unmodified,* 34.

29. Ibid., 39.

30. Ibid., 209.

31. Ibid., 49.

32. Ibid., 209.

33. Ibid., 211.

34. Ibid., 52.

35. In "Feminism and Pragmatism," Rorty acknowledges the "realist" strain in MacKinnon's thought: "We see it as unfortunate that many feminists intermingle pragmatist and realist rhetoric. For example, MacKinnon at one point defines feminism as the belief 'that women are human beings in truth but not in social reality.' The phrase 'in truth' here can only mean 'in reality which is distinct from social reality,' one which is as it is whether or not women ever succeed in saying what has never been heard." (p. 263) In contrast to Rorty, I argue that it is the pragmatist or postmodern strain in MacKinnon's thought that is misguided, and that the realism Rorty laments is just what MacKinnon needs in order to make her argument against pornography.

36. *Feminism Unmodified* is often criticized as an "essentialist" theory in that it makes universal claims (nonlocal claims) about women. In my view, the essentialist criticism is not telling, but it provides more evidence that MacKinnon does not accept a Lyotardian metaphilosophy. For a discussion of essentialism in MacKinnon, see Elizabeth Rapaport's essay in this volume.

37. This essay was hard to write, and it was nursed along by my colleagues in the Philosophy Department at the University of New Hampshire, Durham; I thank in particular Paul MacNamara, Bill deVries, and Ken Westphal. Mark Okrent and Sally Haslanger talked through several issues with me and encouraged me to think that I had something to say.

14

RESURRECTING EMBODIMENT: TOWARD A FEMINIST MATERIALISM

ROBIN MAY SCHOTT

In the *Symposium,* Plato distinguishes between those whose "procreancy is of the body, who turn to woman as the object of their love," and "those whose procreancy is of the spirit rather than the flesh" (*Symposium,* 208e–209a). Love of the pure form of beauty is "unsullied, unalloyed, and freed from the mortal taint that haunts the frailer loveliness of flesh and blood" (*Symposium,* 211e).

The ascetic tradition in Western philosophy has been haunted since its inception by the threat of death inherent in human procreative love and has sought immortality in the quest for pure, ideal forms of knowledge. Women, becoming the symbolic embodiment of the pollution arising from birth and death, were thus excluded from the philosophical community. Socrates's fame rested not on his helping to birth human life but on his role as the "midwife" of ideas. And he sought to transcend human mortality through the philosophical discipline of "separating the soul as much as possible from the body" (*Phaedo,* 67c–d), which provided the only path to immortality.[1] Far from valuing the birth and sustenance of human life as the necessary precondition for philosophical thought, philosophers from Plato to Kant have relegated procreation and child rearing to a lower sphere of human activity. Freed of these responsibilities, the philosopher has been able to seek universal and necessary truths in the realm of pure ideas.

Feminist theory through the 1970s and 1980s has documented what Genevieve Lloyd has termed the "maleness" of reason.[2] Indeed, this historical critique has been so substantial and compelling that many feminists have become impatient with the work of rereading the canon. The time has finally come, it would seem, in which feminist theorists can shift from historical critique to the creative job of defining a new path for feminist theory. In pursuing new directions, however, feminist theorists need to be wary of reiterating assumptions inherited from the ascetic tradition in Western philosophy that they purportedly seek to reject.[3]

In this essay, I will use the lens of pregnancy and birthing[4] to examine the course of contemporary feminist discussions of rationality. I will consider the ways in which radical feminists who reject motherhood and postmodern feminists who deconstruct "women" reiterate a conception of reason drawn from ascetic philosophy from Plato to Kant. Although these feminists seek to critique patriarchal rationality, their own theories become built on a transcendence of the temporal, embodied world—and of women's bodies in particular—that is inherited from their ascetic forefathers. I will begin to explore the possibility of a feminist materialist perspective that provides an alternative to this ascetic tradition and that can help develop "women"-defined images and practices of pregnancy and childbirth.

In debates concerning the distinctively "feminist" contribution to theory, the question of "sexual difference" has been an embattled front. In *Am I That Name? Feminism and the Category of "Women" in History,* Denise Riley argues that the question of sexual difference has vacillated historically within feminism itself.[5] It has been seen as an impediment to change, or as an alternative to the manly values that have perpetuated classism and militarism, or both at once. Similarly, the fluctuations concerning the role of sexual difference in feminism have been mirrored by fluctuations in the treatment of "women's experience," and in particular of women's experience of motherhood.

Radical feminists, for example, have both glorified and denounced motherhood. It has been viewed as a source of a feminine Eros or life force. Huanani-Kay Trask writes, "The 'return to the mother' has meant a simultaneous 'return to the body' where feminists have learned that a mother's love—the love of life—entails a love and acceptance of the body. In this sense, the 'return to the mother' is a return to synthesis because mother-love does not separate body from mind, spirit from form."[6] Motherhood has also been rejected on the grounds that "motherhood is dangerous to women." Jeffner Allen writes, "If [a woman], in patriarchy, is she who exists as the womb and wife of man, every woman is by definition a mother. . . . Motherhood is dangerous to women because it continues the structure within which females must be women and mothers and, conversely, because it denies to females the creation of a subjectivity and world that is open and free."[7] Motherhood is viewed as dangerous not only because the chances are that women sleep with the enemy (though these chances may be reduced by the development of reproductive technology), but also because they run the risk of reproducing the enemy. "*Vous travaillez pour l'armee, madame?*"— the question posed to Adrienne Rich as the mother of three sons—is reiterated throughout her landmark book, *Of Woman Born.*[8]

The fluctuations in the treatment of motherhood follow the same historical logic as the fluctuations of the category of "women." Both romanticization and denunciation of motherhood grow from the critique of women's historical subjugation and the effort to transform it. Standpoint theorists (such as Dorothy Smith and Nancy Hart-sock) and radical feminists (such as Trask) treat women's experience of the dailiness of care as providing a basis for developing an alternative to masculine theory. Others, such as Jeffner Allen, denounce motherhood as itself wholly a product of oppressive conditions. Allen writes, "Freedom is never achieved by the mere inversion of an oppressive construct, that is, by seeing motherhood in a 'new' light. Freedom is achieved when an oppressive construct, motherhood, is vacated by its members and thereby rendered null and void."[9]

The rejection of the *institution* of motherhood is a response to the history in which women's lives have been at the mercy of their childbearing capacities. In *Of Woman Born,* Rich argues that the patriarchal institution of motherhood has ensured that the potential relation of any woman to reproduction and to children has remained under mate control. "Most women in history have become mothers without choice, and an even greater number have lost their lives bringing life into the world."[10] Only since the 1960s has reproductive choice been widespread in the Western world,[11] and this choice has been directly threatened by antiabortion activists and politicians, as well as by eugenicists who force young black women to be sterilized.

But ironically, feminists who reject not only motherhood as a patriarchal institution, but motherhood per se, reiterate the devaluation of motherhood as a source of knowledge and love that has underpinned the ascetic tradition in Western philosophy. In Allen's view, "The moment of birth and the moment of death have, in themselves, no special value. . . . Similarly, I no longer give a primacy to that which I have reproduced. I claim as primary my life and world as I create and experience them."[12] The moments of birth and death have signified historically the irrefutable temporal, embodied character of human existence. It is precisely for this reason that Platonic philosophy sought to transcend these moments, and it was women's link with birth and death that excluded them from philosophical thought. In rejecting the primacy of birth and death for human existence and in defining freedom as the freedom from the material constraints of motherhood, Jeffner Allen unwittingly follows Plato's lead. The self becomes a wholly self-created, self-controlling being, immune to the material conditions that inform individual existence.

Although some radical feminists argue for the evacuation of women from the category of motherhood, postmodern feminists argue more encompassingly for their evacuation from the concept of "women." Just as "woman" has been criticized as falsely asserting an essence to women, so "women" too has come under attack as a falsely homogeneous, normative, exclusionary category. Judith Butter writes,

When the category is understood as representing a set of values or dispositions, it becomes normative in character and hence exclusionary in principle. . . . [A] variety of women from various cultural positions have refused to recognize themselves as "women" in the terms articulated by feminist theory with the result that these women fall outside the category and are left to conclude that (1) either they are not women as they have perhaps previously assumed or (2) the category reflects the restricted location of its theoreticians and, hence, fails to recognize the intersection of gender with race, class, ethnicity, age, sexuality, and other currents which contribute to the formation of cultural (non) identity.[13]

This critique of the category of women is in part motivated by political strife within the feminist movement. Throughout the 1980s, the American women's movement has been charged with racism in treating women's identity as white women's identity, and in particular as middle-class heterosexual white women's identity. Conferences have been called, tears have been shed, and articles have been written. Although some feminists seek to correct the ethnocentrism in feminist theory by talking about women in their heterogeneity,[14] postmodern feminists seek more radically to reject the category of women altogether. For example, although Denise Riley considers it helpful to talk about "elderly Cantonese women living in Soho" instead of generalizing about women, this specification still comes to rest on "women," and it is this isolation that she seeks to question.[15] This deconstruction of gender draws its theoretical arsenal from white male European theorists such as Jacques Derrida, Michel Foucault, and Jean-François Lyotard. These theorists seek to undermine the premises of Western metaphysical thinking by rejecting the view that knowledge can be founded either in the knowing subject or the object of knowledge. They turn instead to the field of language, to the realms of discursive historical formation, as that which constitutes us as subjects and which provides the site of possible resistance.[16] In rejecting foundationalism, they also refuse to treat the body as a starting point or source of truth. The body is itself an effect of discursive practices. In "Nietzsche, Genealogy, History," Foucault writes, "The body is the inscribed surface of events (traced by language and dissolved by ideas), the locus of a dissociated self (adopting the illusion of a substantial unity), and a volume in perpetual disintegration."[17]

In debates within feminist theory, the postmodernist critique has been used to battle the hidden metaphysical commitments of liberal, Marxist, and radical feminists. Both liberal and Marxist feminists are shown to be products of the Enlightenment search for a unitary truth and a complete liberation from domination. They ultimately seek to include women in the "man of reason's" ideals of universality and full emancipation. Radical feminists, along with conservative antifeminists, retain the Enlightenment dichotomies as well. Instead of seeking to join the man of reason, however, they seek to revalorize the feminine side of the dichotomies between male and female, rational and irrational, culture and nature, without recognizing the ways in which the feminine is itself a product of the history of oppression.[18] Postmodern feminism does not seek a "feminist epistemology," for such a term retains the Enlightenment notion of a unitary truth, albeit an alternative, feminist path to truth. A postmodern feminism would "reject the masculinist bias of rationalism but would not attempt to replace it with a feminist bias. Rather it would take the position that there is not one (masculine) truth but, rather, many truths, none of which is privileged along gendered lines."[19]

The postmodern prioritization of discourse as that which constitutes bodies in the field of power relations has a number of consequences for feminist theory. It implies for example, that women's experience of their bodies can no longer be taken as a foundation for feminist theory. Radical theorists such as Andrea Dworkin and Catharine MacKinnon have used women's sexuality—in particular the objectification and exploitation of women evident in pornography and violence against women—as a touchstone for feminist theory. Feminist-standpoint theorists argue that understanding women's experiences can lead to a more complete, less distorted form of knowledge than that grounded in men's experiences.[20] But if women's bodies are thoroughly constituted by the discursive operations of power, they cannot provide a foundation for feminist theory.

It is the failure of either sex or gender to fulfill the dream of a solid, ongoing foundation that leads postmodern feminists to argue that there are no women.[21] Riley poses the question, "How could someone 'be a woman' through and through, make a final home in that classification without suffering claustrophobia? To lead a life soaked in the passionate consciousness of one's gender at every single moment, to will to be a sex with a vengeance—these are impossibilities and far from the aims of feminism." Instead, one should reflect on the question, "At this instant, am I a woman as distinct from a human being?"[22] The postmodern ambivalence regarding women is frighteningly reminiscent of the New Woman of the 1920s, who claimed, "We're interested in people now—not men and women."[23] Donna Haraway takes the logical next step in the deconstruction of women by deconstructing altogether the distinction between human, animal, and machine. "Why should our bodies end at the skin or include at best other beings encapsulated by skin?" she writes in her fantasy of the cyborg.[24]

What are the implications of this deconstruction of women for the historical fate of pregnancy and birth? Apparently, to raise the question is already to be guilty of relying on the categories of oppression that postmodern feminists seek to deconstruct. Like some radical feminists, Denise Riley situates "women's experience" as the product of oppression. "The phrase works curiously, for it implies that the experiences originate with the women, and it masks the likelihood that instead these have accrued to women not by virtue of their womanhood alone, but as traces of domination, whether natural or political."[25] It is true, Riley acknowledges, that women have the capacity for childbearing and therefore can be targeted by natalist or antinatalist plans. But the point is that "only some prior lens which intends to focus on 'women's bodies' is going to set them in such a light. The body becomes visible *as* a body, and *as* a female body, only under some particular gaze—including that of politics.[26]

What is the significance of this refusal of any gaze that focuses on aspects of women's bodies linked to pregnancy and childbirth? Postmodern feminists tend to ignore these issues altogether.[27] When they mention motherhood in passing, they follow Simone de Beauvoir and Shulamith Firestone in wholly identifying it with women's oppression. We have leaped from the philosophical transcendence of pregnancy and birth as a pollution threatening the higher reaches of philosophical thought, to radical and postmodern feminists who treat motherhood strictly as "traces of domination." Both classical and contemporary positions articulate an ascetic mistrust of embodiment, which precludes an affirmation of birthing in philosophical thought.[28]

What we may be witnessing, as Rosi Braidotti points out, is the inability of the postmodern era to come to terms with time.[29] We may need to recognize that it takes time to develop women-centered theories and practices related to menstruation, pregnancy, childbirth, and menopause. By disregarding this historical stage, postmodernism reiterates the classical philosophical desire to transcend the process of temporal change. This philosophical transcendence of time has been rooted in a transcendence of bodily identity, now resurrected in the current deconstruction of women. It is provocative to sweep away the old-fashioned categories of individual and group identity, to seek to define oneself in the radical freedom "which does not follow from any postulation of our nature or essence."[30] And it is certainly true that in the battle for AIDS research, white lesbians have more commonality with white gay men than they do with homophobic women—thereby bypassing any so-called solidarity based on gender. Nonetheless, it remains historically true that the events of menstruation, pregnancy, childbirth, and menopause form significant junctures in women's lives, with varying degrees of intensity. To delegitimate reflection on this sphere of human existence is to reiterate the categories of masculine thought that postmodernism ostensibly seeks to deconstruct.

This move to explode gender and to reject the lens that focuses on women's embodied experience is in part inspired by the criticism of racism, classism, and heterosexism in the women's movement mentioned above. If black women, whether heterosexual or lesbian, do not recognize themselves in the gendered characterizations of white feminist theory, then the emphasis must be taken off the category of women and shifted to other dimensions of "identity"—such as racial experience and sexual choice and the tensions that exist between these junctures. Only then can feminism begin to consider, for example, the particular conflicts faced by black women who criticize sexism and homophobia within black communities while retaining allegiance to them. Only then can lesbians challenge the normative heterosexuality that still exists in the recesses of many feminists' consciousness.

The attempt to account for the insidious operation of racial, class, and heterosexist consciousness within feminist theories and movements should remain primary on our agenda as critics and activists. Yet there are a number of ironies in the manner in which white feminist theorists have sought to do this. As bell hooks points out, "Postmodernist discourses are often exclusionary even as they call attention to, appropriate even, the experience of 'difference' and 'Otherness.'"[31] The vast majority of writings on postmodernism have no reference to black women writers.[32] Theoretically, affirming the recognition of difference does not itself constitute a grappling with racial consciousness—as it exists in the white theorist herself or as it exists among blacks. To come to grips with racism necessitates that whites recognize that their implicit view that to have a race is to be black is itself a racist assumption. As hooks points out, white women often bond on the basis of shared racial identity. A group of white feminists may meet at a conference and feel their solidarity is based on shared political concerns. But if the atmosphere changes when a black woman walks in the room, this closeness is revealed as an expression of their racial identity, which treats nonwhite people as "other."[33] Needless to say, this bonding occurs in theory as well as in practice. To grapple with racism also means to engage with the struggles, writings, and works of art created by blacks. And it means acknowledging that treating a black writer or speaker as special or exotic is itself a sign of patronizing consciousness.[34]

Black writers, like hooks, who are sympathetic to the possibility of radical postmodern consciousness based on a critique of essentialism nonetheless do not abandon concerns drawn from their experience as black women. Angela Davis and bell hooks share the criticisms raised more abstractly by white postmodern writers that the mainstream American women's movement has been exclusionary from its inception.[35] But they abandon neither *black* nor *women* in trying to render the struggle of Afro-American women visible. Rejecting a lens that brings into focus the struggles of black women in pregnancy, childbirth, and child rearing is not progressive; it is a symptom of the lack of racial consciousness of postmodern critics. Rather, a multiracial women's movement needs to focus on issues such as how black women's health is affected by prevailing political conditions. Pregnant black women, uninsured and with no means of paying hospital entrance fees, have been known to give birth in parking lots outside of the hospitals that have refused them entrance. Black women who are subscribers to health plans have been denied treatment because hospital officials have presumed they were lying about their health coverage.[36] In the United States, black infant mortality is twice that of whites, and maternal mortality is three times as high.[37]

Clearly, rather than arguing for an abolition of the family, as many white feminists do, it is necessary to recognize that the family can also be the context for experiencing dignity and self-worth in an exploitative society, as it has been for blacks from the period of enslavement to the present.[38] Rather than devaluing family life entirely, what we may need is a multiracial effort to free it of its exploitative dimensions. We need to ensure, in our theories and politics, that women have the choice to limit the size of their families by access to contraception and abortion or to increase the size of their families by fighting sterilization abuse and poverty.[39]

In reflecting on the postmodern aversion to discussions of pregnancy, childbirth, or child rearing, I cannot help but agree with Susan Bordo's suspicion that it may be a result of women gaining a foothold in the professions that historically have excluded them.[40] The university itself is a historical product of an ascetic Christian tradition,[41] and it still refuses to acknowledge that a scholar may have a personal life as well. It makes me wonder how far we have come from Kant's ridicule of the idea that a woman could be a scholar. Postmodern feminists seem intent to repeat this perception by proving that they are not really "women." Therefore, they pose no danger of raising issues concerning women's role in the generation of life as opposed to the generation of theory.[42]

Instead of abandoning women, feminists may need to consider developing a renewed form of materialism, one that considers the social relations involved in the processes of menstruation, pregnancy, birth, childbearing, and child rearing. Although I am invoking the term *materialism,* I will avoid embarking into the murky waters of definition and justification. There are many versions of materialism and many debates about its nature and method. In fact, seeking to theoretically define materialism may be counter to its critique of abstract and hypostatized thought.[43] Instead, I will use the term to indicate a practical and philosophical orientation, in the spirit of Marx's philosophy, that is opposed both to idealism and to reductionist materialism. In this usage, materialism is committed to concrete, historiographical research and to the significance of human practice in understanding the social world,

I am not the first to call for a feminist materialism. Other writers, notably Shulamith Firestone, Mary O'Brien, and Nancy Hartsock, have embarked on this path.[44] These theorists rely on a metatheory of dialectical materialism drawn from the Hegelian-Marxist tradition but shift the focus to the reproductive sphere, which remained a blind spot in this tradition. However, feminists can no more adopt a full-fledged Hegelian-Marxist methodology than they can adopt a full-scale Foucauldian or Derridian perspective. The political and theoretical crisis in Marxism—since 1968 and with the current disillusion of the socialist dream in Eastern Europe—precludes transplanting a Marxist "method" to feminist problems. But it is fruitful to explore the intersections and tensions that emerge between Marxism and postmodernism, both of which are forms of "oppositional thinking."[45]

The postmodern critique of universality convincingly debunks universalist claims about women's standpoint and reproductive consciousness,[46] as well as the claim that a feminist materialism is the strategy for "opposing all forms of domination."[47] Women's bodies cannot provide a "foundation" for feminist theory, nor can feminist theory serve as a "foundation" for all possible emancipatory strategies. But one can develop materialist insights without subscribing to the dream of a universal revolutionary consciousness that will bring about emancipation from all forms of domination. Minimally, I would argue for the coexistence of a materialist lens with the linguistic lens that has prevailed in the twentieth century, in order to bring into focus the social relations involved in the generation of new life.[48] This approach would revalue both in theory and in practice procreative experiences, in contrast to the postmodern rejection of an analytics of procreation.

One danger with this strategy is that one is faced with the charges of essentialism or biologism. Doesn't developing feminist theories of birth and child rearing merely reiterate the traditional identification of women with these spheres? Doesn't one continue to assert that women's true nature resides in their procreative capacity? Doesn't such a strategy once again reduce women's choices to a biologically determined sexual nature, thereby belittling women who choose to mother as well as those who refuse the choice of motherhood?

It is important to bear these charges in mind, to avoid romanticizing motherhood, and to reject ahistorical, naturalist conceptions of procreation. Postmodernists are valuable in stressing the complex and multiple positions in which individuals find themselves. Thus attempting to understand the historical significance of procreation in a given epoch would include focuses on race, class, ethnicity, religion, technology, and epidemic. A woman is never just pregnant nor just a mother. Even within a racially and nationally homogeneous group of white Danish mothers, a woman's experience of pregnancy and motherhood is refracted through other lenses as well—her age, her educational or job opportunities, her support or nonsupport in child rearing from her partner or extended family, her health and that of her children, her housing, and her emotional configurations. But recognizing that identity is complex does not contradict the observation that vast numbers of women desire to and/or do become mothers; therefore, this phenomenon should remain important on feminist agendas.

Rather than embarking on metatheoretical debates, a feminist materialism should begin with a turn to concrete, historiographical research—one of the methodological contributions of Marx.[49] Such an approach would be attuned to specificity, without eschewing the generality that is inherent in language itself. In describing a postmodern-feminist theory, Nancy Fraser and Linda Nicholson write that it would be "comparativist, rather than universalizing, attuned to changes and contrasts instead of to covering laws."[50] I would add that this description is compatible with a materialist analysis of the social relations of procreation.[51] Emily Martin's *The Woman in the Body* is an interesting contribution to a comparative class and racial analysis of reproduction. Based on interviews with women in Baltimore, Martin explores how class and race inflects the experiences of menstruation and childbirth. She argues, for example, that middle-class white women are prone to accepting a medical model of menstruation, whereas working-class black and white women are apt to talk about what menstruation looks and feels like and what significance it has in terms of life-change.[52] Moreover, Martin notes that the problems of resistance to dominant medical practices change significantly with class position. Whereas middle-class white women may be most concerned to demand birthing rooms, working-class white women need to struggle with the larger issue of managing to pay for prenatal and obstetrical care, and working-class black women also have to struggle against downright mistreatment.[53]

Concrete, historical analyses would enable women to reflect on their own experience as well as to understand the perspectives generated by the experience of other women. Yet one has to be aware of the specific problems involved in drawing on experience. While seeking to be attuned to the "authority" of one's own experience,[54] one must also be aware of the limits of one's locatedness, of falsely generalizing from one's own perspective. Therefore, it is equally necessary to draw on the authority of other women's experience—for example, through conversation and historical and aesthetic works. But white feminist theorists in particular must be aware of the danger of romanticizing or co-opting the experiences of women of color. In trying to overcome the blinders of their own racial consciousness, white women may romanticize black women's experiences as a source of greater authenticity and truth and may even "wish" that they themselves were black as an ultimate expiation of their guilt (knowing that they are safe from realizing this wish, because of the irrefutable fact of their race). White theorists may also "use" or co-opt black women's contributions to prove in the academic arena their own integrity and sensitivity to the issue of race. Both of these responses remain rooted in what Angela Davis has called the "Great White Sister Savior" complex.[55] Yet these dilemmas do not eliminate the necessity for a white theorist to seek to grapple with the multiple authorities of women's experiences, despite the assumptions of privilege in their own consciousness.

In speaking of the "authority" of experience, I am using a concept invoked by standpoint theorists. In my mind, there is something commonsensically true in the claim that people who are most oppressed by structures of power see its effect on them in daily life and do not have the privilege of ignoring it. I was shaken when one of my black students pointed out to me that the readings by black women writers came at the end of the course. Why, she asked, do black writers always appear in the last week or two of a semester? And I had to admit the correctness of her criticism, which had not occurred to me when I planned the course. Yet postmodernists have convincingly criticized standpoint theorists for positing a univocal revolutionary subject that is capable of wholly grasping the "truth" of the social order and of carving a path to total emancipation. A feminist materialism may need, instead, to validate multiple perspectives. But then how does one prioritize perspectives in setting the political agenda for feminist theory? How does one compare the situation of a middle-class mother worrying about the conflict between work and child care with a poor mother's worrying about whether her child will have food for breakfast? In foregoing the dream of a rational foundation for truth or morality, one does not undercut the responsibility of choice. For some feminists, choice will be based on the consciousness of privilege amid inequality; for others, it will be based on the necessity of resistance and the dream of greater freedom.[56]

A "perspectivist" materialism would validate many different avenues for exploring the significance of procreation in women's lives. It would include analyses of the emotional, psychological, and phenomenological dimensions of motherhood, as well as of its social, economic, and political contexts. As for me, trained as a philosopher and having a first child in my middle thirties, I would imagine exploring the implications of pregnancy and motherhood for the traditional philosophical dualisms of mind-body, self-other, subject-object. Postmodernists have criticized these dualisms through a theoretical critique of metaphysics. Marxists have criticized these dualisms through an analysis of the concrete activity of human labor. But new light is shed on these entrenched assumptions through the concrete analysis of birthing. The dichotomy between self and other is inappropriate for understanding the creation of new life. A woman during pregnancy experiences herself as not just one (her bodily integrity) but also as two (the new life within her, dependent yet also separable) and even three (projecting the family that will emerge with the birth). And when a nursing mother's milk "lets down" when her baby cries, even when she is out of hearing range, her body is developing a new "sense" of knowing another human being. This knowledge is not "rational," according to the model of knowledge inherited from the ascetic tradition in Western philosophy. Like the child's knowledge of her/his parents' emotional states, it is a knowledge that displays the sensuous and emotional roots of cognition.

Birthing will also bring into focus the social, political, and economic inhumanity of Western capitalist systems, like the United States, with no adequate welfare net. For example, the lack of any nationally assured maternity leave creates a cruel conflict between work and care in American society. Ironically, some American universities— ostensibly committed to educating the young—still do not provide even six weeks of maternity leave. And six weeks is pathetically inadequate and should be compared with the six months to three years of maternity leave provided to women in Scandinavian countries.[57] Poor and working-class women's experience of motherhood demands attention to the more general issues of social inequality—poverty,[58] unemployment, cutbacks in education and nutrition programs like WIC (Women, Infants, and Children), lack of national health insurance,[59] and lack of child care.[60]

To call for developing a feminist materialist analysis of procreation is not to argue that procreation is the *fundamental* historical dynamic, to identify women's nature with motherhood, or to exclude the perspectives of fathers, nonbiological mothers, and women who choose not to mother. These latter perspectives are also necessary for understanding the significance of procreation. But a feminist materialist perspective does acknowledge that procreation is a precondition for human life and thought and investigates its historical configurations. Western society needs to celebrate and validate the joys of motherhood and to transform its limiting and oppressive features. But if we leap from a Platonic transcendence of human bodies, and women's bodies in particular, to a postmodern deconstruction of human bodies, and women's bodies in particular, we reiterate the devaluation of birthing and motherhood that has marked the ascetic tradition in Western philosophy. Instead, feminists need to face the historically important task of exploring procreation in its emotional, psychological, philosophical, social, technological, medical, legal, and ethical aspects. We live in an era confronting the proliferation of reproductive technologies that can be used to devalue pregnancy and childbirth, to commercialize the creation of children, to create a new class of domestic "surrogate" labor,[61] and to bypass women's bodies altogether. In such times, it is especially urgent for women to develop their own definitions of pregnancy, childbirth, and motherhood in order to resist the increasing technological control over human ends.

Notes

1. See Robin May Schott, *Cognition and Eros: A Critique of the Kantian Paradigm* (Boston: Beacon Press, 1988), chs. 1 and 2.

2. Genevieve Lloyd, *The Man of Reason: "Male" and "Female" in Western Philosophy* (Minneapolis: University of Minnesota Press, 1984).

3. Elizabeth V. Spelman's strategy in *Inessential Woman: Problems of Exclusion in Feminist Thought* (Boston: Beacon Press, 1988), is to point out the ways in which white feminist theorists have repeated in particular the essentialist categories of Western masculine philosophy.

4. I will try to avoid the term "reproduction," which is built on the root "production." This term has been criticized by some feminists as adopting a masculine paradigm of control.

5. Denise Riley, *Am I That Name? Feminism and the Category of "Women" in History* (Minneapolis: University of Minnesota Press, 1988), p. 64.

6. Huanani-Kay Trask, *Eros and Power: The Promise of Feminist Theory* (Philadelphia: University of Pennsylvania Press, 1986), p. 131.

7. Jeffner Allen, "Motherhood: The Annihilation of Women," in Joyce Trebilcot, ed., *Mothering: Essays in Feminist Theory* (Totowa, N.J.: Rowman and Allanheld, 1983), p. 315.

8. Adrienne Rich, *Of Woman Born: Motherhood as Experience and Institution* (New York: W. W. Norton, 1976). See, for example, pp. 30, 192, 193, and 274.

9. Allen, "Motherhood," p. 315.

10. Rich, *Of Woman Born,* p. 13.

11. Jeffrey Weeks, *Sex, Politics, and Society: The Regulation of Sexuality Since 1800* (London: Longman, 1989), p. 260.

12. Allen, "Motherhood," pp. 325–326.

13. Judith Butler, "Gender Trouble, Feminist Theory, and Psychoanalytic Discourse," in Linda J. Nicholson, ed., *Feminism/Postmodernism* (New York: Routledge, 1990), p. 325.

14. Elizabeth Spelman in *Inessential Woman* analyzes the way white Western feminist theory has been as guilty of essentialism regarding the category of woman as Western philosophy has been regarding the category of man. In assuming that one can talk about women as women, who are oppressed as women, and whose gender is isolatable from other elements of identity, white feminists have implicitly assumed a perspective of privilege (p. 165). No black woman, argues Spelman, would seek to separate her experience of oppression from her racial identity in the United States. Spelman thus rejects the language of "difference" because this term itself assumes that difference is difference from a taken-for-granted norm. "The many turn out to be the one, and the one that they are is me" (p. 159).

15. Riley, *Am I That Name?* p. 17.

16. Ibid., p. 5.

17. Michel Foucault, "Nietzsche, Genealogy, History," in *Language, Counter-Memory, Practice: Selected Essays and Interviews,* ed. and tr. Donald F. Bouchard and Sherry Simon (Ithaca, N.Y.: Cornell University Press, 1977), p. 148.

18. Susan J. Hekman, *Gender and Knowledge: Elements of a Postmodern Feminism* (Cambridge, Mass.: Polity Press, 1990), pp. 39–40.

19. Ibid., p. 9.

20. Nancy Hartsock, "The Feminist Standpoint: Developing the Grounds for a Specifically Feminist Historical Materialism," in Sandra Harding and Merrill B. Hintikka, eds., *Discovering Reality: Feminist Perspectives in Epistemology, Metaphysics, Methodology, and Philosophy of Science* (Dordrecht: D. Reidel, 1983), p. 294.

21. Sandra Harding notes that "paradoxically, feminist postmodernists adhere to some powerful Enlightenment assumptions" ("Feminism, Science, and the Anti-Enlightenment Critiques," in Nicholson, ed., *Feminism/Postmodernism,* p. 99). One of these assumptions may be that if there is no sure foundation for concepts (e.g., women), then these concepts should be abandoned altogether.

22. Riley, *Am I That Name?* p. 6. Denise Riley's aversion to the claustrophobia of being a woman is reminiscent of Sartre's discussion of bad faith in *Being and Nothingness.* The waiter who sought to be a waiter in every moment of his existence became, for Sartre, the paradigm of bad faith—of abandoning free human choice by becoming a role, an object. Although Denise Riley would analyze identity in terms of positions or locations, instead of Sartrean choice, she nonetheless retains the language of a philosophy of consciousness. It is the problematic nature of the waiter's consciousness that concerns Sartre, just as it is the consciousness of gender that Riley addresses as the clue to its temporal discontinuity.

But surely being a gender is not merely having a consciousness of being a gender. Although I was not always conscious of my gender in my recent role as student of Danish, I would have to acknowledge that gender was implicated in my willingness to learn yet another language in my thirties because it is my husband's language, in the compulsiveness of my study, and in the eroticization of relations in the classroom. I do not mean to suggest that men do not also become zealous students of new languages as adults. One of my classmates, a man from San Francisco who was "married" under Danish law to a Danish man, was also learning Danish because it was his husband's language. However, his student identity was not compartmentalized from his embodied identity as a gay black American man in a committed marital relationship. Complexity of identity shatters stereotypes, but it does not necessarily entail the fragmentation enlisted in the postmodern account of "nonidentity."

In raising the question concerning the boundaries between being a woman and being a human being, Riley also fails to bring into focus the problematic nature of the concept of human person. Her text is littered with references to "people," "human being," "persons," and even "humanity" (as opposed to "Humanity"), as if she recognizes the need for *some* identifying concepts in order to write. Yet in using "person" as an unexplained reference, she herself falls into the humanist assumptions that she purportedly seeks to reject. The critiques of the concept of "human being" have been so substantial as not to require repetition. Recall Sartre's discussion in *Anti-Semite and Jew* of the hidden prejudicial norms of the "democrat." Think of James Baldwin's critique of the hidden white premises of liberalism in *The Fire Next Time*. And it hardly needs to be mentioned that the concept of person has been one of the central targets of feminist critique of the Western masculine philosophical canon. In a society structured by power relations, the notions of personhood are never neutral.

23. Quoted in Susan Bordo, "Feminism, Postmodernism, and Gender-Skepticism," in Nicholson, ed., *Feminism/Postmodernism,* p. 152.

24. Donna Haraway, "A Manifesto for Cyborgs," in Nicholson, ed., *Feminism/Postmodernism,* p. 220.

25. Riley, *Am I That Name?* p. 99.

26. Ibid., p. 106.

27. Witness the absence of any articles on pregnancy or childbirth in two recent collections: Irene Diamond and Lee Quinby, eds., *Feminism and Foucault: Reflections on Resistance* (Boston: Northeastern University Press, 1988), and Nicholson, ed., *Feminism/Postmodernism.*

28. Of course, postmodernists do not distrust merely the body; all concepts are viewed as intertwined with regimes of power. Foucault's interest in problematics led him to remark, "Everything is dangerous" ("Afterword," in Hubert L. Dreyfus and Paul Rabinow, *Michel Foucault: Beyond Structuralism and Hermeneutics* [Chicago: University of Chicago Press, 1982], p. 232). But Foucault's analysis of body-power has been particularly influential in recent feminist debates. Foucauldians could analyze the medical treatment of maternity in terms of a nexus of power relations. This project would be an important contribution to an analysis of pregnancy and childbirth. Nonetheless, a Foucauldian position could not account for the positive ways in which motherhood contributes to human worth.

29. Rosi Braidotti emphasizes the importance of time in bringing about a "woman-identified redefinition of female subjectivity, of motherhood, of heterosexuality," in "Organs Without Bodies," *Differences* (Winter 1989): 158.

30. John Rajchman's discussion of Foucault's ethics, quoted in Diamond and Quinby, eds., *Feminism and Foucault,* p. xiv. The similarity between this Foucauldian definition of freedom and the existential definition of freedom should be noted. Existentialism has also been problematic in dealing with the materiality of existence.

31. bell hooks, "Postmodern Blackness," in hooks, *Yearning: Race, Gender, and Cultural Politics* (Boston: South End Press, 1984), p. 23.

32. This is true, for example, of the works by Denise Riley and Judith Butler discussed above. Moreover, there are no contributions by black women in the collection *Feminism/Postmodernism*. In my view, this is one more sign of the metatheoretical obsession of this discourse and its divorce from concrete life.

33. bell hooks, *Feminist Theory: From Margin to Center* (Boston: South End Press, 1984), pp. 54–55.

34. hooks speaks frankly of the temptation to be the exotic celebrity in her essay "Third World Diva Girls: Politics of Feminist Solidarity," in hooks, *Yearning*. I have witnessed the phenomenon of a black speaker being treated with a hands-off reverential attitude by white listeners, because of their fear of showing racist sentiment, thus foreclosing the possibility of appropriate intellectual debate.

35. For a history of racism in the American women's movement, see Angela Davis, *Women, Race, and Class* (New York: Random House, 1981).

36. Angela Davis, *Women, Culture, and Politics* (New York: Random House, 1989), p. 55.

37. Ibid., p. 58.

38. hooks, "The Significance of the Feminist Movement," in hooks, *Feminist Theory*, p. 37. See also Angela Davis's discussion of black families during enslavement in *Women, Race, and Class*.

39. In my reading of postmodern feminists, I have been somewhat shocked to discover that references by other feminists to positive features of motherhood are dismissed as naively reviving a conservative familialist ideology (see, for example, Susan Hekman's critique of Sara Ruddick's *Maternal Thinking: Towards a Politics of Peace* [Boston: Beacon Press, 1989] in *Gender and Knowledge*, p. 41). It is true that historically, pronatalists and eugenicists have supported the practice of motherhood. However, eugenicists were also early advocates of birth control and genetic counseling (Weeks, *Sex, Politics, and Society*, p. 136). Surely this is not grounds to reject birth control in contemporary society. Any good genealogy needs to account for the historical transformations of institutions and values and not study first origins in order to ascribe unchanging meaning to these phenomena.

40. Bordo, "Feminism, Postmodernism, and Gender-Skepticism," in Nicholson, ed., *Feminism/Postmodernism*, p. 151.

41. See the discussion of the ascetic origins of the university in chapter 6 of my book, *Cognition and Eros*.

42. The behavior of many academic women unfortunately supports my perception that when a woman becomes a mother, she is immediately suspect as a scholar.

43. Tom Bottomore, Laurence Harris, V. G. Kiernan, and Ralph Miliband, eds., *A Dictionary of Marxist Thought* (Cambridge, Mass.: Harvard University Press, 1983), p. 328.

44. See Shulamith Firestone, *The Dialectic of Sex* (New York: Morrow, 1970); Mary O'Brien, *The Politics of Reproduction* (Boston: Routledge and Kegan Paul, 1981); and Nancy Hartsock, "The Feminist Standpoint: Developing the Ground for a Specifically Feminist Historical Materialism," in Harding and Hintikka, eds. *Discovering Reality*.

45. Barry Smart, *Foucault, Marxism, and Critique* (London: Routledge and Kegan Paul, 1983), p. 135. Michael Ryan's *Marxism and Deconstruction* (Baltimore: Johns Hopkins University Press, 1982) addresses the relation between Marxism and Derrida's thought.

46. For example, Mary O'Brien writes, "The female reproductive consciousness whose historical reality we are attempting to establish is a universal consciousness, common to all women." *Politics of Reproduction,* p. 50.

47. Hartsock, "Feminist Standpoint," in Harding and Hintikka, eds., *Discovering Reality,* p. 283.

48. In choosing the word *coexistence,* I am acknowledging the plurality of theory. This could be interpreted as a postmodern move or it could be viewed as a more commonsense recognition that one can make an argument for just about anything. The point, therefore, is to interrogate the motivating desire or interest in theory. This does not entail relativism or nihilism. Rather, I agree with Sandra Harding that "if one gives up the goal of telling one true story about reality, one must (not) also give up trying to tell less false stories" ("Feminism, Science, and the Anti-Enlightenment Critiques," in Nicholson, ed., *Feminism/Postmodernism,* p. 100).

49. Bottomore et al., eds., *Dictionary of Marxist Thought,* p. 324. Marx's opposition to abstract philosophical reflection, in his critique of idealism, implies that theoretical tools emerge from concrete historiographical research.

50. Nancy Fraser and Linda J. Nicholson, "Social Criticism Without Philosophy," in Nicholson, ed., *Feminism/Postmodernism,* p. 34.

51. The comparison between genealogy, to which Nancy Fraser and Linda Nicholson refer, and materialism is an important topic that cannot be pursued here.

52. Emily Martin, *The Woman in the Body: A Cultural Analysis of Reproduction* (Boston: Beacon Press, 1987), p. 108.

53. Ibid., p. 155. Emily Martin also notes that when there are clear clinical indications of fetal or maternal danger, more white women get a cesarean section, but when the labor is long or the progression is slow, more black women get them (p. 151).

54. This concept, which has played an important role for feminist-standpoint theorists, is reiterated in bell hooks's attempt to understand postmodern blackness (*Yearning,* p. 29).

55. Davis, *Women, Culture, and Politics,* p. 30. Much of white feminist discussion of racial "difference" falls into these traps, perhaps my own discussion here included.

56. I would reject the implications of a Foucauldian view that because power is omnipresent, there is no possibility for joy or dreams of greater freedom. Many blacks criticize the rendering of black history as merely one of oppression. They stress that strength and joy have also been part of the black tradition. And in the Jewish celebration of Passover, one eats charoset—a mixture of apples, honey, and cinnamon—to represent the mortar made by the Jews when they were slaves under Pharaoh. The dish is sweet because it is a reminder that in the most bitter times of slavery, Jews were able to remember the sweet taste of freedom.

57. In Denmark, women receive six months of paid maternity leave. In Sweden, women receive nine months of paid leave and the option of up to six additional months at lower rates of compensation. In Finland, women receive one year of paid maternity leave. They have the guarantee that they will be able to return to their workplace with the same salary and level of responsibilities for up to three years after the birth of a child. If a woman is unable to find a place for her child in a day-care center, she will also receive payment for staying home during this period. Paid leave for fathers varies between two and six weeks. (In Sweden, parents also have the option of dividing the leave more evenly between themselves.)

58. New Haven, Connecticut, home of Yale University, boasts the highest infant mortality rate in the United States. A mobile health clinic has begun to provide prenatal care to pregnant women who do not even have the 75 cents to spend for bus fare to the hospital (Danish Radio's television news report, April 14, 1991).

59. The United States is the only major industrial country in the world outside of South Africa that lacks a uniform national health-insurance plan (Davis, *Women, Culture, and Politics,* p. 60).

60. The Children's Defense Fund reports that perhaps six to seven million children in the United States, including preschoolers, may be left alone at home by working parents who cannot afford day care (hooks, *Feminist Theory,* p. 142).

61. See Katha Pollitt's discussion of surrogate labor in, "When Is a Mother Not a Mother?" *The Nation,* December 31, 1990, p. 844.

SOCIAL AND
POLITICAL PHILOSOPHY

15

FEMINIST
CONTRACTARIANISM

JEAN HAMPTON

*Like any good theory, {a woman's moral theory} will need not to ignore the partial
truth of previous theories. So it must accommodate both the insights men have more
easily than women, and those women have more easily than men. It should swallow
up its predecessor theories. Women moral theorists, if any, will have this very great
advantage over the men whose theories theirs supplant, that they can stand on the
shoulders of men moral theorists, as no man has yet been able to stand on the shoulders
of any woman moral theorist. There can be advantages, as well as handicaps, in being latecomers.*

Annette C. Baier[1]

Is it possible to be simultaneously a feminist and a partisan of the contractarian approach to moral and political theory? The prospects for a successful marriage of these
two positions look dubious if one has read recent feminist criticisms of contemporary
contractarian theories. Moreover, this brand of moral theory has been suffused with
the technical machinery of game theory, logic, and economics of the sort often
thought to attract male philosophers and repel female ones, making such theorizing,
in the words of one feminist philosopher, a "big boys' game" and a "male locker room"
that few female philosophers have "dared enter."[2]

But this seemingly inhospitable philosophical terrain has been my intellectual
home for some years now. And I have been persistently attracted to contractarian modes
of theorizing not merely because such theorizing offers "good clean intellectual fun"[3]
but also because it holds out the promise of delivering a moral theory that will answer to
my political—and in particular my feminist—commitments. This is not to say that par-

ticular contractarian moral theories don't deserve much of the feminist criticism they have received. In this chapter, I will explore and acknowledge the legitimacy of these feminist challenges. Nonetheless I want to argue that one version of this method of moral theorizing offers us what may be the keystone of any truly adequate moral theory.

In a nutshell I will be contending that contractarianism illuminates distributive justice, and this form of justice is required not only in relationships between strangers but also in relationships between intimates, including husbands and wives, parents and children, friend and friend. In making this argument I am opposing conventional philosophical wisdom going back as far as Aristotle, who writes, "If people are friends, they have no need of justice."[4] Among contemporary theorists, David Hume's claim that justice is only necessary in circumstances in which people have limited feelings of benevolence or friendship toward one another has been accepted by virtually every political philosopher since then, including Karl Marx and John Rawls. But I will contend that distributive justice, understood in its deepest sense, is inherent in any relationship that we regard as morally healthy and respectable—particularly in a friendship. Indeed, Aristotle himself hinted at this idea immediately after the passage just quoted—he says not only that those who are just also require friendship but also that "the justice that is most just seems to belong to friendship."[5] The reflection in this chapter might be taken as a way of exploring this enigmatic passage.

Hearing Voices

Recent work by Carol Gilligan has reinforced the general tendency of philosophers to see the concerns of justice and friendship as distinct from one another. Using interviews with older children and adults that address real or hypothetical moral problems, Gilligan attempts to display two different "moral voices"—voices she calls the "ethic of justice" and the "ethic of care"—and finds some evidence (albeit controversial) associating the first with men and the second with women.[6]

Two of her interviews with older children have always struck me as highly interesting. Eleven-year-old Jake, whose answers to the interviewers earned him high marks on Lawrence Kohlberg's moral maturity scale, gave the following answer when asked, "When responsibility to oneself and responsibility to others conflict, how should one choose?" He replied with great self-assurance, "You go about one-fourth to the others and three-fourths to yourself."[7] Contrast the following answer to the same question given by eleven-year-old Amy, whose answers to the interviewers earned poorer marks on Kohlberg's scale:

> Well, it really depends on the situation. If you have a responsibility with somebody else [sic], then you should keep it to a certain extent, but to the extent that it is really going to hurt you or stop you from doing something that you really, really want, then I think maybe you should put yourself first. But if it is your responsibility to somebody really close to you, you've just got to decide in that situation which is more important, yourself or that person, and like I said,

it really depends on what kind of person you are and how you feel about the other person or persons involved.[8]

This rather tortured reply indicates considerable sensitivity and beneficent concern for others. Unsurprisingly, Amy's discussion of other moral problems reveals an interest in maintaining the well-being of others and in keeping relationships intact, which, according to Gilligan, shows that Amy values care. In contrast, Jake's remarks take for granted the importance of following rules that preclude interference in other people's pursuit of their interests, which, according to Gilligan, shows that Jake values justice. When asked to explain his answer to the question about responsibility to himself and others, Jake replies, "Because the most important thing in your decision should be yourself, don't let yourself be guided totally by other people, but you have to take them into consideration. So, if what you want to do is blow yourself up with an atom bomb, you should maybe blow yourself up with a hand grenade because you are thinking about your neighbors who would die also."[9]

As Jake's remarkable example shows, he regards "being moral" as pursuing one's own interests without damaging the interests of others, and he takes it as a matter of moral strength not to allow the interests of others to dictate to him what he ought or ought not to do. ("Don't let yourself be guided totally by other people," he warns.) In contrast, "being moral" for Amy means being responsive to the needs of others who are close to you or to whom you have made a commitment. Each child therefore makes a different assumption about the extent to which any of us is self-sufficient. Jake assumes that we are and ought to be interested in and capable of caring for ourselves, so that interaction with others is likely to be perceived either as interference or as an attempt to compromise one's independence. In contrast, Amy takes it for granted that we are not self-sufficient and that service to others will be welcomed as a sign of care and commendable concern.

Many feminist theorists maintain that the kind of moral voice that Amy exemplifies is clearly preferable to that of Jake. Annette Baier, for example, writes,

> Gilligan's girls and women saw morality as a matter of preserving valued ties to others, of preserving the conditions for that care and mutual care without which human life becomes bleak, lonely, and after a while, as the mature men in her study found, not self affirming, however successful in achieving the egoistic goals which had been set. The boys and men saw morality as a matter of finding workable traffic rules for self assertors, so that they do not needlessly frustrate one another, and so that they could, should they so choose, cooperate in more positive ways to mutual advantage.[10]

Certainly Baier is right that a "traffic rule" perspective on morality is neither a sophisticated nor a mature moral perspective. It appears to derive from the mistaken assumption that each of us is self-sufficient, able and desirous of "going it alone." Amy is surely right that this is false. In contrast, a perspective on morality that emphasizes caring for and fostering the well-being of others appears to be not only a richer, sounder theory of what genuine moral behavior is all about but also a better guide to behavior that enables one to live a life full of friendship and love. Such a perspective is one that women (and especially mothers) are frequently thought to exhibit more than men. Baier concludes, "It would not be much of an exaggeration to call the Gilligan 'different voice' the voice of the potential parent."[11]

Baier's way of responding to Jake's answer makes him into an archetype for a (commonly male) brand of moral immaturity. But one can respond to Amy's answer in a way that makes her an archetype for a quite different (and commonly female) brand of moral immaturity. Consider that Jake's answer is 13 words; Amy's is 109 words, and it is neither clear nor self-assured. *Maybe* she can put herself first, she says, if not doing so would mean losing out on something that she "really, really" wants. But only maybe. Jake is convinced not only that his interests count, but that they count far more than other people's (three-quarters to one-quarter). Amy appears to be having trouble figuring out whether or not her interests count at all. Consider her answer to the responsibility question:

> Some people put themselves and things for themselves before they put other people, and some people really care about other people. Like, I don't think your job is as important as somebody that you really love, like your husband or your parents or a very close friend. Somebody that you really care for—or if it's just your responsibility to your job or somebody that you barely know, then maybe you go first.[12]

Again, note her "maybe." Even in a situation in which she takes her responsibility to others to be minimal, she is having trouble asserting the priority of her own interests. Here is a child who appears very much guided by the interests of other people and takes that guidance to be what "being moral" means. One worries that she will find it difficult to plan a life that takes into consideration what she alone wants, because she is highly susceptible to being at the beck and call of others.

These interpretations are harsh and are probably not fair to the real children. But the fact that they are not only possible but natural shows the immature directions in which each child's thinking tends. Jack is susceptible to a brand of moral immaturity that manifests itself in an insensitivity to the needs of others and a failure to see himself as a fellow caretaker in a relationship. His remarks define a morality only in the most minimal sense: There is too much distance between him and others to enable him to be aware of and responsive to the needs or interests of others. In contrast, Amy is susceptible to a moral perspective that makes her too sensitive to other people, and her concern to meet their needs borders on outright servility. Whereas the authority and importance of others' needs are clear for her, the authority and importance of her own needs appear not to be. Indeed, unlike Jake she can offer no principle upon which to adjudicate the conflict between her claims and the claims of others, presumably because she has difficulty seeing herself as entitled to make any claim at all. And because she is so readily able to appreciate and be responsive to the needs of others, she is potentially a highly exploitable person. Thus if we interpret Amy's remarks as typifying a brand of moral immaturity quite different from that of Jake, they define an "ethic of care" that is really just a mimicry of genuine morality insofar as "caring" actions are generated out of the assumption that the agent is worth less than (and hence the servant of) the people she serves. Such caring cannot be moral because it is born of self-abnegation rather than self-worth.[13]

Although she respects Amy's concern for care, Gilligan herself admits the immaturity of Amy's response (while also stressing the immaturity of Jake's perspective). Moreover, that this brand of caring is an imitation of a genuinely moral response to others has also been noticed by other feminist writers,[14] and it is a surprisingly common theme in literature by women. For example, Charlotte Brontë's heroine in *Shirley* begins the journey to genuine maturity when she comes to question her own propensity to offer to care for others:

> "What was I created for, I wonder? Where is my place in the world?" She mused again. "Ah! I see," she pursued presently, "that is the question which most old maids are puzzled to solve: other people solve it for them by saying, 'Your place is to do good to others, to be helpful whenever help is wanted.' That is right in some measure, and a very convenient doctrine for the people who hold it; but I perceive that certain sets of human beings are very apt to maintain that other sets should give up their lives to them and their service, and then they requite them by praise: they call them devoted and virtuous. Is this enough? Is it to live? Is there not a terrible hollowness, mockery, want, craving, in that existence which is given away to others, for want of something of your own to bestow it on? I suspect there is. Does virtue lie in abnegation of self? I do not believe it. Undue humility makes tyranny: weak concession creates selfishness. . . . Each human being has his share of rights. I suspect it would conduce to the happiness and welfare of all, if each knew his allotment and held to it as tenaciously as a martyr to his creed."[15]

And there is Virginia Woolf's well-known description of "the angel in the house" who threatens to take over and destroy a woman's soul:

> She was intensely sympathetic. She was immensely charming. She was utterly unselfish. She excelled in the difficult art of family life. She sacrificed herself daily. If there was chicken, she took the leg: if there was a draught she sat in it—in short she was so constituted that she never had a mind or a wish of her own, but preferred to sympathize always with the minds and wishes of others. Above all—I need not say it—she was pure. . . . I turned upon her and caught her by the throat. I did my best to kill her. My excuse, if I were to be had up in a court of law would be that I acted in self-defence. Had I not killed her she would have killed me.[16]

Both novelists believe that a genuine moral agent has to have a good sense of her own moral claims if she is going to be a person at all and thus a real partner in a morally sound relationship.[17] She must also have some sense of what it is to make a legitimate claim if she is to understand and respond to the legitimate claims of others and resist attempts to involve herself in relationships that will make her the mere servant of others' desires. Both philosophical and commonsense understandings of morality have been so fixated on the other-regardingness of moral life that they have encouraged us to mistake archetypal Amy's response for a moral response.[18]

What happens when archetypal Jake and archetypal Amy grow up? If they were to marry, wouldn't Amy take it upon herself to meet the needs of Jake and do the work to maintain their relationship (giving up her career if necessary, insofar as she thinks that a job isn't as important as "someone you really love")? And wouldn't Jake naturally take it for granted that his interests should predominate (three-fourths to one fourth) and be ignorant of many of the needs of others around him that might prompt a caring response? I find it striking that these children's answers betray perspectives that seem to fit them perfectly for the kind of gendered roles that prevail in our society. In their archetypal forms, I hear the voice of a child who is preparing to be a member of a dominating group and the voice of another who is preparing to be a member of the group that is dominated. Neither of these voices should be allowed to inform our moral theorizing if such theorizing is going to be successful at formulating ways of interacting that are not only morally acceptable but also attack the oppressive relationships that now hold in our society.

Two Forms of Contractarian Theory

So how do we set about defining an acceptable formulation of morality? The idea that the essence not only of human rationality but also of human morality is embodied in the notion of contract is the heart of what is called the "contractarian" approach to moral thinking. Advocates of this approach ask us to imagine a group of people sitting around a bargaining table; each person is interested only in himself. This group is to decide answers to moral or political questions by determining what they can all agree to or what they would all be unreasonable to reject.

However, both proponents and opponents of this style of argument have failed to appreciate just how many argumentative uses of the contract idea have appeared over the centuries. Arguments that self-consciously invoke a social contract can differ in what they aim to justify or explain (for example, the state, conceptions of justice, morality), what they take the problem of justification to be, and whether or not they presuppose a moral theory or purport to be a moral theory. Thus, even though theorists who call themselves "contractarians" have all supposedly begun from the same reflective starting point—namely, what people could "agree to"—these differences and disagreements among people who are supposedly in the same philosophical camp show that contractarians are united not by a common philosophical theory but by a common *image*. Philosophers hate to admit it, but sometimes they work from pictures rather than ideas. And in an attempt to get a handle on the nature of the state, the reasons for its justification, and the legitimate moral claims each of us can make on our behalf against others, the contract imagery has struck many as enormously promising. But how that image has been translated into argument has varied considerably, and philosophers have disagreed about what political or moral issue that image can profitably illuminate.

A number of feminist theorists reject out of hand the idea that this could be an acceptable approach to defining morality precisely because of what they take to be the unattractiveness of the contract image.[19] Virginia Held, for example, insists:

> To see contractual relations between self-interested or mutually disinterested individuals as constituting a paradigm of human relations is to take a certain historically specific conception of 'economic man' as representative of humanity. And it is, many feminists are beginning to agree, to overlook or to discount in very fundamental ways the experience of women.[20]

And at first glance this way of thinking about morality does seem rather Jake-like. People are postulated to be self-regarding rather than other-regarding and their project is to define rules that enable them to live in harmony—which sounds a great deal like constructing (to quote Baier again) "traffic rules for self assertors."[21] Moreover, their distance from one another seems to prevent them from feeling emotional bonds of attachment or concern that would prompt care without the promise of pay.

I will be arguing that this type of attack on contractarian theory is importantly misguided. But before I can begin that argument, I want to clarify in this section exactly what kind of contractarian argument I will be defending in the rest of the chapter. There are two kinds of moral argument that one contract image has spawned in modern times—the first has its roots in Thomas Hobbes and is exemplified in the work of David Gauthier, James Buchanan, Gilbert Harman, and John Mackie; the second has its roots in Immanuel Kant and is exemplified in the work of John Rawls and T. M. Scanlon. I will review these two forms of contractarian theory and the criticisms to which each is subject before I go on, in the next section, to locate my own contractarian approach in this conceptual space.

Hobbesian Contractarianism

Although Hobbes himself never repudiated a divine origin for moral laws, he and the moral philosophers who followed him have attempted to develop an entirely *human* justification of morality.[22] Hobbesians start by insisting that what is valuable is what a person desires or prefers, not what he ought to desire (for no such prescriptively powerful object exists); and rational action is action that achieves or maximizes the satisfaction of desires or preferences. They then go on to insist that moral action is rational for a person to perform if and only if such action advances the satisfaction of his desires or preferences. And usually, they argue, for most of us the moral action will be rational. Because moral actions lead to peaceful and harmonious living conducive to the satisfaction of almost everyone's desires or preferences, moral actions are rational for almost everyone and thus "mutually agreeable." But in order to ensure that no co-operative person becomes the prey of immoral aggressors, Hobbesians believe that moral actions must be the conventional norms in a community, so that each person can expect that if she behaves cooperatively, others will do so too, and vice versa. These conventions constitute the institution of morality in a society.

So the Hobbesian moral theory is committed to the idea that morality is a human-made institution that is justified only to the extent that it effectively furthers human interests. Hobbesians explain the existence of morality in society by appealing to the convention-creating activities of human beings; they also argue that the justification of morality in any human society depends upon how well its moral conventions serve individuals' desires or preferences. So Hobbesians do not assume that existing conventions are, in and of themselves, justified. By considering "what we *could* agree to" if we had the chance to reappraise and redo the cooperative conventions in our society, we are able to determine the extent to which our present conventions are mutually agreeable and thus rational for us to accept and act on. Consequently, Hobbesians invoke both actual agreements (or rather, conventions) and hypothetical agreements (which involve considering what conventions would be mutually agreeable) at different points in their theory. The former are what they believe our moral life consists in; the latter are what they believe our moral life *should* consist in—that is, what our actual moral life should model.[23]

This means the notion of contract does not do justificational work *by itself* in the Hobbesian moral theory—this term is only used metaphorically. What we "could agree to" has moral force for the Hobbesians not because make-believe promises in hypothetical worlds have any binding force but because this sort of agreement is a device that (merely) reveals the way in which the agreed-upon outcome is rational for all of us. In particular, thinking about "what we could all agree to" allows us to construct a deduction of practical reason to determine what politics are mutually advantageous. Thus the justificational force of this kind of contract theory is carried within but is derived from sources other than the contractor agreement in the theory.

As I've noted, many theorists are attracted to this theory because of its sensible metaphysics: It doesn't base morality on strange, nonnatural properties or objects; nor does it credit human beings with what Mackie calls "magical" powers capable of discerning the moral truth "out there."[24] Instead it sees morality as a human invention that we commend to the extent that it is mutually advantageous for those who would use it. But such a metaphysical foundation is attractive only if what is built upon it counts as a genuine morality. And there are good reasons for complaining that Hobbesian contractarianism yields considerably less than the real thing. When *Leviathan* was originally published in 1651, some readers sympathetic to Aristotelian ideas were shocked by the idea that the nature of our ties to others was interest based and contended that Hobbes's theory went too far in trying to represent us as radically separate from others. Their worries are also the worries of many twentieth-century critics, including feminists, who insist that any adequate moral theory must take into account our emotion-based connections with others and the fact that we are socially defined beings.[25]

But I would argue that what disqualifies it at a more fundamental level as an acceptable moral theory is its failure to incorporate the idea that individuals have what I will call "intrinsic value." It has not been sufficiently appreciated, I believe, that by answering the "Why be moral?" question by invoking self-interest in the way that Hobbesians do, one makes not only cooperative action but also the human beings with whom one will cooperate merely of *instrumental value*. That is, if you ask me why I should treat you morally, and I respond by saying that it is in my interest to do so, I am telling you that my regard for you is something that is merely instrumentally valuable to me; I do not give you that regard because there is something about you yourself that merits it, regardless of the usefulness of that regard to me. Now Hobbes is unembarrassed by the fact that on his view, "the *Value,* or WORTH of a man, is as of all other things, his Price; that is to say, so much as would be given for the use of his Power: and therefore is not absolute; but a thing dependent on the need and judgment of another."[26]

But this way of viewing people is not something that we, or even some Hobbesians, can take with equanimity. In the final two chapters of his book, Gauthier openly worries about the fact that the reason why we value moral imperatives on this Hobbesian view is that they are instrumentally valuable to us in our pursuit of what we value. But why are they instrumentally valuable? Because, in virtue of our physical and intellectual weaknesses that make it impossible for us to be self-sufficient, we need the cooperation of others to prosper. If there were some way that we could remedy our weaknesses and become self-sufficient—for example, by becoming a superman or a superwoman, or by using a Ring of Gyges to make ourselves invisible and so steal from the stores of others with impunity—then it seems we would no longer value or respect moral constraints because they would no longer be useful to us—unless we happened to like the idea. But in this case, sentiment rather than reason would motivate kind treatment. And without such sentiment, it would be rational for us to take other people as "prey."

Even in a world in which we are not self-sufficient, the Hobbesian moral theory gives us no reason outside of contingent emotional sentiment to respect those with whom we have no need of cooperating or those whom we are strong enough to dominate, such as the elderly, the physically handicapped, mentally disabled children whom we do not want to rear, or people from other societies with whom we have no interest in trading. And I would argue that this shows that Hobbesian moral contractarianism fails in a serious way to capture the nature of morality. Regardless of whether or not one can engage in beneficial cooperative interactions with another, our moral intuitions push us to assent to the idea that one owes that person respectful treatment simply in virtue of the fact that she is a *person*. It seems to be a feature of our moral life that we regard a human being, whether or not she is instrumentally valuable, as always intrinsically valuable. Indeed, to the extent that the results of a Hobbesian theory are acceptable, this is because one's concern to cooperate with someone whom one cannot dominate leads one to behave in ways that mimic the respect one ought to show her simply in virtue of her worth as a human being.

Kantian Contractarianism

To abandon the idea that the only value human beings have is instrumental is to abandon the Hobbesian approach to morality and to move in the direction of what I will call "Kantian contractarianism." In his later writings Immanuel Kant proposed that the "ideal" of the "Original Contract" could be used to determine just political policies:

> Yet this contract, which we call *contractus originarius* or *pactum sociale,* as the coalition of every particular and private will within a people into a common public will for purposes of purely legal legislation, need by no means be presupposed as a fact. . . . It is rather a *mere idea* of reason, albeit one with indubitable practical reality, obligating every lawmaker to frame his laws so that they *might* have come from the united will of an entire people, and to regard any subject who would be a citizen as if he had joined in voting for such a will. For this is the touchstone of the legitimacy of public law. If a law is so framed that all the people *could not possibly* give their consent—as, for example, a law granting the hereditary *privilege* of *master status* to a certain class of subjects— the law is unjust.[27]

As I interpret this passage, when Kant asks us to think about what people could agree to, he is not trying to justify actions or policies by invoking, in any literal sense, the consent of the people. Only the consent of *real* people can be legitimating, and Kant talks about hypothetical agreements made by hypothetical people. But he does believe these make-believe agreements have moral force for us, not because we are under any illusion that the make-believe consent of make-believe people is obliging for us, but because the process by which these people reach agreement is morally revealing.

Kant's contracting process has been further developed by subsequent philosophers, such as John Rawls and T. M. Scanlon, convinced of its moral promise. Rawls, in particular, concentrates on defining the hypothetical people who are supposed to make this agreement to ensure that their reasoning will not be tarnished by immorality, injustice, or prejudice and thus that the outcome of their joint deliberations will be morally sound (although not all contractarians have agreed with his way of defining the parties to get this result). The Kantians' social contract is therefore a device used in their theorizing to reveal what is just or what is moral. So like the Hobbesians, their contract talk is really just a way of reasoning that allows us to work out conceptual answers to moral problems. But whereas the Hobbesians' use of contract language expresses the fact that, on their view, morality is a human invention that (if it is well invented) ought to be mutually advantageous, the Kantians' use of the contract language is meant to show that moral principles and conceptions are provable theorems derived from a morally revealing and authoritative contractarian reasoning process or "moral proof procedure."[28]

There is a prominent feminist criticism of Rawls's version of this form of contractarianism. These feminists charge (along with certain Hegelian critics) that

Rawls's stripping people of their socially defined identities and sending them off to an "Archimedean point" to choose among or between moral conceptions asks us to do the impossible—namely, to abstract from our socially defined identities in order to reveal some sort of transcultural truth.[29] Because we are socially defined, these critics contend that any intuitions remaining after people are supposedly stripped to their bare essentials will still be permeated with the assumptions of a sexist society, producing (not surprisingly) "patriarchal outcomes."[30]

There is good reason to think that this feminist complaint is importantly misguided, particularly in view of the feminists' own political commitments (and at least one feminist has already argued this point).[31] Although feminists often insist that our natures are to a high degree socially defined—which means that, on their view, theorizing about what we are "really like" will tend to be informed by intuitions that reflect the society that forms us—it is part of the feminist challenge to our society that some ways in which our society forms us are *wrong*—producing human beings whose development is stunted or distorted and whose connection with other human beings is problematic (because they are either too inclined to want to master others or too likely to wind up being mastered). So although many feminists call themselves "pluralists" who advocate the recognition of many points of view and the legitimacy of many kinds of theorizing about the world, in fact there are some points of view that they reject outright, including sexist and racist views and inegalitarian conceptions of human treatment. Whether or not they explicitly recognize it, this rejection is motivated by an implicit appeal to objective ideals of human interaction and optimal socialization of men and women. The pluralists' vision of a better world, in which the oppression of women does not exist, is a vision of human beings developing in the right—that is, objectively right—way, such that they can flourish and interact well with one another rather than in ways that precipitate oppression or abuse. Accordingly, it is ironic that a Rawlsian Archimedean point is exactly what feminists require to carry out their form of social criticism.

Some feminists will insist that although they do attack some of the practices and points of view in their society, nonetheless the values they use in their criticisms are still authored by their society. Hence, they argue, their society is sufficiently pluralistic to produce mutually inconsistent value-schemes. But even if that is so, what bearing does this sociological fact have on what ought to happen in the sociopolitical arena? In particular, what justifies the feminists in thinking that their values should come to predominate? Merely appealing to consistency or social stability isn't sufficient to justify that predominance, because these reasons could just as easily justify the predominance of racist/sexist values. Feminists not only want their values to predominate, they want them to do so because they are the right values. Hence to argue for their values, they must have an Archimedean point from which to survey and critically assess the value-schemes in their societies. The Rawlsian Archimedean point "forces one to question and consider traditions, customs, and institutions from all points of view"[32] and thus attempts to go beyond mere shared understandings, common beliefs, or social practices that may be oppressive or exploitative. Hence, it seems to offer feminists the perspective they need to be able to identify and attack unjust social practices.[33]

Feminists, however, have an important counterresponse to this defense of the Rawlsian method. They can grant that an Archimedean point would be highly desirable for them given their political agenda, but go on to complain that no Kantian contractarian, including Rawls, has convincingly demonstrated that his contractarian theory provides one, because no contractarian has specified his theory sufficiently such that we can be sure it relies only upon "morally pure" starting points and not the sort of "biased" (for example, sexist or racist) ideas or intuitions that an unjust society can encourage in its citizens. There are two ways in which feminists could charge that these morally suspect intuitions might be intruding into Rawls's theory. First, these intuitions may be covertly motivating the particular constraints, assumptions, or features that are supposed to apply in the contract situation. Feminists are implicitly criticizing Rawls's theory on this basis when they charge that his assumption that parties in the original position are self-interested is motivated by intuitions about what counts as a plausibly "weak" psychology, intuitions that actually derive from a discredited Hobbesian view of human nature. According to these critics, this Jake-like component of Rawls's thinking drives out of his theory both our emotion-based attachments to others' well-being and our other-regarding, duty-based commitments to them, demonstrating the extent to which even this high-minded Kantian appears heavily in the grip of outmoded and distorting individualistic intuitions. Second, suspect intuitions may be illicitly operating within the original-position reasoning procedure and thereby playing a direct role in the justification of Rawls's political conclusions. Critics who charge that Rawls's reliance on the maximin rule cannot be justified will note that if the rule is removed from the argument, only vague intuitive appeals could explain how the parties would reach the political conclusions Rawls recommends, appeals that might not withstand sustained moral scrutiny if they were better understood.[34]

Although Scanlon does not presume that his contract approach defines an Archimedean point, his approach is even more susceptible to the charge that it is covertly relying on ill-defined or ill-defended intuitions. Scanlon argues that (what he calls) the "contractualist" account of the nature of moral wrongdoing goes as follows: "An act is wrong if its performance under the circumstances would be disallowed by any system of rules for the general regulation of behavior which no one could reasonably reject as a basis for informed, unforced general agreement."[35] This definition is intended as "a characterization of the kind of property which moral wrongness is."[36] In this statement of contractualism, the reader is inevitably drawn to the word 'reasonably', yet Scanlon never explicitly cashes out the term. He claims, for example, that a policy A that would pass an average utilitarian test but that would cause some to fare badly is, prima facie, a policy that the "losers" would be reasonable to reject.[37] He goes on to say, however, that ultimately the reasonableness of the losers' objection to A is not established simply by the fact that they are worse off under A than they would be under some alternative policy E in which no one's situation is as bad. Instead, says Scanlon, the complaint against A by the A losers must be weighed against the complaints made by those who would do worse under E than under A. "The question to be asked is, is it unreasonable for someone to refuse to put up with the Losers' situation under A in order that someone else should be able to enjoy the benefits which he would have to give up under E?"38

But on what grounds, or using what criteria, can we provide the right answer to this question? Scanlon gives us no directions for adjudicating the complaints of the two groups in this situation, and one begins to worry that his appeal to "reasonableness" as a way of determining the solution is an appeal to inchoate intuitions. Occasionally, he seems to link the term to the purported desire that people in the hypothetical contract are supposed to have to reach an agreement with one another: "The only relevant pressure for agreement comes from the desire to find and agree on principles which no one who had this desire could reasonably reject."39 But what is this desire? It seems to be more than just the desire to reach an agreement, for Scanlon says later that the desire is one to "find principles which none could reasonably reject."40 So, because the desire is defined in terms of reasonableness, it cannot be taken to explicate it. And if reasonableness is defined using moral notions such as fairness (as in, "It is only reasonable for me to reject proposals that are unfair"), Scanlon's moral project is circular, because on his view moral properties are supposed to be defined by the contract test, thereby precluding a central component of that test that presupposes one or more moral properties.41

So we don't know what is really doing the work in Scanlon's test, and this generates at least three problems for his theory. First, we can't be sure that everyone who uses Scanlon's test will rely on the same conception of reasonableness to arrive at the same answer. Second, unless his conception of reasonableness is fully (and acceptably) explicated, feminists have good reason to worry about what might seem reasonable to people raised in a sexist patriarchal society. And third, unless this conception is fully explicated, those of us loyal to contractarianism as a distinctive form of moral argument have reason to worry that there is so much reliance on intuition in the operation of Scanlon's test that his approach ultimately reduces to some other ethical theory. For example, if these intuitions are understood as foundational, his theory would seem to amount to nothing more than a version of ethical intuitionism. Or if they are understood to be generated by some other moral theory, such as utilitarianism, the contract method would appear to be merely a way of marshaling ideas generated by that other theory. Thus a utilitarian might argue that "reasonable rejection" should be understood as rejection on the grounds that what is being proposed is not utility-maximizing for the group. But Scanlon wants to be able to draw upon and generate antiutilitarian ideas in his contractarian argument through argument rather than through an appeal to intuition alone.42 Because neither he nor, for that matter, any Kantian contractarian has given us any sense of what these ideas are, or why they are appropriate to rely upon, or how they work together to form a nonintuitionistic moral reasoning procedure, we begin to wonder whether or not this or indeed any Kantian's appeal to "what we could agree to" is just a way to fabricate a defense for moral or political conceptions that these Kantian theorists happen to like but for which they cannot provide a valid argument resting on plausible and well-explicated premises.

A Feminist Form of Kantian Contractarian Theory

In view of these criticisms against both Hobbesian and Kantian contractarianism, it might seem that the whole approach is a theoretical dead end not only for feminists but also for any philosopher interested in developing a successful theory of our moral life. But I want to try to rehabilitate this approach in the eyes of its critics by outlining what might be called a "Hobbesian" brand of Kantian contractarianism that is responsible both to the meta-ethical and to the feminist criticisms I have outlined and that holds the promise of being at least part (but only part) of a complete theory outlining a mature morality.

"Private" Relationships and the Contractarian Test

As I tried over the years to determine the source of my own support for the contractarian approach, I found myself increasingly convinced that the contract test was highly appropriate for the evaluation of exactly the kinds of relationships feminists assumed they could not illuminate: personal, intimate ones. It is a testament to the powerful control that the public-private distinction has over even its most ardent feminist critics that they resist the appropriateness of what they take to be a "public" metaphor to evaluate the morality of a "private" relationship. I want to propose that by invoking the idea of a contract we can make a moral evaluation of any relationship, whether it is in the family, the marketplace, the political society, or the workplace[43]—namely, an evaluation of the extent to which that relationship is just ("just" in a sense I shall define below).

A necessary condition of a relationship's being just is that no party in that relationship or system is exploited by another. But exploitation is possible even in the most intimate relationship if one party relies upon the affection or duty felt by another party to use that other party to her detriment. In Gauthier's words, our sociality

> becomes a source of exploitation if it induces persons to acquiesce in institutions and practices that but for their fellow-feeling would be costly to them. Feminist thought has surely made this, perhaps the core form of exploitation, clear to us. Thus the contractarian insists that a society could not command the willing allegiance of a rational person if, without appealing to her feelings for others, it afforded her no expectation of benefit.[44]

As I understand Gauthier's remarks, he is not suggesting that one should never give gifts out of love or duty without insisting on being paid for them; rather, he is suggesting that one's propensity to give gifts out of love or duty *should not become the lever that another party who is capable of reciprocating relies upon to get one to maintain a relationship to one's cost.*

Perhaps this is most deeply true within the family. A woman whose devotion to her family causes her to serve them despite the fact that they do little in return is in an exploitative relationship. Of course, infants cannot assume any of her burdens; fairness cannot exist between individuals whose powers and capacities are so unequal. (Note that this relationship is not unfair either; the infant does not use the mother's love in order to exploit her.) But older children can. Indeed, as children become able to benefit those who have cared for them, it becomes increasingly unacceptable to see them failing to return these benefits. Unless they are encouraged to reciprocate the care they have received as they become able to do so, they are being allowed to exploit other human beings by taking advantage of their love for them.

So our ties (for example, of friendship or marriage) to those who are able to reciprocate what we give to them (as opposed to victims of serious diseases, impoverished people, or infants) are morally acceptable, healthy, and worthy of praise only insofar as they do not involve, on either side, the infliction of costs or the confiscation of benefits over a significant period that implicitly reveals disregard rather than respect for that person.

In order to test for the presence of such disregard, I want to argue that we should apply a version of a contractarian test to the relationship by asking: "Given the fact that we are in this relationship, could both of us reasonably accept the distribution of costs and benefits (that is, the costs and benefits that are not themselves side effects of any affective or duty-based tie between us) if it were the subject of an informed, unforced agreement in which we think of ourselves as motivated solely by self-interest?" Note, first, that the self-interested motivation is assumed for purposes of testing the moral health of the relationship; one is essentially trying to put aside the potentially blinding influence of affection or duty to see whether costs and benefits are distributed such that one is losing out to the other party. Second, note that the costs and benefits that the test inquires about are not ones that come from the affection or duty holding the parties together in the relationship—for among other things, these cannot be distributed and are outside the province of justice. One cannot distribute the pain that a parent feels when her teenage child gets into trouble, the happiness felt by someone because of the accomplishments of her friend, the suffering of a woman because of the illness of a parent. But one can distribute the burdens of caring for an infant or running a household, the costs of correspondence, the work involved in a project jointly undertaken by two friends. These nonaffective costs and benefits that the relationship itself creates or makes possible must be distributed fairly if the relationship is to be just.

But how does this test actually work? In particular, how do we give content to the word 'reasonable' such that it is not just a covert appeal to our (perhaps morally suspect) intuitions?

A simple appeal to equality won't do. Exploitation doesn't loom every time a person gets a present from a friend and then forgets her friend's birthday, or when she pays less in long-distance phone calls than her friend does. Nor would the test be reliable if it relied only upon feelings of "being used"; such feelings are all too likely to be wrong, or exaggerated, or inappropriately weak for us to put full moral faith in them. So I shall now argue that the test must be informed by a set of normative concepts that, taken together, enable us to define exploitation and recognize it when it occurs.

The Concept Behind the Test

I claim that at the base of the Kantian contract theory is not a collection of inchoate and perhaps morally suspect intuitions that might vary among human beings; rather, it is a particular set of defensible concepts composing what I will call, after Rawls, a "conception of the person." As I understand it, in a successful contractarian theory the contract is a (mere) device that, if used in the right circumstances, will call to mind and organize these concepts in a way that will enable us to apply them to diagnose successfully the presence of injustice in a relationship. The contractarian conception of the person includes a list of characteristics of personhood. But it is more than just a list. It also includes two normative conceptions that are central to understanding how we are to respond to a person: namely, a conception of human worth and a conception of a person's legitimate interests.

A conception of human worth tells one what sort of treatment is appropriate or required or prohibited for certain types of individuals on the basis of an assessment of how valuable these individuals are. Some philosophers follow Hobbes in thinking that any assessments of our value as individuals can only be instrumental, whereas other philosophers such as Kant believe that, regardless of our price, our worth is noninstrumental, objective, and equal. Kant also has opponents who, while agreeing that our value is noninstrumental and objective, reject the idea that all humans are of equal value—for example, those who think human beings of a certain gender or race or caste are higher in value (and so deserving of better treatment) than those of a different gender, race, or caste.

I want to argue that animating the contract test is a certain very Kantian conception of human worth. To say that a policy must be "agreed to" by all is to say that in formulating a just policy, we must recognize that none of us can take only herself to "matter" such that she can dictate the solution alone, and also that none of us is allowed to ignore or disregard her own importance in the formulation of the right policy. Therefore, the self-interested perspective each person takes when she uses the test to assess a relationship shouldn't be seen as arrogant selfishness but as a way of symbolizing (as Jake would wish) the proper self-regard each of us should have in view of our worth, in view of the fact that, as Kant would put it, we are "ends in ourselves." However, by requiring that a policy be one that we could all agree to, the contractarian doesn't merely ask each of us to insist on our own worth; he also asks us (as Amy would wish) to recognize and come to terms with the fact that others are just as valuable as we ourselves. So without being an explicit theory of how we are valuable relative to one another, the contract device nonetheless "pictures" that relative value.

It was because the contractarian image implicitly calls forth a certain conception of relative human worth that Rawls was drawn to it as a way of combating the sacrificial tendencies of utilitarianism. The Amy-like insistence of the utilitarian that we should put the group first and accommodate ourselves to the well-being of others even if it would mean substantial and serious sacrifices either on our part or on the part of others has been the central reason why so many have rejected it as an adequate moral theory. If, on the other hand, we evaluate policies, actions, or treatments in any relationship by asking whether each individual, from a self-interested point of view, could reasonably reject them, we are letting each person "count" in a certain way. And I am proposing that we can give content to a Scanlon-like contract test as long as we develop the conception of how human beings ought to count—that is, the conception of human worth that implicitly informs the contract image.[45]

Because the contract image is ultimately animated by this conception of worth, a contractarian doesn't even need to appeal to "what we could agree to" if she has another device that is animated by the same conception. In this regard, it is important to note that although Rawls is called a contractarian, he makes minimal use of the contract device in *A Theory of Justice* and relies on another method of accomplishing the morally revealing representation of relative worth.[46] Although he says that each party to the original position must agree with all the rest on which available alternative is the best conception of justice, in fact that agreement is otiose because each party in his original position follows the same reasoning procedure and reaches the same conclusion—namely, that the Rawlsian conception of justice is preferable to all others. This reasoning procedure requires those who use it to appraise policies, rules, or principles without knowing which person she will become in the society that will be subject to these policies, rules, or principles. But note that, as with the contract device, this "I could be anybody" device requires that I reason in such a way that each person matters, so that I will be reluctant to permit any one of them (who might turn out to be *me*) to be sacrificed for the benefit of the group. So although Rawls relies on a noncontractarian device in *A Theory of Justice,* he is nonetheless a "real" contractarian because the device he uses taps into the same conception of worth as the contract device.[47] And this shows that it isn't the contract device that is the substance of a contractarian theory but the conception of worth that informs that device.

But, the reader may ask, if the conception of the person you're developing is the *real* moral theory and the contract talk only a heuristic device useful for picturing or suggesting this conception, are you really a contractarian?

In a way I don't care about the answer to this question: I am ultimately uninterested in labels, and if my insistence that the substantive roots of my theory are not found in the idea of a contract convinces readers that the label 'contractarian' is inappropriate for that theory, then so be it. But, as I've discussed, every contract theory, whether Hobbesian or Kantian, has used the idea of a contract as a heuristic tool that points us toward the correct form of moral reasoning and has not relied on the idea of contract in any literal way to do any justificatory work. Moreover, there is not enough in the notion of a contract to constitute an adequate moral reasoning procedure in and of itself, as the discussion of Scanlon's theory shows. Hence, in my theory (and, I would argue, in Kant's), the idea of a contract serves as a device that points to, or suggests, the concepts (in particular, the concept of human worth) at the substantive heart of morality. And I would argue that it is because of its suggestiveness that philosophers like me have been persistently attracted to talk of contract and have used the term to label their theories.

Clarifying the Concept

On my view, the way to develop a successful Kantian contractarian argument so that it is not worryingly "intuitive" is to understand and make precise the conception of the person, and particularly the conception of human worth, implicitly underlying the contract image. I regard this as a tough, lengthy and long-term project. Nonetheless, I can at least make a few preliminary remarks here to show how I believe we can read off from the contract image aspects of the conception of human worth that animates it.

The most important idea invoked by the image is the Kantian idea that people have *intrinsic, noninstrumental value* (which is why I take it that Kant himself invoked the image in his political writings). But some readers may wonder why the contract image doesn't imply, instead, the idea that the people involved in the contract, or the services they would provide, are mere commodities. This is the assumption of many Marxists and some feminists: Carol Pateman, for example, has argued that the "logic" of contractual thinking would effect a morally offensive "universal market in bodies and services" in which people would contract for the services they desired (many of which they now get "for free" in a marriage—for example, sex, surrogate parenting, selling human eggs, renting wombs, and so on).[48]

But my understanding of the contract image suggests nothing of the sort. This is because, first, the contract image I invoke is deliberately meant to be an *ideal* agreement between equals. I do not regard the contract test as a morally neutral device (as Rawls, for example, suggests); rather, I see it as an image fed by normative ideas that one is ultimately relying on when using the test to make moral evaluations. And it is not true that in an ideal contract each party responds to the other solely as instrumentally valuable. Think literally about what one means when one says a person is instrumentally valuable: One is saying that the person is valuable in the way that a pen or a typewriter or a hammer is valuable. That person has the value *and the status* of a tool. But in an ideal contract among relative strangers, neither party responds to the other only in that way. I don't get you to paint my house simply by whistling and pointing to the paint, as if you were some kind of automated paint machine. I believe that to get you to paint my house I must get your *consent* to do so, and I also believe (if I think our contractual relationship is ideal and hence just) that I can only get your consent if you are sure that I am not asking you to bear the costs of doing so without any reciprocating benefit from me to you. But note that this attitude implicitly rejects the view that the other person has only instrumental standing. In an ideal contract between equals, each person must respect the wishes of the other in order to achieve the agreement; hence, requiring mutual consent under these circumstances means requiring respect.

So understood, the contract test could be successfully used to disallow the commodization of certain aspects of our person. It could be used, for example, to preclude the commodization of a womb: Before a group of people could even consider the question, "What terms could we reasonably accept for our surrogacy contract?" they would have to ask the question, "Is the very idea of a surrogacy contract something that each of us could reasonably accept?" And it is plausible to suppose that people equally situated and motivated to secure their legitimate interests could not all agree to such a contract (in particular, the prospective surrogate mother could not). Remember that both Kant and Rawls have argued that the contract idea, when invoked, precludes certain institutional structures and social practices (for example, aristocratic social orders or slavery) that are degrading; similarly, I argue for an understanding of the contract test that forbids a variety of social arrangements that are demeaning—that is, inconsistent with the worth of all the parties involved.

As these remarks show, the conception of worth informing the contract device, understood ideally, is an *egalitarian* conception: Contractarians aim to idealize parties in a relationship so that each of them not only is an equal participant in the agreement process but also possesses equal bargaining power. And this is a way of expressing the idea that no person's intrinsic worth is greater than any other's. Finally, it is a *nonaggregative* conception. Although utilitarians grant people value, and can even be called "egalitarians" about value insofar as they allow each person to count equally in the utilitarian calculation, this way of "counting" still isn't good enough for the contractarian, who would note that each person appears in the utilitarian calculation as a number representing how much he contributes to the total good. This means that it is not really the individual so much as the summable units of good that he contributes (and, in the final analysis, represents in the calculation) that the utilitarian takes seriously. Each individual is therefore valued by that theory (only) to the extent that he will respond to any resources by contributing units of good to the total. In contrast, the contractarian gives each person the ability to veto an arrangement that he believes will unreasonably disadvantage him relative to the others, and this reflects the contractarian's view that each of us has a value that resists aggregation and that makes demands on us regardless of how advantageous a group might find it to ignore those demands.

The other component of the conception of the person informing the contract device is the conception of a person's legitimate interests. If one has something of great value, that value requires that one, for example, preserve it, treat it carefully so as not to hurt it, and, if it is sentient, minimize its experience of pain. That is, its value requires that one care for it in view of its importance. These responses presuppose a theory of what a valued object requires such that its value can be both preserved and respected. Human beings' unique and considerable value requires that they be properly cared for. But what does such care involve? I believe that the answer to such a question would involve detailing who we are and what interests of ours are urgent given our nature. These interests would include not only having enough to eat but also have the psychological conditions that allow us to function well and the liberty that, as autonomous beings, we need. To put it in Aristotelian terms, the answer involves constructing a normative theory formulating what is good for human beings (both as a species and as distinctive individuals).[49] This normative theory is, however, connected to the contractarian's theory of human worth. If we regard a certain set of sentient creatures as relatively unimportant, what we take to be their legitimate interests will differ sharply from what we take to be the legitimate interests of those to whom we attribute great worth. Of course, a conception of human good will also be informed by a host of physiological and psychological facts about human beings, but how we respond to those facts is fundamentally dependent upon how we understand human beings to be valuable.

To the extent that we can pin down what our legitimate interests are, we can also pin down some of the ideas to which we are implicitly appealing in the contract test. When we ask, "Could all of us reasonably accept this if it were proposed as the subject of unforced, informed agreement?" we must assume that each of us is consulting interests that we are legitimately entitled to have respected. Rawls's theory is famous for trying to define these interests in a political context, and many critics have noted that despite his demurrers to the contrary, his is a normatively loaded conception. But of course it must be, because not all of our interests are good ones and thus count as grounds for "reasonable rejections." Contractarians have thus far been unable to get philosophical control over the concept of legitimate interests to which they must appeal if their test is going to have real bite; I am proposing that to do so, they must not rely upon vaguely defined intuitions called forth by the contract device but must instead develop and defend in its own right the concept of legitimate interests generating these intuitions.

Contractarianism and Feminist Politics

The development of this theory depends upon the development and defense of the conception of the person informing the contract test. I believe feminist theorizing can be a highly useful resource for this development and defense. Feminist writings have a lot to say about questions surrounding worth, status, and honor. They also have a lot to say about the pain and damage human beings experience when they are considered second class and subject to discrimination and prejudice, or when they are denied not only economic opportunities but decent housing and food. Implicit in these writings, on my view, is a conception of how people can go wrong not only in how they treat others but also in how they regard these others such that this treatment is permitted (and even, at times, encouraged). So both contractarians and many feminists are concerned to clarify the right kind of regard that any human being, in any human relationship, must be paid by others. Once that regard, and the treatment associated with it, are better understood, we will be able to clarify what each party to the contract wants when she is motivated to secure "what is best for her." Feminist theorizing can therefore do much to help the development and analytical precision of Kantian contractarian theory.

But contractarian theory can also help the feminist cause, and it can do so because it unabashedly insists on the worth of each of us. The reliance on self-interest in my formulation of the contract test is not an unfortunate remnant of Hobbes's moral theory; rather, it is a deliberate attempt to preserve what may be the only right-headed aspect of Hobbes's thought—namely, *the idea that morality should not be understood to require that we make ourselves the prey of others.* The self-interested concern that each party to a Kantian social contract brings to the agreement process symbolizes her morally legitimate concern to prevent her exploitation and have the value of her interests and her person respected. My insistence that each party to a relationship take a self-concerned perspective in his or her evaluation of its moral health is really the insistence that each of us is right to value ourselves, our interests, and our projects and right to insist that we not become the prey of other parties in the pursuit of their projects. The contractarian method grants us what Charlotte Brontë in the passage quoted earlier seems to want: a way to be tenacious advocates of ourselves. What has attracted so many to this form of argument and what makes it worthy of further pursuit is precisely the fact that by granting to each individual the ability to be his or her own advocate, this method enables us to conceive of both public and private relationships without exploitative servitude.

Nonetheless, a philosopher's call for all of us to insist that our interests be accorded proper weight in a relationship will sound foolish indeed to a mother caring for three kids alone after her husband has left her and who ends up taking in an aging mother too ill to take care of herself. Women in this society are in trouble largely because society has defined roles for them to play in a variety of relationships that involve them bearing a disproportionately larger share of the costs and receiving a disproportionately smaller share of the benefits than others.

The strength and downright bravery many women display as they endure their burdens is considerable and impressive, but such strength is, in the eyes of one feminist, also a roadblock to ending the abuse: "Certain values described as feminine virtues may get some women through but they do not seem to offer most women the resources for fighting the enemy—for genuine resistance. They do not, that is, push one to 'cripple' or 'damage' or stop the enemy . . . or at least to try."[50] However impressive the heroic service women have traditionally provided—to the extent that it is soul destroying for them and for the women who will follow them—they must develop forms of thinking and acting that prevent their propensity to care from being the source of their abuse and exploitation. Thus it is precisely because its self-interested perspective is so alien to their other-regarding modes of thinking that feminist critics of contractarianism should welcome it as they pursue changes not merely in intimate relationships but in society at large. It is a form of thinking about moral relationships that not only encourages individuals to insist on the acknowledgment of their own interests and concerns but also (as a Rawlsian would wish) encourages them to attack societal and political sources of the exploitative roles in which women find themselves.

The Uses and Limits of Contractarian Moral Theory

I have been arguing that if we understand the structure and role of the contractarian device in our moral thinking, the contract idea isn't in any sense foundational, or even necessary, for effective moral reasoning. It is merely a test that is heuristically valuable for the moral agent in virtue of the fact that it is informed by ideas that are the real source of moral reasoning. In particular, *the contract device is effective at illuminating the nature of distributive justice, which I understand to be the 'distribution of benefits and burdens in a relationship consistent with the contractarian conception of the person.'* Thus exploitation, or distributive injustice, is a distribution inconsistent with that conception. So understood, the concern to realize distributive justice is a species of moral concern generally, which I define as *treating people consistent with the contractarian conception of the person*. In this section I shall explore how and when the contract test works and when it is not appropriate to use it.

There are three different ways exploitation can exist and thus three ways that the contract test can be used to search for it. First, as I've emphasized, exploitation can exist within a relationship when it evolves such that the distribution of nonaffective costs and benefits is unfair. In this situation, there is nothing inherent in the relationship itself that creates the exploitation; instead, the behavior of the parties involved precipitates it. Consider a relationship held together by bonds of affection. Although the contract test is misapplied if someone were to try to use it to evaluate directly those affective bonds (such as love or sympathetic concern), it might nonetheless be instrumental to preserving these affective bonds by enabling the parties to locate and correct ways in which they have been behaving unfairly toward one another. In a good friendship, for example, each friend naturally accords the other noninstrumental value. In response to this value, each is prepared to give gifts to the other. A "pay for service" mentality exists between business partners; but between genuine friends, there is only a concern to serve the other insofar as she is (each believes) the sort of valuable being for whom such service or such gift-giving is appropriate. Note, however, that when both friends take this kind of interest in the other, the gift-giving will be roughly reciprocal, and each will be loathe even to appear to use the other as a means.

In contrast, when a friendship starts to get corrupted, one of the parties begins to enjoy the gifts being given more than he does the giver of those gifts, thereby evaluating the one who is giving the gifts as a gift-giver, as a servant of his desires, as the one who ministers to his needs or desires. And if her affection for him is sufficiently strong to motivate her to continue to give the gifts without being paid, why should he reciprocate? He gets what he wants "for free" (or perhaps with minimal cost on his part). This is an example of the kind of exploitation that, as Gauthier notes, can exist in the context of an affective relationship. One party uses the other party's affection to get her to serve him, according her mere instrumental worth. This is not only unjust; it is also a sign that the love in the relationship has been corrupted.

So although philosophers have generally believed that distributive justice has little to do with friendship or love, in fact a concern to locate and eradicate this kind of exploitation can be understood to derive not only from an interest in securing justice between the parties but also from an interest in preserving a genuinely caring relationship. Or to put it another way, insofar as I am arguing that "being just" in a distributive sense means "distributing benefits and burdens in a relationship such that each person's worth is properly respected," then love and distributive justice so understood are not opposing responses because the former is only possible if the latter prevails.

Second, the contract test can function as a test, not of the operation of a relationship, but of the relationship itself, to determine whether exploitation is inherent in the design of some of the roles played by those involved in it. The master-slave relationship is an example of a relationship that would fail the test, "Could all of us reasonably accept the idea of entering into or remaining in any of the roles in this relationship if doing so were the subject of an informed, unforced agreement in which we think of ourselves as motivated solely by self-interest?" Yet another example is given by Charlotte Brontë's account of society's role for spinster women: "Your place is to do good to others, to be helpful whenever help is wanted." As she notes, this is "a very convenient doctrine for the people who hold it," but one that results in "a terrible hollowness, mockery, want, craving, in that existence which is given away to others, for want of something of your own to bestow it on." It is a good example of a social role that could not be agreed upon by those called upon to assume it were they freed of social pressures and imagined obligations and encouraged instead to consult (and regard as legitimate) their own wishes and aspirations.

Third, even if no injustice would occur within a relationship, it might occur as a result of one's decision to enter into it. A relationship can be nonexploitative in its nature and in its operation but still precipitate exploitation if one's decision to participate in it will result in someone (for example, oneself or third parties) getting less than her due. So the contract test can be used to explore whether everyone involved could agree to one's participation in that relationship. Suppose, for example, that you were considering whether to become a parent, teacher, doctor, or minister. The contract test would evaluate whether, if you took on one of these roles and, as a result, developed obligations and affective connections toward others, you could remain fair to yourself and/or to others toward whom you already had obligations or affection. ("If I have this child, can I still do what I need to do for myself?" "If I adopt this profession, will I be able to give to my family what I owe them?") There may be nothing unjust in, say, a parent-child relationship in and of itself, but there may be injustice in the adult's decision to become a parent in the first place.

There are also times, however, when the contract test is not appropriate to use. In particular, it is not appropriate for morally evaluating relationships between people radically unequal in capacity.[51] There is something absurd about inquiring into the morality of the relationship between, say, a mother and her newborn infant by asking, "What services could each agree to? What would they be unreasonable to reject?" For, so long as this radical inequality prevails, such a relationship is outside the province of distributive justice—in part because an infant or anyone severely infirm is incapable of reciprocating the benefit, making it ridiculous for any moral theory to require it, and in part because such people are not manipulating the situation to extract "free care" from others.[52] The contract test is not useful in helping to determine the obligations parties have to one another in these relationships because there are no issues of distributive justice involved in them. However, the conception of the person animating that device is directly relevant to defining those duties.

As I have discussed, it is part of what it means to respect someone's worth that one attend to her legitimate interests. So a traveler who, like the Samaritan, sees someone bleeding to death on the roadside and refuses to help him is failing to honor that person's worth, and a society that fails to define or develop institutional or social responses to those who are in serious need is failing to respond to the worth of its own citizens effectively. In such "Good Samaritan" cases, we commend the caregivers precisely because they unselfishly provide care for the needy person, without thinking of any benefits for themselves. It is not only permissible but also appropriate to give one's services as a gift to those who are in trouble. But note that what we are concerned about when we test relationships for their justice—namely, that each party's worth is properly acknowledged—is never compromised in these sorts of relationships. We are able to commend the service provided by the Good Samaritan because the person being benefited receives the aid without ever taking advantage of the benefactor's affection for or feeling of duty toward him in order to receive the service. He has a great need to which the Samaritan responds insofar as she is respectful of his value as a human being.

Suppose the incapacitated person regains (or develops) his capacities. Once that happens, the use of the contract test becomes appropriate to determine the response he ought to make toward his benefactor. Normally we say that such a person should feel "gratitude" toward his benefactor and take steps to benefit her in some way in order to thank her for his care. I would argue that gratitude is at least partly generated by a concern to be just: Gratitude contains within it the appreciation of the worth of the person who would provide such care, engendering in the genuinely moral person the desire to give benefits in return as a way of showing that he desires to honor, rather than take advantage of, his benefactor's services. An ungrateful recipient of a Good Samaritan's care is therefore unjust, not because he did anything to manipulate the situation such that he received care for which he did not have to pay, but because he is now acquiescing in the uneven distribution of benefits and burdens that could not have been agreed to by self-interested parties had such agreement been possible before the care. This acquiescence may not be as bad as actions that have manipulated the exploitation, but it is still an unjust reaction to the benefactor—a way of responding to his benefactor solely as instrumentally valuable to his needs and interests.[53]

But let me stress once again that the return needn't be equal to the gift received in order for justice to be realized. Even after one gains capacities roughly equal to those of one's benefactor, an equal return might be impossible. The impoverished widow who gave her mite to the Lord in gratitude surely indicates by her actions that she honors the one who benefited her and does not view him merely as a means. Even a bare "thank you" from one who can give little else may be sufficient to show this person's desire to honor rather than take advantage of the one who helped him.[54] The bottom line for those who use the contract test is not whether the distribution of costs and benefits between them has been equal, but whether the distribution is such that either of them is exploiting the other. Given the complexities of human circumstances, there is no formula applicable in all situations to decide the answer to this question. It is for this reason that Scanlon's imprecise word *reasonable* may be a good one to use to characterize what we are looking for in an acceptable distribution of costs and benefits—assuming, of course, that it is nonetheless given content by the conception of the person defined earlier—because *reasonable* implies both that there is no set of rules we can invoke that decisively determines how to distribute costs and benefits and that there are still right and wrong answers as to how to do it.

Communitarian Concerns

Suppose the conception of the person required by the contract test can be developed successfully. Nonetheless, is this the sort of theory upon which our moral and political theorizing should rest? There are two interesting reasons why certain communitarian political theorists might argue it should not.

Consider, first, Michael Sandel's criticism of Rawls's contract theory as one that presupposes an implausible metaphysical conception of the person. In his recent work, Rawls has tried to back away from grounding his argument in any metaphysical claims at all. So a communitarian might argue that my theory takes on the sort of metaphysical baggage other contractarians don't (and shouldn't) want. I would insist, however, that the metaphysical claims made in my theory are the strength of that theory and not an embarrassment to it. There is nothing in the contractarian conception of the person as I understand it that would deny our deep sociality as a species; indeed, like Rawls, who stressed our sociality as a reason for beginning moral philosophy at the level of the basic structure of society, I agree that it is this structure that plays a primary role in forming us. But I would also insist that, regardless of the society we develop in, we are autonomous beings possessing a worth that is noninstrumental and equal, with certain needs that ought to be met. So on this view, a society that teaches its members to believe that some of them are inherently more valuable than others by virtue of their birth, or gender, or race is importantly *wrong*. I will not dispute that this metaphysical claim requires a defense, and in a forthcoming work I aim to propose one; but I will insist that there is nothing "unattractive" about this metaphysics. Indeed, a communitarian who is ready to embrace whatever views about relative value his culture communicates to him will have to swallow views (for example, about women or people of color) that many of us believe are unacceptable. The driving force behind the contractarian theory is what might be called a "socially responsible metaphysics" that insists on the equal intrinsic worth of all people. I would argue that we owe this idea our allegiance, even as we strive to construct philosophical arguments that develop and defend it.

Which brings us to the communitarian's second concern: Isn't a contract test likely to generate a liberal political theory hostile to the interests of a community? In answering this concern I admit—and welcome—the idea that it would do so, although I do not have time to spell out in detail the structure of the political liberalism it would generate. Nonetheless, it is not a morally neutral form of political liberalism but rather (and quite deliberately) a morally loaded liberalism informed by a conception of the person prescribing the creation and sustenance of institutions that respect the worth and legitimate interests of persons. Thus a society that has an unregulated market economy, or wholesale allegiance to the doctrine of freedom of contract, or patriarchal institutions, or racist practices will not function so that each gets what she is due as a person; accordingly, it would be criticized as unjust by this theory. Of course, individuals, not groups, are the fundamental concern of this theory; in this sense, the theory might be thought anticommunitarian. But insofar as our legitimate needs include the need to function as part of a collective, the interests of a collective will be recognized insofar as they are instrumental to the aims of (intrinsically worthy) individuals. (So, on this view, collectives are protected only to the extent that they have instrumental value for the individuals who compose them.) And the operation of these collectives—the roles they define for people and the institutions they adopt—are the appropriate subjects of a contract test concerned with locating the presence of exploitative injustice, subjects ranging from the monogamous nuclear family to market society, from democratic polities to social practices defining gender. It is a fundamental (and liberal) tenet of this view that a community's practices must answer to the worth of individuals and not the other way around.

Beyond Morality

Let me conclude on a note sympathetic to some of the feminist criticisms I reviewed earlier. Suppose we had a complete moral theory founded on the contractarian's conception of the person and, as part of this theory, a conception of distributive justice effectively revealed by the contract test. Would we have arrived at a fully mature or (perhaps better) genuinely wise perspective regarding how we should live our lives with one another?

I think not, because we would still not understand certain important reasons why individuals forge relationships or the full nature of the affective or duty-based connections holding our relationships together. Contra the beliefs of Hobbesians, in our various relationships with others we are not simply concerned with gaining the advantages of cooperation from people we take to be instrumentally valuable to the pursuit of our own interests. Moreover, even if our relationships are subject to the demands of justice, most of them are not undertaken in order to realize justice. A person doesn't become a parent so that she can be just toward her children. None of us fosters a friendship with another out of a concern to be fair. Joining a church or a charity organization, volunteering in one's community, organizing charities for people in other countries, committing oneself in the manner of Mother Theresa to the needs of the desperately poor, are ways of creating a role for oneself that are prompted by interests that may have a good deal to do with honoring the worth of these individuals but perhaps have much more to do with the love one feels toward others.

I believe that if we begin to theorize in a more complete way about the values inherent in human relationships, we will find that the concepts of justice as well as morality are too limp to help us understand many of the responses we commend when we praise human beings. Consider, for example, the response of a Texas farm woman to a tornado that destroyed her family's home. As the destruction was occurring she sat in a shelter with her family and worked on a quilt, explaining, "I made my quilt to keep my family warm. I made it beautiful so my heart would not break."[55] To describe this woman as "moral" seems evaluatively inept. In fact, there is no traditional ethical theory (except perhaps Aristotle's) that could shed much light on what this woman was aiming at by her actions with respect to her family or herself. Yet here is someone whose response to herself and those around her is impressive and important; the story surely brings to mind memories of what our families and friends have done for themselves and for us, not merely because they were "moral" and concerned to respect us as persons, but because they loved us, and themselves, and those aspects of the world around us that are worth loving. The intrinsic value morality tells us to respect in our dealings with other persons is probably not the only kind of value each of us has, and to love someone may be to appreciate them in a quite special way—to accord them a particular nonmoral value (think of how parents cherish their children, or how people take delight in their friends' company).

Nonetheless, real love can exist only if there is also moral respect. The contract device therefore gives us a way to evaluate one moral component of any human relationship. It helps us to understand what to protect in our relationships with others, but it doesn't tell us all the ways we should respond to human beings in order to build a fine friendship, a loving marriage, a bond with our children. It tells us the harmful emotional responses we must control in order to accord people their worth; it does not tell us the emotions we ought to cultivate if we wish to develop enriching ties to others. And outside of explaining their instrumental value, it can never tell us what our lives, and our relationships with others, are *for*.

So contractarian theorizing is the beginning of wisdom about how we should relate to our fellow human beings—but it is only the beginning.[56]

Notes

1. Annette C. Baier, "What Do Women Want in a Moral Theory?" *Nous* 19, 1 (March 1985): 56.

2. Ibid., p. 54. And see Ian Hacking, "Winner Take Less: A Review of *The Evolution of Cooperation* by Robert Axelrod," in *New York Review of Books,* June 28, 1984.

3. Baier, "What Do Women Want in a Moral Theory?" p. 55.

4. Aristotle, *Nicomachean Ethics,* tr. by T. E. Irwin (Indianapolis: Hackett, 1985), 1155a22 (p. 208).

5. See 1155a27 (Irwin translation, p. 208). It may be, however, that Aristotle is primarily arguing that if one is just, one is also friendly (as part of his concept of civic friendship), whereas I want to emphasize that if one is friendly, one is also just.

6. Carol Gilligan's classic work is *In a Different Voice: Psychological Theory and Women's Development* (Cambridge, Mass.: Harvard University Press, 1982). She has revised and expanded her ideas since then. See a variety of articles about Gilligan's recent work in *Mapping the Moral Domain,* ed. by Carol Gilligan, Victoria Ward, and Jill McLean, with Betty Bandige (Cambridge, Mass.: Center for the Study of Gender, Education, and Human Development, 1988). See also Carol Gilligan, "Moral Orientation and Moral Development," in *Women and Moral Theory,* ed. by Eva Feder Kittay and Diana T. Meyers (Totowa, N.J.: Rowman and Littlefield, 1987), pp. 19–33.

7. Gilligan, *In a Different Voice,* pp. 35–36.

8. Ibid.

9. Ibid., p. 36.

10. Baier, "What Do Women Want in a Moral Theory," p. 62.

11. Annette Baier, "The Need for More Than Justice," in *Science, Morality, and Feminist Theory,* ed. Marsha Hanen and Kai Nielsen (Calgary: University of Calgary Press, 1987), p. 54.

12. Gilligan, *In a Different Voice,* p. 36.

13. See Marcia Homiak's essay in this volume, which discusses the degenerative form of kindness that emerges when one lacks self-love.

14. See, for example, L. Blum, M. Homiak, J. Housman, and N. Scheman, "Altruism and Women's Oppression," in *Women and Philosophy,* ed. by Carol Gould and Marx Wartofsky (New York: G. P. Putnam's Sons, 1976), pp. 222–247.

15. Charlotte Brontë, *Shirley,* quotation taken from edition of Andrew and Judith Hook (Harmondsworth: Penguin, 1987) p. 190.

16. From "Professions for Women" in *The Virginia Woolf Reader,* ed. by Mitchell A. Leaska (San Diego: Harcourt Brace, 1984), pp. 278–279.

17. See Blum et al., "Altruism and Women's Oppression," for a discussion of the way altruism must be accompanied by autonomy if it is going to be a morally healthy response.

18. I take this to be an idea suggested by Susan Wolf in her "Moral Saints," *Journal of Philosophy,* 79, 8 (August 1982): 419–439. Ironically, this fixation has been more the product of theories developed by males (e.g., Immanuel Kant and Jeremy Bentham) than by females. Perhaps such a fixation is the natural result of male dissatisfaction with a Jake-like moral perspective and an attempt to redirect the largely self-regarding focus of that perspective. But theorists such as Kant, who stress the other-regarding nature of morality, invariably start from an assumption of self-worth and personal autonomy. In a paper that celebrates interdependence and connection, Baier notes that Kant thought women were incapable of full autonomy and then remarks, "It is ironic that Gilligan's original findings in a way confirm Kant's views—it seems that autonomy really may not be for women. Many of them reject that ideal" ("Need for More Than Justice," p. 50). But such a rejection may actually be evidence of these women's development into servile and dependent beings rather than free, self-respecting, and claim-making persons. For discussions on this general topic, see the contributions by DuBois, Dunlap, Carol Gilligan, Catharine MacKinnon and Menkel-Meadow in "Feminist Discourse, Moral Values, and the Law," *Buffalo Law Review* 34 (1985): 11ff.

19. Virginia Held, "Noncontractual Society: A Feminist View," in Hanen and Nielsen, eds., *Science, Morality, and Feminist Theory,* p. 111.

20. Ibid., p. 113. For similar criticisms, see Carole Pateman, *The Sexual Contract* (Palo Alto, Calif: Polity/Stanford University Press, 1988).

21. Baier, "What Do Women Want in a Moral Theory?," p. 62.

22. Hobbes believed that moral imperatives were also justified by virtue of being commanded by God. However, his contractarian justification seeks to define the nature and authority of moral imperatives solely by reference to the desires and reasoning abilities of human beings, so that regardless of their religious commitments, all people will see that they have reason to act morally.

23. Hobbes believes he performed the latter project in Chapters 14 and 15 of *Leviathan,* ed. by C. B. MacPherson (Harmondsworth: Penguin, 1968).

24. However, I have argued elsewhere that Hobbesian contractarians implicitly assume the kind of problematic metaphysical ideas they criticize in the theories of others. See my "Normativity and Naturalism," unpublished manuscript.

25. Gauthier himself has been moved by these kinds of worries, inspired, he says, by Hegel. See his "Social Contract as Ideology," *Philosophy and Public Affairs* (1977): 130–164.

26. Hobbes, *Leviathan,* chapter 10, paragraph 16 (p. 42 in MacPherson edition).

27. Immanuel Kant, On the Common Saying: "This May Be True in Theory, But It Doesn't Apply in Practice," in *Kant's Political Writings,* ed. by Hans Reiss (Cambridge: Cambridge University Press, 1970), p. 63. Emphasis in original.

28. Rawls, for example, explicitly compares his original position procedure to Kant's Categorical Imperative procedure (see Rawls, *A Theory of Justice* [Cambridge, Mass.: Harvard University Press, 1971], section 40). And Scanlon suggests that the contractarian form of argument is a kind of proof procedure for ethics that is analogous to proof procedures in mathematics; its basis is in human reason, and we use it to construct moral laws in a way that gives them objectivity. See Scanlon's "Contractualism and Utilitarianism," in *Utilitarianism and Beyond,* ed. by A. Sen and B. Williams (Cambridge: Cambridge University Press, 1982).

29. Sarah Ruddick, for example, writes, "Especially masculine men (and sometimes women), fearful of physicality and needs of care, develop a transcendence based on a 'tradition of freeing the thinking brain from the depths of the most pressing situations and sending it off to some (fictive) summit for a panoramic overview.' From this perch they promulgate views that are inimical to the values of caring labor. They imagine a truth abstracted from bodies and a self detached from feelings. When faced with concrete seriousness, they measure and quantify. Only partially protected by veils of ignorance that never quite hide frightening differences and dependencies, they forge agreements of reason and regiment dissent by rules and fair fights." From Ruddick, *Maternal Thinking: Toward a Politics of Peace* (Boston: Beacon, 1989); quotation in passage taken from Klaus Thewelweit, *Male Fantasies* (Minneapolis: University of Minnesota Press, 1987), p. 364. Ruddick's criticism is similar to those made by Rawls's Hegel-inspired communitarian critics (e.g., Michael Sandel).

30. See Kathryn Morgan, "Women and Moral Madness," in Hanen and Nielsen, eds., *Science, Morality and Feminist Theory,* pp. 201–226.

31. Susan Moller Okin, *Justice, Gender, and the Family,* (New York: Basic Books, 1989).

32. Ibid., p. 101.

33. Indeed, as I have reflected on Archimedean thinking in the literature, it has struck me that it is interestingly akin to a certain kind of thinking of mothers as they raise their children. In the words of one novelist, mothers are "Conscious Makers of People" who strive to develop an environment for their children that will allow them to grow up well (i.e., confident rather than fearful, fulfilled rather than miserable, capable rather than dependent) and try to ensure that the institutions with which their children come into contact will operate in a way that fosters that end. The Rawlsian contractarian also wants us to play a role in shaping the people of our society by asking us to formulate principles that will animate the social institutions that make any of us who we are. Members of a Rawls-like Archimedean position have as their primary concern the development of an environment in which future members of the society can grow up well, and insofar as they are aware of the powerful effect society and its institutions have on shaping the kind of people

any of us become, they are just as interested as any mother in constructing or changing social institutions to foster the development of mature and morally healthy human beings. Far from being antithetical to the perspective of mothering, Rawls's Archimedean point is a way to encourage mothering-like concerns in a political context.

34. For a review of the problems with Rawls's maximin rule, see John Harsanyi, "Can the Maximin Principle Serve as a Basis for Morality? A Critique of John Rawls's *A Theory of Justice*," *American Political Science Review* 69 (1975): 594–606. And for a discussion of these problems from a philosophical standpoint, see D. Clayton Hubin, "Minimizing Maximin," *Philosophical Studies* 37 (1980): 363–372.

35. Scanlon, "Contractualism and Utilitarianism," p. 110.

36. Ibid.

37. Ibid., pp. 123–124.

38. Ibid., p. 123.

39. Ibid., p. 111.

40. Ibid., p. 127.

41. In "Contractualism and Utilitarianism," Scanlon seems to vacillate between regarding the test as defining moral properties and regarding it as a test that presupposes and uses those properties. He begins the essay by pushing the first position, arguing that we should follow Mackie in being suspicious of moral properties that are supposed to be instances of "intrinsic 'to-be-doneness' and 'not-to-be-doneness'" (p. 118), and he proposes instead that moral properties be defined via a reasoning procedure (and in particular, a contractualist procedure) that would define rather than presuppose such properties (making the view the moral equivalent of mathematical intuitionism). But later Scanlon cannot help but appeal to properties that are right- and wrong-making independent of the contractualist agreement test, properties that he relies upon in order to define that reasoning procedure. "There are also right- and wrong-making properties which are themselves independent of the contractualist notion of agreement. I take the property of being an act of killing for the pleasure of doing so to be a wrong-making property of this kind" (p. 118). But immediately after stating this, Scanlon writes, "Such properties are wrong-making because it would be unreasonable to reject any set of principles which permitted the acts they characterise" (ibid.). But now it sounds as if their wrong-making character is *derived from* the contractualist test, such that it cannot be independent of the test after all.

42. Scanlon is prepared to allow that contractarian reasoning might endorse the utilitarian principle, but he would have to insist that it would do so in a "contractarian way"—i.e., a way that was not itself a form of utilitarian reasoning. Hence, he needs to give us the structure of this uniquely contractarian way of reasoning.

43. See also Marilyn Friedman, "Beyond Caring: The Demoralization of Gender," in Hanen and Nielsen, eds., *Science, Morality, and Feminist Theory*, p. 100. I am in substantial agreement with Friedman's arguments that the "justice perspective" properly understood is just as concerned with and relevant to the health of a variety of human relationships— including intimate ones—as is the "care perspective."

44. David Gauthier, *Morals by Agreement* (Oxford: Oxford University Press, 1986), p. 11.

45. Moreover, to make a meta-ethical point, although I am understanding this notion of dignity or worth to be the source of moral rightness and wrongness, it may not itself be a moral notion. So if "reasonableness" is cashed out using this notion, we may be able to interpret the contractarian test as Scanlon wished—i.e., as that which defines moral rightness and moral wrongness while being informed by something nonmoral.

46. See Jean Hampton, "Contracts and Choices: Does Rawls Have a Social Contract Theory?" *Journal of Philosophy* 77, 6 (June 1980).

47. Thus I disagree with Scanlon ("Contractualism and Utilitarianism," pp. 124–128), who argues that Rawls is not a real contractarian because of his reliance on the "I could be anyone" device. Both devices aim to bring others' needs to bear on your deliberations such that your choice takes them into account in the right way. Whether the others are there "in person" around an agreement table in your thought experiment, or whether they are there in virtue of the fact that you are forced to choose as if you were any one of them, does not seem to matter at all in the final result.

48. Carol Pateman, *The Sexual Contract* (Stanford, Calif.: Stanford University Press, 1988), p. 184; see also p. 187. Patemen lays out the peculiarities of the marriage contract on pp. 163–167. Feminist advocates of contractualization include Marjorie Schultz, "Contractual Ordering of Marriage: A New Model for State Policy," *California Law Review* 70 (1982): 207–334.

49. Such an Aristotelian theory needn't say that all of us have the same legitimate interests. This theory could ascribe to us a certain set of interests but insist that the different psychological and physiological natures of each of us generate different needs.

50. Joan Ringelheim, "Women and the Holocaust: A Reconsideration of Research," *Signs* 10, 4 (1985): 741–761; quoted by Barbara Houston, "Rescuing Womanly Virtues: Some Dangers of Moral Reclamation," in Hanen and Nielsen, eds., *Science, Morality, and Feminist Theory,* p. 248.

51. Annette Baier writes: "It is a typical feature of the dominant moral theories and traditions, since Kant, or perhaps since Hobbes, that relationships between equals or those who are deemed equal in some important sense, have been the relations that morality is concerned primarily to regulate. . . . This pretence of an equality that is in fact absent may often lead to desirable protection of the weaker, or more dependent. But it somewhat masks the question of what our moral relationships are to those who are our superiors or our inferiors in power. A more realistic acceptance of the fact that we begin as helpless children, that at almost every point of our lives we deal with both the more and the less helpless, that equality of power and interdependency, between two persons or groups, is rare and hard to recognize when it does occur, might lead us to a more direct approach to questions concerning the design of institutions structuring these relationships between unequals (families, schools, hospitals, armies) and of the morality of our dealings with the more and the less powerful" ("Need for More Than Justice," pp. 52–53).

52. See also Will Kyrnlicka, "Two Theories of Justice," *Inquiry* 33, 109–110: "In an important sense, the 'ethic of care' advanced by recent feminists does reverse these questions, replacing the contractual relationship between adults with the mother-child relationship as their paradigm of a morally responsible relationship. But the conclusion they reach is that our responsibilities to dependents can only be met if we replace the appeal to impartiality with attention to particularity, and replace justice with care."

53. Of course, a person is grateful for what the benefactor did, not for his worth. Gratitude is a reaction to the beneficial deed; but the benefited one feels it to the extent that he appreciates that his benefactor's services came about not because the benefactor was a servant or tool of his desires, but because the benefactor freely chose to bestow these services upon him. So an acknowledgment of that choice—and thus of the noninstrumental standing of the benefactor—is implicit in the emotion of gratitude.

54. There is a reason why those benefited by Good Samaritans may want to benefit their benefactors in return—they desire to preserve their own worth. Those who are in ex-

treme need, although equal in worth to those who help them, are nonetheless not equal in circumstance or capacity, and in this sense they do not have the equal standing necessary for justice to demand that they make a return. But many find this inequality a painful and humiliating experience. They wish to be in a position to return the favor in order to establish themselves as equal in capacity and circumstance to those who benefited them. Thus they want to respond as justice would require in order to show that they have the standing that the demands of justice presuppose. I am told by a family counselor that this attitude of wishing to return the benefits to parents who have freely given their care is frequent among teenagers desiring to manifest equal status with their parents (sometimes even leading them to insist that all future benefits and burdens in the family be the subject of contracts).

55. Sara Ruddick, "Maternal Thinking," in *Women and Values,* ed. by M. Pearsall (Belmont, Calif.: Wadsworth, 1986), p. 344 and footnote 8.

56. Portions of this chapter were read at Texas Technical University, Yale Law School, and the 1991 Pacific Division Meeting of the American Philosophical Association, and I wish to thank those audiences. I also wish to thank the members of the Los Angeles Law and Philosophy Group; the members of my graduate seminar at the University of California, Davis, in the fall of 1990; and Marcia Homiak, for their help during the writing of this chapter.

16

SHOULD FEMINISTS REJECT RATIONAL CHOICE THEORY?

ELIZABETH ANDERSON

1. Three Questions for Feminism and Rational Choice Theory

Should feminists reject rational choice theory? This is the theory economists and like-minded social scientists use to explain behavior. It is typically embedded in particular frameworks representing the constraints and incentives supposedly facing socially situated agents. Thus we find examples of rational choice theory in the theory of the firm, public choice theory, Becker's theory of the family, and so forth.[1] Feminists have diverse grounds for regarding the theory with suspicion. It could be seen as sexist, or, alternatively, as androcentric.

Rational choice theory could be seen as sexist insofar as its particular exemplifications deny to women, or to "feminine" persons, the status of independent rational agents. The theory, in conceiving of rationality in terms of cold, instrumental, selfish, quantitative calculation, relies on a gender polarized conceptual scheme, which counterposes these stereotypically "masculine" qualities with stereotypically "feminine" qualities of emotionality, expressiveness, caring for others, and sensitivity to qualitative differences. The theory thus presumes that only men or masculine persons are really rational.[2] So it is no wonder that Becker's economic theory of the household represents each family by a single consistent preference ordering identical to that of the male head of household. The theory fails to represent female members of male-headed households as rational agents at all: their interests and agency are subsumed under that of the patriarch.[3]

In response, defenders of rational choice theory propose to apply its model more consistently and universally than male economists have typically done. Thus, some theorists analyze the division of labor and consumption within the heterosexual family as the outcome of bargaining by rational self-interested men and women.[4] But another school of feminists objects that this approach to social explanation is androcentric: it views decisionmaking from a male point of view, ignoring the distinctively feminine ways women go about making decisions. Thus, psychologists such as Carol Gilligan affirm the gender polarized dichotomies of reason vs. emotion, self-interest vs. caring for others, and undertake the project of making women's supposedly "feminine" modes of decisionmaking more visible and more valued.[5]

These feminist criticisms of rational choice theory reflect the underlying conflict between "equality" and "difference" approaches to feminism. Is the fundamental problem the exclusion of women from high status positions, such as the status of a rational agent? Or is the problem rather the unjustified devaluation of the positions women already hold—their roles as altruistic, emotional caregivers?

To many nonfeminist social scientists, this feminist debate would probably appear to be confused and even dangerous to objective inquiry. It is confused, because it fails to distinguish facts from values, positive theories from normative ones. On this view, the theory of rational choice is just an empirical theory. The facts must decide whether women behave rationally, not politics. It is a distinct normative question, to which feminists may contribute an answer, whether women *ought* to be rational in the economist's sense. The feminist debate might also be thought to endanger the objectivity of inquiry. It threatens to make inquiry subject to the demands of "political correctness." But ideology may not dictate to science that it must represent women as behaving "rationally." The question with which I began this paper, when understood to apply to the positive theory of rational choice, thus appears illegitimate.

This critique of feminist challenges to rational choice theory raises a second question that feminists need to answer: how could political values possibly bear upon theory choice? Shouldn't theory choice be determined solely by facts and epistemic values, such as predictive power? To answer the question of this paper, we must engage the larger project of considering how and why feminist concerns might legitimately bear upon theory choice. When the theory in question is a theory of rational action, I want to argue that political values, especially feminist ones, have particular relevance. This would be impossible if the validity of rational choice theory were determined solely by empirical facts. So we must ask, thirdly, what is the empirical status of the theory of rational choice?

2. The Empirical Status of Rational Choice Theory

This is a problem internal to the research program of rational choice theory. Most rational choice theorists talk as if it were a purely empirical theory of human behavior. It is supposed to provide the psychological microfoundations of economic theory. Academics engaged in the "imperialist" project of extending the theory to extra-economic domains such as the family and sexuality regard the theory as universally true, capturing deep facts of human nature independent of the particular cultures and social roles they may inhabit.[6] On this empirical interpretation of the theory of rational choice, it is hard to see how political or normative considerations could bear upon whether the theory should be accepted. The only thing that should matter is whether the facts support it.

The trouble with the empirical, microfoundational interpretation of the theory is that it has been massively falsified.[7] One response to this problem is to interpret the theory as conceptually true. The Austrian School of Economics advanced a strong version of this interpretation.[8] Ludwig von Mises argued that the theory is a priori true, because all action is necessarily rational when viewed from the standpoint of the agents themselves.

Interpreted as the inevitable framework of practical reasoning, the theory is false. For we can imagine alternative systems of rational principles from those proposed by the economic theory of rational choice. The economic theory tells individuals to defect in one-shot prisoner's dilemmas, because defection dominates cooperation from a purely self-interested point of view. But Kantian theory tells individuals to cooperate in these situations, because one can't rationally will defection as a universal principle of action. Whichever theory is normatively correct, our ability to imagine an alternative system of rational principles shows that von Mises's system is not conceptually necessary.

We can, of course, *decide* to interpret people's choices *as if* they were always the product of some imagined set of consistent beliefs and desires. This is how a self-conscious behaviorist must see the theory, as "revealed preference theory" does.[9] But this decision comes at two costs. First, the preferences we impute to people may not correspond to what they actually care about. The economist interpreting the Kantian cooperator in a prisoner's dilemma imputes to her a utility function dependent on the utility of her counterpart in the PD, when in fact her utilities are independent but she acts out of commitment to moral principle.[10] The theory thus fails as a psychological explanation. Second, the behavioristic, tautological interpretation fails as a causal explanation, since it does not offer any account of underlying causes (real beliefs and desires) at all.

Donald Davidson is willing to concede, on independent grounds, that the theory of rational choice does not provide a causal explanation of behavior.[11] He defends a weaker version of the Austrian view: it provides, not the inevitable conceptual framework of action, but the fundamental default conceptual framework for explaining action. This position is known as *methodological rationalism*. On the principle of charity, we should try to interpret others' behavior as rational. This means that we should impute those beliefs and desires to individuals that enable us to represent their choices as maximizing their expected utility. Resort to alternative explanations is warranted only if we can't make sense of their action as rational.

The methodological rationalist interpretation of rational choice theory provides a clear entry for feminist critique. For the justification for making a particular theory of rationality the default explanatory framework is that it is normatively correct. Feminists may therefore challenge its default status by challenging its normative credentials. If the theory is normatively unjustified, it could still explain particular behaviors. But it could not offer a complete explanation. For in addition to knowing that an agent followed the theory, we would also want an explanation of why she deviated from the normatively correct path.

Davidson's methodological rationalism seems too strong. Consider the parallel application of Davidson's principle of charity to beliefs. To make sense of the Scholastics' scientific methods and beliefs, do we really need to explain why they didn't follow modern standards of statistical inference? They were not erring by their own lights; they simply had no conception of statistics, as it hadn't been invented yet. Similarly, we can't expect merchants who operated before the invention of double-entry bookkeeping and probability theory to have been maximizing their expected profits. For they had little idea how profitable their activities were, or of what gambles were good bets.[12] If methodological rationalism has any validity, it can't take the theory of practical reason currently regarded as normatively correct as the default. Rather, it should take the theory accepted by agents at the time as the default. We need to understand how agents tried to make sense of their actions by their own lights.

This is Max Weber's point.[13] Social scientists are entitled to assume that agents generally try to adjust their actions to conform to the norms in terms of which they make sense of their actions. So some form of methodological rationalism is right. But the default explanatory framework should be the system of rational norms agents accept. Of course, agents' own rationales and motives for their actions are often inarticulate, confused, and appeal to conflicting systems of norms. So the social scientist's task is to make sense of this mess by sorting out the strands of appeals to different systems of norms, clarifying and rationalizing these, and putting them into perspicuous contrast with each other. This yields a range of ideal types of action. Weber distilled human action into four ideal types. Action in conformity with rational choice theory was just one ideal type (*zweckrational*); an alternative ideal type of rational action (*wertrational*) followed a rigorist version of Kantian morality. In addition, Weber thought that some people sometimes act more or less automatically, without a discernible subjective rationale. Two ideal types of nonrational action deal with these cases—traditional action and emotional action. On Weber's view, the theory of rational choice offers just one among several ideal types of action to which people conform, and people live up to its demands only in particular social and historical contexts.

It might seem that, in relativizing his methodological rationalism to agents' subjective systems of norms, Weber's project insulates positive social science from normative criticism. Weber himself certainly thought so.[14] But the act of classifying the strands of subjective motivation into a range of distinct, internally coherent ideal types of action reflects the value judgments of the classifier. For example, feminists contest Weber's representation of emotional action as indiscriminate, automatic, and lacking purpose or point. This assimilates the loving embrace a mother may give to her child—an expressive action that may be highly nuanced and sensitive to her child's needs, temperament, and conflicting senses of pride and dependence—to the blind lashing out of a person boiling over in rage. In insisting on a sharp distinction between rational and emotional action, Weber prevents us from representing part of what is normatively compelling and admirable about some types of emotional action, particularly those associated with women and "feminine" roles. Some emotions sensitize us to others' needs, rather than just getting in the way of coolly calculated purposes.

One might defend the value-neutrality of Weber's framework by arguing that, from a logical point of view, emotional action has nothing less going for it than rational action—embracing either involves an equally irrational existential commitment. That is cold comfort to the side whose position has lost the ability to represent its appealing features within Weber's ideal typical classification. Weber defends the value-neutrality of his framework from the nihilistic standpoint of the night in which all cows are black. But he constructed his ideal-typical framework in broad daylight, where the normative implications of one ideal-typical representation of action relative to another are as clear as the distinction between a spotted and a belted cow. By representing different types of action in the way he did, Weber loaded the argument in favor of economic rationality.

Let us take stock of the argument so far. Our question was how feminist or any other social values could legitimately bear on theory choice in social science. We have seen that on several interpretations of the theory—rational choice as a simple empirical truth about human nature, as a necessary truth about intentional action, and as a mere tautology of logical behaviorism—it is hard to see the relevance of social values to theory choice. But the first two interpretations of the theory make it false, and the third reduces it to triviality, without explanatory power. On two alternative interpretations of the theory—as the default explanation in methodological rationalism, or as one among several ideal types of rational and nonrational action—social values do play a role in choosing the theory. It merits choice as the default explanation in methodological rationalism only if it is the normatively correct theory of rational choice. It merits a place in the constellation of ideal types of action only if the way it figures in specifying the range of actions available to us highlights rather than obscures our options, and the considerations normatively relevant to evaluating them. Misleading typologies of action are objectionable for misrepresenting or obscuring the merits and demerits of some types of action.

3. Dimensions of Rational Choice Theory

I have argued that social values can play a legitimate role in deciding whether to explain human action in terms of rational choice theory. But how should feminists actually evaluate the theory? We need first to get clear on what the theory of rational choice says. Applications of the theory typically weave together several logically independent strands of thought. Let us distinguish five dimensions of rational choice theory: *instrumental, formal, deliberative, substantive, and rhetorical*.

The *instrumental* theory of rational choice says that people tend to select means that effectively achieve their ends. The *formal* theory of rational choice says that people tend to maximize their utility; that is, that they adopt as their end the maximal satisfaction of their overall scheme of preferences. The theory is formal in that it concerns only the relative rankings of a person's preferences, disregarding the contents of these preferences or the individual's reasons for having them. It says that an individual's preferences fit into a single, complete, transitive ordering, and that individuals choose to satisfy the top ranked preference in that ordering. Under conditions of risk and uncertainty, the formal theory assumes that individuals make choices in accordance with consistent subjective estimates of the probability of different outcomes given their options, and choose the option that maximizes their expected utility.[15]

The *deliberative* theory of rational choice depicts individuals as deciding what to do by undertaking a cost-benefit analysis of their options and choosing the option that yields the greatest net expected benefit. Of course, people rarely think things through as systematically as a real cost-benefit analysis would prescribe. The idea is that people do this more or less inarticulately and half-consciously, and that they would subjectively endorse this way of deliberating about their choices were the process to be made explicit. The deliberative theory supposes that people are ready to accept the formal theory of their behavior not only as correctly identifying their beliefs and desires, but as specifying the norms of practical reasoning they accept,

The *substantive* theory of rational choice says that people rank their options according to how well these options promote their self-interest. Although egoism is logically distinct from the other aspects of rational choice theory, it almost always accompanies them in actual social scientific applications. Jon Elster argues, with some force, that much of the interest of rational choice theory for social science would be lost if it abandoned the presumption that people mainly act out of self-interest.[16]

When we consider actual social scientific explanations of observed phenomena, which of these dimensions of rational choice theory bears the most explanatory weight? Judging by where economists invest their greatest intellectual energies, bestow their highest honors, and take their hardest line of defense when criticized, one might think it was the formal theory of rational choice. It is a poor choice. As I noted above, no dimension of rational choice theory has been more thoroughly disconfirmed.[17] But, as Dierdre McCloskey has persuasively argued, economists misapprehend the real source of power in rational choice explanation, which has little to do with the formalism.[18] She traces economists' misapprehension to their training in discredited positivist theories of scientific explanation, and to the gendered symbolism of scientific prestige. Economists invest themselves in formal, axiomatic, mathematical modes of explanation not because these really explain the empirical phenomena but because ingenuity in deploying these stereotypically masculine modes of reasoning bestows manly prestige on their inventor.[19]

McCloskey (1985) argues that what is really doing most explanatory work in economics is, among other rhetorical devices, the *rhetoric* of rational choice theory, which includes a plausible narrative about how people behave.[20] Like Davidson, she assumes that rational choice theory is the default explanation for human behavior. I want to take the rhetoric of rational choice in a different, Weberian direction, and argue that the rhetorical theory of rational choice has explanatory power precisely because it stands in perspicuous contrast with alternative styles of action—other ideal types, although not necessarily Weberian ideal types. When economic explanations are powerful, it is usually because they explain behavior in terms of a compelling ideal of human agency, familiar and socially sanctioned in a wide range of social settings, *but not all-pervasive*.

Who is this rational agent of economic rhetoric? What kind of character is the profit-maximizing entrepreneur, the bargain-shopping consumer, the rent-seeking lobbyist that populates economists' stories? He (this is popularly coded a masculine ideal) is *self-transparent:* he knows what he wants, and suffers from no unconscious drives that thwart his conscious desires. He is *opportunistic:* he takes the initiative in pursuing his goals, and actively seeks and promptly takes advantage of every opportunity to advance his goals. He is resourceful and enterprising; neither passive nor procrastinating. He is *self-reliant*, and expects others to likewise look after themselves. He is *coolly calculating:* he is good at probability theory and engages in no wishful thinking, self-deception, or superstition in calculating means to his ends.[21] Most importantly, the rhetoric of economic rationality portrays the rational agent as *autonomous* and *self-confident*.

By autonomy, I mean, firstly, that the economically rational agent regards himself as authorized to order his own preferences as he sees fit. He understands himself as having preferences of his own, distinct from the preferences other people have about how he should act, and has *no compunctions* about pursuing those preferences. So he feels no obligation to defer to others' opinions as to how he should behave. He does not bow down to social convention, tradition, or even morality. This does not mean that he will never act in conformity to social norms. He may do so if he feels like it, or if he judges that the payoffs of conformity (in terms of avoiding the sanctions of others or gaining the rewards they offer for conformity) exceed the payoffs of nonconformity.

What he does not do is conform to a norm out of a sense of obligation, from the thought that the norm is right, correct, or legitimate—something that people in his situation *ought* to follow or have reason to follow, even if they don't feel like it. This sense of obligation need not have anything to do with morality. It can attach to expressly nonmoral norms of fashion, etiquette, masculinity or femininity. Action from obligation is not action out of regard for the rewards and punishments contingently attached to the norm: a sense of obligation may motivate conformity to norms even among agents who are certain others aren't looking. Nor is it action from personal preference: people engaged in norm-governed action people feel that if the choice were up to them, they would prefer to act otherwise—but they do not feel that the choice is up to them.[22] By contrast, the rhetorically rational agent always feels that the choice is up to him, even when others rig the incentives in a compelling way.

The second sense in which the rhetorically rational agent is autonomous is that he regards himself as a self-originating source of claims when interacting with others, and expects others to acknowledge his authority to make such claims. This is a logical implication from his willingness to explicitly assume the position of a bargainer in negotiations. Bargainers make claims on their own account, without having to make excuses for refusing to do what others want them to do. They don't feel a need to find some external source of authority licensing their demands on or offers to others. This is what distinguishes the social setting of bargaining from other social settings in which people try to get what they want—for example, servants pleading to their masters, or convicts begging for mercy from the court.

The rational agent of economic rhetoric is *self-confident* in his self-knowledge. His frank acknowledgment to himself of what he wants and what he is doing does not destabilize his preferences or choices or call his own self-image into question. He suffers from no inner conflict, ambivalence, vacillation, or shame over his preferences, or over seeing himself as an active, opportunistic, autonomous agent. He feels entitled to regard himself as a self-originating source of claims, and so need not hide behind a conception of himself as bound by obligations or external expectations in order to justify his own actions before himself. He therefore has no reason to practice self-deception. He stands in an unproblematic relation to his preferences, goals, and agency.

The rhetoric of rational choice theory clearly reaches far beyond the formal axioms of rational choice. The rhetorical theory is psychologically much richer, involving mental contents not present in the formal theory: notably, an agent's representations of and attitudes toward himself, his own choices, other people's attitudes toward him, and other people's preferences over the choices he makes. Why go this far? Why not stick to the parsimonious psychology of the formal theory?

If McCloskey is right, it is the rhetorical aspects of rational choice theory rather than the formal axioms that bear the weight of most rational choice explanations of human events. This becomes clear when we consider the normative uses economists make of rational choice theory. Most economists favor the principle of consumer's sovereignty. This says that social arrangements, including government policies, should be evaluated by the degree to which they satisfy the preferences of individuals, as these are expressed in their market choices.[23] If the concept of "preference" in this principle were understood purely formally, as "whatever people, in fact, choose" or perhaps causally, as "whatever psychological states cause them to choose as they do," then the principle would have little normative force. Why should we think that people choose well, or that what causes them to choose has any normative authority? Economists have only one plausible reply: because, in general, people are *autonomous* choosers, acting on their *own* judgments of good and bad, and individuals are the ultimate normative authorities for themselves. The preferences they reveal in their market choices should be respected because they are autonomous.[24]

Another reason for moving beyond the formal to the rhetorical theory of rational choice is that the formal theory of rational choice at best captures only a part of human psychology, omitting much that may conflict with it. We are not perfect rational choosers. So what are the psychological conditions under which we *can* be perfect rational choosers? One answer might be: if we were stripped of the psychological capacities that make us different from pigeons or rats (who, it appears, are more perfect rational choice machines than we are).[25] But this condition is rarely realized.

Another answer might be: if we had *mastered* the psychological motivations in us that might conflict with our satisfying the formal axioms of rational choice. We can read the rhetorical theory of rational choice as representing *one* set of psychological conditions for people satisfying the formal theory of rational choice, given that we have various tendencies that can move us to formulate preferences and make choices contrary to the theory's predictions. Chief among those tendencies are self-doubt, and heteronomous motivations derived from what others expect or demand of oneself. Consciousness of one's own negative self-assessments, and of others' evaluations of oneself, combined with caring about these evaluations, tends to generate multiple, conflicting, incomplete, intransitive preference orderings. Multiplicity comes from the different points of view one takes on one's own options: the points of view of one's uncritized preferences, of one's unconscious preferences, of what one would want on one's own account, of one's shame or disapproval of one's preferences, of other people's condemnation or approval of those preferences, and so forth. Conflict comes from the fact that these points of view disagree. Incompleteness comes about from irresolution over how to resolve such conflicts. Intransitivity comes from inconsistent attempts to resolve conflicts, first one way, then another. The rhetorical theory of rational choice, taking account of some of the complex ways we might fail to be formally rational, offers one way out of these conflicts. It suggests that a person can *achieve* a single, unified, complete, consistent preference ordering by bringing to consciousness all of his motivations (self-transparency), resolving to evaluate them all from the standpoint of what he would want on his own account, disregarding the conflicting preferences of other people for what his preferences should be (autonomy), and getting comfortable with his own resolution and with the motivations he acts on (self-confidence).

The formal theory of rational choice represents only the shadows of these complex conditions. For example, the formal theory reflects the autonomy condition in the standard assumption that individuals' preferences are independent. But the purely formal representation of independent preference orderings loses information that is crucial to understanding the basis upon which the parties are interacting. Consider two people, Joe and Jane, who have the same preference orderings. Economists conventionally understand this situation, if it isn't coincidental, to be the product of altruism: perhaps Jane loves Joe, and so adopts as her aim the satisfaction of his preferences. But altruism is not the only possible cause of convergent preference orderings. Another possibility is that Jane is married to Joe, and conceives of herself as bound by her vow to obey him. Perhaps the love has gone out of the marriage, but her minister tells her that she is duty-bound by God to obey her husband, and she believes she must obey the word of God. Or perhaps she was so deeply socialized into thinking of herself as feminine and therefore passive that she never thought of framing preferences on her own account, but always waited upon the initiative of intimate others to tell her what she should want. Or perhaps Joe flies into a violent rage whenever she does something he doesn't want her to do, and by sheer terror drives out any motivation she has to resist his will. All of these causes could bring about convergent preference orderings, but they are due to radical heteronomy, not altruism.

It matters a lot whether one person's preferences coincide with another's because of self-confident altruism or because of heteronomous causes. The formal theory of rational choice lacks the means to represent these differences. Nor can it tell us whose utilities may be dependent on whose: that is, whether Jane's preferences coincide with Joe's because she orders him around, because he orders her around, because she cares about him, or he, her, or because they make joint plans together on terms of equality.

But these differences matter. The rhetorical theory of rational choice is superior to the formal theory, because in the context of the field of alternative ideal types of action to which it stands in perspicuous contrast, it lets us distinguish between altruistic and heteronomous "failures" to conform to the assumptions of the theory of rational choice. The capacity to draw this distinction is crucial for feminist projects.

Here, then, we have a straightforwardly political reason for feminists to prefer one articulation of rational choice theory to another: the rhetorical theory is superior to the purely formal theory in its ability to represent real distinctions in the character of human motivation that matter to feminists. The rhetorical theory of rational choice is, then, an apt object for feminist assessment. It doesn't follow from this argument that feminists should rush to embrace the rhetoric of rationality and its theory of human agency. Feminists must still ask whether it draws the distinctions feminists care about in the right way. And here arises the ambivalence of feminism toward rational choice theory. The rhetorical theory of rational choice represents a normative ideal of rational agency, not merely a description of certain people. Is it an ideal we ought to accept?

The rhetorical theory of rational choice arouses ambivalence among feminists because its ideal typical character sits squarely between stereotypically feminine vices and virtues. On the one hand, becoming an economically rational agent can be viewed as a remedy for stereotypically feminine vices—for the sorts of self-effacing, heteronomous character traits that women who internalize norms of femininity find themselves trapped in. Egoism is a virtue compared to feminine self-abnegation, to the feminine thoughtfulness for others that is supposed to entail no regard for oneself. Go-getting assertiveness is a virtue compared with feminine passivity. Self-reliance is a virtue compared with feminine one-sided dependence on those who take their superior status for granted. Calculativeness is a virtue compared with the cult of romanticism about sexuality that discourages women from considering whether their sexual activity is self-destructive. Autonomy reflected in disdain for social convention and traditional moral norms is a virtue compared with internalizing norms of femininity that command one's self-cancellation or servility. The frank, self-confident affirmation of one's own preferences on one's own account is superior to the feminine "niceness" that requires women not to make claims for themselves except as a means to serving others' needs. No wonder that "equality feminists" should be attracted to the rhetoric of rational choice, not just as a normative ideal, but as a tool for diagnosing how women who have internalized submissive norms of femininity end up undermining their own interests. The rhetoric of rational choice articulates a set of virtues that equality feminists would like to see women acquire.

On the other hand, the rational agent of economic rhetoric can be viewed as vicious in comparison to some stereotypically feminine virtues. Egoism is a vice when it is just a form of selfishness, opposed to caring for others. Excessive self-reliance can be just a way to emotionally disengage from the obligations entailed by intimate relations with others. Expecting others to look after themselves is a vice for someone occupying a role of mother or caretaker of dependents. From the perspective of feminine ideals of shared feelings, intimacy, and refined manners, the rhetorically rational agent can be a sorry social clod. His autonomous disregard for others' feelings and preferences is often a poor excuse for inconsiderate behavior. Whatever the rational agent may be, he isn't "nice." His autonomous determination to make claims on his own account can interfere with his making claims on account of "us"—a couple, a family, a neighborhood—and thus renders him dysfunctional for membership in communities. He tends to be uncooperative, untrustworthy, and a free rider whenever he can get away with it. These are the features of the rational agent that make difference feminists, and indeed feminists more generally, want to reject rational choice theory as a normative doctrine as well as a theory of human nature. In representing human behavior through economic rhetoric, the theory of rational choice may blind us to the operations of other, important "feminine" human capacities in the phenomena being explained, and thereby render feminine difference invisible, in women and men alike.

4. Luker's *Taking Chances*: A Case Study of Feminist Rational Choice Research

This sketch of feminist reactions to rational choice theory only opens up questions for exploration; it doesn't settle them. It suggests that rational choice theory in its rhetorically rich version offers both opportunities and pitfalls for feminist researchers. We can get a clearer sense of these issues by studying an example of feminist research using rational choice theory. A particularly fruitful case to consider is Kristin Luker's study of women's decisions about their sexuality and contraceptive use, *Taking Chances*.[26] In this classic study, Luker investigated the sexual and contraceptive choices of 500 women who sought the services of a California abortion clinic in the early 1970s. Her subjects consisted of those women who were voluntarily sexually active, did not want to be pregnant, had contraceptive skills, but were not using effective contraception. They were contraceptive risk-takers. Luker found that the vast majority of women who seek abortions fit into this category.[27] Relatively few women seek abortions because of rape, incest, their own health needs, fetal deformity, contraceptive failure, or contraceptive ignorance—the standard list most Americans allow as morally acceptable reasons or excuses for abortion. Thus, most women seeking abortions are condemned by mainstream American society as foolish, irresponsible, or immoral. Against this view, Luker aims to rationalize the seemingly paradoxical behavior of abortion-seeking women.

Luker's project pursues two feminist aims. One is to refute the sexist assumption that women are irrational, especially with respect to decisions concerning sexuality and reproduction. According to this sexist view, women make self-destructive reproductive choices because they are driven by unreflective emotions or neuroses. By vindicating the rationality of women's sexual and reproductive choices, Luker undermines a demeaning view of women and the paternalistic conclusion that people often draw from it, that women can't be trusted with the freedom to make their own sexual choices.

A second aim is to provide an understanding of the causes of unwanted pregnancy that would enable family planning clinics and health care services to deliver contraceptives more effectively to the women who need it most. Health care institutions assume that if they provide contraceptive knowledge and access, then rational, responsible women who are sexually active and don't want babies will take effective advantage of these services. Those who don't are seen as irrational and hence beyond the reach of the help provided by these institutions. By showing how women are really rational in their contraceptive choices, Luker shifts the blame for unwanted pregnancy from women to the system of contraceptive delivery. The problem is not that women are unresponsive to their own needs, it's that the system is unresponsive to women's needs. If it judged the costs and benefits of contraceptive use from women's points of view rather than its own point of view, it could develop better ways to deliver contraceptive services.

Luker's study is an interesting case of economic "imperialism." It extends the theory of rational choice to a domain of human behavior usually explained by other ideal types of action: emotional, as a reflection of erotic drives or romantic passions; conventional, as governed by moral norms and gender role socialization; biological, as the product of instincts for reproduction; or psychodynamic, as due to neuroses, repression, and inner motivational conflicts. So when we ask whether Luker's subjects are rational in their sexual and contraceptive behavior, it isn't sufficient to consider whether her data can be fit into the rational choice model. We must also ask whether other ideal types of action fit the data better.

Are Luker's subjects rational? On a first analysis, it seems evident that they are not. They have an end, namely, to avoid pregnancy. They all know that sexual intercourse causes pregnancy and know how to use various methods of contraception to prevent pregnancy. They have access to these methods. Yet, they engage in sexual intercourse without using effective contraception. This seems to be a straightforward case of instrumental irrationality, a failure to take appropriate means to an end.

On a second analysis, matters are not so clear. Luker argues, consistently with rational choice theory, that her subjects have multiple, discrete ends. Avoiding pregnancy is just one of these. Thus, rational action isn't just a matter of adjusting means to ends. It is a matter of consistently ordering one's ends. In shifting the focus from instrumental to formal rationality, Luker aims to represent her subjects as choosing the option with the highest net balance of expected benefits over costs. Women who take contraceptive risks must be assigning a high cost to contraceptive use, perhaps some benefits to becoming pregnant, and a low probability of pregnancy from their sexual activities.

One might object that it's hard to believe that the costs, benefits, and probabilities could favor contraceptive risk-taking. Using contraception is less expensive, safer, and more convenient than either abortion or pregnancy. Its emotional costs seem trivial compared with the emotional costs of abortion and pregnancy. If the woman gives birth to an unwanted child, either her entire life is disrupted or she must go through the trauma of giving up the child for adoption. If she has an abortion, she must deal with the humiliation and harsh moral judgment of others, and possible disturbance of relationships with family members who disapprove and partners who refuse to share responsibility for the pregnancy. At the time Luker's subjects were seeking abortions, they also had to undertake mandatory psychiatric examinations and accept a stigmatizing diagnosis of mental disorder before obtaining an abortion. Nor is there much scope for discounting these costs in light of the probability of getting away with risk-taking: in the population at large, 80% of sexually active women who don't use contraception get pregnant within a year.[28]

Luker responds to these objections by invoking the standard economic assumption of subjective value. The cost-benefit analysis of contraceptive risk-taking just offered represents the costs and benefits as judged by outsiders. But rationality must be judged from the point of view of the agents. Nothing dictates that women must judge the emotional cost of getting pregnant and obtaining an abortion higher than the emotional cost of taking the pill, for instance. Her methods don't permit any choice-independent measurement of her subjects' views of the relative emotional and other costs of contraception and abortion. Instead, she applies a Davidsonian principle of charity and imputes to her subjects an assignment of relative costs and benefits of contraception, abortion, and pregnancy that enables her to represent their contraceptive risk-taking as rational.

This second analysis, vindicating the rationality of contraceptive risk-taking women, could be called into question by Luker's own data. Luker reports that most of the women she interviewed expressed regret for their contraceptive risk-taking. They felt stupid and foolish for the behavior that led them to seek an abortion. They saw themselves as irrational by their own lights.[29] Shouldn't this be enough to undermine the applicability of rational choice theory to their behavior?

Luker answers no. She points out that these women's expressions of regret and self-condemnation take place *ex post*. But, as any economist would insist, the proper perspective for judging the rationality of risk-taking is *ex ante*.[30] Moreover, her study population is biased to include only those women who gambled and lost—these are the only women who turned up at the abortion clinic. Luker's study methodology had no way to identify risk-taking women who gambled and didn't get pregnant, or who got pregnant but found this outcome acceptable. Risk-taking cannot be irrational just because we sometimes lose and so regret having run the risk.

Luker's point is well-taken, but not conclusive. There is a difference between merely wishing one hadn't taken a risk and lost, and judging oneself foolish or stupid for having taken the risk. In the latter case, one judges that the gamble itself was irrational. Many of Luker's subjects were judging the gamble, not merely its outcome. Luker argues that her subjects' self-condemnation should not be taken at face value, however. They were expressing their sense of foolishness in an abortion clinic, an institutional context that pressures women to accept the "official" cost-benefit analysis of their behavior, one which regards using contraception a superior option to having an abortion. When Luker heard women kicking themselves for their stupidity, she interpreted them as intimidated by health-care providers, moralists, and public-policy makers into accepting others' ways of framing the cost-benefit analysis of contraceptive use, rather than affirming the way they framed their own choices.[31] Rational choice theory only views the rationality of choices from the point of view of agents' own frames.

Let us consider, then, how Luker's subjects framed their own cost-benefit analysis of contraceptive risk-taking. Luker here appeals to the deliberative theory of rational choice, while allowing that few women articulated the reasons for their choices as explicitly as her account does. For contraceptive risk-taking to be subjectively rational, Luker argues that three calculations must differ from the "official" cost benefit analysis of this behavior: (1) the costs of contraception must be higher than officially assumed; (2) the benefits of pregnancy must be higher; and (3) the subjective probability of getting pregnancy must be lower. Let us consider each of these factors.

Among the costs of contraception Luker's subjects identified, the most interesting concern the symbolic aspects of contraceptive use—that is, what using contraception means to the agent. In using contraception, women admit to themselves that they are sexually active, planning for sex, and thus sexually available to men. Many women find this admission costly, because it conflicts with their feminine gender identity as sexually passive beings, waiting for the man to take the sexual initiative.[32] Sex is something that "just happens" to virtuous women. This is a particularly important consideration for women who have just broken up with their partners. They stop taking the pill because they assume they won't be having sex until they get "serious" with another man again. They don't see themselves as having casual sex, since this would mark them in their own minds as promiscuous, hence "trashy" and cheap.[33] Stopping contraception has the added advantage of giving women additional bargaining power with men they meet. It arms them with an excuse not to have sex with their dates, because of the higher risk of getting pregnant without adequate contraception. Some Catholic women don't use contraception because it is against their religion. Other women don't use contraception because it makes sex feel too cold and calculating, when they feel that sex should be spontaneous, a matter of being overcome by passion rather than directed by reason.[34]

Contraceptive use also expresses certain ideas about a woman's relation to her male partner which Luker's subjects found aversive. Some women fear alienating their partners by getting them involved in contraceptive decisionmaking. Planning for sex and contraception together expresses a mutual understanding between the woman and her partner that they are a couple. This admission can be frightening to both parties, who would prefer to avoid the frank and open communication couplehood entails. In the absence of communication, each partner tends to assume that the other is responsible for taking the initiative in contraceptive decisionmaking. The man assumes contraception is up to the woman, because she's the one who gets pregnant and bears the cost of sex. The woman assumes contraception is up to the man, because he's supposed to be the active partner in the relationship. The result is that couples tend to procrastinate over the decision to contracept.[35] Some of Luker's subjects stopped using birth control pills while still in a sexually active relationship. These women resented the pill because it placed the entire burden on them for preventing pregnancy, while the man was left free to enjoy sex without responsibility. Far from seeing the pill as giving them control over their bodies, they felt as if in using the pill, they were yielding control to their partners. They saw their boyfriends as self-indulgently using them for sex, while remaining unconcerned about the possible consequences of sex for the woman or the relationship. By stopping the pill, these woman saw themselves as restoring equality to the relationship, on the assumption that the man would be forced to take responsibility if she got pregnant.[36]

Luker's subjects also saw some benefits in getting pregnant. Many of these benefits were symbolic, tied to the way pregnancy affirms women's own self-conceptions and ideals for themselves. Many of Luker's subjects saw pregnancy as proving their womanhood. Luker interprets this as a response to her subjects' conflicting feelings over the changing roles of women in the 1970s. At that time women were being expected to take up new roles even as the opportunities for pursuing them were far less than promised. Becoming pregnant allows women to affirm a traditional gender identity and claim its prerogatives. It allows them to avoid taking up the challenges of a new definition of womanhood—assertiveness, initiative, independence—and indulge the traditional feminine virtues of passivity, dependence, nurturance, compliance, and self-effacement. Pregnancy can also enhance a woman's self-worth, by offering the prospect of having someone who will accept the love she has to give.[37]

Pregnancy also has instrumental value to some women who don't intend to continue the pregnancy. Some of Luker's subjects used pregnancy as a plea for help, or as a way to force themselves to confront other problems in their lives by bringing a crisis to a head. The chief instrumental value of pregnancy to Luker's subjects was to prompt changes in the relationships they had with their families and partners. Some women used pregnancy to get attention and aid from their partners or parents. Others used their pregnancy to declare independence from their parents, or to "punish" their parents by doing something that would shock them.[38] Most importantly, a large number of Luker's subjects used pregnancy to test for commitment from their partners. This should be seen more as an information gathering tool than a manipulative one. These women did not want to marry a man who married only out of duty, only because they got their partner pregnant. (Many of Luker's subjects had received an offer to marry, but rejected it because they sensed the man was reluctant or resentful.)[39] Luker's subjects wanted to marry for love. But their partners seemed content to let the relationship drift without commitment. Getting pregnant was a way to force their partner into declaring his intentions and find out whether he was serious.[40] Luker cautions against reading too much deliberateness into these motivations. Few of these pregnancies were deliberate. Rather, Luker's subjects foresaw the risk of pregnancy, considered, however dimly, that getting pregnant might carry some benefits, and thus felt willing to run the risk.

Finally, consider women's calculations of the probability that they would get pregnant. Many women start off believing that a single act of unprotected sexual intercourse carries a high probability of getting pregnant. Each time they don't get pregnant after unprotected intercourse, they reduce their estimate of the probability of getting pregnant. Many of Luker's subjects reported that after having gotten away with contraceptive risk-taking for months, they concluded that they must be infertile. This belief made it rational for them to continue having unprotected sexual intercourse. Gynecologists often prompted or reinforced these women's beliefs in their own infertility, by expressing worries that using the pill might impair their fertility and suggesting that they drop pill use to test their fertility. Many of Luker's subjects thought that they were exceptions to the general rule of fertility among women their age, or that they couldn't get pregnant if they didn't want to be pregnant. If women believe they are infertile, it is not irrational for them to engaging in sexual intercourse without contraception.[41]

5. Critique of Luker's Application of Rational Choice Theory

Do Luker's arguments show that her subjects are rational agents? They do show that it is possible to fit contraceptive risk-takers' reported motivations into the structure of a cost-benefit analysis. One simply tallies every motivation that induced women to engage in contraceptive risk-taking as a cost of contraception or a benefit of pregnancy, and every motivation repelling them from such behavior as a benefit of contraception or a cost of pregnancy. One then uses the principle of charity to impute to women relative weights of these costs and benefits so as to represent risk-taking as the option with the greatest net benefits. Thus, Luker's use of rational choice theory reduces it to an accounting framework applicable to all choices.

This fact undermines Luker's claim to have vindicated the rationality of her subjects. One can vindicate the claim to rationality only under a framework that allows subjects to fail the test. Such a framework need not impose a conception of rationality on subjects that they don't recognize. It need only make room for subjects to offer their own judgments that they acted out of weakness of will or irrational motivations, or that what they held before themselves as reasons for action were mere rationalizations for conduct they couldn't reflectively endorse. The use of rational choice theory as an accounting structure for classifying motivations precludes this, because it fails to ask whether subjects endorse their own motivations as good reasons for action.

We already know that many of Luker's subjects rejected their own motivations as foolish. Luker replied by claiming that in the context of the abortion clinic where she encountered her subjects, they were pressured to adopt the clinic's cost-benefit analysis of their choice over their own. That is, Luker argued that her subject's *ex post* negative assessments of their own rationality were not authoritative, because they were not *autonomous:* they reflected not the subjects' own cost-benefit accounting, but someone else's accounting.

Luker's reply commits her to a stronger conception of rationality than that implied by the formal and deliberative theories she applies to vindicate her subjects' rationality. It commits her to the rhetorical theory of rational choice. This commitment places a greater burden on Luker to substantiate the rationality of her subjects. For if Luker is so ready to deny the autonomy of her subjects' self-assessments in the social context of the abortion clinic, what entitles her to assume that they are autonomous in the social contexts in which they decide to take contraceptive risks?

Fortunately, Luker's data are rich enough to answer this question. But they undermine Luker's exclusive reliance on rational choice theory to explain women's contraceptive risk-taking. Her subjects' reported motivations are radically at odds with the rhetorical theory of rational choice. Women who engage in contraceptive risk-taking are not the self-confident, self-transparent, autonomous, self-reliant, consistent, coolly calculating agents of the rhetoric of rational choice. Let's consider how Luker's subjects depart from each of these characteristics.

The rational agent of economic rhetoric is conscious and assured of what she is doing. The ability to act this way is a reasonable condition on rational agency. Action is behavior one undertakes under a conception of what one is doing. If knowledge of what one is doing undermines one's confidence and willingness to do it, this is powerful evidence that one's action can't survive rational scrutiny. Rationality thus requires confidence in one's ends under knowledge of what these ends are.

Luker's subjects, by contrast, are radically self-deceived. Among the primary "costs" Luker's subjects see in contraceptive use are that they force women to acknowledge what they are doing. Using contraception forces women to admit that they are sexually active, receptive to sexual advances from strange men, taking sexual initiatives, exercising agency with respect to their sexual choices. Luker's subjects don't like to see themselves in this light. But whether they are taking contraception or not, that is what they are.

This self-deception highlights a difficulty in Luker's assumption that her subjects' reasoning can be accurately represented in a cost-benefit analysis. From an agent's perspective, the only considerations that can count as "costs" are those that can be consciously and consistently counted as reasons against doing something in deliberation. Seeing oneself as a sexual agent can't count as genuine cost of contraceptive use relative to contraceptive risk-taking. For in the act of weighing *either* of these alternatives, one necessarily regards oneself as making sexual choices. Luker mistakenly supposes that *every* motivation against doing something is capable of counting as a reason against doing it—as a rationally accountable cost. But some motives repel action without supplying reasons—that is, considerations that can survive conscious scrutiny.

The rhetoric of rational choice represents agents as autonomous in two senses: they don't take the purported validity or obligatory force of social norms as their reasons for action, and they regard themselves as self-originating sources of claims. Luker's subjects, by contrast, are heteronomous. Socially imposed norms of femininity and sexuality drive both their sexual activity and their reluctance to use contraception. Norms of femininity tell them it isn't "nice" to continue taking the pill between serious relationships, as this would signify their readiness to have sex without intimacy. Yet once they meet a new partner, they feel a need to find an excuse for not having sex with him. To represent one's reasons for not doing what one's partner wants one to do as excuses is to concede his presumptive authority over one's actions. One doesn't have to excuse oneself before those who are not entitled to expect certain behavior. So it is ironic that Luker represents her subjects' cessation of birth control as part of a bargaining strategy that affords them an excuse to say "no" to sex. Full-blooded bargainers regard themselves and one another as making demands on their own account. Their reasons for action therefore don't have to be framed as excuses.

I am not claiming that it would be strategically rational for Luker's subjects to "just say no" to sex if they don't want it. *Given* norms of femininity and heterosexual courtship, women must resort to covert means for getting their way. My point is rather that an essential feature of the social setting of heterosexual courtship is that the parties do *not* regard themselves as rational bargainers. Explicit bargaining over sex would mark the woman as a "whore," hence ineligible for serious courtship, even when what she bargains for is not cash. By representing her subjects' interactions as a form of rational bargaining, Luker effaces the vital distinctions between the social settings of courtship and market, and thereby obscures the profound ways in which these settings are governed by distinct social norms. She thus obscures the ways in which women's own norm-governed behavior—the behavior that makes these oppressive norms of femininity exist in the first place—undercuts their autonomy.

Many of Luker's subjects appear to have sincerely *internalized* these norms of femininity. They are not just strategically manipulating them or responding to external sanctions for disobeying them. Thus it appears that Luker's subjects are caught between contradictory norms of femininity: one that tells them it isn't nice to have sex without intimacy; another that tells them it isn't nice to refuse their date's sexual demands unless they have a good excuse. Rhetorically rational agents, not being moved by the obligations of social norms, would never find themselves in this *internal* predicament.

The rational agent of economic rhetoric is self-reliant. By contrast, Luker's subjects are in the grip of norms of femininity that express contradictory expectations of women's self-reliance. On the one hand, women are supposed to be sexually passive, relying on their partners to take the initiative. This would suggest that it is up to the man to make decisions concerning sexuality, including contraception. On the other hand, women are supposed to take responsibility for contraception, since they are the ones who get pregnant. So women are supposed both to not plan for sex, and to plan for it. In practice this contradiction results in a situation in which the woman relies on the man to take the contraceptive initiative, and when he fails to do so, she bears the costs of pregnancy. The right story to tell here is not Luker's tale of rational agents calculating costs and benefits, but of heteronomous agents self-destructively caught between contradictory external norms. The self-reliant, self-interested agents of the rhetoric of rational choice would reject these absurd norms and do what they had to do to protect themselves, without expecting others to do this for them.

The rhetorically rational agent makes choices from a single unified perspective, in accordance with a consistent system of values. Many of Luker's subjects, by contrast, incoherently combined their own priorities with those of the Catholic Church. Many of her subjects refused to use contraception because they were Catholic. Yet Luker found them seeking abortion services! The Catholic Church condemns contraception, but it condemns abortion and premarital sex even more strongly. Luker's subjects report some loyalty to Catholic norms, yet flout the more serious norms while accepting the less serious ones. Self-deception accounts for this bizarre inconsistency. The Catholic Church forgives single sins committed in desperation or out of weakness of will more readily than deliberate, planned, repeated wrongdoing. Contraceptive use by single women requires planning ahead for two sins: contraception and fornication. By refusing to use contraception and reserving the abortion option in the back of their minds if they get pregnant, Luker's Catholic subjects could pretend to themselves that in engaging in premarital sex, they were spontaneously overwhelmed by temptation, and in seeking an abortion, they were merely acting out of desperation.[42] Thus, they can be forgiven for these graver sins so long as they deny their own agency. But there is no forgiveness for planning contraception. Here again, to understand the point of the self-deception, we need to distinguish between behavior caught in the grips of half-accepted heteronomous moral norms and rhetorically rational behavior. The autonomous, consistent agents of the rhetoric of rational choice wouldn't deny their own agency, and would deny any obligation to obey the Catholic Church.

Rational agents calculate their chances with hard-headed logic. They don't indulge in superstition, wishful thinking, or passive rationalization. Luker represents her subjects' calculations of the probabilities of pregnancy as rational, but her data belie this. It is true that on a Bayesian account of belief revision, it is rational for women to reduce their initially high estimates of getting pregnant from a single act of intercourse each time they "get away" with unprotected sex. However, to estimate their chances of getting pregnant over a period of sexual activity, they also ought to *add* the probabilities of getting pregnant from each act of sexual intercourse in that period. Luker's subjects don't do this, because they pretend to themselves that each sex act is an isolated accident, not part of a pattern. Moreover, even a long stretch of sexual activity without pregnancy is insufficient to justify the conclusion that one is infertile. By sheer chance it will take some fertile couples more than a year to get pregnant. The readiness of Luker's subjects to assume their infertility from a period of successful contraceptive risk-taking reflects wishful thinking. (Suppose they had wanted to get pregnant: surely they would not give up trying on the basis of such slim evidence.) Some of Luker's subjects even thought that they couldn't get pregnant if they didn't want to be pregnant.[43]

The rhetoric of rational agency is above all a story of independence, self-command, consistency, and initiative. By contrast, the stories Luker's subjects tell about themselves involve dependency, subjection, ambivalence, and passivity. They seem all-too-eager to *escape* the implications of autonomous agency. Their self-deception primarily involves a denial of their own sexual agency. Their ideal of sex repudiates rational calculation in favor of spontaneous passion. They value pregnancy for the way it affirms their feminine passivity and hence excuses them from the masculine demands of rational agency. Rather than describing their reasons for choice as the products of consistent calculations they made on their own account, they describe themselves as entangled in and paralyzed by contradictory social norms and the expectations of others. No wonder they procrastinate over contraceptive planning, even when they think it is foolish to take risks. How can they be opportunistic, when they are so ambivalent about rational agency itself?

These contradictions appear even in Luker's bargaining theory of domestic partner interactions. This theory offers Luker's best case for regarding her subjects as economically rational agents. She views women's contraceptive risk-taking as a strategic move in a tacit bargain for marriage. In a society where premarital sex is widely available, women face an inherent disadvantage in bargaining for marriage compared to men. Women's assets—beauty, fertility, youth, sexuality, domestic services—either decline over time, or are available to men without the commitments of marriage. Men's assets—income, prestige, and power—tend to increase over time and are hard for women to obtain outside of marriage. Thus, premarital sexual relationships look like a worse investment to women as time goes on. But men have little incentive to move from domestic partnership to marriage, as they are already getting most of the benefits of marriage from their partner without the commitment. Nor do children figure urgently in their short-run plans, since men remain fertile throughout adulthood. Women, with their biological clocks ticking, cannot afford to wait for their partners to declare their intentions on their own. In this context, contraceptive risk-taking is a woman's rational strategy to gather information and force the man's hand in a timely way. If she gets pregnant, he will have to reveal how serious he is about her, and either agree to marry or break off the relationship. She either gains a husband, or the knowledge that he isn't worth further investment plus the freedom to seek a more marriage-worthy partner.[44]

Luker's rational bargaining theory strikes me as a compelling explanation of why many women in premarital relationships engage in contraceptive risk-taking. Yet even here the story works in conjunction with other facts not explicable by the rhetorical theory of rational choice. If the man has such a great interest in avoiding commitment or delaying decisionmaking, then why doesn't he wear a condom, or urge her to contracept? It isn't as if he doesn't know that she is taking contraceptive risks: Luker reports that her subjects' partners often passively colluded with their contraceptive risk-taking.[45] Why don't couples plan for contraception together? Why don't they bargain openly about what they want from each other?

Social norms of heterosexual courtship, which repudiate explicit bargaining, explain this. In planning together for contraception by discussions that avoid the forms associated with bargaining, the parties affirm their *couplehood*. This explains why men, even though they have an interest in contraception, avoid the subject. To raise it is to accept responsibility for it and thereby to accept the obligations of couplehood. For their part, women may see that raising the issue in a context that permits men to disavow couplehood may just drive them away. By contrast, "getting" pregnant is a "passive" way to *force* men to consider matters from the standpoint of the couple. *This behavior is strategically rational only in a context in which all parties view themselves as bound, or bindable, by obligations of heterosexual couplehood.* This entails that they not regard themselves as rhetorically rational agents, since such agents are not moved by conceptions of obligation.

The sexual revolution of the 1960s, in conjunction with the pill and availability of abortion, were supposed to liberate women from repressive norms of sexuality to enjoy sex on the same terms as men. Instead, many women felt that their bargaining power with men was reduced because men could now obtain sex without offering commitment in return. What looked like an expansion of women's choices rapidly turned into a new, unwelcome obligation: now that contraception was available, women didn't have an "excuse" to withhold sex from their partners. Thus, the pill, held forth as a way for women to assume control over their own bodies, was seen by some of Luker's subjects as *yielding* control to their partners, turning them into mere "sexual service stations" for men.[46] The pill, by putting the power to contracept in women's hands alone, entitled men to indulge in sex without responsibility.

Rational choice theory explains part of this story. A person's bargaining position can be weakened if less desirable options are added to her feasible set. However, another part of the story involves the social norms of femininity that have removed some of women's best options, that structure the rules by which covert heterosexual "bargaining" takes place, and that allocate different entitlements, obligations, and responsibilities to male and female partners in heterosexual relationships. Luker's rational choice explanation of women's covert "bargaining" therefore works only in conjunction with background norms that are sustained by behavior not itself explicable by her theory.

6. Lessons for Rational Choice Theory: Social Norms and Social Conditions for Rationality

I want to draw two sets of lessons from this critique of Luker's case study, one for rational choice theory, and one for feminism. Consider first the lessons for rational choice theory.

One common defense of rational choice theory is that there is no alternative theory of human behavior that has comparable scope. This is a good argument only if there is value in having *one* hypothesis explain everything. Thales conjectured that everything was made of water. This may have been the best *single* hypothesis one could come up with about the constitution of things. But chemistry could not progress until it accepted that there was more than one element. A rational choice theorist might reply that the hypothesis that there is more than one element was needed to explain chemical phenomena. But, since it is possible to interpret rational choice theory in such a way that it can explain virtually all behavior, we don't need to entertain alternative hypotheses.

To this reply there are two rejoinders. First, while it is true that, for any observed behavior, one can construct a rational choice model that generates it, it doesn't follow that the model identifies the actual causes of that behavior. Second, what counts as a good explanation of a phenomenon depends on what aspects of that phenomenon one wants to understand. For certain purposes, it is important to be able to capture the difference between an individual acting on her own personal preferences, and her taking other considerations—social norms, say, or other people's preferences—as her reasons for action. For other purposes, it is important to capture the difference between an individual acting on reasons she can reflectively accept, and motives that cannot survive critical scrutiny. Often we need to make conceptual space for representing human capacities for self-criticism, self-deception, procrastination, passivity, weakness of will, and denials of their own agency.

To represent these possibilities, we need to go beyond a conception of rational choice theory as either tautology or universal truth. We need to go beyond the formal theory of rational choice. Considered as one ideal type of action among others, the rhetorical theory of rational choice provides conceptual space for capturing these phenomena. It achieves this advantage over its rivals precisely by restricting its explanatory scope.

We found in Luker's study a stunning example of a radical division between the formal theory of rational choice and the rhetoric of rational choice. The choices of Luker's subjects can be fit into the formal theory, but not into the rhetorical theory of rational choice. This might seem like a victory for the formal theory. But it is achieved only at the cost of effacing distinctions of great interest. While the rhetorical theory of rational choice does not directly explain Luker's subjects, it plays a role in understanding what they are up to. To get a clearer view of an object, we often place it against a contrasting background. By standing in perspicuous contrast with their actual behavior, the rhetorical theory of rational choice helps us see Luker's subjects more clearly. This vindicates Weber's interpretation of rational choice theory as just one ideal type of action among others.

My critique of Luker's study contrasts rhetorically rational agency with norm-governed action. This suggests that we should regard rhetorical rationality and norm-governed action as two distinct ideal types of action. Luker's study also reveals cases in which both types of action are in play at the same time. What might be thought of as strategically rational choice takes place against a background of accepted social norms, and would not make sense unless people were antecedently motivated by obligations to obey social norms.

Rational choice theory in its "imperializing" mode aims to erase the distinction between rational choice and norm-governed action by showing how social norms could be produced by the interactions of agents whose rationality is given. This attempt to represent social action *exclusively* in terms of rational choice theory is doomed to failure, for two reasons. First, social norms are sustained by choices not themselves explicable in terms of rational choice. They are not merely the outcome of everyone following their personal preferences.[47] Nor can they be generated by rewards and punishments that others attach to them. For there is no way to get sanctioning behavior off the ground unless some people accept the validity of the norm in itself, apart from its payoffs, and are ready to take its validity as their reason for obeying it.[48] It would be absurd for people to be punishing one another for failure to conform to norms that they think are improper. The distinction between economic rationality and social norms is fundamental.

The second reason why social norms cannot be explained by rational choice theory is that rationality is not a given to agents, but an achievement. The rhetorical theory of rational choice lets us see this, because it offers a rich account of the psychological conditions needed for an agent's reflective and autonomous judgments of worth to coincide with the motivations that actually generate her choices. It thus opens up a new question: under what *social* conditions can agents achieve the *psychological* conditions for rational agency?

In the context of Luker's study, this question becomes: how might women become rational agents with respect to their own sexuality? One condition seems clear: one needs a conception of oneself as an autonomous, rational agent in order to become such an agent. Otherwise one will find oneself entangled in contradictory, heteronomous norms and feel hopelessly bound by the demands of others. Luker's subjects find themselves caught in contradictory external demands: between traditional femininity and "liberated" sexuality; between feminism and Catholicism; between ideals of romantic love and their partners' sexual demands.

How might women gain genuine autonomy with respect to their sexuality? I suggest that the rhetorical theory of rational choice becomes applicable to oneself only in the context of specific social norms. First, third parties must accept one as autonomous. People need social recognition to understand themselves as entitled to make claims on their own behalf, and to have confidence in asserting themselves as such. Thus, adults must socialize girls into this view of themselves, and women must not be held in contempt for making sexual choices on their own account. Second, the parties with whom one interacts must accept one as a self-originating source of claims. Thus, men must acknowledge that women have full rights over their own bodies, and not demand "excuses" for refusing to have sex with them. People have a joint responsibility in facilitating and enabling each others' autonomy. This is a crucial respect in which the assumption of self-reliance built into rational choice theory undermines the conditions of its own realization.

Thus, far from posing a conception of rational agency that generates all social norms, rational agency is itself an achievement that requires social norms of autonomy to get off the ground. Robust rational agency is a radically problematic condition, achieved only under special social circumstances.

7. Lessons for Feminism: Uses of Rational Choice Theory

Let us now return to the question with which I opened this paper: should feminists reject rational choice theory? In particular, should they use it to explain women's sexual and contraceptive choices? The answer depends on our purposes, and on the aspect of rational choice theory being used.

One feminist aim is to ensure that the health-care system effectively delivers contraception to the women who need it. Luker's use of the deliberative theory of rational choice effectively illuminates the motivations that deter many sexually active women from using contraception, even when they have an interest in doing so. Here, the function of rational choice theory is to make women's choices intelligible in terms of their motivations, so that the health-care system responds to women's needs as they see them. For example, Luker suggests that once health-care practitioners recognize that women have a stake in seeing their sexual activity as spontaneous, and tend to stop contraception between relationships, they can respond by providing drop-in contraceptive services, rather than requiring women to make appointments weeks in advance.[49] This is a sound use of rational choice theory, but one that makes no use of its formal apparatus.

Another feminist aim, as Luker sees it, is to vindicate the rationality of women, so as to counter demeaning representations of women that support paternalistic moves to take reproductive choices out of women's hands. I have argued that the formal and deliberative theories of rational choice are not up to this task. Merely showing that women's choices can be fit into the accounting framework of a cost-benefit analysis is not enough to vindicate women's rationality. Nor should feminists want to rush to judgment on this score. We should be interested in identifying obstacles to the achievement of women's autonomy and rationality, rather than assuming that women face no problems in this area.

With respect to the feminist goal of identifying realizations of, or impediments to, women's rationality, the application of the formal theory of rational choice to women's choices poses an obstacle. It effaces the distinction between action on one's own autonomous preferences, and action governed by oppressive social norms. The problem is not just that the formal theory fails to distinguish between autonomous and heteronomous preferences, and thus fails to mark distinctions of vital interest to feminists. It is that in practice, rational choice theorists take the applicability of the formal theory to a person's actions as a license to describe their actions in terms of the rhetorical theory of rational choice. They thus represent people as acting on their own preferences, when they may just be yielding to the demands and expectations of others, or governed by oppressive or incoherent social norms. This representation legitimates outcomes and conditions of women's agency that feminists need to call into question. Feminists can target internalized sexist social norms for critical attention only if we represent them as factors influencing women's choices that are independent of—and indeed, contrary to—their autonomous personal preferences. Luker's representation of women's sexual agency as rational ignores the numerous social conditions that undermine women's rational autonomy with respect to their sexual decisions.

An antifeminist might try to conclude from my argument that since many women seeking abortions are irrational in their sexual and reproductive choices, others ought to control their sexuality and reproduction. This conclusion gets things backward: it is *because* others are controlling women's sexuality and reproduction through oppressive social norms that women are prevented from exercising rational choice in this domain. The antifeminist draws the wrong conclusion because of the background assumption that rationality is an individual endowment. I would suggest rather than an individual's rationality is partly a function of her place in the social order, and depends on social conditions—in particular, on not being held accountable to contradictory and agency-denying social norms. As one like-minded critic has put the point, the contradictory norms of femininity to which women are subject are oppressive "because they coerce women to avoid moral decisiveness in a social setting in which women are held responsible as moral agents for the consequences of their actions."[50]

I have argued that, so long as we conceive of rational choice in its full-blooded rhetoric, as a contingent achievement, a particular ideal type of action with circumscribed application under special social conditions—not as a behavioristic tautology, a psychological universal, or the inevitable framework of practical reasoning—it has important feminist uses. It can be viewed as a normative standard of action, deviations from which require explanation.

Normative considerations play the same role in this type of feminist inquiry that they do in medicine. Medicine assumes a normative standard of health, deviations from which demand explanation. We seek to understand the causes of disease, of deviations from health, to facilitate the discovery of treatments and cures. Similarly, feminists regard autonomous, self-confident agency as desirable for women. Deviations from this norm demand explanation, so that feminists can identify the obstacles to women's rationality, and seek ways to overcome them. Call this understanding of the proper role of normative considerations in social science *critical methodological rationalism*. Feminist theory is a kind of critical theory, in that it tries to understand the social world so as to enable certain kinds of liberating changes in it. The function of critical social science in seeking understandings that can advance liberatory political purposes justifies its tailoring a standard of acceptable explanation in relation to a normative ideal.

This method does not confuse facts and values or undermine objective inquiry. Normative and factual considerations play distinct roles in critical theory. Normative considerations set the end, deviations from which require explanation. Once the end is specified, it is up to the facts and not wishful thinking or ideology to determine how far people come short, what causes them to do so, and how the gap could be closed.

It makes sense for feminists to require explanations that account for deviations from the rhetorical theory of rational choice only if the rhetorical theory is normatively acceptable from a feminist point of view. We have seen that agents who satisfy the demands of the rhetorical theory of rational choice embody what, from a feminist point of view, are virtues compared to stereotypically "feminine" vices. In particular, feminists should take a normative interest in two aspects of the rhetorical theory: autonomy and self-confidence. Deviations from these ideals demand feminist attention. To the extent that women's oppression is due to their lack of autonomy and self-confidence, the rhetorical theory of rational choice has important feminist uses.

However, other aspects of the rhetorical theory are normatively indefensible from a feminist point of view. In particular, the theory's assumption of universal self-reliance simultaneously ignores and undermines the social conditions of rationality, in ways that particularly damage women. If everyone acted as if everyone held the conditions of their own rationality in themselves, without need of others to support or develop their autonomy, nobody would be autonomous. Nobody would grow up without adults to bring them up! No wonder the agent of the rhetorical theory of rational choice is depicted as masculine: who else has such a stake in (mis)representing himself as self-made, as if his mother had nothing to do with developing his capabilities?

A feminist version of rational choice theory would need to be universalizable, so as to include women, especially mothers, among those eligible to live up to its demands. That is, it would have to prescribe characteristics that are consistent with everyone enjoying the social conditions of rational agency. Among these characteristics are that a rational agent must give due recognition to the social conditions of her own agency, and accept an *obligation* to reciprocate, to do her part to uphold the social conditions for others' rational agency as well. This replaces the assumptions of mutual self-reliance (caveat emptor) and egoism that lead the agent of the rhetoric of rational choice to be such a social clod, a freerider, and an untrustworthy partner in cooperative enterprises.

Thus we see how, in scrutinizing the social conditions under which the rhetorical theory of rational choice could be universally true of human beings, the theory necessarily points beyond itself. It points toward a Kantian theory of rational agency, which conditions rational intentions on their universalizability. This suggests that the better model of rationality for feminists to adopt in critical methodological rationalism is Kantian. I leave it to a future investigation to explore how a Kantian model of rationality would rework the conceptions of autonomy and self-confidence so central to feminist ends.

Notes

I thank Louise Antony, Ann Cudd, Robert Cooter, Sally Haslanger, and Richard Posner for comments on an earlier draft of this paper. Through her undergraduate senior honors thesis, Anna Stubblefield inspired me to consider the study by Kristin Luker that occupies a central place in this paper. Her excellent "Contraceptive Risk-Taking and Norms of Chastity" *Journal of Social Philosophy* 27 (1996): 81–100, takes a distinct but compatible view of Luker's study to mine.

1. Gary Becker, *A Treatise on the Family* (Chicago: University of Chicago Press, 1981).

2. Phyllis Rooney, "Gendered Reason: Sex Metaphor and Conceptions of Reason," *Hypatia* 6 (1991): 77–103.

3. Paula England, "The Separative Self Androcentric Bias in Neoclassical Assumptions," in *Beyond Economic Man*, ed. Marianne Ferber and Julie Nelson, 37–53 (Chicago: University of Chicago Press, 1992).

4. Amartya Sen, "Gender and Cooperative Conflicts," in *Persistent Inequalities,* ed. Irene Tinker (New York: Oxford University Press, 1990), 123–149.

5. Carol Gilligan, *In a Different Voice* (Cambridge, Mass.: Harvard University Press, 1982).

6. See, for example, Gary Becker, *The Economic Approach to Human Behavior* (Chicago: University of Chicago Press, 1976); Gary Becker, *A Treatise on the Family* (Chicago: University of Chicago Press, 1981); Richard Posner, *Sex and Reason* (Cambridge, Mass.: Harvard University Press, 1992).

7. A small sample of such disconfirmations includes Amos Tversky and Daniel Kahneman, "The Framing of Decisions and the Psychology of Choice," *Science* 211 (1981): 453–58; Robyn Dawes, Alphonse van de Kragt, and John Orbell, "Cooperation for the Benefit of Us—Not Me, or My Conscience," in *Beyond Self-Interest,* ed. Jane Mansbridge (Chicago: University of Chicago Press, 1990); Donald Green and Ian Shapiro, *Pathologies of Rational Choice Theory* (New Haven: Yale University Press, 1994); Daniel Kahneman, Jack Knetsch, and Richard Thaler, "Experimental Tests of the Endowment Effect and the Coase Theorem," *Journal of Political Economy* 98 (1990): 1325–1348; Richard Thaler, *The Winner's Curse: Paradoxes and Anomalies of Economic Life* (New York: Free Press, 1992); Daniel Kah-

neman, Paul Slovic, and Amos Tversky, eds., *Judgment Under Uncertainty: Heuristics and Biases* (Cambridge New York: Cambridge University Press, 1982); Daniel Kahneman, Jack Knetsch, and Richard Thaler, "Fairness and the Assumptions of Economics," in *Rational Choice: The Contrast Between Economics and Psychology*, ed. Robin Hogarth and Melvin Reder (Chicago: University of Chicago Press, 1987), 101–116; Maurice Allais, "Le Compartement de l'Homme Rationnel Devant le Risque: Critique Des Postulats et Axiomes de l'Ecole Américaine," *Econometrica* 21 (1953): 503–546.

8. Ludwig von Mises, *Human Action*, 3d ed. (Chicago: Henry Regnery, 1966).

9. Paul Samuelson, "Consumption Theory in Terms of Revealed Preference," *Economica* 15 (1948): 243–253.

10. Amartya Sen, "Behavior and the Concept of Preference," *Economica* 41 (1973): 241–59.

11. Donald Davidson, "Psychology as Philosophy," in *Essays on Actions and Events* (Oxford: Oxford University Press, 1982), 229–39.

12. Thanks to Don Herzog for this point.

13. Max Weber, *The Theory of Social and Economic Organization*, edited by Talcott Parsons, translated by A. M. Henderson (New York: Free Press, 1964).

14. Max Weber, "Science as a Vocation," in *From Max Weber: Essays in Sociology,* ed. H. H. Gerth and C. Wright Mills (New York: Oxford University Press, 1946), 129–156.

15. Economists often interpret the formal theory behavioristically, as claiming simply that people act *as if* they had consistent preferences. This makes the theory equally applicable to inanimate objects such as thermostats. So interpreted, the theory makes no psychological claims and is of no concern to feminists. But this interpretation also provides no causal explanations. I shall consider the formal theory only when it purports to provide causal explanations; that is, when as it claims that the beliefs and preferences it imputes to individuals match their real motives for action.

16. Jon Elster, *Ulysses and the Sirens* (Cambridge: Cambridge University Press, 1979), 142.

17. This is *not* to claim that rational choice theory cannot claim many explanatory triumphs. For example, it provides excellent explanations of why rationing leads to black markets and why bad money drives out good. The question being explored here is which *dimensions* of the theory are carrying the explanatory burdens. In the cases just cited, the conjunction of the hypotheses of self-interest and instrumental rationality do virtually all of the explanatory work. One need not appeal to the formal properties of individuals' preference orderings or any supposed consistency of their estimates of risk to explain these phenomena. In other cases, rational choice theory enjoys explanatory success because it models structural constraints on individual behavior. Gary Becker's famous demonstration that the Law of Demand would still hold in virtue of people's budget constraints, even if they chose randomly, illustrates this point. See Becker, "Irrational Behavior and Economic Theory," in *The Economic Approach to Human Behavior* (Chicago: University of Chicago Press, 1976), 153–168. For a general defense of this structural, antipsychological, anti-individualist account of rational choice theory, see Debra Satz and John Ferejohn, "Rational Choice and Social Theory," *Journal of Philosophy* 91 (1994): 71–87. Structural explanations are important tools for social science, but it seems a misnomer to call them rational choice explanations, since they have nothing to do with choice, much less rationality.

18. D. McCloskey, *The Rhetoric of Economics* (Madison: University of Wisconsin Press, 1985).

19. D. McCloskey, "Some Consequences of a Conjective Economics," in *Beyond Economic Man*, edited by Marianne Ferber and Julie Nelson (Chicago: University of Chicago Press, 1993), 69–93; D. McCloskey, *The Vices of Economists, the Virtues of the Bourgeoisie* (Amsterdam: Amsterdam University Press, 1996).

20. McCloskey, *Rhetoric of Economics.*

21. His "coolness" implies that he does not act on emotion, but rather on account of the payoffs of acting. Emotional action is not attuned to the payoffs in the way required by rational choice, although people disposed to act on emotion may tend to be better off than people not so disposed. For one explanation of this point, see Robert Frank, *Passions Within Reason: The Strategic Role of the Emotions* (New York: Norton, 1988).

22. For a compelling account of this sense of obligation, see Margaret Gilbert, *On Social Facts* (Princeton: Princeton University Press, 1989), 367–427. Such obligations need not be seen by agents as overriding other reasons for action.

23. G. Peter Penz, *Consumer Sovereignty and Human Interests* (Cambridge: Cambridge University Press, 1986).

24. I explain why this is so in "Soberanía del consumidor versus soberanía del ciudadano. Algunos errores en la economía neoclásica del Bienestar," *Isegoría* 18 (1998): 19–46. English-language version available upon request.

25. Raymond Battaglio et al., "Commodity Choice Behavior with Pigeons as Subjects," *Journal of Political Economy* 84 (1981): 116–151; Howard Rachlin, "Economics and Behavioral Psychology," in *The Limits to Action: The Allocation of Individual Behavior,* ed. J. Stadden (New York: Academic Press, 1980), 205–236.

26. Kristin Luker, *Taking Chances* (1975; reprint, Berkeley: University of California Press, 1991).

27. Luker, *Taking Chances,* p. x, reports that 90 percent of her subjects had contraceptive knowledge, skills, and access, yet 57 percent used no contraception at all in the month prior to becoming pregnant, and most of the remainder used contraceptive techniques, such as rhythm and withdrawal, that they knew were less effective than alternatives.

28. Luker, *Taking Chances,* 41.

29. Ibid., p. 17.

30. Ibid., p. 17.

31. Ibid., pp. 17, 78–79.

32. Ibid., pp. 42, 46.

33. Ibid., pp. 48–49.

34. Ibid., pp. 42–44.

35. Ibid., pp. 56–59.

36. Ibid., pp. 127.

37. Ibid., pp. 66–68.

38. Ibid., pp. 71–75.

39. Ibid., p. 135.

40. Ibid., p. 70.

41. Ibid., pp. 87–94.

42. Ibid., p. 45. Richard Posner, in "Social Norms, Social Meaning, and Economic Analysis of Law: A Comment," *Journal of Legal Studies* 27 (1998): 561, attempts to counter this representation in an earlier version of this chapter, which I delivered at the University of Chicago. In his view, it is rational to refuse to commit what one regards as a certain lesser sin at the cost of risking a graver uncertain sin in the future. This rationale fails to capture the self-deception in the Catholic women's self-representations: one can't reserve the option

of abortion in the back of one's mind and also regard oneself as sinning out of spontaneous desperation rather than foresight when one seeks an abortion. Luker's subjects, in evading the implications of their own foresight, thus reject Posner's rationalization of their action. Posner's error is characteristic of rational choice theory: it systematically disregards both the causal and normative roles of subjects' own self-understandings, even when it purports to offer a microfoundational, psychological account of their behavior.

43. Ibid., p. 93.

44. Ibid., pp. 101, 115–116, 121–123.

45. Ibid., p. 133.

46. Ibid., p. 49.

47. For a decisive argument against any such view of social norms, see Margaret Gilbert, *On Social Facts* (Princeton: Princeton University Press, 1989), 315–367.

48. Jon Elster, *The Cement of Society* (Cambridge: Cambridge University Press, 1989), provides powerful arguments against the view that norms can be explained by sanctioning, and in favor of the view that norm-governed action is distinct from economically rational action. I argue against a wide array of different attempts to explain social norms as the outcome of strategically interactions of economically rational agents in "Beyond *Homo Economicus*: New Developments in Economic Theories of Social Norms," *Philosophy and Public Affairs* forthcoming (2000).

49. Luker, *Taking Chances,* 149.

50. Anna Stubblefield, "Contraceptive Risk-Taking and Norms of Chastity," *Journal of Social Philosophy* 27 (1996): 83.

17

RATIONAL CHOICE THEORY AND THE LESSONS OF FEMINISM

ANN E. CUDD

I. Introduction

I want to discuss the claim, found in the philosophical and social science literature, that rational choice theory cannot serve progressive social ends. I am particularly concerned with the version of this claim made by feminists: that rational choice theory is masculinist and inevitably leads to androcentric or sexist politics. Here I want to examine the objections and show that rational choice theory can be salvaged, albeit with a few caveats and an enhanced understanding of its strengths and weaknesses.

My thesis is that there are two interpretations of rational choice theory under which it can serve progressive ends and reveal feminist insights. But feminists and other social theorists have raised some astute criticisms. They have shown that when using this tool for constructing political or social theory or for formulating social policy, one has to take care in several ways not to privilege the status quo. These caveats can be gleaned from an analysis of some of the main findings of feminist theory, what I shall call in this chapter "the lessons of feminism." Some of the criticisms I explore are implicit or explicit in other critiques of standard rational choice theory, and others are unique to feminism. I hope to show that feminist theory provides an illuminating entrée into exploring the interpretation and usefulness of rational choice theory.

After briefly describing the rational choice model, I shall examine the lessons of feminism for all theory, and the feminist critiques of rational choice theory in particular, that are either explicitly given or implicit in the lessons. I shall then give the two interpretations of rational choice theory under which those lessons can be respected.

II. Rational Choice Theory

Rational choice theory comprises three separate theories: decision theory, which is the theory of rationality for agents facing an environment lacking in other rational agents, game theory, which is the theory of rationality for strategically interacting agents, and social choice theory, which is the theory of the rationality of collective choice. I shall focus on game theory because I think that the lessons of feminism apply most forcefully here and because I have concentrated my research on game theory.

In the basic model, agents are assumed to be self-interested and to seek to maximize their self-interest. Rational agents are self-interested in the sense described by Wicksteed (and adopted by Rawls and Gauthier) as "non-tuism," that is, they are not ultimately motivated by, for good or ill, the preferences of those with whom they are interacting.[1] This is not to be confused with selfishness. Selfish individuals prefer their own well-being over that of others; non-tuists do not aim to satisfy or thwart others' preferences when they interact. The well-being of others could enter a non-tuist's utility function, but not as another's utility function. As Gauthier puts it, "Even if one takes no interest in others' interests, one may take interest in states of affairs that cannot be specified except with reference to others."[2] Even less is non-tuism to be confused with hedonism. Non-tuism is methodological atomism, but it does not imply ontological atomism.[3] In assuming non-tuism, rational choice theory assumes only that the preferences of the agents are in principle stable apart from others' preferences. It does not assume that agents do not affect each other or that the well-being of agents does not affect each other's preference orderings. Rational agents are self-interest maximizers, but this does not entail that they are constantly calculating; rational agents might adopt dispositions or habits to behave in certain ways under certain circumstances because those dispositions or habits are themselves maximizing in the long run. They act as if they were calculating their rational self-interest, but this action might be realized by multiple mental or physical states.

Rational agents are ideally rational: they (act as if they) have no limitations in their calculating ability; they don't get bored or tired; they don't suffer cognitive illusions. They have given preferences for a given problem, that is, they don't change their preferences in the middle of a decision situation. Rational agents make optimal use of their information. They are self-knowers: they know what they know. When they interact with other rational agents, they have common knowledge of some features of their interaction. Rational choice theory uses "knowledge" loosely, however, to mean the same as "information" or "belief"; beliefs need be neither true nor justified to constitute knowledge. They just have to be believed or commonly believed for common knowledge.[4]

Rational choice theory construes value subjectively. That is, the preferences whose satisfaction rational agents pursue are theirs as they themselves perceive those preferences. Their preferences are constrained by some existence and consistency conditions. Rational agents should be able to rank order the alternative possibilities. Their preferences should not form a cycle. Their preferences should be consistent with the tenet that more is preferred to less and their preferences over lotteries with the probability calculus. They should not consider sunk costs or "irrelevant alternatives."

In game theory, interacting agents are depicted as playing a game whose rules and possible outcomes are set exogenously and are common knowledge. Rational agents behave according to solutions to the games. In particular, they choose strategies that are optimal based on the assumption that the other agents are behaving according to optimal strategies. There are two fundamental kinds of games: cooperative games, in which players may agree to coordinate strategies and enforce the behavior that the joint strategy prescribes, and noncooperative games, in which players cannot enforce any such agreements. This distinction is only apparent, however, since "enforcement" can also be viewed as offering just another set of outcomes for violation or conformity.

There is a long tradition of employing rational choice theory, or something that might anachronistically be interpreted as a precursor of rational choice theory, in political and social philosophy. Thus we see interpretations of Hobbes's social contract theory, Rousseau's theory of interaction in the state of nature, Hume's theory of contract and convention, and Adam Smith's conception of the invisible hand of the marketplace reconstructed through game theory. In contemporary moral, political, and legal philosophy, rational choice theory is rife. I have myself been engaged in constructing a theory of oppression based in rational choice theory. I am particularly attracted to bargaining theories, as they illuminate the factors that account for and affect the relative distributive shares of goods. My aim is to produce not only a good theory that leads to an understanding of oppression but also a progressive theory that leads to a way out. Some feminists challenge whether this is possible. Let us now examine some of their challenges.

III. The Lessons of Feminism

There is little in the way of consensus among feminist philosophers. Until just a few years ago I could have said[5] that all feminist philosophers ("feminists" from here on) assert the sex/gender distinction (on which more later), but recently some have repudiated this, though from a dialectical position that is considerably advanced by the earlier consensus. Perhaps I can say that feminists share the conviction that the social constructions of gender create a fundamentally unjust imbalance in contemporary social and political arrangements. Not all feminists, though most, agree that abortion is morally acceptable; not all feminists, though most, agree that sexual equality is desirable; not all feminists, though most, agree that sexual harassment and rape are gender-based hate crimes. There is considerably more disagreement on issues such as the moral and legal status of pornography, the definition of sexual equality, or whether androgyny (by which I mean the eradication of gender difference) is a social ideal. Feminist philosophers share a canonical history. I think that the best way to characterize feminism today is by way of describing the dialectical progression of the debates over the social status of women and the philosophical implications of sexual difference. I shall do this by way of discussing what I consider to be four lessons of feminism. Although not all feminists will agree with my presentation of these points, I think that we would agree that they are considered crucial nodes in the debate within philosophical feminism.

1. The Sex/Gender Distinction

The single most important conceptual contribution of feminism is the sex/gender distinction. On the original construal of this distinction, sex is taken to be a biological category. Males and females are the two sexes, though some have argued that there need to be a few more sex categories to include all the varieties of intersexed persons. In humans it is pretty clear that there are biological differences between the sexes beyond production of egg and sperm, but what those differences are remains difficult to discern. There is a lot of scientific work on human sexual difference, but much of it is confused by another main way to categorize humans, that is, by gender.

Gender, in contrast to sex, is a social category; gender is said to be "socially constructed." What this phrase means is that how sexual difference is significant varies across cultures, and indeed the fact that sexual difference has any social significance is believed by most feminists to be a purely contingent, socially determined matter. Men and women are the two genders that are normally found in societies, but many argue that lots of people don't neatly fit into one of them or they fit into both; some societies are said to have more than two. One of the main social functions of the category of gender has been to divide labor or social roles. When we look closely at that division of the human species, we find quite a wide range of meanings and overlap between the genders across societies. Margaret Mead once said that in some societies the men fish and the women weave, and in other societies the women fish and the men weave, meaning that how gender difference is expressed can be completely opposite from one society to the next. All societies practice some segregation by gender in division of labor. One nearly universal fact has been that in every society men are politically, religiously, and economically dominant and women subordinate. As Mead added to her statement about the gendered division of labor, whatever men do is seen as the more valuable activity. Gender is thus not only a social difference but also a social *hierarchy*.

Recently many feminists have begun to question whether sex is a biological category, and propose instead that sex is also socially constructed.[6] Whatever the case is about the biological nature of sex, however, it is clear that sex and gender are not isomorphic. That is, not all females are women and not all males are men, unless that is dogmatically pronounced definitional. For instance, if a woman is someone who wears clothing that is socially classified as women's clothing, walks in a way that is socially classified as a woman's walk, performs labor that consists in caring for the physical and emotional needs of others, is generally unaggressive, and has intimate sexual relationships with men, then there are males who are women. More often in the social class that most philosophy professors inhabit, though, people do some things that are coded as masculine and some as feminine, that is, they represent a mix of genders, even though they have one sex. For example, I am in a male-dominated and masculine-coded profession, I like to play and talk sports, I wear men's clothing whenever I can get away with it, and I never wear makeup or carry an object that is classified as a woman's purse. But I also take primary care of two small children, clean the toilets in my house, and identify with the oppressed condition of women around the globe.

The question that a skeptic about the sex/gender distinction might ask is, Does sex cause gender, that is, is gender redundant with sex as an explanatory category? No, the matter is more complex than that. Although sexual difference is necessary, it is not sufficient for gender; other conditions must exist to make gender possible and desirable for cultures. Primitive conditions of survival and the sexual difference in reproduction and lactation no doubt provided a powerful economic incentive for human societies to invent gender. It would not have been necessary—they could have divided between reproducing/nonreproducing, swift/slow, large/small, or some other classification relevant to their survival needs. But our ancestors, probably because of the strong instinctive salience of sex, endowed great social significance to sexual difference and thereby invented gender. Gender and sex must have begun to come uncorrelated even from the very beginning because of the great variation one finds between individuals of both sexes: some males must have been good at feminine tasks and some females at masculine tasks. Gender norms must have been enforced with strong social taboos, as they were crucial, given no existing alternative norms for dividing labor, to survival. The point here is well illustrated by a simple concept from game theory, namely, the mixed motive coordination game. Although there are a variety of possible norm systems (read: strategy combinations) that would have worked for these early societies, once they arrived at one set it was a stable equilibrium and thus difficult if not impossible to move from. Now that there is no survival need for this distinction, gender has strayed farther away from its connection with sex. It is now, I believe, an ancient relic. Whether or in what form gender will survive the next millennium is an interesting question, and one whose answer may well depend on the outcome of current political and philosophical struggles.

Feminists have shown how the conflation of sex and gender magnifies sexual difference and in turn justifies further enforcement of gender. Like the first lesson of feminism, this one goes way back in the history of feminism. Something like the sex/gender distinction is implicit in Mary Wollstonecraft's claims that encouraging passivity and vanity in women has made them weaker physically and morally than their natures require.[7] Likewise John Stuart Mill argues that we cannot determine what differences there would be between the sexes because socially enforced gender (not his term) differences have exaggerated and distorted sexual difference: "What is now called the nature of women is an eminently artificial thing—the result of forced repression in some directions, unnatural stimulation in others."[8] We have not changed much in this way since Mill's time. Girls of my generation were not as strongly encouraged, as boys were, to play sports, study mathematics, or learn how to fix stereos. When women are consequently much slower and weaker than men on average, score much lower on math exams, or are less able in a physics or engineering lab, this has often given rise to the claim that we as a society are justified in encouraging girls less in those areas, as if the female sex itself determines an inability to run swiftly, prove theorems, or invent gadgets. Thus the first lesson of the sex/gender distinction is to be wary when a theory claims to reveal a difference between the sexes.

There are other, more subtle lessons to be learned from the sex/gender distinction. Feminists have shown three categories of gender-related mistakes that can infect normative or scientific theories.[9] The first is sexism, which is the denigration of one sex or gender, typically females and women. Sexism infects a scientific theory when it asserts that women are inferior to men, that women are properly subordinated to men, that women should be confined to gender-stereotyped roles, or when it asserts a double standard for judging men and women. Sexism can be unconscious, as well as conscious. It can be part of the unstated and unrecognized assumptions of a theory. As I have defined it, sexism involves normative moral, social, or political judgments, that is, value judgments. As such, the official scientific method rules sexism out as illegitimate assertions or assumptions, but that does not mean that they do not continue to affect science.

The second mistake is androcentrism. Androcentrism infects a theory when it assumes that the experiences, biology, and social roles of males or men are the norm and that of females or women a deviation from the norm. Like sexism, androcentrism may be explicit or implicit, conscious or unconscious. Androcentrism in theories reflects the interests of the theorist, but not necessarily as moral, political, or social values. Some androcentrism might be characterized as epistemic values, that is, as assertions of what is most interesting to study. And this kind of value judgment is not ruled out by the official scientific or philosophic method. After all, colleagues, funding agencies, and journal editors make judgments all the time about whether a line of research is *interesting*. The "interest" of a theory or line of research must be judged if the best use of resources is to be made. At least normally, scientific peer evaluation of interest is crucial if a good judgment is to be made. But interest is relative to the objectives of scientists, and there is no value-neutral way to specify objectives. Any reasonable history of science will reveal how the interests of scientists typically coincide with the social and political interests of the dominant social groups, from which the scientists themselves normally come. If the full range of genders and sexes were represented in the disciplines in roughly equal numbers, we might expect that there would be theorists whose interests focus on each group, so that science as a whole would not be androcentric. As this is not the case, since the disciplines are dominated by the dominant gender and sex, the sciences are, overall, androcentric. There are both epistemic and social consequences to androcentrism that are bad, and hence rational choice theory ought to avoid androcentrism.

The third mistake comes about when theories employ gender or sexual symbolism. We often code our ideas, theories, and methods as masculine or feminine, male or female, and this is true of scientific ideas, theories, and methods as well. What I mean by saying that we "code" ideas with gender is that we associate them with the experiences and values that are likewise thought to be somehow gendered, sexed, or sexual. This coding is clearly hierarchical. Whatever is coded masculine is better than feminine, what is coded as normal is better than deviant. Although gender symbolism, like any other kind of symbolism, is not a priori illegitimate, it is easy to allow the social authority of the symbol to carry over to the cognitive authority of the theory, and that, of course, is illegitimate.

In sum, then, the lessons of the sex/gender distinction are these. First, that gender structures society hierarchically and that by conflating sex and gender, sexual difference is exaggerated and gender difference enforced. Second that sex/gender difference or supposed difference can afflict theories in three ways: sexism, androcentrism, and through illegitimate cognitive authority (or lack thereof) from the theory's association with gender or sexual symbols. Let us discuss the impact of these lessons on rational choice theory.[10]

Blatant sexism is rare these days; it's not acceptable. Sexism by insinuation is more common and can be found in rational choice theorist writings.[11] Sexist language is common.[12] Sexist stories for models and stereotypically sexist attributions of preference are not infrequent.[13] I have experienced quite astonishing sexist treatment from male rational choice theorists at conferences. But sexism is not the most interesting topic here. Sexism is bad, unambiguously so. The lesson: see it, expose it, eradicate it.

More interesting because more ambiguous are the androcentrisms and gender symbols of the theory. Two feminist theorists, the philosopher Elizabeth Anderson and the economist Paula England, have directly criticized the androcentrism in rational choice theory. They level three charges of androcentrism and gender symbolism: rational choice theory's conception of autonomy is masculine; its conception of rationality is masculine; and the theory radically (and androcentrically) separates reason and emotion. On the formal rational choice model, an agent is autonomous in the sense that she pursues her own preferences and appeals to her own beliefs about available options and their consequences. Following on the work of Donald (now Dierdre) McCloskey, Anderson argues that there is a rhetorical dimension of rational choice theory that goes beyond the formal statement of the model. This rhetorical dimension of the theory depicts the agent as self-transparent, opportunistic, self-reliant, coolly calculating, autonomous, and self-confident. On this interpretation, an agent is autonomous if he "regards himself as authorized to order his own preferences as he sees fit," which she takes to mean (by the lights of the theory) that "he does not bow down to social convention, tradition, or even morality."[14]

England's criticism of rational choice theory centers on the androcentrism of the model of agency employed by the theory. Feminist theory distinguishes two different and gendered notions of the mature person, one a separative self that is a fully self-sufficient source of moral and legal claims, and the other a connected self that is never fully separable from others on whom the self depends and who depend on that person for physical and emotional well-being. The separative self is the masculine person of the public sphere presupposed by liberal political theory. The connected self is the feminine person of the private sphere. Carol Gilligan's work suggests that most women see themselves as primarily connected and that their moral decisionmaking reflects their connectedness. The women in her study often held that maintaining a relationship was more important than any other duty or principle. They tended to hold virtues of self-sacrifice, patience, and motherly love above more public virtues like honesty, objectivity, or self-determination. Neither most women nor most men are truly unconnected, as the separative model proposes, but most women and most men have some ability to make and enforce some moral and legal claims without considering their impact on intimate relationships. England charges that rational choice theory assumes the separative model of the self.

Are the ideals of autonomy and rationality posited by rational choice theory masculine? As I described it, rational choice theory's agents are self-interested and opportunistic. But this does not entail that they are radically separate or selfish. It may be that this is a common misconception about rational choice theory sometimes held even by its adherents, but it is not a necessary interpretation of the model. The theory's assumption that its agents are non-tuists implies a certain independence of preference from others' preferences. However, rational agents must order their preferences under the influence of social norms. Otherwise they would not be considering all the consequences of their actions. The theory does require that these social pressures cannot be absolute external constraints on preferences, but this does not mean that they cannot be internalized in one's preference ordering so as to constitute an *effective* constraint on action. For example, consistently with rational choice theory, one might for moral reasons prefer to do anything else to killing innocent humans, and this may then result in always *effectively* ruling out killing innocents as a rational action. That is, the preference for acting "morally" could lead to "moral action" being ranked highly in the preference ordering. Morality, tradition, and norms ought to affect the rational person's preference ranking precisely because they make a difference in the outcome associated with one's decisions. Thus the masculinist interpretation of the theory, if it requires one not to internalize social norms, is actually inconsistent with the theory's assumptions. As to the charge that agents must be cold and passionless, again there is no requirement that emotion or passion not be a part of the makeup of agents' preferences. Indeed, I would argue again that, just as the social facts must affect one's rational decisions, one's emotional responses to situations ought to affect rational decisions because they affect the outcomes of actions. Rational choice theory need not, then, be restricted to masculine separative selves. Connected selves, provided that they choose actions by the consequences *for themselves* of their actions on intimate relations or emotional responses, can be seen as autonomous agents of the theory.

Whether or not women can be seen as autonomous rational agents on the rhetorical theory, Anderson objects that it does not postulate a liberating form of autonomous rationality. And as a result of its failure to conceptualize a liberating form of autonomy, rational choice theory does not recommend the kind of social/political changes that would lead to true liberation. She writes, "the theory's assumption of universal self-reliance simultaneously ignores and undermines the social conditions of rationality, in ways that particularly damage women,"[15] since it undervalues the work of caregivers, who are typically women. Masculine dignity, she claims, requires a declaration of independence from all others, especially from one's mother, and hence also from motherly work. Furthermore, it is not a universalizable ideal—if everyone were autonomous there would be no caregiving parents and consequently no nurtured adults. The preconditions for this kind of rational individual would be thereby undermined.

I agree that these would be serious shortcomings for any ideal of rationality, but I would argue that there is nothing in the theory that suggests that one cannot, would not, or ought not spend one's resources on whatever one likes, including children and significant others in need. Children (like disciples—which even the rhetorically manliest of men have never been averse to) are highly gratifying beings; they are luxury goods in economists' terms. Many rhetorically rational men would be willing to spend vast resources to have them and to invest in them. Motherly work can also be gotten from parents of both sexes. What is required is that the job of mothering be highly paid or have lower opportunity costs, and this is socially manipulable by eliminating the wage gap, making workplaces more child friendly, socially subsidizing child care, evening out the income distribution, and so on. Under the right social conditions, conditions that rational choice theory can reveal to us, the rhetorical ideal of rationality could be a sustainable one.

Further I would argue that the rhetorical ideal—as I understand it—is defensible on feminist grounds. It requires agents not to engage in self-deception or weakness of will, but to cultivate self-confidence, opportunism, and self-knowledge. It does not require one to be antisocial, antichild, or antimorality. Nor does it motivate, in itself and without considering any empirical facts about human inclinations, sociality, child rearing, or morality. But such, I would argue, is too much to ask of a theory of rationality alone.

Although England may be right that women tend to be connected selves rather than separative ones, I think that for the purposes of recommending a rational course of action to individual women, we would do better on feminist grounds to model them as separate persons. By treating persons as self-originating sources of moral claims, we take seriously the differences between persons, to borrow Rawls's phrase. If we treat them as the connected selves of Gilligan's study, then we treat them as persons who, at times, sublimate their interests for the sake of continuing a relationship. I see this as a dangerous course, especially for a feminist social theory.

England objects to the rationality assumption of the model because it radically separates reason from emotion. Although England objects to this separation on feminist grounds, there are also nonfeminist epistemic reasons to reject it.[16] I think that, like the selfishness assumption, it sends a precautionary note, but the separation of reason and emotion in rational choice theory is due more to the common interpretation of the model than to intrinsic features of the model itself. Although preference is often associated with emotion and sharply distinguished from cognition, this is an interpretation foisted on the model by philosophical understandings of reason, cognition, passion, emotion, and affect. The model itself has nothing to say about how preferences or beliefs are formed. Hence a rational choice theorist could hold that emotion is a cognitive process and that belief formation is influenced by emotion. One might object that although the formal theory does not separate reason and emotion, the rhetorical force of the theory is to hold them separate. I would argue that this is true only against a background philosophical conception of reason and emotion as separate. The problem is not with the model, but with the background assumptions that (some) modelers might bring to it. The solution is not to draw conclusions that are not warranted by the model.

2. The Personal Is Political

I take it that "the personal is political" is implicit in the feminist literature at least from Wollstonecraft, and you will no doubt recognize it as the central unifying slogan of the second wave of the women's movement, the movement of the 1960s and 1970s for legal sexual equality and recognition of widespread gender discrimination. "The personal is political" has several levels of meaning. Fundamentally it refers to and challenges the public/private distinction that is enshrined in liberalism. Family life, relations among family members, and individual choices concerning home, religion, and matters of sexual and esthetic taste are supposed to be private, personal decisions that are beyond the reach of legitimate government authority. Market work, contracts, relations among nonintimates, and political action are supposed to be realms that are subject to government intervention. Corresponding to the public/private distinction, different virtues and moral principles apply in each sphere. According to classical liberal theory, whereas the public sphere ought to be guided by the principles of justice, equality, and minimal interference in individual choice, the private sphere is to be guided by mercy, friendship, love, charity, and benevolent paternalism. Feminists point out that women have traditionally been excluded, legally, socially, or by the force of moral and religious norms, from the public sphere and relegated to second-class status in the private sphere, where they are the subjects, not the agents, of paternalistic intervention. Thus the slogan is first a demand for equal rights to join the public sphere. Second, it is a critique of the public/private distinction and a recommendation to be wary whenever the distinction is invoked to justify some paternalistic intervention or supposed moral or religious gender distinction. For example, wife beating was considered a private family matter, and so to be tolerated to a much greater degree than other, equally damaging forms of assault. Feminist analyses of the public/private distinction have revealed domestic violence for the crime that it is. Third, the slogan implies that what happens in the public political sphere governs the supposed private sphere as well. For example, feminists have revealed how legal definitions of property, voting rights, labor, and human capital shape family structure.

The lesson for rational choice theory from "the personal is political" is that theorists ought to reject the public/private boundary as a boundary for the theory, and bring public rules of justice into the modeling of the private sphere. Feminist economists have already begun to apply these lessons by modeling household production and distribution using bargaining theory.[17] In these theories spouses are modeled as agents with separate self-interested preferences that they seek to satisfy. Typically the Nash bargaining solution is then appealed to, so that the solution is determined primarily by the outside option, the alternative to a failure to agree on a solution to the bargain. These models have illuminated the causes and effects of inequality within and outside the family on the relative distributions of goods in the household.

3. The Practical Is Theoretical

Feminism has been in the forefront of a critique that has been simultaneously pursued by a variety of other philosophical movements and positions. This is the critique of a priori theorizing, which has been made in various ways by communitarians with respect to moral and political theories, Kuhn-inspired philosophers of science with respect to theories of science, critical legal studies in law, social epistemologists, and others. In science, law, morality, and politics, feminists have shown that by concentrating on theoretical rational reconstructions of science/morality, without considering the practical circumstances of theoretical formulation, fundamental aspects of each may be missed or misconstrued. In the case of rational choice theory, feminist practical concerns have led to new uses of theory and to illuminating discoveries about the way that preference is formed under practical circumstances. Let me illustrate with two feminist examples: the recognition of the family as a site of injustice and intrahousehold bargaining. These examples show that androcentrism in rational choice theory can be revealed in practice, that is, by the practical step of encouraging women to enter the theory-making field.

As already noted, in traditional liberal political theory, the family belongs to the private sphere. Justice is a virtue of the public sphere. Liberal theorists from Hobbes to Rousseau to Locke to Rawls have all taken households to be represented by a single head, and that head has been gendered male. Likewise, economic theory, when it has mentioned the family as a social institution at all, has assumed a single gendered utility function, that of a male head of household. The attitude toward the family is perhaps best summarized by the words of James Mill:

> All those individuals whose interests are indisputably included in those of other individuals may be struck off without inconvenience. In this light may be viewed all children, up to a certain age, whose interests are involved in those of their parents. In this light also, women may be regarded, the interests of almost all of whom is involved either in that of their fathers or in that of their husbands.[18]

The single, gendered utility function is problematic because it internalizes any conflicts and represents only the interests of the male head of household. But, as feminists have pointed out, the family is a primary site of the production and distribution of goods. The norms of family life determine who produces and who gets the primary share of the basic goods of food, shelter, clothing, and leisure. And, as feminists have documented, on any reasonable system of accounts, women get lesser shares than men.[19] Since the entry of women and the development of feminism as a theoretical perspective, in both political philosophy, as exemplified by the work of Susan Moller

Okin,[20] and in economic theory, exemplified by the work of Bina Agarwal,[21] Amartya Sen,[22] Nancy Folbre,[23] and Elaine McCrate,[24] the family is now seen as a primary site of injustice, and hence in need of a theory (and practice) of distributive justice, a task for which rational choice theory is well suited.

One result has been bargaining analysis of household distribution of goods and labor division. However, feminist practical observation and analysis here reveals some gender-related complexity that theorists had not noticed. In her analysis of the use of bargaining theory to model interactions within families, Agarwal claims that these models fall to recognize the gendered psychosocial factors that affect bargaining power. In particular she charges that formal models cannot incorporate the full complexity of gender interactions within and outside of households that affect the outcomes of bargaining.[25] Agarwal's study concentrates on household economics in India, but it has some important problems for household bargaining everywhere. The first problem is that formal models fail to distinguish perceived need and contribution from actual need and contribution. Women's and girls' needs and contributions in household consumption and production are systematically underestimated. As long as the rational choice model uses subjective preference and beliefs, this problem will continue, and it is a serious problem if social and political policies are based on these (under)estimates. However, rational choice theory must assume that agents use *their* beliefs and desires; otherwise, rationality would be opaque to the agents. In my interpretations of rational choice theory, I will have a suggestion to address the problem of perceived need and contribution.

Second, Agarwal raises the problem of the endogeneity of factors determining the outcome of bargaining to the bargaining process. Bargaining theory makes the outside options available to the agents crucial determinants of the outcome, and it takes the outside options to be exogenously determined. But sometimes the outside options are endogenous to the bargaining process itself. An example Agarwal uses to illustrate this point is that having land rights can help women negotiate less restrictive social norms and thus have an effect on inheritance laws, access to education, access to government officials, access to social resources outside of other kin contesting for the land, and legal representation. These factors in turn determine whether women can bargain successfully for land rights. Agarwal discusses the problem of the endogeneity of other social norms to the bargaining process, as well. Gender norms set limits on what can be bargained about. Agarwal points out that because of the accumulated effect of individual bargains over time, gender norms might also be modeled as outcomes of a larger social bargain. Gender norms also set constraints on the use of bargaining abilities that are not modeled by the theory, such as the ability to raise one's voice or threaten the use of force. Bargaining theory models all bargainers as having the same bargaining ability. In cases involving persons with differential social status, however, this assumption is questionable. However, one must remember that there is rarely an actual bargain, with its haggling and negotiating, going on. The bargain is a metaphor for division of goods and labor. Still, men's greater ability to make demands must affect divisions and a feminist use of rational choice theory must take this inequality into account.

Third, Agarwal argues that women may be more motivated by altruism in the household, while men may be more motivated by self-interest. There are two ways of taking this objection. On one construal, altruists would fail to meet the requirements of rational agency set by rational choice theory. But this is not a good interpretation, for if altruists fail, then for the same reason self-interested persons fail: neither is being non-tuistic. The altruist is taking the others' interests into account and trying to serve them, and the self-interested person is trying not to serve them. But if we understand the altruist as taking the others' interests as her own, and likewise the self-interested person as taking no account of the others' interests, then both fit the model of agency of rational choice theory. Still, Agarwal's observation is important for a feminist social theory because it suggests that bargaining will doubly serve men's interests, even as women get what they want. What are the lessons here for rational choice theory? The problems Agarwal raises are not necessarily problems with the theory or its application, but with the reality being modeled. That is, if individual women demand less and are weaker bargainers than individual men, and if individual women really are altruists and individual men really are selfish, then men will get more of what they want in any actual bargain.

4. The Imaginary Domain

Much of feminist work concerns issues of sex and sexuality. Practical legal issues for women, including pornography, sexual harassment, rape, and sodomy statutes, make this concern urgent for all feminist theorists. Some feminists, particularly those inspired by psychoanalysis, are interested in the more esoteric issues of feminine sexuality, feminine difference, and how these are constructed in patriarchal society. In recent work, Drucilla Cornell forges a link between these two sets of concerns with her concept of the imaginary domain.[26] Cornell argues that we are fundamentally and essentially sexual beings, that is, beings who live in sexed bodies, and for whom sex is the most basic motivational drive. However, sex is not to be taken as purely natural. Although we have a natural capacity for sexual interest, how we express it is constructed socially. Social norms for appropriate sexual behavior constrain our sexual expression and our sexual fantasies. Those of us whose sexual fantasies stray from the norm are subjected to sexual shame, and this shame in turn affects sexual desire and satisfaction. Cornell holds that constraints on sexual expression through sexual shame are among the most fundamental invasions of our being. She argues for the freedom of our sexual fantasy life, a psychic space that she terms the imaginary domain. Since this freedom lies at the very foundation of self-respect, it is, she claims, a primary good, a minimum amount of which ought to be guaranteed in liberal societies. Hence, laws that infringe on the imaginary domain are illegitimate (pornography is not to be censored, sexual expression should be allowed in the workplace, and sodomy statutes ought to be ruled unconstitutional), and behaviors that encroach on others' imaginary domain are to be outlawed or discouraged (thus rape and sexual harassment are to be made illegal because they trespass on the imaginary domain).

Although I reject the sexual reductionism of psychoanalysis,[27] I think that the concept of the imaginary domain can provide an important lesson of feminism, especially for liberalism and rational choice theory. I find the concept of the imaginary domain to be an illuminating metaphor for the feminist desire to reinvent society in spite of patriarchal norms that constrain our visions of the future. Like any political philosophy, feminism must offer a vision of the future. Yet, like other progressive philosophies, feminism argues that persons who are constructed under the current repressions are unable fully to conceive the possibilities for liberation. Indeed, given severe enough repression, they may be unable to conceive any alternative world at all. Thus we cannot simply design a future society and take the optimal steps to bring it about. We must be careful what we wish for, as our wishes may unwittingly be for further repression. It is also true, however, that we can imagine life that is different from what we have known, institutions that are less repressive. The imaginary domain accounts for these possibilities. It is our capacity to imagine other ways of being, apart from the social norms that now constrain us.[28] The imaginary domain is the repository from which alternative conceptions of norms and social structures regarding sex and gender might arise. Cornell effectively argues that if we close off this well of options, if we too strongly enforce the current norms and make them appear natural and necessary, then we insist that persons choose within them. Optimization is unlikely in such a circumstance, and to call such conditions "autonomous" is to mock the word. Rational choice theory, then, must respect the imaginary domain.

What I think is the most serious charge against rational choice theory, and this charge has been leveled in various ways by many, including Agarwal, Anderson, England, and Sen,[29] is that its construal of autonomy as simply consistent non-tuism leads to accommodating preferences that are actually nonautonomous in some thicker and more interesting sense. If rational choice theory were to only give us the means to achieve sexist or androcentric ends, then it would thwart the ultimate feminist aim of progressive social change. I am convinced that some systematic, gendered preferences under conditions of patriarchy are not autonomous, not worthy of ultimate respect. Feminists from de Beauvoir to MacKinnon have argued this forcefully and successfully. So there is a serious problem. However, this is a general problem for feminism, no matter what social theory or methodology one employs to formulate policy. It is important to change people's preferences, but also to avoid hurting those persons who have suffered oppression. In the short run, social policies ought to attempt to satisfy the given preferences of the oppressed in order to minimize the immediate damage to victims of oppression. In the long run justice demands that oppression be abolished, however. How can we abolish oppression without violating the preferences of the already oppressed? This goal is further hampered by the fact that it is difficult to see from our perspective what autonomous preferences would look like. Would pornography exist in a feminist enlightened future? It is hard to tell: some would argue that it would be a part of transformative erotic life; others argue that pornography is appealing only because it depicts women as lesser beings, and this will not be erotic in an enlightened future. Since it is impossible to discern which side is right in this debate, we need to make small, transformative steps toward freedom rather than make a direct effort at preference reeducation. It seems to me that rational choice theory has a lot to offer toward a transformative analysis of the social system itself.

Cornell objects to the use of rational choice theory in understanding sex and sexuality. I want to address her objection because I would like to make subversive use of her concept of the imaginary domain, so it is important to show that the concept does not fundamentally contradict the ideal of agency assumed by rational choice theory. The imaginary domain is, for Cornell, the wellspring of the symbolic construction of eroticism. It is, she claims, arational (if not irrational) and hence not amenable to a rational choice analysis.[30] I agree that rational choice theory is unlikely to have anything to say about how the imaginary domain works; that is the bailiwick of cognitive psychology (psychoanalysis, according to Cornell). The imaginary domain is the source of beliefs and desires for the theory, and it is unlikely to be usefully illuminated by any probing of it by the theory. However, rational choice theory must recommend that the imaginary domain be respected, as it is the source of strategies, beliefs, desires, games—it is the fuel on which the model runs.

IV. Toward a Feminist Rational Choice Theory

I want now to assert an interpretation of the model that will serve progressive feminist ends in light of the lessons of feminism. As I see it, rational choice theory can be a tool for progressive feminist social theory on two interpretations of the model. Since models may admit of many interpretations, there is no need to see these as contradictory. On one interpretation the model is about individual rationality, and it prescribes an ideal to which rational persons, including rational women, ought to strive. On the second interpretation, the model is about how social norms, rules, and conventions structure incentives to guide, if not completely determine, individual behavior.

1. Rationality as an Ideal for Individual Women

First, on the individualist interpretation, the model is to be seen as a primarily normative model for individual rational behavior.[31] On this model the theory recommends consistency in beliefs and desires, as well as the single-minded, serious pursuit of non-tuistic self-interest. I take it that the former is good for everyone. The latter recommendation is especially important for women, I believe, in light of the lessons of feminism. For they have revealed that women are more likely to be caregivers and less likely to be care receivers than men. Rational choice theory offers recommendations for maximizing self-interest in such situations. If we understand caregiving behavior as, in Gauthier's terms, constrained maximization and noncaregiving as straightforward maximization, then game theory tells us when it is rational to be a caregiver and when it is rational not to give care, and how it might be better to increase the penalties against noncaregivers in order to increase their numbers in the environment. Game theory suggests that one's disposition is a choice to be caring or to be selfish, and thus that the relative numbers of caregivers and noncaregivers might be affected by how the collective of the caregivers treat the noncaregivers. For women this is an especially relevant and important message, in light of the fact that women do too much of the caring work in society. Recommending to women that they withhold care from men or others who refuse to reciprocate care is a feminist message.

As already noted, however, the fundamental problem with the individual interpretation of rational choice theory for feminism is that it takes the preferences and beliefs about the available options as given. But these preferences were forged under, and our sights are limited by, the social norms and institutions that we now have. Women in our society, for example, seem to want more than men to give care.[32] Hence rational choice theory seems to offer no way out for the oppressed: they will continue to believe that their choices are circumscribed and to choose according to preferences formed under those beliefs. This is the problem that Anderson pointed out, when she argued that women's preferences may be nonautonomous, and that Agarwal alluded to in her criticism that bargaining theory takes social norms as given. Furthermore, the individual interpretation recommends action to individuals, but individuals acting alone are unlikely to change social norms or gendered preferences.

My response to this problem is twofold. First, this is not a problem with the model so much as with reality. It is a fact that persons' beliefs and desires are forged in part by the social norms of the society in which they live. But it is also the case that people sometimes manage to imagine their way to a new social order. Here the feminist lesson of the imaginary domain is helpful. It suggests that we are able, if only occasionally, if only in contrast to what we have learned and in spite of the social enforcement of the status quo, to imagine new ways of being. Rational choice theory takes the possible strategies and outcomes as given. But given by whom? By the modeler, who models the agents themselves. A progressive normative model of rational choice models the possibilities in light of an appreciation of the imaginary domain. Second, however, we must, as Agarwal's critique implies, model the evolution of social norms themselves. To do this we need a second interpretation of the model that rational choice theory offers.

2. Rational Choice Theory as a Theory of Structural Incentives

The structural theory of rational choice[33] assumes that the social environment systematically rewards and punishes behaviors by social groups and thereby induces a preference structure on (most) members. Thus the structural theory of rational choice assesses the objective social rewards and penalties that are consequent on their (inter)actions and their social status and uses these assessments to impute preferences and beliefs to individuals based purely on their social group memberships. For example, a norm of feminine passivity means that women are rewarded for behaving passively and penalized for behaving assertively, and thus these penalties and rewards are part of the outcomes of females' passive or assertive actions. Another example: the gender wage gap means that women can expect lower wages than men can expect, and hence the outcomes expected by women from market work are discounted as compared with those of similarly placed men by the degree of the wage gap. Stereotypical beliefs that attach to members of groups regardless of individual characteristics play an important role in the structural theory as imputed beliefs.

The structural theory of rational choice assumes that agents behave rationally in the sense that they choose actions that maximize their (induced) expected utilities. Hence, it cannot show individuals or women as a group to be rational; it assumes this thin rationality. Furthermore, it would be inappropriate to rest a judgment of individual rationality on this dimension of rational choice, since persons acting to thwart the social system of rewards and penalties might be acting admirably, depending on their reasons for acting, or even rationally in the then formal sense, depending on their idiosyncratic beliefs and desires. In this theory, individuals are interpreted as anonymous members of social groups, which are determined by the reward structures of laws, norms, traditions, and stereotypes that discriminate by group membership. The structural theory of rational choice aims to examine how social structures motivate normal behavior and differentially reward individuals based on their social status. From such analyses, we can see how social structures might be changed to liberate persons from their ascribed, nonvoluntary, group membership, or how to make group membership neutral with respect to their outcomes vis-à-vis other groups. Arguments for changing social structures depend also on moral and political premises that rational choice theory cannot provide. But rational choice theory can recommend the means to those ends.

In this interpretation, rational choice theory takes seriously the first two lessons of feminism, the sex/gender distinction and that the personal is political. It takes the first lesson seriously by supposing that gender divides society into groups that consist of individuals who act according to similar structured incentives. It takes the second seriously by exhibiting personal motivations as the outcomes of social norms and political struggle.

A problem that Agarwal raised for the theory, the problem of perceived need and contribution, can now be addressed. The problem arises in particular in the context of social policy formation, where the structural theory of rational choice is to be used. But here we do not use agents' beliefs but rather impute beliefs. The theorist can then choose to impute beliefs in a given context, depending on how the model is used. If the point is to describe the effect of a policy on the population, then it will be best to impute the beliefs as they are found in the population so that the model accurately predicts how agents' actions will respond to the policy. If, on the other hand, the model is being used to prescribe the just outcome of a bargain or decision, then actual needs and contributions ought to be used to model the agents' beliefs.

Dan Hausman rejects the structural interpretation of rational choice theory because, he claims, on the structural interpretation we cannot interpret the model literally.[34] But this misses the point that models allow multiple interpretations. Game theory already has a well developed interpretation in evolutionary biology, where the optimizing strategies are termed "evolutionary stable strategies" and the game players are species. In this interpretation surely the terms "rationality" and "choice" are metaphors. Here I am suggesting that the institutional stable strategies are played out by social groups. Under the individual psychological interpretation of rational choice theory the mechanism that allows individuals to choose optimizing strategies is rational deliberation, in the evolutionary case it is natural selection, and at the institutional level it is a combination of these mechanisms. In some cases rational deliberation is the appropriate interpretation (collective action, conspiracy); in other cases conventions can be seen to evolve by the fact that less successful strategies are selected out. The individual psychological interpretation just doesn't focus the story correctly when we are asking questions about what social norms, conventions, laws, and the like are optimal or just. Game theory allows at least three interpretations, and two of them are amenable to feminist ends.

Acknowledgements

I thank Elizabeth Anderson, Tamara Horowitz, and audiences at the University of Missouri and the University of Georgia for helpful comments on earlier versions of this paper.

Notes

It seems that the concern about sexist language has become passé.

1. Drucilla Cornell, *The Imaginary Domain* (New York: Routledge, 1995); and Cornell, *At the Heart of Freedom: Feminism, Sex, and Equality* (Princeton: Princeton University Press, 1999).

2. See P. H. Wicksteed, *The Common Sense of Political Economy and Selected Papers and Reviews on Economic Theory*, ed. L. Robbins, 2 vols. (London, 1933). See also David Gauthier, *Morals by Agreement* (New York: Oxford University Press, 1986), p. 87; and John Rawls, *A Theory of Justice* (Cambridge: Harvard University Press, 1971), p. 13.

3. Gauthier, *Morals*, p. 311.

4. In *The Common Mind* (New York: Oxford University Press, 1993) Philip Pettit distinguishes individualism, the thesis that individuals (rather than social groups) are the primary explanatory units of social theory, and atomism, the thesis that individual persons are essentially unaffected by other persons. I use the term "atomism" in this sense; Petit also offers a powerful criticism of ontological atomism as against holism. However, I take it that rational choice theory does not fall afoul of this criticism in assuming methodological atomism.

5. At this point the reader unsympathetic to rational choice theory will begin to question the extreme unrealism of the assumptions, and hence the applicability of the theory. First, I want to point out that a full defense of rational choice theory against this sort of critique, which is not a feminist critique, is beyond the scope of this chapter. Here is a too brief defense: With rational choice theory we are trying to approximately describe action in a way that uncovers one kind of conscious, intentional motivation to action. Let us call tills the economic force. Analogous to the gravitational force in physical phenomena, the economic force is only one of several forces that cause action. What rational choice theorists want to do is not precisely determine the outcome of interactions, but rather to try to isolate economic force. For this purpose we need pure and simple models, models that attempt to abstract away from other motivational forces such as tuistic concerns and psychological forces, both cognitive and affective, such as stereotype belief formation, and shame, pride, and the strive for recognition.

6. For example, Drucilla Cornell, *The Imaginary Domain* (New York: Routledge, 1997). Postmodern feminists like Judith Butler question whether there is any coherent sense of any gender identity. See Donna Haraway, "'Gender' for a Marxist Dictionary: The Sexual Politics of a Word," in *Simians, Cyborgs, and Women* (New York: Routledge, 1991).

7. Mary Wollstonecraft, *A Vindication of the Rights of Women* (Prometheus, 1989).

8. John Stuart Mill, *The Subjection of Women* (Indianapolis: Hackett, 1988), p. 22.

9. As will be obvious, I owe much in this discussion to Elizabeth Anderson; see Anderson, "Feminist Epistemology: An Interpretation and a Defense," *Hypatia*, Summer 1994, pp. 30–84.

10. Related, though different, mistakes occur as a result of the confusion of the biological natures and social constructions of race, ethnicity, sexuality, and, perhaps, class. A thorough feminist critique of rational choice theory would account for these as well.

11. Look at the assumptions about the family in Gary Becker's *Treatise on the Family* or assumptions about female nature in Richard Posner's *Sex and Reason*.

12. See Ken Binmore, *Game Theory and the Social Contract* (Cambridge: MIT Press, 1995); Frederic Schick, *Making Choices* (Cambridge: Cambridge University Press, 1997).

13. Consider the infamous "battle of the sexes."

14. Anderson, "Feminist Epistemology," p. 10.

15. Anderson, "Feminist Epistemology," p. 37.

16. See Catherine Elgin, *Considered Judgment* (Princeton: Princeton University Press, 1997), chap. 5.

17. Some examples of these bargaining analyses of marriage include Shelly Lundberg and Robert A. Pollak, "Non-cooperative Bargaining Models of Marriage," *American Economic Review* 84 (1994): 132–137; Lundberg and Pollak, "Separate Spheres Bargaining and the Marriage Market," *Journal of Political Economy* 101 (1993): 988–1010; Rhona Mahony, *Kidding Ourselves: Breadwinning, Babies, and Bargaining Power* (New York: Basic, 1995); Marilyn Manser and Murray Brown, "Marriage and Household Decision-Making: A Bargaining Analysis," *International Economic Review* 21 (1980): 31–44; Marjorie B. McElroy and Mary Jean Homey, "Nash-Bargained Household Decisions: Toward a Generalization of the Theory of Demand," *International Economic Review* 22 (1981): 333–349.

18. James Mill, as quoted in Nancy Hartman and Heidi Hartmann, "The Rhetoric of Self-Interest: Ideology and Gender in Economic Theory," in *The Consequences of Economic Rhetoric*, ed. Arjo Klamer, Donald N. McCloskey, and Robert M. Solow (New York: Cambridge University Press, 1988), p. 188.

19. Barbara Bergmann, *The Economic Emergence of Women* (New York: Basic, 1988); Martha Nussbaum and Jonathon Glover, eds., *Women, Culture, and Development* (New York: Oxford University Press, 1995), especially the introduction by Nussbaum and "Gender Inequalities and Theories of Justice" by Amartya Sen.

20. Susan Moller Okin, *Justice, Gender, and the Family* (New York: Basic, 1989).

21. Bina Agarwal, *A Field of One's Own: Gender and Land Rights in South Asia* (Cambridge: Cambridge University Press, 1994); and Agarwal, "Bargaining and Gender Relations: Within and Beyond the Household," *Feminist Economics* 3 (1997): 1–50.

22. Amartya Sen, "Gender and Cooperative Conflicts," in *Persistent Inequalities: Women and World Development*, ed. Irene Tinker (New York: Oxford University Press, 1990).

23. Nancy Folbre, *Who Pays for the Kids? Gender and the Structures of Constraint* (New York: Routledge, 1994).

24. Elaine McCrate, "Trade, Merger, and Employment: Economic Theory on Marriage," *Review of Radical Political Economics* 19 (1987): 73–89; and McCrate, "Rationality, Gender, and Domination" (paper presented at the 1992 AEA meetings in New Orleans, January 1992).

25. Bina Agarwal, "Bargaining and Gender Relations," in *Field of One's Own*, p. 2.

26. Drucilla Cornell, *The Imaginary Domain* (New York: Routledge, 1995); and Cornell, *At the Heart of Freedom: Feminism Sex and Equality* (Princeton: Princeton University Press, 1999).

27. For my critique of psychoanalysis, see Ann E. Cudd, "Psychological Explanations of Oppression," in *Theorizing Multiculturalism*, ed. Cynthia Willet; Blackwell, 1998.

28. María Lugones, "Structure/Antistructure and Agency Under Oppression," *Journal of Philosophy*, October 1990, pp. 500–507, nicely states the difficulty for theories of oppression that locate oppression in social structures and recommend liberatory strategies.

29. Amartya Sen, "Rational Fools: A Critique of the Behavioural Foundations of Economic Theory," *Philosophy and Public Affairs* 6 (1976–1977): 317–344.

30. Cornell, *Imaginary Domain*, p. 8.

31. I mean to distinguish sharply normative from empirical models. For more on this interpretation of rational choice theory, see Ann E. Cudd, "Modeling Rationality as a Normative Enterprise" (unpublished manuscript).

32. For example, Victor Fuchs, "Women's Quest for Economic Equality," *Journal of Economic Perspectives* 3 (1989): "On average women have a stronger demand for children than men do and have more concern for children after they are born. In short, there is a difference on the side of preferences, and this difference is a major source of women's economic disadvantage" (p. 38).

33. The external theory of rational choice bears some resemblance in the big picture, if not in the details, to the interpretation of rational choice theory offered by Debra Satz and John Ferejohn, "Rational Choice and Social Theory," *Journal of Philosophy*, February 1994, pp. 71–87.

34. Daniel M. Hausman, "Rational Choice and Social Theory: A Comment," *Journal of Philosophy*, February 1995, pp. 96–101.

18

MINDS OF THEIR OWN: CHOICES, AUTONOMY, CULTURAL PRACTICES, AND OTHER WOMEN

UMA NARAYAN

Specters of the Other Woman: Or How Not to Put Oneself in Another's Shoes

Reflecting on discussions about "cultural practices" pertaining to Third World women that I have both in the classroom and outside it, I believe that two different but connected "specters of the other woman" often haunt these conversations and require philosophical exorcism. I call the first of these two specters the "prisoner of patriarchy." The "prisoner of patriarchy" has various forms of patriarchal oppression imposed on her *entirely against her will and consent*—similar to how a prisoner is subject to constraints on liberty. I believe this specter results from a mainstream American, say a student, imagining herself, the person she currently is with her own values and perspectives, in an Other context where she is subjected to practices such as veiling, purdah (seclusion), or arranged marriage. Endorsing or accepting any of these practices for herself seems inconceivable, and so she imagines these Other women in exactly the same terms.

When this figure of the prisoner of patriarchy is invoked in classroom discussions, other students often react critically by pointing out that the Other woman is unlikely to have the same attitudes to these patriarchal practices "as We do." However, in making this criticism, they often evoke the second specter, one call the dupe of patriarchy. Although patriarchal violence is coercively imposed on the prisoner of patriarchy, it is virtually *self-imposed* by the dupe of patriarchy because she is imagined to completely subscribe to the patriarchal norms and practices of her culture. Her attitudes are envisioned as completely shaped by the dominant patriarchal values of her cultural context.

I believe that these specters are invoked in response to two different kinds of "ethical impulse," which attempt to objectively or rationally come to terms with the situation of the Other woman. With the prisoner, the ethical impulse is to imaginatively understand the experiences of the Other in ways identical to how one would experience an oppressive practice. This impulse follows the common ethical injunction to imagine oneself in the Other's shoes—but imagines one's feet as identical to that of the Other woman, subject to being pinched or hobbled in exactly those places where they would pinch or hobble her feet, failing to imagine what it is like to be the Other woman, with her own feet in her shoes. "Putting oneself in her place" amounts to displacing her and filling her shoes with one's own feet—attributing to her responses and attitudes modeled entirely on one's own.

The second ethical impulse, which summons the dupe of patriarchy, strives to attend to the fact that the Other woman is shaped by differences of circumstances, commitments, and context. It acknowledges a genuine difficulty in "putting oneself in the shoes of the Other woman," since her feet may fit differently into those shoes than would one's own. However, this insight is pushed to an extreme and imagines the feet of the Other woman as *entirely committed to the shape of her shoes*, as feet that either feel no chafing or are committed to wearing those shoes no matter how many they blisters they cause. To avoid imagining the Other woman as identical to oneself fills the Other woman's shoes nevertheless—with a projection of an Other woman who entirely subscribes to the values and practices of her culture.

Each specter displays one problematic pole of a certain "imperialism of the imagination"—the prisoner imagines the Other's responses as perfectly identical to one's own; the dupe projects a totalizing form of "difference" on one's Others. Both specters share the problem of imagining one's Others as *monolithic in their responses*, failing to recognize that one's Others have a *variety* of responses to the practices that shape their lives. They fail to register the real multiplicity of Other women, with different sorts of shoes and feet, and different takes on the fit between them! Attending to the varied responses of real Other women, responses that are often critical of certain aspects of patriarchal cultural practices, even as they endorse or collude with others, enables us to see that most Other women differ from both the prisoner and the dupe of patriarchy, and to recognize that perhaps the most important form of "sameness" these "Other women" share with "Us" is the wide variation in their responses to "patriarchal practices" in their context.

I will proceed to concretely illustrate these claims by examining women's attitudes to veiling. In the prisoner of patriarchy model, the veil is entirely imposed on the woman—she veils only because she must. In the dupe of patriarchy model, she veils because she completely endorses all aspects of the practice. I discuss actual veiled women's responses to veiling, responses which show that these women differ both from the prisoner and dupe of patriarchy, and from each other.

I will focus on the responses of women from the conservative Sufi Pirzada community of Old Delhi, who live in relative purdah (or seclusion) within the home and are expected to veil when they are in public.[1] The range of criticisms about veiling voiced by many of these women would surprise those inclined to view them as completely compliant dupes of patriarchy. Many complain strenuously about the sheer physical discomforts that attend veiling in really hot weather and about how it makes them giddy and faint and about being unable to see properly and tripping into drains. Many even have a wry take on the esthetics of the burqua, commenting with exasperated amusement that it makes them look like water buffaloes!

Many of their complaints go further. They recognize how purdah and veiling are implicated in the more general constraints of their lives. Many talk about how purdah has prevented many of them from learning elementary skills such as crossing heavily-trafficked roads or finding their way around the local streets, and made them embarrassed and frightened to ask directions of strangers. They acknowledge how the lack of these skills keeps them dependent on male kinsmen accompanying them, even when they venture out on minor errands.[2] They recognize how purdah and veiling have limited their access to education and their social mobility in terms of shopping or visiting relatives. They have even kept them ignorant about much that happens in their immediate social world—self-deprecatingly referring to themselves as "frogs in a well."[3] Many older women talk with envy about younger women who have had the luck to be married into families that are not as strict about veiling or purdah; many of the younger women express the hope that they will be married into such families. All these responses collectively show that Pirzada women are not dupes of patriarchy who completely and uncritically endorse the values and practices of their culture.

On the other hand, many of these women simultaneously have a wide range of reasons for continuing to practice purdah and veiling. Outside the home, wearing the burqua signifies womanly modesty and propriety. Many older women admit that despite its discomfort, they would feel naked if they went out without their burqua.[4] For many, wearing the burqua is an integral part of their social identity and sense of self, and the social discomfort they would feel without it outweighs its physical inconveniences. Others shrewdly note the practical and strategic advantages of wearing the burqua—under its cover they can go out in a hurry without changing the old clothes they were wearing for housework, or they can sneak off to the cinema with a friend after telling their husbands they are going to the bazaar, the husbands being none the wiser even if they pass them in the streets. Some younger Pirzada women acknowledge that they veil because of the insistence of strict family elders or because the community would disparage their reputation, hurting their prospects for a good marriage, were they to go unveiled.[5] These reasons, individually and collectively, demonstrate that these women differ from the prisoner of patriarchy, who is forced to veil under *literal coercion*. These women recognize they have *real practical and emotional stakes* in the approval of their family elders and in maintaining their reputation in the community.

For many Pirzada women, the significance of veiling and purdah goes beyond its links to their gender identity—they are also markers of other linked aspects of social identity that the women value. For instance, the Pirzada claim superior Syed status in virtue of being descendants of the Prophet's daughter Fatima. Adherence to veiling and purdah signify their superior standing vis-à-vis other Muslim women, a standing

Pirzada women value. And even as some Pirzada women complain about veiling, they are critical of the "immodesty" of Western women with their hair flying loose, wearing low necklines and flimsy dresses, and of Hindu women who wear midriff revealing saris and light blouses.[6] Thus Pirzada women's complaints about the veil often coexist with veiling to signify their sense of superior modesty and bodily propriety compared with women who constitute their Others. In addition, Pirzada women understand that purdah and veiling have important economic implications. Pirzada men are custodians of a popular local shrine of a Sufi saint and depend on the income that the pilgrims bring.[7] Economic reliance on the shrine provides an important reason for appearing "orthodox"—and veiling and purdah are important markers of such orthodoxy. Their veiling also functions as a marker of visible Muslim presence in the midst of a Hindu majority. In this context it constitutes a public signifier of religious and ethnic identity. Veiling and purdah clearly have significance for the lives of different women even in this one community, making it clear that these practices are not *reducible* to "patriarchal control of women."

Intelligent analogues to our own context can help us better understand Other women's collusions with and resistances to "cultural practices." Compare the veiling of Pirzada women with a less visible and more transparent form of veiling commonly worn here—the different forms of makeup Western women routinely wear in public settings. Both makeup and veiling convey symbolic messages about women's social status; they emphasize that attention to their "outward appearance" matters and that wherever they appear in public, they appear in part as sexualized entities. Western feminists have documented the adverse effects on women of a cultural regime that pressures them to expend great effort in subjecting themselves to various "regimens of beauty" and creates considerable anxiety over different aspects of their bodily appearance.[8] Like many women who veil, many women who wear makeup do not centrally *experience* it as a form of patriarchal oppression. Even many women who understand the patriarchal connotations of wearing makeup continue to do so, for a variety of reasons. For some, wearing makeup is part of their self-image, their sense of femininity, or part of a playful erotic relationship to their own bodies. For others, wearing makeup is part of the way they are expected to look in professional contexts or mediates their attempts to conform to prevailing norms of feminine attractiveness. Westerners might more easily understand why some veiled women feel embarrassment at going out with their heads uncovered, when they think about why many women here would feel mortified going out in public with hairy legs uncovered! Such cross-cultural comparisons help us better understand Other women's responses to cultural practices, as long as we attend to the plurality of women's attitudes to these practices and do not flatten the range of meanings of complex cultural practices.

Patriarchal Contexts, Cultural Practices, and Women's Choices

Many women's decisions to comply with cultural practices such as veiling or wearing makeup can, I believe, be seen as forms of "bargaining with patriarchy"[9] rather than living as prisoners or dupes of patriarchy. There is active agency involved in women's compliance with patriarchal structures, even when the stakes involved in noncompliance and the pressures that enjoin compliance are very high, and the idea of "bargaining with patriarchy" enables us to keep this consideration in mind. The negotiating powers some women have to bargain with patriarchy might be considerable; in other cases their negotiating powers are far less strong. But even in the latter sorts of cases, women avail themselves of whatever room they have to maneuver, and unlike the prisoner of patriarchy, they know they have some *real stakes* in the compliances they do undertake. Pirzada women's compliances, for instance, stem from the fact that they have valued lives deeply rooted in the Pirzada community. They have neither access to nor a desire for ways of life that would sunder them from their community. Some of the compliances they undertake are, while irksome, compromises they make in order to secure the real stakes they have in life within the community. Other aspects of their compliances reflect their noninstrumental commitments to various aspects of their own religious, social, and communal identities.

The decisions many women make with respect to "cultural practices" ought, I think, to be understood as a choice of a "bundle of elements," some of which they want and some of which they do not, and where they lack the power to "undo the bundle" so as to choose only those elements they want. Much of what individuals in general want in life comes in such "mixed bundles" that require resignation to certain tradeoffs as a means to secure goods one values, and it would be both incorrect and dangerous to ignore that choices were in fact being made by women, even where they lacked the power to negotiate some elements of the "bundle." Regarding women's compliances with "cultural practices" it is important for feminists to maintain a dual awareness—seeing *both how the practice imposes constraints on choices and how choices are in fact being made within these constraints.*

Feminists have correctly insisted that patriarchal structures not only pose serious *external* obstacles to the life options available to women; they also *internally* handicap, distort, and impoverish women's expectations, desires, sense of entitlement, and sense of self. But when this insistence is pushed to an extreme (as it arguably is at moments in the work of feminists like Mary Daly, Andrea Dworkin, and Catherine MacKinnon),[10] it results in what I think of as an "engulfing view" of patriarchy and its effects on women's agency. In the engulfing view, women's agency is represented as if it were completely "pulverized by patriarchy"—so maimed that women have no wit, no capacity for critical reflection or resistance, no real stakes in their way of life. They are capable only of zombielike acquiescence to patriarchal norms, beings whose desires and values are patriarchal excrescence not attributable to women as real free agents. This engulfing view portrays women's desires and attitudes as "not really their own" in any meaningful or legitimate sense, reducing them to mere symptoms of their being individuals-subject-to patriarchy. The idea that women's values, attitudes, and choices can be impoverished and distorted by patriarchy should not be used so heavy-handedly as to *completely efface* the value and significance of these choices *from the point of view of the women who make them.* Despite undeniable distortions, these are in fact the values, attitudes, and choices that define for these women the lives they currently have and value, and the selves they currently are and in many ways want to remain.

Such heavy-handed effacement of women's agency under patriarchal constraints seems particularly likely and is especially worrisome in contexts where Western feminists engage with Other cultural practices. Discussing Other women's choices to comply with cultural practices, Susan Okin says,

> What if the "acquiescence" by some in cultural practices stems from lack of power or socialization into inferior roles, resulting in lack of self-esteem or a sense of entitlement? Such is often the case, I submit, within cultures or religions whose female members are devalued and imbibe their sense of inferiority virtually from birth.[11]

I am willing to admit that many Pirzada women's "acquiescence" to veiling is in fact partly an effect of lack of power, of socialization into inferior social roles, and a low sense of entitlement. However, I would want to insist alongside this admission that many of these women are fairly *realistic* in their assessments of their lack of power, and shrewdly aware of the powers they do have to negotiate; they accept their inferior social roles in some ways even as they try to rewrite the scripts of these roles in others; and although their sense of entitlement is low in some respects, they are aware of the entitlements they have as respectable women in the community. When Okin describes their "acquiescence" as due to "lack of power," I would want to add that their lack of power is not akin to the absolute lack of power of the prisoner of patriarchy model of these women's agency. When Okin describes their "acquiescence" as due to "socialization into inferior roles," I would want to add that these women are not total dupes of patriarchy.

Further in the same article, discussing the pressures for "cultural conformity" experienced by women from immigrant groups in the United States, Okin says,

> It is therefore difficult to understand how these young women's cultures could be viewed as providing for them the background enabling them "to make informed decisions about how to lead their lives" "to make choices among various meaningful options" or "to freely pursue the life they see fit"—functions that liberal defenders of multiculturalism ascribe to cultures. Serious constraints, rather than personal freedom or the capacity to make meaningful choices about their lives, make up a major part of their cultural heritage.[12]

This difficulty in understanding worries me—particularly when it concerns Western feminist engagements with Other cultural practices. I have no problem with any feminist judging that the kinds of information and the nature and extent of "meaningful options" that Other women have, and the freedom with which they pursue the life they see fit, are seriously limited in the light of feminist moral and political considerations. However, I think it would be a dangerous sort of blindness if we refuse to simultaneously understand that these women do have, within their horizons, significant amounts of information with respect to the life choices currently open to them, that some choices of options are meaningful to them, and that the lives they pursue are in many respects lives they see fit to pursue.

Okin expresses a widely shared view when she says that she finds it difficult to understand how oppressive cultural contexts could be viewed as enabling Other women "to make informed decisions about how to lead their lives," "to make choices among various meaningful options," or "to freely pursue the life they see fit." I would like to complicate this prevalent understanding of the effects that "oppressive cultural contexts" can have on women's capacities for critical reflection and autonomy. I have no doubt that oppressive constraints can often distort women's critical abilities and their sense of entitlements and options. However, I want to insist that "oppressive cultural contexts," whether familial or communal, can sometimes have the very opposite effect. When the "oppressiveness" of patriarchal practices is blatant and obvious, agents might be more critically aware of it and more realistic about the nature of their choices, than when "oppression" is subtle, and can seem not like oppression at all.

Let me illustrate this by means of an example, which I recognize may be controversial. Many women I knew in India were subject to pretty strong "cultural pressures" to enter into arranged marriages, pressures to which some eventually yielded. It is my considered judgment that some women who did yield to these pressures had a pretty clear-eyed and realistic sense of what they were letting themselves in for, and why. They saw consenting to an arranged marriage as making their parents happy, as providing themselves with a socially sanctioned avenue for sexuality, and with an economic arrangement conducive to having children and a family life. They had no great illusions about the men they were to marry or what they could expect from the lives they were entering. It is also my considered judgment that some of these women in India were more critical and reflective about their choices than some women I know here, who have rushed into unappealing relationships or marriages with vastly exaggerated notions of what these men were like and what kind of treatment they could expect from them. These relationships are explained and justified in the name of "romantic love" and "personal choice," without acknowledgment of the pressures that women here face, from the time they are teenagers, to engage in what, modifying Adrienne Rich, I think of as "compulsive heterosexuality."[13]

I believe that the "rhetoric of choice" functions as a powerful form of cultural ideology, enabling *women to see themselves as "engaging in free choices" by overlooking the "cultural pressures and constraints" that shape their choices*. This includes everything from dieting to breast implants to obsessive involvement with their appearance to relationships with abusive or unappealing men, to be conceptualized and experienced by many women here as "free choices," thus diluting acknowledgment of the "cultural pressures" they are subject to and eclipsing the ways in which the prevalent "rhetoric of choice" influences their conceptualizations of the decisions they make. In addition, I believe that the legacies of colonial history often encourage mainstream Westerners to *overemphasize constraints and underemphasize choice* in Other cultural contexts, while *underestimating constraints and overemphasizing choice* in Western contexts. Such considerations make me cautious about generalizations concerning the effects of particular "cultural contexts" on women's critical ability and choice and prevent me from sharing Okin's generalization that "Western liberal contexts" are more empowering for women's agency and choices than cultural contexts that are Other.[14]

I am sympathetic to Martha Nussbaum's overall position on how feminists ought to deal with the fact that women's preferences and choices are often deformed by their patriarchal socialization and limited opportunities. Nussbaum correctly insists that such deformed preferences should not count against social policies that will empower them to make choices that are currently inconceivable or unappealing, since women can reconsider what they are entitled to and what they should aspire to as the options available to them increase. But Nussbaum cautions that the "central focus" of feminist attempts to change such deformed preferences should be "on persuasion rather than coercion."[15] My sense that women's "deformed preferences" can often also reflect *realistic assessments* of the options open to them to get the things they currently want out of life, and my worries about *inaccuracies* that might beset feminist attempts to make *generalized assessments* about the varied intersections of choices and constraints different women face with respect to cultural practices such as veiling, lead me to share Nussbaum's sense that feminist policies should, for the most part, rely on providing women with more empowering options rather than on using coercion to prevent women from making choices to comply with patriarchal practices. In contrast to Nussbaum, other feminists have been more supportive of the use of state coercion to prevent women from making choices to conform to patriarchal cultural practices, an issue to which I now turn.

Autonomy and "Other Women": State Coercion and "Cultural Practices"

Acknowledging that women's responses to patriarchal cultural practices involve constraints on choices, but also choice within constraints, makes a difference to the kinds of state policies feminists ought to support. I am interested here in one subset of cases of "practices involving Other women": practices involving *adult women* that are not literally coercively imposed on them, where there are strong "cultural pressures" to conform to these practices, where these practices contribute to maintaining women's second-class social status, and where women arguably make choices about conforming to these practices and have a wide range of attitudes to them. I am thinking of practices such as veiling and seclusion but also practices such as arranged marriages in a variety of Indian communities.

With respect to such practices, I believe that it is usually unproblematic if feminists support two kinds of actions on the part of the state. First, the state ought to intervene to protect women in cases of outright coercion, where women are subject to the practice entirely involuntarily, and protect their ability to exit from the coercive situation. Second, the state should actively foster a number of legal and social changes that improve women's powers and opportunities to negotiate their encounters with these practices—providing women with opportunities for education, employment, ownership of property and the like, opportunities that might empower women to re-think, modify, or reject these practices. However, I believe that improving the range of options women have with respect to these practices is vastly different, both morally and politically, from using coercive state intervention to outlaw or illegalize such practices on the grounds that the cultural constraints render women's decisions to comply with such practices "not really choices in any meaningful sense." I am going to argue that feminists should *not* support coercive state intervention against such practices, for a number of reasons.

First, I have serious reservations about state-directed agendas to "save women from cultural backwardness." The history of state-driven attempts to ban veiling in a number of countries shows us that the motives and effects of these policies are deeply problematic. Talking about the State outlawing the veil in Iran and in Turkey in the 1930s, Homa Hoodfar states:

> Although the rhetoric of de-veiling was to liberate women so that they could contribute to build a new modern nation, in reality women and their interests counted for little. Rather, they had become the battlefield and the booty of the harsh and sometimes bloody struggle between the secularists and the modernists on one side, and the religious authorities on the other.[16]

Hoodfar describes the very different effects that deveiling policy had on different groups of women in Iran. Although the policy was welcomed by many women of the urban elites, urban lower-middle-class and low-income women bore the brunt of its adverse effects. Many of these women would not go out without the veil and thus felt compelled to stay home at all times, becoming dependent on male relatives for the public tasks they previously carried out themselves. These women could no longer engage in activities like shopping, going to the public baths, attending the mosque for religious ceremonies, or attending carpet-weaving workshops that gave them both an economically valuable skill and an opportunity to socialize with women outside their families. By state edict, veiled women were denied access to employment in the government sector, denied service in hotels and restaurants, and subject to being chased and harassed by the police if they ventured out with even a head scarf on.[17] State-sponsored "compulsory deveiling policies" expose women to serious state surveillance and terror, no less than state-sponsored policies that compel women to veil. I find it difficult to support the conclusion that one kind of policy is any less "patriarchal" than the other. Imagine the effects of an allegedly "antipatriarchal" policy here that allowed the police to chase women wearing makeup, to threaten them with arrest, and to manhandle them while they scrubbed their faces of any offending marks of their patriarchal oppression!

I am saddened to find that some feminists, whose work I otherwise respect, support coercive state interference in cultural practices affecting Other women, such as veiling, because they fail to make such analogies to similar issues in their own context. Addressing the controversy over the Muslim schoolgirls in France who wanted to veil by wearing head scarves to school, Katha Pollitt says:

An older friend of mine was in Paris while the dispute over Muslim school-girls' head scarves was going on. A gentle, tolerant, worldly-wise leftist, she sided with the girls against the government: why shouldn't they be able to dress as they wished, to follow their culture? Then she came across a television debate in which a Muslim girl wanted the ban to stay because without it, her family would force her to wear a scarf. That changed my friend's view of the matter: the left, and feminist position, she now thought, was to support this girl and ones like her in their struggle to be independent, modern women—not the parents, the neighbors, the community and religious "leaders." I think my friend was right.[18]

I have a number of difficulties with this position. I would argue that someone who is "tolerant and worldly-wise" needs to ask if her "support" for the Muslim girl on television should proceed by advocating state coercion against the choices of other Muslims girls who wanted to wear the head scarf. I find it disturbing that this femi-nist's change of heart proceeds by entirely eclipsing the agency and presence of the girls who wanted to wear the head scarf—juxtaposing the girl on television only to parents, neighbors, community, and religious leaders, and not to those other girls who wanted to veil, suggesting that she now perhaps regards the latter as "dupes of patri-archy" manipulated by their parents, neighbors, and religious leaders. This line of rea-soning questions neither the simplistic equation between wearing the veil and not be-ing "independent modern women," nor the whether the French state's enforcement of the ban would be driven by a concern for its Muslim schoolgirls becoming "independ-ent modern women" or by a less appealing set of motives to do with instigating anti-immigrant sentiments.

Pollitt's article, as well as other antiveiling discussions of this French case I have come across, tend to discount the agency of the girls who initially put on the head scarves—leaving the reader with little sense of the considerations they might have had for so doing. In contrast, Bhiku Parekh provides a sharp sense of their agency when he reconstructs their motivations thus:

In France and the Netherlands, several Muslim schoolgirls freely wore the hi-jab (headscarf), partly to reassure their conservative parents that they would not be corrupted by the public culture of the school, and partly to reshape the latter by indicating to white boys how they wished to be treated. The hijab in their case was a highly complex autonomous act intended to use the resources of the tradition both to change and to preserve it. To see it merely as a symbol of their subordination, as many French feminists did, is to miss the subtle di-alect of cultural negotiation.[19]

Last, but not least, there is no attempt, in the viewpoint endorsed by Pollitt, to consider whether one would support a similar ban on head scarves or veils in our pub-lic schools or colleges in the United States. Such a ban would have the dubious virtue of pitting "the left and feminist position" against many African American Muslim women, women from a variety of immigrant communities, as well as a small but significant number of white women converts to Islam, all of whom might have different reasons for wanting to veil. Such a ban would, I think, correctly be upheld as an unconstitutional infringement of some women's rights to both freedom of religion and political expression.

The second set of reasons I have for opposing coercive state intervention to ban these practices has to do with my belief that deeply entrenched practices and deeply held views about women are more likely to genuinely change for the better when such changes occur via processes that lead people's perceptions, sensibilities, and value frameworks to regard these changes favorably. State-imposed coercion is more likely than not to result in resentment and a "hardening of the categories"—often contributing to backlash and to reactionary rather than progressive changes in attitudes. Iran's use of state power to enforce deveiling, and popular resentments about the hardships these caused some women, undoubtedly assisted in the veil becoming a symbol of resistance to the shah and to his vision of the Iranian nation in the early stages of Iran's Islamic revolution.[20]

What is perhaps my central reason for opposing state-imposed coercion as a means to eradicate these sorts of "patriarchal practices" has to do with my sense that the wide range of desires and attitudes women have with respect to such practices, and wide range of negotiations and choices they may wish to make with respect to various aspects of such practice, should be respected. Here is where I run into an important problem. Much of liberal feminist discourse treats "respect for women's choices" as an important value. However, it often predicates such "respect" on the grounds that those choices can be judged to have been made "autonomously." I have worries about the ways in which some of these positions cash out the notion of "autonomy" in overly demanding ways— that might lend support for the view that many of the desires and the decisions made by "Other women" lack autonomy and therefore do not deserve such respect, since no considerations beside autonomy are advanced to ground respect for choices.

Veiling happens to be one example Marilyn Friedman cites of a practice she would like to protect on grounds of respect for women's procedural autonomy. However, I am unsure whether her *account of autonomy* would in fact shield practices like veiling from coercive state interference. Friedman sets out the following as conditions to be met if women's choices are to be regarded as worthy of respect on grounds of procedural autonomy. She says:

> First, the conditions under which women actually reflect on their situations and decide how to live would have to promote generally reliable choices. In particular, there must be significant and morally acceptable alternatives among which the women can choose. As well, the level of coercion, manipulation and deception must be insignificant. Second, prior conditions must have fostered in women the development of their very capacities to reflect on their situations and make decisions about them.[21]

I have difficulties with two of the conditions for autonomy that Friedman sets out. First is the condition that "the level of coercion, manipulation and deception must be insignificant." In the case of many Pirzada women, for instance, there is a significant amount of situational coercion in their having to veil—their veiling is socially expected and enforced by families, and there would be potentially serious consequences for some of these women were they to refuse to veil. There is a similar situation with some women and makeup in contexts here. There is certainly ample manipulation by media and advertising that construct women's desires for makeup, and there is considerable deception in sales pitches for beauty products that promise wrinkle-free youth and sizzling attractiveness. There is also a considerable amount of peer pressure, and in some cases a fair degree of situational coercion; there would be professional risks in certain contexts for women who refused to wear any makeup. I am unsure as to how to judge whether these manipulations, coercions and deceptions are "insignificant" and concerned about judging these pressures to be "significant" given the potential implication that these "choices" might then not warrant "respect."

I have even more difficulties with another of Friedman's conditions for procedural autonomy, the one requiring that "there must be significant and morally acceptable alternatives among which the women can choose." Consider a younger Pirzada woman who does not wish to veil but lacks "significant morally acceptable alternatives," given her economic and social dependence on her family and community, and her Western counterpart who does not wish to wear any makeup but lacks "significant morally acceptable alternatives" given that she might lose her job if she refused to do so. It is not a "morally acceptable alternative" for the Pirzada woman to be ostracized by her family and community, or for the American woman to lose her present job. But surely these women make clear choices when they conform to these requirements in the absence of acceptable alternatives. They are choices to do something they don't really want to do but would rather do than face the unacceptable consequences of not so doing, and there are benefits to compliance that the agents are aware of and genuinely desire. I am genuinely puzzled as to why such choices are not procedurally autonomous or worthy of respect. Although I have no quarrel with the view that both women might benefit from having more acceptable alternatives available, the lack of such alternatives seems a reason for *respecting* their choice rather than a feature that *counts against* it.

I understand why choice has such a great importance in the liberal lexicon—as agents, there are indeed many situations in which we do value having a range of "morally acceptable choices," and we find our freedom enhanced as a result of the existence of such alternatives. However, I am not inclined to tie an agent's autonomy so stringently to the existence of such alternatives, making the existence of such alternatives a *necessary condition for autonomous choice* as Friedman seems to do. I believe that such a requirement overly inflates the conditions for autonomy, at least for contexts in which coercive interference by the state is at issue. I believe a "thin" notion of autonomy should suffice for respect in terms of state coercion. A person's choice should be considered autonomous as long as the person was a "normal adult" with no serious cognitive or emotional impairments, and was not subject to literal or outright coercion from others. On this account, a person's choice could be autonomous even if made under considerable social or cultural pressure, and even if it were the only morally palatable option open to her. Choices to engage in a "cultural practice," where the woman's values and identity are in part "invested in and served by the practice," even if she does not care for certain aspects of the practice and lacks the power to negotiate modifications, would certainly meet my test for procedural autonomy.

The philosophical literature on autonomy reveals that although it is a widely used and widely relied on notion, the range of meaning ascribed to it is enormous. It is often used as a synonym for everything from free will, sovereignty, dignity, integrity, rationality, independence, responsibility, self-assertion, self-knowledge, critical reflection, freedom from external causation, and freedom from obligation.[22] I think these many connotations are interesting and useful to philosophically reflect on and clarify, a project I am clearly not undertaking in this chapter. I do not wish to suggest that "thicker" notions of autonomy should be given up or serve no legitimate purpose. Thicker notions of autonomy, that measure the degree of autonomy in terms of conditions such as the absence of significant amounts of manipulation and deception, or in terms of the existence of morally acceptable alternatives, have their uses. For instance, they may help in formulating policies that would leave agents freer of manipulation or with access to more alternatives. I merely wish to insist that such "thicker notions" are not the appropriate measure for judging whether individual choices warrant respect in terms of coercive interference by the state. Given the prevalent complexities and unclarities regarding what autonomy amounts to, relying on autonomy as a central consideration with respect to issues of limits on state coercion might be more of a problem than is often recognized.

I believe that liberals have reason to care about *liberty* and not merely about *autonomy*. I believe that considerations of liberty provide stronger limits to coercive state regulations than considerations of autonomy because liberty is both a wider and a clearer notion than autonomy. Leaving individual choices vulnerable to state coercion on the grounds that they are not founded in deep critical reflection or are due to unreflective habits or to the unrecognized manipulation of the agent by media or "cultural pressures" would protect very few of the actual choices of actual individuals from state coercion. Whereas autonomous choices are usually considered to demand an impersonal sort of "respect" because they are the rational choices of rational agents, most of us experience our choices as valuable to us even when they do not constitute robustly "autonomous choices." Many nonautonomous choices arguably have significance to agents because they are "one's own"—they are forms of liberty we enjoy, and resent interferences with, even when we may grant that they are not based on critical reflection or are otherwise robustly autonomous. I believe that liberal states must have substantial reasons to restrict individual *liberty*, even where such restrictions might arguably not reduce autonomy, or even when such restrictions might potentially enhance autonomy. If a liberal position is concerned only with protecting individual autonomy, and not with protecting liberty more generally, I believe that it would paradoxically have profoundly illiberal effects. State policies that protect women against coerced compliance with cultural practices, as well as state policies that improve women's opportunities to reflect on, modify, or reject certain cultural practices by promoting their access to education and employment and by safeguarding their rights, promote *both their liberty and their autonomy*. In contrast, coercive state intervention into cultural practices, such as compulsory deveiling policies, often end up substantially reducing their *actual liberty* in the name of enhancing their *potential autonomy*. I am arguing that feminists need to be extremely wary about endorsing such tradeoffs.

Because the notion of autonomy is both vague and complex, I do not think that autonomy, other than in the extremely "thin" version I previously suggested, should be the central issue in determining whether coercive state interference with individual choices is justifiable. Not only is the degree of autonomy evinced by particular agents often difficult to gauge, it is often difficult to generalize about the degree of autonomy different women enjoy with respect to particular cultural practices. The degree to which different agents who engage in the "cultural practice" regard it as life and self-defining, and the degrees of coercion and constraint that agents experience with respect to the practice, *vary widely*. There are special dangers, I believe, where such generalizations about personal agency, coercion, and autonomy are attempted by Western feminists with respect to cultural practices affecting Other women. I believe that the prisoner and dupe type stereotypes about Other women would make it likely that such generalizations would *underestimate* the significance of the practice to, and degree of autonomy manifested by, many women who engage in the practice, as well as *overestimate* the degree of coercion they face to comply with the practice.

I would like to end by pointing out that my rejection of state coercion to end oppressive cultural practices affecting Other women is not a position that is wedded to supporting any form of "group rights" or "cultural rights." Thus I am sympathetic to Okin's opposition to such rights. However, rejecting "group rights" or "cultural rights" should not be seen as a justification, however oblique, for state coercion with respect to these sorts of cultural practices. I think it is important for both liberals and feminists to recognize that arguments for "respecting the choices of Other women" need not rely on endorsing group rights or cultural rights, but can rest on the uncontroversial and straightforwardly liberal concern to protect a wide range of individual choices made by different groups of women.

Notes

1. My discussion of Pirzada women's attitudes to veiling relies on Patricia Jeffrey's ethnography, *Frogs in a Well: Indian Women in Purdah* (London: Zed, 1979.)

2. Most of these responses are found on pages 149–153 of Jeffrey, *Frogs.*

3. Ibid., p. 11.

4. Ibid., p. 155.

5. Ibid., pp. 153–155.

6. Ibid., p. 109.

7. Ibid., p. 34.

8. See, for instance, Susan Bordo, *Unbearable Weight: Feminism, Western Culture, and the Body* (Berkeley: University of California Press, 1993); and Naomi Wolf, *The Beauty Myth: How Images of Beauty Are Used Against Women* (New York: Morrow, 1991).

9. I borrow this useful phrase from the title of Deniz Kandiyoti's article "Bargaining with Patriarchy," *Gender and Society,* September 1988, pp. 274–290.

10. For instance, see some of the views and their implications in Mary Daly, *Gyn-Ecology: The Metaethics of Radical Feminism* (Boston: Beacon, 1978); Andrea Dworkin, *Pornography: Men Possessing Women* (New York: Penguin, 1981); and Catharine MacKinnon, *Feminism Unmodified* (Cambridge: Harvard University Press, 1987).

11. Susan Moller Okin, "Feminism and Multiculturalism: Some Tensions," *Ethics*, July 1998, p. 675. An earlier version of this piece appeared as "Is Multiculturalism Bad for Women?" *Boston Review*, October–November 1997, pp. 25–28. The Pollitt and Parekh articles cited later are responses to this earlier piece.

12. Okin, "Feminism and Multiculturalism," p. 683.

13. I am modifying Adrienne Rich's term "compulsory heterosexuality." See Adrienne Rich, "Compulsory Heterosexuality and Lesbian Existence," *Signs*, Summer 1980, pp. 139–165.

14. Okin suggests that "Western liberal cultures" have departed further from patriarchal pasts than others and that most cultural minorities in Western contexts are more patriarchal than the surrounding culture. See Susan Moller Okin, "Is Multiculturalism Bad for Women?" *Boston Review*, October–November 1997, p. 27.

15. See Martha Nussbaum, *Sex and Social Justice* (New York: Oxford University Press, 1999).

16. Homa Hoodfar, "The Veil in Their Minds and on Our Heads: Veiling Practices and Muslim Women," in *The Politics of Culture in the Shadow of Capital*, ed. Lisa Lowe and David Lloyd (Durham, N.C.: Duke University Press, 1997), pp. 258–259.

17. Hoodfar, "Veil," pp. 260–263.

18. Katha Pollitt, "Whose Culture?" *Boston Review*, October–November 1997, p. 29.

19. Bhiku Parekh, "A Varied Moral World," *Boston Review*, October–November 1997, p. 35.

20. Hoodfar, "Veil," p. 265.

21. Marilyn Friedman, "Human Rights, Cultural Minorities, and Women" (paper presented at the McDowell Conference on Human Rights, American University, November 1998), p. 6.

22. Gerald Dworkin draws attention to the various meanings of the term; see *The Theory and Practice of Autonomy* (Cambridge University Press, 1988), p. 6.

ABOUT THE EDITORS AND CONTRIBUTORS

Elizabeth Anderson is professor of philosophy and women's studies at the University of Michigan–Ann Arbor, where she teaches courses in ethics, social and political philosophy, and feminist theory. She is the author of *Value in Ethics and Economics* (1993) and is currently working on issues in feminist epistemology and philosophy of science.

Louise M. Antony is professor of philosophy and women's studies at the Ohio State University. Her teaching and research interests are in the philosophy of mind, the philosophy of language, the foundations of cognitive science, and feminist theory. She is coeditor, with Norbert Hornstein, of *Chomsky and His Critics* (forthcoming).

Margaret Atherton is professor of philosophy at the University of Wisconsin–Milwaukee. She teaches courses in early modern philosophy and in the Women's Studies Program. In addition to many articles on early modern philosophy, she is author of *Berkeley's Revolution in Vision* (1990) and editor of *Women Philosophers in the Early Modern Period* (1994).

Annette C. Baier was professor of philosophy at the University of Pittsburgh until retiring to New Zealand in 1996. She is the author of *Postures of the Mind* (1985); *A Progress of Sentiments: Reflections on Hume's Treatise* (1991); *Moral Prejudices* (1994); and *The Commons of the Mind: Paul Carus Lectures Series 19* (1997).

Ann E. Cudd is professor of philosophy and director of women's studies at the University of Kansas. She teaches courses in philosophy of social science, feminist theory, social and political philosophy, and decision theory. She is currently working on a book on the psychological and economic forces of oppression.

Jean Hampton was professor of philosophy at the University of Arizona until her death in 1996. In addition to many articles in ethical and political theory, she was the author of *Hobbes and the Social Contract Tradition* (1986); *Political Philosophy* (1997); and *The Authority of Reason,* edited by Richard Healey (1998); and coauthor, with Jeffrie G. Murphy, of *Forgiveness and Mercy* (1988). She was also coeditor, with David Copp and John E. Roemer, of *The Idea of Democracy* (1993).

Sally Haslanger is associate professor of philosophy at the Massachusetts Institute of Technology, where she teaches courses in philosophy and women's studies. She has published articles in metaphysics and epistemology, and she is coeditor, with Charlotte Witt, of *The View from Home: Philosophical Issues in Adoption* (forthcoming) and, with Elizabeth Hackett, of *Theorizing Feminisms: North American Approaches in Context* (forthcoming).

Barbara Herman is Griffin Professor of Philosophy at UCLA. She is the author of *The Practice of Moral Judgment* (1993); and coeditor, with Andrews Reath and Christine Korsgaard, of *Reclaiming the History of Ethics: Essays for John Rawls* (1997). She has also written many articles on Kantian ethics, moral psychology, and the social bases of ordinary moral practice.

Marcia L. Homiak is professor of philosophy at Occidental College, where she teaches philosophy, women's studies, and ancient history. Her research interests are in classical ethics, the history of ethics, and moral psychology. A recent article on feminist ethics, "On the Malleability of Character," appeared in *On Feminist Ethics and Politics,* edited by Claudia Card (1999).

Karen Jones is assistant professor of philosophy at Cornell University, and research fellow in the philosophy program at the Australian National University. She is the author of articles on trust in both its moral and epistemic dimensions. She is currently working on a book about the emotions, entitled *Emotional Rationality as Practical Rationality.*

Genevieve Lloyd is emeritus professor in philosophy at the University of New South Wales Sydney, N.S.W., Australia. She is author of *The Man of Reason: "Male" and "Female" in Western Philosophy* (1984; 2d ed., 1993).

Helen E. Longino is professor of women's studies and philosophy at the University of Minnesota. She is author of *Science as Social Knowledge* (1990) and *The Fate of Knowledge* (2001), as well as numerous articles in feminist philosophy, philosophy of science, and philosophy of the behavioral sciences.

Uma Narayan is associate professor of philosophy at Vassar College. She has research and teaching interests in social and political philosophy, ethics, and feminist theory. She is the author of *Dis-locating Cultures: Identities, Traditions, and Third-World Feminism* (1997); and coeditor, with Sandra Harding, of *Decentering the Center: Philosophy for a Multicultural, Postcolonial, and Feminist World* (2000).

Elizabeth Rapaport is professor of law at the University of New Mexico. She teaches courses in jurisprudence, professional ethics, and criminal law and procedure. Recently she has written on women and crime, gender and capital punishment, and executive clemency.

Naomi Scheman is professor of philosophy and women's studies and associate dean of the graduate school at the University of Minnesota. She is the author of *Engenderings: Constructions of Knowledge, Authority, and Privilege* (1993).

Robin May Schott is associate research professor of philosophy at the University of Copenhagen, and director for the Philosophy on the Border project. She is the author of *Cognition and Eros: A Critique of the Kantian Paradigm* (1988); coeditor of *Forplantning: Køen og teknologi* (1995); and editor of *Feminist Interpretations of Kant* (1997).

Charlotte Witt is professor and chair of philosophy at the University of New Hampshire. Her teaching and research interests are in ancient philosophy and feminist philosophy. She is the author of *Substance and Essence in Aristotle*; and coeditor, with Sally Haslanger, of *The View from Home: Philosophical Issues in Adoption* (forthcoming).

Rachel Zuckert is assistant professor of philosophy at Rice University, where she teaches courses in eighteenth- and nineteenth-century German philosophy and esthetics. She is currently working on a book about Kant's *Critique of Judgment.*

INDEX